HE FRANKISH KINGDOMS UNDER THE
CAROLINGIANS
751–987

THE FRANKISH KINGDOMS UNDER THE CAROLINGIANS, 751–987

ROSAMOND MCKITTERICK

LONGMAN
London and New York

Longman Group Limited
Longman House
Burnt Mill, Harlow, Essex, UK

*Published in the United States of America
by Longman Inc., New York*

© Longman Group Limited 1983

First published 1983

British Library Cataloguing in Publication Data

McKitterick, Rosamond
The Frankish kingdoms under the Carolinginans,
751–987.
1. Franks – History
I. Title
944′.01   DC70.A4/

ISBN 0-582-49005-7

Library of Congress Cataloging in Publication Data

McKitterick, Rosamond.
The Frankish kingdoms under the Carolingians,
751–987.
Bibliography: p. 340.
Includes indexes.
1. Carolingians.   2. France – History – To 987.
3. Franks – History.   I. Title.
DC70.M3   1983   944′.01   82-8944
ISBN 0-582-49005-7 (pbk.)   AACR2

Printed in Singapore by
Singapore National Printers (Pte) Ltd.

Contents

List of Figures

List of Genealogical Tables

List of Maps

Preface

Previous work on the Carolingians has either given undue prominence to Charlemagne at the expense of his predecessors and successors, has sketched their history in the general context of European developments in the Middle Ages, or has concentrated on particular themes, regions or small portions of the period. My aim has been, rather, to provide a political narrative and analysis concerning the Carolingian kings, the aristocracy and the church in their social context. I have presented the Carolingian kings, from Pippin III (751–68) to Louis V (986–7), not as a line of kings who made and failed to preserve an Empire, but as a succession of, for the most part, able rulers who raised themselves above their peers and who extended their authority and landed wealth, but whose exercise of authority and influence was gradually eroded by others among their contemporaries in similar bids for power. Because studies of Carolingian Italy and the history of the east Franks and Germany after 800 have been or are being written, I have more or less confined myself after 843 to the west Frankish kingdom.

The practice of kingship and government, the kings' policies towards the church, the continuous struggle between king and nobles and the development of the territorial principalities are principal themes in this book. I have devoted particular attention to the foundation of Normandy, Brittany and Flanders and the emergence of the Robertian (or Capetian) family. Subsidiary themes are the developments in learning, culture and the religious life. Wherever possible I have examined the source, both in manuscript and print, afresh. While I have been able to include my own research in many sections of this book, I have also drawn extensively on recent Continental scholarship on the Carolingians with the intention of making it more generally available to the English reader.

Citation of primary sources is to be found both in the text and in the notes in an abbreviated form. Reference to secondary material has had to be kept, for reasons of space, to the minimum. I have thus usually only cited the most essential contribution to a particular issue in the notes. The spelling of personal names in the early medieval period always presents problems; I have adopted throughout, with the exception of such accepted name forms as Charlemagne, either anglicized forms of names where English equivalents exist (for example, Louis rather than Hludowicus) or simplified forms of the Latin names (for example, Walafrid rather than Walahfridus). There being no generally current spellings of Viking names, these too have followed the Latin forms given in the primary sources.

I am indebted to a great many friends, colleagues and students for their help while I have been writing this book: to Ian Wood and Edward James who encouraged me to write it in the first place and to Christopher Brooke for his valuable advice; to Giles Brown, Edward James, Janet Nelson and Patricia McNulty who read most, if not all, of it and to Simon Keynes, Jonathan Shepard, Julia Smith and Janthia Yearley who read sections of it; to my students, especially Rhiannon Bell, Sarah Foot and Jacqueline Smith who kindly acted as guinea-pigs and who were a constant reminder of those for whom I was writing the book; to David Dumville, J. C. Holt, Michael Metcalf, Ray Page and Eleanor Searle for answering my queries on particular points; to Edmund Poole for his bibliographical assistance for my discussion of early medieval music; to the Principal and Fellows of Newnham College for their support; to Joan Townsend for producing an immaculate typescript and to the staff at Longman who saw it through the press. I am profoundly grateful to them all and none is in any way responsible for any errors or infelicities that remain. My most heartfelt thanks are for my husband David for his never-failing encouragement and comfort as well as his practical assistance at every stage of this book's production. My father and mother too, as always, have been a constant source of strength and good sense; it is the least I can do to dedicate this book to them both.

Cambridge, 2 February 1982   ROSAMOND MCKITTERICK

Acknowledgements

We are grateful to the following for permission to reproduce copyright material:

Edward Arnold Ltd for an extract from *The Reign of Charlemagne* by Loyn and Percival, from Documents of Medieval History Series; Arts et Métiers Graphiques for our Figs 5, 6 and 7 from *L'Ecriture Latine de la Capitale Romaine à la Minuscule* by J. Mallon, R. Marechal, and C. Perrat, 1939, Numbers 69, 68 and 75; Bibliothéque Nationale for our Fig 2; Oxford University Press for our Fig 4 from *Codices Latini Antiquiores* V No 579 by E. A. Lowe; Edizioni Di Storia E Letteratura for an extract from *Handwriting* by E. A. Lowe.

List of Abbreviations

Böhmer–Mühlbacher	J. F. Böhmer and E. Mühlbacher, *Regesta Imperii* I. *Die Regesten des Kaiserreichs unter den Karolingern* (Innsbruck 1908)
Bouquet, *Recueil*	M. Bouquet, *Recueil des Historiens des Gaules et de la France* (Paris new ed. vols i–xix under the direction of L. Delisle, 1869–80)
BEC	*Bibliothèque de l'Ecole des Chartes*
BL	British Library
BM	Bibliothèque Municipale
BN	Bibliothèque Nationale, Paris
Clm	Codices latini monacensis, Bayerische Staatsbibliothek, Munich
DA	*Deutsches Archiv für die Erforschung des Mittelalters*
Ep(p)	Epistola(e)
EHR	*English Historical Review*
Ganshof, *Carolingians*	F. L. Ganshof, *The Carolingians and the Frankish Monarchy*, trs. J. Sondheimer (London 1971)
HJ	*Historisches Jahrbuch*
HZ	*Historisches Zeitschrift*
KdG I–IV	W. Braunfels (general, editor) *Karl der Grosse. Lebenswerk und Nachleben* (Düsseldorf 4 vols, 1965) I *Persönlichkeit und Geschichte*, H. Beumann ed. II *Das Geistige Leben*. B. Bischoff ed. III *Karolingische Kunst*, W. Braunfels and P. E. Schramm ed. IV *Das Nachleben*, W. Braunfels and P. E. Schramm eds.

Loyn and Percival	H. Loyn and J. Percival, *The Reign of Charlemagne* (London 1975)
McKitterick, *Frankish Church*	R. McKitterick, *The Frankish Church and the Carolingian Reforms 789–895* (London 1977)
MGH : AA	*Monumenta Germaniae Historica : Auctores Antiquissimi*
: *Cap.*	: *Capitularia*
: *Conc.*	: *Concilia*
: *Dip. Kar.*	: *Diplomata Karolinorum*
: *Epp.*	: *Epistolae*
: *Leges*	: *Leges*
: *Poet.*	: *Poetae aevi Karolini*
: *SS*	: *Scriptores*
: *SS i.u.s.*	: *Scriptores in usum scholarum*
: *SS rer. merov.*	: *Scriptores rerum merovingicarum*
MA	*Le Moyen Age*
MIOG	*Mitteilungen des Instituts für Österreichische Geschichtsforschung*
PL	J. P. Migne, *Patrologia Latina* (Paris 1844–55)
Rau, *Quellen*	R. Rau (ed.), *Quellen zur karolingische Reichsgeschichte* (Darmstadt 3 vols, 1974–75)
RhV	*Rheinische Vierteljahrsblätter*
Settimane	*Settimane di Studio del Centro Italiano di Studi sull'alto Medioevo* (Spoleto)
TRHS	*Transactions of the Royal Historical Society*
Vat.	Bibliotheca Apostolica Vaticana, Rome *Zeitschrift für Kirchengeschichte*
ZRG: GA	*Zeitschrift der Savigny Stiftung für Rechtsgeschichte: Germanistische Abteilung*
: *KA*	*: Kanonistische Abteilung*

All sources have been cited in an abbreviated form; the full title of each work is to be found in the Bibliography of principal sources, listed in alphabetical order of author where this is known, or of title in the case of anonymous works.

To my parents

CHAPTER ONE

The Sources

The sources extant for the two and a half centuries during which the Carolingians ruled as kings over the Franks are of great richness and diversity. Not only are there the narrative sources, annals, chronicles, biographies and saints' lives, the histories of abbeys and of bishoprics; there are also many letters, both official and unofficial, poems, theological and didactic treatises, and all the legal sources, charters, conciliar decrees, royal legislation and the Germanic law codes. All these, with a few exceptions, are written in Latin; the vernacular languages were only beginning to be written down in the late eighth and the ninth centuries, and most of what vernacular source material survives is religious in content. Excellent surveys have been made of the types of both Carolingian and medieval source material, such as those of Wattenbach and Levison, Monod, Molinier or Van Caenegem, which describe the principal editions of printed material.[1] Most of the sources have been printed in one form or another, though in many cases the only editions available are those of the sixteenth and seventeenth centuries and are inadequate by modern standards. There remains, however, unstudied and unedited manuscript material to be explored. Coins,[2] archaeological remains and manuscripts also provide important insights into the history and culture of the Carolingian period. It is often purely fortuitous that much that has survived has done so. The *Codex Epistolaris Carolinus* for example, a vitally important collection of papal letters addressed to the first Carolingian rulers, Charles Martel, Pippin III and Charlemagne, survives in one manuscript in Vienna, a late ninth-century copy of the collection Charlemagne ordered to be made of these letters in 791. This copy seems at one time to have been in the possession of Willebert, archbishop of Cologne from 870 to 889, and may even have been made for him, but nothing more is known of the manuscript until it turned up in 1554 and was acquired by Caspar Niedbruck for the Imperial Library in Vienna.[3]

The greater proportion of the extant Carolingian material dates from the first three-quarters of the ninth century. The comparative paucity of sources for the eighth and tenth centuries, however, need not necessarily reflect a decline in political and cultural life; the problems of survival from such an early period make it unwise to infer too much from a lack of evidence or type of evidence.

1

Much of the evidence on which the following chapters are based will be discussed in its proper context; a consideration of all the legal sources, for example, will be included in the chapter on Carolingian government and administration. It is useful, however, to gain not only a general familiarity with the types of evidence available for the different stages of Carolingian rule in the Frankish kingdoms, but also an awareness of the difficulties of dealing with some of this evidence. To take but one instance, what kind of narrative sources are there for the Carolingian period, and why and for whom were they written?

Of the narrative sources the annals are the most essential. Annals first appeared as short notes of an event or events in a year. The year 715 in the *Annales Sancti Amandi*, probably the earliest of the Frankish annals, is the year 'when the Saxons devastated the land of the Chatuariori' (the region between the Rhine and the Meuse rivers) and 720 the year in which 'Charles waged war against the Saxons'.[4] At first these notes were written between the lines or in the margins of the Easter tables. These tables, of which probably every monastery possessed a copy, were drawn up on the basis of the astronomical calculations to determine the date of Easter made in Rome in the sixth century by the Scythian monk Dionysius Exiguus. He adopted the old Alexandrian method of calculating Easter in relation to the first full moon after the vernal equinox, and formed a cycle of 532 years from 28 cycles of 19 years. All these years were carefully tabulated in the Easter tables, usually at first with a cycle of nineteen years to each page. The earliest tables included columns for the year of the Incarnation, the Indiction, the Epacts, concurrents and lunar cycles as well as the dates of Easter and days of the moon. Their purpose was solely to fix the day of Easter and no room was left for notes, which was why they had to be crammed between the lines and in the margins. The Stuttgart manuscript of the Annals of Weingarten is typical of such an arrangement.

ANŃ DŃI	INDICT.	EPACT̄	CONC̄.	CYCL̄. LUŃ.	
dcclxxviiii	II	NULLE	IIII	XVII	Iterū Karol' in saxoniā fames magna et mortalitas in Francia
dcclxxx	III	XI	VI	XVII	Saxonia capta est

After a while the notices of events became more important and other parts of the table less essential, so that tables were drawn up containing only the year of the Incarnation on the left and the date of Easter on the right, with the space in between left blank for the insertion of notes. Gradually the nineteen-year cycle to a page arrangement was modified, years without notes were omitted, and the notes themselves became much fuller and more detailed and in time developed into a form of historical writing in their own right. The notes had no historical pretensions however, but were simply a memorandum, either contemporary or near contemporary, of events. Entries continued to be random in the earlier Frankish annals; notices concerning famine, the death of an abbot, the new campaigns of a king and an eclipse of the sun follow one another in rapid succession.

Annals appeared on the Continent for the first time in the eight century, and although the manuscripts containing the earliest are from the Rhine–Meuse region where the Carolingian family was strongest, there is no necessary connection between the appearance in time or place of these early compilations and that of the annal as a form of historical writing. Because the Roman method of calculating Easter devised by Dionysius Exiguus was accepted by the Synod of Whitby in 664 and Bede subsequently wrote *De temporibus* and *De temporum ratione* which both made clear to the clergy the principles underlying the calculation of the date of Easter and did much to introduce the practice of dating events by the year of the Incarnation, and because Bede's two works and the Easter tables were probably brought to the Continent by the Anglo-Saxon missionaries, the beginning of annal making has also been ascribed to them. How much influence, if any, Anglo-Saxon or even Irish annal writing had on the Frankish, cannot be determined. Certainly Easter tables with annal entries and Bede's *De temporum ratione* are often juxtaposed in the manuscripts, as in the ninth-century Valenciennes BM 343 (though the entries in this case date from the middle of the tenth century). Nevertheless, the habit of making annal entries need not have been introduced by the Anglo-Saxons. The early annal entries are so terse, based so exclusively upon events impinging upon the life of the abbey, that they may have been no more than natural reactions (like the commemoration of the death of an abbot or the recording of some items of news received from a passing traveller) to events of local importance.

Frankish annals may be divided into two main groups, the minor or little annals which were the more primitive form, and the major annals, displaying a more sophisticated form of historical writing. The most representative of these are the Royal Frankish Annals and their successors. The little annals for the most part cover a good deal of the eighth century and the early years of the ninth, and a very few were continued down to the tenth century. They can be divided into four main groups according to their probable place of origin: those from the region of Cologne and Trier (for example *Annales Sancti Amandi* 687, 703–810, *Annales Tiliani*, 708–867, and *Annales Laubacenses* 708–926), those possibly from Metz (for example *Annales Mosellani* 703–98 and *Annales Petaviani* 708–99), those for the Murbach region, Alsace and Swabia (for example *Annales Guelferbytani* 741–805 and *Annales Nazariani* 708–90), and annals from the Salzburg and Bavarian areas (for example *Annales Salisburgenses* and *Annales Invavenses*). None of the original manuscripts of these annals is extant; most have come down to us in later copies, and some, as in the case of the earliest of them, the *Annales Sancti Amandi*, in the seventeenth-century edition made of them.[5]

Moreover, we cannot be sure when the annals were written and by whom. In other words, there is no obvious way of telling how near in time the annals are to the events they describe. A further problem is the close resemblance of the many collections of annal entries (Monod listed forty-one of varying importance in 1898) to each other. The same incidents are recorded in similar language each year. Monod and most historians after him have attributed this to their method of composition. It is suggested that Easter tables containing annalistic material circulated between abbeys and churches to provide information and to be copied and that numerous 'copying mistakes', such as mis-spelling, the use of a different tense or person of a verb and the insertion of adjectives or alternative words are to be explained by this manner of compo-sition. An image is thus evoked of zealous and historically minded monks trav-elling between their monasteries carrying annals with them to copy. The notion is unsatisfactory. The identity of annal entries in two collections from different monasteries would clearly suggest communication between the two, but even then one monastery may have copied from another's collection at a much later date. The similarity of an account of any event, however, is not enough to suggest constant copying, though it does not rule out oral communication of contemporary news, Writers of annals with the same education, the same lim-ited, miserable, vocabulary, governed moreover by conventions of expression, living in the same region and recording the same event for any one year, are bound to sound very similar. Hoffman's reminder that the annalists' limited command of Latin and their use of stock phrases make it dangerous to seek their identity should warn us too against assuming too readily that similarities between sets of annals proves their affiliation.[6] Resemblances between the minor annals have also made some scholars ask whether they are dependent on one another or on a third 'lost work'.[7] In recent years the 'lost work' theory has lost favour as being too contrived a solution. The uncertainty concerning the annals' value as historical evidence would increase if the possibility of unknown sources had to be taken into account.

The minor annals' chief value as an historical source is that although they were probably not written year by year they are generally either very close in time or contemporary with the events they describe. The years 785–798 of the *Annales Mosellani*, which run from 703 to 798, are a contemporary report. So too the famous Lorsch Annals, not from Lorsch but written in Alemannia, are not only contemporary with the years they describe, 794–803, but also survive in the original manuscript, now in Vienna. In this manuscript each year is entered by a different hand, so that there is neither one scribe nor necessarily one author. The Lorsch Annals are of great interest because of the independent account they give of the coronation of Charlemagne in 800.[8] Sometimes too annals may provide insight into events or even just the outlook of a particular region, as is the case with the *Chronicon Moissiacense* compiled in Aquitaine. As a group, the importance of the minor annals is diminished by the fact that the compilers of the Royal Frankish Annals and other annal compilations made in the ninth century drew on them for details concerning the eighth century to such an extent that there are only a few instances where the evidence of the minor annals is at variance with the information contained in the Royal Frank-ish Annals. These too acted as a source for compilers. The *Annales Mettenses Priores* for example, which cover the years 678–830, draw on various minor annals up to the year 802, the account for 803–5 is the author's own, later interpolated, and from then until 829 he depends on the Royal Frankish Annals.[9]

The Royal Frankish Annals, or *Annales regni Francorum*, are the most important single narrative source for Carolingian history. Originally called the *Annales Laurissenses maiores*, their name was changed when von Ranke drew attention to their 'official' nature and the Carolingian point of view they express. The annals run from 741 to 829 and are then continued separately in the west and east Frankish kingdoms from 830. The western continuation, the Annals of St Bertin, is continued to 882 and the eastern, the Annals of Fulda, to 887 with a further addition taking it to 901. The entries are far more detailed than those of the minor annals but are still organized on a yearly basis. That the Royal Frankish Annals drew on earlier 'minor' annal entries for its own notes as far as 788 or so, and that from that date to 793 the entries represent a first-hand account is now generally accepted. The eminent French scholar Louis Halphen, however, wished to reverse the relationship and suggested that the minor annals were simply later abbreviations of the Royal Frankish Annals, a suggestion which also put the date from which the annals could be considered as a contemporary account back to 768, but this view has not received much support.[10] It is possible that more than one hand worked on the section between 788 and 793, and that between 793 and 807 is also not a unified record by one single author, although the Latin has a definite style. In the next section, from 808 to 829, there seems to be a change of author at 820, and the entries for the following nine years are thought to be by Hilduin, abbot of St Denis, who became archchaplain at the court of Louis the Pious at Aachen, and left in disgrace in 830 because of his opposition to Louis' second wife Judith. Malbos suggested that Helisachar, archchancellor to Louis, collaborated with Hilduin on this section, on the grounds that the arguments in favour of Hilduin's authorship would also fit Helisachar.[11] No agreement has been reached about the authorship of this or the earlier sections. During the reign of Louis the Pious a revised version of the entries from 741 to 812 was made; the Latin style was improved and the account was augmented from other now lost or unknown sources which do not appear in other annals and which included some details about the less happy moments of Charlemagne's reign. The entries for the years 741, 746, 747, 753, 755, 769, 775, 778, 783, 786, 790, 793 and 799 are either completely or largely altered, and most editors indicate the contribution of the reviser in their texts. The revision was once attributed to Einhard but is now attributed to no one with any certainty, although its author was probably someone from the court circle of Charlemagne.

The manuscript tradition of the Royal Frankish Annals is rather complicated. There are five different groups of manuscripts containing the text, numbered A to E by most editors, each identified by the variant readings of the text common to members of its group. The members of group C are the most important and include Leningrad F.v.IV.4, a tenth-century collection of historical texts including the annals and Einhard's Life of Charlemagne, copied from a copy made for Charles the Bald, and St Omer 706, the only manuscript in the tradition which contains the complete annals to 882. The revised version is contained in the manuscripts belonging to group E. The Poet Saxo had a text covering the years 772–801 from this group before him from which he drew the material for his historical poem in celebration of Charlemagne.[12] None of these manuscripts is the original.

It is now generally agreed that from 788 the Royal Frankish Annals were composed under the aegis of the palace chaplain. When Hilduin of St Denis was disgraced, Fulk, abbot of the monasteries of St Hilary of Poitiers, St Wandrille and St Remigius at Rheims, a partisan of Louis and (after Ebbo of Rheims' deposition) suffragan bishop of Rheims with the administration of the diocese in his charge, seems to have taken over and written the entries for 830–5. These form the first section of the continuation to the royal annals known as the Annals of St Bertin, because St Bertin is the provenance of the earliest manuscript, St Omer 706. The entries from 835 to 861 are the work of a well-read man; they are written in a clear style which always refers to the towns by their classical names. Hincmar of Rheims tells us that Prudentius, bishop of Troyes, was responsible for this section of the annals.[13] After Prudentius' death in 861 Hincmar himself continued the annals until his death in 882, and inserted letters and *acta* either in their entirety or in part throughout his account. Hincmar's political acumen and his position in the kingdom make his account very valuable. For the period 840–82 therefore, the Annals of St Bertin provide a rich source for Frankish history, particularly for the reign of Charles the Bald. The western annals are more informative and more critical of the king's policies, particularly when Hincmar was writing them, than the eastern annals, which were continued as part of the Annals of Fulda up to 887. These are a much more personal account and are connected with the archbishops of Mainz rather than with the court and the archchaplain of the east Frankish kings. Unfortunately, like the Royal Frankish Annals, the Annals of St Bertin and the Annals of Fulda are no longer extant in the original manuscripts. The oldest manuscript of the Annals of St Bertin, St Omer 706, dates from the mid-tenth century and was probably written at Rheims. A seventeenth-century copy of the annals for 839–63, BN Mélanges Colbert 46,2 ff 283–313, made by Rosweyd and sent by Bolland to André Duchesne in 1638, preserves a much better text, which is thought to have been taken from either Hincmar's own copy or a copy of it.

After the Annals of St Bertin, history writing was no longer directly related to the Carolingian rulers. Richer, a monk of Rheims, wrote a history covering the period 888–995 during the archepiscopate of Gerbert (afterwards Pope Sylvester II), and presented it as a continuation of Hincmar's annals. It is, however, rather different in style and method from the annals, the influence of Sallust is evident, and its main preoccupations are no longer the fortunes of the Carolingian kings.[14] Regino of Prüm in Lotharingia also wrote a Chronicle for the years 876–906; it is not an official account and he added a universal chronicle beginning with the Incarnation, but it does portray the particular 'aristocratic ethic' of the Franks which had not appeared in Christian and Latin literature hitherto.[15]

It is the close association between the development of the annals and the rise to power and success of the Carolingian kings which make them such an important source, as well as, of course, a biased one. Nearly all the annals are pro-Carolingian; the take-over by the Carolingians from the Merovingians is seen as a matter of good sense. As the Carolingians became more firmly established, patriotic annalists wished to record the earlier stages of their rise to power. The *Annales Mettenses Priores*, for example, were compiled to glorify the Carolingian house, and to interpret their success as a natural development from the achievements of their noble ancestors.

This long account of the annals has been given not only because they are the most informative and coherent of the narrative sources for Frankish history, but also because the difficulties of their interpretation, their undoubted bias in favour of the Carolingian rulers, the uncertainties and disputes over dating and provenance, the problems of origin, authorship and revision and the complexities of the manuscript tradition typify the problems of nearly every piece of Frankish written source material. In most cases a consideration of what manuscripts are extant, how old they are, their origin and the reasons for their production are of crucial importance.

As well as the narrative sources directly related to the Carolingian rulers, there are a number of independent chronicles and histories which provide information about particular regions as well as slightly more objective references to the kings themselves. The most important of these are the histories of abbeys and bishoprics, inspired by the *Liber Pontificalis*, a collection of biographies of the early medieval popes, which is particularly full of detail for the eighth and ninth centuries; after the seventh century it was written up by papal biographers from time to time so that the entries are roughly contemporary with the events they describe.[16] The oldest history of a Frankish bishopric is Paul the Deacon's history of the bishops of Metz, *Gesta Episcoporum Mettensium*, composed after 783, and the oldest and most interesting abbey history is that of the abbey of St Wandrille or Fontanelle, *Gesta sanctorum patrum Fontanellensis Coenobium*, which covers the years 649–850. It provides information about the Carolingians and the monastery's relations with them as well as details about the abbots of St Wandrille. The history also preserves invaluable documents and notes concerning gifts to the abbey such as those given to the abbey by Abbot Wando (742–7) and the will of Abbot Ansegisus (823–33), the abbot famous for the collection he made of the royal capitularies in 826. The history was written in four sections and was never completed; the last section was written between 850 and 867.[17] Other abbey and episcopal histories are also of considerable importance, such as Folcuin's *Gesta abbatum Sancti Bertini Sithiensium*, Flodoard's History of Rheims or Aldric of Le Mans's *Gesta* of the bishops of Le Mans, all of which to a greater or a lesser extent make the narrative a framework for charters, letters and *acta* relevant to the history of the abbey or see. Flodoard's History and his annals are among the main narrative sources for the tenth century in the west Frankish kingdom.

There are, too, a number of monastic annals of the ninth and tenth century, the most important of which are the Xanten Annals, discovered by the German scholar Pertz in a manuscript in the British Library, and the Annals of St Vaast d'Arras, both of which contain much material concerning the raids of the

Northmen in the second half of the ninth century. One vivid eye-witness account of the raids of the Northmen is the description in verse by Abbo, a monk of St-Germain-des-Prés, of the siege of Paris in 885–6. Historical poems such as this, the 'Paderborn epic' or the poem on Louis the Pious by Ermold the Black add colour to the drier content of the annals.[18] The few biographies extant also provide a rather more intimate knowledge of some of the Carolingian rulers; Einhard's Life of Charlemagne retains its value despite its obvious debt to Suetonius,[19] and Notker's account of the deeds of Charlemagne, while adding little that is certain to the knowledge of Charlemagne, is nevertheless of great interest for the picture it presents of the ideal Frankish king and the implications it has for the political atmosphere at the end of the ninth century.[20]

But the best insight into the character of some of the Franks is to be gained from their correspondence. A great many letters have survived, sometimes only one or two from a particular writer, but there are also a number of large collections of great interest for the Carolingian period, the most important of which are the letters of Boniface of Mainz, Alcuin, Lupus of Ferrières, Hincmar, archbishop of Rheims, and Gerbert of Rheims. It is important to remember that letters in the Middle Ages were almost public literary documents; they were written not only to inform or to entertain someone else, but also to be communicated to a wider audience and with the possibility of future collections and 'publication' in mind. This presents obvious difficulties for the historian.[21] The letters of the Merovingian Bishop Desiderius of Cahors were collected together in the Carolingian period by a monk who also wrote his life, Boniface's letters were collected together in both England and the Frankish kingdoms, and the collection of papal letters made at the Carolingian court in 791, the *Codex Carolinus*, has already been mentioned.

It seems that Alcuin made a collection of his own letters for himself, and his letters were certainly used afterwards as models of epistolary style as well as being preserved for their didactic content and as a source for meditation and inspiration. Two such collections of Alcuin's letters are to be found: BL Cotton Vespasian A XIV, comprising twenty-four letters in all, and a further collection made for his friend Arno, bishop of Salzburg, which is in Vienna (MS 795) and contains in addition to the letters, many of which are expositions of some part of the Scriptures, a personal selection of the exegesis of Augustine, Jerome and others, mostly on the Epistles of St Paul, which was compiled in about 799. It is a very fine codex and interesting too for the light it sheds on Arno's interests, quite apart from the texts it contains. Most of Alcuin's letters were written in the last few years of his life, and the ones that have survived are those he wrote once he had settled in the Frankish kingdom. They tell us much of the literary and theological preoccupations of his day, as well as a personal view not only of Charlemagne himself, but also of the court and kingdom as a whole.[22]

The letters of Lupus of Ferrières have been closely studied for what they suggest about his interest in classical literature and learning, but there is much in them concerning monastic affairs and his involvement in the political life of the kingdom. His relationship with Charles the Bald appears to have been similar to that between Alcuin and Charlemagne, so that Lupus' letters are a useful source for the history of that reign. Hincmar's letters, too, are of vital importance and reveal a strong, rumbustious and argumentative character embroiled in the affairs of the kingdom and the church. Gerbert's letters are a rich source for the late tenth century, particularly for what they reveal of the relations between the east and west Frankish kingdoms at this time.

Apart from letters and biographies, direct evidence for the Franks·as individuals is rare and has to be culled from a wide variety of sources. One treatise, however, which acquaints us with a Frankish noblewoman of the mid-ninth century is the Manual of Dhuoda, written at Uzès in Aquitaine by Dhuoda, wife of Count Bernard of Septimania between 841 and 843 and addressed to their eldest son William. The Manual sets out to direct Dhuoda's son's life and morals, to instil the manners and piety essential for a man of his rank, and to urge him to be loyal both to the king and to his God. Dhuoda, to judge by her writing, was remarkably well read and cultured. Her Manual, like the extant catalogues of the libraries of three lay aristocrats, provides some notion of the interests and level of culture of some at least among the laity.[23] For the most part, information such as this is rare; most of the source material is ecclesiastical in origin.

Even the greater part of the architectural and archaeological evidence for the Carolingian period has to do with the church; little is known about domestic architecture and daily life, and what is known is derived for the most part from literary rather than archaeological evidence. Not many Carolingian buildings have survived. There are a number of churches, the finest of which of course is the great palace chapel at Aachen built during Charlemagne's reign, [24] but most of them were pulled down or transformed during the great years of cathedral building in the eleventh, twelfth and thirteenth centuries. Excavation work becomes difficult if not impossible, and again resort has to be had to the literary sources to fill out the archaeological evidence, with the many pitfalls of interpretation that this can entail, archaeologists supporting their findings from the literary sources and historians interpreting their literary sources in light of the archaeological evidence!

Perhaps the best known of the Carolingian churches is the abbey of St Denis, the first definitely dated Carolingian church. Construction to replace the Merovingian church of St Denis was probably begun during Pippin's reign, so that it is likely that Pippin was crowned in 754 in the old church of St Denis, a fact which emphasized the link between Merovingian and Carolingian rulership. Like the Merovingian kings, many of the Carolingian kings were buried in St Denis. According to a diploma of Charlemagne the new church was dedicated in 775. Fulrad was abbot at the time of the consecration of the new church, and some of the structure of Fulrad's church was excavated before and after the last war, as was the chapel of Hilduin, abbot of St Denis, added in about 832. Only a portion of the ground plan of St Denis is known with any certainty and there is almost no literary evidence concerning the appearance of the Carolingian abbey of St Denis until the time of Abbot Suger, who was the architect of the rebuilding of the abbey in the eleventh century and who referred in passing to various features of the older building in his account of the construction of the new one. Excavation to establish the details of St Denis has been made extraordinarily difficult, not only by the destruction of or additions to the structure of the Carolingian church made from the eleventh to the thirteenth centuries and the damage wreaked during or as a consequence of the French Wars of Religion, but also by the various works of 'restoration' and alteration in the eighteenth and nineteenth centuries which have undermined and often completely transformed the earlier structures, even that of the abbey of Suger. The main restoration work of the nineteenth century was carried out by Viollet le Duc, who did much valuable work and left plans and drawings of what he found and what he did. It is thanks to him that St Denis still stands today, but he created a great number of problems for the archaeologist nevertheless.[25]

The Carolingian period was a most productive one for the construction of both palaces and monasteries. Construction of the palace complex at Aachen began in about 792 and the chapel at least was more or less completed by 805. The complex (a model of it was built by Hugot for the Council of Europe exhibition on Charlemagne in 1965) included buildings to accommodate the royal household, royal officials and guests, gardens, a menagerie, and baths fed by Aachen's hot springs. The largest of the baths could hold 100 bathers. The crowning glory of Aachen was the magnificent vaulted and octagonal chapel designed by Odo of Metz and decorated with rich mosaics, marble columns and bronze parapets. Charlemagne's throne was set in the west gallery facing the altar. The palace chapel at Aachen still survives in all its splendour, though it was restored in 983 and 1881. Another important complex of buildings was the royal palace at Ingelheim near Mainz and the Rhine, begun under Charlemagne (his first recorded stay there is in 774) and completed under Louis the Pious, for whom it was particularly important. Louis usually spent the summer at Ingelheim and the winter at Aachen. The range of buildings comprised two courts, the smaller of which was semicircular, with a great hall and large chapel. All the buildings were connected by arched galleries. Ermold the Black provides us with a vivid description of the magnificence and labyrinthine scale of Ingelheim; the great hall was decorated with frescos or mosaics (we are not sure which) of the great heroes of Greece and Rome, including Remus, Hannibal and Alexander the Great, with on the opposite wall the no less great barbarian heroes Theodoric, Charles Martel, Pippin and Charlemagne. Excavations started before the First World War at Ingelheim by Clemen and continued in the 1950s, 1960s and 1970s by Sage and others have uncovered a great range of buildings which accord with Ermold's description. Not all their functions can be determined and many of them were added after the first phase of building had been completed under Louis the Pious. After Louis' death, Ingelheim ceased to be of such central importance to the Carolingian kings for some decades, but it became a favourite centre for the Saxon kings in the tenth century.[26]

There is information in some of the texts concerning the churches of St Peter at Fontanelle or St Wandrille, Centula-St Riquier, Fulda, Corbie, St Germigny-des-Prés, and St Martin at Angers among others. A drawing of the three churches and cloister of St Riquier made before the reconstruction work of 1071–97 survives in an engraving made of it in 1612, so that we have some idea of what a complete Carolingian church looked like, as well as those parts of buildings which survive.[27] All Carolingian churches reflect developments in the liturgy as well as developments in architecture, with such innovations as the Westworks, ambulatories, and the provision of altars and little side chapels to answer the needs of the growing cult of relics. But because little is known except in bare outline about late Carolingian building and still less about Merovingian churches, there is still considerable uncertainty concerning the development of Carolingian architecture. One ground plan of a monastic complex once supposed to be an actual builder's blueprint is the 'St Gall' plan, extant in St Gall Stiftsbibliothek 1092, which was sent by Haito, bishop of Basle, to Gozbert, abbot of St Gall, in about 820.[28] The plan is very detailed and appears to be a direct copy of the original. It was drawn with red ink on five pieces of parchment sewn together, and every aspect of the life of a monastery seems to have been catered for, from the abbey church down to the beds in the monks' dormitory and the coops for the hens and geese. The monastery was expected to be virtually self-sufficient, and was provided moreover with guest house, schools, infirmary, cemetery and herb garden. Each part of the plan is carefully labelled and its scale is on a ratio of 1 : 192, that is, one-sixteenth of a Carolingian inch corresponds to a Carolingian foot (about 34 centimetres). The plan is now accepted as a representation of the ideal monastery, a visible expression of monastic life according to the resolutions made at the Council of Aachen in 817, for it reflects that council's interpretation of St Benedict's Rule. The plan is nevertheless drawn with sufficient precision to suggest that it could be used as a building blueprint and is thus a testimony to both Carolingian aspirations for the monastic life and Carolingian technical skill.

Manuscripts themselves can be informative about the Franks not only for their content but because of the way in which they were written and the person or abbey to whom they may have belonged. The development of the script known as Caroline minuscule will be discussed in detail in Chapter Six; here I simply wish to stress how important a type of historical evidence script can be in itself. Caroline minuscule had its origin in the west Frankish kingdom; it started to emerge in the second half of the eighth century and developed rapidly in the early years of the ninth. Many important centres in the kingdom not only adopted the fine clear Caroline script but developed distinct types based upon its elements; in other words the script was far from being uniform despite its basic similarity, so that it becomes possible in many cases to distinguish which books were written in which centres, or at least in which part of the country, simply on the basis of the type of Caroline minuscule used.

The scripts of Tours, Cologne, Corbie, Lyons, Rheims, Laon and St Amand, for example, have been identified in the western region, as have those of many centres in the east, such as Lorsch, St Emmeram at Regensburg, Freising, Tegernsee, Murbach, Augsburg and Salzburg.[29] There are about 7000 Latin codices surviving from the ninth century in Western Europe as a whole compared to 1811 for the period up to AD 800 and the majority of these were written in the Frankish kingdoms. Among them are about 250 manuscripts from Tours, 200 or so from Corbie, 150 from Rheims, which had 2 or 3 *scriptoria*, 80 from Regensburg and 90 from Salzburg. At least 60 other scriptoria are known to have been active and a few exceptional libraries had over 300 books by the end of the ninth century, although generally the numbers are much smaller.

To be able to determine the date and also to identify the origin of a manuscript from its handwriting is of the utmost importance when dealing with a text. Our knowledge of Carolingian manuscripts is still far from complete and such exactitude is not always possible, but Bernhard Bischoff of Munich is preparing a descriptive catalogue of all the ninth-century manuscripts extant which, added to the invaluable catalogue of E A. Lowe for Latin manuscripts prior to AD 800 already published, will be of inestimable value for Carolingian studies. Quite apart from the precision the palaeographical study of a manuscript can give to knowledge of a text, the production of manuscripts in different centres sheds a great deal of light on the importance, wealth and intellectual activity of those centres and on the process and progress of education and learning in the Frankish kingdoms.

On the basis of the clues yielded by the script and content of a manuscript, it is possible to work out the particular interests of a centre, what sort of books they read and copied, how large the scriptorium was and, in the cases of annotated manuscripts, who read the books and what was found interesting in them. Many Carolingian manuscripts remain in the places where they were written even today, as in the case with the books of Cologne, Laon, St Gall or Lyons. But it is not always so; codices from a particular centre may now be scattered far and wide, and be very difficult both to trace and identify. In some cases the books may simply have been moved, as is the case with many French monastic libraries, from the monastery to the nearest municipal library or else the National Library as a result of the secularization of church property. The manuscripts of St Amand, for example, were moved from the abbey to the municipal library at Valenciennes in 1790 and the books belonging to the monasteries of Bavaria were moved to the then Königliche Bibliothek in Munich, now the Bayerische Staatsbibliothek. Codices from libraries may also have left the centre in which they were produced long before they were acquired by the state. Twenty books from St Amand were taken by the archbishop of Rheims, Le Tellier, in 1700 and some of them later found their way into the Bibliothèque Nationale in Paris, but St Amand also produced manuscripts for export to other monasteries and sees in the ninth century, so that products of the scriptorium are now scattered in ones and twos as far afield as Cambrai, Copenhagen, Douai, Ghent, London, Leningrad, Munich, New York, Oxford, Paris, Rheims, Rome, Stockholm, Stuttgart, Tours, Troyes and Vienna.

The provenance of a manuscript, that is, the place where it now is or was once for a time, can sometimes be a clue to its origin. Many of the manuscripts of Lorsch, for example, were at one time in the Palatine library at Heidelberg which went to the Vatican in 1623. Some of the Lorsch manuscripts are in Oxford as part of Archbishop Laud's collection, acquired as a result of the same war which brought them into the hands of the Elector Palatine. In some cases there are early catalogues of the libraries extant, which assist in identifying manuscripts from the scriptorium. There are for instance four ninth-century catalogues extant of the Lorsch library. Other means of identification are the ex-libris notes on some books which are of assistance in determining provenance at least, but ultimately it is the physical features of the books themselves, of which a well-established style of script is the principal criterion, which determine their origin. Not that complete certainty can always be reached; there are many manuscripts whose attribution remains doubtful, whose handwriting does not quite conform to the known 'house style' of a centre, or which reveals characteristics of another centre's house style which may be evidence of association between the two. Nevertheless, the Frankish codices extant are the richest, most valuable and certainly the most fascinating of the sources for the Carolingian period.

It has only been possible to give a brief description of part of the wealth of material available concerning the history of the Franks, as well as some of the problems involved in the study of it. How the sources may be interpreted will be evident from the chapters which follow.

NOTES

1. W. Wattenbach, W. Levison and H. Lowe, *Deutschlands Geschichtsquellen im Mittelalter* (Weimar 1953–): G. Monod, *Etudes critiques sur les sources de l'histoire carolingienne* (Paris 1898); A. Molinier, *Les sources de l'histoire de France* (Paris 1901); R. C. van Caenegem, *Guide to the Sources of Medieval History* (Oxford 1978): L. Genicot, *Typologie des sources du Moyen Age* (Turnhout 1972–).
2. See P. Grierson, *Monnaies du moyen âge* (Fribourg 1976) and 'The coinage of Charlemagne', *KdG* I, 501–36.
3. F. Unterkircher, *Codex epistolaris Carolinus*, Österreichische Nationalbibliothek 449 (Graz 1962) (Facsimile). Text ed. P. Jaffé.
4. *MGH SS* I, 6.
5. Published by André Duchesne from an unidentified manuscript in 1638. Text reprinted in *MGM SS* I, 6–14. See M. McCormick, *Les Annales du Haut Moyen Age* (Turnhout 1975).
6. H. Hoffmann, *Untersuchungen zur karolingischen Annalistik* (Bonn 1958).
7. For example, F. Kurze, *Die karolingische Annalen bis zum Tode Einhards* (Berlin 1913).
8. F. Unterkircher, *Das Wiener Fragment der Lorscher Annalen, Christus und die Samariterin und Katechesa des Niceta von Remesiana* (Graz 1967) (facsimile).
9. B. von Simson (ed.) (Hannover and Leipzig 1905), and see I. Haselbach, *Aufstieg und Herrschaft der Karlinger und der Darstellung der sogenannten Annales Mettenses Priores* (Lubeck 1970) and compare Hoffmann, *Untersuchungen*.
10. L. Halphen, *Etudes critiques sur l'histore de Charlemagne* (Paris 1921). Compare

R. L. Poole, *Chronicles and Annals* (Oxford 1926), who summarizes the debate to 1925.

11. 'L' annaliste royal sous Louis le Pieux', *MA*72 (1966), 225–33.

12. B. Bischoff, 'Das Thema des Poeta Saxo', *Speculum Historiale. Festschrift J. Spörl* L. Boehm, C. Boehm, C. Bauer and M. Müller (eds.) (Munich 1965), 198–203.

13. J. L. Nelson, 'The Annals of St Bertin', *Charles the Bald: court and kingdom* J. L. Nelson and M. T. Gibson (eds.) (Oxford 1981), 15–36. On Fulco's identity see P. Grierson, 'Abbot Fulco and the date of the *Gesta abbatum Fontanellensium*', *EHR* 55 (1940), 275–84. See also F. L. Ganshof, 'Notes critiques sur les *Annales Bertiniani*', *Mélanges dediés à la memoire de Félix Grat* (Paris 1949), 159–74.

14. R. Latouche, 'Un imitateur de Sallust au xe siècle, l'historien Richer', *Annales de l'Université de Grenoble* 6 (1929), 289–305.

15. H. Lowe, 'Regino von Prüm und das historische Weltbild der Karolingerzeit' *RhV* 17 (1952), 151–79 and K-F. Werner, 'Zur Arbeitsweise des Regino von Prüm', *Welt als Geschichte* 2 (1959), 96–116. See also E. R. Labande, 'L'historiographie de la France de l'Ouest au xe et xie siècles', *Settimane* 17 (1970), 751–91 and R. H. Bautier, 'L' Historiographie en France au xe et xie siècles', *Settimane* 17 (1970), 793–850.

16. L. Duchesne, *Etude sur le Liber Pontificalis* (Paris 1877).

17. F. Lot, *Etudes critiques sur l'abbaye de Saint-Wandrille* (Paris 1913) and see Grierson, art. cit., *EHR* 55 (1940) and W. Levison, 'Zu den *Gesta abbatum Fontanellensium*', *Revue Bénédictine* 44 (1934), 241–64.

18 H. Beumann, F. Brunhölzl and W. Winkelmann, *Karolus Magnus et Leo Papa: ein Paderborner Epos vom Jahre 799* (Paderborn 1966).

19. F. L. Ganshof, 'L' Historiographie dans la monarchie Franque sous les Mérovingiens et les Carolingiens. Monarchie franque unitaire et Francie occidentale', *Settimane* 17 (1970) 631–85.

20. L. Halphen, 'Etudes critiques sur l'histoire de Charlemagne. IV Le moine de Saint-Gall', *Revue Historique* 128 (1918). 260–98, and H. Lowe, 'Das Karlsbuch Notkers von St Gallen und sein Zeitgeschichtlichen Hintergrund', *Schweizerische Zeitschrift für Geschichte* 20 (1970), 269a–302.

21. G. Constable, *Letters and Letter Collections* (Turnhout 1976).

22. C. Chase, *Two Alcuin Letter Books from the British Museum MS Cotton Vespasian A.XIV* (Toronto 1975); F. Unterkircher, *Alkuin-Briefe und andere Traktate im Auftrage des Salzburg Erzbischof Arnum 799 zu einem Sammelband vereinigt.* Codex Vindobonensis 795 der Österreichischen Nationalbibliothek (Graz 1969) (facsimile).

23. P. Riché, 'Les bibliothèques de trois aristocrates laïques', *MA* 69 (1963). 87–104.

24. G. Bandmann, 'Die Vorbilder der Aachener Pfalzkapelle', *KdG* III.424–62: F. Kreusch, 'Kirche, Atrium und porticus der Aachener Pfalz'. *KdG* III, 463–533 and L. Hugot, 'Die Pfalz Karls des Grossen in Aachen', *KdG* III, 534–72.

25. S. McK. Crosby, *The Abbey of St Denis* (New Haven 1942), and J. Formigé, *L'abbaye royale de St Denis; recherches nouvelles* (Paris 1960).

26. On palaces see P. Riché, *Daily Life in the World of Charlemagne* trs. J. A. McNamara (Philadelphia 1978), 41–7; J. Autenrieth (ed), *Ingelheim-am-Rheim* (Stuttgart 1964); W. Sage, 'Zur archaelolgischen Untersuchung karolingischer Pfalzen in Deutschland', *KdG* III, 323–35 and *idem.* 'Die Ausgrabungen in der Pfalz zu Ingelheim am Rhein 1960–1970', *Francia* 4 (1976) 141–60.

27. K. Conant, *Carolingian and Romanesque Architecture, 800 –1200* (Harmondsworth

1973), 43–6: illustrated in J. Hubert, H. Porcher and W. Volbach, *The Carolingian Age* (London 1970), facing p. 1.

28. E. Born and W. Horn, *The Plan of St Gall* (Berkeley 1979) and their references.

29. See for example B. Bischoff, *Die Südostdeutsche Schreibschulen und Bibliotheken in der Karolingerzeit*, 3rd edn. (Wiesbaden 1974), and *Lorsch im Spiegel seiner Handschriften* (Munich 1974).

CHAPTER TWO

From *major domus* to *rex francorum*: the Emergence of the Carolingians

By 613, when the Arnulfing or Carolingian family is mentioned for the first time in the Chronicle of Fredegar, the ruling dynasty of Frankish kings, the Merovingians, had ruled a mixed population in Gaul, mostly composed of Franks and 'Gallo-Romans' for over a century. Gaul had become an important, and rich, province of the Roman Empire after its conquest by Julius Caesar, and since that time many Romans, aristocrats, army veterans and civilians from south of the Alps had settled or had been settled there. They mingled with the indigenous Celtic population to some extent and a mixed Roman and Gallic ruling class emerged, of which the senatorial aristocracy and the bishops were the acknowledged leaders. The Franks, a confederacy of Germanic peoples of obscure origin, make their first appearance in the literary sources in the third century. They are mentioned in the context of the great barbarian invasion of Gaul during the reign of Gallienus; Aurelius Victor and Eutropius, for example, say the Franks crossed the Rhine near Cologne in about 257. The Franks were probably made up of small groups of those German tribes described in Tacitus's *Germania*. The Frankish people comprised several subgroups, the most important of which were the Salian Franks, who probably settled first in Belgium and who were permitted to occupy the region west of the Rhine as far south as the Loire, probably as *foederati*. (That is, they occupied Roman land on condition that they would only use their armies in the service of Rome.) Gregory of Tours in his history of the Franks provides meagre information about different groups of Franks under 'subkings' who were conquered by Clovis;[1] little remained of the distinction between groups of Franks by the Carolingian period.

In their position east of the Rhine in the third and fourth centuries the Franks had been in close contact with Roman civilization, a civilization they also encountered in Gaul as they occupied it gradually. The Gallo-Roman people had been assimilated into the Frankish by the mid-eighth century, and the Franks in their turn had adopted much that was Roman after their occupation of Gaul, an adaptation assisted perhaps by the fact that the Franks were in the minority. The most significant feature of their adaptation to Roman ways was the use of Latin both for official business and literary writing; even the Germanic customary laws were codified in Latin. The part the church played in the assimilation of Roman or at least Gallo-Roman culture by the Franks was crucial. Latin was the language of the church and of the Christian faith in the west and the Franks were converted to the Catholic creed of Christianity at the turn of the fifth century. The special position of the church and its clergy in relation to the Franks and in particular to the Frankish ruler was to be a vital factor in the subsequent development of the nation.

At the end of the fourth century the majority of the Franks were still east of the Rhine but by about 500 most of them had moved to the western side of the river. The territory ruled by Clovis, son of the first known Merovingian ruler Childeric, at his death in 511, included the whole of the region between the Loire and the Rhine as well as Aquitaine. The vast estates of the old Roman imperial fisc became the royal domain of the Merovingian kings and formed a considerable adjunct to their authority. The sons and grandsons of Clovis added Provence and Burgundy, Rhaetia, Alemannia and Thuringia. By the mid-sixth century the Franks ruled, or claimed to rule, the whole of Gaul except for Brittany in the west and Septimania in the south. They had extended their rule south of the Loire by means of a series of campaigns conducted by Clovis against the Visigoths between 496 and 507. Until the mid-sixth century the border between the Gothic and Frankish spheres of influence south of the Loire fluctuated; it was some time before effective royal control was established by the Merovingians in the area, and Aquitaine remained on the periphery of Frankish affairs throughout the sixth and seventh centuries. Merovingian kings who made their capitals in the south were Chramn (d. 561?), possibly Gundovald (583–5) and Charibert, who ruled from Toulouse between 629 and 632.[2] Much of the administration of the church and of the region south of the Loire as a whole seems to have been left in the hands of the Gallo-Roman aristocracy to a greater extent than elsewhere in the Frankish kingdom. Aquitaine was not included in the partition of rule between Pippin and Carloman, the sons of Charles Martel, in 741, and was not brought fully under Frankish control until 768.

In the first century of Merovingian rule in Gaul, Paris, Orleans, Rheims and Soissons had been the most important cities and were the centres of the kingdoms formed on Clovis' death. Metz and Chalon were also prominent. The partition of the Merovingian lands in 561 created the kingdoms of Austrasia, Neustria and Burgundy, a division of Francia or the Frankish heartland which was to endure throughout the seventh and first part of the eighth century. Occasionally one king, such as Chlothar II (583–629) or Dagobert I (621–37) ruled over all three kingdoms. Austrasia comprised the lands between the Seine (though it did not extend to the river) and the Rhine and included the Meuse and Moselle river valleys. The area later to be distinguished as Flanders, the northern Meuse region and Holland were included in Austrasia. It came of the fusion of the old kingdom of Soissons with the kernel of the kingdom of Paris after 567 (see Map 1). It was in the Moselle–Meuse region, moreover, that the landed wealth of the Carolingians was based. Neustria extended between the Seine and the Loire; possibly already by the seventh century Neustria was dominated by a dukedom centred on Le Mans which in 748 Pippin gave to his half-brother Grifo. In 790 Charlemagne gave it to his son Charles and in 838 Louis the Pious gave it to Charles the Bald. Burgundy consisted of the Rhône–Saône valley as far north as Toul and extending east into present-day Switzerland. It had developed from a combination of the kingdom of Orleans and the former territory of the Burgundians, conquered by the sons of Clovis. The region's main cities were Lyons, Vienne, Autun, Chalon and Sens.

Apart from the regions of Austrasia, Neustria and Burgundy which remained the principal divisions of the Frankish kingdom until the middle of the eighth century, some of the lands outside the Frankish territory were annexed in the course of the eighth century, mostly through the efforts of the Carolingian mayors of the palace. Bavaria before 788, for example, when Charlemagne defeated his cousin the Agilolfing Tassilo of Bavaria, had been in a state of some sort of dependence upon the Franks, but the ties were not strong and it is uncertain what they meant in terms of jurisdiction and political influence. After 788 however, Bavaria became a province of the Frankish kingdom, a fief of the Carolingian king, and all the Bavarian magnates were bound to the king by oath. Alemannia had been invaded by the Merovingian rulers and their armies; it had preserved some measure of independence, a manifestation of which was the production of a law code, probably under Duke Landfrid (d. 741), but the Etichonen dukes of Alemannia were finally vanquished by the Carolingian Pippin III.[3] Tribute had been received by the Franks from the Saxons in the form of 400 cows a year. This tribute ceased with Dagobert II in 631 but in 747–8 it was renewed, and paid to Pippin III, the mayor of the palace. The Saxons were eventually subdued by Charlemagne. The exact relationship between the Franks and the Bretons up to the ninth century is obscure. In 635 King Judicaël of Brittany submitted to Dagobert I, and according to the Chronicle of Fredegar undertook that he and his kingdom of Brittany should always acknowledge Dagobert and the Frankish kings as their lords. There is no evidence, however, that the Bretons took much notice of the undertaking. There is also little information about contact between the Bretons and the Franks until the former were defeated by the armies of Louis the Pious in 818.

The population of the Frankish kingdoms was clearly very diverse, and this diversity contributed to a richness and heterogeneity of culture which distinguished the Franks from the other barbarian peoples of Europe. As well as the surviving and eventually transformed Roman civilization and the religious and cultural influence of the Christian church, Germanic traditions remained a strong element in Frankish culture. Some distinctions between peoples, moreover, were preserved. The Burgundians, Alemannians, Bavarians and Saxons lived under their own laws, and these distinctions, political, cultural, economic and linguistic, as well as historical, were never entirely lost. The various regions of the Frankish kingdoms retained a certain sense of identity, which in time was to forge new political units as the hold of the Carolingian family over their huge domain became weaker.

It remains to consider the meaning of the term 'Francia' and to what it referred geographically or politically. Francia at first referred not to the whole kingdom of the Franks but only to that part of the country in which the people had settled as a compact group and which was the political centre of the kingdom. In other words it referred to the heartland of the Frankish kingdom, and comprised, roughly speaking, Austrasia and Neustria. The Merovingian partitions split Francia, but the partitions made in 768 by Pippin III no longer corresponded to the Merovingian division so that after 771 and the death of Charlemagne's brother Carloman Francia was united once more: a process Charlemagne assisted by leaving the heartland intact in the partition of 806, but creating a new division by giving the lands north of the Loire and Danube to his eldest son Charles. Austrasia and Neustria in the partition of 806 acquired a new meaning; they designated the two neighbouring Frankish lands which later on were sometimes called 'Francia media'. By 800 the extent of Carolingian Francia was settled and included the ecclesiastical provinces of Rheims and Trier but excluded the west of the diocese of Tours. The name Francia was also used in the chancery of Charles the Bald after 843 to signify the west Frankish kingdom formed at the partition of Verdun. The *Annales Bertiniani* mirror the terminology used in the charters issued from the royal chancery. Prudentius of Troyes, for example, used the name Francia only in the regional sense of the northern half of the west Frankish kingdom and so did Hincmar, archbishop of Rheims. The shrinkage of the west Frankish kingdom from the time of Odo (888–98) onwards probably increased the tendency to understand the name Francia as referring to the western kingdom north of the Loire.[4]

At the death of Charles Martel in 741, the Frankish kingdom extended north to the mouth of the Rhine and included the towns of Deventer, Utrecht, Dorestad and Nijmegen; to the east it included Thuringia and Alemannia as far as the river Lech and the cities of Eichstätt and Augsburg; to the southeast it extended to the Alps; in the south the kingdom reached to the Pyrenees but did not include either Septimania or Aquitaine; except for Brittany it reached west to the English Channel. Saxony, Bavaria, Lombard North Italy, Aquitaine, Gascony and Brittany were to be added later. Even at this point, however, it was a vast region to be controlled and administered.

Very little is, or can be, known about the size of population in the Frankish kingdoms before the ninth century; before about 800 there are too few surviving documents of any kind to say anything specific about the density of settlement or its distribution. Even after 800 information is derived from a few surveys, or polyptychs, of the great estates of the royal domain in the region between the Loire and the Rhine, such as the survey of the abbey of St Germain-des-Prés, the Polyptych of Irmino, compiled between 802 and 829, the survey of the abbey of St Bertin (844–8) or the *Capitulare de Villis* concerning the royal estates, issued by Charlemagne in 807.[5] Thus there is only evidence about some pockets of settlement within a limited area. That these estates were almost certainly the best endowed and most efficiently run of the Carolingian estates make it even more difficult to use the surveys as representative evidence for Carolingian economic and social life as a whole. Duby, Latouche, Riché and

Bloch should all be consulted for clear discussions of this evidence and its implications.[6]

Nevertheless, we know from what evidence there is, and from the testimony of the landscape itself and what it tells us of settlement patterns, agricultural practices and vegetation, that Frankish economy was primarily rural; the land and the demesne manor were the centre of economic and social life. Agriculture was carried out in small areas of cleared land surrounded by great tracts of forest, wilderness, heath and marshland, generally termed the 'waste'. The wilderness and forest were used for the pasturage of cattle, pigs and sheep, and the forest in particular was inhabited by wild animals of various kinds which provided both food and skins to supplement what could be gained from the arable. The forest was also the source of fuel, charcoal and building materials, wild fruit and wild honey. Large areas of land were assarted from the waste, that is forest and scrub land were brought under cultivation, particularly in the ninth century.[7]

Literary sources occasionally give glimpses of the wilderness of the forests, the poor communications and roads between one area of settlement and another, and the ever-present threat of robbers. The population as a whole was almost certainly small, mostly very sparse or concentrated in the cleared areas. Some information about the density of settlement in the Paris basin can be computed from the Polyptych of Irmino, which describes a population of twenty-six human beings to the square mile for the village of Palaiseu and thirty-five at Vernères both in the region of Paris, but even this may mean simply the number of workers rather than the number of people. Diet for the bulk of the population was both meagre and deficient if the slim surplus yield of crops at Annapes may be taken as representative. The bulk of each crop was required for the following years' seeding.[8] The fear of famine and its attendant disease was constant and often realized; the annals often refer to famine, terrible hunger, failed crops through drought or frost, and pestilence. Agricultural techniques were woefully inadequate. An unsatisfactory wooden plough without a mouldboard (the latter an essential addition for turning heavy soil) seems to have been the most commonly used piece of equipment for tilling the soil. Inventories of farm implements, even on the best run of the Carolingian estates such as those for which the *Capitulare de Villis* was intended, show that little iron was used in the manufacture of agricultural tools; most were made of wood. Not much is known about what the Franks ate (the only Carolingian cookery book surviving is a copy of the Roman author Apicius made at the abbey of St Martin of Tours, now Vatican Urb. lat. 1146), and most of our information is from monastic sources. Bread, made from rye, spelt, corn and oats as well as wheat, and other products of the grain such as ale, were the mainstays, with pulses, beans, cheese, eggs and perhaps chicken to supplement the diet.[9] There was meat and fish if the hunting and fishing were good, and on the larger estates, both secular and ecclesiastical, vegetables (legumes and roots), fruit, wine, honey and spices, were enjoyed as well. The diet of the majority was almost certainly deficient and the infant and female mortality rate high, but there is little specific or reliable evidence. The great estates tried to be self-sufficient, everything they needed being produced on their own lands. Clothes for example were spun, woven and sewn by the women from wool and flax produced on the estate.

Frankish society in the early Carolingian period was thus a poorly equipped agrarian society in which a great deal of labour was expended to scratch a bare living from the land, a society in which the ruling classes, both secular and ecclesiastical, probably had the best of it. Duby rather bitterly defined the man of power in the period as 'the man who could always eat as much as he wished'.[10] The lack of evidence which prevents us from knowing exactly how the peasants fared, however, is also an obstacle to knowledge of the 'lords'; any indictment of the latter on the basis of such meagre evidence would seem to be unwarranted. Most of the lay population on the estates was occupied in some pursuit related to agriculture, from the tilling of the soil to the manufacture of tools. The census of the town of Centula-St Riquier in 831, however, listed the *vici* or quarters in the town occupied by householders according to occupation: there were soldiers, cobblers, butchers, bakers, vintners (who supplied both wine and oil) merchants and innkeepers.[11] Not all the population therefore was tied to the soil; even though the Centula census is some eighty years after the period being considered in this chapter, the occupations are those to be expected in any predominantly rural society in which the people who were not agricultural labourers served a wide area with their crafts and trades. There are references elsewhere to stonemasons and carvers, builders, wood-carvers, furniture makers and carpenters, artisans and smiths of all kinds, even workers in precious metals, gold and silver, not to mention the artists and scribes, not always monks or nuns, who wrote and illuminated books, of whose work many splendid examples survive.

The question of the existence of towns in the Carolingian period is a difficult one. Too little evidence concerning many of the settlements of the eighth and ninth centuries survives to allow us to call them towns and we have little idea what they were like.[12] It is only in the tenth century that the evidence for mercantile activity in towns and for greater density of urban population increases appreciably. With the barbarian invasions the towns had ceased to be the central focuses of economic life; the manorial estates took their place, and it was sometimes only as a diocesan centre that a town continued to exist from the Gallo-Roman to the Carolingian period. This ecclesiastical character was intensified in the eighth and ninth centuries: sometimes a large proportion of a town's population could consist of priests and monks. Many of the more important episcopal sees such as Rheims, Sens, Paris, Tours, Orleans, Lyons, Worms, Mainz and Trier, had markets and mints and were the nuclei of the larger settlements which developed in the tenth and eleventh centuries. The population of these settlements in the eighth and ninth centuries was never more than a few thousand and probably very much less. The Carolingian kings lived in the country far more than in such towns as existed, and administered the country from rural palaces; Attigny, Ponthion, Herstal, Aachen and Thionville were among the new rural residences favoured by the Carolingians and only in the town of Worms is a royal residence attested. The Carolingians also created new centres of power in the north, such as Frankfurt, Nijmegen and above all, Aachen, as well as adopting some of the Merovingian palaces as their residences. Paris, the most important of the Merovingian residences, and its region became relatively insignificant. Quierzy, unimportant to the Merovingians but where the mayors of the palace Grimoald and Charles Martel had lived, features prominently in the itinerary of Pippin III, as do Verberie, Compiègne, the rural palace *par excellence* of the last Merovingian kings, and Ver, the former residence of Pippin II. Even with the Carolingians there were shifts in the concentration of power and different centres became important. Under Pippin III the centres of the kingdom were Soissons, Noyon and Laon, and Quierzy was one of the most favoured palaces, but after 768 the 'Mosan' region became increasingly important; Herstal, and then Aachen, took the place of Quierzy.[13] After 843 in the western kingdom, the early Carolingian residences were favoured once more. Under Charles the Bald, for example, Compiègne and Quierzy were the favourite royal palaces. These rural palaces became in time the nuclei of urban settlement.

I

The seventh and eighth centuries in the Frankish kingdoms were years of great change and political reorganization. From the reign of Clovis until the end of the sixth century the Merovingian kings had ruled and governed the kingdom. The nobility served the kings but their position was ambivalent; the king's position did not depend entirely on noble support but the nobles were nevertheless both servants and potential enemies of the king. With the accession of Chlothar II (583–629) in 613 however, the relationship between king and nobility began to change. Chlothar's victory over Queen Brunhild and her greatgrandsons, by which he succeeded to the whole kingdom, was won with the assistance of Warnachar, mayor of the palace in Burgundy, and the Austrasian *optimates* or magnates, led by Arnulf, later to become bishop of Metz, and Pippin I, the ancestors of the Carolingians.[14] Chlothar's success was gained at the price of guaranteeing the position and strengthening the power of many of his aristocratic helpers. He swore for example that Warnachar should never be deposed from his office of mayor of the palace during his lifetime. It was from this time, moreover, that the function of the mayor of the palace was extended from that of a mere court official in control of palace affairs to that of governing both palace and kingdom; from at least as early as 626/7 the mayor had the authority to rule in the king's absence. Warnachar himself exerted almost complete control in Burgundy and in 626 or 627 convoked a synod of bishops. Adalgisel, duke in Austrasia 'governed palace and kingdom' and the same was said of Aega (d. 642) the Neustrian mayor.[15] The power of the mayor was also of course dependent on aristocratic support.

Indeed, the mayor was usually the leader of one of the great noble families, a tradition so well established that Einhard commented in the 830s that 'the office of mayor was usually given by the people only to those who exceeded all others in the distinction of their families and in their wealth.'[16] As well as the mayor's direct rule from the centre, there were the *duces* and *comites*, who administered the provinces. On the periphery of the Frankish kingdom a few dukes developed their regions to almost independent status, into a *principatus*.[17]

A further contribution to the increase of both the mayor's power and that of the magnates, and as a corollary, to the weakening of the Merovingian position, was the fact that from Chlothar II's reign, each of the three kingdoms, Austrasia, Burgundy and Neustria had its own palace and mayor but not necessarily its own king. Chlothar II, for example, succeeded to all three kingdoms but Warnachar was the effective ruler in Burgundy and in 622 the Austrasians persuaded Chlothar to make his young son Dagobert king, or rather subking, in Austrasia, where he was subjected to the influence of his noble advisers. Similarly, Dagobert himself, ten years later, having succeeded in his turn to an undivided kingdom, 'on the advice of his bishops and lords and with the consent of all the great men of the kingdom, placed his own son Sigibert, an infant, on the throne of Austrasia and allowed him to make Metz his headquarters'. Cunibert, bishop of Cologne and Adalgisel, duke of Austrasia, were chosen 'to control the palace and the kingdom'.[18] Dagobert's action also had the effect of securing Austrasian zeal in defending the north-east frontier of the Frankish kingdom. On the birth of a second son to Dagobert, Clovis II, it was agreed that Sigibert should have Austrasia and Clovis Neustria, an arrangement which placed the magnates in a position, as far as the throne and the effectiveness of a central authority were concerned, they were not slow to exploit.

A contributory factor in the growth of the magnates' power, the alteration in the balance of authority and the increasing assertiveness of Austrasia, was the fact that many of the kings who succeeded Chlothar II and Dagobert came to the throne as minors, achieved little and died young, so that either the mayor of the palace or one of the magnates was able to serve king, kingdom and his own interests at once. Seventh- and eighth-century sources often describe the mayors in similar terms to those used for kings. Aega, Grimoald and Erchinoald, for example, are described as *pius, modestus* and *iustus*; Charles Martel, like Clovis II, is *elegans*. The strongest magnate or the mayor often acted in association with the king's mother. Nantechild, the mother of Clovis II, ruled in Neustria with the support of Aega, the mayor of the palace, during her son's minority, and Balthild ruled with the support of her mayor Erchinoald, and after his death in 638/9 with that of Ebroin, for her son Chlothar III. The Arnulfings or Carolingians were not the only nobles who both supported the Merovingian kings and undermined their position; Warnachar, Adalgisel, Cunibert, Pippin and Arnulf and their fellow magnates were successful in establishing a substratum to royal power. Werner's study of the nobility and the 'non-royal principalities' has made it quite clear how the emergence of the Carolingians was made possible by the accretion of power both by the nobility and by the mayor of the palace.[19] It is in this context that the rise of the Carolingians is to be understood.

One major difficulty in assessing both the Carolingians and the last Merovingian kings is the bias of the sources; most of the narrative sources for the eighth and early ninth centuries are pro-Carolingian. While the fourth book of the Chronicle of Fredegar is written from the Burgundian point of view, the second and third Continuations were written for Pippin III's uncle and cousin, Childebrand and Nibelung, and cover the years 736–68. The anonymous *Liber Historiae Francorum* on the other hand, probably written at the monastery of St Denis before 727, has a clear Neustrian bias and contains some refreshing criticism of the Carolingians or at least records some of the deeds of some among those who were not their loyal supporters. Some independent and very interesting information concerning Pippin II, Charles Martel and Pippin III is to be found in the *Annales Mettenses Priores*, yet even these were concerned to glorify the Carolingian house. The Royal Frankish Annals begin with Charles Martel's death in 741. A number of saints' Lives are also useful, such as the *Vita Leodegarii*, while charters can often provide supplementary information about individuals and institutions and the grants of land made to or by them. The Carolingians themselves seem to have encouraged histories about their house. Charles the Bald, Charlemagne's grandson, certainly possessed Einhard's Life of Charlemagne, Nithard's History of the Sons of Louis the Pious and a verse history of the Franks, and it was in the ninth century that a number of false king-lists and genealogies were drawn up to the Carolingians' advantage. Preserved in a late ninth-century manuscript in the Bibliothèque Nationale in Paris is the life of Arnulf, saint and bishop of Metz, the exemplar of which had apparently been copied by Jerome, a son of Charles Martel, when he was nine years old (BN lat. 5327 ff. 181^r–186^v). A further famous account of the last Merovingian kings is that of Einhard at the beginning of his life of Charlemagne. Einhard painted a vivid if slightly ridiculous portrait of the Merovingians, describing, rather unconvincingly in view of the fact that most of the kings were little more than children, their long hair and flowing beards, their helplessness and their dependence on the mayors of the palace for their title, estate and the means of support. We shall be returning to Einhard's account a little later on in this chapter.

Who were the Carolingians? Arnulf and Pippin I, the ancestors of the Carolingians mentioned earlier, supported Chlothar's bid for the kingdom in 613. Pippin, described by Fredegar as 'of all men the most careful, a true counsellor, a man of unshakeable fidelity and beloved of all for that passion for justice he had prudently instilled into Dagobert'[20] continued as mayor of the palace in Austrasia into the beginning of Sigibert's reign there as subking. He appears to have been removed from political life for a time, but on Dagobert's death in 638 Pippin as mayor and the other magnates supported Sigibert in Austrasia, and Pippin and Cunibert bishop of Cologne 'with suitable blandishments drew the Austrasian notables into their orbit, ruled them generously, won their support and knew how to keep it'.[21] Aristocratic rivalry is well illustrated by the plot instigated by Pippin and Arnulf against the Agilolfing Chrodoald (the Agilolfings were an ancient Frankish noble family whose power was centred in Bavaria). Dagobert's mind was poisoned against Chrodoald and the latter was killed on Dagobert's orders by Berthar. In Burgundy too there was opposition to dominance by the king or his mayor. This at least would seem to be the explanation for the decision of the Burgundian nobles on the death of Warnachar the mayor to have no other mayor but to be dealt with directly by the king. That the nobles were not entirely behind Dagobert is indicated by the deputations he sent into Neustria and Burgundy on his father Chlothar's death, in order to confirm his position on the throne. Charibert, Dagobert's brother, also competed, unsuccessfully, for the throne, but Dagobert allotted him Aquitaine and Gascony as his kingdom. Barontus, another aristocratic rebel, had been charged with bringing Charibert's treasure back to Austrasia on Charibert's death, but he and his supporters embezzled it. Austrasia, too, showed signs of weaning itself from the central authority, and was not entirely helpful in resisting the Slavs. A further example of aristocratic moves towards independence is Radulf of Thuringia's revolt against Sigibert in 639. Radulf's victory over Sigibert's army meant in the words of Fredegar that 'he did not in so many words deny Sigibert's overlordship but in practice did all he could to resist his power' and styled himself king of Thuringia.

Pippin I died in 640 but was succeeded in the office of mayor by his son Grimoald, after a short struggle with a rival in the office called Otto. Grimoald was, according to Fredegar, as beloved by the people as his father Pippin. The fortunes of the Pippinids (so called after Pippin I) foundered under Grimoald. Grimoald's own son, with the Merovingian name Childebert, appears to have been adopted by Sigibert when the king himself had no other son; he subsequently did have a son of his own who became in due course Dagobert II, but on Sigibert's death in 656 it seems to have been Childebert the adopted son who was set on the throne by his real father Grimoald, while Dagobert was tonsured and sent into Ireland. Dagobert may well have sat on the throne for some years before being removed. The chronology is very difficult and the details of the incident almost impossible to unravel. The years between 656 and 662 in Austrasia have to be accounted for; the Chronicle of Fredegar makes no mention of Grimoald's career after he had seized his office from Otto. The only narrative account is in the *Liber Historiae Francorum*, and it is quite explicit in saying Grimoald deposed Dagobert and placed his own son on the throne.[22] There are also some charter evidence[23] and some perplexing king-lists, one of which, in the Diptychon Barberini, was thought to provide a key to the chronology of Grimoald's coup but has more recently been ascribed to an earlier date and significance.[24] Some favour the years 660–2, others 656–62 for the duration of Childebert's reign. The general view is that Grimoald wanted to secure the throne for his family, deposed Dagobert, and gave out that Sigibert had adopted Childebert as his heir, but that loyalty to the legitimate house proved too strong and Grimoald was executed by outraged loyal magnates in 662.

There has been a suggestion that even the Grimoald coup was part of Merovingian family politics, as the Pippinids themselves may have had Merovingian blood, but the evidence is too flimsy to make this interpretation tenable.[25] Any Merovingian blood came into the family later, in the early eighth century, with Pippin III's marriage to Bertrada III, granddaughter of Charibert of Laon, thought by some to be of Merovingian descent. The fact moreover that Wulfetrud, Grimoald's daughter and abbess of the Pippinid foundation of Nivelles, had to face an attempt made by the Merovingian kings and queens to remove her from office 'out of hatred for her late father and their family's enemy' hardly suggests that the Merovingians had understood Grimoald to be fighting for their cause.[26] The struggle is nevertheless indicative of a move to displace the Merovingians on the throne and symptomatic of the ambitions of the aristocracy, as well as of the more general problem of the clash of interests between rival factions in Austrasia, Neustria and Burgundy. Royal manoeuvring was also important. On Childebert's death, Grimoald was in a very insecure position. This may have prompted him to assist Queen Balthild to promote her interest in Austrasia on behalf of her son Childeric; Balthild's policy culminated in arranging Childeric's marriage to Dagobert's sister Bilichild.[27] Grimoald may have hoped to be able to control the young king and continue to enjoy his power, but it is clear that at this point he became expendable and was executed. It should be stressed that Grimoald never sought to rule as king himself, but only to control the king and kingdom, and thought to do it most satisfactorily within his own family.

Mayors of the palace from Pippin II's time onwards were in a very similar position to Grimoald as far as control of the king was concerned, despite the fact that the king remained a Merovingian. Grimoald's coup is sometimes described as a precedent for Pippin III's takeover in 751, but this is reading too much into the affair. Grimoald after all belonged to a different branch of the family, and there is certainly no specific evidence for Schieffer's statement that the memory of Grimoald's 'premature' bid for the throne overshadowed the political decisions of the next three generations.[28] It is simply an instance of the expression of a particular family's ambitions in the late Merovingian political world.

Arnulf's son Ansegis had married Pippin I's daughter Begga (Grimoald's sister) and it is from this union that the Arnulfings or Carolingians are descended. In no source is Pippin II referred to as anything but the son of Ansegis, so that to describe him, as Halphen does, as the grandson of Pippin I, though genealogically correct, misrepresents the historical significance of that relationship. Later accounts of the Carolingian descent, the earliest of which is included in Paul the Deacon's *Gesta Episcoporum Mettensium* written in 785, are only interested in the descent in the male line.[29]

As the twenty-ninth bishop of Metz, Arnulf took over the leadership of the church of Metz, a man shining brightly with the light of his holiness and the distinction of his parentage. He was descended from a highly born, honourable and brave Frankish family and was of such standing in the church that he was also an adviser to the royal palace. This deeply revered man had married in his youth and fathered two sons, Ansegisus and Chlodulfus. Ansegisus begat Pippin (II) . . . and Pippin's son was Charles Martel who must be described as the most courageous among men, to say nothing of the great campaigns which he waged. He so destroyed the Saracens that that godless and fierce people today shrink with horror before the Frankish might. Charles fathered Pippin III who was distinguished both for his intelligence and valour. Among other achievements he subdued and subjugated the rebellious Aquitainians together with their leader

Waifar, who had long resisted Frankish rule. His son in turn is the great king Charles who enlarged the kingdom of the Franks to a greater extent than ever before.

Begga by her marriage became an Arnulfing, and her children Arnulfings, yet the name Pippin remained an important one in the Arnulfing/Carolingian family. Little is known about her husband: a charter of Sigibert III for Stavelot–Malmédy dated 648 lists him as a *vir illuster* and *domesticus* in Austrasia with extensive estates.[30] It was his son, Pippin II, who was the real founder of Carolingian power. Pippin II is mentioned for the first time in the first Continuation of the Chronicle of Fredegar, when he was embroiled in the disputes of the rival factions in Austrasia, Neustria and Burgundy. Pippin and Duke Martin, who may have been related to Pippin, ruled jointly over Austrasia after the death of Wulfoald.[31] To understand how Pippin was able to bring all three kingdoms under his control, it is necessary to rehearse the events in Neustria which enabled Pippin to emerge as victor.

Dagobert I on his death-bed in 637 had commended his queen Nantechild and his son Clovis to Aega, mayor of the palace in Neustria. Aega died in 642 and was succeeded by Erchinoald. It was at this time that Grimoald I was mayor of the palace in Austrasia and in 643 Queen Nantechild visited Burgundy and 'by choice of all the bishops and dukes raised the Frank Flaochad to the dignity of mayor of the palace'.[32] Flaochad's personal enmity towards Willibad, a Burgundian patrician probably of Gallo-Roman descent, involved the magnates of both Burgundy and Neustria in a bitter struggle; Ewig has suggested that Burgundian resentment at having a Frank imposed on them as mayor may have been an element in the feud. Clovis married the Anglo-Saxon Balthild (Baldechildis) and had three sons, Chlothar, Childeric and Theuderic. When Clovis died, Chlothar was made king under the 'regency' of his mother and Ebroin, whose ambition rivalled that of the Carolingians, was chosen to succeed Erchinoald as mayor. He made a bid for power which ultimately brought about the end of the pre-eminence of Neustria.

An important rival was Leudegar, bishop of Autun 611–79.[33] Leudegar was educated at the court of Chlothar II and was chosen as bishop of Autun by Balthild. When Chlothar III died in 673 and was succeeded in Neustria by his youngest brother Theuderic, Leudegar and the Austrasian Duke Wulfoald supported the claims of Childeric his other brother, who had been made king in Austrasia in 662. Leudegar, however, also fell out with Childeric. The Continuator's account at this point gives a brief insight into how far these magnates were prepared to go in the furtherance of their ambitions. The Franks in Neustria, burdened by Ebroin's cruelty and no doubt jealous of his influence over the king, plotted against Ebroin, deposed Theuderic, tonsured both of them and Ebroin was sent to the monastery of Luxeuil in Burgundy. Childeric was then made king of the entire kingdom, Neustria, Austrasia and Burgundy, but he antagonized the Franks with his 'frivolous and imperious behaviour', and he and his pregnant queen Bilichild were murdered in the forest of Livry by a group of nobles. Wulfoald fled to Austrasia and Leudegar and his party were now left in control. Leudesius, son of Erchinoald, was made mayor and Theuderic presumably was restored to the throne, though no source says as much specifically. Ebroin chose this moment to return, bringing with him his own band of supporters. Leudesius was killed, Theuderic set on the throne for the third time and Leudegar and his brother Gaerinus were executed. Leudegar's surviving supporters fled into Gascony. Conditions were thus ripe for a determined man and his Mafia to win the whole kingdom; the king was ineffectual to say the least and the disaffection among the Franks in Neustria meant potential support for anyone who chose to make a bid for power. It is at this point that Pippin II appears. He is described as ruling over Austrasia 'after the death of Wulfoald and the disappearance of the kings'.[34] Pippin went to war against Ebroin and Theuderic, but was defeated. It was a group of dissident Neustrians who assassinated Ebroin and then went and joined Pippin in Neustria. Waratto was chosen by the remaining Neustrians to succeed Ebroin, and he made peace with Pippin.

Neustria's troubles, however, were still not over. Waratto's son Ghislemar deposed his father and earned Pippin's enmity, but Ghislemar died and Waratto was restored to his position, being succeeded on his death by his son-in-law Berchar, a man of 'small ability, light minded and impetuous'. He managed to alienate many Neustrians who deserted to join Pippin. Pippin now took action. He led his warbands against Berchar and King Theuderic and defeated them in a great battle at Tertry in 687. Pippin secured Theuderic and the royal treasure, settled Neustrian affairs and returned to Austrasia.

The battle of Tertry has been described, with some exaggeration, as the decisive moment for the Carolingian house and the assurance of Austrasian ascendancy over Neustria. It was certainly a resounding success for Pippin, but it was to be another forty-six years before Carolingian power was firmly established. Nevertheless, the first step towards Carolingian dominance of the Frankish kingdoms had been achieved. It has been customary to see the fortunes of the mayor of the palace from this date onwards in terms of an opposition to both king and noble, but it would be more accurate still to think in terms of a struggle for dominance among the magnates, in the course of which the king became a person of little consequence. When in 690–1 Theuderic III died, his son Clovis III, still an infant, succeeded him but died after a short reign of four years and was succeeded by his younger brother Childebert II, who died, still a young man, in 711. Childebert's young son Dagobert III succeeded him but died in 715.

It was Pippin II who developed the office of mayor of the palace, already a position of great power, into a means of achieving dominance over the whole kingdom. A small but important piece of evidence concerning the extent of Pippin II's dominance over the Merovingian king is to be found in a charter dated 13 December 695, drawn up in Childebert's name. On the face of it this charter might be evidence that the king still retained authority within his chancery, with a will to exert as far as donation or grant were concerned, at least with respect to St Denis. Yet the note in notarial shorthand written by the notary under the signatures states that he was ordered to draw up the charter by Pippin.[35]

Pippin II's first wife was Plectrud, daughter of a magnate called Hugobert from the middle Moselle region. Hugobert appears to have had five daughters, while his wife Irmina was the foundress of the monastery of Echternach. Pippin II's grandson married Bertrada II, granddaughter of another daughter of Hugobert, Bertrada I. Bertrada I's husband Herbert or Charibert of Laon was founder of the abbey of Prüm and had lands in the middle Moselle and Eifel region. Plectrud thus brought with her in all probability a considerable inheritance of land in the Moselle region and on the Eifel river near Trier, Echternach and Prüm. This land, combined with the wealth already possessed by the Arnulfings in the region of Metz, provided the material basis for much of the Carolingian exercise of power.[36] The wealth of the Arnulfings was based on extensive family lands in the north and north-east of the kingdom, particularly in the Meuse – Moselle region; the biggest concentrations of land were round Metz, originally the family possessions of Arnulf, the region of Fosses, Namur and Nivelles and Stavelot – Malmédy, the two Pippinid family monasteries. (Pippin I's daughter Geretrud founded Nivelles.) Some of this land must have come with Begga on her marriage to Ansegis, probably due to the change in the inheritance laws in the sixth century under Chilperic I, which enabled females to share in the inheritance of ancestral land, although none were admitted to the exclusion of male heirs.[37] While male heirs existed females would not in theory inherit land, but in practice estates were often divided between son and daughter; the foundation of monasteries by women and donation of lands to these foundations by women bears this out. It should be stressed how important the family monasteries were; their structure was adapted to the land-based familial structure and the monasteries were influential supporters of the family's interests.

Some of the east Frankish lands may have been Carolingian from the beginning of the eighth century, inherited from the family in the Echternach region. There seem to have been some lands they possessed round Würzburg and Hammelburg, but the evidence is not clear. The *ducatus Austrasiorum* which Pippin administered apart from his duties in the kingdom was territory traditionally assigned to the duke, and seems to have been equivalent to the *ducatus regni* of the late ninth and tenth centuries which Hugh the Abbot and, after him, the Robertians possessed. Champagne and the bishoprics of Rheims, Laon and Châlons remained outside the limits of the Austrasian dukedom, and when Pippin made his son Drogo duke of Champagne, the bishoprics of Sens and Rheims were still outside his jurisdiction. With the success of Pippin at Tertry in 687, the *dux Austrasiorum* became the *princeps francorum*.

In an attempt to establish an hereditary right to his power, Pippin made his sons by his first wife Plectrud, Grimoald and Drogo, mayor of the palace in Neustria and duke of Champagne respectively. Both his sons, however, died before him, and Grimoald's young son Theudoald was made mayor in place of his father. It is perhaps an indication of the strength of the Carolingian position that a young and inexperienced son (it is possible, however, that Theudoald was of age) under the protection of his grandparents, and after Pippin's death of his grandmother Plectrud, could be placed in the office which had hitherto required a grown man capable of administering the kingdom. There is an obvious parallel here with the young Merovingian kings.

Pippin II's settlement for his kingdom and the consequent long-drawn-out struggle on the part of Charles Martel to gain power have most recently been analysed by Semmler who has demonstrated conclusively that Charles's position was not assured until 723.[38] Pippin II died in 714, leaving his grandsons Theudoald, mayor of the palace in Neustria, and Arnulf to rule under the leadership of Plectrud probably based in Cologne, while a third grandson, Hugh, had already entered the church. As far as Plectrud was concerned however, Pippin's son Charles by another wife or concubine Chalpaida, was not eligible for any position or any portion of his father's power and she had him imprisoned. The third party in the struggle for power in Neustria was the Neustrian magnates who were opposed to Carolingian dominance and, ostensibly at least, supporters of the Merovingian king. In 715 the Neustrians revolted gainst Plectrud and Theudoald, and those of the Arnulfing supporters who recognised Theudoald's authority. Arnulf, probably ambitious for himself, supported none of the parties contending for power. Theudoald escaped from the field of battle and probably died shortly afterwards; the rebels chose Ragamfred, a Neustrian noble whose ambition was equal to that of Ebroin, as their mayor of the palace. Ragamfred's greatest opponent, however, was not any supporter of the claims of Pippin II's grandsons, but Charles Martel, who had managed to escape from Plectrud's custody and gather round him a band of followers. Meanwhile Dagobert III had died and had been succeeded by Chilperic II, whom the *Liber Historiae Francorum* describes as formerly a monk called Daniel. One would surmise from this and the subsequent paucity of suitable candidates for the throne (Charles Martel reinstated Chilperic II after his own choice of puppet king had died) that the Merovingian blood royal was in very short supply; Theuderic IV was also taken from a monastery, so was Chilperic III and to it he returned when deposed by Pippin III in 751.

In 716 the Frisians, with whom the Neustrians had allied themselves, attacked Charles in the region of Cologne and inflicted great losses on his forces. Chilperic and Ragamfred now appear to have received material aid from Plectrud who was apparently backing what she thought, or hoped, to be the winning side. In September 717 Charles and Ragamfred joined battle at Vinchy and this time Charles emerged the victor and Ragamfred and Chilperic fled. Charles Martel at this stage had little real power in Neustria and retired to Cologne where the *Liber Historiae Francorum* reports that he 'discussed matters with the lady Plectrud.' It may be that at this interview Charles persuaded Plectrud that she would be well advised to support him as the leader of the Carolingian family and promoter of its interests, and that Ragamfred had no intention of reinstating any of the Carolingian family in the mayoralty. Certainly, while Arnulf, who had not assisted Plectrud or Theudoald, did nothing to help Charles, his brother Hugh did much to consolidate Charles' authority in Neustria, and Plectrud herself surrendered her husband's treasure to Charles; the sources thereafter do not record any further attempt on Plectrud's part to undermine her stepson's position. Charles now felt himself strong enough to

30

set up an administration; he placed a Merovingian king of his own, Chlothar IV, on the throne and set about strengthening his position in the middle Rhine region, largely by buying support with gifts of land and offices to both the secular and ecclesiastical *optimates*.

Ragamfred and Chilperic in the meantime sought the aid of Eudo, duke of Aquitaine, and in return for any assistance he might render, promised him independent status in his duchy. Eudo's army moved against Charles but was forced to retreat rapidly beyond the Loire, taking King Chilperic with him. Ragamfred fled to Paris. When Chlothar IV died, however, partly because there seems to have been no other suitable candidate, but also perhaps to win Neustrian loyalty, Charles retrieved Chilperic II from Eudo in Aquitaine and made him king again. In 721 he was succeeded by Theuderic IV. For the next four years Charles concentrated his efforts on ousting Ragamfred. Some indication of the spheres of influence of Charles and Ragamfred may be calculated from the charters recording gifts of lands and privileges which issued from the chancery of each in the names of Chlothar IV and Chilperic II respectively between 715 and 719. Ragamfred acquired the Merovingian royal chancery along with Chilperic, while Charles was obliged to form a new chancery. Ragamfred's territory included Compiègne, Paris, Rouen, and the Paris basin, the lower Loire, Amiens, Abbéville, Thérouanne, Ghent, Cambrai and the bishoprics of Paris and Soissons. Among the peripheral principalities, Provence, Aquitaine and Frisia were allied to the Neustrian mayor. Ragamfred made gifts for example to the hitherto Carolingian monastery of St Wandrille, weaned the monks away from their former allegiance and made his own nominee abbot. Charles' region where he could count on support was at first confined to the Ardennes and Eifel regions, the Meuse and middle Moselle river valleys and northern Alsace. Among the peripheral principalities, only Thuringia was sympathetic; Bavaria went its own way under the Agilolfing dukes.

After 718, however, Charles was able to begin to make his claim to his father's power a reality. He was greatly helped by alliances with a number of important bishops, abbots and aristocrats. Echternach, a Carolingian foundation, remained, unlike St Wandrille, loyal to Charles. Milo, bishop of both Trier and Rheims, Gewilib, bishop of Mainz, and the abbots and monasteries of Stavelot – Malmédy and Maastricht were his supporters. His most active accomplice was his nephew Hugh; it was Hugh who did much to establish Charles in Neustria. The abbot placed at St Wandrille by Ragamfred, who had distinguished himself in Ragamfred's service, was banished by Charles to Maastricht; the former abbot was reinstated but after 723 was replaced by Hugh. Hugh also became abbot of Jumièges, La Croix and Saint-Leufroy, and held the bishoprics of Rouen and Paris, and according to the episcopal lists, of Bayeux, Lisieux and Avranches as well. This shameless pluralism meant that Hugh's region extended over the whole ecclesiastical province of Rouen and the west of the province of Sens, and that Carolingian enclaves were studded all over Neustria. Other loyal supporters were granted abbacies and bishoprics or at least the use of the incomes and estates pertaining to these offices. Agatheus, count of Nantes and Rennes, for example, received monastic foundations at each of these places, Eucherius, Charles' personal nominee, was made bishop of Orleans, and by 723 Ebbo of Sens and the bishop of Cologne were also among Charles' supporters. With the defeat of his other nephew Arnulf in about 723 Charles' position as both the head of the Carolingian family and the ruler of the Franks, *princeps francorum*, was assured.

His position in the Frankish kingdom itself established, Charles Martel was much occupied for the rest of his life in extending the authority of the central government to the principalities encircling the kingdom, and conducted campaigns against the Frisians, Saxons, Alemans and Bavarians. Eudo of Aquitaine called on Charles Martel to help him fight off the Arabs.[39] The army of Abd-ar-Rahman was defeated by Charles at the famous battle of Poitiers in 732. The battle not only halted further Arab advance northwards but enabled Charles to enter Burgundy, establish his authority there and parcel out the lands of the Lyonnais to his loyal followers. On Eudo's death Charles also attempted, without much success, to take over Aquitaine, though he laid waste great tracts of the country. The accounts of Charles' campaigns in the Continuation of Fredegar and the *Annales Mettenses Priores* comment on the spoils and plunder won by Charles and his armies. The wealth thus gained, augmenting his already considerable resources in family land and treasure, as well as those derived from control over much of the Merovingian royal fisc, must have done much to bolster Charles' power and prestige. Charles had also received all Pippin's treasure from Plectrud and this probably included the Neustrian portion of the Merovingian royal treasure over which Pippin II had assumed control in 687. After Charles' siege of Angers he returned home with 'much booty'; he carried back great treasure from Bavaria, he was laden with spoils after his campaign against the Frisians in 734 and again from Burgundy in 736 he returned 'with gifts and much treasure'. From the Saxons he extorted taxes and hostages, and from the Arabs in 732 and 737 he won great 'spoil, booty and many prisoners'. In the sources Charles appears as a hero on a biblical scale; Avignon, for example, fell to Charles as Jericho did to Joshua.[40] Charles' campaigns south of the Loire did much to subdue the country materially and economically; great areas of the countryside were laid waste, Nîmes, Agde, Béziers and Avignon were razed to the ground; crops and villages were burnt.

Charles' martial help was even sought by Gregory III, who in 739 sent an embassy to Charles bearing many precious gifts, including the keys to the tomb of St Peter and a link from his chains, and begged with great eloquence that Charles come and defend Rome and the church from the onslaughts of the Lombards. Charles sent Grimo, abbot of Corbie, and Sigibert of St Denis to Rome, but the Continuation of Fredegar does not relate what answer Charles gave. It was undoubtedly negative; Charles had received Lombard support against the Arabs and might have to call on it again. Close *rapprochement* between the Papacy and the Frankish kingdom was not attained for another fifteen years.

When Theuderic IV died in 737, Charles, no doubt sure of his position, did not bother to set up another puppet king on the throne but ruled by himself as king in all but name. Shortly before he died, Charles divided the effective rulership of the country between Carloman and Pippin, his two sons by his first wife Chrotrud. Claims may also have been made on behalf of his third son Grifo by Grifo's mother Sunnichild, Charles Martel's second wife, for provision of some sort, the details of which are not known, was also made for Grifo. The partition is reminiscent of the earlier Merovingian partitions. A letter survives written by St Boniface to each of the brothers shortly after Charles Martel's death, asking for protection for his mission in Thuringia from whichever one of the three heirs gained the authority over that region.[41] Carloman received Austrasia, Alemannia and Thuringia, Pippin was allotted Burgundy, Neustria and Provence. It may be that it was to consolidate his position in Neustria, not traditionally the home ground of the Carolingians, that Pippin married Bertrada, a member of a noble Neustrian family whose lands extended as far east as Prüm. Neither Bavaria nor Aquitaine was included in the partition owing to the greater independence they had achieved.

II

Charles Martel died at Quierzy in October 741 and was buried at St Denis, the necropolis of the Merovingian kings. The first opposition to the authority of Carloman and Pippin was from Grifo. Whether or not Grifo's ambition was fired by his mother, Pippin and Carloman chose to contest Grifo's claims to a portion of the kingdom; possible dissension between the two brothers was thus diverted by their common ambition and common dislike of Grifo. Grifo's rebellions and the apparent ease with which he could gather supporters, particularly in the peripheral principalities of the Frankish kingdom, attest to the strong anti-Carolingian feeling and the uncertain position of the Carolingian rulers.[42] Only the *Annales Mettenses Priores* and the revised version of the Royal Frankish Annals describe Grifo's activities in any detail. On Charles Martel's death Grifo occupied Laon and declared war on his brothers but was defeated, and imprisoned by Carloman. It was not until Carloman's departure for Rome that Pippin could release Grifo. There may be some indication of antagonism between Pippin and Carloman here. Had Pippin come round to the idea of using Grifo to dislodge Carloman? Grifo promptly fled, first to the Saxons and then to Bavaria. His half-sister, Chiltrud, against her brothers' advice, had married Odilo duke of Bavaria. Odilo himself had rebelled against his brothers-in-law (an incident ruefully recalled some years later by the 'Astronomer' in his life of Louis the Pious[43]) and on Odilo's death, Grifo seized power and, allied with Lantfrid, duke of the Alemans, attacked the Franks in 749. On his defeat by Pippin, a result of which was Pippin's installation of his nephew Tassilo as duke of Bavaria, Pippin magnanimously gave Grifo twelve counties in Neustria. Grifo, however, remained discontented, and, disinclined to be fobbed off with a few counties, he joined forces with Duke Waifar of Aquitaine in order to aid Waifar in his bid for independence from the Carolingians. It was in Aquitaine that he was killed in 753, when he was, according to the hostile Continuator of Fredegar, on his way to Lombardy to stir up trouble against Pippin.

It was not just those principalities or dukedoms incited by Grifo which rebelled against Carolingian authority. The Gascons of Aquitaine rebelled under their leader Chunoald or Hunuald, son of Eudo. They and the Etichonen dukes of Alemannia were dealt with by Pippin and Carloman, and Pippin quelled Odilo of Bavaria's revolt in 743, while Carloman subdued the Saxons. At this point Childeric III, after an interregnum of six years, was placed on the throne. It may be, as some historians have suggested, that this was an admission of weakness on the part of Pippin and Carloman. It could on the other hand have been a canny ploy on their part in order to disarm potential loyalist or legitimist opposition. Levillain suggested another interpretation and argued that Childeric's elevation is evidence that there was still a loyalist party in the Frankish kingdom, headed by Carloman, who did not wish to make the break with the Merovingian line final.[44] It is certainly Carloman to whom Childeric refers in his charters as instrumental in gaining him his throne. In a diploma for Stavelot–Malmédy, for example, Carloman is cited as the man *qui nobis in solium regni instituit*.[45] That Carloman was instrumental in re-estab-lishing a Merovingian on the throne rather than Pippin would fit with the tension we have already noted between the two brothers, but the action, whether or not inspired by loyalty, undoubtedly served as a symbol to con-solidate Frankish rule, and the two mayors were able to shield their real power behind the nominal power of the shadow king.

Pippin's power was further strengthened when he was left as sole ruler on his elder brother Carloman's decision to relinquish his worldly state and enter a monastery. The Annals record that no campaigns were mounted in 746, because Carloman was preparing for his departure, and in the following year Carloman left the Frankish kingdom bound for Mount Soracte near Rome, and committed his rule and his young son Drogo (about whom we hear nothing more) to the care of his brother Pippin. During the next three years Pippin was preoccupied with the rebellion led by Grifo already mentioned and with the consolidation of his position both at home and in the principalities he had already subdued by means of a judicious monastic policy which will be dis-cussed at greater length in the following chapter.

It was in 750 that Burchard, bishop of Würzburg, and Fulrad, abbot of St Denis, were sent to Rome with the famous request to Pope Zacharias, whether it was right that the king of the Franks should wield no power and whether he that did wield the power should be called king. The Royal Frankish Annals give credit to Zacharias for advising Pippin that it was better to call him king who had the royal power 'in order to prevent provoking civil war in Francia', and that Zacharias 'by virtue of his apostolic authority commanded that Pippin should be made king'. In the following year Pippin was elected king of the Franks, anointed and raised to the kingship at Soissons, while Childeric was tonsured and relegated to the monastery once more. Fredegar's Continuator, more contemporary with events than the Royal Frankish Annals, gives a rather different account, for there the request was made to the Holy See on the advice and with the consent of all the Franks, and simply the sanction of the Pope was gained. Pippin was 'chosen king by all the Franks in accordance with ancient tradition, consecrated by the bishops and received the submission of all the great men'.

The elevation of Pippin to the kingship naturally enough raises a great number of questions. The first difficulty is that all the accounts of Pippin's take-over are written from a Carolingian point of view; it was not the writers' aim to present the Merovingians in a favourable, or the Carolingians in an un-favourable, light. The accounts that do survive moreover, are little more than laconic statements of fact. Many have seen the accession of Pippin as the trium-phant outcome of a century and a half's inevitable progression towards the throne. Such an interpretation does not accord with the evidence; the Carolin-gians were opportunists and no opportunity of acquiring the crown presented itself until 737; even then anti-Carolingian opposition was still strong and Charles Martel was content simply to rule rather than assume the title of king.

It was Pippin whose ambition made him aspire to the title as well as the fact of royal power. Pippin actually deposed the king set up by his brother Carloman, albeit no doubt with Pippin's own compliance. That Pippin could so dispose of the legitimate line of kings says a great deal for his estimate of his own strength and for the loyalty he felt he could command. Pippin asked for sanction from the Pope for his action. There is no evidence that he did so because he did not wish to repeat the failure of his forebear Grimoald I. Obviously a higher, non-Frankish, sanction of some sort was needed to condone what amounted to oathbreaking, usurpation and theft; that it was the Pope who was requested to give this sanction accords with the tradition already established of the Pope's authority carrying some weight in the Frankish king-dom, especially in measures which involved the church. In 747, for example, a synod of Frankish bishops sent to Rome a declaration that they would main-tain the Catholic faith and unity and the subjection of the Frankish church to the Roman church of St Peter and the Pope.[46] The year before, the magnates, bishops and abbots of the kingdom had sent a questionnaire to Pope Zacharias asking his advice on a number of points. The Pope had moreover long been interested in the missionary work in Frisia and Germany being carried out with the protection of the Frankish mayors of the palace. Ecclesiastical support within the Frankish kingdom had become so essential to Pippin that it was clearly in his interests to seek ecclesiastical sanctions to confirm his political authority. The oil of unction with which Pippin was anointed by the Frankish bishops in 751 may well have made up for the long hair of the Merovingian kings, but it also symbolized the pact between the Carolingian ruler and the church and the relationship which had developed between the two since the time of Pippin II. The growth of the Austrasian and German missionary church and reform of the church with Carolingian support, meant that the church was indeed the decisive factor in the transference of rule to the Carolingians, and this aspect of their activity will be examined in the following chapter. The Pope was really the only possible provider of sanctions for the transference of the title of ruler, but one wonders whether the Pope really understood the complications of Frankish political structure and the position of the mayor of the palace. It may have been with some surprise that Zacharias received the query about their position, for for some time Charles Martel, Pippin and Carloman had been referring to the domain under their control as 'our kingdom' and the popes had been addressing them as *subregulus*, *princeps*, *dux* and *patricius*, which may have been attempts simply to describe their power in the face of the known existence of a king.

If the takeover in 751 is viewed in the context of the political developments discussed in this chapter it is in fact less of a revolution than is sometimes thought. Filial succession to the Merovingian throne had been maintained only in the interests of the nobility since the beginning of the seventh century, but by the time Pippin III inherited his father's power such an expedient could simply be dispensed with. We tend to assume that the laws of hereditary succession were well established, but it was in fact still an age where hereditary claims had to be made good. Even the Merovingians when still powerful had often had trouble pressing their claims and some of them had been deposed and murdered by rival factions.[47] Not only had Zacharias recognized political reality in granting his sanction, but the nature of Frankish kingship was still such that a *rex inutilis*, a powerless and useless king, such as the Merovingians had become, was simply a contradiction in terms; the ruler had still to be a warlord, a defender of the faith and a governor of his people.

Einhard represents papal authority as the decisive factor which constituted Pippin king, but it must be remembered that Einhard was writing some eighty years after the event, owed everything to the Carolingians and was interested in magnifying the memory of Charlemagne. Riché argues that in order to extirpate the belief that one ought to remain loyal to the Merovingian family, Pippin had to find a new principle of legitimacy.[48] Einhard says nothing of this necessity; he conveys the impression of an evolution, without resistance. From the brief accounts in Einhard, the annals and the Continuation of Fredegar, we have no exact idea of events. Reuter has pointed out the part Boniface played in enhancing the position of the Pope in Frankish eyes.[49] Zacharias also, it should be remembered, did not approve for nothing; the Lombards at this stage threatened to conquer the papal states. Pippin could be a protector, and for the Papacy there were precedents for seeking Frankish protection and intervention. Yet in seeking Frankish support against the Lombards, would not this have put Pippin in a similar position to Charles Martel, of attacking traditional allies, for Pippin had been 'adopted' by Liutprand? On the other hand, he may have felt no sense of obligation to Liutprand's successor, for Aistulf was no relation. Einhard omits to mention Pippin's unction, a curious omission if it was as significant an innovation as later historians have supposed. Einhard seems to have wished to convey the impression that it was the Pope who really invested Pippin with the kingship. Rather than describing a historical incident, he may well have been making political statements more relevant in the context of the early ninth century.

Generally too much emphasis is placed on Pippin's policies, his request to

the Pope and his coronation, and too little attention paid to the gradual accumulation of power, landed wealth and treasure, and of followers, by Pippin II,
Charles Martel, Carloman and Pippin III, a wealth which formed the basis of
Carolingian power and made them for some time virtually invincible. Their
monastic policy, already referred to briefly with reference to Charles Martel,
built up a large number of 'royal monasteries' over which they had considerable
control and on which they could rely for support. Monasteries in territories
brought under Carolingian control were particularly liable to become 'royal
monasteries'. Those of the Etichonen dukes of Alemannia, for example, were
taken over by Pippin III after the defeat of the Alemans. Church lands could
also be secularized or appropriated for the mayor or monarch's use; Charles
Martel's secularization of many ecclesiastical estates and the granting of benefices and lands to loyal followers won him ill fame among the ecclesiastical
writers of the later ninth century. The habit of confiscation, secularization and
the rewarding or buying of followers with land was something Pippin III too
followed, and emasculation of a powerful group could also be achieved by this
means. In 742 for example, Pippin III, according to the *Gesta episcoporum
Autissiodorensium*, deprived the bishops of Auxerre of the power and possessions
which had practically formed a principality for them in northern Burgundy,
and as such constituted a threat to Pippin's authority.[50] Pippin rewarded those
who had served in his chancery with abbacies. Fulrad his chaplain, for example,
was given the abbacy of St Denis, Widmar that of St Riquier and Baddilo was
made abbot of Marmoutier. Other followers were granted monasteries, or their
lands, in the provinces of Sens, Rheims, Châlons-sur-Marne, Autun and
Nevers. But Pippin could benefit monasteries; Prüm was restored and richly
endowed and both St Denis and St Martin at Tours were granted privileges and
lands.

As well as their own family lands and the lands acquired by extortion, confiscation, conquest or gift, the Carolingians came in 751 into possession of
what was left of the Merovingian estates. It is difficult to ascertain just how
extensive these were. Einhard would have us believe that the king had been
reduced to the position of a pathetic dependent on the Carolingian mayors, in
possession of only one small estate with only a few servants and an allowance
from Pippin III as his sole means of support. There is reason to believe, however, that he exaggerated. Some continuity can be traced between Merovingian
and Carolingian possessions and of these many may have come to the Carolingians only in the eighth century, and some only on their acquisition of the
royal title.[51] Despite the inadequacy of our knowledge of the *palatia*, manors
and itineraries of the Merovingian kings, places such as Lille, Compiegne,
Soissons, Servais, Quierzy, Ver, Attigny and Ponthion in the Marne, Oise and
Aisne river valleys are known to have been favoured possessions of the Merovingians; all became part of the Carolingian domain. Later documents of the
ninth century provide details of Carolingian property, such as the Capitulary
of Aachen in 802, the *Divisio regni* of 806, the *Capitulare missorum Wormatense*
of 829 or the *Capitulare de Villis*, but by this stage it is not possible to determine
which lands were originally Carolingian and which they had taken over from

the Merovingians. While it is undoubtedly true that the later Merovingians had less land and less treasure than their predecessors, it is not at present possible to establish how much less. Whatever the size of their estates however, Pippin added considerably to his already extensive properties.

The 'revolution' in 751 was completely successful. No attempts were made, as far as we know, to reinstate Childeric III; he died in about 753 and his son was never king. Nor did Grifo succeed in challenging his brother's rights and we have seen that other attempts to displace the Carolingians were suppressed. The Carolingians, a noble, ambitious and powerful family, with considerable wealth and ability at their command, had struggled with other noble families to gain a position of supremacy in Frankish Gaul. They were Frankish aristocrats just like any other Frankish aristocrat, but with harder fists and sharper elbows; they were to stay on the throne for the next two centuries.

NOTES

1. Gregory of Tours, *Historia Francorum*, II, 40–3.
2. Ibid. IV, 9 and VII, 26; Fredegar, IV, 57 and compare M. Rouche, *L'Aquitaine, des Wisigoths aux Arabes, 418–781. Naissance d'une région* (Paris 1979).
3. See J. Semmler, 'Pippin III und die fränkischen Klöster', *Francia* 3 (1976), 88–146 especially 97–9.
4. E. Ewig, 'Divisio Franciae', *KdG* I, 143–77.
5. *Capitulare de Villis* ed. *MGH Cap.* I, 83–91 (trs. Loyn and Percival 64–73); see B. Fois Ennas, *Il 'Capitulare de Villis'* (Milan 1981).
6. G. Duby, *The Early Growth of the European Economy* (London 1974), and idem, *Rural Economy and Country Life in the Medieval West* (London 1968); R. Latouche, *The Birth of the Western Economy* (London 1961); P. Riché, *Daily Life in the World of Charlemagne* (Philadelphia 1978); M. Bloch, *Feudal Society* (London 1962).
7. Duby, *Early Growth*, 80–2 and compare Riché, *Daily Life*, 138–40.
8. *MGH Cap.* I, 254, and see Duby, *Early Growth*, 28. Duby may well be too extreme in the inferences he draws.
9. See Riché, *Daily Life*, 171–7.
10. Duby, *Rural Economy*, 38.
11. F. Lot (ed.), *Chronique de l'abbaye de Saint Riquier* (Paris 1894), 306–8.
12. G. Duby (ed.), *Histoire de la France Urbaine I La Ville Antique* (Paris 1980) and compare M. W. Barley (ed.), *European Towns. Their Archaeology and Early History* (London 1977).
13. E. Ewig, 'Résidence et capitale pendant le haut moyen âge', *Revue Historique* 230 (1963), 25–72.
14. Fredegar, IV, 40.
15. Ibid., IV, 80.
16. Einhard, *Vita Karoli*, c. 1.
17. K. F. Werner, 'Les principautés périphériques dans le monde franc du viiie siècle', *Settimane* 20 (1973), 483–514.
18. Fredegar, IV, 75.
19. Werner, 'Les principautés périphériques'.

20. Fredegar, IV, 61.
21. Ibid., IV, 85.
22. *Liber Historiae Francorum* c. 43; compare Eddius Stephanus, *Vita Wilfridi* c. 28.
23. The *Vita Nivardi*, c. 6, *MGH SS rer. merov.* V, 163, records that Nivard, bishop of Rheims (650–673) obtained from king Childebert an exemption from tolls.
24. The regnal lists show a Childebert succeeding Sigibert, and one of these records that he was the son of Grimoald. On the Grimoald coup, see J. L. Nelson, 'Queens as Jezebels: the careers of Brunhild and Balthild in Merovingian history', *Medieval Women* D. Baker (ed.) (Oxford 1978), 31–77 especially 48–50 and her references. See also H. Thomas, 'Die Namenliste des Diptychon Barberini und der Sturz des Hausmeiers Grimoald', *DA* 25 (1969), 17–63 and K. A. Eckhardt, *Studia Merovingica* (Aalen 1975) 151–83 and 262–79.
25. L. Dupraz, *Le royaume des franques et l'ascension politique des maires du palais (656– 680)* (Fribourg 1948). E. Hlawitschka, 'Studien zur Genealogie und Geschichte der Merowinger und der frühen Karolinger', *RhV* 43 (1979), 1–99; R. Schieffer, review of Eckhardt, *Studia Merowingica, DA* 33 (1977), 270–1, and E. Hlawitschka, 'Merovingerblut bei der Karolingern?', *Adel und Kirche Gerd Tellenbach zum 65. Geburstag dargebracht*, J. Fleckenstein and K. Schmid (eds); (Fribourg, Basle and Vienna 1968) 66–91.
26. *MGH SS rer. merov.* II, 460.
27. Nelson, 'Queens as Jezebels', 49.
28 T. Schieffer, *Winfrid-Bonifatius und die Grundelegung von Europas* (Freiburg 1954 and reprint Darmstadt 1972), 25.
29. E. Hlawitschka, 'Die Vorfahren Karls des Grossen', *KdG* I, 51–82.
30. *MGH Dip. Kar.*, Nos. 22, 23.
31. Fredegar, Continuation 3.
32. Ibid., IV, 89.
33. Compare *Vita sancti Leudegarii, MGH SS rer. merov.*, 249–362 and L. Levillain, 'Les comtes de Paris à l'époque franque', *MA* 3rd series, 12 (1941), 137–205.
34. Fredegar, Continuation 3. On Ebroin, however, see the illuminating thesis by P. J. Fouracre. 'The career of Ebroin, mayor of the palace *c.* 657–680' (London, Ph.D. thesis, 1981).
35. Facsimile of original, Archives nationales K3, No. 8; P. Lauer and C. Samaran, *Les diplômes originaux des Merovingiens* (Paris 1908), No. 24, transcription 17.
36. W. Metz, *Zur Erforschung des karolingischen Reichsgutes* (Darmstadt 1971) and E. Hlawitschka, 'Zur landschaftlichen Herkunft der Karolinger', *RhV* 27 (1962), 1–17.
37. *Edictum Chilperici* c. 3, *MGH Cap.* I, 8 and compare F. L. Ganshof, 'Le statut de la femme', *Société Jean Bodin* 12 (1962), 5–58.
38. J. Semmler, 'Zur pippinidisch – karolingischen Suksessionskrise 714–723', *DA* 33 (1977), 1–36.
39. M. Rouche, 'Les Aquitains ont-ils trahi avant la bataille de Poitiers? Un éclairage "événementiel" sur les mentalités', *MA* 23 (1968), 1–26.
40. Fredegar, Continuation 20.
41. Boniface, Ep. 48.
42. H. Wolfram, 'Der heilige Rupert und die anti-karolingische Adelsopposition', *MIÖG* 80 (1972), 4–34, and K. F. Werner, 'Bedeutende Adelsfamilien im Reich Karls des Grossen', *KdG* I, 83–142; Eng. trs. T. Reuter, *The Medieval Nobility* (Amsterdam, New York and Oxford 1978), 137–202.
43. Astronomer, c. 21.

44. L. Levillain, 'L'avènement de la dynastie Carolingienne et les origines de l'Etat pontificale 749–757', *BEC* 94 (1933), 225–95.
45. J.-M. Pardessus, *Diplomatae, chartae, epistolae leges aliaque instrumenta ad res Gallo-Francicas spectantia* (Paris 2 vols, 1843–49), II, No. DLXXV, 387.
46. *MGH Conc.* II, i., No. 6, 46–8.
47. I. Wood, 'Kings, kingdoms and consent', *Early Medieval Kingship*, I. Wood and P. Sawyer (eds) (Leeds 1977), 6–29.
48. P. Riché and G. Tate, *Textes et documents d'Histoire du Moyen Age, V^e–Xe siècles* (Paris 1974), 249–83 especially 281. Compare L. Levillain, 'De l'authenticité de la *clausula de unctione Pippini*', *BEC* 88 (1927), 20–42, and E. Caspar, *Pippin und der römische Kirche* (Berlin 1914).
49. T. Reuter, 'Saint Boniface and Europe', *The Greatest Englishman* T. Reuter (ed.) (Exeter 1980), 69–94. But Boniface did not anoint Pippin king.
50. See Semmler, 'Pippin III und die fränkischen Klöster', especially 95–7, and K. F. Werner, 'Les principautés périphériques'.
51. H. Pirenne, 'Le fisc royal de Tournai', *Mélanges F. Lot* (Paris 1925), 641–8.

CHAPTER THREE

Conquest and Consolidation: Pippin III and Charlemagne

There is little to distinguish Pippin's mayoral from his royal policies and activities. While his campaigns in Saxony, Alemannia and Aquitaine can be seen as a continuation of the aims of Charles Martel, the relationship Pippin formed with the Frankish church, especially the monasteries, and with the Papacy, are distinctive features of his reign which had far-reaching consequences for his successors. The customary view of Pippin is of a king zealous in promoting reform and the church's interests, and the man responsible for the small beginnings of his son Charlemagne's great achievements. Recent research, however, has substantially modified this view. Pippin's reign was characterized by a ruthless and single-minded utilization of every possible means, including religious ones, of furthering his political ends.[1] His monastic policy in particular, fully integrated into his political activities, was extraordinarily complex, and was either directed at effecting political change or the outcome of it.[2]

I

By the eighth century, aristocratic families, and the bishops among them, dominated the church in the Frankish kingdoms.[3] In the course of the seventh century entrenched local families had acquired control of bishoprics; and independent monasteries and churches, themselves often founded by aristocratic saints, were brought under the direct administration of the bishop. The massive spoliation and secularization of church property in the first part of the eighth century, for which Charles Martel was blamed by Hincmar in the second half of the ninth century,[4] was in fact carried out by a great many Frankish noble families, including the Arnulfings (or Carolingians), who thus came to wield the power of ecclesiastical appointment and with it the possibility of despoiling churches from within. Sees and abbacies were kept in the family. The Widones, for example, possessed the wealth and occupied the sees of Rheims and Trier, as well as the monasteries integrated into the territories of these two bishoprics.

41

At Trier, Basin (d. 705) was succeeded by his nephew Liutwin (d. 717) who in turn was succeeded by his son, the doughty sportsman Milo (d. 757), whose fondness for hunting angered St Boniface[5] and who was, according to a later story, gored to death by a boar when out hunting; not really a seemly end for a man of the cloth. Similarly Gewilib, bishop of Mainz, was deposed after seeking vengeance for his father Bishop Gerold of Mainz's death. The Etichonids, the ducal family of Alemannia, controlled a number of monasteries in their region; they were the founders of Moutier Grandval (640), Münster im Gregoriental (660), St Stephen in Strasbourg (c. 700), Honau and Murbach, and to others, such as Remiremont and Weissenburg, they granted a form of immunity. Some of these bishops, including Gewilib of Mainz, Milo of Trier and Ainmar of Auxerre, owed their position to Charles Martel, for they had supported him loyally; Ainmar had fought by Charles's side at the battle of Poitiers.[6]

Given their background and tradition, it is not surprising that a great many of these bishops were worldly, cared little for the sees or monasteries under them except as sources of wealth to be tapped, and possibly neglected the Christian religion. Nevertheless some missionary work was undertaken in the seventh and eighth centuries, and many monastic communities living in conformity with one or a number of the monastic rules current at the time, were established, such as Echternach, Prüm and Lorsch. Emmeram and Corbinian, both Franks, evangelized much of Bavaria; from the see of Cologne missions were sent to Westphalia and parts of Frisia, and from Worms, Rupert went to Salzburg.[7] In the seventh century Aquitainian missionaries had been active north of the Loire and Seine in converting Franks. Amand, for example, was active in Flanders and the region round Valenciennes, and was the first bishop of Maastricht. The monasteries and bishoprics established by him and his followers and colleagues – Vedast (St Vaast), Bertin, Bavo and Omer – in Ghent, Arras and north-east France led to a growth in the number of Christians and the development of the church in this area which continued in the eighth century, little disturbed or even encouraged by the Carolingians until the reign of Louis the Pious.[8] The most important missionary in the early part of the eighth century was Pirmin (d. 753). He came from Septimania or southern Aquitaine and had been taught in his youth by Bishop Fructuosus of Braga. His *Scarapsus*, a rule for Christian conduct (incidentally the earliest document containing the Apostles' Creed in its present form) enjoyed some popularity. Pirmin's chief missionary work was in Alemannia, Rhaetia and Alsace. The most important of the monasteries he founded was Reichenau (724), but all his foundations became in due course centres of religious and cultural activity. Pirmin enjoyed the protection of both Charles Martel and Pippin and became an important agent for the furthering of Pippin's monastic policy in Alemannia.

Many of the aristocratic bishops combined the episcopal office with the abbacy of the monastery of the same city or region. David, bishop of Strasbourg, was abbot of Weissenburg, and Milo, bishop of Trier, was an apparently conscientious abbot of Mittlach. Other associations of abbacies with bishoprics include St Vaast and the see of Cambrai–Arras, St Medard and the see of Soissons, St Emmeram and Regensburg, and St Peter's and Salzburg. Not all of these associations came about by choice. St Gall for example had been grasped greedily by the bishops of Constance with the collusion of counts Warin and Radulf, and St Calais monastery became an appendage of the bishopric of Le Mans and was controlled by the counts of Maine who possessed the bishopric.[9]

The aristocratic bishops constituted the principal threat to Pippin's position, his authority and the future of his house. They were classic examples of the overmighty subject. Pippin mistrusted the power of these bishops and of the families who backed them, and set out systematically to destroy it. He did this by means of a monastic policy which went hand in hand with his series of campaigns.

Charles Martel had exiled the family of Eucharic of Orleans, who controlled the bishopric of Auxerre, to Hesbaye and installed his own man, Ainmar, in the see. Ainmar naturally enough subsequently used the resources to hand to extend his influence over what amounted to an episcopal principality in Burgundy. Pippin in 741 simply confiscated all the episcopal estates except for 100 manses, thereby ensuring that the impoverished bishops would not again be able to achieve such influence. In other words, although the bishop was left in charge of the spiritual welfare of the diocese, the temporal, that is, the estates and revenues, would be granted to loyal followers, usually laymen. In the case of Auxerre military protection was accorded to the region and a count appointed to administer it. The church of Auxerre was excluded from the main group of foundations and abbots to whom independent administration was ceded. The monasteries of St Julien and St Germain of Auxerre were granted privileges of immunity as well as administrative and military independence. The abbots became Pippin's men. The monasteries of Saints Gervase and Protasius, Martin, Eusebius and Marian were also lost to the bishopric. Charlemagne later restored all these monasteries to the bishopric except St Julien, which remained in royal hands until the end of the ninth century. In the case of Auxerre then, Pippin gained control of the monasteries as a means of strengthening his own position. This entailed in Auxerre, as it was to do in many other dioceses, the substitution of royal for episcopal dominance of certain monasteries. The policy, though drastic, was effective, but the religious scruples of his successors undid many of the measures Pippin had taken to safeguard the Carolingian position.

Pippin's conquest of Alemannia and the submission of the Etichonen dukes also brought about a realignment of the Alemannian monasteries. At the fall of the Etichonids, the abbot of Honau commended the abbey and its community of monks to Pippin,[10] and thereby secured his protection. Soon all the other Etichonid monasteries had followed suit, and by 750 all were Carolingian. Similarly when Count Wulfoald, an Etichonid, was defeated, his own foundation St Mihiel was granted immunity and became a royal monastery; Count Wulfoald's private lands were confiscated and given to the royal monastery of St Denis. Pippin then placed Alemannia in the hands of two nobles, counts Ruthard and Warin: Ruthard and the missionary Pirmin acted together as agents of the Carolingian house, working to make other monasteries in the region, such as Arnulfsau and Gengenbach, independent of any bishop and instead dependent on the goodwill of the king.

St Gall was to suffer from the interference of Ruthard and Warin. Abbot Otmar of St Gall had given the monastery a firm organization but had not been able to avoid coming under the influence of the Alemannian dukes. Pippin of course took over, and obliged the monks of St Gall to follow the Rule of St Benedict as a model; he also strengthened the monastery's economy with the gift of lands. The monastery was further enriched by the gifts or grants *in precaria* of land and property made by the pious among the inhabitants of Alemannia. This meant the donor could retain the use of his or her property till he or she died. The original charters recording all these gifts are still in the St Gall archive.[11] Monks were dispatched from St Gall to form communities at Füssen and Kempten. Yet the relative self-sufficiency of St Gall seems to have been a thorn in the flesh of Ruthard and Warin. In 756 Pippin actually acquiesced in the removal of Abbot Otmar; Otmar was imprisoned by the counts and his successor as abbot was John, bishop of Constance. For nearly a century St Gall was attached to the see of Constance; Reichenau and Säckingen also came within the control of that diocese.

This development was at odds with Pippin's general policy of reducing the wealth of the bishops and the extent of episcopal control of monasteries. Either Pippin agreed with his counts' assessment of the potential threat posed by St Gall or else the counts simply took advantage of Pippin's preoccupation in the west of his kingdom and strengthened their own position in the king's name. If the latter interpretation is correct it is a telling reminder of the underlying weakness of Pippin's authority. His success depended on the loyalty of his men. Pippin also found time, once Odilo was defeated, to interfere in the monastic development of Bavaria. Both Pippin and Carloman granted privileges to Benedictbeuren, and Gisela their sister shared their interest in this abbey and in its daughter convent at Kochel. The biggest dent Pippin made in the ecclesiastical power of the Bavarian dukes was at Tegernsee, founded in 762–5 by Autgar and Adalbert. Autgar came under Pippin's wing and Adalbert remained as abbot. Tegernsee became the first Bavarian royal monastery.

The bishops of Sens, Châlons-sur-Marne, Rheims, Autun and Nevers all lost the power of disposition over some of the monasteries attached to their sees.[12] On the other hand, Pippin did nothing to hinder the bishops of Mainz, Autun, Toul and Metz who wanted to found or revive monasteries. Chrodegang, bishop of Metz, was especially favoured among the Frankish bishops, one of the few exceptions in Pippin's anti-episcopal campaign. But Chrodegang was, after all, a bishop of a different stamp. He was a churchman, devoted to reform. Born of noble parents, Chrodegang had acted as referendary in the chancery of Charles Martel and in 742, at the early age of thirty, he was consecrated bishop of Metz. After 747 he appears to have been closer to Pippin in reforming matters than Boniface. He introduced the Roman form of liturgy and chant and wrote the *Regula canonicorum*, a rule for the daily conduct of the canons regular attached to the cathedral of Metz which was widely adopted in the Frankish kingdoms as an alternative form of conventual life. After Boniface's martyrdom in 754, Chrodegang succeeded to the title of archbishop and was entrusted with the ecclesiastical affairs of the whole Frankish kingdom. As a reforming bishop, he was much involved in the revival of monastic life in the Metz region. He acquired relics in Rome for the monasteries with which he was most concerned: Gorze, St Avold and Lorsch. The last of these was a foundation of his relatives the Rupertines and Chrodegang seems to have had a hand in its affairs. Gorze was made into the exemplary monastery of his diocese by Chrodegang, and it is significant that this episcopal foundation was backed by Pippin. At Compiègne in 757 Chrodegang presented the privilege of Gorze for signature by all the bishops present. It was an episcopal monastery; the bishops of Metz had important disciplinary powers over it and the election of its abbots needed his consent. Already by 761 monks from Gorze had been sent to set up Gengenbach, and when Lorsch was founded in 764, it was again monks from Gorze who were sent to establish the community.

It is in accordance with Pippin's general monastic policy that he made only a few gifts of land to Tours and to monasteries in the Paris basin, of which St Denis, as the surviving charters indicate, got the lion's share. Fulrad, abbot of St Denis, through systematic acquisition of lands in Alsace, built up the basis from which after 768 St Denis established daughter monasteries in the dioceses of Strasbourg and Metz and east into Alemannia. Pippin confirmed monastic ownership on a grand scale; he conferred on an impressive number of monasteries, including St Wandrille, Stavelot–Malmédy, St Bertin and St Oyen, various rights such as the privilege of immunity, freedom of election for abbots, independence from the *dominium* of the bishop of the see and freedom from dues on goods imported into the monastery. Pippin restored Prüm, founded thirty years before by his wife's grandmother, had a church built and gave it land out of his own and his wife's personal property, as well as considerable possessions elsewhere, especially in the regions of Le Mans and Rennes. Private donors increased the monastery's wealth. Prüm became a family monastery of the Carolingians; it was accorded royal protection, the choice of abbot was to be confirmed by the king and the monastic community was bound to be loyal to the Carolingian family.

II

The first of Pippin's campaigns as king was occasioned by a revolt of the Saxons against Carolingian authority in 753. According to the *Annales Mettenses* the Saxons were obliged to permit Christian missionaries to enter the country. Again the sources attribute religious motives to Pippin's aggrandizement. The Saxons also agreed to pay an annual tribute of 300 horses. The same source records that in the same year Pippin conducted a successful campaign in Brittany. [13] Whether this campaign really took place is doubted by some historians, but that Pippin was in the vicinity of Brittany in 753 is attested by the material relating to the history of the diocese of Le Mans.

In Maine, the Count Rotgar and his son Charivius gained control of the see of Le Mans. After the death of Herlemund (724) the see remained vacant for a number of years and the counts administered the possessions, monasteries and *cellulae* of the bishopric.[14] Rotgar then made his second son Gauciolenus, described as an illiterate and ignorant cleric, bishop, with the connivance of the bishop of Rouen, rather than of the metropolitan of the region, the bishop of Tours. Bishop Gauciolenus lived a secular life for half a century and the diocese went to rack and ruin. In 748 or 749 Pippin made his first move and installed his brother Grifo as count of Maine. What the position was between Grifo, Gauciolenus and Charivius is not known, but in all events Grifo went to Aquitaine in 753. Did the count and bishop drive him out? It is at this stage that Pippin arrived in the region. Gauciolenus and Charivius shut the gates of Le Mans against Pippin and the king retaliated by devastating the region round Le Mans, taking care however, to preserve the monasteries from harm. St Calais and its community of monks was taken under Pippin's protection and lordship and granted immunity; Abbot Sigebald commended himself and his community to the king. Pippin then got rid of the suffragan bishops of Le Mans but Gauciolenus appears to have been left as incumbent, for he is among the signatories of the foundation privilege of Prüm and the confraternity book of Attigny in 760.[15] Many *villae* were lost to the diocese and the king appropriated the monasteries; it was impoverished and its power emasculated, much as the diocese of Auxerre had been ten years earlier. Until their restitution by Louis the Pious the monasteries of St Vincent and Notre Dame du Mans were part of the imperial fisc. It is possible that the subjection of Maine was confused by the 'Metz annalist' with a subjection of Brittany. If the Breton campaign took place, it must have been earlier in the year than the Saxon one, for it was on Pippin's way home from Saxony in November that news was brought to the king in his villa at Diedenhofen or Thionville, that the Pope had arrived in the Frankish kingdom and was on his way to meet Pippin.

III

Fredegar's Continuator records that Pippin sent his son Charles (then probably only six years old[16]) together with some of his leading magnates, including Duke Rothard and Fulrad, abbot of St Denis, to meet the Pope and bring him to his residence at Ponthion.[17] The *Liber Pontificalis'* story that Pippin came out from Ponthion on foot to meet the Pope and led the Pontiff's horse back as if he, Pippin, were a groom, can probably be discounted as no more than the author's opinion of how Pippin should have behaved; none of the Frankish sources add this detail.[18]

What had brought about the Pope's visit to the Frankish kingdom? The Lombards' aggressive expansion within Italy and into the Exarchate of Ravenna had goaded the Pope into seeking help from Charles Martel; the latter, mindful of the Lombards' aid against the Arabs, refused. The fact that his son Pippin had spent some time as an honoured adopted son at Liutprand's court was also, no doubt, an important consideration. An association between the Papacy and the Franks had, however, been formed in the ecclesiastical sphere, largely due to the work of the Englishman Boniface and Frankish reform councils of the 740s. This association reached a climax in 751 when the Pope was asked to give his sanction to the Carolingian *coup d'état*.[19] Pope Zacharias, quite apart from his promotion of the association with the Franks, had had some success in restraining the Lombard kings, Liutprand, Ratchis and Aistulf, from conquering the cities of the Exarchate of Ravenna, and had imposed a forty-years peace on Aistulf, a peace broken by the Lombard king four months after its confirmation by Zacharias' successor, Stephen II, The Exarchate had fallen into Lombard hands in 751–2; the imperial legates from Byzantium offered advice and exhortation but little material assistance, and embassies were despatched from the papal to the Lombard courts with appeals for the return of the Exarchate. Aistulf's response was to invade papal territory.

Early in 753, alarmed by Aistulf's seizure of the Exarchate of Ravenna and invasion of the duchy of Rome, Stephen II appealed to Pippin through a Frankish pilgrim. Pippin commissioned Droctegang, abbot of Jumièges, to go and take stock of the situation and assure the Pope of his willingness to help. Chrodegang, bishop of Metz, and Duke Autchar were assigned to the Pope as escorts and the party first sought audience with Aistulf at Pavia in order to beg him to deliver up the cities. Aistulf proved obdurate, and the party continued on its way over the Alps and reached Ponthion, where Epiphany was celebrated with much festivity and rejoicing.

What happened at Ponthion is not at all clear. Pope Stephen probably asked for aid and for protection of the church's interests in Italy. According to the *Liber Pontificalis*, Pippin's response was the so-called Donation of Pippin, an oral promise on Pippin's part to restore the territories of the Roman state seized by the Lombards. This was perhaps given in written form at Quierzy on 14 April 754 rather than at Ponthion. The *Vita Stephani* states that Pippin granted the Exarchate and Roman duchy to the Papacy.[20] The *Vita Hadriani* records that Charlemagne confirmed this grant in 778 and renewed the promise, pledging the whole peninsular of Italy; a promise confirmed again in 817.[21] But what Charlemagne and Louis confirmed may well have been not the oral promise attributed to Pippin at Ponthion but the charter of donation of the cities of the Exarchate and Pentapolis and the provinces of Emilia and Narnia which Fulrad delivered to Rome after Pippin's second campaign in Italy in 756.

There can be little doubt that Pippin made some promise of restitution and that he gave little thought to any possible Byzantine claims on the territories in Lombard hands. It is equally certain that the Roman *Curia* itself provided the legal, historical and written justification for, as well as the details of, this promise in the spurious document known as the Donation of Constantine, first exposed as a forgery by Lorenzo Valla in 1439.

It is not actually certain for whom the document was intended. According to it, Constantine gave Pope Silvester Italy and the West to be under his rule: 'so that the papal crown may not be despised but adorned with glory and influence beyond the dignity of the earthly empire, we hand over and relinquish our palace, the city of Rome, and all the provinces, places and cities of Italy and the western regions to the blessed pontiff and universal Pope Silvester; and we ordain by our pragmatic constitution that they shall be governed by him and by his successors and we grant that they shall remain under the authority of the holy Roman church'.[22]

Unfortunately it is impossible to date the document precisely, and its correct interpretation depends on its date. One theory is that the Pope prepared the forgery for the Frankish king as proof of his claim to the Exarchate,[23] or even to encourage Pippin to make his promise.[24] Some have attempted to make it a later, Carolingian, forgery. Max Buchner, for example, suggested that it was produced at Rheims in 816,[25] and Ohnsorge that the Franks produced it in 806 in order to justify Charlemagne's position.[26] Caspar saw in the document a move against Byzantium, but the anti-Byzantine element is probably of secondary importance.[27] The weight of opinion now, however, is that the document was forged in the papal *Curia* in Rome in about 756, perhaps with the cognizance of the Pope, in order to represent what may have been imagined to be legal rights; and that it was then presented to the king.[28] But this view would only make sense if the forgery was made at the latest before 14 April 754, when Pippin consulted his magnates at Quierzy as to whether an Italian campaign should be mounted. A further important body of opinion dates the Donation to before Stephen set out on his journey to the Frankish kingdom.[29] On the other hand, the document may not have been intended for the Franks so much as to serve as a general papal justification of its position and the Franks' actions.

After the festivities at Ponthion, Pippin installed Pope Stephen at St Denis for the rest of the winter, and an embassy was sent to Aistulf demanding that he restore the territories he had taken. Aistulf's refusal was lent added weight in 754 when Pippin's brother Carloman was sent on the order of his abbot, Aistulf's man, to beg Pippin not to comply with the Pope's request. The sources give little idea of Pippin's reactions to this extraordinary reappearance of his brother, nor is there any hint of foul play; the facts are bald enough. Carloman was detained in the Frankish kingdom and died at Vienne the following year; his two sons were subsequently tonsured.[30] Two years later the Pope demanded that the monks of Monte Cassino who had accompanied Carloman should be freed, and it was only when Pippin himself was on the point of death in 768 that he made gifts to Fulda and St Denis for the good of his brother's soul. Was this remorse?

In July 754 Pope Stephen reanointed Pippin king, and anointed Pippin's two sons Charles and Carloman and his queen Bertrada, declaring the Carolingians to be the legitimate rulers of the Frankish kingdom. Pippin, Charles and Carloman were all accorded the title *patricius*, that is, protectors of Italy and the see of St Peter – the highest secular and honorary post the Pope could bestow. The account in the *Liber Pontificalis* is corroborated by the *Clausula de unctione Pippini*, a text now accepted as an eye-witness account despite the doubts cast upon it by Buchner and others.[31] The Papacy thus not only reaffirmed its position as a supporter of the Carolingian house and the Frankish ruler's obligations towards the Papacy; it also set an important precedent for the confirmation of Carolingian royal power, a precedent followed to its logical conclusion with the coronation of Charlemagne in 800.

Pippin seems to have encountered some opposition from his nobles to the prospect of war against the Lombards. Two meetings appear to have been held to discuss the possibility of forcing Aistulf to give back the stolen territory, though the first may simply have been a consultation with his chief advisers which resulted in the fruitless embassy to Aistulf referred to above. At the *placitum* in 755, the Franks agreed to mount a campaign against the Lombards. The latter were defeated in the valley of Susa and the Frankish army marched on Pavia. They captured much treasure, equipment and tents, and Aistulf begged for terms. According to the Royal Frankish Annals and the Continuation of Fredegar, Pippin obtained hostages and solemn oaths from Aistulf that he would never again enter the territories of the Papacy. The *Annales Mettenses* add that Aistulf also promised to return the cities of the Pentapolis and Narnia and pay an annual tribute. Aistulf was little inclined to keep any promises he made, and the treaty was broken in the following year. Not only had he failed to restore so much as a hand's-breath of land to the Papacy; he besieged Rome itself for three months and ravaged the Roman countryside. Again the Pope sent pathetic messages to Pippin, and again Pippin set out with his army, this time accompanied by his nephew, the young Duke Tassilo of Bavaria. Again Pavia was besieged and Aistulf forced to submit, and again he was let off with terrible oaths that this time he would make amends. It seems that near Pavia Pippin was met by the Byzantine legate who asked that Ravenna and the Exarchate be handed over to Byzantium but Pippin thought only of the Papacy.[32] The Byzantine interventions in these years were remarkably ineffectual. Pippin took greater care to see that the cities were restored to the Papacy. Fulrad, the Frankish palace chaplain, accompanied by Aistulf's representative, entered every city of the Pentapolis and province of Emilia, received hostages from each and sent them, together with the keys of each city and a charter of donation to the Pope. Aistulf died shortly afterwards leaving no obvious heir. The succession was disputed. An attempt was made by the ex-king Ratchis to emerge from his monastery and reascend the throne, but Desiderius, duke of Tuscany, succeeded in gaining papal and Frankish support, and assumed the royal title in March 757. No further campaigns were conducted by the Franks for the remainder of Pippin's reign. Pope Stephen II died in 757 and his successor Paul I reported to Pippin that the Empire, represented by the legate George, and the Lombards had come to an agreement.[33] In 758 Desiderius marched on Spoleto and Benevento and destroyed the independence of both the dukes. From 762–7 the Pope himself was forced to take refuge in the catacombs of Naples, but continued in spite of his discomfort to strengthen the ties with the Franks, mostly in a very small way in the religious sphere by means of the gift of books (most of them in Greek so they would have been of little use to the Franks) and the grant of the monastery of Mount Soracte which Pippin 'gave back' as the fact that it was in Lombard territory made it difficult to administer.

The Lombard campaigns had had the effect of forging a strong political connection between the Frankish rulers and the Papacy where before there had been little more than a pastoral interest. The Papacy had found the protector it needed, not only to make up for the deficiencies and lack of interest of the Eastern Empire but also to offset the aggression of the Lombards. At more or less the same time as the agreement reached between the Lombards and Byzantium, the latter sent an embassy to the Frankish kingdom, bearing princely gifts, including an organ, and relations between the Franks and Byzantium remained ill-defined. There is a sense in which the difficulties of the Papacy had brought the Franks irrevocably to the fore in the political developments in the West.

IV

The most concerted opposition to the extension of Carolingian rule came from Aquitaine and occupied Pippin for the remainder of his reign. There was only one year between 759 and 768 in which Pippin did not conduct a campaign in this region. Duke Waifar was not the only intransigent opponent of Pippin in Aquitaine, for there are some indications of local noble opposition and, unlike the hostility encountered from the counts of Maine, the aristocratic bishops of Auxerre, the dukes of Alemannia or Bavaria, this opposition was almost entirely secular. Nevertheless, Pippin's original and ostensible motive for mounting his offensive against Aquitaine was to protect ecclesiastical interests. Yet the fact he had established some authority in Septimania between 752 and 759 should also be taken into account. The sources state that he was an unwilling aggressor, goaded into action by Duke Waifar's refusal to restore to the churches and monasteries in Pippin's kingdom the lands in Aquitaine which belonged to them, or to respect the immunity Pippin had bestowed upon these same establishments.[34] The religious motive should not be discounted entirely. There was no need to trump up such an excuse for an act of aggression, and it is possible that Pippin was simply being consistent in his policy of protecting the interests of the church so long as it served his own.

Since the death of Charibert in 632, Aquitaine had enjoyed a state of semi-independence *vis-à-vis* the Frankish rulers. The *Annales Mettenses* record that Hunuald, son of Eudo, promised loyalty to Charles Martel and his son and recovered the duchy of Aquitaine. Thus Aquitaine was excluded from the partition made between Carloman and Pippin on Charles Martel's death, and almost immediately a conspiracy seems to have been formed between the dukes of Aquitaine and Bavaria, both averse to Carolingian dominance. In 742 Carloman and Pippin conducted a campaign to Aquitaine and split the region, which it could hardly be said they had conquered, between them, even though they reached no further than Loches, some 32 miles south of Tours. References to Aquitaine are rare in the narrative sources. The *Annales Mettenses* give an account of the burning of Chartres by Hunuald at the instigation of the Bavarian Duke Odilo in 743, his later retirement into a monastery and the succession of his son Waifar. And the Chronicle of Moissac records that Waifar 'the prince of Aquitaine' devastated the region of Narbonne in 751 and that in 753 Grifo had taken refuge in Aquitaine.

Pippin's annual raids in Aquitaine were essentially directed against fortresses.[35] Apart from the urban stronghold of Clermont, most of the fortresses attacked by Pippin's armies were rural strongholds such as Escorailles, Chantelle, Turenne, Carlat or Ronzières, the remains of many of which are still to be seen. At the close of the campaign Pippin took sanctions against those who had defended these fortresses, and as late as 820 Louis the Pious published a capitulary designed to regulate the type of benefits accruing to the defenders of the fortresses taken by Pippin and ruled that only those who had continued the resistance should forfeit their lands.[36] One defendant had been made a slave but obtained his freedom from Louis (he must surely have been the son or grandson of the man originally enslaved). Some of the fortresses may have been built in the late Roman period, but it is not clear from the archaeological evidence whether the Aquitainian troubles increased the number of fortified strongholds in Aquitaine. If this is the case, it suggests that the local and aristocratic resistance to Carolingian rule in Aquitaine was strong enough to make defensive building possible; indeed, in Saxony the forts of Siegburg and Buraburg were constructed in similar circumstances. In other words, Pippin's strategy and tactics – short forays, raids on forts, burning and looting and a 'scorched earth' policy – suggest that it was not just a recalcitrant Duke Waifar with whom he was dealing but a widespread reluctance to acknowledge the Carolingian as overlord to which Waifar's defiance had given teeth. The history of Remistian, uncle of Waifar, provides one example of the way loyalties could be swayed. After the campaign of 762, Pippin gave the fortress of Argenton-sur-Creuse and half Berry into the care of Remistian, who had joined Pippin's army. Remistian stayed on Pippin's side for the next few years, all through the terrible destruction Pippin wrought in Aquitaine. But in 767 after the king had taken Toulouse, Albi and Javols, Remistian defected back to Waifar. This did him little good, for in the following year Remistian was captured by Pippin's men and hanged at Bourges.

It seems that once an area with fortified sites had been subdued, the Carolingians retained only a limited interest in this form of military organization, though the nature of the archaeological evidence prevents certainty about this. Town walls were not repaired or rebuilt; indeed, they were often destroyed for the sake of the masonry. The Carolingian rulers may have felt that fortified places in a region recently conquered or subdued could be a dangerous weakness in case of revolt and that frontier defences were more important. The relative paucity of maintained fortifications in the Frankish kingdoms may account in part for the success of the Northmen's raids. The Carolingian rulers preferred social, religious and political means of establishing and exerting their authority. After his gradual conquest of Poitiers, Limoges, Saintes, Périgueux, Angoulême and Bourges, Pippin installed his own representatives to administer these regions, and abbots loyal to him were placed at the head of many of the principal Aquitainian monasteries. Such a policy would presumably have put the local magnates' and ecclesiastics' noses severely out of joint. St Hilary of Poitiers became a royal monastery and was granted an immunity. So did St Croix at Poitiers, Noirmoutier and St Maixent. The last of these served for the provision of the count of that area and the lands of St Savin-sur-Gartempe were granted to Baddilo, Pippin's chancery notary, to enable him to endow a college of clerics.[37] In the Clermont region Pippin took St Julien of Brioude, and other monasteries were granted to new counts. Menat became the morning gift to the wife of the Aquitainian subking. The revenues of St Victor of Marseilles and St Chaffre de Monastier in the diocese of Le Puy were also granted to counties.[38] Pippin made little attempt to interfere in the organization of the Aquitainian monasteries or to care for their religious welfare; he simply used them to bolster his own power.

In 761 Pippin led an expedition into Burgundy and devastated the country as far as Chalon-sur-Saône, helped by Hunibert, count of Bourges, and Bladin, count of the Auvergne, the first among many Aquitainian nobles who defected to Pippin as his success became more assured. Pippin then crossed the Loire to Nevers, took Bourbon and Clermont and devastated parts of Aquitaine. His conquest was methodical; he started by establishing his power in the districts close to the frontiers – Berry, the Auvergne, the Touraine, and expanding from there. Waifar ordered the dismantlement of the fortified strongholds such as Poitiers, Bourges, Limoges, Saintes, Périgueux and Angoulême and retired ever further south and closer to the bases of his power. Pippin pursued him relentlessly, and captured Agen, Poitiers and Limoges. When he arrived in the Garonne valley he received oaths of loyalty from the people. Waifar took refuge in the forest of Ver, Pippin still in pursuit. The war ended abruptly with the assassination of Waifar by his own men, possibly at the instigation of Pippin. It was the end for some decades of the independence of Aquitaine. In the *Capitulare Aquitanicum* drawn up in April 768, the king set out his first decisions regarding the province. The secular clauses dealt for the most part with administration of justice. The right of appeal to the king was established and the principle of the personality of law upheld, in that each national group, Roman, Frank or whatever, was accorded the right to be judged by its own law. The six clauses concerning the church extended the reform which had already begun in the church north of the Loire to the south. Abandoned churches were to be restored, canonical life for bishops, abbots and abbesses was prescribed, and regulations were made concerning the disposition of ecclesiastical property.[39]

Pippin's strategy in Aquitaine appears to have been at first to create a new march, with the annual campaigns forming a second stage. No text tells us precisely what the limits of Pippin's conquests were, but it seems certain to have been the Garonne and Bordeaux, a limit to Frankish expansion which remained until the tenth century. The diocese of Bordeaux extended along the right bank of the Garonne only. Under Louis the Pious, who from 781 was the subking of Aquitaine, the archbishop of Bordeaux was the only one among the Gascon bishops to receive the canons of the Council of Aachen (816–17), and to be named in the circular issued by Louis and Lothar in that year.[40] Ten years after the death of Pippin the kingdom of Aquitaine established by Charlemagne stopped at the Garonne and Lupus was the leader or duke of Gascony. In 836 Gascony was considered to be separated from the kingdom of Aquitaine, the northern part of it probably forming a marcher region like the march of Brittany. The campaign supposedly conducted in Brittany by Pippin may also have been a strategic establishment of a marcher region round Vannes.

Before he died at St Denis in September 768, Pippin divided his hard-won kingdom between his two surviving sons Charles and Carloman. The division is not at all clear; surviving charters indicate that there was some overlapping of the brothers' jurisdiction in Neustria. Aquitaine was included in this partition. Either Charlemagne got the whole of Aquitaine[41] or it was divided between the two princes.[42] When Hunuald, son of Waifar, raised a revolt in Aquitaine, however, it was Charles who dealt with it and 'even went so far as to ask his brother for help',[43] at a time when the relations between the two brothers were strained. Charlemagne chased Hunuald as far as the Garonne, but Lupus surrendered the luckless fugitive to Charlemagne. Aquitaine and Gascony seem to have been subdued, but in 778 the *Wascones* (Gascons) wreaked much havoc in the van of Charlemagne's army on his return from Spain, a tragic but minor skirmish immortalized in the *Chanson de Roland*. In 781 Louis was made subking of Aquitaine; it was a very astute move on Charlemagne's part, and Aquitaine remained for three-quarters of a century part of the Frankish kingdom.

Political background & ambitions of King

V

Because Pippin made so much use of the monasteries as the foundation of his power, he was more or less obliged to do something about the internal organization, discipline and religious observance of these establishments. It was also clearly in his own interests as well as those of the kingdom and of the church. It is in this light that to a considerable extent his reform activities should be viewed, and it should be noted that many of his actions had important implications for his office as king as well as for royal relations with the church. The policies of Charles Martel and Pippin undoubtedly weakened both the independence of the church and its pastoral activities. The bishop whose diocesan lands had been misappropriated had little means of promoting the Christian faith, assisting or supporting his clergy or organizing his diocese. There was a definite decline in the quality of the clergy and the activities of the church.

The English missionary Boniface's accounts of his difficulties in the mission field and the situation he encountered in the Frankish church are usually accepted as a faithful description of what Frankish religious life was like at this time.[44] Although there can be no doubt that the church was at a low ebb, Boniface's picture is limited, not only by his own prejudices and preoccupations but also by the sphere of his own activities; he was simply not familiar with a large area of the Frankish kingdom. Working from the names of the bishops known to have been present at the various councils of the Frankish church held in the mid-eighth century, Ewig has pieced together the evidence for defining the geographical spread of Boniface's activities.[45] The zone of Boniface's influence, that is the area in which the sees adhering to Boniface's methods and procedures lay, was north of a line between Paris and Strasbourg, perhaps as far west as Rheims and Sens, east into Germany and the Rhineland, south-east to Bavaria, but excluding the provinces of Trier and Worms, which remained staunchly Frankish and aristocratic. Boniface's opinion about the parlous state of the church in Bavaria and the province of Trier, furthermore, may well have been coloured by the opposition or at least coolness he encountered there.[46] For too long we have been regarding the eighth-century Frankish church through the eyes of this English missionary.

How instrumental was Boniface in effecting a reform of the Frankish church? It has been noted above how many of the Frankish bishops in the Rhineland – Cologne, Mainz, Worms, Speyer and Strasbourg in particular – were active in both missionary and colonizing work. Collections of charters such as those surviving in the St Gall archive bear witness to the pious participation of the laity in the religious life of a region through gifts of land and offerings for the sake of prayers. In the eighth century moreover, largely as a result of Pippin's monastic policy, but also because of missionary activity on the part of Frankish and Irish saints such as Kilian, Rupert, Corbinian and Emmeram, monasteries begin to emerge as religious, cultural and political centres of considerable importance. The monasteries played a vital part in ensuring the continuity of religious life.

The Anglo-Saxon mission in the person of Willibrord had confined itself at first to Frisia. Willibrord's successor was Boniface and whereas the former had sought protection from Charles Martel, Boniface went to Rome and there received his pallium or insignia of office from the Pope, together with papal authorization to undertake missionary work. Boniface's work in Germany and Frisia was largely a reorganization of the Christian church already established, however shakily, in these regions. Bavaria was divided into four dioceses centred on Passau, Eichstätt, Regensburg and Salzburg, and monasteries and bishops loyal to Boniface were established along the Rhine and east into Germany, the see of Mainz and the monastery of Fulda being the most important.

Yet we are not so much concerned with Boniface's work in Germany as with the light his letters and activities throw on the Frankish church at this time. Conditions in the eighth-century church can be guessed at from the nature of the attempts to reform it. Boniface's efforts at reform are recorded in the decrees of the synods presided over by him and the ruler of the region in which the synod was held. The first of these was the *Concilium Germanicum* of 742 or 743, held in Austrasia with the support of Carloman. The ecclesiastical provinces involved – the Bonifacian bishops of Germany together with the Austrasian bishops of Cologne and Strasbourg – indicate that the effects of the council would have been limited to a small area.[47] The second council was again held in Austrasian territory, this time at Estinnes in 744. In the same year another was held at Soissons, under the auspices of Pippin III. Twenty-three bishops attended; we do not know from which sees, but those of the provinces of Sens, Rheims and Rouen have been suggested as the most likely. Reforms proposed at these synods included the appointment of bishops to vacant sees; the decision to hold a synod every year so that the laws of the church might be re-established and the Christian religion purified; the restoration of church revenues to the church (this is probably a reference to the expropriation of church property by laymen); the denial of church incomes to false priests or 'adulterous and lustful deacons'; a prohibition against priests carrying arms, fighting, joining the army, hunting or keeping hawks and falcons; the subjection of every priest in the diocese to his bishop; and the duty of every bishop to ensure that the people desisted from their pagan foulnesses such as sacrifices to the dead, casting of lots, divination, amulets and auguries, incantations or offering of animal sacrifices 'which foolish folk perform in the churches according to pagan custom'.[48]

In these conciliar decrees, in the correspondence of Boniface and the biographies of him and of his contemporaries, we learn of the continued prevalence of pagan beliefs, the ignorance of the clergy and the enormous difficulties not only of pulling the established church in Neustria and Austrasia into better shape, but also of establishing the church in the wilder regions to the west and north. It is also of significance that these conciliar decrees were issued in the name of Carloman and Pippin, lending them the character of royal legislation, and thus helping to establish a particularly enduring relationship between the Carolingian ruler and the church. Yet this evidence does apply to a specific sphere of influence and cannot be taken as a description of the status quo everywhere. For example, the famous reference by Boniface to a priest 'so ignorant that he could only produce a garbled version of the baptismal formula: in nomine patria et filia et spiritus sancti',[49] refers to the peculiar position in which Boniface found himself in the diocese of Salzburg, ruled then by the eccentric Bishop Virgil, and should certainly not be understood as a general comment on the learning of the clergy in the whole of the Frankish kingdom. Boniface also stated that no synod had been held in the country for seventy years; an exaggeration, since the period was probably nearer forty. As the synod was the forum where legislation, decisions concerning organization and discipline within the church and judgement of appeals took place, it means that there had been no strong centralized church government for a generation. This does not mean that some dioceses did not function better than others and maintain a higher level of religious life, and there may well have been occasional diocesan synods about which neither we know nor Boniface knew anything. Further, and perhaps more important, surely we do not have to believe that the main impetus to reform of the Frankish church came from a foreigner? Were there no Frankish efforts to reform the church before the arrival of Boniface or the legislation of Charlemagne?

Apart from the work of Pirmin in Alemannia, the Frankish reform move-

55

ment centred on Metz and was led by none other than Bishop Chrodegang. Schieffer has also emphasized the importance of the young Frankish generation which augmented and continued the work of Boniface.[50] Chrodegang was consecrated bishop of Metz in 742. Apart from the foundation of his exemplary monastery at Gorze and patronage of Lorsch and St Avold, Chrodegang's most enduring work was his *Regula canonicorum*, a rule for canons intended primarily for the cathedral clergy at Metz which was introduced at the Synod of Ver in 755 and became an alternative set of directives for the religious and communal life throughout the Frankish kingdom. The Rule draws on those portions of the Rule of St Benedict which pertain to communal life, as well as on Frankish synodal law.[51] It was also popular in England, and was translated into English in the tenth century. Chrodegang was instrumental in the adoption of Roman liturgical forms by the Frankish church in 755; Metz became a centre for Roman chant, but the main efforts towards establishing liturgical uniformity in the Frankish kingdom took place in the reign of Charlemagne.[52] Chrodegang's sphere of influence differed from that of Boniface. It extended between the Loire and the Seine and after 754 embraced also the Bonifacian bishoprics of Germany, as well as Cologne, Rouen, Sens, Toul and Trier, Besançon, Alemannia and as far as east as St Gall and Wessobrun, but excluding Mainz which was still dominated by Lull, Boniface's successor at Mainz. Altogether, including those sees within Pirmin's sphere of influence, there were six groups of cities over the whole kingdom, which after 768 included Aquitaine, active in reform.[53]

Chrodegang of Metz seems to have emerged as the most prominent bishop of the Frankish Kingdom after Carloman's retirement from the throne in 747. Carloman had certainly been more inclined than Pippin to patronize Boniface, and with his sympathetic support withdrawn, Boniface appears to have confined his activities to Germany and Frisia and to have been no longer centrally involved in the affairs of the Frankish church. Passages of Boniface's *Vita* by Willibald imply this, although Boniface's retirement may have had as much to do with his personal commitment to returning to missionary work in the last years of his life. The *Annales regni Francorum*, written many years after the mid-eighth-century events they describe, assert that Boniface was present at the anointing of Pippin in 751. The more contemporary accounts, the *Vita sancti Bonifacii*, the *Clausula de unctione Pippini* and the Continuation of Fredegar's Chronicle do not mention Boniface's participation in the anointing but refer simply to bishops. From the little that we do know, it would be a mistake to assume that Boniface was there, and there is absolutely no evidence that Zacharias commissioned Boniface to anoint Pippin. It is much more likely that Chrodegang and other bishops loyal both to the Frankish reform and to Pippin, would have anointed the new king. There is no need to posit alienation, or opposition to Boniface's work from Pippin and his supporters, but there is a possibility that Pippin's policy, directed at gaining adherents within the church and controlling the monasteries, was antipathetic to Boniface's plans and purpose. Boniface's close circle of monasteries associated with Fulda furthermore constituted a large bloc outside Pippin's control and not even within his sphere of influence. This situation was speedily remedied after Boniface's death.

The foundation of Fulda was initiated by Boniface and enriched by an endowment from Carloman and other gifts from nobles in the area. Sturm was made the first abbot and Boniface sought a papal privilege for the monastery so that the danger of Fulda becoming an episcopal monastery integrated into a diocese, like so many Frankish monasteries, would be removed. Donations were also made enabling daughter monasteries such as Kitzingen (a nunnery with Thecla as abbess) and Ohrdruf (with Wigbert as abbot) to be established. The Englishwoman Lioba became abbess of Taubersbischofsheim and after Boniface's death had close connections with Fulda. Fritzlar, Eichstätt, Heidenheim and Neustadt-am-Main were all associated with the original Bonifacian group of monasteries.

Pippin's first chance of penetrating this closed circle was provided by a revolt against Sturm by some of the monks at Fulda. The majority of the monks at Fulda thought that Lull was responsible for the secession, and it may be that Lull was seeking to make Fulda an integrated episcopal monastery in the see of Mainz, directly contrary to his predecessor's wishes, and that the move was resisted by Sturm and some of his monks, loyal disciples of Boniface. Sturm was exiled to Jumièges and Lull established his own man as abbot. Enraged, the monks at Fulda threw the upstart out and forced Lull to grant them freedom of election, whereupon they chose a young monk to act as deputy for Sturm. At this point, according to Eigil's Life of Sturm, Pippin intervened; he was 'reconciled' to Sturm and Sturm was reinstated. But the outcome of Pippin's intervention was that Fulda too was brought within the sphere of Carolingian influence without having anything to do with the see of Mainz; Pippin released the abbey *ab omni dominio Lulli episcopi* and put it under his protection. Fulda became a royal monastery and later Hersfeld and Fritzlar followed suit. Although it is not know how, Kitzingen, Neustadt-am-Main and Amorbach also became royal monasteries, while other foundations in the Fulda circle, such as Holzkirchen or Wenkheim, gradually came much more under Fulda's control. Fulda itself developed into one of the most important monasteries in the Frankish kingdom.

After Boniface's martyrdom in 754, Chrodegang of Metz received the title of archbishop and was entrusted with the ecclesiastical affairs of the whole Frankish kingdom. He was thus able to continue on a far wider scale the reforming activity he had begun in Metz. The Frankish councils which had lapsed on the departure of Carloman were renewed and held at Ver (755), Verberie (756), Compiègne (757) Attigny (760–2) and Gentilly (767), all under Chrodegang's presidency and most of them assemblies of the leading laymen and clerics. Chrodegang continued the programme of Boniface, above all that which aligned the Frankish church to Rome. He concentrated in particular on regularizing liturgical practice, on the restoration of ecclesiastical discipline, the reorganization of ecclesiastical provinces and the dioceses within them (though the renewed attempt to re-establish the metropolitans failed), the duties and prerogatives of bishops and the Roman laws for Christian marriage. At Gentilly the question of iconoclasm came up, apparently for the first time, though it was not until 794 that the Franks were to provide their definitive statement on the matter. The privilege of Gorze was confirmed at the Synod of Compiègne in 757; the signatories to this document attest to the presence of nineteen bishops of whom twelve can be identified.[54] According to the Lorsch Annals, Tassilo of Bavaria made his oath of fidelity to Pippin at this assembly. Perhaps the most interesting document from this succession of councils was the confraternity list of Attigny, extant in Vatican Pal. lat. 577, which contains the names of twenty-three bishops and twenty-one abbots present at the assembly who bound themselves together in a brotherhood of prayer.[55] The text would be of great importance for an examination, long overdue, of the relationship between monastic and clerical groups in the Carolingian period. In 765 Pippin made a significant contribution to parish organization in his letter to the Frankish episcopate. In it he imposed the payment of the tithe; and asked for prayers for a year of fertility and abundance after the lean period that had been endured.[56]

The decrees of the Synod of Ver in particular are a comment on Pippin's monastic policy. They were designed to revive discipline, and were destined for those monasteries and bishoprics which acknowledged Pippin as their protector. Laymen were not to be permitted to have their own private monasteries on their estates (*Eigenklöster*), abbots were to provide soldiers but refrain from going to war themselves and stability was required of monks and nuns. Monks and nuns had to renounce all personal property, but nevertheless it is clear that many possessed it, the most famous example being Fulrad, abbot of St Denis, who left all his personal property – lands, mills, herds, gold, silver, books and bronze *ornamenta* – to St Denis in 777.[57] Only the Bonifacian group of monasteries appears to have been strict in their observance of this rule, but even Lioba, abbess of Taubersbischofsheim, spent the last years of her life in a villa the king had given for her personal use. The abbots of the monasteries over which Pippin gained control considered the king as their lord; to him they owed their office and dignity. Pippin could rely on these men, and one of the distinctive features of his administration is the extent to which clerics, and in particular, monks, were employed in the king's service. Those who had served in his chancery were often rewarded by Pippin with abbacies. Widmar received the abbacy of St Riquier, Baddilo that of Marmoutier and Pippin's chaplain Fulrad was made abbot of St Denis. Abbots sometimes guarded state prisoners for the Carolingians; St Amand was the prison for Desiderius, king of the Lombards, and Childeric III was immured in St Denis. The heads of St Denis, St Germain-des-Prés, Jumièges, St Riquier and St Martin of Tours undertook missions on the ruler's behalf.

The distinction between the *ordines* of monks and canons emerged for the first time at Ver, and remained one of the main themes of the early Carolingian monastic ordinances. Monks and nuns were required to opt for a monastic rule, preferably that of St Benedict, or Chrodegang's *Regula canonicorum*. The acceptance of the latter would not, in practice, have made an enormous difference to the way of life in the monasteries. That the *ordo canonicorum* permitted the possession of personal property was probably one reason why many communities, such as St Denis, St Maur des Fosses and Stavelot–Malmédy, chose to follow it. The Benedictine Rule remained a directive for communal living rather than a law, despite Boniface's efforts to establish the Rule of St Benedict as the core of monastic life. A 'mixed rule' reflecting the rich monastic traditions of the Frankish kingdoms in which the Rule of St Benedict was certainly an important component prevailed in many Frankish monasteries until the reforms of Louis the Pious in 816 and 817, although an attempt was made in 802 to assert the priority of Benedict's Rule (see Ch. 5). Some monasteries then opted for the *Regula canonicorum*, but others chose to live according to the Rule of St Benedict. Only under Louis the Pious therefore was the work of Pippin, Boniface and Chrodegang completed. The interdependence of king and clergy in the second half of the eighth century and the drive for reform remained, moreover, important features of the reigns of Pippin's successors.

The first genuine capitulary of Charlemagne advocating reform in both the religious and secular spheres and in which he demonstrated that he was following in his father's footsteps was the Capitulary of Herstal, dated 779. Clauses in this capitulary concern the organization of metropolitan and suffragan bishops (see Map 3) and a renewed and, within three decades, successful attempt to revive the metropolitans,[58] the conduct of life in the monasteries, episcopal authority within the dioceses, the paying of church tithes, the taxing of church property and the administration of secular justice. Pippin's requirements for the introduction of Roman liturgical forms, especially for baptism, and for Sunday observance were also repeated by Charlemagne.[59] The position of archbishop and papal legate held by both Boniface and Chrodegang seems to have died out and it was perhaps replaced as far as the Frankish church, though not the Papacy, was concerned, by the archchaplain, the chief adviser to the king in ecclesiastical affairs and head of the palace clergy. A full programmatic declaration for the reform of the church and kingdom was not formulated until 789 in the *Admonitio Generalis*, and this decree, together with the general capitulary of 802 and the decrees of the reform councils of 813 convoked by Charlemagne, had, as I have argued elsewhere, considerable influence on subsequent reform and pastoral activity within the Frankish kingdom.[60] Of great importance too was the synod of Frankfurt of 794, attended by representatives from most of the re-established metropolitan provinces of the Frankish church – Provence, Vienne, Arles, Aquitaine, Gaul and Germany – as well as the papal legates, Theophylact and Stephen. The synod was convened primarily to discuss and condemn Adoptionism, the heresy formulated by the Spanish bishop Felix of Urgel, and to approve the Frankish statement on iconoclasm embodied in the *Libri Carolini* of Theodulf of Orleans. Tassilo of Bavaria also made his submission before the assembly and a few clauses dealt with the price of corn and bread, the regulation of weights and measures, the bishop's right to administer justice in his diocese and the extent of the bishop's jurisdiction.[61]

Like Pippin, Charlemagne's relations with the church were interwoven with his political activities and ways of conquest, but there were significant discontinuities as well as continuities between the policies of the father and son.

Charlemagne in some respects seems to have missed the point of the careful 'balance of power' that Pippin had tried to create between kings, bishops, abbots and lay magnates. He was undoubtedly a more devout and convinced Christian than Pippin, and it is ironic that the protective and supportive policies of both Charlemagne and Louis the Pious towards the church were ultimately to weaken the political position of the king.

A feature of Charlemagne's monastic policy as evidenced in his charters is the comparatively little attention he paid to the monasteries of the Frankish heartland. Only about ten monasteries were favoured, and some of these favours, such as the gift to St Arnulf where his queen, Hildegard, was buried, or the new buildings for St Riquier, have the character of personal and unstrategic gifts. St Denis' position on the other hand was strengthened by gifts of land in Alsace, Alemannia and Italy, as well as by having new buildings built and old ones restored. St Martin of Tours and St Maurice of Agaune also received land in Italy and it is supposed that these links promoted the spread of Frankish influence in Italy. Similarly, lands given to Echternach were to promote the Saxon mission, as were the lands granted to monasteries east of the Rhine such as Hersfeld and Fulda, which were also actively involved in missionary work.[62]

During Charlemagne's reign, any monasteries which became royal monasteries were in Aquitaine, Septimania and east of the Rhine, and it is clear that for Charlemagne these foundations served to aid his particular interest in and aspirations for, on the one hand monastic reform and the promotion of the Rule of St Benedict, and on the other, missionary work among the heathen. It could be argued, however, that his policies indicate a simple ambition to gain control of these monasteries, and he sometimes abused his position. Monastic lands, for example, were granted to his followers as benefices, and he installed loyal followers, members of his family or even, briefly, himself, as in the case of Echternach and Murbach, as heads of important monastic communities.[63] Hugh, an illegitimate son of Charlemagne, was made abbot of Novalese, Charlemagne's daughter Theodrada became abbess of Argenteuil in the diocese of Paris and of Schwarzach on the Main, and his daughters Gisela and Rothad were abbesses of Notre Dame of Soissons and Faremoutiers respectively. Only exceptionally did Charlemagne accord freedom of election to particular institutions.

By 775 Charlemagne had all the most important monasteries between Worms and Hesse under his control, and this was of great importance for the officially promoted evangelization of Saxony. The monasteries were also used by Charlemagne to open up land; they had, in other words, a colonizing function. Monasteries in the Rhineland, Hesse, Franconia and Bavaria such as Fulda, Hersfeld, Niederaltaich, Kremsmünster and St Peter's Salzburg were active in opening up land; all were royal monasteries and all promoted missionary work. St Amand may also have participated in the Saxon mission, for it was Bishop Agilfrid of Liège, also abbot of St Amand, who founded the first church of Osnabrück. The monasteries were cherished by the missionary bishoprics as nurseries of missionaries and bases for the evangelization of the surrounding countryside.

Yet by the third decade of the ninth century, missionary work had largely petered out. Semmler associates this with the promotion of the Benedictine Rule and the relinquishment of the old Frankish monastic tradition. Frankish monks thought themselves no longer obliged to venture among the heathen. Strictly speaking, the Benedictine monk did not give up anything essential to the monastic life by refusing or by ceasing to be a missionary. That no monastery in the peripheral regions of the Frankish kingdom became a royal monastery after 800 has been connected by Semmler with the cessation of monastery-based evangelization at about this time and Charlemagne's consequent lack of further interest in the monasteries. Missionary work thereafter was left to the episcopal hierarchy and non-Benedictine establishments.[64] Charlemagne bought support with the monasteries as much as with any other means at his disposal, and promoted any institution so long as it served its purpose or his interests. Fortunately his interests were not always political and his enlightened promotion of learning and education will be discussed more fully in Chapter Six. Missionary work was also strongly backed, and as Büttner has demonstrated, it went hand in hand with Charlemagne's wars of conquest, particularly those against the Saxons.[65]

The intention of the campaign in Saxony seems to have been at first no more than to enforce recognition of Frankish overlordship in the form of tribute, and ensure peace in the frontier region between Saxony and the rest of the Frankish lands. During the long and bloody war against the Saxons, however, conquest and the spread of the Christian faith became the principal objectives. As far as the sources are concerned, the conquest of Saxony was Charlemagne's greatest achievement, for he manifested both singular abilities as the warrior king and, by his promotion of the Christian faith, a zeal to fulfil his obligations as Christian ruler. The Frankish army, moreover, became the most efficient military machine in Europe. The military progress of the Saxon campaigns has also a number of parallels with Pippin's conquest of Aquitaine. Between 772 and 785 hardly a year passed without Charlemagne or his deputies leading an expedition into Saxony; in 784 the Royal Frankish annalist noted that the Saxons rebelled again 'as usual'. With each campaign more was undertaken. In 772, during the first major expedition, the Irminsul was destroyed and in 775 the castle of Siegburg was occupied and reorganized as part of a system of defence which included the castle of Eresburg and another, unnamed, on the river Lippe, as well as the creation of a marcher region.[66] At Paderborn in 777 an assembly was held which inaugurated the ecclesiastical organization of Saxony; the country was divided up into missionary zones and a large number of Saxons were reputed to have been baptized. Willehad was made responsible for the region of Wigmodia between the Weser and the Elbe and Bishop Gregory of Utrecht and Liudger were active in Frisia.

Missionary work was disrupted, however, by the rising of the Saxons under Widukind, a valiant Westphalian noble who took advantage of Charlemagne's absence in Spain in 778. Two campaigns were mounted by Charlemagne in 779 and 781, but the Frankish army under Adalgisus, Geilo and Worad was routed by the Saxons led by Widukind in the Sütel mountains, and Charlemagne's savage reprisal at Verdun, in which all the Saxons responsible for the revolt (reputed to number 4500) were beheaded, had the effect of stiffening Saxon resistance rather than cowing Widukind's followers into submission. By 780 Charlemagne had reached the Elbe, and in 782 the country was divided into counties to be administered by Saxons. At Attigny, Widukind and his son-in-law Abbi submitted to Charlemagne and baptism, with Charlemagne standing as godfather. Saxony was pronounced conquered. Many Saxons were absorbed into the Frankish army and thereafter fought for the Franks against the Sorbs and Avars. Many more were baptized, and such baptisms were rather statements of political realignment than affirmations of religious faith. At Paderborn in 785 a general assembly was held and decisions on the organization of Saxony were taken by all present and recorded in the draconian *Capitulatio de partibus Saxoniae*.[67] Most offences against the secular authority and Christianity or the church and its clergy, even resisting baptism, were punishable by death or prohibitively heavy fines. Reference is also made to the law of the Saxons, according to which Saxons were to be judged in some cases, such as perjury, and it is probably to this period that the compilation of the *Lex Saxonum* is to be dated. The decree also assumes that the church has already been established for some years and makes extensive provision for the establishment of churches and clergy in the country.

From 785, Charlemagne promoted a systematic evangelization of Saxony. Christianity had been established in the first stages of the campaign by force, and even in 796 allegiance to the church and the tithe in particular were being demanded with such rigour that Alcuin was moved to protest.[68] Willehad was consecrated bishop at Worms and re-established in Wigmodia; he made his episcopal seat at Bremen and further sees were created at Paderborn (799–806), Werden by the end of the eighth or early ninth century, Münster (802–6) and Osnabrück by 803. Liudger, consecrated bishop in 805, was sent to Westphalia as bishop of Münster with jurisdiction over Westphalia and Frisia. In 790 Erkenbert is described as a bishop *de Saxonia* in the Weser region near Minden, and was succeeded by Haduard in 830, but very little is known about either of these bishops or their activities. Thus the group of missionary areas established in Saxony in 785 had, by the beginning of the ninth century, become bishoprics, and the special activities of a missionary church played an important role in the arrangements for the administration of the diocese.

A tenth-century charter from Bremen, cited by Büttner, states that 'the Saxons were not so much conquered by the Franks as by God'.[69] Yet the Saxons were still not completely quelled or Christian after 785. In the absence of convenient opportunities for rebellion, and the lack of an effective leader now that Widukind was no longer a rebel, the Saxons quietened down for a few years but revolted again in 793. Not until after Easter and the Synod of Frankfurt in the following year were Charlemagne and his eldest son Charles able to lead two detachments into Saxony, upon which the Saxons capitulated, apparently without a struggle, only to revolt again in 795 and be dealt with mercilessly. In 797 another Frankish expedition resulted in the submission of the 'whole Saxon people' and from Aachen was issued the *Capitulare Saxonicum*, a more moderate decree than the early *Capitulatio*, although there is nothing to suggest that the earlier decree was no longer valid.[70] A further measure designed to subdue the population was the wholesale transfer of considerable numbers of Saxons to other parts of the Frankish kingdom; archaeological evidence of this policy, such as mounds and ditches, is still to be seen in some parts of Germany, such as in the area near Diesenhofen in Bavaria. The confiscated land was given to bishops, Frankish counts and royal vassals and had the effect, if nothing else, of increasing the proportion of Franks in the population of Saxony. Furthermore, the new Saxon bishoprics retained their links both with the missionary areas in which they were situated and with the Rhineland monasteries and the older Frankish ecclesiastical provinces. Friesland, for example, kept in contact with the see of Utrecht, Westphalia with Münster, Osnabrück and Bremen with Cologne and Paderborn, and Werden with Mainz.

The conquest of Saxony by 797 and the annexation of Bavaria in 788 made it possible for the Franks to extend their political conquest as well as their missionary activities into Carinthia and further east and north into Avar and Slav territory. As early as the mid-eighth century a connection had been established between Carinthia and the Bavarian bishoprics of Passau and Salzburg during Virgil's occupancy of the see; Virgil dispatched Bishop Modestus with priests and clerics to Carinthia. Virgil, an Irishman, had been much favoured by Pippin III and spent some time at Quierzy before being sent to Odilo, duke of Bavaria. Odilo conferred on Virgil the abbacy of St Peter's Salzburg, and subsequently the bishopric of that city, although Virgil was not actually consecrated bishop until 767. Boniface had made a certain John bishop of Salzburg and resented Virgil's installation because his opinion and consent had not been asked. The famous garbled baptismal formula which forms the subject of one of Boniface's letters is an episode in the quarrel between Virgil and Boniface; Boniface rebaptized the person over whom the formula *In nomine patria et filia et spiritus sancti* had been said. Virgil refused to allow this rebaptism and his judgement was upheld by the Pope. Boniface attempted to have Virgil unfrocked by claiming that Virgil advocated not only the existence of the Antipodes but also that they were inhabited by humans. Yet, despite him, Virgil continued active in Salzburg. Löwe thinks that Aethicus Ister, author of the Cosmography which conveyed a knowledge of ancient geography from classical literary sources, and Virgil are one and the same person, and that Virgil invented Jerome's translation from the Greek of Aethicus Ister in order to take literary revenge on Boniface.[71]

Tassilo, Odilo's successor as duke of Bavaria, also took some interest in the missionary enterprise in Carinthia and founded the monastery of Innichen, which eventually became attached to the see of Freising. The church in Bavaria was active under Tassilo and well favoured by the duke. Donations from Tassilo, for example, considerably enriched the monasteries of Mondsee, Chiemsee and Kremsmünster, while the ecclesiastical magnates exerted a considerable influence in the government. It is possible that the compilation of the *Lex Baiuuuariorum* is to be attributed to Eberswind, first abbot of Niederaltaich (741–3), and churchmen certainly acted as ducal legates in the negotiations with Charlemagne and the Pope. Bavaria's ecclesiastical organization appears to have been relatively independent, but after 788 the Bavarian church was fully integrated into the Frankish church. After the death of Chietmar, the pro-Christian duke of Carinthia, in 772, Tassilo asserted his authority in the area, so that the Bavarian Christian mission and extension of Bavarian political influence were closely related. At the synods of Dingolfing and Neuching, called and attended by Tassilo, particular attention was paid to the instruction of the clergy working in the mission field and Clm 6241, a manual of texts suitable for the missionary cleric and written in Bavaria, may well represent a book designed to equip a missionary in Carinthia.[72] In 785, Arno succeeded Virgil at Salzburg. He appears to have been a Bavarian and was educated at the cathedral school of Freising. He went to St Amand as abbot in 782 and from there to Salzburg where he assumed the leadership of the Carinthian mission. After Tassilo had been deprived of his duchy and Charlemagne had appointed Count Gerold as administrator, Gerold and Arno worked together, and sent Bishop Deoderich to the eastern alpine region and Carinthia. By 811, the quarrel between the dioceses of Aquileia and Salzburg over which see should direct missionary work in Carinthia and Pannonia (Aquileia's interest in the area dated from the fourth century) was referred to Charlemagne and the Pope, with the result that the area was split between the two sees.

VI

The opposition Pippin III had encountered in establishing Carolingian authority was a problem for Charlemagne as well, though the pro-Carolingian bias of the sources makes it difficult to determine the precise details and motives for the resistance to Carolingian rule. A number of attempts were made in the second half of the eighth century to resist the imposing of Frankish rule or, more particularly, to oust Charlemagne.

Relations between Charlemagne and his brother Carloman had soured very quickly after Pippin III's death. Charlemagne's junior by about four years, Carloman received in 768 the regions of Burgundy, Provence, Gothia, Alsace, Alemannia and probably half of Aquitaine, and in October 768 was raised to the throne and consecrated king at Soissons (see Map 2). In Neustria however, their jurisdiction appears to have overlapped. Little survives concerning Carloman's activities in the three short years of his reign, but his fifteen surviving charters suggest that his monastic policy resembled that of his father. Echternach was taken under his protection, Novalese was granted freedom from dues, various grants of land were made to St Denis and in 771 the villa of Noviliacum was conferred on the church of Rheims for use as a cemetery.[73]

In 769 Carloman refused to help his brother deal with the rebellion of Hunuald in Aquitaine. There seems to have been a wish on Carloman's part to undermine Charlemagne's position; this may well have been through fear for his own. The revised version of the Royal Frankish Annals mentions a mysterious meeting between Bertrada, mother of the two brothers, and Carloman at Seltz in 770, after which Bertrada travelled to Italy 'in the interests of peace'. Bertrada was presumably either allaying the fears of Carloman or persuading him to be more co-operative towards his elder brother. Bertrada visited Bavaria on her way to Italy and she may have aimed there at a reconciliation between her sons and Tassilo.[74]

In Italy Bertrada arranged Charlemagne's betrothal to Desiderata, daughter of the Lombard King Desiderius, but Charlemagne repudiated her after a year; it is not clear whether he actually married her and repudiated her because she failed to produce a child within the year, or whether she never in fact left the Lombard kingdom.[75] The alliance with the Lombards may have alarmed the Pope, and Carloman might have seen his opportunity to ingratiate himself with the Pope as well as visions of becoming sole Frankish ruler. On the other hand, the subsequent repudiation by Charlemagne of Desiderata may have meant that there was then a possibility of the Lombard king and Carloman joining against Charlemagne and the Pope. In Rome, the leader of the clerical party, Christopher, had certainly entered into some sort of negotiation with Carloman. Whatever the nature and intent of, or justification for, Carloman's undoubted animosity towards Charlemagne, the potential threat he presented was nullified by his death at the villa of Samoussy on 4 December 771. The Annals report that Charlemagne received the leading men of Carloman's kingdom at Corbeny – Wilchar, bishop of Sens, Fulrad, Carloman's chaplain, counts Warin and Adalhard and the other bishops, priests and magnates. Carloman's wife Gerberga and her sons fled to the Lombard court, a 'needless' departure as far as Charlemagne was concerned who 'bore it patiently'.[76] But it does suggest that Gerberga felt she and her sons had something to fear and that the Lombards were Carloman's allies, however lukewarm. The *Liber Pontificalis* states that when Gerberga and her sons arrived at the Lombard court, Desiderius sought to use the boys for his own ends and proposed to compel the Pope to anoint Carloman's two sons as kings, and thus divide Charlemagne's Franks and the Pope.

After Charlemagne's conquest of Pavia and the Lombard kingdom in 774, Gerberga and her sons, who had taken refuge during the war in Verona, surrendered, or were given up to Charlemagne, and disappear from the sources. Carloman's sons should have inherited their father's kingdom, but Charlemagne made no bones about depriving them of their birthright and was left as sole ruler of the Frankish kingdom. When in 781 Charlemagne's eldest son Carloman, aged three, was made king of Italy, Charlemagne had his name changed to Pippin. It is possible that the child's original name had been a public gesture to honour his brother's memory and thus quell any rumours about his treatment of his brother's children. The change could also have had some connection with the revolt of Pippin the Hunchback.

Again Charlemagne, following Pippin's example, seems to have made his own rules in his annexation of the duchy of Bavaria. The Agilolfing family in Bavaria, of Frankish stock, had originally administered Bavaria as agents of the Merovingians, but Agilolfing loyalty had presumably been forfeited when the Carolingians assumed the throne. There is certainly no reference in the Carolingian sources to the old relationship between the Agilolfing dukes and the Merovingian kings. Tassilo III, duke of Bavaria, came into his inheritance when Carolingian influence in Bavaria was strong, for the attempt by Grifo after Duke Odilo's death in 748 to seize the duchy for himself, and Grifo's defeat by Pippin had enabled the latter to establish some semblance of overlordship in Bavaria, whether or not the duchy was conceded by Pippin to the eight-year-old Tassilo as a *beneficium*. The Bavarians had to swear not to rebel against Pippin and Pippin's name appeared in Bavarian charters. Yet Bavaria remained legally, administratively and ecclesiastically distinct from the rest of the Frank-ish kingdom. Tassilo was made duke by Pippin under the regency of his mother Chiltrud until her death in 754; thereafter Tassilo probably ruled for himself, yet some sort of relationship with Pippin is suggested by the fact that Tassilo and his army participated in the Frankish expedition into Italy.

In 757 Tassilo commended himself into vassalage and took oaths to be a vassal to Pippin; some of his magnates present at Compiègne where Tassilo swore his oath to Pippin and his two sons, Carloman and Charlemagne, con-firmed what had taken place. How should this oath to be a vassal of Pippin be interpreted? Odegaard, in an unaccountably neglected study, observed that Tassilo is the only great magnate of whom it is said that he commended himself into vassalage. It was a highly unusual event.[77] Odegaard defined the vassals as a category of men distinct from bishop, abbots and counts and inferior to these in rank. A vassal was not a royal functionary like the count, bishop or abbot, he had no territory assigned to him as an administrative portion of the kingdom, and could serve men other than the king. He was a man who com-mended himself to his lord to serve as a warrior, a properly equipped and trained fighting man. Odegaard rejected the suggestion that the case of Tassilo necessitated a broader definition of vassalage, and suggested that Tassilo was indeed forced by Pippin to undergo the humiliation of taking the oath to serve the king in the inferior capacity of vassal. The oath certainly did not establish Tassilo's right to rule in Bavaria for he appeared at Compiègne as *dux baiu-uuariorum*. In other words, Pippin had no right to demand a vassal's service from Tassilo. It was unprecedented for a man of Tassilo's rank to occupy such a position. One of the vassal's obligations was to attend the mustering of the Frankish host, but Tassilo refused to do so after 763; worse, he committed, according to the Franks, the crime of *harisliz* or desertion, for he returned home in the middle of Pippin's fourth campaign in Aquitaine and thus broke the oath he had made six years earlier.

The view taken of the nature of Tassilo's oath and Pippin's behaviour deter-mines the interpretation of Charlemagne's actions in annexing Bavaria. Pippin did not take any further steps towards forcing Tassilo into submission, real-izing, perhaps, that his position was ambivalent. When Pippin's kingdom was divided in 768, Bavaria was not included in the partition, and it retained its independence until after Charlemagne had conquered the Saxons and the Lom-bards. Strategic considerations concerning control of the alpine passes into Italy as well as greed played a part in Charlemagne's next moves. It is difficult to believe that outraged feudal sensibilities were anything other than a convenient excuse; indeed it is possible that Tassilo's case became the precedent for making the obligations of the oath of fidelity rather more precisely defined, though it should be remembered that Charlemagne's move against Tassilo started before the imposition of a general oath in 785. In 781, Charlemagne persuaded the Pope to join him in warning Tassilo and impressing the old oath of 757 upon Tassilo. We do not know what threats may have been relayed by the papal and royal emissaries, but Tassilo came before Charlemagne at Worms, 'renewed his oaths and gave twelve hostages', though this time nothing is said in the sources about vassalage. But Tassilo did not, according to the Royal Frankish Annals, keep the promises he had made and in 787 Arno of Salzburg and Hunric, abbot of Mondsee, arrived in Rome and asked the Pope to act as intermediary between Tassilo and Charlemagne; the Pope, to his credit, did make a move and he would hardly have done so had Charlemagne's case been clear-cut. Yet the Frankish king managed to sway the Pope in his favour. Charlemagne wanted to settle with the Bavarian emissaries in the Pope's presence, but the emissaries refused on the grounds that they could not commit themselves without consulting their duke. Charlemagne was clearly asking too much. Pope Hadrian then threatened to excommunicate Tassilo and his supporters unless they renewed and kept their oaths to Charlemagne and Tassilo was commanded to appear before Charlemagne at Worms. He refused. Charlemagne promptly mustered three armies to march on Bavaria from three different directions 'to protect his rights'.[78] Tassilo was surrounded on all sides and, to make matters worse, some of his own Bavarians had transferred their loyalty from him to Charlemagne. Thus beset, Tassilo appeared before Charlemagne and was obliged to eat humble pie and declare himself a vassal of the Frankish king, renew his oaths and give twelve hostages including his son Theodo, as well as return the duchy committed to him by Pippin and admit that he had acted against the law.

Tassilo evidently found his position unendurable; in desperation he opened negotiations with the Avars, seeking their help to win back his duchy. Einhard states furthermore that it was Tassilo's Lombard wife Liutberga who had encouraged him to seek the Avars as allies. The Avars, however, were defeated and 'loyal Bavarians' informed Charlemagne what was going on behind his back, for Tassilo had also, apparently, instructed his followers to have mental reservations when giving their spoken oath to the king.[79] Tassilo was charged with his crimes at Ingelheim in 788 and condemned to death by the assembly, but Charlemagne was inclined to be merciful; Tassilo, his son, his wife and daughters all entered monasteries and those Bavarians still hostile to Charlemagne were exiled. We last hear of Tassilo in 794 when he came to the Synod of Frankfurt and renounced his duchy.

With Bavaria successfully annexed to the Frankish kingdom and the administration of the country committed to count Gerold, Charlemagne could concentrate on the Avars. From 791 to 793 he was based at Regensburg and his armies destroyed the Ring (the system of fortification) of the Avars and carried the stupendous Avar treasure with them back to Aachen. By 796 the Avars had submitted and their territory was brought within the sphere of Frankish jurisdiction.

Besides the opposition to Frankish or to Carolingian rule demonstrated by Carloman and his supporters, Hunuald of Aquitaine, Tassilo of Bavaria, the Saxons and the Bretons, and his efforts to exert his authority in Spain, Charlemagne had to contend with what were potentially two major Frankish revolts against him. Both are referred to very briefly in the revised version of the Royal Frankish Annals and by Einhard. In 785 or 786 a conspiracy formed in Thuringia and led by Count Hardrad was discovered and ruthlessly suppressed. What the aims of these rebels were is not known. Einhard adds the detail that it was the cruelty of Queen Fastrada, Charlemagne's fourth wife, which was the cause both of this conspiracy and that of Pippin the Hunchback, Charlemagne's eldest illegitimate son. It is not clear what Einhard meant, but Fastrada is also held accountable by the reviser of the Royal Frankish Annals for the plot in 792 against the king's life by Pippin the Hunchback and various members of the Frankish aristocracy, among whom only the name of Count Theobald is known. The plot was disclosed by the Lombard Fardulf, who was rewarded with the abbacy of St Denis. Most of the plotters were put to death, but Pippin entered the monastery of Prüm where he died in 811. It is possible that he had been but the tool of a party of aristocrats opposed to the Carolingian house. Charlemagne subsequently held a winter assembly at Regensburg and lavishly rewarded those who had kept faith. Such a step suggests that this revolt was much more serious than the sources would have us believe.

It was after the conspiracy of 786, moreover, that Charlemagne insisted on all freemen of the kingdom renewing their oaths to him. The plots against and resistance to Charlemagne, both within and without his kingdom, indicate that the Carolingian position was by no means secure or fully supported, and this latent hostility undoubtedly manifested itself more forcefully in the reign of Louis the Pious. Such was Charlemagne's strength, however, that he was able to quell the opposition to his authority and use his successes to forge an enormous Empire. His conquest of Lombardy in 774 in particular set the seal on Pippin III's campaigns in Italy. It established the close Frankish involvement in Italian and papal affairs which was to lead to the symbolic triumph of Charlemagne's coronation as Emperor, and remain an intermittent but vital factor in Frankish politics for the next century.

The need to avert the threat of a possible Lombard alliance with a Frankish anti-Charlemagne party which had Carloman's two sons as their mascots and *raison d'être* was no doubt a consideration in Charlemagne's conquest of the Lombard kingdom. But it was also a crucial step in tightening the link between the Frankish ruler and the Pope and was undertaken primarily in response to an appeal for help against the Lombards from Pope Hadrian. The campaign was conducted swiftly and efficiently during the winter of 773–4. Pavia was besieged and captured and Charlemagne assumed the title of king of the Lombards. Lombardy was not annexed as Saxony and Bavaria had been annexed, but preserved as a separate kingdom. In 781, Charlemagne made his son Pippin the subking of Italy. Pippin ruled in Charlemagne's name and in 810 was succeeded by his son Bernard. A number of Frankish counts were installed in Lombard territory. Charlemagne also conserved the secular and ecclesiastical legislation of the Lombards. He, and after 781, his son Pippin, published capitularies especially for the Lombards and convoked assemblies in Lombard territory in which the Lombard lay magnates and bishops participated. Some general capitularies, such as the Capitulary of Herstal of 779, also appear to have exerted some influence or at least to have been applicable to the Lombards, for some Italian manuscripts reproduce the collections of Lombard capitularies together with other legislation by Charlemagne.[80] A letter of 779–81 addressed to civil officials in Lombardy complained that tithe was not being paid and the bishops were impeded by the nobles of the kingdom, who put strangers in the churches as priests rather than the men chosen by the bishop.[81] The capitularies concerning ecclesiastical matters extended the Frankish reform to Italy, as well as the authority of the king to intervene in the affairs of the church, a situation with which the Lombards had hitherto been relatively unfamiliar.

All the territories usurped by the Lombard King Desiderius in 772 were restored to the Pope, together with Bologna and Imola, but not till 777 did Ravenna acknowledge the Pope's overlordship. Spoleto maintained a wish to acknowledge the Frankish king rather than the Pope as overlord, and after 789 became part of the Frankish kingdom of Italy. A number of Lombards resisted the imposition of Frankish rule. In 775 for example, Hrodgaud, the Lombard duke of Friuli, installed in office by Charlemagne, broke faith and was killed. Thereafter, Friuli and the marcher region were administered by Frankish counts. In 787–8, Charlemagne went again to Italy to obtain the submission of Arichis, duke of Benevento. The Pope had claimed Spoleto, Benevento, Tuscany and Corsica but he was obliged to renounce any pretensions to jurisdiction over Spoleto and Tuscany. Duke Arichis of Benevento seems to have been negotiating with Byzantium for assistance in maintaining his position, and in 787 sent an embassy, headed by his son Romuald, to Charlemagne in Rome insisting on his loyalty but demanding that Charlemagne keep out of Benevento. Charlemagne ignored the demand, but appears to have permitted Arichis to retain his position while retaining his younger son Grimoald as a hostage. It is likely that Charlemagne was trying to divert Arichis from an alliance with the Greeks. After the death of Arichis and Romuald later in the same year, Charlemagne installed Grimoald as duke of Benevento, and Grimoald then led an army of Lombards and Franks against a Byzantine force and defeated it. Charlemagne had acted in his own political interests in supporting Benevento and going against the wishes of the Pope. Thereafter Benevento retained its autonomy. The Byzantines were clearly anxious to promote their interests in the Italian peninsular, and at a later stage Charlemagne clashed with them over the provinces of Venetia and Dalmatia. Desiderius' son Adalgis had, furthermore, taken refuge in Byzantium and almost certainly intrigued with the Greeks to regain his father's kingdom. Certainly Pope Hadrian believed he had discovered a conspiracy against Charlemagne organized by Adalgis, the dukes of Friuli, Spoleto, Chiusi and the Greeks.

The Byzantine position in Italy and the relations between Byzantium and the Papacy as they developed in the second half of the eighth century underlie the creation of Charlemagne as Emperor in the West by the Pope. During this period Byzantine imperial authority dwindled to nothing, but it had also become apparent by the reign of Pope Stephen III that the Byzantine Emperor was but a frail and reluctant supporter of the Papacy.[82] In 787, the betrothal between Charlemagne's daughter Rotrud and the Byzantine Emperor Constantine VI had been broken off by the latter's mother, Empress Irene. The Carolingian conquest of Lombardy and support of the Papacy cannot have endeared the Franks to the Byzantines, and iconoclasm created a further rift between Rome and Byzantium. At the same time, while the Papacy became increasingly independent of the Eastern Empire, it became ever more familiar with the reality and effectiveness of Frankish power in Italy and the protection afforded the Pope himself by the Franks.

VII

In 795 Leo III succeeded to the papal throne, but was beset by a strong and hostile party of aristocrats. Their enmity erupted in April 799 when the Pope was ambushed and an attempt made to gouge out his eyes and tongue. Leo fled to the Frankish kingdom and met Charles at Paderborn. The latter was on his way to launch another offensive against the Saxons, and rather than interrupt his campaign he commissioned Arno, bishop of Salzburg and Hildebald, archbishop of Cologne, to re-establish Leo in Rome and initiate an enquiry into the accusations against him. The proceedings began in the church of St Peter on 1 December 800; Charlemagne arrived in Rome on 24 November. The Pope was required to clear himself of charges of adultery and perjury with an oath, to which he finally submitted on 23 December.[83] It was common knowledge that the oath had been forced upon him by the Frankish bishops in Rome and the Frankish king. Two days later the Pope made an attempt to assert his superiority and crowned Charles Emperor of the Romans in the church of St Peter according to Byzantine usage, with adoration by the Pope and the acclamation of the people. There seems little doubt that it was primarily a move on the part of the Papacy to attempt to bind to itself yet more closely the Frankish monarch. The account of the Royal Frankish Annals, in which the Roman people assembled in the great church of St Peter roared their acclamation according to a traditional formula: 'To Charles Augustus mighty and peaceable emperor of the Romans crowned by God, long life and victory' suggests that they had been rehearsed.[84] The Lorsch Annals, a contemporary account, certainly attribute the move to the Pope and his advisers. For the Papacy Charlemagne's coronation was a restoration of an Emperor in the West and Charlemagne was the obvious candidate for the post. It is possible that Charlemagne was not taken completely by surprise, however much he may have affected to resent the precipitousness with which he had been crowned,[85] for

70

the Pope may well have discussed the matter with him when they met at Paderborn. The Lorsch Annals certainly imply that the king was asked whether he would accept the imperial title, and the Paderborn epic is redolent of the imperial majesty of Charlemagne, even if the poem is to be seen as hyperbole rather than as a significant comment on events which took place six months after it was written.[86]

The full implications of the new Emperor's obligations towards the Papacy and involvement in Italian affairs can have been only vaguely comprehended by the Franks and, one suspects, by the Pope and his advisers as well. To the modern historian they have appeared abundantly clear, perhaps misleadingly and anachronistically so. The significance of Charlemagne's coronation emerged only with the full accumulation of medieval legend and history to enhance it, and against the backcloth of the political world of the nineteenth and early twentieth centuries, in which Empire and Emperor represented the acme of political achievement. It is clear that Charlemagne himself did not acquire as Emperor any lasting or extra power in any real sense, nor were his rights substantially extended in any sphere. Charlemagne remained the master; the inhabitants of the papal states had to swear loyalty to Charlemagne as well as to the Pope. If we examine all the sources, the only positive move Charlemagne made as Emperor was his restoration of the church of Rome to peace and concord, yet the fact that Leo III had appealed to the Frankish king to assist him in this task before Charles was crowned Emperor must mean that this cannot be regarded as a peculiarly imperial act.

Indeed, if we try and determine what the event meant to contemporaries in 800, little seems apparent apart from a sense of the glory and honour of the great warrior and Christian king who received the grand title of Emperor. It may be that a little of the thinking behind Charlemagne's elevation resembled that which prompted Pippin III's usurpation of the kingship. Alcuin's letter of 799 undoubtedly influenced Charlemagne's conception of his obligations and responsibilities as Christian king,[87] but Ganshof is surely right when he suggests that Charlemagne and most of his Franks did not really grasp what Alcuin meant by the imperial dignity.[88] Alcuin's own views may have been influenced by Anglo-Saxon notions of *imperium* as overlordship. What possible meaning could the Roman Empire in the West, moribund since the fifth century and only dimly remembered, have for a vigorous barbarian nation except as a vague dream of glory and widespread authority? Charlemagne no doubt did not mind being called Emperor, but it is doubtful whether he would ever have taken the decisive step himself. Presumably Leo III wished to create the illusion that the Emperor had his power from the Pope, but he had in fact nothing to do with the power actually wielded by Charlemagne, and was too poor a statesman to have made good use of it even if he had had. One can fully appreciate why the Eastern Emperors did not think much of the Pope's creation of a rival Emperor in the West, an Emperor moreover renowned for his military conquests.

In the contemporary sources, Charlemagne's coronation is described as if there were no preparation for it on the part of the Frankish king. Nevertheless, Charlemagne did accept the imperial title. Einhard implied that the title made some difference to Charlemagne's own conception of his office when he associated the making of the king and emperor with the discovery by Charlemagne that reform and reorganization of the laws of the Franks was much needed. The Lorsch Annals and the Capitularies of 802 corroborate that an assembly was held in 802 and a reorganization of the administration in both the ecclesiastical and secular spheres, and a new formulation of the oath of fidelity to the Emperor (which also acquired a religious emphasis) were undertaken by Charlemagne after his coronation in Rome.[89] Yet it must be asked how much this reorganization constituted a 'programme of imperial government' and how much it was a royal programme continuing the work begun with the *Admonitio Generalis* of 789 and coinciding with Charlemagne's strengthened position and a short period of relative peace and stability after three decades of campaigns, conquest and revolt. Should not the legislative activity of the Frankish king after 800 be regarded rather as the ordinary culmination of royal rule than being particularly imperial? Charlemagne's use of the imperial title in his charters and in his Class IV coins of the period 806–14,[90] his seal which is supposed to have borne the legend *renovatio Romani imperii*, and the conferring of his title upon his son Louis in 813 are all reminiscences of imperial glory, with connotations of great power and territorial jurisdiction. But the title was not of any practical importance. It is difficult indeed to see the imperial title as anything more than a bold attempt by the Papacy to describe the achievements and stature of Charlemagne, cock a snook at Byzantium, and define the peculiar relationship that had evolved between the Papacy and the Frankish rulers over the preceding century. A strong argument in favour of this view is the *Divisio regni* of 806, which is devoid of any idea of Empire, let alone of unity, and cheerfully splits Charlemagne's vast realm into kingdoms for each of his three sons.[91] No reference is made to the imperial title. The acquisition of the imperial title in 800 simply added a name rich in tradition to a well-developed theory of Christian kingship, of which the duties of protection of Rome and the Pope were a part, and which was itself largely the outcome of the actual practice of the early Carolingian kings. Only under Louis the Pious was a theory of Empire and imperial office elaborated.

NOTES

1. See the articles on Pippin III's reign by Fournier, Gasnault, Hubert, Lafaurie, Mordek, Oexle and Schmid, and Riché in *Francia* 2(1974), J. Boussard, 'L'Ouest du royaume franc aux VIIe et VIIIe siècles', *Journal des Savants* (1973), 3–27 and F. Prinz, *Klerus and Krieg im früheren Mittelalter* (Stuttgart 1971).
2. Discussed by J. Semmler, 'Pippin III und die fränkische Klöster', *Francia* 3 (1975), 88–146.
3. A number of instances are discussed by J. M. Wallace-Hadrill, 'A background to Boniface's mission', *England before the Conquest*, P. Clemoes and K. Hughes (eds) (Cambridge 1971), 35–48, F. Prinz, *Frühesmönchtum im Frankenreich* (Munich 1965), T. Schieffer, *Winfrid-Bonifatius und die Grundlegung von Europas* (Freiburg

1954) and E. Ewig, 'Milo et eiusmodi similes', *Sankt Bonifatius Gedenkgabe* (Fulda 1954), 412–40.

4. Hincmar, *PL* 126, col. 15, Ep. 7.

5. Boniface, Ep. 87 and compare Ewig, 'Milo et eiusmodi similes', A. Angenendt, 'Pirmin und Bonifatius. Ihr Verhältnis zu Mönchtum, Bischofsamt und Adel', *Mönchtum, Episkopat und Adel*, A Borst (ed.) (Sigmaringen 1974), 251–304 and *Monachi Peregrini* (Munich 1972).

6. *Gesta episcoporum Autissiodorensium*, c. 27.

7. H. Wolfram, 'Der heilige Rupert und die antikarolingische Adelsopposition', *MIÖG* 80 (1972), 4–34, and see P. Barton, *Frühzeit des Christentums in Österreich in Sudostmitteleuropa bis 788* (Vienna 1975).

8. H. Platelle, *Le temporel de l'abbaye de Saint-Amand* (Paris 1962).

9. H. Frank, *Die Klosterbischöfe des Frankenreiches* (Münster in Westphalen 1932).

10. Semmler, 'Pippin III und die fränkischen Klöster', 98–9 and 101.

11. A. Brückner and R. Marichal, *Chartae Latinae Antiquiores*, I and II (Olten and Lausanne 1954 and 1956), and A Bruckner, 'Die Anfänge des St Galler Stiftsarchivs', *Festschrift Gustav Binz* (Basle 1935), 119–31.

12. Discussed by Semmler, 'Pippin III und die fränkischen Klöster', 91.

13. *Annales Mettenses Priores*, *s.a.*, 753.

14. Discussed by W. Goffart, *The Le Mans Forgeries* (Cambridge, Mass. 1966).

15. *MGH Conc.* II,i, 72–3. See K. Schmid and O. G. Oexle, 'Voraussetzungen und Wirkung des Gebetsbundes von Attigny', *Francia* 2 (1974), 71–121.

16. K. F. Werner, 'La date du naissance de Charlemagne', *Bulletin de la Société des Antiquaires de la France 1972* (Paris 1975), 116–42.

17. Fredegar, Continuation 36.

18. *Liber Pontificalis* XCIIII, 447 (*Vita Stephani* c. 25 and 26).

19. L. Levillain 'L'avènement de la dynastie carolingienne et les origines de l'état pontifical 749–757', *BEC* 94 (1933), 225–95 and W. Levison, *England and the Continent in the Eighth Century* (Oxford 1948), 78–94.

20. *Liber Pontificalis* XCVII, 498 (*Vita Hadriani*, cc. 41 and 42). Compare F. Lot, C. Pfister and F. L. Ganshof, *Les destinées de l'Empire en Occident de 395 à 888* (Paris 1928), 410 and A. Hauck, *Kirchengeschichte Deutschlands*, 2nd ed. (Leipzig 5 vols 1904–1920), II (3–4), 23–4.

21. *Liber Pontificalis* XCVII, 498 (*Vita Hadriani*, c. 41).

22. Donation of Constantine, K. Mirbt (ed.), *Quellen Zur Geschichte des Papsttums* (Freiburg 1895), No. 228, 107–12. Eng. trs. S. Z. Ehler and J. B. Morrall (eds) *Church and State throughout the Centuries* (London 1954), 16–27. See also S. Williams, 'The oldest text of the Constitutum Constantini', *Traditio* 20 (1964), 488–561 and his references.

23. P. Scheffer-Boichorst, 'Neuere Forschungen über die Konstantinische Schenkung II', *MIÖG* 11 (1890), 128–46.

24. W. Levison, 'Konstantinische Schenkung und Silvester-Legende', *Miscellanea F. Ehrle* (Rome 1924), II, 159–247.

25. M. Buchner, 'Rom oder Reims die Heimat des *Constitutum Constantini?*', *HJ* 53 (1933), 137–68.

26. W. Ohnsorge, 'Die Konstantinische Schenkung, Leo III und die Anfänge des kurialen römischen Kaiseridee', *ZRG GA* 68 (1951), 78–109.

27. E. Caspar, *Pippin III und die römische Kirche* (Berlin 1914), 185–9.

28. P. E. Schramm, 'Die Anerkennung Karls des Grossen als Kaiser. Ein Kapitel aus der Geschichte der Mittelalterlichen Staatssymbolik', *HZ* 172 (1951), 449–515;

W. Holtzmann, review of Ohnsorge (n. 26 above), ibid., 173 (1952), 408–9; H. Lowe, review of Ohnsorge, *DA* 9 (1952), 579; H. Fuhrmann, 'Konstantinische Schenkung und abendländisches Kaisertum', *DA* 22 (1966), 63–178. The view of W. Gericke, 'Wann entstand die Konstantinische Schenkung?', *ZRG* 74 *KA* 43 (1957), 1–88, that the document was put together in stages between 754 and 756 is generally not accepted.

29. Lot, Pfister, Ganshof, *Les destinées de l'Empire*, 409, n. 21 for references to Hauck and others. Compare E. Meissner, *Die Entwicklung des weströmischen Staates und Pippin der Jüngere* (Bischberg, Oberfranken 1973).

30. *Annales regni Francorum*, s.a., 755.

31. *MGH SS rer. merov.*, II, 465–6.

32. *Annales Mettenses Priores*, s.a., 756. *Liber Pontificalis* XCIIII, 452 (*Vita Stephani*, c. 44).

33. *Codex Carolinus*, Ep. 16. Compare P. Llewellyn, *Rome in the Dark Ages* (London 1972), 218.

34. Fredegar, Continuation 41. Waifar was also to pay Pippin the wergild of the Goths he had killed.

35. G. Fournier, 'Les campagnes de Pépin le Bref en Auvergne et la question des fortifications rurales au VIIIᵉ siècle', *Francia* 2 (1974), 123–35.

36. *MGH Cap.* I, No. 145, c. 2, 296.

37. *Acta translationis S. Savini martyris*, E. Martène and U. Durand (eds), *Veterum scriptorum et documentorum amplissima collectio* VI (Paris 1729), 808.

38. *Vita Benedicti Anianensi, MGH SS* XV, 213, B. Guérard, *Cartulaire de l'abbaye de Saint Victor de Marseilles* I (Paris 1867), No. 31, 43–6, and Pippin II of Aquitaine, charter 51 respectively.

39. J. Boussard, 'L'Ouest du royaume franc aux VIIᵉ et VIIIᵉ siècles', *Journal des Savants* (1973), 3–27.

40. *MGH Cap.* I, No. 169, 338.

41. *Annales regni Francorum*, reviser's addition, s.a., 769; compare Einhard, *Vita Caroli*, c. 3.

42. Fredegar, Continuation 53.

43. Einhard, *Vita Karoli*, c. 5.

44. For example, Boniface Epp. 50 and 51.

45. E. Ewig, 'Chrodegang et la réforme de l'église franque', *Saint Chrodegang* (Metz 1967), 25–53 and 'Beobachtung zur Entwicklung der fränkischen Reichskirche unter Chrodegang von Metz', *Frühmittelalterliche Studien* 2 (1968), 67–77.

46. E. Ewig, 'Milo et eiusmodi similes', *Sankt Bonifatius Gedenkgabe* (Fulda 1954), 412–40 and J. M. Wallace-Hadrill, 'A background to Boniface's mission', *England before the Conquest*, P. Clemoes and K. Hughes (eds) (Cambridge 1971), 35–48.

47. *MGH Conc.* II,i, 2–4.

48. *MGH Conc.* II,i, 3, and compare *MGH Conc.* II,i c. 4,35.

49. Boniface, Ep. 68.

50. Schieffer, *Winfrid-Bonifatius*, 276–8.

51. G. Hocquard, 'La règle de Saint Chrodegang', *Saint Chrodegang* (Metz 1967), 55–89.

52. See C. Vogel, 'Saint Chrodegang et les débuts de la romanisation du culte en pays franc', ibid., 91–109, and compare McKitterick, *Frankish Church*, 115–54.

53. E. Ewig, 'Chrodegang et la réforme de l'église franque'.

54. *MGH Conc.* II,i, No. 11, 60–3.

55. See the discussion by Oexle and Schmid (n. 15 above).

56. *MGH Cap.* I, No. 17, 42.

57. M. Tangl, *Das Mittelalter in Quellenkinde und Diplomatik* I (Berlin 1966), 540–81 (texts 572–81).

58. *MGH Cap,* I, No. 20, 47–51; compare *MGH Cap.* I, Nos. 71 and 72, 161–4.

59. *MGH Cap.* I, No. 23, c. 23 and c. 35, 64; compare No. 22, c. 80 and c. 81, 61.

60. McKitterick, *Frankish Church,* 1–79.

61. *MGH Conc.* II,i, No. 19, 110–71.

62. J. Semmler, 'Karl der Grosse und des fränkische Mönchtum', *KdG* II, 255–89.

63. Compare Notker's comments on Charlemagne's ecclesiastical policy, *Gesta Karoli Magni,* I, c. 13.

64. Semmler, *KdG* II.

65. H. Büttner, 'Mission und Kirchenorganisation des Frankenreiches bis zum Tode Karls des Grossen', *KdG* I, 454–87.

66. See E. Kleber, 'Herzogtümer und Marken bis 900', *DA* 2 (1938), 1–53.

67. *MGH Cap.* I, No. 26, 68–70; trs. Loyn and Percival, 51–4.

68. *MGH Epp.* IV, Nos. 107 and 110; trs. Allott, Nos. 59 and 56.

69. Büttner, *KdG* I.

70. *MGH Cap.* I, No. 27, 73–8; trs. Loyn and Percival, 55–6.

71. H. Lowe, *Ein literarischer Widersache des Bonifatius, Virgil von Salzburg und die Kosmographie des Aethicus Ister* (Wiesbaden 1951), but there are good grounds for doubting this identification. See W. Stevens, review of K. Hillkowitz, *Zur Kosmographie des Aethicus* II (Frankfurt-am-Main 1973), *Speculum* 40 (1976), 752–5.

72. H. Wolfram (ed.), *Conversio Bagoariorum et Carantanorum* (Vienna 1979).

73. *MGH Dip. Kar.* I, Nos. 48, 47, 53, 43, 44, 46, and Flodoard, *Historia Remensis ecclesiae,* II, 17, respectively.

74. Böhmer–Mühlbacher, 59. See *Codex Carolinus,* No. 46, *MGH Epp.* III, No. 44, 561, and H. von Sybel, 'Die karolingische Annalen', *HZ* 42 (1879), 260–88 especially 274.

75. Einhard, *Vita Karoli,* c. 18 and compare *Vita Adalhardi,* c. 7.

76. *Annales regni Francorum,* reviser's addition, *s.a.,* 771.

77. C. E. Odegaard, *Vassi et Fideles in the Carolingian Empire* (Cambridge, Mass. 1945), 24–31 and Appendix IV, 90–6.

78. *Annales regni francorum, s.a.,* 787. On Tassilo's position in Bavaria see *Lex Baiuuariorum.* II, 89, *MGH Leges Sect.* II, 5, 302.

79. *Annales regni Francorum, s.a.,* 788 and compare Einhard, *Vita Karoli,* c. 11.

80. *MGH Cap.* I, No. 20, 47–51 and see C. de Clercq, *La législation religieuse franque* (Louvain 1937), 160–3.

81. *MGH Cap.* I, No. 97, 203–4.

82. P. Classen, 'Karl der Grosse und Byzanz', *KdG* I, 537–608.

83. L. Wallach, *Diplomatic Studies in Latin and Greek Documents from the Carolingian Age* (Ithaca 1977), 299–352.

84. E. Kantorowicz, *Laudes Regiae* (Berkeley and Los Angeles 1958), 65–111.

85. Einhard, *Vita Karoli,* c. 28.

86. H. Beumann, F. Brunhölzl and W. Winkelmann, *Karolus Magnus et Leo papa; ein Paderborner Epos vom Jahre 799* (Paderborn 1966).

87. *MGH Epp.* IV, No. 110; trs. Allott, No. 56.

88. F. L. Ganshof, *The Imperial Coronation of Charlemagne. Theories and Facts. The David Murray Lecture* No. 16 (Glasgow 1949).

89. *Annales Lauresbanenses, s.a.*, 802, and *MGH Cap.* I, No. 33, c. 2, 90; trs. Loyn and Percival, 44–5 and 74 respectively. Compare C. E. Odegaard, 'Carolingian oaths of fidelity', *Speculum* 16 (1941), 284–96.
90. P. Grierson, 'Money and coinage under Charlemagne', *KdG* I, 501–36.
91. *MGH Cap.* I, No. 45, 126–30; trs. Loyn and Percival, 91–6.

CHAPTER FOUR

The Means of Ruling

The power of the Carolingian kings depended on the respect the ruler inspired by right and by tradition and on the actual government of the people. Thus the vast kingdom acquired by the Carolingians required careful administration to render their authority effective (see Map 4). The rulers appear to have recognized the magnitude of the task of governing the realm, and Charlemagne in particular, whatever his shortcomings in external policy, did much to provide the means of ruling. Yet the administration's total dependence on the efficiency, loyalty and support of his subjects meant that the means ultimately proved insufficient, or rather, that they were effective in providing administration by lesser officials who became increasingly independent. The relative novelty of the comprehensive and ambitious scheme of Carolingian administration in the barbarian kingdoms of Western Europe, however, as well as the actual achievements of the Franks in the administrative sphere, must be borne in mind when assessing the effectiveness and significance of Carolingian government. Early Carolingian administrative institutions had important consequences for the subsequent political development of the Frankish kingdom.

The Carolingian king was head of the administration both within his household and throughout the kingdom. He exercised the *bannum* or the right to rule and command over all his subjects. He was the guardian of justice and peace and acted as the final court of appeal in judicial matters. He made the decisions and promulgated the legislation, probably at the general assembly and in the form of the capitularies, for the ordering of his kingdom, though in this activity he was undoubtedly helped and guided by a group of advisers.[1] He acted as protector and patron of the church, and champion of the poor and weak. Perhaps his most important function was that of warlord. The ideal king of the early medieval period was the man who extended the kingdom, and brought nations and their wealth under his control. Alcuin wrote to Charlemagne's son Pippin that a king should be strong against his enemies, humble to Christians, feared by pagans, loved by the poor and judicious in counsel and maintaining justice.[2] In the seventh century and early eighth century the mayors of the palace and the Carolingian kings had added perceptibly to what was expected and permitted of a king. Thus, when Pippin deposed Childeric III

77

in 751, he acquired the office and mystique of kingship as it had developed under the Merovingians, as well as the power and functions of the mayor of the palace. That the Carolingians themselves were wealthy landowners was an important feature of their kingship. By the time of Pippin moreover, they were pre-eminently Christian kings. What the early Carolingians made of the royal office provided a model for future kings. Their aims, actions and ideals became the ideal to be striven for by their successors.

I

Between 714 and 814 only seven years are noted by the annalists as being years of peace; in every other year the Frankish host mounted campaigns, whether against rebels within the kingdom or against non-Franks and pagans. Military expeditions brought wealth in the form of booty, tribute, slaves, land and new fields of endeavour for the Christian church; society was geared to war, and considerable resources were expended on its successful waging. Energy and resources do not seem to have been diverted on any appreciable scale to peaceful activities such as government and administration. It is an indication of the rapid evolution of early medieval society under the Carolingians that emphasis was increasingly placed on government, the administration of justice and legislation. The actual workings of this shift in emphasis are not always entirely clear, but by examining the development of some of the most important Carolingian institutions of government the innovations made by the Carolingians for the ordering of their society may be better understood.

The framework of Carolingian institutions was one aspect of the attempt made by Pippin, Charlemagne and Louis the Pious to organize kingdom, church and nobility around their persons. The central administration of the Carolingian monarchy was extremely rudimentary. To the king was attached his household, many members of which had duties and responsibilities that extended beyond the palace. The household was not just a court, but an organ of administration. Except for the last few years of Charlemagne's reign, the king and his household were itinerant; they travelled from palace to villa to monastery to *civitas*. There was no one place where the king could be expected to be at any one time, albeit a number of royal residences, Ingelheim, Herstal, Attigny, and after 796 Aachen, were more often favoured with the king's presence than others.

The sources concerning the royal household and its functions are often ambiguous and imprecise. Hincmar of Rheims' *De ordine palatii* used to be regarded as a description of the king's household. The work was written in 882 in the form of an exhortation addressed to the young King Carloman, but Hincmar stated in the treatise that his description of palace government was based on an earlier work by Adalhard of Corbie (d. 826) as well as on what he himself had observed in his youth. Adalhard's treatise, if it ever existed, is no longer extant, and Hincmar provides the sole contemporary reference to it.

Whether or not Hincmar was using a treatise by Adalhard, it is clear that the smooth functioning and harmony of the government he portrays is idealized.[3] There is much that he could have told us in detail about the functioning of the palace officials, but he refers to many very briefly, simply as part of his portrait of harmonious government. There is, on the other hand, no reason to suppose that Hincmar was inventing all the officials he describes, and any doubt that some of them may not have existed in the early ninth century is dispelled by occasional references to them in other sources. Hincmar's description of the issuing of capitularies, however, applies more to the reign of Charles the Bald. Used with due caution therefore, and notwithstanding Perroy's views that *De ordine palatii*'s value as historical evidence is well nigh worthless, the bare bones of the treatise provide useful information.[4]

Hincmar describes one of the two chief functionaries in the palace as the chaplain, who had charge of all ecclesiastical affairs within the kingdom. Some measure of the importance of the office of chaplain may be obtained from the stature of the men who filled the office; Hincmar states that Fulrad, abbot of St Denis, Angilramn, archbishop of Metz, and Hildebold, archbishop of Cologne, acted as chaplains under Pippin and Charlemagne. The *comes palatii*, count of the palace, was the most important secular official; we know one incumbent of this office, Count Wigbod, from Theodulf's mocking description of him, with his great belly and waddling gait.[5] The count exercised some of the functions of the old Merovingian office of mayor of the palace. He had complete control over the running of the household and under him were all the other officials in charge of the various departments. These included the chamberlain who was primarily responsible to the queen, and both queen and chamberlain acted as housekeepers on a grand scale; the seneschal (head of table), wine steward, count of the stable, marshal and *mansionarius* (master of lodgings) were subordinates of the count of the palace. Between them were divided the responsibilities of arranging accommodation and board for the itinerant royal household and ensuring that there was enough fodder and water for the horses wherever the royal household was. Hincmar also tells us that there were four chief hunters and a falconer, as well as a number of lesser officials and servants who assisted the above named. The Plan of St Gall provides an indication of the expectations of a monastery as far as a visit from the king's retinue is concerned. It makes provision, with its elaborately furnished and heated 'house for distinguished guests' for the accommodation of the king and his household. The guests were provided with their own kitchen, bakery and brewing house separate from those of the monastery, not unlike a self-catering youth hostel. Another building may have been provided on the plan for the warriors in the king's retinue, and there was certainly a separate house with nine privies for the use of the royal servants.[6]

Often the functionaries of the palace are found elsewhere in the service of the king. Adalgis the chamberlain, and Geilo, the count of the stable, were among the leaders of the army in the campaigns against the Saxons, during which Adalgis was killed. In 786, Andulf the seneschal was required to lead an expedition against the Bretons; Eggihard, his predecessor as seneschal, and

Anshelm, count of the palace, were killed with Count Roland of the Breton march, in the ambush in Roncesvalles. The king always seems to have had a small group of advisers with him. An anecdote in the Cartulary of Lorsch describes Charlemagne calling together all his advisers, explaining the problem, letting them express their views and then deciding against the advice he had been given. Fustel de Coulanges, commenting on this story, thought that there may have been a certain obligation rather than a right to offer the king advice.[7]

Associated with the chaplain in the palace was the *cancellarius* or chancellor, head of the writing office. This writing office is not to be understood as a permanent institution like the later medieval chancery. It was rather a group of notaries who redacted the documents but who almost certainly performed other functions in the palace as well. There is still a great deal of uncertainty about the position of the writing office within the palace, its relation to the personnel of the palace chapel and the actual process of redaction of the documents themselves. The Carolingian chancery developed slowly and attained its complete form under Louis the Pious. When the Empire split in 843, so did the chancery. The chancery is only alluded to in very general terms by Hincmar, but its activities are amply documented by the charters which survive. The stress on written instruments to validate claims to property, record exchanges, confirm privileges, grant immunities and give land is an important instance of the growing importance of the written word in Carolingian administration. Proposals for administrative innovations and organization within the kingdom were also committed to writing in the form of capitularies.

Were the Merovingian chancery and chancery practice taken over by the Carolingians in the eighth century? The mayors of the palace under the Merovingians used a form of charter more like the private charter. In other words, it was a very simplified version lacking most of the protocol of the Merovingian royal charter and with few of the variations in content. Charters, by the eighth century, were probably drawn up by the mayor's notaries, and the formulae for signatures are similar to those of the dukes of Alemannia and Bavaria, with no authentication other than the signatures. The only notary known by name is Aldo, who wrote and subscribed a charter for St Willibrord for Charles Martel in 726.[8]

A change seems to have come about between 737 and 743 when a mayor's writing office was instituted under Charles Martel. There is only one extant charter, dated 14–27 September 741, produced for Charles Martel from the period, and it is still closer in form to the private charters than to the royal charters, except that like a royal charter it is not only written and signed by a notary, it also has a recognition note: *Chrothgangus iussus hanc epistolam donationis recognovi.*[9] With such a note the signatory assumes responsibility for the validity of the document, and in this case Chrothgangus is none other than Chrodegang, later bishop of Metz, who is described by Paul the Deacon as a referendary to the mayor of the palace before his elevation.[10] It seems that while Charles Martel ruled without a king, the mayor's writing office acted instead of the royal one. As far as we can tell, it was not the case that the Carolingian mayors took over the royal chancery. This impression is reinforced by the evidence from Pippin III's reign. Although with the elevation of the last Merovingian king to the throne a royal writing office appears to have been established, the mayor's 'chancery' continued an independent existence. Two charters of Carloman survive, and from Pippin's mayoral writing office three referendaries are known by name – Rodegus, Wilecharius and Wineramnus.

New names are associated with Pippin's writing office after 751 and Pippin's ascent to the throne; the chancery became more highly organized under Pippin and a change in its structure was effected in that a *cancellarius* emerged. These changes may readily be attributed to the dependence of the Carolingians on particular noble and clerical support; the office of chancellor and posts for notaries within the writing office may have been one means of promoting influential followers. Widmar, Eius and Baddilo were prominent from 757; Widmar and Eius both seem to have left the chancery by 760 and are replaced by Hitherius and Berneric, both of whom supply the *recognitio* in Baddilo's name. Hitherius succeeded Baddilo in about 766 and stayed into Charlemagne's reign till 776. Ercambald, the chancellor from 797 to 812, was described by Theodulf of Orleans as carrying two wax tablets about with him on which he wrote down the king's orders and hummed them over to himself under his breath.[11] Baddilo, the first sole head of Pippin's chancery, was called *summus sacri palatii cancellarius* or *sacri palatii archinotarius*. Hincmar of Rheims in 882 called the head of the chancery *summus cancellarius* and this term, or *archicancellarius*, was used in the tenth century.

Hitherius is the first chancery official who can with certainty be described as a cleric, and from this time onwards, in contrast to the writing office of the Merovingians, no chancery officials were laymen. The notaries were also in orders. This development may have been connected with the change of dynasty and the importance of ecclesiastical support for the Carolingians.

With the changeover from Merovingian to Carolingian rule there is thus a change, rather than continuity, in the structure and personnel of the chancery, developing from the mayor of the palace's writing office. But in the actual form of the charters there is considerable continuity between the Merovingian and Carolingian royal documents. From the example given below one can see what form the early Carolingian document took.

A gift to the monastery of St Denis, 25 February 775
Charles, by the grace of God king of the Franks and Lombards, to all our faithful subjects both present and future.
Seeing that the scriptures admonish us that each man ought steadfastly so to prepare himself that when he comes into the sight of the Judge on high he may deserve to hear of his Lord those words of kindness in which all just men through their good acts will rejoice, for this reason we have made, we believe, a salutary decision, that from those earthly possessions with which the Divine Grace has seen abundantly to endow us in this life we should make donations, however small they may be, to the end that we may so obtain mercy of the Most High.
Wherefore, to the church of St Denis, where that precious master rests in bodily remains along with his fellows, and where the venerable Fulrad is abbot, and which

we ourselves with Christ's favour have built anew and have ordered lately to be dedicated with great honour, we give, and wish to be given in perpetuity for the salvation of our soul, two villas, the one in the place called Luzarches, which is situated in the district of Paris on the river called *Folunca*, together with the church in honour of St Cosmas and St Damian, and the other in the place called Messy, which is situated in the district of Meaux, both these villas with all their bounds and appurtenances, that they may be used for the increase of the said monastery and the monks that serve there, for the furnishing of the church itself and for the maintenance of the poor.

These we give in their entirety, that is to say, with their lands, houses and other buildings, their tenants, slaves, vineyards, woods, meadows, pastures, waters and water courses, flour mills and all movable and immovable belongings. All this, as we have said, the monastery and those in charge of it are for their part to have, hold and possess, and shall have licence to do with as they wish both now and for the future, so long as it shall please these servants of God earnestly to pray both day and night for the Lord's mercy upon us and our descendants.

And that this our authority may be more strictly observed and better maintained throughout the years, we have directed that it be confirmed hereunder in our own hand and sealed with our ring. Mark of the most glorious king Charles.

I, Wigbald, witnessed and signed on behalf of Hitherius.

Issued the twenty-fifth day of February in the seventh and first years of our reign; enacted in the monastery of St Denis; in the name of God, so be it.

Most charters followed this format. The use of the chrismon or symbolic invocation at the beginning, the address, the format, the appreciation and the script form a continuous line of development with the Merovingian charters. Some innovations were made, such as the added epithet of *vir inluster* to Pippin's title, and the form of the date formula. The script, originally very similar to Merovingian chancery hand, under the influence of Caroline minuscule became much clearer, evolving into a type of writing known as Carolingian royal chancery hand. In addition to the signatures of the king and the notary, the seal was announced. For the royal signature a distinctive monogram was used from the time of Charlemagne onwards, made up of the letters of the king's name, Karolus, Hludovicus and so on. Later kings bearing the same name employed the same monogram. Nearly all charters had a wax seal (some were of metal) affixed at the bottom of the text, above the date clause and to the right of the chancery subscription. The barbarous Latin of the Merovingian charters steadily improved, and was correct by the reign of Louis the Pious. In the initial protocol the chrismon or symbolic invocation is present, and from 800 a verbal invocation such as 'in nomine Dei . . .' is added.

The title of the king used in the charter varied according to political circumstances and can thus be a useful means of dating. Charlemagne was called in succeeding charters: *Carolus gratia Dei rex, vir inluster; Carolus gratia dei rex francorum et langobardorum atque patricius romanorum; Carolus serenissimus augustus.* The text of the charter expresses the sovereign's will, and the formulae at the end of the charter are essential for its legal validity and authenticity. The formula of corroboration announces the seal, and the chancery subscription and *recognitio* give the name of the notary responsible for the redaction and the validity of the charter. On a single line at the bottom of a charter the date was written, in book hand rather than the chancery cursive. The place where the charter was drawn up was part of the date clause. The places most often mentioned are the royal residences or *palatia*, sometimes a *civitas*, monastery, villa or similar resting place. This information is invaluable for establishing the itinerary of the monarch.

The *recognitio* (recognition) was given the charter by the chancellor or notary. Validation was effected by the royal monogram and seal. The absence of the royal monogram may mean the king never saw the document. In other words the monogram is not essential for its validation. Only the king had the power to authorize a document to be issued with his signature and seal, but he alone did not give the necessary orders for the expedition of the diplomas; these orders were passed on to the chancery by officials called *ambasciatores* or *impetratores* or by the archchancellor or head of the notaries. Most of the charters do not mention the immediate motive for their redaction. Sometimes a decision is presented as done with the advice and consent of the king's entourage, but it is exceptional until the second half of the tenth century and only becomes more common under the Capetians. Many charters resulted from pleas and requests, often to restore ancient, real or imagined rights, grants of immunity from the interference of royal officials, protection and so on. A significant proportion of the Carolingian charters simply renew the precepts and grants of their predecessors.

We have 40 charters of Pippin, 12 from the reign of Carloman, 262 of Charlemagne and 350–400 of Louis the Pious. After Charles the Bald – we know of 500 of his charters – the number decreases. Because of the relative abundance of originals among these charters, many of which have been preserved in monastic archives, it has been possible to establish a number of rules and principles for chancery methods and for the detection of forgery and interpolation. Most of what we know about the Carolingian chancery is in fact deduced from the internal evidence provided by the documents. A further source of information is the formulary. Sample charters for various purposes were put together into collections. These formularies contain more types of document than we have surviving examples of, so formularies are important for illustrating a range of written record. Because they were destined for no one in particular, however, they lack the extra historical interest that a true legal document possesses. The most important formulary is the Formulary of Marculf dedicated to a Bishop Landri (650–67?), possibly written by a notary at St Denis. If not used by the Merovingian royal officials, it was certainly used by the mayors of the palace and the first Carolingian kings. An extensively revised collection of formulae was produced during the reign of Louis the Pious. The *Formulae imperiales e curia Ludovici Pii* was an official collection of fifty-five formulae thought to have been compiled under the direction of Fridugis, chancellor from 819 to 832. It remained in use until the beginning of the tenth century. The sole surviving manuscript containing this formulary, BN lat. 2718, was written almost entirely in tironian notes, the notarial shorthand, and is said to have been written at Tours. If the manuscript is indeed from Tours it raises the question of the relationship between Louis' chancery scribes and those of his principal monasteries, especially in view of the comments Keynes has made with regard to the Anglo-Saxon royal chancery.[12]

The types of document issued from the Carolingian writing office or 'chancery' are known either from extant examples, or from their formulae in the formularies. There are donations, restitutions and confirmations of benefits. Gifts of personal ownership were exceptional before 814 and increase after that as a means of ensuring loyalty and increasing the number of loyal followers. A great many donations of this kind were made by Charles the Bald. There were also many gifts to ecclesiastical establishments, precepts granting protection, exemption from tolls, privileges and assignments to benefices, confirmations of exchange, *tractoria* (documents giving free passage and right to hospitality from the king's subjects), mandates and a type of document called *pancarta*, that is reallocation of rights and possessions lost due to the loss of documents. The Viking invasions necessitated many of these. There was also the precarial grant, by which an individual could make a grant to an institution yet retain the use of the land or dwelling during his lifetime.

In the early years of the Carolingian chancery, under Pippin and Charlemagne, chancellors had been recruited from the notaries and were professionals. Louis the Pious changed this. Chancellors were appointed by the king from among his chief advisers and supporters rather than being raised through the ranks from notary status. Helisachar, chancellor to Louis in Aquitaine, may well have started his career as a notary, but his successors, Fridugis, abbot of Tours, Theoto, abbot of Marmoutier, and Hugh, abbot of St Quentin, were all installed in office by Louis and took no personal part in the drawing up of documents. At first the archchancellor had charge of the royal seal, but notes in notarial shorthand on a charter of 821 indicate that the chief notary had sealed the document rather than the chancellor, and from 827 it is certain that the notary always did it. Until 819 the *recognitio* of the charters was made and the control of the regularity of the charters exercised by the chancellor himself, but after that it was a subordinate's job, and a new official emerges, the master of the notaries, who signs the documents *ad vicem*. In a charter of 815, for example, Durandus, the head of the notaries, acts as Helisachar's deputy. The chancellor continued for some time to exercise administrative control and discipline in the writing office, but in time the archchaplain took over the duty. The archchancellor also supervised the palace archive which is only occasionally referred to in the sources. A number of Louis the Pious' mandates, for example, such as the *Constitutio de Hispanis* refer to copies of a document being sent out and a further copy being retained in the royal archive.

A number of notaries, possibly attached to the royal chapel, served under the chancellor. Notaries often achieved high ecclesiastical office, so it would seem that they cannot be regarded as mere clerks. Many of them came from important noble families. To be a notary in the royal writing office became an important means of advancement within the ecclesiastical hierarchy. After Fridugis' term of office, one notary emerged as more important than the others with the title *magister notarius*, and it was he who kept the seal. The chief notary increased in importance as the involvement of the archchancellor in the work of the chancery decreased.

It remains to consider the relationship between the *capella* or chapel of the palace and the writing office. The chapel personnel were the palace clergy appointed to look after the *cappa* or cloak of St Martin. Under Pippin the chaplains' duties were to perform the holy rites in the palace chapel; the clergy also assisted in this.

In the early years the relationship between chancery and chapel had been, according to Sickel, that of two separate institutions, but Tangl, Kehr, Klewitz and others have thought otherwise.[13] It was Klewitz who went so far as to suggest that the redaction of documents was one of the duties of the chapel personnel. This would certainly account for the fact that all the notaries were clerics, and reinforces the impression that too well-defined an institution should not be assumed. It is thought that some of the chapel personnel, and thus some notaries, were itinerant with the king, while some of the others stayed in one of the palaces, and possibly after 802 at least, at Aachen. Wala, once a royal official and later abbot of Corbie (d. 836) averred that the 'army of clerics' at the palace (that is, the chaplains) was not a proper ecclesiastical order, and that the chaplains served for no reason other than for the sake of profit and the advantages of this world.[14] Until the time of Louis the Pious, the head of the palatine chapel was called the archipresbyter, *custos capellae* (guardian of the chapel) or *premicerius capellae* (head of the chapel), but from Louis' time he was called *archicapellanus* (archchaplain). The archchaplain acted as the king's personal counsellor on all ecclesiastical matters, he had all the palace clergy under him and was thus also the ecclesiastical superior of the notaries in the writing office, if indeed they and the palatine clergy of the chapel were not one and the same. Evidence from the reign of Charlemagne and Louis the Pious suggests that the archchancellor and notaries were subordinate to the archchaplain, but the archchancellor gradually became more important. In the east Frankish kingdom after 856 the archchancellor and archchaplain were the same person, but this does not appear to have been the case in the western kingdom. There, the office of archchaplain ceased after Hilduin and nothing more is known of the western chapel or its officials.

II

The Carolingians were possessed of considerable personal wealth, in the form for the most part of vast landed estates, many of which were concentrated in the Meuse – Moselle river valleys. The *Capitulare de Villis* and the *Brevium exempla* provide some notion of the extent and prosperity of a royal estate, and it is to be assumed that the Carolingians actually lived off their own estates.[15] More conventional sources of income for the king and his government, however, were irregular, unsystematic and far from universal. There was, for example, no land tax as such, but instead a series of customary dues on land and persons, tributes related to occupation of royal land, tolls, compulsory gifts and fines which provided some sort of revenue. To this must be added the treasure plundered from conquered peoples, as much a part of Carolingian warfare as it had been under the Merovingians, as well as the slaves captured, land confiscated and tribute extorted. The Avar treasure was the most celebrated haul made by the Frankish host; its richness left all who saw or heard of it agape. Gifts from visiting dignitaries were also of some importance; rich gifts are often mentioned in the annals, though the famous elephant 'Abul-Abaz' sent by Haroun-al-Raschid to Charlemagne, would not exactly be regarded as a source of revenue![16]

Only rarely are there references in the sources to taxes or dues. The *donum publicum* was an obligatory gift required from the magnates, and ecclesiastical establishments. The Annals of St Bertin and the *Gesta abbatum Fontanellensium* state that the gift was generally made at the general assembly held each year.[17] No fixed amount or nature of the gift is stipulated; it could be in money or in kind. Some attempt was made to revive any existing taxes, for in 812 Charlemagne asked his *missi* to search out all the ancient taxes due to the king, in the hope of reviving them.[18] We know that some taxes and dues were levied on landholding, simply because charters exist granting immunity from them. The direct taxes such as tolls and custom dues (*teloneum*), a wheel tax, a bridge tax and port tax could be levied and the proceeds went to the king, but sometimes the receipt of these could be bestowed on a magnate or an ecclesiastical establishment. The *mansio* or *parata* represented the obligation of all landowners to give bed and board to the envoys of the king,[19] and a set tariff of what a legate should receive was sometimes set. This obligation was often dodged and collection of the other direct or indirect taxes was hardly regular or well organized. Profits from the exercise of justice provided revenue for both the king and the counts, his representatives in local courts, for , of the composition fines (*fredum*) two-thirds went to the king and one-third to the count. The penal fines, such as the *heribannum* (a fine for refusal to perform military service) were also shared between the king and the count. For allowing certain privileges to merchants the king could receive some payment, and there was also seigneurage, the small percentage taken by the king on every coin minted; in contrast to the Merovingians, the early Carolingian kings exercised considerable control over the minting of coinage.

The gradual debasement of Merovingian gold coinage culminated in its replacement with silver in the eighth century, and from then until the twelfth century is regarded as a period of silver monometallism, that is, coinage was entirely of silver. The silver penny or *denarius* was virtually the sole coin in use; although it was known that there were twelve *denarii* or pennies to the *solidus* or shilling and twenty *solidi* to the *libra* or pound, there were no coins in the Carolingian period to represent either the *solidus* or the *libra*. By Charlemagne's time the silver coins were thin and ill-formed, but under Charlemagne a reform of the coinage was effected and a heavier, better-struck silver coinage introduced. Most historians make a strong distinction between the silver 'medieval' coinage of Charlemagne and the gold coinage of the Roman Empire, forgetting to stress what a gradual development the change was in which Charlemagne's reform represents a culmination. Grierson considers Charlemagne's change of the weight of the penny from 1.3 g to 1.7 g in about 793–4 to have had no particular economic rationale and to be unrelated to the silver supply in Europe at this time; the heavy penny, he argues, simply marked the transition from a weight system based on the barley grain to one based on the wheat grain, a system which persisted thereafter for some centuries.[20] In 803 and 805 Charlemagne attempted to centralize the issue of coinage and the Carolingians maintained reasonably firm control of minting until the end of the ninth century. Gold coinage was introduced on a minor scale by Louis the Pious, but numismatists are still making up their minds about the function, if any, of gold coinage in this period.

III

However well organized the royal household may have been, the real test of the Carolingian kings' success in ruling their domain was the extent to which their authority over their agents and subjects was effective. In which regions and how were the Carolingians able to enforce their authority? How did the king communicate with his agents and subjects? In what circumstances was public justice exercised? The two principal types of official for representing and enforcing the king's authority in the kingdom were the count and the *missus dominicus*.

The whole kingdom was divided into counties or *comitati*. These were adapted to the older divisions of *pagus* and *civitas* and usually comprised the *civitas* and its surrounding region. In the course of the eighth century the county became a geographical term. Estimates of the number of counties in the Frankish kingdom under the Carolingians have varied between 110 and 600.[21] The latter figure seems the more likely. The *ducatus* or duchy by contrast was not a fixed region until towards the end of the Carolingian period. In the eighth and ninth centuries the *ducatus* was to be understood much more as a command temporarily entrusted to a person who had under him a number of counts, and whose functions were primarily military. A Carolingian innovation in administrative districts was the march or marcher region, an area on the frontier whose counts, for example the counts of the marches of Spain, Benevento, Friuli, Brittany and Septimania, had particular responsibilities for defence. The county itself was divided up into *centenae* or vicariates, the heads of which were the *centenarii* or vicars. They assisted the count and acted for him in minor judicial cases.

To the administrative district of the county was assigned the official called the *comes* or count. Originally a count was appointed and sent out to administer a region, but it gradually became customary for the local magnate in a district to be appointed count. Some counts served in the king's household rather than administering a county. We find examples of local magnates acting as counts as early as 802. The responsibility to act as count was conferred by the king and could, at least until Charles the Bald's reign, be revoked by him. In theory, moreover, the count was temporary and removeable, but in practice the same count remained in office for as much as thirty years in the same district, and the office gradually tended to remain in the family, such as the family of Count Gerard (see p. 90 below) in the county of Paris. It was probably not until the late ninth or the tenth century, however, that countships customarily became hereditary.

Through the count the king transmitted his will to his subjects. Diplomas were generally addressed to counts and other agents. Each count was supposed to receive a copy of a decree from the king, make known its contents to the people in his region, and see to its implementation.[22] Alternatively, as and when counts attended on the king each year they could take the opportunity to obtain new orders.[23] Viscounts acted for the counts in their absence. As king's delegate the count judged legal cases, received dues and tolls, and levied military forces. He also had to supervise the upkeep of roads, bridges and any public buildings, and work was required from all free men to this end. Counts were also subject to inspection by the royal *missi*. They were not paid a salary. Although a proportion of the composition fines and judicial dues was for the count, his principal benefit was the lands attached to his office from which he received one-third of the revenues. The count's assistant was the viscount, nominated by the count himself.

The oath of fidelity was an important means of establishing a relationship of mutual dependence between king and subject. The count or *missus dominicus* received the oaths of fidelity from the king's subjects and recorded the names of the oath-takers. Three of these oath-swearers' lists are extant: one with 180 names is probably to be dated to the last years of Charlemagne's reign while the others are later, and seem to have been drawn up in Rheims and Italy in 854.[24] The oath of fidelity was to be sworn by every freeman over the age of twelve. In 792, Charlemagne enumerated all those who were to take the oath: bishops, abbots, archdeacons, canons, parish priests, clerics and monks, counts, royal vassals, vicars, *centenarii* and 'all the people'.[25] Thus the oath was not the custom of a particular class of men, race or region; it was an obligation imposed by the Frankish king. The formula of the oath of 789 is recorded and is generally associated with the renewal of oaths after the revolt of 786. The conspirators apparently insisted that they had not sworn an oath of fidelity to the king. Every man was required to swear: 'I promise that I am and shall be faithful to my lord Charles the king and his sons all the days of my life without deception or deceit.'[26] In 802, after Charlemagne had been crowned Emperor, all Franks were required to renew the oath, and a new formula was supplied. Every man was to promise to be faithful to Lord Charles with regard to his kingdom and his rights 'just as a man rightly should be to his lord'.[27] The import of the 789 oath was that a subject promised to be loyal. The oath of 802 is more specific in requiring subjects to be obedient, but also not to interfere with the commands, property, taxes, army and courts of the king.

Charlemagne explained in his capitulary for 802 what an oath of fidelity entailed. It was not simply a profession of loyalty to the king but also a promise to serve God, respect royal property, church property and the poor, to take proper care of any benefice held of the king, to obey the summons to war, promote and carry out the orders of the king, and ensure the proper conduct of judicial procedure. The ideas of the faithful of the church and the *fideles* of the Empire were conflated.

The county system operated over most of the Frankish Empire apart from Bavaria. That counties were of manageable size was one of the virtues of the system, and certainly in theory the counts were well placed to relay royal power. In non-Frankish regions the counts represented foreign rule. They assured order and the rule of justice. In other words they performed a vital social function and were not necessarily the instruments of repression or oppression. Like any administrative system, that of the counts was open to abuse, but to the extent that the counts ensured order, public peace and security, they were excellent propagandists for the benefits of fidelity to the Carolingians.

But to what extent did the counts ensure public order and security? This unfortunately cannot be answered satisfactorily. Although we are fully informed about the tasks the count was required to fulfil, it is clear from the references to abuses committed by counts abounding in the capitularies and other written sources (such as going hunting on the very day they were supposed to hold court, accepting bribes, sending small farmers to war so that their crops were ruined and deflecting serf labour from royal estates to their own land), that some counts were far from exemplary, but it is impossible to say whether these abuses were the rule rather than the exception. Dhondt suggested that in the ninth century there was an absence of a sense of the public welfare among the great comital families, but again it is difficult to substantiate or contradict this view, especially as the royal legislation made a concerted effort to inculcate a sense of public welfare.[28]

Very little information survives about individual counts to enable us to form some picture of their stature and function. Count Eric of Friuli and Gerold of Bavaria were both killed fighting the Avars and both had their prowess celebrated in verse. Eric was a friend of Paulinus, bishop of Aquileia, and Alcuin and received the *Liber Exhortationis* from the former. He had led the Frankish host against the Avars, despoiled the Avar Ring of its treasure and sent it to the king. Gerold was brother-in-law to Charlemagne through the latter's first wife Hildegard. He may have acted as a *missus* and his gifts to Reichenau where he was buried, and to St Gall, survive in charters. He left no direct heirs.[29]

A close examination of the history of the county of Paris, one of the better-documented counties, reveals both the sparseness of our knowledge and a little about the count's activities. The count of Paris was one of the most important in the system, partly because of the religious, political and military importance of the Paris basin. The first count about whom anything much is known is Guerinus or Warin, who belonged to a Frankish family resident in Burgundy and who was brother to Leudegar, bishop of Autun. He appears for the first time in a diploma dated 22 June 654, confirming a privilege of Landri of Paris in favour of St Denis. The counts of Paris remained involved, in one way or another, with the abbey of St Denis and the surviving charters witness to their disputes with the abbots. No text tells us who succeeded Warin, but in a private charter from the Paris region the will of a woman called Irmintrude, dated c. 700, was witnessed by a Count Mummolus. Levillain thought his name permitted the conjecture that he was from a family of Gallo-Roman origin.

Because of Paris' strategic importance, the county had to be in the hands of a staunchly loyal man, and we next hear of the countship when it is in the hands of the mayor of the palace, Pippin II, though there is nothing to suggest that the countship of Paris was personal property. Pippin II delegated the mayor's power to Nordebert (689–96) and then to his own son Grimoald who as count initiated moves against the rights of St Denis once more. When Grimoald was assassinated in 714 his son Theudoald succeeded him as count and mayor, but after 714 the Neustrians revolted, Theudoald was killed, Ragamfred was elected and he managed to stay in control of the Paris region until 719. He then disappears from the sources. When Charles Martel became mayor he delegated his Neustrian responsibilities to someone else. When the countship is next mentioned it appears to have been merged with the office of mayor of Neustria and Grifo seems to have been the count. A diploma of 8 July 753 refers to taxes Grifo had imposed on the merchants going to St Denis and which were lifted by his successor Gerard. It is probable that Grifo's nomination to the county dated from the partition of the rest of the kingdom in 741 between Carloman and Pippin, and that a tradition was developing according to which the county of Paris was an apanage of the Carolingian house. As count, Grifo subscribed to an act conceding the domain of Clichy-la-Garenne to St Denis.[30] When Grifo after his rebellion in Bavaria was made head of twelve counties in Neustria it is possible that the county of Paris was among them.

It was not until well after Pippin was made king that we hear again of a count of Paris. This time it is Gerard, one of Pippin's *fideles*. The names of his wife, daughter and granddaughter, all Carolingian feminine names, suggest that the count married into the Carolingian royal family. The countship remained in the hands of this aristocratic family of Gerard, connected to the royal house by ties of blood, for a century. It is conjectured that this family originally came from the Rhine – Alsace region, that is, from Austrasia, but this may simply be Levillain's maintenance of the old view that the Meuse – Moselle nobility were dominant in the Carolingian Empire. Little is known of Gerard's activities; he may have given some land to monasteries, but the identification is not certain. Gerard I's successor was almost certainly Stephen and probably his son. He is the first count of Paris after Gerard attested by genuine documents. In 802 he was designated *missus dominicus* with Abbot Fardulf of St Denis, and in 811 he was one of the fifteen counts who witnessed Charlemagne's will. In this year he and his wife Amaltrude gave to the church of Paris the lands they possessed in the Paris region. Stephen died probably before 816, for by June of that year the count is Bego. Bego seems to have served the young King Louis in Aquitaine and in 800 is mentioned raising troops and serving under the command of Count William of Toulouse. Bego may have succeeded William as count of Toulouse and probably followed Louis to Aachen in 814. He was probably made count shortly thereafter and died in October 816. He married a daughter of Louis the Pious.

Not until 838 do we hear again of the counts of Paris. Gerard II took the oath to Charles the Bald when the latter's kingdom was established, but defected to Lothar in 840. Gerard II could have been a grandson of Bego, or a son, but the relationship is not clear. He did, however, marry into an influential family. His wife's sister Irmingarde married the Emperor Lothar. There is no reference to the counts of Paris from 840–79: the countship had presumably been forfeited by Gerard's family. Adalhard or the Welf Conrad (brother of the Empress Judith) may have had the post but lost it to Odo of Paris, who subsequently became king of the Franks in 888. The county became part of the Robertian or Capetian house and the first landed estate on which that family built its fortunes.[31]

Sometimes another official, the duke, was introduced between palace and counts. From the mid-ninth century this became more common. There were also the subkings, Pippin, king of Italy, and Louis the Pious, king of Aquitaine, who, though made subkings as children, became effective rulers of their particular regions as adults. The Carolingian subkings supported the purely dynastic interests of the ruler. For Charlemagne the subkingship was a source of strength and made a region closer and more intimately connected with the central power and the ruling house.[32]

IV

In about 769, Charlemagne reformed the local system of administering justice, instituted the *scabini* (possibly because of abuse in the counts' courts) and reduced to two (later increased to three) the number of court sessions to be held in a year. Under Louis the Pious frequent court sessions were also frowned upon. As well as the counts' regular courts and those of the *centenarii*, courts were held by the count while on tour through the county and by the *missi dominici*. They were probably held in spring, summer and autumn; there were prohibitions about holding courts on Sundays or other holy days and there seems to have been no set location. The administration of justice was all important. The *scabini* replaced the Merovingian *rachimburgii*, to whom they were similar in function, probably before 780, but they are first mentioned in the capitularies for 802. Their function was that of assessors; they accompanied the count on his judicial circuit, they declared the law, questioned litigants and witnessed documents. *Scabini* were to be chosen by the *missus* in consultation with the count and the people. They appear to have been chosen from a class of small landowners. In the sources they are referred to as *boni homines*, *boni viri* and *nobiles viri*, and the courts at which they appear are very close to the land they own. The *scabini* Adalbertus, Ambaldus, Arlulfus, Aynin, Bererius and Uuichardus who served in the court at Mâcon, for example, all owned property within 12 miles of Mâcon and all are referred to as *boni homines*, while Uuichardus is called *fidelis*. In other words, it is clear that just as the count was normally a local magnate, so the *scabini* were local small landowners hearing cases arising within their own locality.[33] In the *mallus* or court it was expected that every plaintiff or defendant should make known his national law, and the judge was supposed to know which was applicable to the case and to be familiar with it. Counts and lesser officials, presumably the *scabini*, were exhorted in the royal legislation to gain a knowledge of the law.

Theodulf of Orleans in his famous poem *Ad Iudices* warned judges against accepting bribes, partiality, indolence and pride. He described the rich presents he was offered, including a silver flask carved with the labours of Hercules which a man offered Theodulf as a bribe if he would annul the enfranchisement of all his parents' slaves. Another offered an Arabian tapestry. Theodulf was concerned that he would not have been offered these gifts had not his predecessors accepted them. His journey took place in 798; in the company of the *missus dominicus*, Leidrad, bishop of Lyons, Theodulf visited the Rhône valley and Septimania, carrying out the king's order of inspection and holding court. Towns they visited included Avignon, Nîmes, Maguelonne, Agde, Béziers, Narbonne and Carcassonne, Narbonne being the principal target of their journey. Theodulf presents the court at Narbonne – it may not perhaps have been a typical Frankish courtroom – taking place in an ancient basilica or curia, outside which a crowd of plaintiffs waited beside the door. Before going to court the judge should have prayed for God's guidance and help to enable him to judge justly. Theodulf also admonished the judge not to drink or eat too heavily at the banquet prepared in his honour the night before, 'lest he be sluggish and slow coming to court'. The judge advances, accompanied by his secretary. If a poor person has come from a long distance and needs his case heard early enough to enable him to return home before dark, he is to be heard first. The doorkeeper is urged to refrain from charging the poor people an entrance fee. Once inside the court where he remains all day, the judge seats himself and around him are the leading men, the *senatores*, of Narbonne. The judge selects a group of assessors (not called *scabini* in the south) to assist him. The judge is the supreme authority; he assigns penalties, and directs the debate and the procedure. The judge's task is made more difficult by the multiplicity and uncertainty of the witnesses. Theodulf takes the opportunity to inveigh against the Germanic system of oaths. He prefers to weigh evidence and reach a proper decision, arriving at the truth by judicial enquiry with witnesses.[34]

What sort of cases would be brought before this tribunal? Theodulf mentions cases of murder, theft of animals, property and inheritance disputes, and arguments over the enfranchisement of slaves. Theodulf condemns the illogically heavy penalties for theft and the light ones for murder which can be appeased with a fine. He is especially revolted by the punishments wrought on the poor and despises those who retreat behind the law and say it is the law which treats the guilty thus. He is thus refreshingly aware that the law he administers is man made. Civil offences could also be brought before the judge.

Cases brought include the man already mentioned above who wanted all his parents' slaves disenfranchised; another wanted to deprive his brother and sister of their inheritance. The cases evidently gave all sorts of opportunities for corruption; the capitularies of 789 c. 63, 802 c. 4, 809 c. 7 and the *Capitulatio de partibus Saxoniae* c. 28, for example, speak strongly against the judges and other officials who accept bribes.[35] Theodulf warned too against the blandishments of the judge's wife, who might persuade her husband into favouring a wrongdoer. Justice remained venal. Agobard of Lyons accused both ecclesiastics and secular judges of bending the law in return for silver and favouring the sins of the rich more than the rights of the poor. Theodulf's poem is in effect a lament on the corruption of the judges and the abuses they permitted. He was probably an official of the best sort, with a keen sense of justice and sympathy with the poor. His instructions to judges were practical and humane.

An innovation of the Carolingian judicial system was the *inquisitio*, a means of gathering information for the king. It involved taking depositions on oath from subjects upon matters affecting the king's fiscal prerogatives, and the use of local representatives neither as oath helpers nor as judgement finders, but simply as witnesses. Each local community was responsible for social order, and it fell to it to see that lawbreakers were brought to justice. *Notitiae*, the records of suits heard to decide questions of ownership and rights of ownership, are important legal records, whose interest has been largely ignored.

V

One of the first administrative measures initiated by Charlemagne after his return from his imperial coronation in Rome was to reorganize the *missi dominici*. Whether these two things were actually related causally is doubtful. *Missi dominici*, in the sense of royal legates for extraordinary missions, had existed under the Merovingians, but Charlemagne made a regular and vital administrative institution out of an intermittent one, and by so doing provided the most effective means of exerting his authority and supervision within his kingdom. His reorganization in 802 of the *missi* is recorded in the Annals of Lorsch as well as in the *Capitulare missorum specialia* of that year.[36] The reason was probably the proven corruptibility of the royal vassals and Carolingian fear of their acquisition of undue power. In order to cancel out both it appears that Charlemagne decided to use only the *potentes* of the kingdom; that is, he used the nobility and placed them in positions of honour and influence but as agents of his own authority. The part-time nature of the job meant that the *missi* could perform their normal functions at the same time. Yet to do so effectively, it was essential that the *missi* be in direct contact with their own localities.

The *missi dominici* were royal agents. They could judge cases in a court of law, punish offenders, redress wrongs, receive the oath and survey all aspects of royal administration. They were required to make the royal will and the capitularies known throughout the country. Sometimes, like the counts, they raised armies. It was not only justice that the *missi* were to administer. Landri, abbot of Jumièges and Count Richard, for example, visited the abbey of St Wandrille in order to make an inventory of that abbey's estates for the king. At the time of Theodulf's journey down the Rhône, the institution of the *missi dominici* was not as highly organized as it was to become after 802; the *missi*'s missions before the great capitulary were still irregular and often of much longer duration than the journeys of one month each, four times a year, advocated for *missi* after 802. Even then, one suspects that all these journeys would rarely have taken place. After 802, if not before, the customary combination of *missi* was one layman and one cleric. It may be that the granting of office of *missus* to a count was to the person concerned, rather than to the office, whereas the appointment was to the office in the case of bishops.

Each pair of (or under Charles the Bald group of four) *missi* was responsible for a region called a *missaticum* (see Map 5). The principal evidence for the *missatica* and activities of the *missi dominici* is the *Capitulare missorum specialia* of 802 which exists in three versions (printed by Eckhardt in parallel columns).[37] The first version, which survives in two tenth-century manuscripts, Vat. pal. lat. 582 ff. 13^v–14^v and BN lat. 9654 ff. 10^v–11^v, was intended for the Orleans region, the *missi* appointed being Magnus of Sens (801–18) and Count Godefridus. The description of the *missaticum* is in terms of its extent rather than of the districts it comprises, so the boundaries are uncertain. The Leiden version, in Leiden Voss lat. 4° 119, ff. 134^v–135^r, is almost certainly of Aquitainian provenance and must go back to a copy executed for an Aquitanian *missaticum*. A third version is on ff. 28^v–$29^v$of BN lat. 4995, and records two different exemplars. The first was intended for a *missaticum* which included the counties of Paris, Meaux, Melun, Provins, Estampes, Chartres and Poissy, that is the northern part of the ecclesiastical province of Sens, with the *missi* Abbot Fardulf of St Denis (d. 806) and Count Stephen of Paris (d. 814–15). The second *missaticum* comprised a large part of the ecclesiastical province of Rouen (mentioned in c. 10 of Frankfurt 794); Rouen's *missi* were charged with the extra duty of maintaining coastal defences and harbours. The *missi* appointed were Magenaud, archbishop of Rouen, and Madelgaud, probably a count and probably the same man who is mentioned in c. 7 of Thionville 805.

A further version of the Capitulary for 802 is to be found in Flodoard's History of Rheims, II. 18, where Wulfar, archbishop of Rheims, is described as the king's *missus* in a *missaticum* which made up the south-east portion of the ecclesiastical province of Rheims. Wulfar was later a royal legate in Rhaetia and in 813 attended the Council of Rheims. In 814 he held a synod at Noyon for his bishops, abbots and a few counts, and died on 18 June 816. The name of his secular colleague is not known. Eckhardt also discovered traces of a sixth version of the *Capitulare missorum specialia* of 802 in the capitulary collection of Gerbald of Liège compiled in 806.[38] This referred to a *missaticum* which may have extended from Arras and Vermandois to Liège. Thus the *missatica* of 802 covered a region extending from Brittany to Paris and Sens, Rheims and as far east as Liège. From references to copies being made of this capitulary in later years, as well as the evidence for copies being made in 802, one can conclude with Eckhardt that copies of the all-important Capitulary of 802 were prepared in the royal chancery for circulation to individual *missi dominici*.[39] Eckhardt, furthermore, thinks that the redaction of capitularies was the duty of the chancery officials, with the proviso that some officials had to have their own copies made; some of the provisions of the capitularies for the *missi* may have resulted from general assemblies and perhaps never went through the chancery.

The Capitulary of 802 undoubtedly provides the clearest evidence of the *missatica* regions, but from the activities of the *missi* during the reign of Charlemagne other districts may be identified. Few *missi* are mentioned before 802; there are twenty-three examples in all, the earliest being Sindolf, who in 771 was in Mainz to investigate a claim. In 782, Walter, Adalbert, Fulco and Gibuin were in Narbonne to deal with a property dispute, and in 786 *missi* were sent to Italy, Neustria and Thuringia to receive the oaths of defeated Thuringians. In 789 other *missi* were sent forth into the kingdom to administer justice. The two *missi* whose names we know in Aquitaine were Mancio and Eugenio. Others referred to between 750 and 802 are in Poitiers, Passau, Melun, Freising, Spoleto and Saxony, and in 798, as has been discussed above, Theodulf, bishop of Orleans, and Leidrad, bishop of Lyons, travelled their circuit in south-east Gaul, travelling from Lyons to Avignon, Carcassonne, Arles, Marseilles, Aix and Narbonne. In 799 Wirund, abbot of Stavelot, and Winegis, duke of Spoleto, acted as Charles' legates to Rome. Of some of the *missi* before 802 we hear more than once. Kerolt and Meginfrid, probably counts, were in Freising in 791 and later that year were with Bishop Arno of Salzburg and Wolfholt in Lorch-am-Wartburg to settle a dispute. Wolfholt appears again as *missus* in Bavaria 784–800 and Arno acts as *missus* several times. Mancio is referred to in 789 in Aquitaine and in Spoleto as Abbot Mancio in 798, though it may not be the same person.[40]

To the *missi* and *missatica* of 802 discussed by Eckhardt should be added Arno, bishop of Salzburg and Kiselhard *iudex* (probably a layman) who operated in the area near Passau. Arno is frequently referred to as the king's *missus* in Bavaria between 791 and 806, his main centres of activity being Passau, Freising and Regensburg. A seventh *missaticum* therefore was probably in that region. Arno also went on missions to Lucca and Pistoia in Italy. After 802 other missions from *missi* are recorded, some of them in the newly conquered regions, such as the visits Madelgaud, Heidi, Aito and Audulf made to towns in Saxony and east of the Rhine, charged with negotiating with Slav merchants. Numerous visits were made by Adalhard of Corbie to Italy between 781 and 814. In about 806, Adalhard was also among the group of four *missi* who inspected the diocese of Gerbald of Liège, a visit which elicited a response in the form of the episcopal statutes of Gerbald, written *c.* 805–6.[41]

As far as we can tell the *missi* were attached to the particular districts they looked after by the other office or offices they held or by their origin; this was the case for both the ecclesiastical and the lay *missi*. Whereas Krause and most other scholars in his wake asserted that 'ordinary *missi*' were not attached to their own districts and that it became a feature of the decline of the office of *missus* after the reign of Charlemagne, it seems certain, as Eckhardt has stressed, that the *missi* did indeed act on their home ground. We have only to look at the *missi* appointed in 802, Magenaud of Rouen in the Rouen region, Fardulf of St Denis and Count Stephen of Paris in the Paris basin, Magnus of Sens in the southern part of Sens province and Wulfar of Rheims acting in a *missaticum* of which Rheims was the centre, to see that this was the rule rather than the exception. In newly conquered areas or in *missatica* where a *missus* died suddenly and a suitable replacement could not be found, this was not the case. We may add to this evidence from a letter of Alcuin dated 801–2, according to which Guy or Wido, Count of the March of Brittany, was *missus dominicus* of Tours. At this stage the ecclesiastical province of Tours included eastern Brittany.[42] In 802 at least the *missatica* took no notice of the borders of the bishoprics, but by 825 archbishops and counts functioned as *missi dominici* and covered the *missaticum* within their own metropolitanate. The districts of a bishop or count generally comprised one *gau*, and that of the *missaticum* several. Abbacies, however, had no official region under their influence apart from their own estates, so it is not particularly relevant whether the abbey of a *missus* lay in the *missaticum* or not, though it usually did so.

The system of *missi dominici* meant that the best strength of the imperial aristocracy was used for administrative purposes. Werner has argued that different types of nobility survived into the Carolingian period – families of senatorial rank, nobles of Roman origin, cadet lines of the Merovingian house, old Frankish families such as the Agilofings, holders of principalities and the chief families of the Neustro-Burgundian region. He states that the Carolingians' great achievement was to win over a significant section of the Merovingian nobility (from which they themselves emerged) and bind it to itself in order to overcome the remaining part. The administration thus both favoured and depended upon the nobility.[43]

In a recent and characteristically excellent article, Werner has stressed that the *missatica* system was one which evolved gradually and at the same time as the Carolingian chancery was developing, and that it was functioning fully throughout the reigns of Charlemagne, Louis the Pious and Charles the Bald. He noted that both Charlemagne and Louis the Pious had recourse to archbishops to act as *missi* and that by Louis' reign almost all the *missatica* had the archbishop as first *missus*, with the *missaticum* more or less coinciding with the boundary of the ecclesiastical province. Further, he states that the *missatica* answerable to the central government as far as we can tell from the 802, 825 and 853 capitularies, only existed in the Frankish heartland, that is in the old three kingdoms of Austrasia, Neustria and Burgundy. That is, that Provence, Septimania, Gascony, Aquitaine, Brittany, Frisia, Saxony, Thuringia, Bavaria, Alemannia and Italy were not part of the *missatica* system immediately dependent on the centre. Werner argues that most of these peripheral regions were organized politically and administratively into small *regna* (from which the duchies later developed); that is, areas which kept their territorial and non-Frankish integrity. Italy, Aquitaine, Bavaria, Neustria, Provence, Alemannia, Frisia, Saxony and Lotharingia all come into this category, and to administer them the king could either install a subking, usually one of his sons, with his own court and Frankish officials to help him who as often as not were the young subking's wife's relatives, or he could install a magnate, as Gerald was installed in Bavaria by Charlemagne, to govern the region on the king's behalf, or the counts of the region could be considered as a group responsible collectively for the administration of the region. *Missi* could be appointed to visit the *regna* or they could be appointed from the local aristocracy and episcopate as was the case in Bavaria and Brittany. These *regna* also tended to be militarily coherent in that they would be represented in the army. Warriors they sent to the Frankish army would be distinguished as Bavarians, Saxons and so on. The marcher regions in their turn were subordinate to the *regna*.[44]

Thus there were three principal administrative divisions in the structure of the Carolingian kingdoms: the heartland supervised directly with the aid of the *missatica* system, the intermediary *regna* which were the non-Frankish territories governed with a Frankish type of administration, and the peripheral marches which increasingly in the course of the ninth century were integrated into the neighbouring *regna*.

VI

The other important instrument of government was the public assembly (*placitum*). The assembly seems to have been variable in its function and make-up. The three main reasons for calling an assembly appear to have been to gather the Frankish host together before going on campaign, to discuss political or ecclesiastical matters concerning the kingdom and to act as the assembly at which judgements were made. This does not mean that the assembly had a judicial function – judgements could be made during the assembly, not necessarily by it. Nor was it a legislating body. Under the Merovingians we hear only of military assemblies and the military element remained until the reign of Charles the Bald the principal *raison d'être* of the institution. It was customary for a *conventus* to be held at least once a year; it never met without the order of a king or in his absence and dissolved only on his command. The king also fixed the date and time. The place chosen was variable but it was usually near a royal palace or villa such as Attigny, Worms, Frankfurt, Thionville, Duren, Aachen, Quierzy and Ingelheim. That is, it took place on land owned by the king. The Frankish freemen, lay and ecclesiastical magnates, counts and warriors had an obligation to attend; usually the men attended accompanied by their retinues. It was at the assemblies that legates and ambassadors were received, news communicated, campaigns and the public affairs *de salute patriae* and *de utilitate regni* were discussed. Here too the king received advice and his instructions were given to his agents, who may also have been selected and appointed at these assemblies. Smaller local assemblies might also be convened by the count. Under Louis the Pious assemblies were held two or three times a year in the early part of his reign. It may be that he wished thereby to establish and maintain contact with the far-flung regions of his empire. While the monarchy was strong the assembly provided effective leadership, but it gradually became to much greater an extent a forum for discussion and the agreement or refusal to cooperate on the part of the nobles.

Rosenthal defined the public assembly as 'the public means for the transaction of royal or national business'.[45] Some assemblies under Louis the Pious were composed of nobles from the entire Empire. Others were provincial or regional in nature. But Rosenthal considered military assemblies to be simply collecting points for men going to war, and claimed that public business was almost never transacted at the military rendezvous. Yet some, such as Worms in 787, undoubtedly considered other matters. Financial affairs were generally handled outside the assembly. Public acceptance on questions of succession or partition such as the *Divisio regni* of 806 did not have to come from a public assembly but an assembly was the most convenient and accepted place in which to gain it.

The preamble to the Capitulary of Herstal refers to an assembly of bishops, abbots, counts and the king; decisions were made and then recorded in the capitulary. Most capitularies in fact mention that they are the record of deliberations or decisions on the part of an assembly. The Capitulary of Mantua, for example, is a memorandum made known to all at Mantua, and the *Capitulatio de partibus Saxoniae* is a set of stipulations agreed on at an assembly held at Ingelheim. In 797 the assembly at Aachen is also explicitly referred to in the preface to the *Capitulare Saxonicum*, while the Synod of Frankfurt in 794 is described in a preamble to the *acta* as an assembly comprising Charles and all the bishops and priests of the kingdom of the Franks, Italy, Aquitaine and Provence. This synod discussed, as well as the fines for Saxons to be included in the Salic law, Adoptionism, iconoclasm, the position of Tassilo of Bavaria, the price of corn, grain and bread, the responsibilities of bishops for justice in their parishes and various other matters concerning individual monastic provisions.

VII

How was Carolingian legislation implemented? The Carolingian period witnessed a great effort to record the law in writing, and the authority of the written word itself increased. In 802, according to the Lorsch Annals, Charlemagne made provision for the revision where possible of existing texts of the laws: '. . . the emperor also summoned together all the lawmakers and had all the laws of the kingdom read to them; each man was given a national law and where necessary laws were amended and the changes written down'. Charlemagne thus effectively upheld the validity of the Germanic codes and gave the written texts some status. Surviving law books containing the text of these laws are for the most part scruffy, small, well thumbed, the texts often imperfect and incomplete. These imperfections and omissions have given some historians cause for alarm and despondency. They cannot see how such incomplete texts could have been of any use to the Franks in the day to day administration of justice. Yet we are confronted in the sources by repeated urgings on officials of the necessity to use the books of written law.

Although there is rarely an official code of Frankish royal law available in the Carolingian period, the revisions of the *Lex Salica* must be regarded as an attempt to produce such an official code. Also, the situation alters under Louis the Pious. Thereafter there are many instances of the use of written law.

The customary law code of the Franks is known as the Salic law, though another Frankish law code, the Ripuarian code, is of importance. The first issuing of the Salic law is associated with the last years of the reign of Clovis, that is *c.* 511, but there is no specific evidence to confirm either that the *Lex Salica* was promulgated by the king or that it was compiled by his officials. The *Lex Salica* is extant in no less than five versions, the first three of which were produced in the Merovingian period. The fourth version, the so-called 100-Title text, simply abbreviated and reorganized the 65 Titles of the earlier redactions of the code. It was completed by 763–4 and was possibly drawn up during the reign of Pippin III. Some have associated it with Pippin's ascent to the throne. The fifth version, the *Emendata Karolina*, reduced the number of sections to seventy titles and was made during the reign of Charlemagne, probably in 798.[46]

The prologue to *Lex Salica* affirming the king's authority in issuing the laws was not added until the eighth century under Pippin III. Although the *Lex Salica* was originally a personal law, because of Frankish success the law acquired greater authority, and probably, with the additions made by Charlemagne and Louis the Pious, acquired territorial status. Its provisions are similar to those of the other barbarian codes, with the same system of wergild and composition, but there is a greater concentration on the authority of the king. Table companions of the king for example have a higher wergild than ordinary men. Fines are set for most offences, and as we have seen, these fines were divided between the king and the count. The burden of apprehending a criminal is placed on the community; there is no policing; the king's representatives simply administer justice. A few Roman ideas, such as the concept of a royal fisc or land belonging to the office of the king, the concept of confiscation, and the Roman position on marriage with or between slaves, were incorporated into the Frankish law.

From the number of families of the text of *Lex Salica* and the younger development of Frankish law known as the Ripuarian code that was in circulation at the same time as the Salic code, it seems that there was a lack of uniformity in the redaction of either the Salic or the Ripuarian collections of titles. This lack of uniformity, however, does not seem to have mattered much, an odd state of affairs according to our modern notions of order and precision in legislation. It must give us pause to consider what the function of these codes could have been. Wallace-Hadrill goes too far when he suggests that compilations of Salic and Ripuarian law were designed solely for consultation and study by the clergy.[47] Or perhaps not far enough, for why should the clergy study law? If they wanted to teach it, that implies that there were other people besides the clergy who wanted to know about the law. And even if only the clergy read about the appropriate fines for pig stealing, surely it was because they wanted to apply these rules? There is evidence in the capitularies of counts, *missi dominici* and judges being advised to possess copies of the law. The wills of counts Eberhard of Friuli and Eccard of Mâcon indicate that they possessed law books;[48] Eberhard possessed a copy of all the barbarian codes and bequeathed it to his eldest son, and Eccard left two copies of the Salic law to one of his friends. Manuscripts of compilations of barbarian law, moreover, show signs of having been read and presumably therefore, used, by secular officials (for example, Berlin Phillipps 1761, BN lat. 4628, 4417, 4418, etc.).

Other problems in assessing the importance and function of the barbarian law codes in general have been raised by recent studies of the Visigothic and Lombard codes, and by discussions on the nature of early medieval legislation. It is obviously the case that the laws present a society as it should be rather than as it was. That is, the laws that survive may not represent the laws that were obeyed. Many clauses in the codes are out of date, are based on the single occurrence of a crime, or reflect ideals about the relationship between authority and subject. The systematization of the laws can be somewhat artificial, presenting a rather more rigid social structure than that which actually obtained. In the absence of other evidence one can only be aware of this problem. To some extent the main text of the laws do not allow for change and development in society. Only rarely do we have successive alterations in a code such as the royal capitulary additions so that one may see how society has changed.

It is difficult to be certain to what extent the texts we have are the original. None of the codes survives in anything but manuscripts considerably later than the first compilation, so that the possibilities of emendation, interpolation, rewording and so on have to be considered.

The connection between the Christian concept of kingship and the issuing of laws, as well as between barbarian kingship and the Roman Emperor's function as legislator is fundamental to the development of written law in the barbarian kingdoms. Every barbarian kingdom was subject either to Roman or Christian influence before any one of them produced a law code. Whether lawmaking was an exclusively royal prerogative before Roman examples existed as precedents is difficult to ascertain, but the little evidence we have suggests the contrary; that is, that the law was made by the *Volk* or people and responsibility for upholding it was shared within the community. The barbarian kings furthermore had a memory and a precedent for a kingdom ruled by law in the Roman Empire, and it was Roman law, the Vulgar Roman Law of the provinces, which served in most cases as the initial impetus for lawmaking. It was seen by the barbarians that a sole ruler governed with, and made, his kingdom's law. Legislative activity, moreover, enhanced a king's status in all eyes, particularly those of the church.

Wormald has suggested recently that it is difficult to understand the production of the law codes simply in terms of the administration of justice because the legislation is generally too selective, confused and carelessly produced and would not have been much use to a judge sitting in court 'even supposing that they could have read texts which were nearly always in Latin . . .'.[49] This is simply to misunderstand the nature of early medieval lawmaking as it is illustrated by the codes. Some provisions there are simply *ad hoc*; they are made to provide for a particular incident, and we find this in canon and conciliar law as well. As a crime occurred which was not in the book it would be entered if it was thought it might occur again. Early medieval legislators were living in a society that was changing its mores and aims. The very earliest redaction of the *Lex Salica* deals almost solely with the problem of a predominantly agrarian society. Provisions that are other than those of folk custom, a basic set of rules that evolved within a community, are those of king's law. When a ruler emerged as the sole leader of a community, once, perhaps, regulated other than by a single chief, new provisions were necessary to cater for royal authority and its exercise. That the laws were 'inadequate' can hardly, surely, be judged by us. In most communities even now we are barely aware of the law in day to day living; our code of ethics and moral sense is something we grow up with, and it is not just a law which enables us to distinguish right from wrong. Now, too, the law may not provide for every contingency or redress every injustice and is still in the process of development and adaptation. I see no reason why the law should have impinged any more strongly on the people of the early Middle Ages, especially when so many societies and communities had their own locally accepted rules of behaviour and looked to themselves for the maintenance of order. It is precisely with the development of a strong central authority that law becomes an important element of it. This is why barbarian kings endeavoured to establish official codes of written law, and why with the Carolingians, law, at least in theory, attained considerable importance. We should not therefore argue against the intention or even the reception of what the law implied and contained. If it did not at first meet all contingencies, it did in time. Only by trying a code out could its deficiencies be realized.

Pierre Riché has set out the evidence that those administering justice could read Latin and knew their law;[50] we have seen that one judge when acting for a king in the south of the kingdom was no less a person than Theodulf of Orleans, and his knowledge of Latin is not in question. Manuscript evidence also, as I have suggested, supports the view that the law was taught to and known by lay magnates. Undoubtedly, much legal business was still conducted orally, but it should be stressed that Carolingian society was one in which the status of written law was growing rapidly. Law was primarily practical rather than ideological in its inspiration. Local needs determined what proportion of the laws available would be used; the codification of these laws depended in great measure on personal initiative. Laws were based on precedent. A count would judge according to a case, consult the codes and see if there was a stipulation covering it. If there was not, then he would have to decide by himself to appeal to the king, in which case a provision might be formulated to cope with the particular issue. In other words, the law codes are to be understood as working drafts, subject to alteration and addition.

The second category of Frankish legislation is that of the capitularies.[51] These were decrees divided into *capitula*, comprising injunctions and provisions agreed upon by the king and his advisers or the assembly covering administrative matters in both the secular and ecclesiastical spheres. Sometimes they are full descriptions of measures to be taken; at other times they are little more than lists of headings, serving simply as *aides-mémoire*. Nevertheless some of the documents classified as capitularies in modern editions are of great importance for our knowledge of Carolingian administration and government. Reference has been made through this and the two preceding chapters to the capitularies and the evidence they provide for particular aspects of royal policy towards the church, the counts, the poor, the economy and so on. The Capitulary of Herstal, for example, set out a number of corrections to be made in ecclesiastical and secular affairs; the 802 Capitulary effected a complete reorganization of the *missatica* system. Capitularies were issued concerning the administration for, and the behaviour required of, the Saxons after they had been conquered. Statements were made on theological issues as well as on the introduction of new standards of weights, measures, prices and coinage in the Capitulary of Frankfurt in 794, and the *Capitulare de Villis* made various recommendations and requests for the management of the royal estates. The actual implementation of these decrees depended on the *missi* and the counts; the contents of the capitularies were to be made known to all the people by reading them out aloud at a meeting as Count Stephen read out a new law at a *mallus publicus* in 803.[52] For this purpose moreover, translations may have been made of the Latin text into the vernacular; Werner has remarked on the significance of the number of juridical and administrative texts which survive in Old High German.[53]

One problem in assessing the importance of the Carolingian capitularies, and indeed of the conciliar decrees of the church, is that their function and the effectiveness of their distribution are not always clearly defined. There is but meagre evidence for official collections being made of secular, royal or ecclesiastical law in the Frankish kingdom, though I shall argue in the following chapter that Ansegisus, abbot of St Wandrille, made such a collection for Louis the Pious. Many surviving capitulary texts were included in larger codices containing canonical, penitential, catechetical and legal material of various types destined for consultation. Lay magnates and royal agents may well have possessed legal handbooks which contained not only some of the royal capitularies but also the Breviary of Alaric and a selection from among the barbarian law codes. Other smaller collections are volumes such as Wolfenbüttel MS Helmstedt 254, containing a few capitularies dealing with estate management, and there are also the small collections in the episcopal handbooks, most of which concern ecclesiastical matters.[54]

It has often been argued that the kingdoms or Empire ruled by the Carolingians was an unwieldy structure, too large to be effectively governed, and that it was inevitable that it should collapse. Although, as we have seen, much depended on the effectiveness of the head of the centre of the Carolingian administrative structure, it was in fact divided into smaller regions, the *regna*, the *missatica* and the counties or *pagi* which could be ruled effectively at the local level. Certainly until the end of the reign of Charles the Bald there is evidence that this complex system was working, and still to the king's advantage, but under the later Carolingian kings it ceased to do so, and was turned to the service of aspiring local magnates.

NOTES

1. The preface to the Capitulary of Herstal (779), *MGH Cap*. I. No. 20, 47, and the account of the Aachen legislation of 802, *Annales Laureshamenses*, *s. a.*, 802, for example, mention advisers.
2. *MGH Epp*, IV, No. 119; Eng. trs. Allott, No. 61.
3. J. Schmidt, 'Hinkmars "De Ordine Palatii" und seine Quellen', Diss. Phil., Frankfurt 1962, and J. Devisse, *Hincmar, archevêque de Reims* (Geneva 1976), 992, n. 172. See also L. Halphen, 'Le "De ordine palatii" d'Hincmar', *Revue Historique* 183 (1938), 1–9; for further references see the bibliography in Gross and Schieffer's edition.
4. E. Perroy, *Le monde Carolingien* (Paris 1974), 192–3.
5. Hincmar, *De ordine palatii*, c. 5, line 345 and compare Theodulf, *MGH Poet*. I, No. 25, 483–9 at lines 205–10.
6. W. Horn and E. Born, *The Plan of St Gall* (Berkeley 3 vols, 1979), II, 146.
7. Fustel de Coulanges, *Histoire des Institutions de la royauté de l'ancienne France. Les transformations de la royauté pendant l'époque carolingienne* (Paris 1892), 347.
8. J. M. Pardessus, *Diplomata, chartae, epistolae leges aliaque instrumenta ad res Gallo-Francicas spectantia* (Paris 2 vols, 1843–49), II, No. DXXXVII, 347–8. On the development of the Carolingian chancery, see G. Tessier, *La diplomatique royale française* (Paris 1962) and his references. See also F. L. Ganshof, 'Charlemagne et l'usage de l'écrit en matière administrative'. *MA* 57 (1951), 1–25 (Eng. trs. in Ganshof, *Carolingians*) and A. Dumas, 'La parole et l'écriture dans les Capitulaires carolingiens', *Mélanges Louis Halphen* (Paris 1951), 209–17.
9. Pardessus, *Diplomata*, II, No. DLXIII, 380.
10. *Gesta episcoporum mettensium*, *MGH SS* II, 264.
11. *MGH Poet*. I, No. 25, 487, lines 145–50. There seems to be no reason to attribute the changes to, or use the emergence of a chancellor as evidence for, Pippin III's illiteracy as Bresslau does, nor is there any reason to suppose that Pippin was illiterate. He was, after all, educated at both St Denis and the Lombard court.
12. S. Keynes, *The Diplomas of King Aethelred 'the Unready' 978–1016* (Cambridge 1980), esp. 79–83.
13. The problem is discussed at length, with full bibliographical references, in J. Fleckenstein, *Die Hofkapelle der deutschen Könige* I (Stuttgart 1959). See also M. Jusselin, 'La chancellerie de Charles le Chauve d'après les notes tironiennes', *MA* 33 (1922), 1–89.
14. Paschasius Radbert, *Epitaphium Arsenii*, 5.2. Compare the *Visio Wettini*, lines 327–35, *PL*, 104, cols. 1070–1A and Lupus, Ep. 25.
15. Compare F. L. Ganshof, 'Les traits généraux du système d'institutions de la monarchie franque', *Settimane* 9 (1961), 91–127; Eng. trs. Ganshof, *Carolingians*, esp. 95–101.
16. *Annales regni Francorum*, *s.a.*, 802 and 810, P. Grierson, 'Commerce in the Dark Ages: a critique of the evidence', *TRHS* 9 (1959), 123–40.

17. For example, *Annales Bertiniani*, s.a. 833 and *Gesta abbatum fontanellensium*, c. xi, 1.

18. *MGH Leges* I, 175–80.

19. *MGH Cap.* I, No. 33, c. 28, 96; trs. Loyn and Percival, 76.

20. P. Grierson, 'Money and coinage under Charlemagne', *KdG* I, 501–36.

21. See the discussion by K. F. Werner, '*Missus-Marchio-Comes*. Entre l'administration centrale et l'administration locale de l'Empire', *Beihefte der Francia* 9 (Munich 1980), 190–239, at 191 n. 2.

22. *MGH Cap.* I, No. 33, c. 34 and c. 40.

23. See Werner, '*Missus-Marchio-Comes*', and *MGH Cap.* I, No. 54.

24. For example, *MGH Cap.* II, 278. On the oath see C. E. Odegaard, 'Carolingian oaths of fidelity', *Speculum* 16 (1941), 284–96 and 'The concept of royal power in the Carolingian oaths of fidelity', *Speculum* 20 (1945), 279–89.

25. *MGH Cap.* I, No. 25, c. 2, 66.

26. *MGH Cap.* I, No. 63, c. 18.

27. *MGH Cap.* I, No. 34. c. 19, 192; trs. Loyn and Percival, 81–2.

28. J. Dhondt, *Le Haut Moyen Age* (Paris 1968), 42–4 and compare W. Ullmann, 'Public welfare and social legislation in the early medieval councils', *Studies in Church History* 7 (Cambridge 1971), 1–39.

29. J. B. Ross, 'Two neglected paladins of Charlemagne: Erich of Friuli and Gerold of Bavaria', *Speculum* 20 (1954), 212–35.

30. Pardessus, *Diplomata*, II, No. DLXIII, 380.

31. L. Levillain, 'Les comtes de Paris à l'époque franque', *MA* 3rd series, 12, (1941), 137–205.

32. G. Eiten, *Das Unterkönigtum im Reiche der Merowinger und Karolinger* (Heidelberg 1907).

33. F. N. Estey, 'The *scabini* and the local courts', *Speculum* 26 (1951), 119–29.

34. *MGH Poet.* I, No. 23, and see H. Liebeschutz, 'Theodulf of Orleans and the problem of the Carolingian Renaissance', *Fritz Saxl 1890–1948* D. J. Gordon (ed.) (London 1957), 77–92.

35. *MGH Cap.* I, Nos. 22, 33, 61 and 26; trs. Loyn and Percival (Nos. 26, 75 and 54).

36. *MGH Cap.* X, No. 34; Eng. trs. Loyn and Percival, 79–82. For a full discussion of the *missi dominici*, see V. Krause, 'Geschichte des Institutes der missi dominici', *MIÖG* 11 (1890), 193–300.

37. W. A. Eckhardt, 'Die *Capitulare missorum specialia* 802', *DA* 14 (1956), 495–516.

38. W. A. Eckhardt, *Die Kapitulariensammlung Ghaerbalds von Lüttich* (Berlin 1956).

39. *MGH Cap*, I, No. 100, c. 26. and No. 88, c. 8. Ganshof opposed this view, though he acknowledges the exceptions of the *Praeceptum pro Hispanis* (ibid., No. 76) the *Divisio regni* 806 (ibid., No. 46) the *Ordinatio imperii* of 817 (ibid., No. 136); see Ganshof, 'L'usage de l'écrit' (n. 8 above).

40. See Krause's tables, *MIOG* 11 (1890), 258–300, for full references.

41. Eckhardt, *Ghaerbald von Lüttich*, and see McKitterick, *Frankish Church*, 50–2.

42. *MGH Epp* IV, No. 249.

43. K. F. Werner, 'Bedeutende Adelsfamilien', cited above, Chapter 2, n. 42.

44. K. F. Werner, '*Missus-Marchio-Comes*'.

45. J. T. Rosenthal, 'The public assembly in the time of Louis the Pious', *Traditio* 20 (1964), 25–40.

46. K. A. Eckhardt (ed.), *Die Gesetze des karolingerreiches 714–911* (Weimar 3 vols, 1934).

47. J. M. Wallace-Hardrill, 'Archbishop Hincmar and the Lex Salica', *The Long-Haired Kings* (London 1962), 95–120.
48. The wills of Eberhard and Eccard are printed in P. E. Schramm and F. Mütherich, *Denkmale der deutschen Könige und Kaiser* (Munich 1962), 93–4. Compare R. McKitterick, 'Some Carolingian law books and their function', *Authority and Power: Studies on Medieval Law and Government*, P. Linehan and B. Tierney (eds) (Cambridge 1980), 13–27.
49. P. Wormald, 'Lex scripta and *Verbum regis*: legislation and Germanic kingship, from Euric to Cnut', *Early Medieval Kingship*, P. Sawyer and I. Wood (eds) (Leeds 1977), 105–38.
50. P. Riché, 'Enseignement du droit en Gaule du VIᵉ au XIᵉ siècle', *Ius Romanum Medii Aevi*, pars I.5.b.bb. (Milan 1965).
51. F. L. Ganshof, *Was waren die Kapitularien* (Darmstadt 1961). See also McKitterick, *Frankish Church*, 18–21, 23–5, and R. Schneider, 'Zur rechtliche Bedeutung der Kapitularientexte', *DA* 23 (1967), 273–94.
52. Werner, '*Missus-Marchio-Comes*', 119–20 and n. 29.
53. Ibid., 119, n. 27.
54. McKitterick, 'Carolingian law books', and *Frankish Church*, 45–79.

CHAPTER FIVE

Louis the Pious and the Christian Empire

I

In 781 the two-year-old Louis the Pious was crowned and anointed king of Aquitaine by Pope Hadrian I, at the same time as his elder brother Pippin was made king of Italy. Louis, whose twin brother had died at birth, was the third of Charlemagne's sons by his wife Hildegard, and his installation in Aquitaine proved an effective means of administering the region. After Pippin's conquest of Aquitaine, Charlemagne had installed loyal Frankish officials in the counties, bishoprics and abbacies and Arnold acted as chief minister in Aquitaine during Louis' minority.

Charlemagne appears to have interfered but little in Aquitainian affairs thereafter, either during his son's minority or after his coming of age. The *Divisio regni* of 806 clarified Louis' position; he was to have Aquitaine as an independent kingdom after his father's death. In about 794, Louis, 'lest he be led astray in satisfying the natural desires of the body' married Ermengard, the daughter of Count Ingramn.[1] At this time Charlemagne appears to have tried to make some provision to ensure that Louis and his entourage did not constitute a burden on his Aquitainian subjects. Four *villae* – Doué, Chasseneuil (Louis' birthplace), Angéac and Ebreuil – were established as royal residences and they alternated in maintaining Louis and his household. The Astronomer's account suggests that Charlemagne had some difficulty in ensuring even this minimal provision owing to encroachments on the royal fisc by the local magnates. Military supplies were not to be requisitioned from the populace and the people of Albi were dispensed from paying their tribute of wine and grain. Louis' principal administrative centre, as distinct from his residences, appears to have been Toulouse. Throughout his period of rule in Aquitaine, Louis was in constant communication with his father, accompanying him on some of his campaigns or spending the summer or the winter months with him. His first recorded visit to Charlemagne was four years after he had been installed as king; he was brought to Paderborn, dressed in Gascon clothes. In 790 Louis wintered with his father at Worms and again in the following year at Regensburg. He participated in the expedition led by his brother Pippin into Italy in 793, and in the campaign against the Saxons in 799 and 804. Charlemagne never visited his son Louis in Aquitaine; the closest he came was to Tours in 800.

Of the four principal sources which recount the course of Louis' career, the first book of Nithard's History of the sons of Louis the Pious, the biographies of Thegan, suffragan bishop of Trier, and by the Astronomer,[2] and Ermold the Black's poem on Louis the Pious, only the two latter provide information concerning Louis' activities in Aquitaine before he succeeded his father as Emperor in 814. The 'Astronomer's' account is the fullest, for although he wrote his Life of Louis after the Emperor's death, he drew on a now lost account of Louis' early years by a monk called Adhemar who had known Louis since birth, or said he had. Modern historians have had perforce to follow their main sources in paying little attention to Louis' career before he became Emperor at the age of thirty-six. Yet despite the paucity of the sources, and the confusion of the Astronomer's chronology, some aspects of Louis' reign as king in Aquitaine, in particular his military activities and his promotion of monastic reform, are of significance for his subsequent policies as Emperor.

Aquitaine was in effect a march; for much of Louis' reign as subking he or his officials were occupied in quelling Gascon revolts and launching offensives into Spain. Unrest had never completely died out in the frontier region of the Pyrenees, since the annexation of Aquitaine in 768, and more especially after the disastrous ambush of the Frankish vanguard in Roncesvalles in 778. In about 788, Chorso, duke of Toulouse, had been ignominiously captured by a Gascon named Adelric, and then released after being forced to swear an oath of loyalty to the Gascon, or Basque, leader. An assembly was subsequently held at Mors Gothorum (Mourgoudon) to discuss the affair, but Adelric refused to appear. The following year he was summoned before Charlemagne and Louis at Worms and banished from the kingdom, while Chorso was removed from office and replaced by William, a cousin of Charlemagne and founder of the monastery of Gellone. William succeeded in subduing the Gascons for the time being. In 801 they revolted against the imposition of a certain Liuthard (undoubtedly a Frank) in one of their counties, but this and a subsequent revolt in 812 were quelled.

Both the Astronomer and Ermold are fulsome in their praise of Louis' prowess in the Frankish battles in Spain. Despite the space both sources devote to the Spanish campaigns, however, neither yields much information concerning the reasons for the offensive against Spain or indeed the eventual outcome. Charlemagne may have wished to impose some kind of Carolingian superiority in the country as well as to respond to the Muslim attacks on the Frankish kingdom; Louis in this respect acted as his sword.

In 793, the Saracens invaded Septimania, burnt the suburbs of Narbonne and marched on Carcassonne, but in 795 Louis received emissaries from Bahlul-ben-Machluc (Bahaluc) who sued for peace. Evidently the Franks kept the upper hand for the time being; they retained control over the county formed by Vich, Cardona and Casena, and organized their defences along the Aquitainian border. On his own initiative in 797 Louis launched a successful attack against Lerida and Huesca before returning to Aquitaine for the winter. Between 800

and 813 Louis conducted several more expeditions into Spain, the most important of which was the famous and successful siege of Barcelona in 800, conducted by Count Rotstagnus of Gerona. Subsequent campaigns resulted in the
capture of Tortosa, Huesca and Pamplona, but for all the gallant efforts of
Louis and his captains Frankish influence never reached further south than the
Ebro. Links were, however, formed with the kingdom of the Asturias as well
as with the smaller Christian administrative areas.

Louis was also active in promoting the religious life in Aquitaine. The
Astronomer describes his activities in this sphere. He stresses the king's piety
and devotion to the church. Louis had many monasteries repaired and rebuilt,
and founded, or patronized the foundation of, new communities in Aquitaine
and Septimania, of which the most important were Aniane and Gellone.[3] Only
four of Louis' charters relating to monasteries have survived from his early years,
one of which was authorized by Charlemagne. They record the bestowal of
immunity, land and freedom from tolls respectively for Nouaillé, a cell of St
Hilary of Poitiers, Gellone and St Martin of Tours, while a group of religious
from the canons' foundation at St Hilary of Poitiers, who wished to live according to the Rule of St Benedict, was permitted by Louis to settle at Nouaillé;
this subsequently became a royal monastery and was taken under Louis'
protection.[4] Reform of the church and especially of the monastic life proceeded apace in Aquitaine under Louis' energetic patronage, presumably
with his father's approval; but the real leader of this reform was Benedict of
Aniane.

Benedict, or Witiza, of Aniane was a Gothic nobleman. He had become a
monk at St Seine at Langres but left the community in 780 and founded a cell
on his father's land which developed into the monastery of Aniane. Benedict
was an ascetic, and broke with the variegated Frankish monastic tradition in
order to follow, to the exclusion of every other form of monastic observance,
the Rule of St Benedict. He and his followers spread the strict observance of
the Rule among many Aquitainian and Septimanian monasteries, the most
important of which were Goudagnes, Casa Nova, Gellone, Mar, Cormery,
Fleury, Ile Barbe at Lyons and Aniane itself.[5] By 814 this reform movement
had reached the Loire. It is notable that the decrees of the reform councils of
Arles and Chalon-sur-Saône in 813 reflect the pride of the bishops of these
provinces in the healthy monastic life in Lyons, Aquitaine, Septimania and the
Spanish march; indeed, smug fears were expressed that the monasteries of the
region would be unable to support the great number of those seeking the monastic life.[6] By this time Louis had become sole heir to Charlemagne, for his
brothers Pippin and Charles had died in 810 and 811 respectively. On the
advice of a number of close associates, Charlemagne summoned Louis to
Aachen, and on 13 September 813, Charlemagne crowned his son Emperor and
made him heir to all his lands and responsibilities. Charlemagne died five
months later and Louis, losing no time, accomplished the journey to Aachen
in thirteen days, and there was received, in spite of his forebodings of opposition to his accession, as Emperor.

II

On Louis' accession to the Empire in 814, the monastic reform begun in Aquitaine was extended to include the entire Frankish kingdom. Frankish monasticism at the beginning of the ninth century was very diverse, owing to the reception of different forms of monasticism in Gaul during the Gallo-Roman and Merovingian periods. To understand the significance of the 'anian-ischen' reforms of Benedict of Aniane and Louis the Pious, it is necessary to survey the development of monasticism in Gaul, and then, in rather more detail, the evidence for the promotion of the Rule of St Benedict under the Carolingians.

Monasticism is usually recognized to have existed in Gaul from the mid-fourth century, probably even before the arrival of St Martin, though the earliest attested foundation is that of the monastery of Ligugé *c*. 360.[7] Thereafter many groups of men and women retreated from society into a form of collective solitude in the wilderness. These rural communities were probably not organized according to any rule, nor would their organization have been uniform. The monasteries founded (for the most part in the towns) by John Cassian, Honoratus and their followers on the other hand, seem to have been regulated. Certainly a rule is attributed to Honoratus of Lérins. In these regular monasteries the emphasis was on obedience and discipline rather than on solitude; the life of the holy hermit was thought to be a development beyond life in a community which few would ever attain. No Gallic monastic rule survives from before the sixth century, though the Rules of Augustine and Basil were known. It is likely moreover that as much before as after 500 many rules, whether written or oral, were in use, and no one rule was predominant. Some rules would be complete in themselves and could be adopted entire by other communities, as Radegund adopted the Rule of Caesarius of Arles for her convent at Sainte Croix in Poitiers. Others would be personal amalgams of selections from a number of different rules, designed for a particular establishment. To this diversity of monastic forms the arrival of Columbanus *c*. 590 and the foundation of his monasteries of Annegray, Luxeuil and Fontaines, added an influential element. The strict and ascetic discipline observed in their communities by the Irish monks and the Franks they inspired, and prescribed in the Rules and penitential attributed to Columbanus himself, were adopted by many Frankish houses as part of their customs.[8] The Columbanian Rules seem rarely to have been adopted as the sole guide in a community; even at Luxeuil under Abbot Waldebert (629–70) they were joined with the Rule of St Benedict.

Benedictine monasticism was the last major form to arrive in Gaul and had done so by at least the early seventh century. It is unlikely that Benedictine monasticism was much known outside Monte Cassino until after its sack by the Lombards in 581, when the monks were dispersed. The legend that Maurus, Benedict's disciple, brought Benedictine monasticism and the Rule with him to Gaul in 543 and founded the monastery of Glanfeuil is a ninth-century fabrication.[9] Nor is there sufficient evidence to warrant the introduction of the

Rule being associated with Columbanus. The earliest reference to the Rule of St Benedict in Merovingian Gaul is the compilation made by Donatus of Besançon, a monk of Luxeuil, from the Rules of Columbanus, Caesarius of Arles and Benedict, which he presented to the nuns of Jussamoutier in 620.[10] Five years later the monastery of Altaripa in the diocese of Albi was specifically obliged by its founder, Venerandus, to observe the Rule of St Benedict exactly, and a copy of it was sent for safekeeping to Constantius, bishop of Albi.[11] The Rule was well enough respected in the diocese of Autun for a synod held there in 670 to prescribe only the Rule of St Benedict for all abbots and monks. Elsewhere there remained a preference for the old ways; the monks of Lérins are reputed to have killed their abbot in 677 because he tried to introduce the Rule of St Benedict into the community there. Like the Columbanian Rule, the Rule of St Benedict became simply another element in the Frankish monastic tradition, rather than being adopted as the sole guide in any one house.

In the eighth century a further complication was introduced into the organization of religious communities. At the Synod of Ver in 755 the *Regula canonicorum* of Chrodegang of Metz laid down a clear way of life for cathedral clergy.[12] Although canons had been known in Gaul at least since 567 – they are mentioned in the decrees of the Council of Tours for that year[13] – the distinction between the *ordines* of monks and canons emerged fully for the first time at Ver, and remained one of the principal themes of Frankish monastic ordinances. Monks and nuns were required to opt for a monastic rule, preferably that of St Benedict, or Chrodegang's *Regula canonicorum*. The acceptance of the latter would not, in practice, have made an enormous difference to the way of life in the monasteries. That the *ordo canonicorum* permitted the possession of personal property was probably one reason why many monastic communities, such as St Denis, St Maur des Fosses and Stavelot – Malmédy, chose to follow it.

The Anglo-Saxon missionaries who arrived on the Continent in the eighth century did not introduce a more orderly system; they merely added to the diversity of the monastic tradition in the Frankish kingdoms, despite Boniface's efforts at Fulda to establish the Rule of St Benedict as the guide for what monastic life should be. It used to be thought that the Anglo-Saxon missionaries to the Continent were to be credited with the successful promotion of Benedictine monasticism there. This assessment, however, rested on a belief, now questioned, that Benedictinism had been brought to England by Augustine of Canterbury, and that Anglo-Saxon monasticism in Wessex was fully fledged Benedictinism when Boniface set out for the Continent.[14] This was not the case, and Boniface himself added or substituted practices derived from other sources to his own observance of the Rule. Thus the Rule of St Benedict remained one of many directives for the monastic life in the eighth century. Attempts were made to assert its priority at the Frankish reform councils of the mid-eighth century and again by Charlemagne in 802,[15] but little progress in ousting the *regula mixta* seems to have been made. Charlemagne indeed met with forceful opposition to the Rule of St Benedict from members of the 'old guard' such as Adalhard of Corbie, who were attached to their mixed tradition.

By the beginning of the ninth century therefore, the Frankish monasteries and communities of canons were following a variety of rules and customs. From charter evidence and reports of reform carried out later in the ninth century it is possible to identify the type of rule followed by some of these religious houses.[16] Between 768 and 814, for example, some of the monasteries associated with the ancient basilicas – St Martin's at Tours, St Denis, St Hilary at Poitiers, St Bénigne at Dijon, St Martial at Limoges and many others – had adopted an *ordo canonicorum*. Many nunneries, including the important royal and aristocratic foundations of Nivelles, Faremoutiers, Jouarre and Chelles, turned into houses of canonesses. Other convents such as Remiremont and Notre Dame at Soissons, retained their monastic character, as did the basilican monasteries of St Germain at Auxerre, St Medard at Soissons, St Germain-des-Prés, St Vaast at Arras and perhaps also St Maximin at Trier. Other basilican monasteries, St Lupus at Troyes, St Arnulf's at Metz and St Symphorien at Autun had discarded their monastic character at an early stage and were supervised by the regular clergy attached to the cathedral. In Bavaria the ecclesiastical communities in Salzburg, Regensburg and Freising appear to have been mixed; only in the mid-ninth century did the monks separate themselves from the canons in these cathedrals. As far as we can tell, these basilican monasteries had little that was Benedictine in their organization (see Maps 6 and 7).

Some of the monasteries of the Frankish kingdom outside the *civitates*, many of them founded during the seventh century in a non-Benedictine tradition (which in a few cases owed something to Columbanus' foundation at Luxeuil), adopted the canons' *ordo* in the course of the eighth century. St Maurice of Agaune, St Wandrille, Ferrières, Lobbes, St Bavo's and St Peter's at Ghent, Echternach and St Hubert are the best-known examples. Other Merovingian foundations adhered to a *regula mixta*, in which St Benedict's Rule and that of Columbanus were elements. It is probably the case that some houses followed a set of customs based on the Rules of St Benedict and Columbanus alone. No text survives of such a mixed Columbanian and Benedictine Rule, but there is late evidence that St Amand followed such a rule before its reform in 821. St Wandrille possessed the Rule of St Benedict and of Columbanus in one codex rather than a rule comprising a blending of the two. Even in the houses most closely associated with Luxeuil, the Rule followed was not exclusively Columbanian. Corbie, for example, seems to have included the *Regula Magistri* in the guides it followed, judging from the practices described as those of Corbie by Hildemar of Corbie in the ninth century, many of which correspond to clauses in the *Regula Magistri*. The two oldest copies of this text (BN lat. 12205 and 12634) are both from Corbie. Not much is known about the Rule followed by the communities founded by Irish *peregrini* such as Péronne, nor that of the new monasteries founded east of the Rhine after 768. Most of the latter were small and short-lived aristocratic foundations at Neustadt-am-Main, Amorbach, Holzkirchen, Kempten, Ottobeuren, Tegernsee and Chiemsee; they soon came under the control of the king, a bishop or some larger monastery.

Although we can determine in a number of cases which type of rule, whether monks' or canons', a religious community followed, we know tantalizingly little about the precise difference between the customs of different houses. Most of what we do know appears in the context of the effort made to reform all Frankish religious communities in the early years of the reign of Louis the Pious. The reform ordinances promulgated at Aachen in 816 and 817 in particular were not only the first successful attempts to promote the Rule of St Benedict in the Frankish kingdom as the sole norm for the monastic life; they, and the opposition they encountered, also reveal something of monastic practice. It is useful therefore to consider these reforms in some detail.

On Louis' accession to the Frankish Empire in 814, Benedict of Aniane was installed as his chief adviser in religious matters, and the monastery of Inden, later Cornelimünster near Aachen, was founded for him and consecrated in July 817. Louis and Benedict then proceeded to extend the Aquitainian reform to include the entire Frankish kingdom. Two councils were held at Aachen; one in August 816 and one in July of the following year, to discuss the reform of monastic life. The 817 decrees were more moderate in some respects than those of 816, and are understood to be the outcome of protracted discussion in the face of opposition or of the arguments of those in favour of less radical changes. The results of the deliberations of 816 were published in the three decrees: the *Institutio canonicorum* and the *Institutio sanctimonialium* intended for canons and canonesses respectively, and the monastic ordinances.[17] The *ordines* for canons and canonesses were designed to replace their precursor, Chrodegang's Rule (where it was used) and make canons' observance uniform. Sources for the clauses for the canons were predominantly patristic, with precepts culled from the letters of Jerome, Augustine and Leo, from the early church conciliar decrees, Isidore of Seville's *De ecclesiasticis officiis* and *Sententiae*, Taio of Saragossa's excerpts from Gregory the Great and Julianus Pomerius' *De Vita Contemplativa*. Work, reading and prayer were to fill the canon's day, and as with Chrodegang's Rule, a close relationship with a cathedral was envisaged. Lothar, Louis' eldest son, published similar decrees in Italy. The *Institutio canonicorum* survives in sixteen ninth- and tenth-century manuscripts from a wide range of centres, quite apart from later copies. This suggests that it was disseminated, if not used, quite widely. Two letters from Louis the Pious to Arno, bishop of Salzburg, Magnus bishop of Sens, and Sicharius, bishop of Bordeaux, survive. Louis sent them a copy of the canon's rule and asked them to see that it was broadcast in their dioceses and that it was observed and correctly copied. Louis also announced that he would be sending his inspectors to their dioceses later in the year to see that his wishes had been carried out.[18] These letters seem to be the remains of a circular letter addressed by Louis to all the bishops in his kingdom. The rule for canonesses drew on a number of Jerome's letters to his women friends who aspired to devote their lives to Christ, as well as on Cyprian's *De Habitu Virginum*, Caesarius of Arles' *Sermo ad sanctimoniales* and pseudo-Jerome's *De laude virginitatis*. There is not much evidence for the reform of nunneries on the basis of the canonesses' *ordo*, and only five manuscripts are extant.[19]

Until Semmler's articles on the Aachen decrees were published in the early 1960s, their promulgation was always dated to 817. Semmler's preparations for the new edition of the decrees in *Corpus Consuetudinum Monasticarum*, however, brought to light new sources for the 816 and 817 decrees which dated the first version quite explicitly to 23 August 816.[20]

Although the purpose of the 816 decrees was to urge the observance of the Rule of St Benedict on all Frankish monasteries, and all abbots were required to procure copies and read it regularly to their monks, it is clear from the provisions that in some cases current practice was substituted for Benedict's regulations, and that in some others, the decrees of Aachen set themselves against the well-entrenched monastic tradition that had developed in the preceding four centuries. There was probably no question of Benedict's general principles being rejected. The Rule had divided up the monk's day into periods of prayer, reading, manual work, rest and refreshment, and the points of difference in the ninth century were on these practical matters such as the authority of the abbot, the liturgy to be observed, what the monks were to eat, drink and wear, when the monks should pray, work, read, sleep and wash, and the frequency of customs such as foot washing, alms giving and hospitality. The third chapter of the 816 Capitulary, for example, recommended that the Office described in the Rule of St Benedict should be used. Two problems were involved here. In the first place, many monasteries in Frankish Gaul had developed their own forms of liturgical observance, including the *laus perennis*, and were reluctant to relinquish them.[21] In the second place, an attempt to make Frankish liturgical observance both uniform and in accord with current Roman practice had been under way since the mid-eighth century. Benedict's Office, reflecting sixth-century usage, bore little relation to this. To impose the Benedictine Office would simply have added to the confusion, and some monasteries refused to do so. Semmler has noted that there were still monasteries in the second half of the ninth century observing the old liturgical forms. Yet the 816 Capitulary also proposed an innovation in Benedict's Office in stipulating that the use of Alleluias in the Office should cease from Septuagesima until Easter. St Benedict's Rule had stated that it should be discontinued from Quadragesima. The former usage appears to have been customary only since the time of Pope Hadrian I; in this case therefore, the 816 decrees endorsed a relatively recent practice. Benedict of Aniane also introduced into his reformed monasteries the practice of *Trina Oratio* and a visit to the altar three times a day. That is, before Matins five psalms and a collect each were offered for the living, the dead and the recently deceased. Schmitz has pointed out that whereas Benedict of Nursia left private prayer to the individual, Benedict of Aniane did his best to organize it.[22]

The relationship between liturgical observance, manual labour and fasting was a close one; some monasteries absorbed all the monks' time, when not eating or sleeping, in prayer and chant, and manual labour was done by laymen. The 816 decrees, however, affirmed that manual labour was an integral part of the monastic life and forbade the *laus perennis*. Manual labour, cooking and cleaning was to be done by the monks themselves with a rest at midday which was only to be sacrificed if the work to be done was urgent. The period for work was shortened by an hour compared with the time allowed in the Rule of St Benedict in order to allow mass to be said before Vespers and dusk.[23] Hours of work were also to be shortened on work-days in the fasting periods. Wednesdays and Fridays were kept as fast-days throughout the year, whereas in St Benedict's Rule, these days were fast-days only from Whitsun to 13 September, while 14 September to Easter was a half-fast period with only one meal a day. Hildemar tells us that there was a tendency in Frankish monasteries to extend the fasting season to 1 October. Thus as far as work, fasting and the daily mass were concerned, the 816 decrees incorporated, for the most part, later Frankish customs. Even more important were the eight chapters which dealt with the ordering of the day and the customs of the liturgical year. Hitherto these had been anything but uniform. Chapter 5 of the 816 decrees, for example, followed the Rule in forbidding the monks to go back to the dormitory to sleep after the Night Office. This was contrary to the custom of the Frankish communities, the Roman monasteries of the eighth century and the *Regula Magistri*, all of which allowed a pause for sleep at this point. Hildemar commented that a pause for sleep was permissible if dawn had not broken by the end of the Vigil. From Easter to 1 October, Benedict had allowed his monks to go to sleep or read after Sext. Already in Monte Cassino in the eighth century the time was sometimes used by the monks for private prayer. Thus it was in keeping with current practice that the Aachen regulations of 816 said that the monks could use the time after Sext for sleep or prayer.

Cleanliness was not thought to be next to godliness in the ninth century. Indeed, washing the body was considered a moral danger for monks. In Chapter 8 of his Rule, Benedict had warned against the (healthy) monks taking too many baths. The 816 decrees allowed the monks to take baths twice a year, at Christmas and Easter, while the 817 amended decrees put the frequency of baths at the discretion of the head of each community. Hildemar of Corbie endorsed the 816 rule in affirming that at Corbie two baths a year were considered adequate, and lashed out at abbots who permitted monks who did very dirty work to take baths more often. No doubt the natural body oils so preserved would have been material in withstanding the cold, and every brother would have been as dirty and would have smelt as much as his neighbour, but to the modern observer, the lack of personal cleanliness seems distinctly unhygienic. We do not know, of course, whether those who did not live in monasteries had baths more often. As far as privies are concerned, however, the Plan of St Gall and surviving archaeological evidence from later medieval monasteries indicate that sensible provision with suitable drainage away from the main water supply was made.[24] Yet the *necessaria* on the St Gall Plan were provided only for the abbot, monks, students and distinguished guests; herdsmen and workmen shared the animals' accommodation in every respect. In the matter of shaving, the 816 decrees seemed to go against older monastic tradition; monks were to shave once a fortnight, but in Lent on Holy Saturday only. At Monte Cassino in the eighth century, particular days, possibly related to the liturgical calendar, were set aside for shaving just as they were for haircutting, and at Reichenau the monks shaved themselves in the middle of Lent. The 816 decrees also opposed the tendency to set aside particular days for a general bloodletting, and required that bloodletting was to be determined by the health requirements of the individual monks.

The *Mandatum* or washing of feet with its clear associations with the Last Supper was an important part of monastic ritual. Benedict refers to the *Mandatum* to be given to the guests, but is vague about its frequency; the *Regula Magistri* advocated stopping the practice during Lent, and Boniface and Columbanus kept the washing of feet as a daily custom. The 816 decrees seem to advocate the *Mandatum* as a daily custom throughout the year as well; it was to be performed after supper and an antiphon was to be sung.

The Rule of St Benedict had prescribed reading during Lent, and the borrowing of books from the monastic library was controlled by the abbot. The 816 decrees adopted this practice but left it to the discretion of the abbot whether to distribute any additional volumes to any monk. Hildemar describes how each monk at Corbie had to sign his name when borrowing a book, and sign again on returning it.

One of the most contentious issues debated in 816 appears to have been the relationship between the abbot and the rest of the community, though it manifests itself in the decrees only in the arrangements made for the abbot's sleeping and eating. Whereas St Benedict's Rule said that the abbot should eat with the guests and that food for them was to be prepared in a special kitchen, it was decided in 816 that the abbot was to have and to be content with whatever the monks had and was to receive no special privileges. He was forbidden to eat apart with his guests; both the abbot and the visitors were to eat in the refectory with the rest of the brethren. Hildemar suggests that this departure from the Rule was due to abbots being tempted to eat and drink too much and too richly when extending special hospitality. There is other evidence too that abbots were inclined to be too worldly, and some of course were laymen. In 817, the 816 decrees were amended so as to take laymen out of the refectory, but in the winter council of 818/19 bishops, abbots, canons and nobles were permitted to eat in the refectory; all other laymen were still excluded. Again this went against the old Frankish customs. Abbot Adalhard of Corbie on the other hand retained the custom of dining privately with rich or noble guests.

A much bigger role for the *praepositus* or prior was envisaged (c. 29) in 816 than had been the case in the Rule of St Benedict. This probably had everything to do with the monastic policy of the Frankish kings,[25] even Louis the Pious, who appointed lay magnates or court chaplains as abbots of the most important monasteries in the kingdom. The abbot in such cases would have been an absentee for much of the time, and the prior would have acted as the head of the community. The prior was next in rank to the abbot, both within the monastery and on its estates. He was to be selected from among the brethren.

The entry of the novices was also provided for in a way that reflected current practice and abuse. The 816 decrees agreed with St Benedict's Rule in requiring an intending monk to stay for a short period in the guest house, but departed from the Rule in stipulating that there should be a probationary year after which the novice renounced all his worldly goods and these goods were then to be given up to his parents and relatives. Many Franks thought a novice's possessions should benefit the monastery, but already in 794, the Synod of Frankfurt had lamented that unscrupulous abbots were enticing novices into their monasteries in order to seize the innocents' goods.[26] At 816 the assembly further determined that the tonsure and monastic habit would be granted with the profession, thus condemning the old Frankish custom which made the novices assume the tonsure and habit before their probationary period.

There were a number of minor matters of discipline and organization covered at Aachen in 816 which differed slightly from St Benedict's Rule. Benedict (cc. 35 and 38), for example, had suggested that the servitors and lector, who had to wait until after the brethren had finished eating before receiving their own food, might be given some bread and a drink beforehand to stave off the pangs of hunger. Benedict of Aniane in 816 withdrew this bonus. In 816 the Frankish custom that had developed by the eighth century, namely, that a monk was to report on those of his fellows who had erred or sinned, was endorsed; monks were forbidden to travel by themselves, and c. 14 forbade them to act as godparents or kiss women. One wonders whether this had been a part of old Frankish monastic custom as well.

St Benedict's Rule had forbidden the eating of quadrupeds, but it was not clear whether this prohibition extended to the use of animal fat in cooking. This complication probably never occurred to Benedict who no doubt would have used oil. Benedict of Aniane tried to forbid the use of animal fat in his reformed foundations in Aquitaine, but gave up. This relaxation for practical reasons is evident in the 816 decrees, for apart from Fridays, the twenty days before Christmas and from Quinquagesima to Easter, food could be prepared with animal fat. St Wandrille, Fulda, St Germain-des-Prés and St Denis are all known to have used it, but Corbie eschewed it according to Hildemar. This is puzzling, for Corbie, according to Adalhard's statute of 822, killed 600 pigs for the cellar each year. The implication is that some at least of this bacon was eaten by the monks; Adalhard notes, moreover, that there were eighty-six days of the year in which meat eating is not actually prohibited. In 816 eating poultry was prohibited as well, though St Benedict's Rule had not been specific about this. The 817 amendments, on the other hand, allowed birds to be eaten at Christmas, Easter and the Easter octave, as well as the main feasts of the year. Apples were only to be eaten at mealtimes.

Only one canon of the 816 decrees deals with the administration of monastic estates, and this attempted to reduce the part the monks took in managing their wealth. Abbots, for example, were to decrease the number of visits to the *villae* on the monastery's lands, and monks were not to be sent out at all. Fulda was one of the many communities that protested at this clause, arguing that it was much more appropriate for the estate administration to be in the hands of the monks. Rather than employing lay bailiffs in fact, most monasteries entrusted various responsible officials from among the brethren, usually the prior, the treasurer and the *vestiarius* with the supervision of particular estates.

In nearly all its provisions therefore, the monastic regulations made at Aachen in 816 either differed from the Rule of St Benedict in some slight way in order to accord with more recent custom, or else set themselves against the old ways in order to get nearer Benedictine observance. They were obliged to modify Benedictine custom not only because of opposition, but also in recognition of the different geographical and political circumstances of the Carolingian monasteries. There was the added complication in the Frankish kingdom of the close relationship between the monastery and episcopal church, and between the monastery and the king and his nobles. Benedict could not have made provision for this. Yet it is clear that not all the provisions of the 816 and 817 decrees were followed. It was more perhaps in its promotion of the Rule of St Benedict that the Aachen Council's success lies. What evidence is there that the Aachen Council achieved some success in this respect? The manuscript transmission of the 816 and 817 decrees permits us to suppose that the effort to promote the unified observance of the Benedictine Rule within the Frankish kingdoms was widespread, for the manuscripts come from an area extending from Werden to Monte Cassino and from Salzburg to Limoges.[27] Yet a systematic investigation of the monasteries from which the manuscripts come, and from which we have other evidence that the Aachen regulations were adopted, is needed to enable us to see how effective the legislation was. A few such studies have already been made. Lesne, for example, interpreted the *Notitia de servitio monasteriorum*, a list of monasteries which had various public charges imposed upon them, such as military service and the *dona annua*, as an index to the progress of the 'anianischen' reform.[28] Semmler has studied the cases of Fulda, Corvey and Herford.[29]

The Fulda case is known from the *Supplex Libellus*, a long complaint addressed to Charlemagne and subsequently to Louis the Pious by the monks of Fulda concerning their abbot Ratger. Ratger had been the monk in charge of building work at Fulda under Abbot Baugulf, and when he himself succeeded as abbot he rapidly became completely obsessed with the construction of the new church at Fulda, a building his unsympathetic monks described as *aedificia immensa atque superflua*. All his efforts and those of his community were to be devoted to the construction of this grandiose building. His schemes and his method of putting them into effect earned him the enmity of the brethren. Ratger shortened all the liturgical services and converted a number of holy days into work-days to make more time for the monks to build. He dragged monks away from library, kitchen, bakery, brewery and garden, and put them to build. Disregarding the rules for the Novitiate completely, he accepted many new monks and turned them into builders, and extended the right of asylum for fugitives from the law to get yet more labour. The enormous cost of the building meant that the clothing and food allowance of the monks was curtailed and the provision of hospitality and care of the elderly and sick neglected. Those monks unable or resistant to being made to work were exiled to outer cells, and laymen were introduced to do the domestic chores and manage the estates. An epidemic in 806 killed off a number of overworked monks and Ratger was blamed for this. By 810 the monks were in open revolt and a group of them sought out the Emperor. Ratger beat them to it to deliver his version of events at Fulda. Ironically, he invoked Benedict's emphasis on the authority of the abbot to vindicate his activities. Another complaint was lodged by the monks between August 816 and August 817 and Louis the Pious finally relieved the Fulda monks of their despot. The text of this complaint, the *Supplex Libellus*, is invaluable for the light it throws on Fulda's place within the Benedictine tradition, and the influence on it of the 'anianischen' reform. The complaint appears to reflect the monks' knowledge that Ratger was acting against the provisions of 816, such as that which said that the property of the novices should go back to the parents and not be kept by the abbey. They also made particular reference to the Rule of St Benedict. Some of the wrongs they described moreover were the very abuses which Louis and Benedict aimed to correct.

With Ratger's departure, the way was clear for the 'anianischen' reform to be brought to Fulda. Two monks were sent to Fulda by Louis to instruct the monks, and after a year the monks were permitted to choose their new abbot, Eigil.

Corvey and Herford provide another test case of the progress of the 'anianischen' reform. In the first decade of the ninth century, Adalhard, abbot of Corbie, had conceived the idea of founding a new monastery in Saxony, but Adalhard's exile at Noirmoutier meant that the task had to be undertaken by his successor, Adalhard II. In 816 a group of monks set out from Corbie under Hugbert and established a cell at Hettis in lower Saxony which was moved to the site of 'New Corbie' or Corvey in 822. Brothers from Corbie swelled the ranks, and Louis the Pious gave the new foundation the relics of St Stephen and a Gospel book. In July 823 Corvey was granted immunity, royal protection and the status of a royal monastery. By 822, Corbie itself seems to have accepted most of the 816 decrees, though the abbot still dined with his guests apart from the monks, the brethren were allowed to sleep after the Night Office, no animal fat was used in cooking and silence was observed during the *Mandatum*. In 826, Warin became abbot of Corvey, and the abbey became an important centre for the missions to the Saxons and the Danes. Because it had accepted the 816 provisions, Corvey was also instrumental in promoting them and the Rule of Benedict among the new monasteries and convents in Saxony, such as Wendhausen, Essen, Gandersheim and Neuenheerse.

Herford was the female counterpart of Corvey. In about 800 Waltger, a Saxon nobleman, had established a convent at Herford on his own land and the fourteen nuns there were headed by his daughter Suala. Herford remained a family foundation until the Reform Council of Aachen in 816, when Waltger gave the convent into Louis' *dominium*. Louis extended his protection to the convent and Adalhard and Wala of Corbie were deputed to organize Herford. Fortunately, Corbie had long had a close relationship with the convent of Notre Dame of Soissons, for Adalhard's sister Theodrada was the abbess. Theodrada's help was enlisted and many nuns from Soissons went to Herford. Thus Corbie, Notre Dame at Soissons, Herford and Corvey were all ruled in their early years by members of the same family (all were Charlemagne's first cousins). In its early history Notre Dame of Soissons is described as following the Rules of Columbanus and St Benedict, but in 816 the convent opted for the new monastic regulations rather than for the Rule for canonesses. Thus it is likely that the monastic organization established at Herford from 816 was also based on the Rule of St Benedict and the 816 decrees. At St Denis in 817 Abbot Arnulf of St Philibert's monastery at Noirmoutier and Benedict of Aniane arrived to impose the reform and St Benedict's Rule on the monks of the abbey. The brethren resisted. A few were permitted to leave the abbey and follow the Rule elsewhere. It was only in 829 or 830 that another enquiry was held at St Denis, and the Benedictine observance was finally established there in 832.[30] This sort of incident was reproduced elsewhere in the kingdom.

In order to promote his new regulations and see that they were introduced into the Frankish monasteries, Louis the Pious appointed special inspectors or *missi* whose duty was to inspect the monasteries and instruct the brethren in the aims of the reform. St Amand was one of many abbeys subject to such inspection and reform. A charter of Louis dated 29 June 821 provides the information that Adaleodus, abbot of St Amand, and the Emperor's *missus*, Aldric, abbot of Ferrières, were directed to effect a reform at the abbey and enforce the Rule of St Benedict.[31] The Benedictine Rule was also imposed on Landévennec in Brittany, and the document preserved in the Cartulary of Landévennec orders that the Rule be observed and followed all over Brittany.[32]

A further source of information concerning the application of the reform decrees of 816 and 817 is the Plan of St Gall, a building plan of a complete monastic complex drawn *c.* 820 at Reichenau and sent to Abbot Gozbert of St Gall (816–38). The Plan appears to embody features which implement specific provisions of the decrees, and more particularly, they correspond to Abbot Haito of Reichenau's comments on the provisions contained in the *Statuta Murbacensia*. There are in fact a number of buildings – a room for washing the guests' feet, a separate house for the abbot, special quarters for visiting monks, the separate bath houses for the monks (two baths), novices, guests and the abbot, and an external school – that are referred to or implied by the more moderate measures agreed upon in 817.[33]

The evidence from the manuscript transmission of the Rule of St Benedict and other Rules, and from ninth-century library catalogues is rather more ambiguous concerning the status of the Benedictine Rule in the Carolingian monasteries. The earliest extant copy of the 'pure' text of the Rule of St Benedict, St Gall Stiftsbibliothek 914, has been closely associated with the reforms of 816 and 817.[34] The text, written in a Reichenau hand of the early ninth century, is generally regarded as a copy of the 'Aachener Normalexemplar', that is, it is thought to be a copy of the text of the rule that Charlemagne was sent, sometime before 797, by the monks of Monte Cassino; Charlemagne's copy had been made from the supposed autograph manuscript of Benedict himself. Paul the Deacon says in his *Historia Langobardorum* that in 581 the monks of Monte Cassino fled to Rome, taking with them the autograph of the Rule.[35] At the restoration of Monte Cassino under Abbot Petronax (717–47), Paul records that Pope Zacharias gave books to the monks, among them the precious text of St Benedict's Rule 'written by his own holy hand'.[36] Whether this really was the autograph cannot be determined; it was certainly of the sixth century, for the St Gall copy is sixth century in its language and syntax.[37] The supposed autograph was probably consumed in the flames which destroyed Teano in 896, whence the monks of Monte Cassino had fled after their monastery had been sacked by Arabs in 883.

The earlier portion of St Gall 914 contains the Rule, a martyrology and a calendar. According to Gilissen, in the tenth century more quires were inserted containing material relating to the 816/17 reforms, including the Capitulary of 817, notes on the observance at Monte Cassino, and the all-important letter of the Reichenau monks Tatto and Grimald.[38] Tatto and Grimald had probably been sent to Benedict of Aniane's monastery at Inden by their abbot, Haito, bishop of Basle, in order to be instructed in the standard observance promoted by Benedict. According to their letter, the librarian of Reichenau, Reginbert, had requested them to make a copy of St Benedict's Rule. Tatto and Grimald describe how they had striven to make a careful and exact copy of the Rule, and that they had noted variants from other copies of the Rule corrected by 'modern masters'.[39] The authenticity of this letter, and thus of the view that the St Gall copy was made by Tatto and Grimald, has recently been questioned by Gilissen. Because he thinks the text is a tenth-century insertion into St Gall 914, he asserts that it is also a tenth-century fabrication. But the script can be dated to the ninth century and Gelissen has omitted to note the entry in the Reichenau library catalogue for 835–42, which lists the books written by Reginbert, written on his orders, or given to him. It reads as follows: 'in the twentieth volume is the Rule of St Benedict the abbot... which Tatto and Grimald gave me'.[40] St Gall 914's contents correspond to this description, with the exception of the Ambrosian hymns. If not Grimald and Tatto's own transcript, then St Gall 914 is probably a copy of it made at Reichenau and sent to St Gall (perhaps when the Plan was sent by Haito to Abbot Gozbert?).

Needless to say, the genuineness of the letter from the abbot of Monte Cassino concerning the copy of the Rule has been disputed, but for reasons which are more telling as an argument against Charlemagne's part in promoting the Rule of St Benedict than against his having been sent a copy of it.[41] In all his legislation, for example, only one attempt by Charlemagne is evident to raise the Rule from the position it held as one element of the Frankish monastic tradition, and that was his Capitulary for 802. The use of the Aachen exemplar of the Rule is attested unequivocally in one case only, that of the gift Charlemagne made to the Frankish monks in the monastery on Mount Olivet in Jerusalem.[42] The person for whom Abbot Theodemar of Monte Cassino undoubtedly did describe the customs of his monastery was Count Theoderic, brother of Count William of Toulouse. These doubts remain unresolved.[43]

At present St Gall 914 is still accepted as the closest relative to the supposed Aachen copy and to the autograph original by Benedict. It would seem that the 'pure' text was not known in Frankish Gaul until about 800. While Benedict of Aniane, Smaragdus of St Mihiel and Hildemar of Corbie all use it, and it was the text promoted by the 816 reforms, Chrodegang of Metz and Theodulf of Orleans use the 'interpolated' or early revised version which was produced at the end of the sixth century, and whose earliest extant representative is Bodleian Hatton 48, written in England, ss. VII/VIII. There are few Carolingian manuscripts of this 'pure' text. There are in fact as many Carolingian texts of the interpolated version, and indeed of other rules entirely, such as the ninth-century manuscripts containing the Rule of Columbanus and the thirty-five copies of Benedict of Aniane's collection of different rules which included the *Regula Magistri*.[44]

That different rules continued to be copied suggests at least that they were respected if not followed, and that monastic observance was by no means uniform, even after the reforms of Louis the Pious and Benedict of Aniane. The extant Carolingian library catalogues and surviving manuscripts provide further indications of the continuing diversity of the monastic tradition. Corbie, for example, possessed copies of the Rule of St Basil (Leningrad F.v.I. 42 *c*. 700), Cassian's Collations (Leningrad O.v.I. 4 *c*. 730), the *Regula Magistri* (BN lat. 12205 s.vi^med and BN lat. 12634 s.vi^ex), Effraem's *Admonitio ad monachos*, and the Rules of Serapion and Augustine. The books given by Abbot Wando of St Wandrille to his monastery's library *c*. 747 included the Rules of Augustine, Serapion, Pafnutius and the two Macharii, as well as a volume containing the Rules of St Benedict and Columbanus and a martyrology. Abbot Ansegisus (823–33) added the Rule of Basil and another copy of St Benedict's Rule.[45] Staffelsee listed a Rule of Benedict in its inventory of church treasure in 812 and Murbach possessed only Cassian's Collations and Julianus Pomerius on the contemplative life in the mid-ninth century. St Riquier's inventory of 831 included six copies of St Benedict's Rule and the Rules of Augustine, Fructuosus and Isidore in one volume.[46] The most comprehensive collections of monastic rules were possessed by the monasteries of Reichenau, Fulda and St Gall. The Reichenau catalogue of 822 lists most of its collection under a separate headiing; it possessed the Rule of Basil in two volumes and the Life of St Anthony, four copies of Cassian's Collations and Julianus Pomerius on the active and contemplative lives. Under the heading *De regulis*, it listed five volumes containing eleven different monastic rules.[47] Between 823 and 838 two priests presented 'rules' to the monastery of Reichenau. I have already mentioned the copy of St Benedict's Rule given to Reginbert of Reichenau by Tatto and Grimald; Reginbert also possessed a volume containing the Rule of Pachomius and the rule of 'Saint Isidore and other holy fathers'. Fulda in the catalogue dated to *c*. 850 recorded nine volumes of monastic rules.[48] St Gall's collection was rather more modest, though it included Benedict's pure text (the item in the catalogue cannot definitely be identified with St Gall 914) and the Old High German interlinear version of the Rule (St Gall 916, also not mentioned in the catalogue).[49] Benedict of Aniane himself made a collection of no less than seventeen monastic rules.[50]

It may be that these books were simply intended to be reading matter for the monks rather than guides for a particular monastery's organization and discipline. Even if this be so, it implies an eclectic approach to the spiritual and cenobitic life and the realization that these different statements on the monastic life had something to offer the monastic reader, on the part of the houses that possessed these books. We cannot assume that after 816 all Frankish monasteries became completely Benedictine. Indeed, there are a number of factors which prevent us from doing so.

It is disconcerting for example that the first well-attested lay abbots are associated with Louis, and that it was Louis the monastic reformer who tolerated the appointment of laymen, that is, of men who were neither priests nor professed monks, to abbacies. Einhard, for example, received the abbacies of St Peter's Ghent in 815, St Bavo's Ghent between 816 and 821, St Wandrille in 816 and St Servais of Maastricht in 819 or 821. Count Warin received the abbacy of St Marcel of Chalon, Count Matfrid that of St Lifard and the Seneschal Adalhard was made abbot of St Martin's at Tours. In 819, it was decreed that priors were not to be laymen, but no such prohibition was extended to abbots.[51] The capitularies and conciliar decrees by implication acquiesce in the creation of lay abbots, especially if they cared for the material well-being of the monks in their charge. Lay abbots, as Felten has pointed out in a recent appraisal, were not necessarily a bad thing.[52] Historians such as Voigt have tended to criticize the institution of the lay abbots from a moral point of view, and for that matter, from the standpoint of later ecclesiastical norms, have seen it in terms of the modern idea of the development of political power within a state. Felten contends that the historical circumstances and necessities of the Carolingian period are the proper context for the lay abbots and that there is ample evidence that many of them were of positive benefit to the foundations of which they were the heads.

Rather than lay abbacies, it was alienation of church land that was most severely criticized at all the synods held during Louis' reign – at Aachen in December 818/January 819, at Paris in 825, Ingelheim in 826, Paris, Mainz, Lyons and Toulouse in 829, Thionville in 835 and Aachen in 836. In 819 Louis relinquished the Carolingian practice, laid down by the reform councils of the mid-eighth century in an attempt to break down the massive build-up of power and wealth by aristocratic bishops, of granting ecclesiastical land to laymen in return for an annual rent to the church who owned the land. As Goffard puts it: 'The Carolingians had extended their control over church property in the first place . . . to guarantee to a purified church the resources it required.'[53] This practice meant that the bishopric or abbacy would retain enough land for its maintenance and provision of necessities, but no more. Some of the church lands held de verbo regis, however, were not restored to the church during the reign of Louis the Pious, and the monarch's power to dispose of some ecclesiastical lands for a rent ad nonas et decimas (a ninth and tenth part of the estate's produce) was preserved.[54] In other words, although forceful opposition was mounted by such Carolingian churchmen as Agobard, bishop of Lyons, and Wala, later abbot of Corbie, to the king's control of ecclesiastical benefices in the 820s and 830s – a control that had been established with such energy by Pippin III – the king hung on to some of it, and the scale of the distribution of abbacies and bishoprics like honores or countships seems to have been undiminished.

That monasteries still sought the king's full commitment to their interests is evident from Louis' 400 or so extant charters, the greater proportion of which comprise confirmations of grants of land and privileges to Carolingian monasteries made by Louis' predecessors, or his own grants of royal protection, freedom from customs dues and tolls, immunity and the freedom of election for abbots.[55] The texts are full of prohibitions against alienating or exchanging church property without royal permission. It would have suited the church no more than the king for the former to have been fully emancipated from the latter. There is much indeed concerning the role of the monasteries and bishoprics during the reign of Louis the Pious, as well as Louis' monastic policy itself which needs to be studied in detail and analysed. My impression from reading the extant charters and the ecclesiastical legislation of his reign is that Louis had failed to realize the full implications and political logic of Pippin III's policies towards the church, not because he was stupid, but because he had a different conception both of the king's relationship towards the church, and the church itself. More work is needed to substantiate this.

A further factor which prevents us from describing the Frankish monasteries in the ninth century as fully Benedictine, is that the principal monasteries of the Frankish kingdom were powerful institutions in both secular and ecclesiastical politics. Their rulers were among the leading men of the kingdom and played a crucial part in its administration. Their estates and possessions involved them perforce in worldly concerns and their devotion to learning and book production was a far greater and more important aspect of the lives of their communities than Benedict of Nursia, or even Benedict of Aniane, would have countenanced. The foundation and development of Cluny, as we shall see in Chapter Eleven, saw an attempt once more to return to the original Benedictine ideal, and there were to be many more attempts in subsequent centuries. Yet Cluny itself bore the stamp of the reforms of 816 and 817. What evidence we have suggests that the reforms of 816 and 817, promoted by the secular authority, cannot be regarded as a simple return to the original Rule of St Benedict, and that the work of Louis the Pious and Benedict of Aniane, together with Carolingian monastic customs, provided the basis for later attempts to establish the Rule of St Benedict as the sole norm for the monastic life. The legislation of the synods held after 817 was designed to 'promote the honour of the church and the stability of the kingdom' by completing the work of reform begun in the cathedral chapters and monasteries. The *Capitulare ecclesiasticum* issued in 819 for example, turned its attention to correcting abuses in and providing direction for the secular church. It dealt with the safeguarding of church estates from lay control, tithes, the election of bishops, the ordination of priests and the latters' conduct, and many other matters concerning the administration and discipline of the secular church.[56] Later synods echoed this concern, and there is some evidence to suggest that their decrees were circulated to all Frankish bishops, and that the recipients were enjoined to put the decrees into practice. Two circular letters from Louis survive concerning the correction of abuses in the diocesan church according to the precepts formulated in 818/19; the letters are the same in content and were addressed to Bishop Berno of Besançon and Bishop Hetti of Trier respectively in 821. Similarly, letters recommending the decrees of the Synod of Paris to the attention of Bishops

Jeremy of Sens and Jonas of Orleans were sent by Louis, and it is possible that similar letters were sent to his other bishops.[57]

That Louis the Pious' massive reform undertakings were part and parcel of a predominantly Christian and theological interpretation of the function of the Emperor and the meaning of the Empire has been argued persuasively by Semmler.[58] That is, Louis attempted to realize the *renovatio* and unity of the Frankish Empire on the institutional and secular levels as well as on the monastic level. This argument is reinforced by Noble, who makes a strong case for the relationship that existed between Louis' attraction to monastic values and his statecraft and principles. The moral, spiritual and administrative features of the office of abbot as defined in the Rule of St Benedict provided Louis with a model for ruling. The *Proemium Generale* of 818/19, as Noble points out, makes this comparison quite explicit. 'Since each person will render account for his deeds, and we especially who stand equal to others in our mortal condition but who greatly surpass them in dignity of rule, are going to render account not only for our graver commission but also for our words and deeds.' This echoes St Benedict's Rule which had stressed that the abbot should realize that from him to whom more is entrusted, more is expected. Louis, like an abbot, wished to teach by good example.[59]

III

While acknowledging Louis' contribution to monastic reform and to the idea of a Christian Empire, historians have long regarded Louis' reign as the beginning of the 'decline' or 'break-up' of the Carolingian Empire. Such an assessment seems to take into account only a few years of Louis' reign, the years in which his plans for his realm were fiercely opposed by his sons. The principal narrative sources have encouraged this tendency, for all of them, the Royal Frankish Annals, the Annals of St Bertin, the history of Nithard, and the biographies by Thegan and the Astronomer, concentrate for the years 830—40 on the struggle between Louis and his three elder sons. That there is a break in the annals after 829 — the Annals of St Bertin start in 830 — has accentuated this division. Recently Ganshof in a brief but penetrating reconsideration of Louis' reign,[60] Noble in an examination of Louis the Pious' relations with the Papacy, and Schieffer in an ideological re-evaluation of the period[61] have presented a more positive account of Charlemagne's successor, but it is high time that Louis received a full-scale and thorough reassessment. That the Empire split into separate political units after Louis' death is certainly true; but to condemn this development, and the events that led up to it as a decline and Louis consequently as a miserable failure is to ignore not only Louis' very real achievements but also the significance and interest of the political fragmentation itself. That the Frankish kingdoms ceased to be the Carolingian Empire is not necessarily such a disaster as is usually supposed. Louis' achievements in the ecclesiastical sphere were undoubtedly important, but we need now to consider his career in administration and government, and the particular difficulties with which he contended, both within and without his kingdom.

During Louis' reign, many improvements and alterations were made to the structure of Carolingian administration, particularly in the palace chapel and chancery. Some of these witness to Louis' efforts to make his administration more efficient. Louis' closest advisers in Aquitaine, Benedict of Aniane and Helisachar the chancellor, accompanied the Emperor to Aachen and replaced Charlemagne's personnel; Helisachar became head of the palace chancery. Some continuity with Charlemagne's administration was ensured in that Hildebold, archbishop of Cologne and Charlemagne's archchaplain, held that office under Louis the Pious until his death in 819, and some if not all of the notaries of the chancery and the chaplains in the palace chapel (who may well have been one and the same) remained.[62] It was Hildebold's successor, Hilduin, abbot of St Denis, St Medard of Soissons, St Germain-des-Prés, St Ouen and Salonnes who changed the title of the head of the palace chapel to *sacri palatii archicapellanus*, and the office continued to be one of the utmost importance in the affairs of the kingdom. With the defeat of Lothar, Hilduin, who had supported him, lost his job and was succeeded by Fulk, abbot of St Wandrille, Jumièges and St Remigius in Rheims. After Louis' reinstatement in May 834, Drogo, bishop of Metz and the king's half-brother, was made archchaplain; it is not known whether Louis managed or even tried to secure the exemption from episcopal residence for Drogo as Charlemagne had done for his archchaplains Hildebald, archbishop of Cologne, and Angilramn, bishop of Metz. Drogo functioned as an *ambasciator*: that is, as the intermediary between the king and the notary who drew up documents, he took the field with the Emperor, presided at synods and accompanied the king on many of his journeys. Yet he seems to have continued as bishop of Metz and certainly officiated in his cathedral on the main religious festivals. The appointment of a Carolingian to the office of archchaplain may well be a reflection of the importance the office had acquired, as Fleckenstein avers, though it is more likely that Louis simply felt more secure with one trusted half-brother in the job and another, Hugh, also appointed in 834, at the head of the chancery.

As noted in the preceding chapter, Louis effected a number of important changes in chancery practice and structure on his accession in 814, a year which also marks a definite watershed in the development of Carolingian diplomatic. Thegan tells us that Louis decided to inspect and to renew all the grants that his predecessors had made to churches. The pattern of issue of Louis' charters is instructive. From the surviving charters 108 date from the years 814, 815 and 816. Apart from the 25 issued in 819 and 27 in 825, the average number of charters extant for each of the remaining years of the reign is 12, and only 6 each survive from 830 and 837. The proportion of new grants as against confirmation of old ones is greater for the years after 817; the charters for the years 814, 815 and 816 therefore testify to the energy with which Louis' intentions, as reported by Thegan, were carried out. This massive undertaking was accompanied by the reworking of the old formulae to make them better organized and more grammatical, and the incorporation of new formulae into the collection known as the *Formulae Imperiales*. Louis' charters also indicate that donations of complete ownership of land increased during his reign, whereas they had been rare under Charlemagne, and that the notions of *mundium* or royal protection and immunity were amalgamated after 814.

It is interesting to note how the lamentable vicissitudes of Louis' reign are reflected in the protocol of his charters. In 825, for example, Lothar appears in the subscription, signature and date clause beside Louis. In the few diplomas issued after the assembly of Worms in 829 Lothar's name disappears; it appears again in 830 but is gone by the end of the year. For the period June 833 to May 834 we have only one charter from Louis. After this the formula for subscription becomes *Hludowicus divina repropitiante clementia imperator augustus* and the epithet *piissimus* generally replaces that of *serenissimus* and *gloriosissimus*.

Another instance of the work Louis did to organize his legislation and administration is the capitulary collection made by Ansegisus, abbot of St Wandrille, in 827. The collection, divided into parts containing secular and ecclesiastical capitularies issued by Charlemagne and Louis the Pious, incorporated all those capitularies on which Ansegisus had been able to lay his hands. Of the ninety capitularies known to have been issued between 768 and 827, however, Ansegisus used only twenty-eight. Hitherto historians, including myself, have described Ansegisus' capitulary collection as a personal rather than as an official one, and attributed its lacunae either to the inadequacy of the resources at St Wandrille (and thus by implication the ineffectiveness of the distribution of capitularies by the royal writing office) or to the deficiencies of the palace archive.[63] The latter charge is the more probable. Ganshof suggested that Ansegisus may have had access to the palace archive and even that Louis may have 'encouraged' him in his undertaking.[64] The evidence seems to me to suggest much more than that, namely, that the Ansegisus capitulary collection was an official one, commissioned by Louis, and is to be seen in the context of the creation of the Imperial Formulary and the legislation for the reform of the monasteries and the houses of canons, for the latter of which Ansegisus himself has been proposed as the author. For most of his career, Ansegisus was an official at the palace, despite the fact that he held the abbacies of St Wandrille, Luxeuil, St Sextus in Rheims, St Memmius in Châlons-sur-Marne, and St Germer de Flay. He was a chaplain in the palace chapel under Charlemagne and stayed on to serve Louis the Pious. He worked as *exactor operum regalium* in Aachen and assisted Einhard the 'palace architect'.[65] Ansegisus distinguished in his text between capitularies relating to ecclesiastical affairs and those dealing with secular matters and this is precisely the distinction Louis himself made in his capitularies for 818/19. Further, Ansegisus' collection was used in official circles; Louis cites from it at Worms,[66] Charles the Bald also refers to it. Of the many extant manuscripts of it, attesting to its wide distribution, one in particular, now Yale Beinecke Library MS 413, appears to have been copied for Charles the Bald himself.[67]

Louis the Pious therefore did much to make his administration more effective. His secular legislation, particularly his instructions to his *missi dominici*, and the *De disciplina palatii* of 814, indicate that he was doing the best he could

126

to maintain law and order through his vast domain.[68] The *missi* continued to be important extensions of royal authority and in 825 many new ones were named; the new *missi* between them covered the whole of the old three kingdoms of Neustria, Austrasia and Burgundy.[69] For the region of Besançon, Bishop Hermin of Besançon and Count Monogold were appointed; for Mainz, Bishop Heistulf of Mainz and Count Ruodbert; for Trier, Archbishop Hetti of Trier and Count Adalbert; for Cologne, Archbishop Hadubold of Cologne and Count Egmund; for Rheims, Châlons, Soissons, Senlis, Beauvais and Laon, Archbishop Ebbo of Rheims (or in his absence Bishop Rothad of Soissons) and Count Hruotfrid; for Noyon, Amiens, Thérouanne and Cambrai, Bishop Ragnarius of Noyon and Count Berengar; for Sens, Archbishop Jeremy of Sens and Count Donatus; for Rouen, Archbishop Willibert of Rouen and Count Ingobert; for Tours, Archbishop Landramn of Tours and Count Hruodbert; for Lyons, Tarentaise and Vienne, Bishop Alberich of Langres and Count Richard. The only ecclesiastical provinces not covered are those of Italy, Aquitaine and Bavaria, and it is possible that Louis left the organization of these to his sons in their position as subkings. It would be easy to dismiss this network of inspectors as inefficient and ineffective, and many have done so. Yet there are shreds of evidence that the *missi* were doing their job. Several charters issued by Louis concerning disputes and the rightful allocation of property were made as a result of investigations by *missi dominici*. Missi acted for example in the dispute between the monastery of Farfa and Spoleto in 820, land was restored to Würzburg and to Piacenza as a result of imperial intervention through the *missi* for the region, and a villa restored to St Gall in 821.[70] The *missi* were also responsible for the mobilization of the army; lists of the forces available in each *missaticum* had to be drawn up.[71] The public assemblies also increased in number under Louis; there were usually two and sometimes three a year, and legislation concerning the day to day order of the kingdom was usually produced as a result.[72] These are all indications that Louis' administration was as effective as that of his illustrious father, if not more so, and that Louis was a ruler of no mean energy and ability.

IV

These qualities are particularly evident in Louis' dealings with the nations who lived on the fringes of the Frankish kingdom, though rather less so as far as internal Frankish affairs are concerned. Like his father Charlemagne, Louis had to contend with both opposition to Frankish control or influence and opposition to his own personal rule. In coping with the Danes and the Bretons in particular, Louis was remarkably successful, as we shall see in the context of the development of Brittany and of Normandy in Chapter Nine. He also managed to retain the upper hand over another important group of neighbours, the Slavs.

A number of groups of Slavs make an appearance in the annals for Louis' reign but their exact relationship to the Frankish ruler is not clear. Charlemagne had made some attempt to extend Frankish control east of the Elbe, and it is possible that some of the Slavs had made their submission to Charlemagne and Louis. That the sources, all Frankish, refer to the Slavs as if the Franks were their overlords may not be conclusive; nevertheless it is significant that it is Louis who is called upon to arbitrate in Slav internal disputes and who set native rulers over the tribes just as he did in the case of the Bretons. Let us take a particular example. Milegast and Cealadrag, kings of the Wilzi and sons of Liub quarrelled. Milegast was the elder and had been made king on his father's death (by the Franks?), but the Wilzi deposed him and conferred the kingship on his younger brother. Both kings came to the assembly at Frankfurt in May 823 and appealed to Louis; Louis, after consulting the wishes of the Wilzi, decided in Cealadrag's favour. Another case concerns the Slavonic Sorbs who lived to the east of the Obodrites. They refused obedience to the Franks in 816 but were beaten into submission by the Saxons and east Franks. Other Slavs, such as those who threatened invasion in 822, were clearly not under Frankish control, and the defences on the Saxon border had to be strengthened against them.[73]

The Slavonic group whose affairs impinged most strongly on those of the Franks were the Obodrites, for their territory in Holstein bordered on that of the Danes. The Franks appear to have been their overlords. In 815 the Obodrites with the Saxons were requested by the Emperor to assist Harald the Dane in his bid to regain the Danish throne. The Saxon and Obodrite army marched into the land of the Northmen under the *missus* Baldrich, where they did little but lay the country waste, as the sons of Godofrid, the rulers of the Danes, refused to fight. Then in 818 the Obodrites revolted, apparently because the Franks had imposed the joint rule of Sclaomir and Ceadrag son of Thrasco on the Obodrites, and Sclaomir, who had ruled alone after the former king Thrasco's death, resented this interference. It seems to have been a case of the Franks imposing their own ideas of filial succession on a nation with different inheritance patterns for the kingship. Sclaomir's response was to make friends with the sons of Godofrid and encourage them to attack Saxony. Their sortie was routed, and Sclaomir was taken to Aachen in 819 where not only the Franks but his own Obodrite nobles charged him with 'many crimes'. Sclaomir was exiled and the Obodrite kingdom given to Ceadrag. In 821 Ceodrag in his turn was charged with treachery and conspiracy with the Danes; Sclaomir was recalled from exile and reinstated as king, he received baptism on his return to Saxony and died that same year. Ceadrag resumed the throne. Two years later Ceadrag was accused of infidelity to the Franks and appeared at Compiègne in November 823 to answer the charges against him 'and gave an acceptable explanation of his conduct'. The same charges were levelled against Ceadrag in 826 and this time Louis sent his envoys to the Obodrites to ascertain whether they really wanted Ceadrag to rule them. Their reply was somewhat comic, namely, that they could never make up their minds whether they did or not, but on the whole were in favour of him. The Emperor consequently restored Ceadrag to his kingdom. The Obodrites and Wilzi remained quiet until 830 but the annals for that year report an expedition against them which reduced them to submission after they had 'renounced their allegiance'. Another campaign was mounted for the same reason against the Sorbs, Wilzi and Obodrites in 840. Evidently, neither side was strong enough to resolve the situation completely; the Franks could not, or did not wish to, conquer the Slavs as they had conquered the Saxons, and the Slavs were unable to assert their independence.

The ambition of Ljudevit, duke of lower Pannonia and ruler of the Dalmatian Slavs, involved the Bulgars and Byzantium as well as the question of Frankish overlordship. Frankish suzerainty over Pannonia and Croatia dated from about 795, when the Croat chieftain Vojnomir accepted baptism, and over Dalmatia from about 803. The area became a Frankish march and was under the secular jurisdiction of the margrave or duke of Friuli, while the ecclesiastical authority emanated from Aquileia Cividale. Borna, leader of the Dalmatian Croats, and Ljudevit leader of the Pannonian Croats, affirmed their loyalty to Louis the Pious in 814. Borna remained loyal, Ljudevit did not. The annals describe Ljudevit as an 'agitator and schemer'. He revolted in 819 and tried to unite the neighbouring peoples with his own in an attempt to assert his independence. A long struggle ensued, with successes on both sides, the most valuable being those won by the loyal Duke Borna. In 820, 821 and 822 the Franks marched against Ljudevit; Ljudevit fled to the Serbs, murdered the duke who had given him refuge and seized his city. The following year Ljudevit himself was murdered. Dalmatian Croatia remained within the Frankish sphere of influence until 877, but Pannonian Croatia, because of its geographical position, became an object of interest to the Bulgars. In 824, the king of the Bulgars sent an embassy to the Emperor with the aim of determining the borders between Frankish and Bulgar territory. Louis prevaricated about making a decision or treaty with the Bulgars, but in 827 the Bulgars took the initiative, sent an army up the Drave and appointed a Bulgar governor in Pannonia. Thus Pannonian Croatia passed under Bulgarian protection. As a result Baldrich, the duke of Friuli who had failed to prevent this from happening, was deprived of his office.

Other Frankish overtures to the Slavs were made by the church. Some conversions to Christianity in the 820s are recorded, including that of Sclaomir the Obodrite, and Hamburg became the centre of evangelical work in the north of Germany under Anskar, its first bishop. In 834 Anskar was appointed papal legate to 'all Swedes, Danes, Slavs and other northern peoples'.[74] Hamburg itself was destroyed by a Danish raid in 845 and the bishopric was transferred to Bremen; in 864 the sees of Hamburg and Bremen were united under one bishop. Christian missions in Carinthia and Pannonia were conducted from Salzburg, Passau and Aquileia, and between 818 and 825 Mojmir, the Slav dynast in Moravia, was converted to Christianity; Moravia and Bohemia were thereafter rapidly opened up to Frankish penetration. Louis the Pious' policy of conquest for the pagan fringes of his Empire seems in fact, as Hauck noted, to have been the opposite of that of his father, for Louis tried to get them converted before conquering them.[75] It must be said that he was more successful at the former than the latter. In 826 a mission was sent to the Danes, but the only major conversion achieved was the spectacular one of Harald the Dane, his wife and nobles. Generally, Louis retained the upper hand in his relations with the Slavs; only in the dispute with the Bulgars over the Pannonian Croats did he lose it. In all other cases he was served by excellent commanders and directed operations satisfactorily; he was clearly the acknowledged ruler of Western Europe, the counterpart to the emperors in the East.

Charlemagne's relations with Byzantium had been soured by disputes over Venice and Dalmatia. Peace was finally negotiated between the Franks and the Greeks in 810; Charlemagne came to terms with the Emperor Nicephorus and gave Venice back to Byzantium. The peace was ratified by the envoys of the Emperor Michael in 812, who addressed Charlemagne, no doubt to his satisfaction, as *basileus* (Emperor). Subsequent embassies between the Frankish and Byzantine courts from 812 to 839 were simply successive ratifications of this peace treaty.

As king in Aquitaine, Louis the Pious had been active campaigning in Spain and quelling the insurrections of the Basques or Gascons. His son Pippin, succeeding his father as king in Aquitaine, inherited the Spanish and Basque problems, the most troublesome region being the Spanish march. As with the Slavs, we are hampered by inadequate information about the nature of the problem; it seems principally to have been a simple matter of the Franks attempting to extend their control and territory in Spain and maintain their hold on the region they had already annexed north of the Ebro, and resisting at the same time the attempts made by the Moors occupying Islamic Spain from encroaching on territory held by the Franks. Hostility to Frankish suzerainty may also have been an element. As in all border regions, there was a certain amount of flexibility in the loyalties of some of the inhabitants, who could be tempted to support the side they thought would assist their own interests the most. Some of the people of the march, for example, defected to Aizo who was probably a Septimanian nobleman and who was assisted in his revolt by the Moors. Louis sent Abbot Helisachar, a native of the region, and counts Hildebrand and Donatus to quell Aizo's rising. Abumarvan, a general of the Emir Abd-ar-Rahman in Spain, led an army of Saracens against them. To assist the army led by Bernard, count of Barcelona, Louis sent Pippin to defend the Frankish borders against Abumarvan's forces. The leaders of Pippin's army, counts Hugh and Matfrid, proved negligent and the army arrived too late to prevent Abumarvan from laying waste the area round Barcelona and Gerona. At the Frankish *post mortem* on this disaster held at Ingelheim in February 828, the commanders of the army were deprived of their commands. It is from this that Hugh's and Matfrid's resentment of Louis dates. They were to prove dangerous enemies, for they were the instigators of the first serious threat to Louis' position in 830. After the disaster in the Spanish march the Moors drew in their claws, and the only other reference the annalist makes to Spanish affairs is in 834, when at the assembly held at Attigny in June the marcher territories of Spain, Septimania and Provence were 'set in order'.

V

Louis' political dealings with Italy apart from the Papacy were conducted first through Bernard of Italy and, after his death, by Lothar, Louis' eldest son. Louis himself made a treaty with Grimoald, duke of Benevento, 'like that of Charlemagne' to the effect that the Beneventans should continue to pay an annual tribute of 7000 *solidi* in return, presumably, for being left to their own devices.[76] This arrangement remained undisturbed, despite Grimoald's murder shortly afterwards by Sigo, who took Grimoald's place as duke. With Rome and the Papacy, however, Louis' relations were close and complex, and they need to be considered in some detail.

Louis the Pious' relations with the Papacy were very closely connected with his interpretation of his office and the idea of Empire. Charlemagne had never clearly defined the imperial office or his rights, if any, in Rome. His title after 800, *Carolus serenissimus augustus a Deo coronatus magnus et pacificus imperator Romanum gubernans imperium, qui et per misericordiam Dei rex Francorum et Langobardorum* was designed, particularly the Roman formulation *Romanum gubernans imperium*, as Classen has convincingly argued, to include the Romans within the Frankish realm without centering the Empire upon them.[77] In others words, Charlemagne wanted to stress the royal and Frankish bases for his power. As regards Charlemagne's relations with the Papacy, these too were left undefined, but it is significant that when Charlemagne crowned his son Louis Emperor in 813, he did it himself, without any assistance from, and not even in the presence of, the Pope. All the sources, papal as well as Frankish, refer to Louis as Emperor from then onwards.

There were, and are, a number of questions to be raised in the relations between the Frankish Emperor and the Pope during the reign of Louis the Pious. First, it has to be decided by modern historians whether the Pope's coronation of Louis and Lothar as Emperors actually constituted them emperors, and was necessary for them to assume the title, or whether a papal coronation simply sanctified the title and gave it extra dignity. Secondly, did the imperial title imply a special obligation towards the Papacy? The distinct relationship that had existed between the Eastern Emperor and the Papacy might have prompted the Pope to expect similar things from the new Western Emperor. Thirdly, the Franks had for nearly a century acted as protectors of the Papacy; the title of Emperor simply enhanced this function. Then there was the question of the rights the Emperor might have in Rome and the papal states and over the Frankish church, and conversely, the Pope's jurisdiction, if any, over the Frankish church. Not all these issues were resolved during Louis' reign, but it was Louis who defined for the first time the Emperor's rights with regard to Roman territory. Not only that: whereas Charlemagne had emphasized the title of Emperor, Louis began to emphasize the responsibility of the office. The office came from God; the church was identified with the Empire and the imperial office became a *ministerium*, with the welfare, spiritual and physical, of the people in its charge. Noble has identified several episodes in the development of imperial–papal relations during the reign of Louis the Pious. He argued that in the first few years, Louis had the initiative, but that the Papacy seized it after about 824 in an attempt, not wholly successful, to assert its spiritual prerogatives.[78]

In 815, Louis was informed that some Roman nobles had conspired to murder Pope Leo in Rome and that the ringleaders had subsequently been butchered on the Pope's orders. Louis dispatched his nephew Bernard to investigate and envoys from the Pope came to satisfy the Emperor concerning the charges against Leo. The Pope died in May the following year, Stephen IV was elected as his successor, and, according to the Royal Frankish Annals, set out to see Louis, sending two envoys ahead to report his consecration to the Emperor, and taking the unprecedented step of making the Romans swear an oath of loyalty to Louis. At this stage it should be noted that the Franks never claimed or exercised any rights in papal elections, though in 827 Gregory IV was not ordained Pope until the Emperor's *missus* had ascertained that his election was regular.[79] Louis met Pope Stephen IV at Rheims, and 'after the customary solemn masses had been celebrated, Pope Stephen crowned the Emperor by placing a crown on his head . . . after making other arrangements of benefit to the church, the Pope and the Emperor went their separate ways'.[80] Two principal questions arise about this incident: did the Pope come to Francia to crown Louis or for some other reason? Of what significance is the coronation of Louis?

The official papal history, the *Liber Pontificalis*, tells us that Stephen went to Francia to 'confirm the peace and unity of the holy church of God' and to negotiate about a number of Roman exiles who were being held in Francia. Stephen in fact obtained the release of the exiles, confirmation of papal and Frankish friendship and a document defining papal and imperial rights in Rome and its environs. Frankish sources say Stephen obtained 'everything he had sought', but was the coronation one of these things?[81] Nowhere are we told that Stephen went north to crown Louis. Stephen also left Rome in great haste, more as a supplicant and fugitive than as a confident prelate. Some scholars have argued that the Pope sought to make the Pope's part in the Emperor-making process a vital one and bring it within church law. Others think Louis wanted to enhance the imperial dignity. Noble has analysed the proceedings between Louis and the Pope afresh, and comes to the conclusion that the coronation of Louis by Pope Stephen on Sunday 5 October at Rheims was, at the very least, orchestrated by Louis and the coronation *ordo* itself was drawn up at Rheims. Yet, as Noble says: 'Louis was setting a dangerous precedent by associating the papacy with the conferral of imperial dignity.'[82] There seems little doubt that Louis used the Pope for his own purposes, even if the latter remain rather obscure. Much too has been made of the crown the Pope brought with him as a present for Louis and which was used in the coronation ceremony.[83] I am not sure any importance should be attached to this crown. It was a standard regal gift to make to kings; it would have been courteous of Louis to use his new crown on such an occasion.

The document drawn up in 816 mentioned by Ermold the Black, which defined imperial and papal rights in Rome, is no longer extant, but the *Pactum*

Ludovicianum granted to Pope Paschal I, Stephen IV's successor, in the first few weeks of 817, is thought to be similar to it and its origin is now accepted as Frankish.[84] Noble has interpreted this document as the first attempt by the Carolingians to define their rights in and around Rome, and an initial effort to integrate the Papacy into the institutional framework of the Empire. Most of the document constitutes an inventory of the property of the Roman church, the so-called papal states. It marks the end of papal territorial expansion, for the papal states remained more or less the same in extent until 1870. In the ninth clause of the *Pactum*, Louis promised to defend the lands, cities, towns, castles and revenues listed in clauses two to eight, promised not to intervene in the papal states unless expressly asked to do so, and made provision for dealing with fugitives from the papal states. With Louis' churches and monasteries in the Frankish kingdom, the protection and immunity he extended to them involved a certain amount of *dominium* as well. Similarly, the protection accorded Rome provided Louis with the means of intervening in its political affairs, and a royal *missus* was based in Rome.

A coherent extension to the policies begun by Louis in 816 was the *Constitutio Romana* of 824.[85] As well as claiming the right to guarantee free and canonical elections to the Papacy and to oversee the administration of justice, an oath of loyalty to the emperors Louis and Lothar was imposed. The *Constitutio* marked a high point in the imperial position. Thereafter the Papacy began to extend its spiritual role in the Frankish kingdom, one of its first moves being to assume the leadership of the mission to the Danes. A further occasion for asserting papal authority was the 'second' iconoclastic controversy. In 825, the Frankish bishops had met at Paris to discuss the image question once more, and the bishops of Cambrai and Metz, Halitgar and Amalarius, were sent to Louis with a copy of the proceedings of the synod. This was then forwarded to the Pope. The Pope, however, refused to accept the Carolingian theology on icons, and in the following year he tried to regain the direction of church reform, without much success as far as the Frankish church was concerned.

Louis' next confrontation with the Pope, Gregory IV this time, was in 833. Lothar and his brothers brought Gregory from Rome, apparently as a tool, though this is not how Gregory would have seen it. Many Frankish bishops were opposed to his coming and wrote him a fierce letter, accusing him of meddling in Frankish affairs and bringing his office into disrepute, and threatening him with excommunication. Their letter is lost, but fortunately Gregory's reply to it, in which he explained the reasons for his intervention, is not.[86] Gregory asserted that he wished to restore peace in the Christian world and the provisions of the *Ordinatio Imperii* (see below) and to recall Louis and his supporters from their sinful ways which were destroying the peace and unity of the Empire. It is the reference to sin which is crucial here. Gregory was seeing the events of 833 in religious terms and the remission of sin, rather than in secular ones; this served as the pretext for his intervention. That he defined the disturbance of the Christian world as a sin was a move which Noble regards as fraught with significant implications for the 'papal political hegemony in the West'.[87] But the papal strength thus asserted proved illusory and ineffectual. Although Gregory and Louis met, it has never been discovered what agreement, if any, they reached. Gregory was sent ignominiously back to Rome by Lothar. His practical effect had been negligible and his spiritual influence in the Frankish kingdom severely limited. Relations between the Franks and the Papacy at this stage were still based on realities rather than theories.

VI

On his accession, Louis the Pious moved swiftly to remove the possibility of opposition to his rule; first, he exiled his cousins, the offspring of Bernard, Pippin III's half-brother. The influence of Bernard's children had become strong in the last years of Charlemagne's life. Count Wala and Adalhard, abbot of Corbie, served the king in various capacities, notably as his emissaries, and were joined at court by their younger brother Bernhar after 810.[88] Gundrada their sister was also at court – a letter on Adoptionism was addressed to her by Alcuin – and another sister, Theodrada, was made abbess of Notre Dame at Soissons in 810. In 814, Louis obliged Wala to become a monk at Corbie, Adalhard was exiled to Noirmoutier to be held there in custody by the abbot, an ally of Benedict of Aniane; Bernhar returned to Lérins and Gundrada had to retreat to St Radegund's convent of Sainte Croix in Poitiers. Only Theodrada was left unmolested. Semmler has suggested that Benedict of Aniane had something to do with the precipitate exit of Adalhard and his siblings from the palace, for Adalhard was known to oppose Benedict in his views on monastic reform.[89] It may indeed be more than coincidence that all the children of Bernard were restored to favour as soon as Benedict of Aniane was dead.

As well as the potential rivalry of his cousins, there seems to have been other dissension at court, of which the details are obscure. The Astronomer describes how Louis purged Aachen of all those suspected of disloyalty to the Emperor, including a Count Hodoin, who was killed while resisting arrest. Other dissidents or conspirators were blinded. All Louis' sisters were required to quit the palace and retire to their own estates. The Astronomer attributes this unbrotherly act to Louis' fear of history repeating itself and what had happened through Odilo and Chiltrud (parents of Tassilo of Bavaria) happening again. In other words, the Astronomer is suggesting that Louis feared mischief from possible alliances that his sisters might yet make with the rulers of the peripheral territories of the Frankish kingdoms. Very few of Charlemagne's chief personnel were permitted to remain. Einhard was one of those who was, possibly because he had been, according to Ermold the Black, one of those who had advised Charlemagne in 813 to associate Louis with him as Emperor.[90] Einhard was rewarded on 11 January 815 for his 'fidelity, devotion and obedience' and some of the land Einhard donated to the monastery of Lorsch had been given him by Louis.[91] These signs of royal favour and the many abbacies he was given, all indicate that Einhard stood high in Louis' regard in the early years of his reign.

Thus far, Louis had shown himself to be as ruthless and single-minded in the establishing of his authority as his father and grandfather, and he was no less so on the occasion of his nephew Bernard's revolt. Bernard was almost certainly a tool in the hands of a group of malcontent magnates, much as Pippin the Hunchback had been twenty-five years earlier. Indeed a tradition of conspiracy is recorded. The ringleaders of Bernard's revolt were Eggideo, Reginhard and Reginhar, whose maternal grandfather Hardrad had once conspired in Thuringia against Charlemagne.[92] It may be stretching the evidence too far, but it is possible that Hardrad and Reginhar belonged to a family of Frankish aristocrats who had never become reconciled to Carolingian rule. Anshelm, bishop of Milan, and Theodulf, bishop of Orleans, were also accused of being involved, though in Theodulf's case at least there is no evidence either to support or contradict this.

That Bernard was not mentioned at all in the *Ordinatio Imperii* of 817 (in which Louis divided his kingdom between his three sons, and made provision for the ruling of the Empire) even though Bernard's actual position would not have been altered one whit by the decree's provisions, may have been sufficient cause of grievance to encourage Bernard to revolt.[93] When later in 817 Louis was informed that Bernard, king of Italy, was planning to set up an unlawful, that is, an independent regime, the annalist comments that the report was only 'partly true'. Bernard himself surrendered to Louis and in 818 the ringleaders, including Bernard, were blinded and the rest were exiled or tonsured. Bernard died as a result of being blinded. Almost as a reflex action, Louis had his three younger half-brothers, Drogo, Hugh and Theodoric, tonsured and confined in monasteries, so as to remove all possibility of their emulating Bernard's example. At this stage of his career Louis showed no signs of the clemency and mercy for which he is praised by his biographers, but by 821 Louis emerges as a milder and rather more interesting personality, a man with a conscience. Louis then repented of his harshness four years before, pardoned many of the conspirators who had been implicated in the revolt of Bernard, restored their possessions, recalled Adalhard of Corbie from exile and made him abbot of Corbie and permitted Bernhar to return to Corbie from Lérins. The following year his brothers too were released from their monastic custody. Drogo was later made bishop of Metz and Hugh was given the abbacy of St Quentin; both served the Emperor loyally in his administration after 834. Louis also made a public confession and did public penance for what he had done to his relatives – brothers, nephew and cousins. The penance was compared with that of Theodosius by contemporaries, but Louis' penance this time was in fact voluntary rather than forced upon him.[94] Ambrose had forced Theodosius to do penance. Even the hostile *Epitaphium Arsenii* regarded Louis' public penance as a positive rather than a negative move on Louis' part. Evidently by 821, Louis felt his position secure enough to permit him to be magnanimous. Yet the pardon extended to so many dissident magnates, in light of subsequent events, was a serious mistake. Louis appears to have underestimated the strength and ambition of some of his magnates and played right into their hands by making his sons jealous of each other and of their positions, and unscrupulous in their efforts to maintain them.

Three sons were born to Louis by his first wife Ermengard: Lothar, Louis (the German) and Pippin. At an assembly at Aachen in 817 Louis made provision for his sons' inheritance, both for immediate implementation and after his death. Oddly enough, the Royal Frankish Annals' account of this event is laconic and the other narrative sources do not mention it at all. Fortunately the document drawn up at this assembly, the *Ordinatio Imperii*, has survived, and it makes provision for the division of Louis' Empire between his three sons, as well as embodying Louis' own concept of his Empire. The issuing of the *Ordinatio Imperii* was based on the success of Charlemagne's division of his Empire into three parts which Louis himself had experienced (see Map 8). Louis says as much in his preface to the *Ordinatio Imperii*; just as Louis had been more or less independent in Aquitaine, so his sons were to administer the territories put into their charge. Whereas Charlemagne had been silent on the subject of the Empire, Louis was eloquent and explicit about the necessity of preserving its unity. In his preface he states that the unity of the Empire preserved for Louis by God should not be destroyed by men and that Louis had therefore devised a way of preserving that unity. Lothar was given the title of Emperor, as co-ruler with his father at once, made heir to the Empire, and appointed king of Italy in the event of his father's death. Bernard, then king of Italy was not mentioned (this was before his revolt) but the implication is that Bernard would be subordinate to Lothar should Louis die. Pippin and Louis the German were made kings of Aquitaine (plus Gascony, Toulouse, Carcassonne, Autun, Avallon and Nevers) and Bavaria (plus Carinthia, Bohemia, the lands of the Avars and Slavs and the royal manors of Lauterhofen and Ingolstadt) respectively.

The younger brothers were granted power of their own, with exclusive jurisdiction within their territories, but were subordinate to Lothar and required to meet their elder brother each year in order to 'promote friendship and matters of common interest'. In the event of a brother dying and leaving legitimate children, only one son was to succeed the father, so that the territory would not be split any further. The arrangement was neat, and all contingencies catered for, save the one that happened. After his first wife's death Louis married the beautiful Welf, Judith, and in 823 she gave birth to a son. He was called Charles, and it is clear that Louis was as fond of him as Jacob was of his Benjamin.

NOTES

1. Astronomer, c. 8.
2. P. Fournés, *Etude critique sur la vie de Louis le Pieux par Thegan et l'astronomer* (Paris 1907).

3. Astronomer, c. 9. Compare Ardo, *Vita sancti Benedicti*, c. 43–c. 46.
4. Bouquet, *Recueil* VI, 452–4.
5. Ardo, *Vita sancti Benedicti*, c. 58. See S. Dulcy *La règle de St Benoît d'Aniane et la réforme monastique à l'époque carolingienne* (Nancy 1935), and J. Semmler, 'Die Beschlusse des Aachener Konzils im Jahre 816', *ZfK* (1963), 15–82 and his references.
6. *MGH Conc.* II, i, No. 34, c. 8.
7. C. Courtois, 'L'évolution du Monachisme en Gaule de St Martin à St Colomban', *Settimane* 4 (1957), 47–72. See also F. Prinz, *Frühesmönchtum im Frankenreich* (Munich 1965), and *Askese und Kultur: vor and früh benediktinisches Mönchtum an der Wiege Europas* (Munich 1980).
8. G. Walker (ed.) *Sancti Columbani Opera* (Dublin 1970).
9. *Vita Mauri, AA SS* 15 Jan. and compare *AA SS O.S.B.* (1668) 274–98 and VI (1680) 165–84; see J. McCann, *Saint Benedict*, 2nd edn. (London 1979) 274–81.
10. See L. Traube, 'Textgeschichte der Regula Sancti Benedicti', (2nd edn H. Planckers) *Abhandlungen der königlichen Bayerischen Akademie der Wissenschaften*, Philos.-Philol. und Hist. Kl. 25 (Munich 1910), 34–5.
11. Ibid., 35.
12. *MGH Cap.* I, No. 14, c. 11, 35.
13. C. de Clercq (ed.), *Concilia Galliae A.511–A.695* (Turnholt 1963), c. 13(12), 180.
14. C. Holdsworth, 'Boniface the monk', *The Greatest Englishman* T. Reuter (ed.) (Exeter 1980), 49–67.
15. *MGH SS* I, 39, *Annales Laureshamenses*, 802.
16. I here follow J. Semmler, 'Karl der Grosse und das fränkische Mönchtum', *KdG* II, 255–89.
17. *MGH Conc.* II, i. 307–464.
18. *MGH Leges* I, 219 and see Böhmer-Mühlbacher, Nos. 678, 679, 680.
19. A. Werminghoff, 'Die Beschlusse des Aachener Konzils im Jahre 816', *Neues Archiv* 27 (1902), 605–75.
20. K. Hallinger (ed.), *Corpus Consuetudinum Monasticarum* I (Siegburg 1963), 423–82.
21. See McKitterick, *Frankish Church*, 115–54.
22. P. Schmitz, 'L'influence de Saint Benoît d'Aniane dans l'Histoire de l'ordre de Saint Benoît', *Settimane* 4 (1957), 401–15.
23. Hildemar, c. 8.
24. See the discussion by W. Horn and E. Born, *The Plan of St Gall* (Berkeley 3 vols, 1979), II, 300–13.
25. K. Voigt, *Karolingische Klosterpolitik* (Stuttgart 1917), but see F. Felten, 'Laienäbte in der Karolingerzeit. Ein Beitrag zum Problem des Adelsherrschaft über die Kirche', *Mönchtum, Episkopat, Adel zur Gründungszeit des Klosters Reichenau* A. Borst (ed.), (Sigmaringen 1974), 397–432, and idem, *Äbte und Laienäbte im Frankenreich* (Stuttgart 1980).
26. *MGH Conc.* II, i., No. 19G, c. 16, 168.
27. J. Semmler, 'Zur Überlieferung der monastischen Gesetzgebung Ludwigs des Frommen', *DA* 16 (1960), 309–88.
28. E. Lesne, 'Les ordonnances monastiques de Louis le Pieux et la *Notitia de servitio monasteriorum*', *Revue d'Histoire de l'Eglise de France* 6 (1920), 161–75, 321–38, 449–93.
29. J. Semmler, 'Studien zum *Supplex Libellus* und zur anianischen Reform in Fulda', *ZfK* 69 (1958), 268–98, and 'Corvey und Herford in der benediktinischen

Reformbewegung des 9. Jhts', *Frümittelalterliche Studien* 4 (1970), 289–319.

30. Bouquet, *Recueil* VI, 575–8.
31. Ibid., 530–1.
32. Ibid., 513–14.
33. Horn and Born, *The Plan of St Gall*, I, 20–5.
34. For a description of the manuscript, see Traube, 'Textgeschichte der Regula Sancti Benedicti', 49–50.
35. Paul the Deacon, *Historia Langobardorum*, IV, 17.
36. Ibid., VI, 40.
37. See B. Linderbauer, *S. Benedicti regula monasteriorum* (Bonn 1928).
38. J. Gilissen, 'Observations codicologiques sur le codex Sangallensis 914'. *Miscellanea Codicologica F. Masai Dicata*, P. Cockshaw, M. C. Garand and P. Jodogne (eds) (Ghent 1979), 51–70.
39. P. Meyvaert, 'Towards a history of the textual transmission of the Regula sancti Benedicti', *Scriptorium* 17 (1963), 95–100.
40. P. Lehmann, *Mittelalterliche Bibliothekskataloge Deutschlands und der Schweiz* I (Munich 1918), 260.
41. J. Winandy, 'Un témoignage oublié sur les anciens usages Cassiniens', *Revue Bénédictine* 48 (1938), 254–92.
42. *MGH Epp.* V, No. 7, 64–6.
43. Hallinger, *Corpus Consuetudinum Monasticarum* I, 125–57 and compare Traube, 'Textgeschichte der Regula Sancti Benedicti', 25.
44. Walker, *Sancti Columbani Opera*, 122–80.
45. *Gesta abbatum Fontanellensium*, c. IX.2 and XIII.4.
46. Hariulf, III, c. 3.
47. Lehmann, *Mittelalterliche Bibliothekskataloge* I, 251.
48. G. Becker (ed.), *Catalogi Bibliothecarum Antiqui* (Bonn 1885), No. 13, and see P. Lehmann, 'Fuldaer Studien', *Sitzungsberichte der Bayerischen Akademie der Wissenschaften*, Phil. Hist. Kl. (Munich 1925), 6–10.
49. Lehmann, *Mittelalterliche Bibliothekskataloge* I, 77.
50. Hallinger, *Corpus Consuetudinum Monasticarum*, 501–36.
51. *MGH Cap.* I, No. 138, 275–7.
52. Felten, cited n. 25 above.
53. W. Goffard, *The Le Mans Forgeries* (Cambridge, Mass. 1966), 11.
54. G. Constable, *Monastic Tithes from their Origins to the Twelfth Century* (Cambridge 1964), 31–56.
55. Böhmer–Mühlbacher provide a calendar of these; the texts are printed in Bouquet, *Recueil* VI. A new edition is badly needed.
56. *MGH Cap.* I, No. 138, 275–81.
57. Böhmer–Mühlbacher, No. 818, *PL* 104, col. 1316.
58. J. Semmler, 'Reichsidee und kirchliche Gesetzgebung', *ZfK* 71 (1966), 37–65.
59. T. F. X. Noble, 'The monastic ideal as a model for Empire: the case of Louis the Pious', *Revue Bénédictine* 86 (1976), 235–50, and compare idem, 'Louis the Pious and his piety reconsidered', *Revue Belge de Philologie et d'Histoire* 58 (1980), 297–316.
60. F. L. Ganshof, 'Louis the Pious reconsidered', *History* 42 (1957), 171–80.
61. T. F. X. Noble, 'Louis the Pious and the Papacy: law, politics and the theory of Empire in the early ninth century', Ph.D. diss., Michigan State University, 1974, and T. Schieffer, 'Die Krise der karolingische Imperiums', *Aus Mittelalter und Neuzeit: Festschrift für Gerhard Kallen*, J. Engel and H. M. Klinkenberg (eds) (Bonn 1957), 1–15.

62. J. Fleckenstein, *Die Hofkapelle der deutschen Könige* I (Stuttgart 1959), 51–74.
63. See the discussion in McKitterick, *Frankish Church*, 18–21.
64. Ganshof, 'Louis the Pious reconsidered', 178.
65. Fleckenstein, *Hofkapelle*, 105–8.
66. *MGH Cap.* II, No. 191, c. 5 and c. 9, 134; No. 192, c. 1 and c. 8, 14–15; No. 193, c. 1, c. 5, c. 8, 18–20.
67. K. Christ, 'Die Schlossbibliothek von Nikolsburg und die Überlieferung der Kapitulariensammlung des Ansegis', *DA* 1 (1937), 281–322.
68. For example, *MGH Cap.* I, No. 141, 289–92, No. 146, 298, No. 148, 300–2; *MGH Cap.* II, Nos. 187 and 188, 9–11, No. 192, 14.
69. K. F. Werner, '*Missus-Marchio-Comes*. Entre l'administration centrale et l'administration locale de l'Empire', *Beihefte der Francia* 9 (Munich 1980), 190–239.
70. Böhmer–Mühlbacher, Nos. 719, 715 and 735.
71. See Ganshof, 'Louis the Pious reconsidered' and *Frankish Institutions under Charlemagne* (New York 1970), 59–70.
72. See. J. L. Rosenthal, 'The public assembly in the time of Louis the Pious', *Traditio* 20 (1964), 25–40.
73. *Annales regni Francorum, s.a.*, 822. On the Slavs see A. P. Vlasto, *The Entry of the Slavs into Christendom* (Cambridge 1970).
74. *Vita Anskarii* and E. de Moreau, *Un missionaire en Scandinavie au IX siècle: saint Anschaire* (Louvain 1930). Compare the account of Adam of Bremen.
75. On Louis' policy of conquest, see A. Hauck, *Kirchengeschichte Deutschlands* (Leipzig 5 vols, 1904–20), II, 690.
76. Astronomer, c. 23.
77. P. Classen, 'Romanum gubernans imperium', *DA* 9 (1951), 103–21.
78. Noble, 'Louis the Pious and the Papacy'.
79. Compare the election of the Popes recorded in *Annales regni Francorum, s.a.*, 817, 824, 827.
80. *Annales regni Francorum, s.a.*, 816.
81. Ermold the Black, *In honorem Hludowici*, lines 1040–7; Astronomer c. 26, Thegan, c. 16 and *Annales regni Francorum, s.a.* 816.
82. Noble, 'Louis the Pious and the Papacy', 102.
83. Ermold the Black, *In honorem Hludowici*, lines 1074–5.
84. *MGH Cap.* I, No. 172, 353–5.
85. *MGH Cap.* I, No. 161, 322–4.
86. *MGH Epp* V, 230–1 and compare the letter from Agobard, bishop of Lyons, *MGH Epp* V, 227.
87. Noble, 'Louis the Pious and the Papacy', 335.
88. L. Weinrich, *Wala, Graf, Mönch und Rebell* (Lübeck and Hamburg 1963), and Paschasius Radbert, *Epitaphium Arsenii* and *Vita Adalhardi*.
89. Semmler, 'Die Beschlusse des Aachener Konzils im Jahre 816', 76–82.
90. Ermold the Black, *In honorem Hludowici*, lines 682–97.
91. Bouquet, *Recueil* VI, 473, and see A. Kleinclausz, *Eginhard* (Paris 1942), 58–67.
92. *Annales regni Francorum, s.a.*, 817, and see K. Brunner, *Oppositionelle Gruppen im Karolingerreich* (Vienna 1979).
93. *MGH Cap.* I, 270–3; trs. B. Pullan, *Sources for the History of Medieval Europe* (Oxford 1966), 37–42.
94. Astronomer, c. 49. and L. Halphen, 'La pénitence de Louis le Pieux à Saint Médard de Soissons', *Bibliothèque de la Faculté des Lettres de Paris* (Paris 1904), 177–85.

CHAPTER SIX

The Foundations of the Carolingian Renaissance

Very closely related to the political, ecclesiastical and legal developments of the eighth and ninth centuries that have been discussed in the preceding five chapters, was the burgeoning of intellectual and cultural life usually described as the 'Carolingian Renaissance'. What forms this 'Renaissance' took, its origins and principal exponents, need to be more closely defined.

I

It is now generally recognized that in Gaul, with Spain, the British Isles and Italy, an intellectual and cultural tradition common to the whole of Europe developed in the course of the sixth, seventh and eighth centuries. It was a tradition shaped in the barbarian kingdoms from both Christian and classical sources. In England the new culture developed by the Anglo-Saxons was largely based on that imported by Christian missionaries from both the Mediterranean and Ireland; but in Gaul, Spain and Italy there was a far greater element of continuity with the civilization of the late Roman Empire. In the context of Merovingian and Carolingian cultural development, moreover, to concentrate on the Carolingian achievement is to attach too little importance to the formative influence of the Merovingian period. By the mid-eighth century, when the Carolingian Pippin ascended to the throne, many of the principal centres of culture and lines of development were already established.

In Roman Gaul the educational system of classical antiquity with its emphasis on grammar, dialectic, the work of the great poets and dramatists and the professional treatises on law, medicine and technical subjects had been taught.[1] The centres of culture had been in the towns, such as Arles, Marseilles, Avignon and Vienne, and the Gallo-Roman senatorial families such as the Leontii, the Sulpicii and the Apollinarii had felt themselves to be responsible for the preservation and transmission of the old Roman Latin culture from generation to generation.

In the fifth century this classical secular culture was still dominant, but in the course of the sixth century a distinctly Christian and ecclesiastical culture began to emerge. Arles under the great preacher Caesarius (469/70–542) became a centre of religious culture; the cities where a series of church councils was held under the auspices of the Frankish kings – Orleans, Tours, Clermont, Lyons and Mâcon – assumed prominence. The bishops who attended these councils came from the provinces of Bourges, Sens and Lyons and were still for the most part Gallo-Roman aristocrats and men of letters in the old secular manner. Gregory, bishop of Tours, writing at the end of the sixth century, took it for granted that bishops would have studied the authors of the old Roman curriculum, yet he himself, although a member of a family which included many senators and bishops among its members, was of a new order; Gregory had been educated and trained in an episcopal establishment, and while he took steps to acquire a knowledge of the classical authors in later life, his primary sources of inspiration and language were Christian. The episcopal schools such as those which probably existed at Bourges, Poitiers, Clermont and possibly Lyons were still modest affairs, but they too are signs of a new order; they offered a professional training in the reading of Scripture, chant and the administration of the sacraments of the church. Riché has noted how the predominantly secular culture of Gallo-Roman Gaul had become by the seventh century a predominantly ecclesiastical culture in which only a minority possessed a knowledge of the classical authors and a rather larger minority was versed in Christian texts.[2] Yet, to judge a civilization by the extent to which it did or did not preserve the culture of classical antiquity is surely misleading. That a Christian and religious culture should become dominant is one aspect of the transformation of the intellectual and cultural tradition of early medieval Europe rather than its principal characteristic. The barbarians of the Frankish kingdoms were in fact shaping an entirely new culture and a new society.

II

A major problem in tracing the development of the new Christian and ecclesiastical culture in Gaul is one of evidence. We can learn a little from the surviving manuscripts. Some 300 manuscripts or fragments of manuscripts written between about 500 and 750 in Gaul survive.[3] The production of these books and the evolution of a minuscule script (to be discussed in detail below) argue the existence of centres which could produce books and had a sufficient interest in their contents to do so. Very few classical works were copied and apparently none at all in the eighth century.[4] There are copies of the Theodosian code, biblical and liturgical books and the works of the Christian fathers such as Augustine, Jerome and Gregory the Great, as well as 'local' authors such as Hilary of Poitiers, Avitus of Vienne and Faustus of Riez. Book production never actually ceased in Gaul, but it is difficult to locate manuscripts exactly to the place of origin in the early period. There were a number of centres round Lyons in the sixth and seventh centuries and Luxeuil had a flourishing scriptorium from the second half of the seventh century until its sack in 732.

It is possible to trace a geographical progression, linked to the chronological, from south to north of the surviving Merovingian codices; by the eighth century the main centres of book production are north of the Loire, with the principal scriptoria in the great monasteries in north and north-east France. One reason for the emergence of the northern centres, apart from the concentration of Frankish power in the region, was the destruction of the south in the course of the campaigns waged by Charles Martel and Pippin III. Aquitaine, Provence and Burgundy suffered greatly, and the cultural pre-eminence the region had enjoyed in the Gallo-Roman and Merovingian periods was lost. The northern monasteries became the new centres of learning. It was in the monasteries that the teachers and scholars were trained and that the books they needed were written and copied; it was there that some of the clergy were taught as well as the sons of kings and nobles.

Again it is the manuscript evidence that reveals most about the emergence of different centres in the second half of the eighth century. Scriptoria or writing centres at Lyons, Autun, Flavigny and other unidentified centres in Burgundy, Cambrai, the nunnery at Chelles, Corbie, Fleury, the centre responsible for the 'az-type' of script, Meaux, Metz, various centres in the north and north-east, a scriptorium closely associated with the royal court, St Amand, Tours and a number of monasteries in Germany – Echternach, Freising, Regensburg, Salzburg, Augsburg, Reichenau, St Gall and Würzburg – were all producing books by the end of the eighth century and the number of active scriptoria was to increase rapidly in the course of the ninth century. The subject-matter of the books these centres produced is similar to that of the Merovingian centres. Books of the Bible, liturgical books, canon law and patristic texts predominate, but there is already a good sprinkling of school texts.[5] Yet the Carolingians produced far more books than the Merovingians; in the course of the ninth century the range of books copied or written was extended widely, and classical authors were copied again.

It is not only with the production of books that the emergent Frankish culture is to be identified. As well as copies of the works of earlier authors, some native works are known from the seventh and eighth centuries. A great number of saints' Lives were composed at this time, some of which were reworked in the ninth century, such as the *Vita sancti Richarii* and the *Vita sancti Vedasti*. The activities of missionaries in Alemannia, northern France and Flanders were recorded in the saints' lives, as were the deeds of aristocratic and royal founders and foundresses of monasteries. Saints Amand, Vedast, Germanus of Auxerre, Genofeva, Chrothild, Caesarius of Arles, Chlodovald, Germanus of Paris and Radegund (both these written by Venantius Fortunatus) Eligius of Noyon, Audoen of Rouen, Balthild, queen to Clovis II, Leudegar of Autun, Bavo of Ghent, Geretrud of Nivelles, Wandregisil and Ansbert of Fontanelle, Amatus, and Sadalberga of Laon are among the Merovingian men and women commemorated in this way.

Other literary genres also survive. At the monastery of St Medard at Soissons, Numidius in about 695 had the homilies of Caesarius of Arles copied, and in *c.* 700 Defensor, a monk at Ligugé, compiled the *Liber Scintillarum*, a collection of extracts from the Old and New Testaments, Augustine, Jerome, Gregory the Great, Isidore, Hilary of Poitiers and Basil the Great on various matters germane to the monastic life. Theofrid of Corbie composed a rhythmic abecedarian verse on the Creation and the six ages of the world, a monk of St Cyran wrote the *Visio Baronti*, a strange vision of hell, and there were also collections made of letters such as the *Epistolae Austriacae*, the letters of Desiderius of Cahors (d. 655) and the letters of Frodebertus or Chrodebert (653–74) to Importunus of Paris. Seventh- and eighth-century historiography is represented by the so-called Chronicle of Fredegar and its Continuations and the *Liber Historiae Francorum*, probably written at the monastery of St Denis in about 727. In Germany the evidence for literary production is rather more sparse, but there are again a number of saints' Lives, such as the *Vita Hrodoberti*, founder of St Peter's Salzburg, and the *Vita Corbiniani* by Arbeo, bishop of Freising. Literary activity has been associated with the circle of Arbeo of Freising and Virgil of Salzburg; to the latter has been attributed the weird Cosmography by Aethicus Ister.[6] The Latin of most of these works is far from polished, and in some instances is hardly Latin at all. Writers of the seventh and eighth century knew well what style and rhetorical figures were but lacked sufficient basic training in Latin grammar and composition to be polished in their literary effort. Whether one reads the barbarian law codes, the saints' Lives, the poetry or the treatises of this period, the language is undoubtedly vigorous but is very different from that of the late Roman writers, let alone Cicero.

Many of the monasteries which emerged as centres of literary activity or book production in the second half of the eighth century enjoyed royal or aristocratic patronage, and it is patronage which emerges as one of the most important features of the Carolingian Renaissance. Corbie, for example, had been founded by Queen Balthild, and its first abbot and group of brethren came from Luxeuil at her request. Literary activity is attested there from the seventh century, and, as we shall see, it was at Corbie that the earliest example of Caroline minuscule was written. Echternach, St Denis and Tours were among the many monasteries favoured by the Carolingians. That these monasteries assumed such prominence in both the political and cultural life of the kingdom is largely due to the strong position in which they were placed by the Carolingians.

Not much is known, however, of the extent to which Pippin's court itself was a centre of culture. The Merovingian court had been in the seventh century a centre of education in the broad sense of the word, in that young aristocrats were sent there to be trained; it is probable that the palace of the mayor also acquired this function. There is evidence furthermore to suggest that not all aristocrats were illiterate. In the Lyons region, two ladies, Constantina and Justina, owned copies of a selection of Christian tracts, now Lyons Bibliothèque de la Ville MSS 426 and 604. Ragyndrudis, daughter of Arthuolf, had the Synonyma of Isidore copied for her (now Fulda Codex Bonifatius 2) and the

Gundohinus Gospels (Autun Bibliothèque Municipale MS 3) were written at the request of Fausta in 754. All these were women, but signatures on charters indicate that some of the men too were literate. The sons of Charles Martel were the first Frankish princes (if we exclude Dagobert II) that we know to have been educated in a monastery. Pippin III was educated at St Denis, and one of Charles Martel's illegitimate sons, Jerome, at St Amand. Pippin remained closely associated with St Denis; one of his principal advisers, Fulrad, was abbot there, it was there that he built a new church, and there that he, and many of his successors, were buried. Riché conjectures that it was in Lombardy, at King Liutprand's court at Pavia whence Pippin was sent at the age of twenty-one, that Pippin would have observed a cultured court and perhaps learnt to regard it as one essential feature of a royal establishment.[7] There is no evidence that Pippin actually took any personal initiative in promoting letters at his Frankish court, but his promotion of religious culture, ably assisted by such men as Chrodegang of Metz, has already been discussed in Chapter Three.

In the judicial sphere too, the court was a centre of activity; the language and protocol of the charters improved and a number of *Formulae* collections were compiled (though not all these were produced at court) as well as a new redaction of the Salic law. The relations with the Papacy and the number of foreign – mainly Byzantine and Italian – emissaries is thought to have had some effect in widening the cultural horizons of the Franks. Even though young aristocrats and protégés of men of influence were probably sent to Pippin's court to be trained to serve the king in some capacity, whether in the chancery, the chapel or at arms, it was not until some years after the accession of Charlemagne to the throne that the cultivation of letters and scholarship became associated with court life.

An important event for the development of Carolingian culture in the eighth century was the arrival of the Anglo-Saxon missionaries on the Continent, and in particular, the work of Willibrord, Boniface and their disciples and the monasteries they founded. Although their primary impact was on the religious life of Frisia and Germany, Boniface was active in promoting reform in the Frankish church as well. The Anglo-Saxons brought with them a number of ancient codices such as the Laudian Acts and introduced the writings of a number of earlier scholars, possibly unknown or forgotten hitherto on the Continent, such as the poems of Porphyrius, the minor works of Tacitus, the histories of Ammianus Marcellinus and the *De Architectura* of Vitruvius; they also imported the work of English authors, especially Bede and Aldhelm. Bede's biblical exegesis and his treatises on time, rather than his Ecclesiastical History, were of great importance, and it was Bede's works which were responsible for the popularization of the custom of dating according to the year of the Incarnation. The earliest extant manuscript of Bede's Ecclesiastical History, written in about 737, now Cambridge University Library MS Kk.v.16 (the Moore Bede) was at Charlemagne's court at the end of the eighth century. Boniface procured books from England and Alcuin too, as we shall see later, sent to York for books to be sent to him at Tours. Northumbria, Mercia, Kent and

Wessex had a well-developed religious culture by the end of the seventh century. It is usually assumed that this religious culture was a distinctive and different one from that on the other side of the Channel, and that it was brought to the Continent by the Anglo-Saxon missionaries, but it has yet to be established in what way, and what particular elements of Anglo-Saxon culture were transplanted to the Continent.[8] Study of the Continental manuscript tradition of English authors in the Carolingian period would be one way of testing a long-held assumption.

III

Both Alcuin and Einhard praised Charlemagne for his efforts which had brought about a 'rebirth' of knowledge and erudition. We have seen, however, that a distinctive Christian culture had been developing in the Frankish kingdoms since the fifth century, so we need to ask, in the face of these ninth-century assertions, exactly what contribution Charlemagne made to this development.

The two most important declarations of the wishes and aims of Charlemagne and his advisers as far as learning and education are concerned are the *De litteris colendis* and the *Admonitio Generalis* of 789. The *Admonitio Generalis* is quite specific in its seventy-second chapter: 'let schools be established in which boys may learn to read. Correct carefully the Psalms, grammar, calendar and so on in each diocese, because often some desire to pray to God properly but they pray badly because of their incorrect books.'[9] The *De litteris colendis* was written, possibly at Charlemagne's dictation, between 780 and 800, and addressed to Baugulf, abbot of Fulda.[10] Various attempts have been made to date the letter more exactly; the composition of the original letter can possibly be attributed to Angilramn, bishop of Metz, and can thus be dated between 781 and 791, the dates at which Angilramn came to serve Charlemagne in the royal chancery and the year of his death respectively.[11] It is by the merest chance that we know about this letter at all. It survived in only two manuscripts, one of the twelfth century which was destroyed in a bombing raid in 1944, and the other which was found in an eighth-century Oxford manuscript, Bodleian Laud misc. 126, by Paul Lehmann in 1927. Although the letter is addressed to Baugulf, abbot of Fulda, Charlemagne directed that extra copies of it were to be made and distributed to every abbey and bishopric in the kingdom. The letter states that it is Charlemagne's wish that monasteries and bishoprics should devote themselves not only to the observance of monastic discipline and the practice of the religious life, but should also cultivate learning and educate the monks and secular clergy so that they might reach a better understanding of the Christian writings. That the king should make a personal appeal to a number of individuals underlines one of the essential characteristics of the Carolingian 'Renaissance'; it was supported by individuals who worked together with a common purpose and sometimes common methods.

It will be evident that both the *De litteris colendis* and the *Admonitio Generalis* are quite explicit about the primary purpose of the revival of learning. It was to facilitate understanding of the Scriptures and the major Christian writers; it was to enable people to praise God and pray to him in a proper manner; the learning encouraged is a Christian learning and the scholar and teacher are to be men of Christian letters. With his patronage and encouragement of learning and education Charlemagne accelerated and gave form to the development which had had its slow beginnings in the fifth century.

Evidence about the schools of the Carolingians is sparse and ambiguous; generally there are only references to schools rather than precise information about them. Theodulf of Orleans in his episcopal statute recommended to his clergy that schools be set up in the towns and villages for the 'children of the faithful'. At these schools, letters, that is, reading and possibly writing were to be taught. Theodulf was firm that the instruction given should be free. The teachers were to be the clergy, and he urged that they should neither demand, expect nor accept payment. The priest's reward would be the wisdom the children acquired. Theodulf also recommended the schools to which 'relatives' of the clergy could be sent. He lists the schools in his own diocese of Orleans: the schools in the church of the Holy Cross, in the monasteries of St Aniane, St Benedict and St Lifard, or any of the schools in other monasteries which came under the episcopal authority of Theodulf.[12] Theodulf has mentioned two different sorts of school: one offering elementary education to the children of the faithful in the towns and villages, the other education in a monastery for the 'relatives' of the clergy. It may well be the case that these two types of school are really one and the same, for probably many people could claim to be a 'relative' of the clergy. That is, the so-called 'parish schools' were actually accommodated in the nearest monastery.

Another text gives us some more information. In the History of the Abbey of St Riquier, written in the eleventh century, is included a description of a liturgical procession written by Angilbert abbot of St Riquier in the early years of the ninth century. After the seven crosses and priests, deacons, subdeacons, acolytes, exorcists, lectors, *ostiarii* (doorkeepers) and the monks came the boys of the lay school and of the abbey school.[13] This suggests that there were indeed two types of school to which one could go. Angilbert does not make it clear whether one had to belong to a certain class or intend to join the church to go to one or another. The *Admonitio Generalis* said that schools were to be set up for boys from every station in life, but in 817 Louis the Pious decreed that only those intending to be monks should be taught in the monastic schools.[14]

At this point we can bring in another piece of evidence. The St Gall Plan, St Gall Stiftsbibliothek MS 1092, written *c.* 820, makes provision for two schools, an external school, a little removed from the main cluster of the monastic buildings, and the inner school, or Novitiate, east of the church. The provision for schools on the Plan seems to carry out the requirements of Louis the Pious' reform legislation; it has been suggested by Walter Horn that the decree refers to the Novitiate; that is, the external school was for the instruction of laymen and future priests, and the internal school for the instruction of future monks.[15] There is a further clarification of this suggestion to be made, and this has to do with what was actually taught in the schools. In a narrative account of the history of St Gall, there is a reference to the time of Abbot Grimald 841–72, when the Irish monk Marcellus was placed in charge of the inner school and the monk Iso in charge of the outer school. Later teachers, Ratpert, Notker Balbulus, Notker the Physician and the four Ekkehards, are referred to as teaching in both. It may therefore be that the external school was the elementary school where everyone would be taught the rudiments regardless of their eventual vocation, while the internal school offered a more advanced education for those who had decided to withdraw from the world. They would also be involved in the work of the scriptorium and library. Those who had stayed in the world could receive further training at court or in a cathedral school.

Cathedral schools were probably similar to the monastic schools, at least in the education they offered. Arno, bishop of Salzburg, insisted on the theological education of his priests and the maintenance of the cathedral schools; every bishop was to set up a school in his city and learned men were to teach there according to the 'Roman tradition'.[16] The cathedral school at Metz became famous for its chant, and at Laon students by the second half of the ninth century could achieve an advanced level of learning in philosophy, theology, Latin, Greek and music. According to the decrees of the assembly held at Attigny in 822, the work of general education seems to have fallen to the episcopal and cathedral schools, though we have seen that the bishop could also have a say in the monastic schools.[17] The bishops at Attigny insisted on the necessity for providing at least one school in every diocese, or two or three schools if the area were exceptionally large. At the synod at Paris in 829 the bishops also requested that royal 'public' schools be established; they insisted that they were responsible for the suitable education of the clergy and that every bishop ought to include a school in his cathedral establishment.[18] The request for royal 'public' schools was not implemented so far as we know.

Although so little is known about Carolingian schools, rather more is known about the curriculum. It was similar to that of the early Christian schools and those of Merovingian Gaul and eighth-century England. Basic arithmetical knowledge was taught by means of a *computus*, which gave instruction in understanding the calendar, calculating the phases of the moon, the feasts of the Christian year – particularly that of Easter – and rules of simple arithmetic. There is some doubt, however, as to whether arithmetic as distinct from the basic chronology taught in the calendar *computus* was actually a subject for schoolboys. Murray thinks it more likely that arithmetic was studied only by a handful of mature students and that they found it difficult. He has argued that there was very little interest in arithmetic in the early Carolingian period though it began to develop, as we shall see, in the course of the tenth century. Elementary studies could also include geography, and the study of the climate and could lead to astronomy, a useful thing to know for agriculture, navigation and even medicine. In a world ruled by the elements, the sun and the moon, where the rhythm of the seasons was known from sense and observation and where hardly anyone would possess a clock, some familiarity with the measurement of time, as well as a modicum of numeracy, was a sophisticated and necessary subject to be learned.[19] Writing may have been taught generally at a basic level, but this is by no means certain, and there is no information about it. Reading on the other hand was certainly taught, and was made more difficult for the young Franks in the Germanic-speaking regions at least, in that they did not learn to read the language they spoke every day, but had to learn to read and write in a second language, Latin. Latin was the language of the church, of administration and of learning; no school-books were written in the vernacular until the tenth century, and then only in the eastern part of the kingdom.

The first reading matter in any school was the Psalter. St Benedict's Rule had stipulated that the entire Psalter should be sung through every week. Anyone at a monastic school would probably have known the Psalter by heart before he understood a word of it. As a young boy, Gregory, bishop of Utrecht, was questioned on the meaning of the Psalter passage he had read to Boniface, but was forced to admit he had read it without understanding it at all.[20] The Psalter is often recommended for use in the schools, every monastery had at least one, and some houses possessed multiple copies, though these would also have been used in the church. The library catalogue of Reichenau, for example, dated 821, lists no less than fifty Psalters.[21] Some manuscripts of the Psalter moreover, according to Bernhard Bischoff, were set out as school-books rather than as books for church use. That is, the text was written in large letters, like an infant's reading book, and there were points between each word to make them clear.

The grammars of Donatus and Priscian were the other two most important books for instruction in reading Latin, even though both books are much more concerned with providing definitions for, and commentary on, the parts of speech than explaining Latin grammar as it would be explained in a modern textbook. Both the grammars of the fourth-century grammarian Donatus, the *Ars Minor*, which is merely a framework of a grammar (it only conjugates one verb and declines only first-declension nouns), and the *Ars Maior* were particularly widely used in the ninth century and are listed in a number of ninth-century library catalogues. Reichenau, for example, possessed four copies, as well as a book of excerpted definitions of the various parts of speech from Donatus and the *Institutiones Grammaticae* of Priscian.[22] Priscian's grammar, written in the sixth century, seems to have become more popular in the Frankish kingdom as a school-book after about 820. The manuscript tradition of both authors' works attests to their use. So do references to them by Carolingian scholars. Lupus of Ferrières for example, cited Donatus' opinion on the pronunciation of words, and whether the penultimate syllable of a word should be pronounced long or short. He wrote: 'I still have difficulty with the problem, not being certain whether one should observe nature, whether the penultimate syllable should be pronounced long, as it is, or whether on account of the Rule Donatus gives.'[23] Lupus' letter highlights the problems of a Carolingian scholar endeavouring to get things right and to find his way in a whole new realm of knowledge.

One manuscript of Donatus' *Ars Minor* that I have discussed elsewhere can even tell us a little about the teaching procedure,[24] as can the St Gall Priscian, St Gall Stiftsbibliothek 904, which has been studied by Maartje Draak.[25] Draak has followed in her study of this manuscript 'the direction of thought of an Irish grammarian at the monastery of St Gall in the ninth century, when reading and expounding Priscian's Latin grammar to some of his Irish pupils there'. These students' native tongue was Old Irish, a language very different in its structure and word order from Latin. The manuscript is packed with little signs – ticks, commas, letters of the alphabet – and if these are investigated, they prove to be the way the Irish teacher explained the word order as it would have been in an Irish sentence, so that his students could 'unpack' it.

Most of the frequently used school texts for elementary instruction in the Carolingian period were concerned either to paraphrase the Bible or to discuss the Christian and saintly virtues. With some knowledge of the Psalter, grammar and arithmetic, the student could then proceed on the one hand to a study of Christian didactic texts, written for the most part in the fourth and fifth centuries as an alternative to the classical pagan educational tradition and its texts, and on the other hand to the didactic treatises and manuals composed by the Carolingians themselves. When we consider the Carolingian curriculum we are in fact looking at what was to be the basis of a cleric's or layman's schooling for the whole of the Middle Ages. The books which formed the core of this curriculum have been identified by Detlef Illmer and other scholars, so that it is now possible to define a canon of the school texts used in the Carolingian period.[26]

Many older Christian didactic texts were included in this canon. In the course of the fifth century some Christian grammarians and rhetors had transformed the Old and New Testaments into epic poems according to the classical rules of poetry. The books of the Bible, for example, were adapted into hexameters; Avitus of Vienne (d. *c.* 500) wrote a biblical epic in which the theme of Paradise Lost made its first real appearance in Latin poetry; Juvencus, a fourth-century Spaniard, wrote a Gospel Harmony in verse by conflating the stories of Christ related in the four Gospels; the *Paschale Carmen* of Sedulius, a poet from southern Gaul, told of the Old and New Testament wonder stories relating to Christ's coming and the Resurrection; Arator, a scholar from Liguria in the service of the Visigothic King Athalaric, made a Latin epic out of the Acts of the Apostles, and Paulinus of Pella produced a hexameter verse paraphrase of the Psalms. All these texts were popular with the Carolingians, and their moral emphasis was particularly influential. Augustine in his *De doctrina Christiana* had defined the principles of education as designed to deepen a man's religious culture, and this was something the Carolingians believed as well. Saints' Lives appear to have been an important part of Carolingian school education, and from my own study of some manuscript collections of saints' Lives I think it is possible that copying them out was a writing exercise for aspiring scribes, and that these manuscripts provide important evidence for the process of learning to write in the Carolingian period; I have yet to present the full case for this. The most widely read moral treatise was the *Psychomachia* of Prudentius (d. 465), written in the form of an account of a pitched and bloody battle between personified vices and virtues. Some Carolingian copies of this poem are illustrated with lively drawings.

The *Disticha Catonis*, a collection of sayings and aphorisms of predominantly moral content dating from the fourth century, was also well known. Some history was read in the schools, but it was the History of the church by Eusebius and Orosius' Seven books against the pagans rather than their own native history which was read by the Franks.

More advanced learning was based primarily on the works of Isidore of Seville, Martianus Capella and Boethius. The dramas of Terence and collections of extracts from the classical authors were also used for teaching Latin and versifying. Isidore's *Etymologiae* and the *De natura rerum* were handbooks of contemporary knowledge of the world, and Martianus Capella's extraordinary On the Marriage of Mercury and Philology was used as a reference book on all subjects of the 'seven liberal arts'. It established the divisions of knowledge for the curriculum of the medieval schools and later the medieval universities. The term *trivium* for the first three liberal arts, grammar, dialectic and rhetoric, was first employed by the Carolingians. The term *quadrivium* referred to the last four liberal arts, geometry, music, arithmetic and astronomy. The final stage in the educational system lasted for the rest of the scholar's life. Having acquired all the knowledge I have described so far, he was at last equipped to study the Bible and the writings of the church fathers, Augustine, Ambrose, Jerome, Gregory the Great, Leo the Great and many more, and to venture for himself into the rich pastures of exegesis and theology.

In this context the text of the Bible itself was of the greatest importance. In the fourth century, Jerome, a Christian scholar from Strido near Aquileia, had set himself to provide a Latin Bible whose books were translated from the original languages concerned (Hebrew, Greek, Aramaic) into simple and straightforward Latin. The texts of the Bible in existence before Jerome included the Hebrew Old Testament which hardly any non-Jews could read; Origen's *Hexapla*, an elaborate edition of the Old Testament with Hebrew, Hebrew transliterated into Greek letters and four Greek versions in parallel columns; the *Septuagint* or Greek text of the Old Testament translated from the Hebrew at Alexandria probably in the first century BC (reputedly by seventy scholars) which was greatly respected because of its antiquity; the Old Latin version or *Itala* used in the West from before the end of the second century and probably of far from uniform origin. Jerome changed all this, at least as far as the western Mediterranean and Western Europe were concerned, by translating the Old Testament from the Hebrew into Latin and the Gospels from Aramaic and Greek into Latin to produce the Vulgate version of the Bible. All Jerome's translations did not become the only ones in use straight away. The Old Latin version remained current for some time, but by the seventh century the new Vulgate was on the way to being the dominant version.

As a result of local liturgical usage and local familiarity, slightly variant text types (sometimes no more than different spelling or word order) developed. Among these were the southern Italian type introduced into Northumbria, and the Spanish, Anglo-Saxon, Irish, Swiss, Gallic and Aquitainian types. Some regions also preferred different translations of particular books of the Bible such as some of the Old Latin translations and alternative translations Jerome had made of the Psalter (he made three). This meant that by the Carolingian period there was considerable confusion, with no one standard collection of the different books of the Bible generally accepted. Revision was undertaken by Alcuin at Charlemagne's request. The southern Italian text type transmitted to Northumbria (represented by the *Codex Amiatinus*) formed the backbone of his work. Alcuin's aim was to provide a correct text of the Scriptures and his editorial activity was largely devoted to cleaning up errors in punctuation, grammar and orthography and selecting the translations of each book of the Bible which were to be included. Jerome's Gallican Psalter (the second attempt Jerome had made, which was a radical revision of the Old Latin version based on the *Hexapla* texts), for example, was selected rather than the Hebrew or Roman versions. Alcuin's revision was presented to Charlemagne as a Christmas present in 800. The Vulgate Bible in use henceforth was Alcuin's text and became the one in general circulation until it was revised again in the thirteenth century. The Visigoth Theodulf of Orleans also revised the Vulgate. His work was eclectic and not executed according to any determined principles; it suffered from competition with Alcuin's version and its influence was not great. Many of its inherited interpolations, however, were taken up into the thirteenth-century scholastic 'Paris Bible'.

What additions did the Carolingians make to the accepted canon of school texts they had inherited? One of the most celebrated of the early Carolingian masters was the Englishman Alcuin, from York, who was invited to Charlemagne's court (where he seems to have acted as a sort of private tutor to the king) and who stayed in the Frankish kingdom, apart from a visit to England between 790 and 793, until his death as abbot of Tours in 804. Einhard described Alcuin as the most learned man anywhere to be found;[27] it was above all for his teaching, as Edelstein has stressed, that Alcuin was celebrated.[28] Among the didactic works usually attributed to him are a short treatise on orthography, dialogues on rhetoric, dialectic and grammar and a series of questions and answers couched in the form of riddles and arithmetical puzzles called Propositions to sharpen the minds of the young, though the last of these is no longer thought to be by Alcuin. These treatises illustrate very clearly Alcuin's teaching methods and their scope. The dialogues all have in common a love of enigmatic and allegorical definitions as a way of expounding problems.

As well as the didactic treatises for use in the classroom, there were theoretical treatises on education and how the clergy in particular should be trained. The most important of these was the *De institutione clericorum* of Hraban Maur, a student of Alcuin, which drew heavily on the principles outlined in Augustine's *De Doctrina Christiana*. Rules of metre were taught by means of short treatises on versification. Other books provided glossaries for the more difficult words a student might encounter in a text. A number of books of this nature were in the cathedral library at Laon. Laon Bibliothèque Municipale MS 468, for example, provides an introduction to the life of Virgil and a glossary of the more difficult vocabulary in the poetry of both Sedulius and Virgil. Another composite school-book is Paris, BN lat. 2796, dated 813–15. It contains a collection of miscellaneous pieces of information, of a more or less scientific nature, mostly less. It includes formulae for letter writing, prescriptions for medicine, the names of the men who discovered the alphabet, observations on the length of human life, a discussion of the age of Abraham, the names of certain ancient doctors, the number of Roman provinces, an enumeration of the known varieties of snakes, selections from the Bible, the liturgy, canon law and *computus*, some arithmetic and a grammar. Such a magpie collection of miscellaneous knowledge is common in ninth-century school-books; they varied in their emphasis, some were geographical or grammatical, some mainly theological and moral, some legal, some hagiographical. There were also collections of florilegia, ragbags of pithy sayings and definitions and extracts from the most respected authors on all manner of subjects, which were gradually organized into a distinct genre of writing.

Library catalogues and surviving manuscripts indicate that the classical authors, or some of them, were read, copied and emulated. Carolingian copies form a vital part of the transmission of many classical authors, such as Juvenal, Persius, Cicero, Seneca, Ammianus Marcellinus, Suetonius, Tacitus, Pliny the Younger, Aulus Gellius and Columella.[29] With so much emphasis on Christian education and Christian learning one is bound to ask what attitude the Frankish scholars of the Carolingian period had towards the pagan writings of classical antiquity. The obvious objection to the classical authors was their paganism; added to this was the different moral sense and ethic they imparted. The Carolingians inherited the patristic attitude towards the classics in regarding them as a means to an end and as models for imitation in style. Hraban Maur summed the attitude up when he stated that 'the useful elements in the secular poets are so much grist to the human mill; what is not obviously useful we wipe from our minds, and that applies above all to any mention of the heathen gods, love, or care of worldly things'.[30] A few scholars were violent in their opposition to the classical authors; other Carolingians, such as Hadoard of Corbie, Sedulius Scottus of Liège and Lupus of Ferrières loved the classics and did their utmost to obtain copies of them. Charlemagne's palace library had a relatively large collection of rare classical texts and Bischoff has noted the correlation that exists between these books and the authors copied at Corbie in the mid-ninth century.[31] One branch of classical learning in which the Carolingians were interested in for its content rather than for its language and style was the technical branch. The practical manuals on agriculture, gardening, architecture, astronomy, cookery, medicine, herbs and military affairs by Columella, Palladius, Vitruvius, Arator, Apicius, Galen, Dioscorides and Vegetius were copied and, as far as we know, read. A monk at St Denis in the ninth century for example, took careful note of the recommendations for planting asparagus given by Palladius (now CUL Kk.v. 13).

IV

The most important factor which affected every branch of medieval education was a shortage of books. At the end of the eighth century the production of books began to increase rapidly, and in the *Admonitio Generalis*, the *De litteris colendis* and the reform councils of 813 very definite proposals were made with regard to the provision of books. Various complaints were also made about the shortage of books. Alcuin for example in 796 said that he needed at Tours some of the rarer learned books he had had in his own country and suggested that students should be sent to Britain to copy and fetch books for use in the Frankish kingdom. Some abbots of the seventh and eighth centuries are recorded bringing back books from Rome. There was an obvious need to copy books on every subject, but there was also the emphasis the Carolingians placed on the written word, and on the provision of books containing royal and customary law and the canons of the church, the books of the Bible, liturgy and theology.

What did these books look like? The pages were made of parchment or vellum, that is of sheepskin or calfskin, that had been prepared in a special way. This entailed steeping the skin in a lime solution which loosened the hair and fat, then scraping it clean and soaking it in lye, after which it was stretched on a frame to dry. The quality of parchment could vary considerably, and it is some indication of the wealth of a particular centre if the parchment produced is particularly fine or coarse. The books were usually bound with wooden boards, sometimes covered with leather, and there are even a few examples of blind stamped tooling on some of these leather bindings.[32] Occasionally a wealthy patron commissioned a carved ivory, bejewelled, gold or silver book cover. Some of these splendid works of art still survive. The ink used in Frankish manuscripts varies from a dark brown to almost yellow, but it was probably black when first applied. Some later medieval recipes for ink which survive list ingredients such as gall apple, vitriol, soot, or squid ink, mixed with wine, vinegar or water.

Writing was a highly skilled process and a laborious one. One supervisor of the scriptorium at St Gall in the ninth century said that he usually set his less bright students to copy manuscripts. Often there are indications of a scribe at work. Pembroke College Cambridge MS 308, for example, comes from Rheims and belonged to Archbishop Hincmar. The manuscript was divided up to be written by several scribes, and their names were written at the beginning of their allotted portions. Other scribes at St Gall, such as the Irishmen Maelpatricc, Coirbbre, Finguine and Donngar wrote their names on the parts of the manuscript they had copied and added comments in Old Irish such as, 'O my hand', 'That is a hard page and a weary work to read it', 'Nightfall and time for supper'.

Most of the manuscripts from the Carolingian period are written in the clear, rounded and elegant script known as Caroline minuscule. Caroline minuscule was neither a reform nor an invention, but the result of a steady evolution over three centuries, completed during the second half of the eighth century. The

Franks had inherited the Roman script system, in which one form of writing, 'late Roman cursive', (Fig. 1), was used for documents, and other forms, uncial, (Fig. 2), half-uncial (Fig. 3) and capitals, for books. Different letter forms begin to make a steady appearance from the seventh century onwards whose bases are either the old Roman cursive or the old Roman book hands.

Only exceptionally, however, before the Carolingian period, were a number of scribes in one centre trained to write a similar sort of script, that is, a 'house style'. Such an exception is Luxeuil, active from *c.* 669 to the early eighth century. In the Luxeuil script it can clearly be seen how the Merovingians modified the Roman script system and developed a distinguished calligraphic minuscule based on the elongated Merovingian charter hand, in its turn based on late Roman cursive (Fig. 4). Early examples, a fragment in Trier (*s.n.*) and BL Add.29972, illustrate the close connection between Luxeuil minuscule and

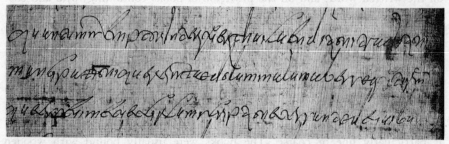

Fig. 1.   Late Roman cursive (from BL Add. MS 5412, AD 572) Reduced from 118 mm × 35 mm

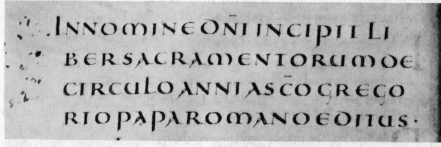

Fig. 2.   Uncial (from BN lat. 2291 f. 19ᵛ. Ninth century, though this kind of script was written from the fifth century onwards) Reduced from 198 mm × 55 mm

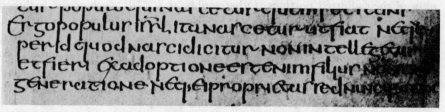

Fig. 3.   Half-uncial (from Rome, Archivo di S. Pietro D. 182. AD 509/510) Reduced from 163 mm × 30 mm

Merovingian charter hand. The sack of Luxeuil in 732 by the Saracens may well have prevented Luxeuil minuscule from developing as the standard Frankish book hand, but its influence can nevertheless be discerned in some Burgundian manuscripts and in the 'Laon az' script (Fig. 5). The influence Luxeuil

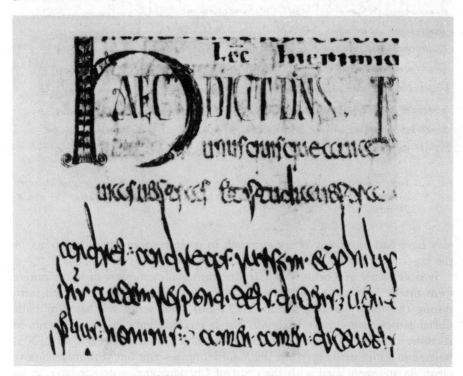

Fig. 4.   Luxeuil minuscule and display capitals (from BN lat. 9427 f. 97. Late seventh to early eighth century) Reduced from 118 mm × 94 mm

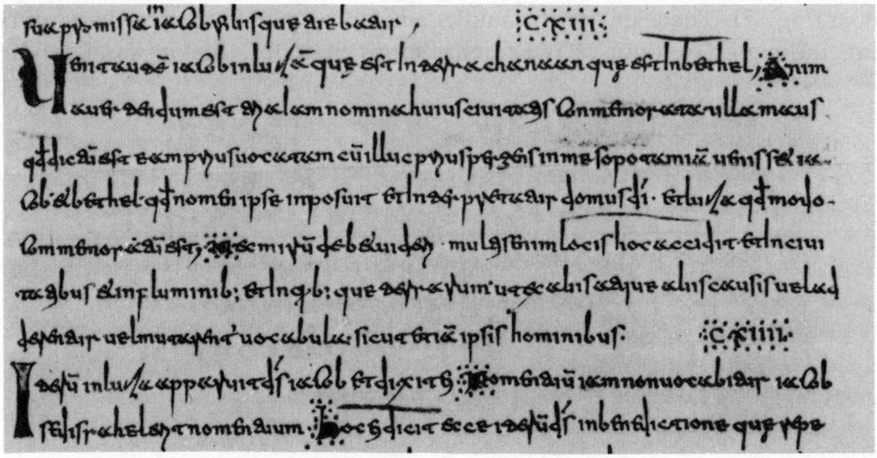

Fig. 5.   Pre-Caroline minuscule; the 'Laon az type' (from BN lat. 12168, f. 20. Eighth century) Reduced from 137 mm × 70 mm.

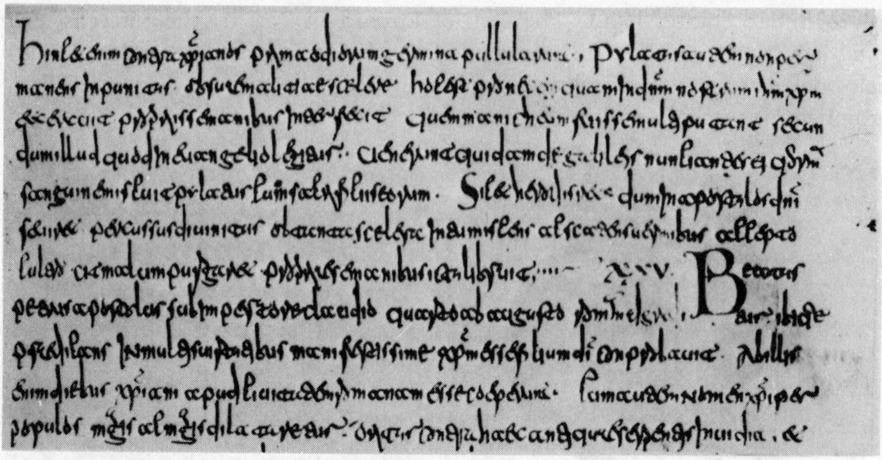

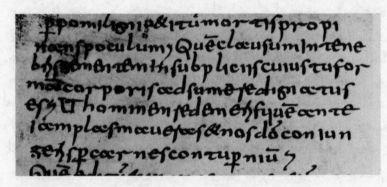

Fig. 6. Early minuscule script from Corbie, showing the influence of Merovingian chancery cursive script (from BN lat. 17655, f. 10. Seventh century) Reduced from 153 mm × 76 mm

may have had on Corbie is not so much in its letter forms but in the fact of the experiment it made and the notion of a 'house style' (Fig. 6).

It is certainly at Corbie that Caroline minuscule emerged in its primitive form in the Leuchtar script between 744 and 768 and in its perfected form during the abbacy of Maurdramnus (771–80). This script was based on half-uncial rather than cursive lettering, but it retained some cursive elements in its minuscule. The appearance of the Godescalc Lectionary (BN n.a. lat. 1203) written in a minuscule very like the Maurdramnus script but with more cursive elements and associated with the court of Charlemagne, a decade later, is an indication that the process of adapting and experimenting with known script types towards Caroline minuscule was going on elsewhere in the Frankish kingdom (Fig. 7). There are other examples among the manuscripts produced during the eighth century of transitional forms of script, but it was Caroline

Fig. 7. Pre-Caroline minuscule from Alemannia (from St Gall, Stiftsbibliothek MS 2, p. 562. AD 761)

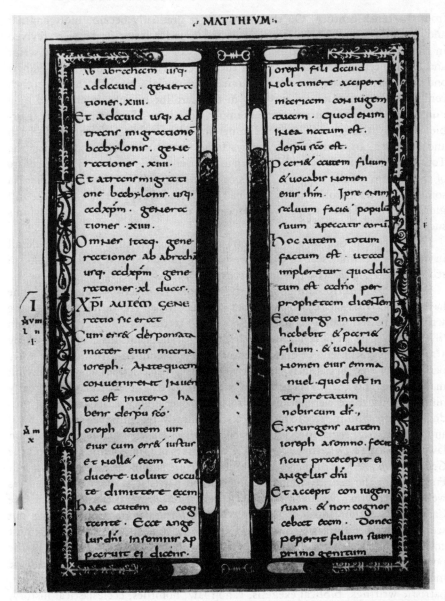

Fig. 8. Caroline minuscule, late eighth century (from the Ada Gospels, Trier Stadrbibliothek MS 22, f. 17) Reduced from 310 mm × 240 mm

minuscule, first perfected at Corbie, which became the standard form of writing for books in the Carolingian period (Fig. 8).

The subsequent spread of Caroline minuscule in its basic script type was due to the increase in intellectual activity and to royal, noble and ecclesiastical patronage of book production from the second half of the eighth century onwards. Caroline minuscule was used in Italy from about 820 and in England

157

from the tenth century. On the Continent it gradually became more angular and developed into Gothic script, but the rounder letter forms were revived in the fifteenth century and became the basis of the Italian humanistic script and Roman type. Caroline minuscule therefore had its origin in western Francia and was based primarily on the old Roman half-uncial script. By the late eighth century different styles are apparent in the Caroline minuscule produced by a number of different centres in the Frankish kingdom – St Amand, Tours, Corbie, Rheims, Cologne, Fleury, St Emmeram at Regensburg, Freising, Murbach and Salzburg, to mention only a few. It has sometimes been argued that the Tours scriptorium, directed by Alcuin at Charlemagne's urging, was the centre of the 'reform' of the script.[33] This is utter nonsense. Alcuin arrived in Francia some time after Caroline minuscule had made its first appearance, and the full glories of the Tours script were produced during the abbacies of Alcuin's successors.

Let us look at one or two scriptoria and a monastic library in some detail in order to see what sort of books were being produced and read by Frankish scholars in the early years of the Carolingian period.

Studies of the script and books of the cathedral church of St Peter at Cologne have been carried out by L. W. Jones. He has traced the development of the script from Archbishop Hildebold (785–819) to the incumbency of Hermann (890–923). The earliest books written under Hildebald are characterized by a normal development of eighth-century pre-Carolingian script. In the early period there were apparently thirty-two or thirty-three scribes at work copying manuscripts and the books produced were primarily theological. By the early ninth century there were, according to Jones, over eighty scribes at work, producing a great number of those books specifically recommended in the royal and ecclesiastical legislation, such as the *Dionysio-Hadriana* collection of canon law, Augustine's *De doctrina christiana*, the letters of Gregory the Great and the *Gesta Pontificum Romanorum*.[34] Works by Alcuin and Bede were also copied. Further into the century more theological and patristic works were copied, as well as Vitruvius' *De Architectura*, Priscian's *Institutiones Grammaticae* and the Carolingian author Jonas of Orleans' *De institutione laicali*. Cologne does not seem to have been greatly concerned with the liberal arts; the library is almost entirely made up of theology and patristic works. A list made in 833 of the possessions of Cologne reinforces the impression given by surviving Cologne manuscripts. It is divided into sections according to subject – bibles, liturgy, patristic writings, biblical exegesis, canon law, homilies, ecclesiastical history, ascetic treatises, and at the end a small section of books on philosophy, grammar, medicine and law. It may be that the cathedral scriptorium at Cologne was primarily concerned with producing books to assist the clergy in their daily functions and to augment the Christian learning of the abler canons.

A similar picture is presented by the manuscripts surviving from Rheims.[35] We might expect that a monastic library or monastic book production would present a practical selection of volumes rather less oriented towards the work of the secular clergy. To some extent this is true. In the 821 catalogue of the library of the monastery of Reichenau 415 volumes were listed, all under categories according to author or subject, with a selection of school texts at the end. The catalogue included books of the Old and New Testaments (36 items – it was very rare to have a whole Bible in one volume in the ninth century), Augustine (24 items), Jerome (27), Gregory, Cyprian, Eusebius, Hilary, Basil, Athanasius, the *Vitae Patrum* and various saints' Lives, a treatise on the origin of the Trojans, Vitruvius' *De Architectura*, Josephus' History of the Jews, Roman law, royal capitularies and barbarian law codes, Gregory of Tour's *Historia Francorum*, German poems, a map of the world, 8 volumes of scientific treatises, a cartulary, 18 sacramentaries, 11 lectionaries, 9 antiphonaries, 8 books of offices and 50 Psalters. In the section of school texts were listed Ambrose's *Hexameron*, John of Constantinople, Orosius, Cassian, Julianus Pomerius, Isidore of Seville, Bede, Cassiodorus, Primasius, Eugippius, Paterius, Aldhelm, Boethius (*De Arithmetica* and *De Geometrica*), Arator and Alcuin, 8 books of canon law and books of homilies, 7 different monastic rules, 4 collections of Passions of the saints and 4 glossaries of 'various things', Donatus, Priscian, Juvencus, Sedulius (*Paschale carmen*) Virgil's *Aeneid* and Aldhelm's *De Virginitate*. [36]

It is quite apparent from the manuscripts produced in the various scriptoria and listed in the library catalogues that library contents and book production were very closely related to the particular needs of a school. [37] The scriptoria in the time of Charlemagne and Louis the Pious laid the cornerstone for the development of medieval intellectual life. The royal library in particular seems to have served as a source of exemplars for the formation of collections elsewhere. Charlemagne probably possessed Augustine's City of God and two other books referred to as *historiae* and *antiquorum res gestae* by Einhard. Alcuin asked to borrow Charlemagne's copy of Pliny's Natural History and refers to the letters of Augustine as being in Charlemagne's possession. The king also owned at least one sacramentary or Mass book, sent him by the Pope, the *Dionysio-Hadriana* collection of canons, a Latin translation of the canons of the Council of Nicaea in 787, the *Liber Pontificalis* and the Rule of St Benedict. From surviving letters we know that he had various computistical texts and biblical commentaries, and it is also possible that he had the sixth-century illustrated copy of Virgil now in the Vatican. [38] Bischoff has also identified a list of books contained in a Berlin manuscript of the late eighth century (now in Tübingen) as nothing other than the catalogue of part of Charlemagne's library. It contains a great number of classical authors, including Lucan, Statius, Juvenal, Tibullus, Horace, Claudian, Martial, Cicero, Sallust, Cato, Servius and Julius Victor. [39] Such a varied and specialized library would have been a great attraction to scholars. We have already noted that there is a remarkable correlation between the titles on this list and the books produced at Corbie later in the century, during the reign of Louis the Pious and Charles the Bald.

Because Einhard tells us that Charlemagne had requested in his will that his great collection of books should be sold at a reasonable price to anyone wishing to buy them, and the money gained given to the poor, and the Astronomer tells us that Louis the Pious carried out his father's testamentary wishes (without mentioning the books), it is usually assumed that Charlemagne's library was scattered to the four winds, and that Louis the Pious had no interest in them. But this raises some questions: when, for example, did Corbie obtain the palace exemplars of the books they copied there in the mid-ninth century? We should note too that Bischoff, in his work on the library of Louis the Pious, has argued that Louis did not in fact carry out the provisions of his father's will as far as the books were concerned, for some of the books known to be in Charlemagne's library – the Rule of St Benedict, the *Libri Carolini*, books by Alcuin, a *mensuratio orbis* – were also used at Louis' court.[40] Hincmar of Rheims refers to the great quantity of books at the palace in 829. Other books are referred to as being presented to Louis or in his possession. The royal library seems in fact not to have lost its importance during Louis' reign. Angilbert of St Riquier gave Louis the *De doctrina christiana* of Augustine, the Emperor Michael of Byzantium sent him the works of pseudo-Dionysius the Areopagite, for which Louis himself commissioned a translation into Latin from Hilduin of St Denis. Theodulf of Orleans gave him the treatise *De Spiritu Sancto*. Poets and scholars, including Hraban Maur, Ermold the Black and Einhard dedicated works to Louis and Judith as they had to Charlemagne. Louis also had a librarian, Gerward, referred to before 828 as the *palatii bibliothecarius*. Louis himself gave rich books to monasteries. Bischoff thinks that some of the manuscripts of the two schools of book painting (to be discussed in Chapter Eight) associated with the court of Charlemagne, have been dated too early, and that some of them could have been produced in the early years of Louis the Pious. Bischoff has also identified a group of scribes working for Louis and his court, and other manuscripts have been associated with Louis' court on palaeographical grounds; these include both Christian and classical texts. Bischoff's research has put Louis the Pious and his place in the patronage emanating from the royal court in a completely new light. The royal library, as he suggests, was not just for the king's pleasure, but was used by scholars for their work not only in the reign of Charlemagne but also in that of Louis the Pious. The use of the library by scholars was a remarkable development which seems not to have been revived after the time of Charles the Bald until the reign of St Louis. Thus the palace library acted as a centre, a receiver and a disseminator of learning continuously for nearly a century. The court also had this function, at least during the reign of Charlemagne.

V

A variety of sources provide information about the court of Charlemagne. Einhard reports that Charlemagne paid the greatest attention to the liberal arts and had the deepest respect for the men who taught at the palace, bestowing on them high honours and office. 'When learning the rules of grammar he was taught by Peter of Pisa, but on all other subjects he was taught by Alcuin . . . the emperor spent much time and effort in studying rhetoric, dialectic and especially astrology. He applied himself to mathematics and traced the course of the stars with great attention.'[41] From this it would seem that scholars were invited to court in the first instance in order to teach the Emperor himself.

It is difficult to describe this court culture with any accuracy. Accounts of Charlemagne's court tend to exaggerate the formality of the intellectual life there and even go so far as to talk in terms of a 'school'. No doubt the sons of aristocrats and others seeking to serve the government in a notarial or judicial capacity were trained at court, as they had been at the courts of the Merovingians and the palace mayors. Charlemagne himself learned from the scholars who visited his court; probably a number of such scholars were always present. But the character of the gathering remains elusive. This has not prevented historians from imagining what such a school might have been like, and they have built on what they have imagined as if it were fact. Some historians, for example, say that Alcuin the Englishman was called by Charlemagne to be 'head of his palace school'; there is insufficient evidence to support such an interpretation. The 'school' can mean no more than a circle of scholars closely associated with king and court and enjoying the king's favour. Scholars rarely stayed at the court for more than a year or two but many of them received favours in the form of abbacies and bishoprics. Alcuin for example, though only a deacon, was made abbot of Tours; Angilbert, probably still a layman, was made abbot of St Riquier, Theodulf of Orleans received the abbacy of Fleury and the bishopric of Orleans, and Einhard, a layman, the abbacy of Seligenstadt.

The court seems to have become a haven for scholars of all nationalities – Lombard, Visigoth, Anglo-Saxon, Irish and Frankish – after the conquest of Lombardy, that is, in the mid-770s. If, as Brunhölzl suggests, Charlemagne considered the patronage of learning to be one of the obligations of royalty, it seems nevertheless that he did not embark on his programme of reform and the revival of learning until his position in the Frankish kingdom seemed fairly secure, and scholars had been associated with the court for some time. Peter of Pisa is thought to have arrived after 773–4, Paulinus of Aquileia was probably there by 776, Paul the Deacon, also a Lombard, arrived at court in 782 not, as is usually supposed, attracted there by its reputation for learning, but to seek the release of his brother taken prisoner in 774. Nevertheless he stayed at the court for four years. Alcuin arrived in 782 and Theodulf of Orleans in the 780s. Angilramn of Metz took up his position at court in 781. All had left by about 796. The chronology suggests in fact that Charlemagne had first to learn what learning and religion were from the scholars he invited to his court, and what his priorities ought to be, before he could decide to promote learning and religious reform on a larger scale. The court did not become a centre of learning in the sense of a focus of intellectual activity until the late 780s and early 790s.

The poets of the court circle, among whom were Alcuin, Joseph the Scot, Peter of Pisa, Candidus, Paul the Deacon, Angilbert and Theodulf of Orleans tell us something about court life at this time. The poets were a learned élite, accomplished in the composition of Latin verse. It was a skill that raised them from the barbarian state and brought them closer to the ancient classical culture

161

they strove to emulate. From Angilbert's *Ad Carolum regem* and Theodulf's poem of the same title, come a few thumb-nail sketches of the court circle. Charlemagne is portrayed surrounded by his courtiers, learned men and poets, while Alcuin – there is a hint of malice here – would sit 'ever on the point of uttering pious words and freely partaking of food with lips and hand'. All Charlemagne's children were youthful and beautiful, they brought presents to their father and received loving kisses from him. The king's sister Gisela discussed some scriptural point with him; Einhard, his little body inhabited by a mighty spirit, scurried hither and thither, bringing big books and literary arrows to slay 'the Scot' (probably Dungal); Count Wigbod, with his great belly and shaking knees, got the sharp edge of Theodulf's tongue. Alcuin, possibly copying Horace, endowed many at court with classical and biblical nicknames. Charlemagne was David; Pippin, Julius; Gisela, Charlemagne's sister, was Lucia and Gisela his daughter Delia; Adalhard was Antonius; Einhard, Bezaleel; Angilbert, Homer; Fredugis, Nathaniel; Arno, Aquila; and Alcuin himself, Flaccus Albinus. The use of nicknames in poems and letters became a literary convention and was adopted by others among the Carolingian poets. They lend an element of self-consciousness and preciousness to the court culture, and suggest an intimacy which in reality the court probably did not possess at all.

The poetry of these scholars is of some importance. It has often been criticized for its monotonous conformity to certain models from among both the classical and early Christian poets, and unfavourably compared with them. Despite the accusation of derivative writing, a modern suspicion that would have made little sense to a Carolingian, the poetry for the most part is attractive, vigorous, sometimes rude and sometimes quite elegant. It expresses, despite its classical forms and metres, a distinctly Christian piety. It was modelled on the styles of the classical poets, with the greatest fidelity being shown to Virgil, and took various forms – laments, debates, verse epistles, panegyric, idyll, elegy, eclogue and moral–didactic verse.

The Carolingians made two contributions to the writing of poetry; they increased the use of rhythmic verse, particularly in octosyllabic and quindecasyllabic lines, and, more important, they produced narrative or elegiac poetry either wholly religious or didactic in its purpose. Alcuin wrote lyrical and some mystical verse and a number of inscriptions and epitaphs as occasional pieces, though his most famous poems, the *De sanctis Eboracensis ecclesiae* and possibly *Conflictus Veris et Hiemis* were composed before he left England. Theodulf of Orleans often wrote in a satirical vein; his best-known poem is the *Versus contra Iudices* (see Ch. 4). Paulinus of Aquileia, Paul the Deacon, Modoin and Angilbert all made notable contributions; Angilbert used to be credited with the authorship of the epic poem *Karolus Magnus et Leo Papa*, though there does not seem to be any firm evidence in his favour and Brunhölzl has discounted it. Other edifying poems were made from older prose saints' Lives. The Carolingians were also fond of experimenting with new forms of verse, found in the works of the classical poets. Paul the Deacon, for example, tried his hand at sapphic metre, and the acrostic poems of Porphyrius were very popular as models. The attempts of Alcuin, Theodulf and Joseph the Scot to write poems in the manner of Porphyrius survive in a manuscript now in Berne (Burger-bibliothek MS 212), written at the royal court. The poets of Louis the Pious' reign stressed sacred themes and the moral–didactic genre even more, but a major difference between the poets of Louis' reign and that of Charlemagne is that there is no evidence that there was a group of poets closely associated with the court; poets wrote in their monasteries and sent their works to Louis. Hra-ban Maur, for example, writing at Fulda, wrote rather weak imitations of his master Alcuin's verse; Ermold was in exile when he wrote his *In honorem Hlu-dowic* in an attempt to regain favour, and Theodulf of Orleans continued to write in exile. Walafrid Strabo, tutor to the young Charles the Bald, was a poet of some power. His *De imagine Tetrici* was a poem intended for public recital at court and was about the Emperor and his entourage, similar to the poems by Theodulf and Angilbert. Walafrid also wrote the *Carmen de visionibus Wettini* which depicts many of the great men of his day suffering in hell for their various sins and crimes. His best-known and most charming poem is the *Hortulus*. It gives an account of his garden (to which the modern visitor to Reichenau in Lake Constance is still directed) and describes twenty-two of the different herbs and plants which grew there, and their healing properties.

The scholars of the court were also interested in theological questions. Among these were the questions concerning Adoptionism and iconoclasm. The heresy of Adoptionism was dealt with at Regensburg in 792 and again at Frank-furt in 794 and one of its authors, Felix, was anathematized by the Pope in 799. The heresy, according to which Christ is the adoptive rather than the true son of God, was formulated by Elipand, bishop of Toledo and Felix, bishop of Urgel. Alcuin in his treatise *Contra Felicem* made the most notable contri-bution to the debate. The most important of the theological disputes of the Carolingian period, however, was that over the worship of images, known as the iconoclast controversy. At the Synod of Nicaea in 787, the bishops of the eastern church met to discuss the reinstatement of images; some eastern the-ologians and churchmen thought that pictures of Christ and the saints might be confused with the immaterial things they represented and that worship might be offered the image. Images were nevertheless restored to the Frankish church. In 794 the Franks met at the Synod of Frankfurt and made a public declaration on both Adoptionism and iconoclasm. Their official response was the treatise composed in Charlemagne's name in 791 known as the *Libri Carolini*. It is a treatise immensely rich in its patristic, biblical and classical learning and has a number of interesting comments on art and its function. It contained an attempt to define the western position on the image question and outlined an advanced theory of Charlemagne's prerogatives as king and his ecclesiastical powers; the king is presented as a defender of the faith and spokesman of the western church.

The *Libri Carolini* also emphasized the importance of the decorative and aes-thetic function of art, and the potential attractiveness of a work of art as a piece of fine craftsmanship, regardless of content. On the other hand the author of the *Libri Carolini* argued firmly against the idea that a painting could possess any magical or spiritual qualities. The didactic and educative value of art was stressed, and this undoubtedly owed much to the teaching of Gregory the Great, who had affirmed that painting was admirable in churches because those who were unlettered could 'read' by seeing on the walls in churches what they were unable to read in books. Examples of such pictures can be seen in the scenes of the Life and Passion of St Stephen in the crypt of St Germain of Auxerre or the Old and New Testament scenes in the frescos in the church of St John, Müstair. The *Libri Carolini* explicitly condemned the use of classical representations in wall paintings, that is, such pagan imagery as river gods, earth gods, personifications of the sun and moon, monsters or naked and semi-naked figures; these were vigorously attacked because they were pagan and contrary to the Scriptures. Such imagery may well have been excluded from church walls, but it certainly turns up in manuscript illuminations, and in liturgical books at that. The best examples of river gods are in the Utrecht Psalter.

Most discussions of the image question had not considered the aesthetic as distinct from the ecclesiastical function of statues and portraits of Christ and the saints, but the author of the *Libri Carolini* paid expert attention to the aesthetic side of the problem. The author of the treatise emphasized the worldly nature of the artist's craft and argued that art had no intrinsic piety; experience rather than inspiration was the artist's teacher. The logical outcome of this view of the artist's function is that painting and the image produced by the artist also had no mystic function, and this of course was the western position as far as the images were concerned. It is now generally believed that Theodulf of Orleans, a prominent member of the group of scholars associated with Charlemagne, was the author of the *Libri Carolini*.[42]

The debate on images at the end of the eighth century had repercussions during the reign of Louis the Pious. The whole subject was revived at the Synod of Paris in 825. Claudius of Turin, a Visigoth who lived in Lyons (d. 827) won himself many enemies for his hostile views on images; his bishop, Agobard, took his part and wrote against the veneration of images. Jonas of Orleans (780–843) underlined in his *De cultu imaginum* the didactic importance of images, and Dungal, an Irish monk at St Denis (d. 827), wrote a polemical treatise against Claudius of Turin: this included a subtle discussion of the many different degrees of veneration which could be accorded images of the saints and their relics besides the actual worship of God. His discussion had some affinities with the more moderate line pursued in the *Libri Carolini*. Generally there was some ambivalence in the ninth-century Carolingian attitude towards representational art in relation to the holy and the teaching of the Christian faith. Representational art came to be valued above all for its didactic function. One school of thought also regarded art as one expression of one's faith and love of God, and much of this spirit was to imbue later medieval art.

VI

There are a number of reasons for arguing that the court of Charlemagne was important in the growth of Carolingian culture. In the first place it was a centre of learning; there was a library containing the rarer books and other scholars with whom to converse, and there was a king interested in, and favourable towards, the pursuit of knowledge for its own sake. The court also served as a training ground for officials and administrators; legislation and administrative measures were issued from the palace. Not only this; the court circle did not consist solely of poets and vain scholars, or even simply of theologians discussing abstruse points of doctrine among themselves; it also included *ministri* or palace officials, notaries and chaplains, military leaders, doctors and musicians. Scholarship and practical ability went very closely together. The scholars were also the men of affairs who ran the kingdom. The learned bishop and abbot were of great social and political importance in the Frankish kingdom. The court offered possibilities for patronage and preferment. It was the centre for the revival of religious life, particularly during the reign of Louis the Pious, and it undoubtedly possessed a certain glamour and richness which made it the place to be for any one who wanted to get on in the world. Yet the question remains as to whether the court continued to have all these functions under Louis the Pious. It is usually assumed that it did not, but we have already seen that in administrative and religious matters and as far as the library was concerned, there is considerable evidence for continuity. Let us see what the sources tell us about Louis in relation to learning.

In his preface to Einhard's Life of Charlemagne, Walafrid said that in his own time, the thirst for knowledge was disappearing again and becoming rarer. Walafrid was probably writing at the end of Louis the Pious' reign; there is no reason to doubt him, but what may have been true of the last few turbulent years of Louis' reign, may not necessarily be true of Louis' reign as a whole. Nevertheless, his view is apparently confirmed by that of Lupus of Ferrières, writing between 829 and 836, who stated that learned men were no longer being patronized and men were no longer so zealous in their pursuit of learning. In both Walafrid and Lupus there may be an element of regarding a past age as better than their own simply because it was past, but it does seem as if Louis might not have been so active a patron of learning as his father. Notker Balbulus depicted Louis as devoting all his energy to works of religion, prayer and charitable activities, listening to lawsuits and making just legal decisions. No reference is made to the encouragement of learning. The Astronomer's Life of Louis, written *c.* 840, gives us a similar picture, as does Thegan. In his narrative poem, Ermold the Black presented Louis as a Christian prince, devoted to religious reform. There were scholars associated with Louis' household, but they were there to perform specific tasks. Walafrid Strabo acted as tutor to Louis' youngest son Charles the Bald; Benedict of Aniane was Louis' chief adviser on religious matters. Hilduin of St Denis was the first Carolingian scholar to attempt, at Louis' request, a translation of the *opera* of pseudo-Dionysius the Areopagite, and was Louis' archchaplain; and Einhard, Charlemagne's biographer, was favoured at court by Louis until about 830, after which Einhard retired to Seligenstadt. The encouragement of learning and the presence of a few scholars at court, however, may have been due to Judith, Louis' second wife, who was possessed of a considerable reputation for learning, and whose private chaplain was Walafrid Strabo.[43]

The implications of the evidence are that Louis was not interested in the pursuit of learning for its own sake, but much more interested in the application of knowledge and its devotion to the service of the Christian faith. 'How much ardour for divine worship he bore in the depth of his heart' [44] is manifest in his achievements within the sphere of monastic and ecclesiastical reform. This was where his primary interests lay, and thereby Louis in fact made a vital contribution to the Carolingian Renaissance. Christianity was, as we have already seen, an integral feature of Carolingian culture. Louis the Pious did much to enhance and strengthen the religious life of the Franks. He did not actually discourage learning, but it seems to be the case that the court ceased for a time to be the main focus of intellectual activity as it had been during the reign of his father. Instead, many scholars were active away from the court and learning was diffused among the great monastic and episcopal centres of the Frankish kingdom, in Corbie, Rheims, Tours, Lyons, Reichenau, Lorsch and Fulda. The role of these centres in the development of Carolingian culture will be discussed fully in a later chapter. In this chapter I have been very much concerned with beginnings. Discussions of the Carolingian Renaissance often manage to convey the impression that all activity ceased after Charlemagne's death. As we shall see, however, it was after the reign of Charlemagne that the Carolingian Renaissance came to full flower.

NOTES

1. H. Marrou, *Histoire de l'Education dans l'Antiquité*, 2nd edn. (Paris 1965); Eng. trs. of first edition of 1948 (1956).
2. P. Riché, *Education et culture dans l'Occident barbare VIe–VIIIe siècles* (Paris 1972); Eng. trs. with updated notes and bibliography by J. J.Contreni (1976).
3. See R. McKitterick, 'The scriptoria of Merovingian Gaul: a survey of the evidence', *Columbanus and Merovingian Monasticism*, H. B. Clarke and M. Brennan (eds) (Oxford 1981), 173–207.
4. L. R. Reynolds and N. G. Wilson, *Scribes and Scholars*, 2nd edn. (Oxford 1974), 76.
5. For a full description of all these early manuscripts, see E. A. Lowe, *Codices Latini Antiquiores* I–XI and Supplement (Oxford 1935–71), esp. VI and Introduction.
6. See, however, the references and comments in Ch. 3 above, n. 71.
7. P. Riché, 'Le renouveau culturel à la cour de Pépin III', *Francia* 2 (1974), 59–70.
8. For example G. Greenaway, 'Saint Boniface as a man of letters', *The Greatest Englishman*, T. Reuter (ed.) (Exeter 1980), 31–46.
9. *MGH Cap.* I, No. 22, c. 72.
10. P. Lehmann, 'Fuldaer Studien', *Sitzungsberichte der Bayerischen Akademie der Wissenschaften*, Phil. Hist. Kl. 1927, 4–13.
11. On Angilramn see, J. Fleckenstein, *Die Hofkapelle der deutschen Könige* I (Stuttgart 1959), 48–51 and 238.

12. *PL* 105, cols 191–210, c. 19 and c. 20.
13. F. Lot (ed.), Appendix VI, p. 300 in his edition of Hariulf.
14. *MGH Cap.* I, No. 170 c. 45, 346.
15. W. Horn, 'On the author of the Plan of St Gall and the relation of the Plan to the monastic reform movement', *Studien zum St Galler Klosterplan*, J. Duft (ed.) (St Gall 1962), 103–27.
16. *MGH Conc.* II, i, No. 22C, c. 4.
17. *MGH Conc.* II, ii, No. 42. c. 3 and compare *MGH Cap.* I, No. 150, c. 6.
18. *MGH Conc.* II, ii, No. 50, c. 30.
19. A. Murray, *Reason and Society in the Middle Ages* (Oxford 1978).
20. Liudger, *Vita Gregorii*, c. 2.
21. P. Lehmann, *Mittelalterliche Bibliothekskataloge Deutschlands und der Schweiz* I (Munich 1918), 248.
22. Ibid., 252.
23. Lupus, Ep. 5.
24. R. McKitterick, 'A ninth century schoolbook from the Loire valley: Phillipps 16308', *Scriptorium* 30 (1976), 225–31.
25. M. Draak, 'Construe marks in Hiberno-Latin manuscripts', *Mededelingen der Koninklijke Nederlandse Akademie van Wetenschappen* 20 (1957), 261–82 and 'The higher teaching of Latin grammar in Ireland during the ninth century', ibid., 30 (1967), 107–95.
26. D. Illmer, *Formen der Erziehung und Wissensvermittlung im frühen Mittelalter* (Munich 1971); G. Glauche, *Schullekture im Mittelalter* (Munich 1970), and B. Bischoff, 'Die Bibliothek im Dienste der Schule', *Settimane* 19 (1972), 385–415.
27. Einhard, *Vita Karoli*, c. 25.
28. W. Edelstein, *Eruditio et Sapientia: Weltbild und Erziehung in der Karolingerzeit* (Freiburg-im-Breisgau 1965).
29. Reynolds and Wilson, *Scribes and Scholars*, 84–94.
30. Hraban Maur, *De institutione clericorum*, 3, 16.
31. B. Bischoff, 'Die Hofbibliothek Karls des Grossen', *KdG* II, 42–62. See too his 'Panorama der Handschriftenüberlieferung aus der Zeit Karls des Grossen', *KdG* II, 233–54.
32. J. Vezin, 'Les reliures carolingiennes de cuir à décor éstampé de la Bibliothèque Nationale de Paris', *BEC* 128 (1970), 81–113 and P. Needham, *Twelve Centuries of Bookbindings 400–1600* (New York and London 1979), 55–61.
33. For example by S. Morison, *Politics and Script* (Oxford 1972), 170–1, and in 'Notes on the development of Latin script', *Selected Essays on the History of Letter Forms in Manuscript and Print*, D. McKitterick (ed.) (Cambridge 2 vols, 1981), I, 253–6.
34. L. W. Jones, *The Script of Cologne from Hildebald to Hermann* (Cambridge, Mass. 1932).
35. F. L. Carey, 'The scriptorium of Rheims during the archbishopric of Hincmar', *Classical and Medieval Studies in Honor of E. K. Rand* (New York 1938), 41–60.
36. Lehmann, *Mittelalterliche Bibliothekskataloge* I, 244–52.
37. Bischoff, cited above n. 26.
38. B. Bischoff, *Lorsch im Spiegel seiner Handschriften* (Munich 1974), 56.
39. Bischoff, 'Die Hofbibliothek Karls des Grossen'.
40. B. Bischoff, 'Die Hofbibliothek unter Ludwig dem Frommen', *Medieval Learning and Literature*, M. T. Gibson and J. J. G. Alexander (eds) (Oxford 1976), 3–22.
41. Einhard, *Vita Karoli*, c. 25.

42. A. Freeman, 'Theodulf of Orleans and the *Libri Carolini*', *Speculum* 32 (1957), 663–705 (and continued in *Speculum* 40 (1965), 203–89 and *Speculum* 46 (1971), 597–612. See the objections by L. Wallach, *Diplomatic Studies in Latin and Greek documents from the Carolingian Age* (Ithaca 1977). See also E. Dahlhaus-Berg, *Nova antiquitas et antiqua novitas* (Cologne 1975).
43. F. von Bezold, 'Kaiserin Judith and ihre Dichter Walahfrid Strabo', *HZ* 130 (1924), 375–439.
44. *MGH Conc.* II, i., No. 39, 312.

CHAPTER SEVEN

Charles the Bald and the Defence of Carolingian Kingship

The birth of Charles the Bald in 823 did not at first excite the jealousy or rivalry of his elder brothers. In 829 Charles was granted the region of Ale-mannia, Rhaetia and part of Burgundy, and though there was no statement at this stage about Charles' eventual inheritance, the grant made it clear to all concerned that Louis' youngest son was not to remain portionless. It is import-ant to remember the ill-defined nature of Charles' position in 829 in view of the motives attributed to the rebels against Louis the Pious in 829 and 830 by the sources and by modern historians. There has been a tendency to see Louis' reign after 823, or at least after 830, almost solely in terms of settling the inheritance for his sons and the consequent 'break-up of the Carolingian Empire'. That our main sources for the period, Thegan, the Astronomer and the Annals of St Bertin are all almost completely preoccupied with the struggle between Louis, his sons and the magnates in the years from 829 to 840, and that Nithard's one purpose in his History was to provide a personal view, increasingly jaundiced, of the quarrels between the sons of Louis the Pious, has obviously increased this tendency. Some indication of the rivalries and hatreds involved can also be gleaned from the *Epitaphium Arsenii*, Paschasius Radbert's life of Wala, abbot of Corbie. There the bias against Louis is strong, though not unqualified; the tract vilifies the Empress Judith and misrepresents Louis as a weakling who admitted his unworthiness to be king to the rebels.

It is in fact possible to be far more positive about the last ten years of Louis' reign; the principal cause of the dissension was not the efforts of Louis and Judith to provide their son Charles with an inheritance (this only really became an issue in 838), but the growing strength and self-interest of the magnates. This is clear from the annal entry for 829 which reports Louis' uneasiness at the news of a nobles' conspiracy against him, and his appointment of Bernard of Septimania as his chamberlain and personal protector, a move which infuri-ated the magnates further. Some of them of course, such as Matfrid of Orle-ans, had a personal grievance against Louis. Others in all probability were members of noble families who had never entirely reconciled themselves to Carolingian rule. As we have seen, this latent opposition occasionally became apparent in the reigns of Pippin III and Charlemagne, and from 830 it becomes even more so. As a result of the increasing power and strength of the magnates a new political structure was eventually to emerge, and it is the process by which it did so that will be examined in the remaining chapters of this book.

I

The struggle between Louis the Pious and his magnates falls into three main stages: 829-30, 833-4, 837-40. The leaders in the first stage were Lothar, the king's eldest son, Count Hugh of Tours whose daughter Lothar had married, and Count Matfrid of Orleans. Both the last two named had been deprived of their offices, for incompetence, by Louis the year before. Open rebellion broke out in February 830. Louis had decided to lead an army against the Bretons but the Franks refused to go. The Annals of St Bertin state that the magnates weaned the army away from its loyalty to the Emperor and induced Pippin I of Aquitaine and Lothar to join them, with the intention of deposing Louis, eliminating Judith and murdering Count Bernard of Septimania. In other words, in the first phase of the struggle, Louis' sons proved willing tools for the magnates. Louis the German does not seem to have been involved at this stage and seems also to have had a following largely independent of that of his brothers. Count Bernard fled to Barcelona but Louis travelled to Compiègne to meet the magnates and his son Pippin. There Pippin, with Lothar's consent (the latter was still in Italy) deposed Louis and incarcerated Judith in St Radegund's convent at Poitiers; Lothar arrived after Easter and took charge. By October, Louis had regained control and at an assembly held at Aachen in February 831 the conspirators were tried and treated very leniently. Judith was reinstated after purging herself of the charges against her of adultery with Count Bernard with an oath. (It is significant that among the entire company at Aachen, no man was willing to accuse her.) Count Bernard was acquitted of the charges against him at Thionville later in the year. Within a few months Lothar had been received back into his father's favour and Pippin, Louis and Lothar were permitted to return to their kingdoms. Yet they continued to behave in a curmudgeonly fashion for the next two years. As a result, Pippin's kingdom of Aquitaine was given to Charles and Louis the Pious assembled an army against his son Louis (who had been encouraged to attempt to annexe Alemannia by Count Matfrid of Orleans) and obliged him to swear never to conspire again against his father.

In 833 the storm broke. It is important to note that it is Louis' sons who were now regarded as the leaders of the rebellion, aided and abetted by their factions of magnates. Nithard associates the rebellion of 833, by implication at least, with the loss to Pippin of the kingdom of Aquitaine. Whatever the cause, Louis' sons and enemies formed an alliance against him. Louis mustered an army of his own and the two parties met at the 'Field of Lies'. There Louis' army was inveigled into deserting their king. Louis, Judith and Charles were captured, Lothar seized power, and Pippin and Louis the German returned to

Aquitaine and Bavaria respectively. Lothar took his father with him to Soissons, but sent his stepmother into exile in Italy and the young Charles to the monastery of Prüm, 'something which grieved his father exceedingly'. Lothar thereupon acted as the sole ruler of the kingdom and forced Louis to do penance for his 'crimes'. Louis languished in Lothar's clutches for ten months before a rescue was organized, either by Louis the German (Annals of St Bertin), by 'many magnates' (Nithard) or by Count Eggehard, Constable William and the king's half-brothers Hugh and Drogo (the Astronomer). There is no reason to doubt Louis the German's part in his father's rescue, or that of the other magnates mentioned, for the latter had remained throughout staunch supporters of the Emperor. By February 834 Louis was reinstated and in an emotional scene in Metz cathedral he was ceremonially reinvested with his regalia. In an expedition mounted against Lothar's party soon afterwards a number of prominent Franks were killed; Lothar himself capitulated without a fight (a habit of his) and was dispatched back to Italy with those of his supporters who cared to follow him. The rebel bishops Ebbo, archbishop of Rheims, and Agobard of Lyons were deposed.

In 837 Louis the Pious made a positive move to provide for Charles. With the agreement of the envoys of Louis the German and Pippin, Charles was given the land west of the Meuse, Burgundy, Chartres and Paris together with all the bishops, abbots, counts and royal vassals who held benefices in these territories.[1] A portion of Neustria was added in 838 and on Pippin's death Louis made Charles king of Aquitaine. It was with the latter provision that Louis went against the agreement of 817 for the first time, for he disinherited Pippin I's son Pippin II. A further division of the kingdom was made in 839 between Lothar, now fully restored to favour and Charles, with Lothar choosing to have the area east of the Meuse, Rhône and Saône rivers and Charles having the western area and Provence. Louis the German was left Bavaria but otherwise excluded from this arrangement and consequently, with some cause for grievance, revolted against the partition; but his father quelled the rebellion and forced his son to return to Bavaria. It was on his return from this expedition that Louis died at Ingelheim on 20 June 840.

There has been some attempt to read into these rebellions against Louis high-flown aspirations for the Empire and ideals of unity.[2] Kleinclausz, for example, has posited the existence of a stalwart group of magnates – Hugh, count of Tours, counts Lambert and Matfrid, Hilduin, abbot of St Denis, Helisachar the chancellor, Adalhard, abbot of Corbie, and his brother Wala, and Agobard, bishop of Lyons – who, from the time of Louis' elevation, formulated and maintained the new ideas of unity and Empire as against the old notion of the partition of the kingdom between male heirs. The 'imperialists' were responsible for the *Ordinatio Imperii*, and behind the provisions of the *Pactum Ludovicianum* and the *Constitutio Romana*; it was their ideals of unity which were compromised by the events of 829–30. It was thus the 'imperialists' and partisans of the constitution of 817 who rebelled and theirs was a truly disinterested zeal for the unity of the Empire.[3] This argument is both weak and ill-founded. For one thing, Kleinclausz and his advocates assume rather than prove that the 'imperialists' were responsible for the content of the *Ordinatio Imperii*, the *Pactum Ludovicianum* and the *Constitutio Romana*, and ignore both the long tradition of opposition to Carolingian rule and the concerted efforts each Carolingian king had been obliged to make to maintain his authority. That theories about the unity of the Empire were formulated is not denied, but advocates of the 'imperialists' have been too much influenced by Paschasius Radbert's version of the sufferings of his righteous heroes, Wala and Adalhard of Corbie, their selflessness for Emperor, Empire, Christendom and the Christian faith, and Radbert's presentation of the 830 and 833 rebellions as pious moves for the Emperor's good to rid his palace of adultery and witchcraft. The *Ordinatio Imperii* of 817 was a useful hook on which the rebels could hang their revolts; preservation of the inheritance of Louis' sons was an excuse for the nobles to begin to assert themselves.

It attests to the strength of Carolingian kingship moreover that the magnates were obliged to work within the existing political structure rather than break away from it. Above all, as far as Louis the Pious was concerned, he was not destroying the unity of the Empire by making territorial provision for his son Charles. Not once was Lothar's position as heir to the Empire and title of Emperor withdrawn, or the idea of a confederation of subkings abandoned. That Lothar was sent in disgrace to Italy does not mean he was deposed as co-Emperor, nor was Charles himself made a subking until 838. The revolts were nothing less than the nobles flexing their muscles and using the sons' greed, ambition and self-esteem to further their own interests. This is fully borne out by the events in the three years following Louis' death, in which the ability to command the loyalty of the nobles became the determining factor for the success of each brother, and the nobles themselves managed to strengthen their positions and increase their wealth at the expense of their kings.

II

On Louis' death, Lothar had galloped back from Italy and taken up arms against his brothers. The fraternal quarrel in its fiercest and most sustained phase, as chronicled by Nithard, lasted from 840 to 843, with contributions from Pippin II of Aquitaine, the Bretons and different groups of nobles, some of whom changed sides — from choice or from necessity — in the course of the struggle. It was only Lothar's defeat at the bloody Battle of Fontenoy and the alliance between Charles and Louis, sealed at Strasbourg in 842 with the famous oaths sworn by each brother and his army in the vernacular (the earliest written record of the west Frankish dialect) that tipped the scales in their favour against Lothar and forced him to come to a settlement.[4] With the treaty of Verdun in 843, some agreement was reached about the territories each brother was to have for his kingdom. Charles was to rule a western kingdom, including Aquitaine; Louis the German was confined to the region east of the Rhine apart from the cities and wine-growing district of Speier, Worms and Mainz on the west side of the Rhine; and Lothar remained Emperor and king of the middle kingdom between his brothers' territories, a kingdom which extended from the lands between the Meuse and Scheldt down the Rhône – Saône valley into Italy; he took up residence at Aachen.

A case has been made for the division between the brothers being made on economic and geographic principles, in that each portion was supposed to contain a similar variety of land and be economically as prosperous as the next. Certainly a written inventory of *mansi*, benefices, offices, rights and lands was drawn up. Ganshof, however, argues that the partition was effected without Aquitaine, Bavaria or Italy (where each brother was the acknowledged king) and that each portion had to join one of these regions; hence the tripartite division ran north and south. Whatever the reasoning behind the divisions, the decisions taken at Verdun largely determined the future shape of Europe (see Map 9).[5] Verdun in fact gives the lie to the 'imperialist' theory for it was far more akin to the *Divisio regni* of 806. In a sense Louis the Pious got his own way after all. Lothar, however, was in no sense the overlord of his brothers. The position of Emperor became a nominal overlordship with real responsibilities in Italy and in relation to the Papacy, but with little power in the Frankish kingdoms apart from his own. After protracted negotiations, the brothers met at Yütz near Thionville the following year to decide the principles upon which the future relations between the kingdoms created at Verdun and between the three brothers were to be conducted. Although the text of this agreement does not survive, it was discussed in the Annals of St Bertin and at a synod held in the same year. The brothers agreed on the principle of confraternity and peace within their confederation of kingdoms; each pledged the other to assist him in the preservation of peace and order in his kingdom.

For the next eleven years, relations between the three independent kingdoms of Lothar, Louis the German and Charles the Bald were dominated by Lothar's attempts to secure his position in the middle kingdom, prevent his brothers from allying themselves against him, and to assert his superiority over them. Twice Lothar attempted to assert his authority through the church. Apparently at his request, Pope Sergius II appointed Drogo archbishop of Metz as the vicar apostolic of the provinces of Gaul and Germany with the right to convoke councils or synods in all three kingdoms, control provincial councils, and act as an intermediate court for appeals to Rome. The Frankish episcopate, however, refused to recognize Drogo's status and he never seems to have acted upon it. Lothar's move to reinstall his protégé Ebbo (deposed in 834 for his part in the rebellion against Louis the Pious) as archbishop of Rheims was also forestalled with the election in 845 of Hincmar, formerly a monk of St Denis. Ebbo retreated to Lothar's kingdom and was eventually given refuge by Louis the German who conferred on him the bishopric of Hildesheim, which he held until his death in 851.

Charles the Bald's position was more precarious than that of his brothers after Verdun. Unlike his two brothers, who had been established as rulers in at least part of their territories for most of their father's reign, Charles, many years younger than they, entered his kingdom virtually as a stranger. In no part of the country did he have roots (though he quickly formed an affection for particular places) and he was obliged to set out to win the loyalty of his people, and in particular of the nobles and the church. In the first three years as king he had gained the support of the Franks in the region between the Meuse and the Seine, Neustria and northern Burgundy, but parts of Aquitaine and the Bretons remained resistant to his rule. Forced to compromise, or else making a realistic decision to deploy as effectively as possible the strengths he possessed, Charles came to an agreement with Pippin II of Aquitaine, according to which Pippin swore an oath of fidelity 'as a nephew should to his uncle'. Pippin was permitted to issue his own charters, and Charles became in effect Pippin's overlord.[6] Unfortunately Pippin seems to have been a charming hot-head and the arrangement was short-lived. The Aquitainians were probably finally roused to oust Pippin after he had failed to do anything to prevent the Vikings burning Bordeaux. At Orleans in 848, the magnates, bishops and abbots of Aquitaine elected Charles the Bald as their king and had him anointed by Wenilo, archbishop of Sens. Pippin II was captured, tonsured and imprisoned at St Medard of Soissons; his younger brother Charles had also been tonsured and committed to Corbie.

Aquitainian and Breton affairs occupied Charles fully for the three years after Verdun, but the first disturbance of the brotherly pact of concord was in 846. In that year Gilbert, a vassal of Charles, absconded with one of Lothar's daughters and married her. Lothar seized his opportunity and accused Charles of complicity;[7] Louis the German was also obliged to swear he had had nothing to do with it. Lothar thereupon embarked on a campaign of annoyance. The lands in Lothar's kingdom belonging to the church of Rheims were pillaged by Lothar's vassals. Lothar also intrigued in Rome on ex-archbishop Ebbo's behalf, and sheltered Charles of Aquitaine who had fled to Lothar's kingdom. Louis the German did his utmost to reconcile his two brothers and Lothar finally agreed to come to the Colloquy of Meersen in 847. Here the pledge of brotherly concord and co-operation was renewed by both the brothers and their *fideles*. Nevertheless, Lothar, decidedly cool and passive in his observance of this agreement, was active in trying to disrupt it. He attempted, without success, to persuade Louis the German to abandon Charles the Bald and form an exclusive alliance with him. Undaunted by Louis' rebuff, he turned to Charles and was rather more graciously received. Charles and Lothar were formally reconciled at Péronne in 849 and to mark the occasion, Lothar commissioned a resplendent Gospel book from Tours, decorated with many beautiful pictures including a full-page portrait representation of Lothar himself. It is surely also with this occasion that the beautiful 'Lothar Crystal' in the British Museum, with its depiction of the story of Susannah and the Elders should be associated. Charles the Bald would undoubtedly demand from his brother Lothar an acknowledgement of his mother Judith's innocence of the charge of adultery brought against her by Lothar in 830. The choice of subject for the crystal, commissioned by *Lotharius rex francorum* would be even more appropriate in this context than for that of Lothar II and his accusations against his wife Theutberga with which the crystal is usually associated.[8]

At the same time as he became reconciled with Lothar, Charles renewed his pact with Louis the German. Another conference between the three brothers was subsequently held at Meersen in 851 to reaffirm the resolutions taken at Yütz; brotherly love and common cause against the enemies of God and against rebels was promised by each to each. As relations between Lothar and Charles became more cordial, those between the latter and Louis cooled. Lothar and Charles met at Valenciennes and at Liège to promise each other mutual aid and support for the other's heirs and Lothar became godfather to Charles' daughter Gisela. Louis the German in the meantime had received overtures from some Aquitainians asking him to send one of his sons to Aquitaine to rule over them and in 855 Louis made the first decisive break in the pact of fraternal friendship and dispatched his second son Louis the Younger into Aquitaine. As a counter move, Charles may have resorted to releasing Pippin II from his imprisonment at Soissons. At any rate, Pippin sped to Aquitaine where some of the nobles rallied to him and Louis the Younger was packed off back to Germany. As usual, enthusiasm for Pippin II was short-lived and by October Charles the Child, son of Charles the Bald, had been designated king of Aquitaine and anointed at Limoges. Within a year he in his turn was spurned, Pippin II was set up again, only to change places once more with Charles the Child, though there remained a group of Aquitainian nobles who remained loyal to Pippin. With his Danish and Aquitainian followers (Pippin was even said to have turned pagan himself[9]) Pippin plundered Aquitaine at will. Such violent vacillations in the Aquitainian nobles' affections for Pippin II cannot simply be attributed to his character. It may be that the Aquitainian aristocracy, or a faction within it, were prepared to back any ruler who seemed unlikely to dominate them, but we should not think in terms of Aquitainian separatism or underestimate the force of the Carolingians' own struggle for power which focused on Aquitaine and divided the nobles' loyalties.[10] In the crisis of 858 when Louis the German invaded the west Frankish kingdom, the Aquitainians allied against Charles the Bald but soon transferred their loyalties back to the subking Charles the Child. Pippin himself was captured in 864 and imprisoned at Senlis. Thereafter he disappears from the sources.

After 855, the government of Aquitaine underwent radical transformation. Before 840, it had been conducted by a virtually autonomous king, ruling in person from one of his rural palaces. The sons of Charles the Bald however (Louis the Stammerer succeeded his brother Charles in Aquitaine in 866), were but nominal rulers; they did not rule in person, they had no chancery and could issue no instruments; they were no longer empowered to bestow privileges on their subjects, endow religious establishments or dispose of royal property. All rights were vested in Charles the Bald who tried to rule Aquitaine directly from his own court and make the Aquitainian nobles directly dependent on him for favours. Charles' itinerary, however, indicates that after 855 he never resided in Aquitaine and may not even have visited the region. As the king lost the ability to enforce his will in Aquitaine, so it became apparent that this policy of centralization would not work and the nobles gradually gathered the substance of royal power into their own hands.[11]

The Emperor Lothar retired to the monastery of Prüm on 22 September 855 and there, six days later, he died. Reaffirming the old principle of partition, Lothar's kingdom was divided between his three sons (see Map 10). Lothar II received Lotharingia, Louis II received the imperial title and the kingdom of Italy, and the sickly Charles was made king of Provence. It was Lotharingia which became the object of the territorial ambitions of the rulers of east and west Francia for the next century. Louis the German and Charles the Bald, temporarily reconciled on Lothar's death, soon renewed their quarrel; Lothar II in his turn renewed his father's alliance with Charles and Louis the German turned to the Emperor Louis II.

III

Of all the three kingdoms created at Verdun in 843, that of Louis the German was the most successful in achieving stability.[12] Although it was as heterogeneous as the other two kingdoms, its tribes of Bavarians, Swabians, Rhine and Main Franks, Thuringians and Saxons became far more integrated into the kingdom than, say, the Aquitainians were into the west Frankish kingdom. The personal authority of the king was strong and Louis had to contend to a much lesser extent with disaffected nobles or the weakening of royal authority through concessions to counts and higher clergy. He also seems to have managed to avoid being dependent on one or other aristocratic party. That campaigns against the Slavs were still being mounted no doubt contributed to the relative stability of the kingdom, for there was still room for expansion. Only in Saxony, Thuringia and the marcher regions was Louis less active, and in consequence some families in these areas, such as the Liudolfings and Liutpoldings, rose to prominence. Louis the Younger was married to Liutgard, daughter of Liudolf, the head of the Liudolfing family, and before 861 Louis the German had married his other two sons to the daughters of leading magnates: Carloman of Bavaria wed the daughter of Duke Ernest of Bavaria and Charles the Fat married Richardis, daughter of Erchangar, a Frankish count. Louis' own wife was the Welf Emma, sister to his stepmother Judith. This marriage policy seems to have been designed to keep the nobles loyal and while Louis the German was alive it was reasonably successful. After his death however, factions quickly formed. In the event it was Louis' own sons who proved Louis' most determined opponents; they chose as their supporters other nobles and groups of neighbouring Slavs. Carloman, for example, formed an alliance with Ratislav of Moravia against Louis. In order to settle the problem of his sons' insurrection, Louis defined the succession for his three sons and tried to do so in terms of national groups and the distribution of the royal fisc. Carloman was allotted Bavaria and the marcher region bordering Moravia and Bohemia, Louis the Younger's portion consisted of Franconia, Thuringia and Saxony, and Charles the Fat was given Swabia and Rhaetia. When it suited them however, as is clear from the Annals of Fulda, Louis' sons were active in the assistance they rendered their father.

Louis the German, basing himself in Regensburg and Frankfurt, maintained the palace administration of his father though he ceased to issue capitularies and the *missatica* and county system was gradually transformed. Louis had a chancery and a chapel, but from 854 the posts of archchaplain and archchancellor were held by the same person: first Grimald, abbot of Weissenberg and St Gall, and then after 870, Liutbert, archbishop of Mainz (863–89). Louis made the learned abbot of Fulda, Hraban Maur, archbishop of Mainz in 847, and at the king's request Hraban held a general synod in Mainz in the year of his consecration. This council renewed the decisions taken at the Reform Council of 813 and promoted the Frankish church reforms in the east Frankish kingdom. Further assemblies and synods of secular and clerical leaders were held, though little is known of what these meetings achieved.

Politically and ecclesiastically Louis the German was closely involved in Slav affairs, and continued his father's policy of interfering in Slav internal politics in order to establish Frankish overlordship. Pribina, the Moravian ruler, for example, was baptized at Salzburg in 835 and granted the Slovene area on the Zala and Lake Balaton by the Frankish ruler. Pribina was driven out by Duke Mojmir who in his turn was overthrown by his Christian nephew Ratislav with the help of Louis the German. Ratislav, however, remained an enemy of Louis and tried to throw off Frankish suzerainty in both the political and religious spheres. Ratislav's capture in 870 by Louis the German put an end to his war of independence but his nephew and successor Svatopluk carried on the fight, so that by 874 Louis the German recognized Moravian independence in return for an annual tribute. Arnulf in 890 moreover acknowledged Moravian dominance in Bohemia.

As far as church matters were concerned, the mission to the Slavs conducted from Salzburg and discussed in Chapter Three had since the 830s expanded into Bohemia, Moravia and Croatia, and this region became part of the ecclesiastical province of Salzburg. Moravia, however, was anxious to be separated from the Frankish diocese of Salzburg. To this end, Ratislav appealed to Byzantium to send him some priests and the following year the Greek missionaries Cyril and Methodios arrived. These two men were later to become renowned for their work in Bulgaria, but their work in Moravia was no less important. In Moravia, the Greek missionary enterprise was supported by the Popes, Hadrian II and John VIII. The missionaries translated the Bible and the Roman liturgy into Slavonic and created for the purpose the Glagolitic script based on Greek minuscule. The Pope consecrated Methodios archbishop of Sumium (Mitrovitza near Belgrade) in 870 and created a new ecclesiastical province for the Serbo-Croatian, Slovene and Moravian missionary territory. This move inevitably led to a collision with the Bavarian church and Methodios was brought before a Bavarian synod to account for himself, and imprisoned. Pope John VIII obtained Methodios' release and continued to give his support to the Moravian church. Soon after Methodios' death however, the Moravian church collapsed. [13]

Disaffected nobles in Neustria and Aquitaine sent an appeal to Louis the German in 856, asking him to come and take charge of the west Frankish kingdom. At this stage Louis was too preoccupied with the Slavs to move westwards. Charles the Bald had appointed his eldest son Louis the Stammerer, not the most competent or intelligent of young men, as subking in Neustria. The magnates of Neustria and the Bretons together rejected Louis and in July 858 they sent Abbot Adalhard of St Bertin and St Amand and Count Odo of Orleans to ask Louis the German to invade the western kingdom and put an end to the tyranny of Charles the Bald.[14] The request was supported by some of the Aquitainians. The Annals of Fulda, sympathetic towards Louis, report his great perturbation of spirit and his perplexity as to what course he should take, and how he decided finally to save the Frankish people from the oppression of one man. As an attempt to absolve Louis from any designs on his brother's kingdom it is not convincing, especially in the context of the deteriorating relations between Louis and Charles since 851. It is possible, however, that without the request from the west Frankish nobles and the promise of support from Neustria and Aquitaine, Louis would never have made such a decisive step westwards. Louis penetrated deep into west Francia and at Attigny he issued a charter dated to the first year of his reign in his brother's kingdom.[15] The invasion came just as Charles was besieging, with some success, a party of Vikings entrenched on the island of Oscellus in the Seine. Charles was obliged to raise the siege and go to meet his brother. It was not Charles who foiled his brother, however, but the bishops of the provinces of Rheims and Rouen. Louis, ensconced at Attigny, felt he needed consecration to legitimize his rule and asked the west Frankish bishops to come to Rheims on 25 November 858, presumably to crown him. The bishops, however, politely refused to co-operate and in a masterly letter composed by Hincmar, archbishop of Rheims, questioned the legality of Louis' actions.[16] Early in 859, Charles, having rallied his forces, left Auxerre with his troops and marched into the Laonnais. Louis retired into Germany and peace was finally concluded between the two brothers at Koblenz. All took oaths in their native dialects to preserve the peace. The independence of the east and west kingdoms was affirmed, and for the next decade it was the affairs of the middle kingdom, and in particular the question of Lothar II's divorce which occupied the attention of Charles the Bald and Louis the German.

On his father's death in 855, Lothar II had been proclaimed king at Frankfurt and anointed. The same year he had married, apparently for political reasons, Theutberga, a Lotharingian noblewoman, even though for some years he had been living with a woman called Waldrada, by whom he had had at least two children. By 857 Lothar II sought to dissolve his marriage to the still childless Theutberga so that he could marry Waldrada instead and have their children legitimized and recognized as his heirs. Lothar's motives for wanting a divorce are of some importance. His anxiety to have Waldrada accepted as his wife was not just his attachment to her (which seems to have been genuine) but the fact that she had already borne him a son. With both uncles quite clearly breathing down his neck and with their beady eyes on his kingdom, a legitimate heir who could command some support would have meant Lothar had some chance of preserving his inheritance. From 858 until 869 Lothar battled to get rid of his wife. His uncles, the church and the Pope himself took sides and the divorce question developed into a full-scale quarrel over the fate of Lotharingia.[17] Lothar had been supported by his own bishops, and archbishops Gunther of Cologne and Theutgaud of Trier went so far as to annul the marriage and declare the liaison with Waldrada a real marriage from the beginning. When the archbishops travelled to Rome to report their decision to Pope Nicholas I, however, they received a rude shock. Nicholas set aside the decision, deposed them both and made Lothar take Theutberga back. In the meantime Louis the German and Charles the Bald had agreed to divide Lothar II's kingdom (augmented in 863 by half Charles of Provence's territory) between them on Lothar's death. When Pope Nicholas I was succeeded by Pope Hadrian II, Lothar renewed his appeal in the hope that the new Pope would be more compliant. Hadrian agreed to raise the matter again, but it was too late; Lothar died at Piacenza on 8 August 869 and his son Hugh remained illegitimate and without an inheritance.

Taking advantage of Louis II's absence in Italy and his brother Louis the German's illness, Charles the Bald sped to Lotharingia as soon as news of his nephew's death reached him, and on 9 September was crowned and anointed king of Lotharingia in Metz cathedral by Bishop Adventius of Metz and Archbishop Hincmar of Rheims. It is with this event that the gift of two magnificent books from Charles the Bald's library are connected: his First Bible, written at Tours in 846 and his Psalter, written and decorated in the 'palace school' atelier.[18] Both contained royal portraits. Charles installed himself at Aachen, but he was unable to maintain his position and Charles was obliged to come to an agreement with Louis the German at the Colloquy of Meersen in 870. There they settled new boundaries for their kingdoms by dividing Lothar's into two (see Map 11). The lands were divided according to the number of counties, bishoprics and abbeys rather than to natural boundaries or language. Louis' portion included the *civitates* of Cologne, Trier, Metz, Strasbourg, Basle, and part of Toul and Liège. Charles received part of Toul and Liège and the *civitates* of Cambrai, Besançon, Lyons and Vienne.

V

Thereafter the most pressing problem for all three kingdoms was the question of the imperial title. Louis II had been crowned king of the Lombards by Pope Sergius II in 844 and operated from Pavia as subking under his father the Emperor Lothar. Louis had his own chapel, held assemblies and issued capitularies. After his coronation as Emperor at Easter 850 Louis ruled Italy more or less independently from Lothar with imperial powers in Rome. That is, in relation to the Papacy the Emperor retained the right to intervene in papal elections and imperial consent was necessary before a new Pope could be consecrated. After Lothar's death Louis II succeeded him as Emperor, but his real power was as king of the Lombards, with the duty to protect Rome. The Saracens presented the most urgent problem both to Louis and to the Papacy, and in fighting off repeated Saracen attacks, Pope and Emperor worked together.

Louis had no male heirs, and the question of who should succeed him involved his territory on the one hand and his imperial title on the other. Louis the German had arranged with Louis II that Carloman of Bavaria should be Louis' heir in Italy. Popes Hadrian II and John VIII, however, favoured Charles the Bald's claim, and as soon as Louis II died, on 12 August 875, Charles hurried to Italy, made a truce with Carloman (who had also travelled over the Alps), and received the imperial crown from Pope John VIII on Christmas Day 875. That this choice of Emperor was made by the Pope and the Roman church is of some significance. Charles was not acclaimed by the Frankish people, nor was he designated heir by the existing Emperor. From 875 onwards coronation by the Pope was the constitutive act for a legitimate Emperor and the Emperor in his turn gave his oath to protect the Holy See. An assembly at Pavia in February 876 acclaimed Charles as *protector et defensor* and king of Italy. To act as his *dux* and *missus* in Italy, Charles appointed Boso, who promptly married Louis II's daughter Ermengard. There was considerable resentment among the nobles of west Francia about Charles the Bald's involvement in Italy, but at Ponthion an assembly of the nobles of Francia, Burgundy, Aquitaine, Septimania, Neustria and Provence gave their consent to the decisions made at Rome and Pavia, and envoys from Louis the German also acknowledged Charles' position.

Charles tried to assert imperial authority over all the the Frankish kingdoms. Ansegis, archbishop of Sens, was made apostolic vicar for Gaul and Germany (a move which met with as little success as the appointment of Drogo of Metz to a similar position thirty years earlier) and after Louis the German's death in August 876, Charles tried to annexe some of his elder brother's kingdom. He marched to Aachen and Cologne but Louis the Younger inflicted a humiliating defeat on Charles at Andernach and destroyed for ever any aspirations Charles may have had to rule the Empire from Aachen. Nor was he long to enjoy his imperial title. John VIII summoned Charles back to assist him in Italy. After settling the affairs of his kingdom in the event of his death,[19] Charles recrossed the Alps. The expedition ended in disaster. Carloman of Bavaria was advancing on Italy, the Frankish nobles and Boso refused to assist and Charles, left with too small a force to achieve anything, was forced to return to Francia. He died on the way home on 6 October 877. It was rumoured that he had been poisoned, but it seems that he died from a severe form of dysentery, for his corpse stank so much that his retinue was obliged to bury it long before they reached St Denis.[20]

The series of events sketched in above, although important to know for an understanding of the history of the Frankish kingdoms in the second half of the ninth century, form but the general historical context for the far more radical transformations in relationships between monarch, nobles and the church within the Frankish lands, particularly in the kingdom of Charles the Bald. These we must now consider.

VI

Nithard's history of the quarrels between the sons of Louis the Pious make two things absolutely clear. The first is how essential the church and the nobility were to each contestant, and the second is the price Lothar, Louis the German and Charles the Bald had to pay to secure their position. Followers were bought with land, benefices, treasure and honours.[21] Others were compensated with new land (having lost theirs in another brother's kingdom) or were promised new land in restitution, for no one was allowed to hold benefices in more than one kingdom. Affiliation in many cases, especially in the area between the Meuse and Seine rivers, was determined by the position of a particular noble's holdings and whether he stood to lose all he had by throwing in his lot with Lothar or Charles. Sometimes two different men were bought with the same piece of land by two different kings. Even Charles the Bald's marriages were dictated by such considerations. He married Ermentrude, daughter of Odo, count of Orleans (d.834) and niece of Adalhard, a powerful noble whose support Charles needed, on 14 December 842 because 'he believed that with Adalhard's help he could win over a large part of the people to him'.[22] He subsequently married Richild after Ermentrude's death in 869 in the hope of winning support from their Lotharingian family, though other Lotharingian nobles were alienated by the promotion of Richild's family.

How Charles the Bald tried to establish a following and ingratiate himself with the higher clergy is evident from the charters from the first three years of his reign (and after). These confirm precepts made by Louis the Pious to particular important monasteries – St Mesmin de Micy, Ferrières, Fosses, Corbie, Tours – and bishoprics such as Nevers and Vienne; they make new grants of land from the royal fisc to monasteries such as St Arnulf's at Metz and to individuals such as Landri granted land in the Mâconnais, Roclin given twenty-two manses in Avallon, Nivelong conceded benefices in Auxerrois and Gâtinois, Sicfrid given possessions 'in recognition of his service' in Urgel, and so on. Other individuals were granted the revenues from particular monastic lands or made lay abbots. How much distress and resentment this could cause is evident from the case of the cell of St Josse. St Josse had been given by Charlemagne to Alcuin in about 792 to provide hospitality to strangers, especially pilgrims on their way from England to Rome; and Louis, on Judith's intercession, had ceded the cell to the monastery of Ferrières, with the understanding that whatever revenues afforded by the cell and not consumed for the care of the pilgrims should be for the use of the monks of Ferrières. Lothar then chose to grant St Josse to one of his followers.[23] In 843, Charles the Bald granted Ferrières protection from lay encroachment and promised to restore St Josse, now in his kingdom. He did so, but almost immediately seized it again and granted all the revenues and estates to Count Odulf.[24] For the next eight years, Lupus besieged the king, Louis his chancellor, Hincmar, archbishop of Rheims, and many others (nineteen letters concerning St Josse are extant) begging for the restoration of St Josse.[25] Lupus gave a heart-rending description of the poverty of the seventy-two brethren of St Josse and the community of Ferrières as a result of the deprivation of their income,[26] and suggested to Hincmar that he should point out to the king what difficulties ensued when laymen were given church property.[27] At last, in 852, St Josse was restored to Ferrières.[28]

Charles the Bald's attempt to win support with the gift of lands, honours and comital office severely weakened his position as king, not only as far as his personal wealth was concerned, but also because the aristocracy was indispensable to the maintenance of royal power at the same time as it presented a potential threat to it. It used to be thought that the Arnulfings/Pippinids eliminated other rival families in Austrasia and conquered Neustria and Burgundy supported by a small group of allied families from the Meuse and Moselle region who subsequently consituted the new Carolingian imperial aristocracy and replaced the old nobility, just as the new Carolingian dynasty replaced the Merovingians. Werner, however, has argued that there was considerable continuity between the great noble families of the Merovingian period and those of the Carolingian era.[29] Although the origins of the most important noble families under Charlemagne and Louis the Pious can be traced to the region of the Moselle and Meuse river valleys, many of the older Frankish, Neustrian and Burgundian noble families survived and assumed prominent positions, participating fully in legislative activity, privileged by birth and estates and with a preferential claim to high office, for it was from the noble class that officials were chosen.

Charlemagne had been careful, as far as we can judge, to control the power of the nobles. He appointed successors to the counties in an ultimately futile effort to prevent the office becoming hereditary and the development of dynasties in possession of positions of influence. Under Charlemagne and Louis the Pious these officials nevertheless formed a powerful group, taking an increasingly prominent part in the affairs of the kingdom. They gradually gained a footing in certain regions, both in Francia and in the newly conquered territories, with the offices tending to become hereditary in practice if not yet in principle, or else accumulating in the hands of one person.[30] Under Louis the Pious for example, Lambert administered the Nantais and Anjou, Warin the Mâconnais and Charnois, Bernard of Septimania Bitterois, Nîmes and Barcelona. This tendency continued and was even encouraged by Charles the Bald. At the time indeed, it was probably the best thing to do. Collections of counties, particularly in the marcher regions, were entrusted to one man, often a stranger in the region he was to administer, whom the king felt he could trust and rely upon to defend the region against external attack, suppress internal rebellion and exercise justice. Count Ingelram in 853 for example administered the counties of Tournai, Ostrevant, Pévèle, and Melantois; Robert the Strong was count of Angers, Blois, Tours, Autun, Auxerre and Nevers; Eccard of Autun also administered Charnois and Mâcon; Bernard of Gothia was successively count of Barcelona, Narbonne and Roussillon between 865 and 878 and also may have been count at some stage of Autun and Berry. Bernard Hairyfeet (Plantevelue or *Plantapilosa*) held some of his father Bernard of Septimania's offices (his father had been executed on Charles the Bald's orders in 844) acting as count of Toulouse from 872 and Narbonne from 878 as well as count of the Auvergne and Limousin. Vulgrin administered the Angoumois, Périgord, Agenais and possibly Saintonge. The Welf Hugh the Abbot, already master of the abbey of St Germain d'Auxerre, received after the death of Robert the Strong most of the honours and offices held by Robert, including the counties of Tours, Blois and Angers.[31]

The examples given above are those of the more prominent nobles and many of them were able to develop their power still further after the death of Charles the Bald, using the immense resources Charles the Bald had put at their disposal. In other words, the new principalities which emerged towards the end of the ninth century were not founded by rebel aristocrats but established by the king himself for sound political reasons.[32] Most of these nobles stayed loyal to Charles during his lifetime, but Bernard Hairyfeet and Bernard of Gothia, for example, were among those who rebelled against the king in 877. With this consolidation of several counties in the hands of one man Charles may well have been trying to streamline his government and ensure he had contact with all his chief administrators by reducing their numbers.

The counts' functions did not alter at first but the office tended to be passed from father to son, brother or nephew, so that certain families gained possession of lands, titles and offices with the danger that they would in time refuse to acknowledge the king's suzerainty. The famous clause in the Quierzy Capitulary of 877 has sometimes been regarded as formal recognition of the right to hereditary succession, for in it Charles the Bald decreed that should a countship fall vacant during his absence in Italy, the count's duties were to be assumed by his eldest son or by a group of the former count's chief officials and the local bishop until the king should return to appoint a new count. The interests of an heir still in his minority or the heir absent on campaign were to be protected by the family and members of the ruling group of officials.[33] The clause can be interpreted as a recognition of the existing state of affairs but it was not necessarily sanctioning its permanence. In Dhondt's view Charles the Bald reserved his right to dispose of counties, though he certainly could not dispose of them with the freedom of his predecessors. The Coulaines provisions were the most sensible to make, given the circumstances, and much the simplest to administer. Some have argued that Charles the Bald's policy of conferring an accumulation of counties on a few individuals was a desperate measure, but Dhondt pointed out long ago that most of these appointments were made when Charles' authority was at its strongest. He argued that there was a consistency in the form of administration Charles devised and that the king obviously regarded these moves as the best safeguards he could make for royal authority.

An interesting light has been thrown on the Quierzy provisions by Collins on the basis of evidence from Carolingian Catalonia.[34] From about 870 offices were retained in Catalonia on an apparently hereditary basis and this was not just a question of the continuity of tenure of office in the hands of a few families. The very nature of the comital office and the basis of its local power seems to have altered significantly in this period. The counts appointed were native to the region (and we know this was happening elsewhere in the west Frankish kingdom) and would obviously enjoy a stronger position in local society as a result. From a charter granting lands to Oliba of Carcassonne moreover, it seems that lands once administered for the king became Oliba's private property instead. This may well have happened on a larger scale south of the Pyrenees and perhaps further north, and could explain how the landed wealth of the local counts increased.

Charles the Bald's relations with particular nobles are often difficult to unravel from the laconic references to them in the sources, but it seems clear that from very few did he have complete and unswerving loyalty for the whole of his reign, and that for many others among the nobility rapid realignments according to circumstances (such as the crisis of 858) were common. The most prominent of the magnates were often related by marriage to the Carolingians, either through the ruler marrying a woman of noble family or through the ruler's daughters and sons marrying into the nobility.[35] There were also a number of direct descendants of the Carolingians of which the most notable examples are the counts of Vermandois, descended from Bernard, king of Italy. Charlemagne had married daughters of Frankish counts, as had Louis the Pious, and the Welf family of Louis' second wife Judith played an increasingly important role in the politics of the later ninth century. The Welfs were one of the aristocratic factions supporting Charles the Bald, and received many favours at his hands. Similarly Charles received valuable assistance from the family of his first wife Ermentrude and of his second wife Richild at crucial stages in his career, though in neither case was the family support long-lasting. Charles, in his turn promoted his second wife's relatives. His brother-in-law Boso, for example, became lay abbot of St Maurice of Agaune in 869, count of Vienne in 871, and was appointed *dux* in Italy by Charles the Bald in 876.

The marriages and liaisons of the daughters of Charlemagne and Louis the Pious were especially fruitful for the nobility. Gisela, Louis' daughter, for example, married Eberhard of Friuli, whose descendants were powerful in both north-east France and in Italy, and one, Berengar, even became Emperor in 915. The family of Ramnulf, count of Poitou, was descended from Hildegard, daughter of Louis the Pious; Ramnulf himself married into the Rorgonids, the descendants of Count Rorico or Rorgo.[36] The first reference we have to Rorgo is *c.* 800 when he was at Charlemagne's court. In 819/20 he was made count of the Breton march and in 832 count of Le Mans. From a liaison with Charlemagne's daughter Rotrud was born Louis, abbot of St Denis and archchancellor to Charles the Bald, while Rorgo's other children included Rorgo II, killed fighting the Vikings in 865, Gauzfrid, active in the Loire region, Bilichild who married a Bernard (their son was Bernard of Gothia) and Gauzlin, who succeeded his half-brother Louis as archchancellor to Charles the Bald. Relationship with the ruling house could raise expectations from the family of preferment, or of grants of land; and particular prizes such as the abbacy of a monastery long associated with the family may well have been regarded as that family's prerogative. If the king then chose to give that office to a member of another family resentment both towards the king and the rival family would ensue. Werner cites the instance of the ousting of Rothild, Charles the Simple's aunt, from the abbacy of Chelles by her nephew, who gave it to a Lotharingian called Hagano.[37] Rothild also happened to be the mother of Hugh, count of Maine and a daughter who had been the first wife of Hugh the Great. Offence was taken and the Robertian Huge could thenceforth count on the support of the counts of Maine!

Recent prosopographical research has made it possible to trace the political careers and family relationships not only of the descendants of the Carolingians but also of other nobles. Odo, count of Troyes, for example, first appears in a charter of Charles the Bald dated 1 October 845. During the troubled years of 842–3, Odo seems to have been granted a portion of the estates of the church of Rheims, and when these lands were restored to the archdiocese in 845, Odo received, probably in compensation, the domaine of Bannay. He married Guandimold and by 846 had been appointed count of Châteaudun, for it was with that title that he with his wife gave some land to the monastery of St Martin of Tours (an interesting document in itself, for it contains the names of twenty-three of his vassals in the witness list). In 851 Odo was made count of Angers, but this countship was given to Odo's close relative Robert the Strong the following year, and Odo was made count of Troyes instead. In the Troyes region he acted as *missus* in 853. At the beginning of 858 when Robert the Strong and other Neustrian nobles rose against Louis the Stammerer, Odo was one of them (due no doubt to his relationship with Robert) and it was Odo who, with Adalhard, abbot of St Amand (not Adalhard of St Quentin), went as envoy to Louis the German to invite him to invade the west Frankish kingdom. In consequence of the support he had rendered Louis, Odo was deprived of his county (Troyes was given to the Welf Rudolf) and rejoined Robert the Strong. By 861 both Robert and Odo had been received back into favour. Odo died on 10 August 871. Odo count of Troyes' career has long been erroneously conflated with that of Odo son of Harduin, a younger man who was one of Louis the Stammerer's party and an enemy of Robert the Strong.[38] It was Odo son of Harduin who gave his sister Ansgard in marriage to Louis the Stammerer in 862. After the defeat of Louis the Stammerer's party by Robert the Strong (acting for the king), Odo son of Harduin was also received back into the king's favour.

The granting of Odo of Troyes' lands to a Welf (and Robert the Strong's honours were for the most part given to the Welf Hugh the Abbot) and the existence of another opposing faction round Louis the Stammerer are some of the large number of indications we have that a number of aristocratic factions had formed during the reign of Charles the Bald. The most important of these factions were the Robertians, the family of Robert the Strong, who were possibly related to Charles the Bald's first wife Ermentrude, and the Welfs, the family of the Empress Judith, Charles' mother. The 858 crisis was as much an internal conflict between these two opposing factions as a revolt against Charles the Bald, though the disillusion and loss of faith and confidence in Charles the Bald as a leader in consequence of his failure to deal effectively or conclusively with the Vikings should not be underestimated. The rebels were the Robertians and their supporters, mostly from the region between the Seine and the Loire where the Viking attacks had been the most destructive and where Charles the Bald's reprisals against particular nobles (such as the beheading of Gauzbert of Maine in 853) had caused deep resentment. Charles the Bald was supported by the Welfs. Two important letters by Hincmar of Rheims to Rudolf, Charles the Bald's Welf uncle, indicate that there was a lot of far from friendly rivalry between the parties of aristocrats and that Charles the Bald himself was caught between two hostile parties.[39]

Once the existence and influence of these noble factions is recognized, much of the political development of the second half of the ninth century becomes much clearer. These factions took it in turns to enjoy the king's favour and were the only instruments with whose help the king could form and carry out policy. Even Charles the Bald's power to depose or instate counts was successful only when a noble faction approved the move and it was done in their interest. After receiving large bribes from Acfrid (Egfrid), for example, Charles the Bald took away the county of Bourges from Gerald and gave it to Acfrid. The latter was attacked and killed by Gerald's men and Gerald reinstalled himself in the county. In 863, Humfrid, marquis of Gothia, took the county of Toulouse after killing the king's appointee.

Another faction of nobles seems to have been involved in the revolt of Carloman, Charles the Bald's youngest son, though their identity remains unknown. Carloman, born in 848, had been tonsured in 854 as part of his father's deliberate policy of avoiding partition of the kingdom by removing his younger sons from the line of succession and destining them for the church instead. Carloman was ordained deacon in 860 and in the subsequent decade was made abbot of St Médard of Soissons, St Germain of Auxerre, St Amand, St Riquier, Lobbes and St Arnulf (Metz). Carloman resented being made a cleric and after the death of two of his brothers in 865 and 866, seems to have begun to cherish ambitions to be a warrior and have some part in the kingdom of his father. By 870 he seems too to have gathered together a band of sympathizers and supporters, among them certain disaffected nobles in Lotharingia and Flanders. Before his revolt had achieved anything, Carloman was captured, tried and imprisoned at Senlis. Pope Hadrian II attempted to intervene on Carloman's behalf, but the latter took matters into his own hands by escaping to Flanders where he mustered his followers. Early in 871, the Frankish bishops met under Hincmar of Rheims' presidency at Compiègne and declared any of the rebels normally under the jurisdiction of the province of Rheims to be excommunicate. One bishop, Hincmar of Laon, refused to agree to this, and McKeon has suggested that there might have been a stronger connection between Hincmar of Laon and Carloman, and more support for Carloman's revolt, than the sources would indicate.[40] Carloman and his supporters continued to present a threat to Charles the Bald, but in 873 Carloman was tried again and blinded; he fled to the kingdom of Louis the German and died there in about 877.

In relation to the nobles therefore, Charles the Bald's power and royal authority were seriously weakened. Whereas the lay aristocracy was divided in its loyalty to Charles the Bald, the bishops and the church backed him strongly, and it is time now to consider the importance of Charles the Bald's relations with the church and the extent to which the church and the higher clergy bolstered or undermined royal power.

VII

From Nithard's History it is clear how much part the church had already taken in determining the course of events in the first three years of Charles the Bald's reign, and how essential their support had become. Like the nobles, the higher clergy used the precariousness of Charles' position to assert an authority and a function that they had not exercised before, insisting on the necessity for their participation in all deliberations about the future of the kingdom and in the maintenance of their lands, rights and privileges. This was no empty formula. Charles' attempt to win military support had resulted in a wholesale granting out of church land to his royal vassals, so that he began his reign after Verdun under pressure not only to restore ecclesiastical property (twenty-four charters witness to his attempt to do so on quite a large scale), but also to acknowledge the higher clergy's 'rightful' position in relation both to the king and to the government of the kingdom. In this context, the agreement made in the king's name at Coulaines in November 843 (reiterated in rather more specific terms at Pîtres in 869) had crucial implications. The church was to retain all honours and wealth received from Charlemagne and Louis the Pious and, in return for loyalty and obedience, Charles promised to protect and promote ecclesiastical interests, with the unspoken understanding that the said loyalty and obedience would be withheld if he did not. Coulaines not only involved an undertaking with regard to the church; it was a landmark in the development of reciprocal relations between king and *fideles*. Charles promised to rule according to justice. He said that he wished all his subjects to be assured that henceforth he would not deprive anyone, of whatever condition or dignity, of the *honor* to which he was entitled, that he would not despoil anyone on a whim, nor as a result of evil counsel, nor from greed, but that he would act in accordance with reason, justice and equity. He confirmed the personality principle of the law by guaranteeing to each man the maintenance of his own law.[41] In effect his kingship was made conditional; all were to honour the church and clergy and honour and serve the king; but the king for his part had to honour all his subjects. What Nelson has termed a 'working partnership between king, clergy and people' was created.[42]

A careful balance had to be struck between exploiting the great material wealth of the church and promoting the church's interests. But the king was obliged to continue to grant ecclesiastical benefices to his followers and excuse himself to the clergy on the grounds of necessity. Charles increased markedly, for example, the granting of lay abbacies, particularly after 858. Lay abbacies were received by many of his nobles, as well as members of the royal household such as Adalhard the seneschal, Vivian his chamberlain, Warin, one of his military commanders, and Gauzlin his archchancellor.[43] Two of his sons were actually tonsured and received a number of abbacies – Lothar was made abbot of St Germain of Auxerre and possibly St Jean of Réomé as well, while Carloman at one stage, as we have seen, was abbot of no less than six monasteries. Charles himself became abbot of St Denis in 867, and Louis the Stammerer was the lay abbot of St Martin of Tours, Marmoutier and St Crépin of Soissons.[44]

On the other hand, Charles used an extensive exercise of patronage to secure the support of his clergy. This manifested itself not only in the granting of land, immunity, royal protection and privileges (such as the right to mint coins, hold markets and receive tolls) to episcopal churches and monasteries, as his surviving charters richly attest, but also in the preferment of individuals to bishoprics and abbacies. Of the 42 bishops assembled at the Synod of Tusey in 860 for example, 11 were royal appointees and 7 more had been put forward as candidates by Hincmar of Rheims and were therefore likely at that stage to be king's men as well. A significant number of the most politically and strategically important bishoprics and abbacies were in the hands of loyal ex-officers of the palace, nominated by the king.[45] This had the effect of making closer the connections between the royal monasteries, dioceses, palace chapel and chancery and the king.[46] Charles the Bald's patronage was in fact exercised very cannily.[47] Out of what might have become a dangerously weak position in relation to the church after 843 he made one of mutual dependence. In return for their enjoyment of his favour the church offered the king a number of essential services – warriors for his army, the annual gift and, most important of all in the material sphere, hospitality to the king and his household.[48] From the clergy, moreover, were recruited notaries for the chancery and clerics for the chapel; and individual members of the higher clergy such as Hincmar, archbishop of Rheims, and Ansegis, archbishop of Sens, acted as close advisers to the king on both ecclesiastical and secular matters.

Hincmar of Rheims, in particular, dominated Frankish ecclesiastical affairs for nearly forty years.[49] Born in 806 in the north of the country, Hincmar was brought up at the abbey of St Denis, where his mentor and teacher was Abbot Hilduin. He also spent some time at the court of Louis the Pious at Aachen and by 830 was taking part in the public affairs of the Frankish kingdom. Hincmar remained loyal to Louis the Pious throughout the decade from 830 to 840. In 845 he was consecrated archbishop of Rheims (the see had been vacant for a decade) and seems to have made the restitution of the property of the archdiocese of Rheims, granted out to secure support from his followers by Charles the Bald, a condition for his accepting the archbishopric. It was Hincmar who composed the splendid letter to Louis the German in 858, and after

858 the archbishop played an increasingly active role in public life, though he and the king fell out when Charles tried to trespass on what Hincmar regarded as ecclesiastical prerogative. His successful attempt in 866 to appoint Wulfad to the important see of Bourges was, for example, sharply contested by Hincmar, on the grounds that Wulfad was one of the priests ordained by the deposed Ebbo. At the Synod of Savonnières in 859 all Ebbo's priests, deacons and sub-deacons had been deposed by Hincmar. The appointment of Ansegis, archbishop of Sens, as vicar apostolic was also opposed. Hincmar regarded the creation of a primate as a threat to the position of the metropolitans. It was in response to this that he wrote his treatise *De iure metropolitanorum* and the Life of Remigius designed to demonstrate the superiority of the churches of Rheims over all other churches.[50] Hincmar's wish to preserve the superiority of the metropolitans, to resist interference from Rome and from the Frankish king was dramatically challenged with the case of Hincmar of Laon.

Hincmar of Laon (835/8–79) had been made bishop of Laon in 858 by his uncle Hincmar of Rheims, and had supported Charles warmly in the 858 crisis by placing the lands of Laon diocese at the king's disposal and receiving a large number of royal vassals (more than the diocese could afford) on these lands. In gratitude, Charles restored some property to Laon in 860. Hincmar of Laon himself soon became an important figure, acting as *missus* on a number of occasions. By 867, however, his greed had got the better of him and complaints were received by the king from his vassals that the bishop had seized their lands unjustly. The king upbraided Hincmar of Laon and required him to appear before a royal court. All the property of the diocese of Laon was confiscated and Charles forbade Hincmar to receive any services or income from it. Hincmar of Rheims, zealous for the rights of the church (though not by then quite so warmly in favour of his nephew personally) remonstrated with Charles, declaring it was a bishop's right to be tried by a proper metropolitan's tribunal. In the face of Hincmar's secret appeal to Rome and papal intervention Hincmar of Rheims decided to support the king. At the Synod of Douzy in 871 Hincmar of Laon was deposed. Thereafter he sided openly with Carloman against Charles the Bald. He was captured and imprisoned in 873, blinded in 875 and died two years later.[51]

If Hincmar of Rheims and his contemporaries were clear about what the king should not do they were equally productive in their interpretation of the king's role as a *ministerium* and in providing a theory of kingship. Their treatises on kingship (the *Fürstenspiegel* or Mirrors for Princes) and on government and administration reveal that the roles of king and clergy that had obtained in the first half of the ninth century were reversed. Then the king had proffered advice on the organization and reform of the church; now a bishop offered admonitions and counsel concerning the government of the kingdom. Hincmar's treatises, *De regis persona et regio ministerio* and the *De ordine palatii*, and the other Frankish *Fürstenspiegel* show how absolutely and unequivocally the king's office was interpreted as a Christian one and that Christian kingship was the predominant concern of Carolingian political thought. What evolved in the course of the ninth century and reached its fullest expression in the writings of Hincmar of

Rheims was a clearly enunciated theory of Christian kingship in which the power to govern was a gift and responsibility given by God.

VIII

Charles the Bald's achievements in the administrative sphere have often been neglected, or even ignored, yet they witness to the maintenance of the Carolingian administrative system and the continued exercise of royal authority through the *missi dominici* and the counts. One important indication of the survival of a system of communication between the king and his officials is the speed and efficiency with which the instructions for collecting the tribute for the Northmen in 845, 860–1, 862, 866 and 877 were issued and the tribute itself collected. In 845, 7000 pounds of silver was demanded in April and paid by July, whether as a result of a general levy or not is not known. An evaluation of church property was carried out in 853, with written inventories being returned to the king, and this has sometimes been associated with the king's need to assess the kingdom's resources against the necessity of further payments. The sum of 3000 pounds of silver (this was later raised to 5000) was demanded by Weland the Viking in 860–1 in return for driving another band of Vikings away from the Seine. His fee was raised by taxes on church treasure, on *mansi* (the portions into which estates were divided) and the property of merchants. Grain and wine were added to the payment. A further payment of 6000 pounds of silver was made to the Vikings by Robert the Strong. How he raised it is unknown, but he could only have drawn on his own resources and those of other Neustrian nobles. To raise the tribute of 4000 pounds of silver in 866, a complicated levy was imposed throughout the kingdom followed by a series of 'topping-up' taxes: each *mansus* contributed, according to the status of its occupant, sums ranging from half a *denarius* to six *denarii*; a tenth of the value of their property was required from the merchants and priests were asked for as much as they could afford, and the military tax of *heribannus* was asked of all free Franks. An extra *denarius* was then demanded from every *mansus*, whether free or unfree, and a payment in wine and silver was contributed from the magnates.[52] The sum was raised in five months and no more tribute had to be paid until 877. Then it was levied in a similar way, though the merchants were not called on this time. Only a very well organized administration could have succeeded in collecting these payments. It should be noted too that the magnates seem to have been called on to contribute only as a last resort; the church, the merchants and the *mansi*, in that order, were levied first.

It is not known to what extent these payments of tribute actually diminished the royal treasury or how much they can be associated with the sudden increase in the number of mints striking coins after 864. There seems to be no strong evidence to warrant the assumption that the treasury was milked dry and the economy greatly strained, though this has not prevented such an assumption being made.[53] Metcalf's comments on the currency in the reign of Charles the Bald indeed question the assumption.[54] Coinage under Charles the Bald was struck in very large quantities (though Metcalf's suggested figures seem improbably large) in parts at least of Gaul, and it circulated widely. The circulation of coinage and the consequent possibility of the existence of a money economy have prompted some numismatists to suggest that Gaul had reached a much higher level of commercial development in the second half of the ninth century than used to be supposed.

The Edict of Pîtres of 864 which announced a massive reorganization and renewal of the coinage in an attempt to establish a uniform type of coin listed ten mints, including 'the palace' (possibly Compiègne), at Chalon-sur-Saône, Melle, Narbonne, Orleans, Paris, Quentovic, Rheims, Rouen, Sens. Only these centres were to be authorized to mint coins, and they were to mint new coins with a cross and the name of the mint on one side and the royal monogram and king's name on the other. In fact, the coins issued are the so-called GDR type bearing the inscription GRATIA D-I REX instead of the king's name. Instead of the 10 mints listed in the Edict moreover, no less than 100 active mints are known. Lafaurie suggested that the 10 mints were where the coins were struck, whereas the 100 active 'mints' represent the cities from which the coins were issued.[55] Grierson does not accept this, and argues that the great proliferation of mints after 864 was due to the need to achieve the transformation of local plate into coin in order to pay the Vikings. This is an odd argument. Vikings were surely interested in the total weight of silver of the coins rather than in having the coins themselves. Nor have significant finds of Frankish coins yet been found in Scandinavia. Metcalf asserts that the number of mints of Francia and Flanders are of a piece with the great volume of currency and the rapid monetary circulation in these regions. The Edict is in fact an invaluable indication of the organization of Charles the Bald's government. It provided that deniers in circulation at the time of the publishing of the Edict were to remain legal tender until 11 November 864 but from Martinmas (11 November) only the new coins (that is, the GDR coins) were to be legal tender and anyone trying to use the old coins was to forfeit them. The king's officials were to ensure the law was observed, moneyers were to be appointed by the count to the region in which there was to be a mint and were to be punished (by amputation of the hand) for any abuses of their position. Other provisions were made in the Edict for the supply of silver bullion for new coinage, the means for detecting forgery, and commerce in precious metal. Strict control of the issue of coinage was stressed as essential.[56]

The chancery of Charles the Bald was well organized; both his archchancellors, Louis, second cousin to Charles and abbot of St Denis (840–67), and Gauzlin, abbot of St Amand (867–882), were men of high calibre, and the chancery proved a nursery for the higher clergy, for many of them were made bishops. Of the 354 genuine charters from Charles the Bald's reign, 111 survive in the originals; the rest are mostly transmitted through the archives of ecclesiastical establishments. The richest deposits of diplomata are those relating to St Denis, St Maur des Fosses, St Martin of Tours, Châlons-sur-Marne, St

Germain of Auxerre and St Philibert. The principal geographical areas in which Charles the Bald's grants to monasteries are concentrated are on the one hand, Francia, Neustria and Burgundy, and on the other, Septimania and the Spanish march; Aquitaine is relatively neglected. Whether the standards of professionalism remained as high in Charles the Bald's chancery as they had been in that of Louis the Pious is open to question. On the evidence of notarial competence in using tironian notes – the notarial shorthand – which were very rarely used by the third quarter of the ninth century, Tessier has suggested there may have been less technical instruction offered in the later Carolingian chancery, though this does not necessarily mean that the chancery itself declined as an institution.[57] It is worth noting in this respect that the volume of instruments issued by the royal chancery decreased rapidly after 877. Charles the Bald's chancery produced a massive output of grants of immunity, exemption from tolls, freedom of election of abbots, and royal protection, but the light this charter evidence throws on Charles' reign has still to be studied in detail.

Capitularies valid for the whole kingdom were issued by Charles the Bald, though he drew extensively on the capitulary collection by Ansegisus drawn up in his father's reign, and many of his own capitularies make a point of citing those of his predecessors. Of the thirty-eight capitularies identified by Boretius, nine are proclamations announcing decisions taken at such meetings as that between Louis the German and Charles the Bald at Koblenz (860), Tusey (865), Metz (867) and Meersen (870), or the announcement of Charles' election as king of Lotharingia. Other capitularies comprise extensive administrative arrangements such as the Capitularies of Pitres of 862 and 864 on the construction of fortified defences on the Seine, other matters 'to be observed as the law throughout his kingdom', and on coinage (discussed above), the arrangements for the government of Aquitaine in 844, the organization of the Spanish march (844), the capitularies containing instructions to the *missi* of 844, 853, 860, 861 and 864 (*missi* continued to be employed for regular inspection as well as on special assignments and were chosen from among the local notables), and the final arrangements for the administration of the kingdom and the disposition of his possessions in the event of his death made before his departure for Italy in 877.

Some indication of how Charles the Bald's orders were transmitted is given by the Annals of St Bertin in 869. Hincmar of Rheims reports that the king had dispatched letters to the abbeys, abbots and bishops in every part of his kingdom, requesting them to make inventories of their estates and the number of manses each possessed by 1 May in the following year. The royal vassals were to write descriptions of the lands held by counts in virtue of their office and the counts were to do the same for the lands, and the buildings on them, held by their vassals. Charles also ordered that for every 100 manses one man was to be sent to Pîtres, and for every 1000 manses a cart with two oxen was to be sent. The young men were to complete the work on the fort at Pîtres and man it when it was built. A written report on markets had been required in 864. This wholesale assessment of his resources may well have had a specific object rather than a general one, but this is not clear.

Not only were his orders dispatched to all parts of his kingdom; the king himself was constantly on the move, though not necessarily for administrative purposes. Nevertheless his presence was undoubtedly felt, and could be of positive benefit to his hosts in the patronage he extended and in the business the presence of the royal household stimulated in a region.[58] Charles' itinerary shows that he hardly ever stayed in any one place for more than a few days and very rarely for as long as two or three months, apart from the winters he spent at his palaces at Compiègne and Quierzy.[59] A few residences and monasteries north of the Loire – St Médard at Soissons, St Quentin, Tours, Rheims, Servais, Attigny, St Denis, Compiègne and Quierzy – were more favoured than any others. Single visits are recorded at a great many other places and it is notable how relatively seldom Charles stayed in centres in Aquitaine, particularly after 855. Charles the Bald's evident ability as an administrator and legislator is an important aspect of his career as king and helped somewhat to compensate for his deficiencies as a charismatic war-leader; it deserves to be studied more fully. Just as the king's activity as legislator enhanced the royal authority, so Charles appears to have taken steps to enhance kingship in spheres other than the indications of wealth and trappings of royalty one might expect.[60]

IX

The obligations and sacred character of the king became more clearly defined and expressed in the liturgy of the royal inauguration ceremonies in the second half of the ninth century.[61] Until then, the blessing of the church in the king-making process was a relatively minor aspect of the inauguration ritual, a ritual which could comprise a number of different traditions – none of them constitutive in itself – such as election, enthronement, celebratory feast, elevation and so on. Anointing seems to have become part of the Frankish kingmaking ritual for the first time in 751, and was probably introduced by members of Pippin's entourage in an attempt, not only to give the royal office an extra mystery and call down God's blessing on the new ruler, but also to provide churchmen with a role in constituting a king. It is significant that anointing had been introduced into the rite for ordination to the priesthood in Francia at about the same time as Pippin was anointed. Yet anointing did not become necessary for legitimate kingship or part of the accepted sequence of ritual acts which together constituted a king for another century. The authority of un-anointed kings was never questioned, and no ecclesiastical rite accompanied the raising to the subkingship, for example, of Louis the Pious, Charles his brother or Charles the Bald. In 848 at Orleans however, Charles the Bald was anointed and crowned king of Aquitaine by Archbishop Wenilo of Sens, in a ceremony probably at least supervised by Archbishop Hincmar of Rheims. As anointing had not hitherto been a necessary part of the kingmaking ritual, the event has been regarded as possessing particular significance, though for different reasons. Some think Charles asserted his newly established authority at last in 848;

others that it was a desperate attempt to secure his position by elevating the monarchy to a sacred office appointed by God.[62] Whatever the reasoning behind the 848 ritual, two things need to be stressed. In the first place, the sacred character of the king's office was emphasized, the king was consecrated to God, his duties were clearly defined and a special benediction for the king to enable him to carry out his royal functions was conferred. In the second place, the bishops asserted their claim to take an indispensable part in the kingmaking process. Hincmar, archbishop of Rheims, the principal initiator of the new rites, stressed that the anointing of Charles the Bald in 848 constituted him king. With his anointing and coronation the king undertook to fulfil certain obligations as ruler. He promised to uphold the Christian faith, the privileges of the church, the secular laws of the kingdom and the welfare of his people; a formal oath to this effect was incorporated into the coronation *ordo*. The anointing of the king by bishops and the fact that the rite became constitutive of course raises the question of the kind of relationship thus created between king and clergy. Inevitably, each side took a different view. Hincmar of Rheims, who composed the four earliest coronation *ordines* to survive (from 856, 866, 869 and 877), may well have intended the king to be in a sense under episcopal jurisdiction, though he did not go so far as to assert the right of bishops to depose kings. The king in his turn was committed to upholding ecclesiastical rights and privileges and acknowledged how essential the church was to his royal character.[63]

Although the bishops assumed, through the liturgy, a crucial role in the inauguration ritual, the ecclesiastical initiative should not be overemphasized. Charles the Bald himself was probably as much responsible as Hincmar of Rheims for the elaboration and introduction of the anointing ritual. Obviously he consented to participate in the liturgical rites because he thought he stood to gain from it. Nor should we be overly cynical about his motives. What else we know about Charles suggests that he took very seriously his kingship as a *ministerium* ordained by God, and his role as a Carolingian, next in a line of a series of great kings. Charles the Bald's political circumstances and the threat to his position from the nobles of Neustria and Francia moreover meant that any move to enhance his dignity and emphasize aspects of his kingship other than those of warlord and legislator would have met with his approval and encouragement. It is no coincidence that all the anointing ceremonies occur at critical moments in his reign or in the working out of his policies. Thus in 848, Charles was crowned and anointed king of Aquitaine not only to exalt him in the eyes of the Aquitainian and Frankish nobles but also to provide an extra, and holy, sanction for taking the kingdom of Aquitaine from Pippin, about whose legitimate rights there remained some doubt. The subsequent coronation of the eight-year-old Charles 'the Child' at Limoges was a similar move. The coronation of Charles the Bald at Metz was quite clearly intended to add legitimacy to Charles' seizure of the kingdom of Lotharingia, and it should be remembered that Louis the German had himself wished to be consecrated king of west Francia in 858. Louis the Stammerer's anointing in 877 moreover constituted a vital strengthening of a precarious position. Judith, Charles the Bald's daughter, was crowned and anointed on the occasion of her marriage to king Aethel-wulf of Wessex in 856. Aethelwulf conferred on Judith the title of queen, which according to Prudentius of Troyes was 'not customary to him or to his people'.[64] Judith's anointing may have been intended in part as a form of protection. She was after all the first Carolingian princess to be married to a foreign ruler, and she was at twelve years of age marrying an elderly man with a clutch of sons older than herself. The marriage itself has been associated with Charles the Bald's need for English assistance against the Vikings.[65] The coronation of Queen Ermentrude, Charles the Bald's wife, in 866 on the other hand has the character of a fertility rite. The order of service asked God to bless her with children.[66] Ermentrude had in fact already produced a number of children, including six sons, but none was satisfactory as far as Charles the Bald was concerned. By September 866, four of them were dead, Carloman had been tonsured in 854 and the eldest, Louis the Stammerer, seems to have been a weakling. Charles the Bald's second wife was also crowned and blessed, in 870, and crowned Empress by the Pope in 877. Hyam thinks that the ceremony for queens may have been carried out because of the queens' desire for special designation to help them maintain their positions.[67] It may also have been in the king's interest to have his queen so distinguished. Queens fulfilled an important function in the royal household (they played a part in controlling the treasury), as well as bearing future heirs. They could act as patronesses, and were often concerned in land grants to monasteries, and on a number of important occasions acted as intermediaries between king and the Pope, the clergy and other Carolingian rulers.

Other means of enhancing his dignity as king were exploited by Charles the Bald. He was an active patron of culture and learning; scholars dedicated their works to him and he was presented with many fine books.[68] Many monasteries benefited from his munificence and he himself became the abbot of St Denis in 867. In imitation of Charlemagne's palace chapel at Aachen, the chapel of St Mary at Compiègne was consecrated in 877.[69] Charles requested that all royal anniversaries be commemorated in the churches and monasteries of the kingdom and prayers offered up for every member of his family.[70] That a number of portraits of Charles were painted in books presented to or commissioned by him, is a further indication of the image of the king becoming more elaborate and more public.[71] The imagery of most of these portraits is quite complex. That in the Vivian Bible for example (BN lat. 1) recalls the depictions of King David and reinforces the idea, often expressed by Hincmar of Rheims and other Frankish authors of the *Fürstenspiegel*, that the Frankish kings were the successors to the monarchs of the Old Testament, just as the Franks were the new chosen people of God. The portrait in Charles' Third Bible (the Bible of San Paolo fuori le Mura) stresses the king's earthly might, his personal goodness and his divine appointment, while the representation of Charles in his Psalter (BN lat. 1152) added to these kingly attributes Charles' functions as lawgiver and judge. In his Prayer book (now in the Schatzkammer der Residenz in Munich), Charles is portrayed in an attitude of proskynesis before the foot of the cross. Prayers before the cross were part of the Good Friday liturgy in the mid-ninth century and Deshman has therefore related this portrait of Charles to the Good Friday liturgy in which Charles participated at St Denis after 867. No other portrait of Charles illustrates quite so clearly the bond between the church and the ruler and the king's personal piety. The king is depicted as the 'exalted servant' supplicating Christ, and an association is made in the iconography between Christ the king and Charles the king whose power comes from God.[72] Portraits of the king with inscriptions proclaiming his greatness may have been intended for his eyes only (though he presented both his First Bible and his Psalter to the cathedral church of Metz).

But however idealized, these portraits, painted on parchment, carved in ivory or sculpted in bronze, are an expression at least of Charles' and his artists' attitude towards kingship; they complement the liturgical affirmation of the king's functions. The coronation *ordines*, the commemoration of royal anniversaries, the new interest in royal genealogies and the royal portraits together constitute a religious and public enhancement of kingship at precisely the time when the king's real power was being challenged. It was an expression of an ideal, an ideal that, however removed from reality it might become, remained a factor in Frankish politics and contributed to the survival of kingship as a political institution.

NOTES

1. *Annales Bertiniani, s.a.*, 837.
2. On the idea of Empire, see R. Folz, *L'idée d'Empire dans l'occident du Ve au XIVe siècle* (Paris 1953); Eng. trs. 1969, and U. Penndorf, *Das Problem der 'Reichseinheitsidee' nach der Teilung von Verdun* (Munich 1974).
3. A. Kleinclausz, *L'Empire Carolingien* (Dijon and Paris 1902), 263–80.
4. Nithard, III, 5, and see J. Knight Bostock, *A Handbook on Old High German Literature*, 2nd edn. (Oxford 1976), 187–89.
5. F. L. Ganshof, 'Zur Entstehungsgeschichte und Bedeutung des Vertrags von Verdun (843)', *DA* 12 (1956), 313–30; Eng. trs. Ganshof, *Carolingians*, 289–302. See also P. Classen, 'Die Verträge von Verdun und von Coulaines 843 als politischen Grundlagen des westfränkisches Reiches', *HZ* 196 (1963), 1–85.
6. See Pippin II of Aquitaine, *Recueil*.
7. *Annales Fuldenses*, 846.
8. P. E. Schramm and F. Mütherich, *Denkmale der deutschen Könige und Kaiser* (Munich 1962), No. 31, 125–26.
9. *Annales Bertiniani, s.a.*, 864.
10. J. Martindale, 'Charles the Bald and the government of Aquitaine', *Charles the Bald: Court and Kingdom*, M. T. Gibson and J. L. Nelson (eds) (Oxford 1981), 109–35.
11. Ibid., and see her references to earlier work on Aquitaine.
12. Owing to the forthcoming study of the east Frankish kingdom after 800 by T. Reuter, I have confined my comments on Louis the German and his successors to the minimum, but see T. Schieder (ed.), *Handbuch der Europäischen Geschichte* I (Stuttgart 1976), 596–640, 665–707.
13. A. P. Vlasto, *The Entry of the Slavs into Christendom* (Cambridge 1970), 20–85,

and J. Bujnoch, *Zwischen Rom und Byzanz*, 2nd edn. (Vienna and Cologne 1972) – a collection of sources on the Slav missions in German translation.

14. *Annales Bertiniani, s.a.*, 857.
15. Böhmer–Mühlbacher I, No. 1345; *MGH SS* XXI, 363.
16. Recorded by Flodoard, *Historia*, III, 20.
17. *Annales Bertiniani*, 863; see P. McKeon, *Hincmar of Laon and Carolingian Politics* (Urbana, Chicago and London 1978), 39–56 and J. A. McNamara and S. F. Wemple, 'Marriage and divorce in the Frankish kingdom', *Women in Medieval Society*, S. M. Stuard (ed.) (Philadelphia 1976), 95–124.
18. R. McKitterick, 'Charles the Bald (823–877) and his library: the patronage of learning', *EHR* 95 (1980), 28–47.
19. *MGH Cap.* II, 358–9.
20. *Annales Bertiniani, s.a.*, 877.
21. See for example *Annales Bertiniani, s.a.*, 842, where Lothar breaks up a great silver plate in order to pay his followers.
22. Nithard, IV, 6.
23. Lupus, Ep. 19.
24. Lupus, Ep. 32.
25. Lupus, Epp. 19, 32, 36, 42, 43, 45, 47, 48, 49, 50, 60, 62, 65, 82, 84, 86, 87.
26. Lupus, Epp. 42 and 47.
27. Lupus, Epp. 49.
28. Lupus, Epp. 86 and 87.
29. K. F. Werner, 'Bedeutende Adelsfamilien', (cited above Ch. 2 n. 42).
30. See K. Brunner, *Oppositionelle Gruppen im Karolingerreich* (Vienna 1979), 96–109.
31. J. Dhondt, *Etudes sur la naissance des principautés territoriales en France* (Bruges 1948), 231–58, discusses these developments in detail.
32. Dhondt argues this, ibid., 213–14.
33. *MGH Cap.* II, 358–9.
34. R. Collins, 'Charles the Bald and Wifrid the Hairy', *Charles the Bald: Court and Kingdom*, 169–89.
35. K. F. Werner, 'Die Nachkommen Karls des Grossen bis um das Jahr 1000', *KdG* IV (1965), 403–84, with tables.
36. K. F. Werner, 'Untersuchung zur Frühzeit des französischen Fürstentums 9–10 Jht I', *Welt als Geschichte* 18 (1958), 256–89.
37. Ibid., 282–3.
38. L. Levillain, 'Essai sur le comte Eudes fils de Harduin et de Guerinbourg 845–871', *MA* (1937), 153–271. Compare Werner, 'Untersuchung . . . II,' *Welt als Geschichte* 19 (1959), 152.
39. Recorded in Flodoard, *Historia*, III, 26 and see J. Calmette, *La diplomatie carolingienne* (Paris 1901), 40–8.
40. McKeon, *Hincmar of Laon*, 120–31.
41. *MGH Cap.* II, No. 254. Compare P. Classen, 'Die Verträge von Verdun und von Coulaines 843 als politische Grundlagen des westfränkischen Reiches', *HZ* 196 (1963), 1–85.
42. J. L. Nelson, 'Kingship, law and liturgy in the political thought of Hincmar of Rheims', *EHR* 92 (1977), 241–79 especially 255.
43. K. Voigt, *Die Karolingische Klosterpolitik* (Stuttgart 1917), 86–100.
44. J. L. Nelson, 'Charles the Bald and the church in town and countryside', *Studies in Church History* 16 (1979), 103–18.

45. J. Fleckenstein, *Die Hofkapelle der deutschen Könige* (Stuttgart 1959), 106–7.
46. Also commented on by D. Ganz, 'The literary interests of the abbey of Corbie in the first half of the ninth century', Oxford D. Phil., 1980, 385. I am grateful to Dr Ganz for allowing me to read his thesis.
47. J. F. Lemarignier, for example, has drawn attention to the concentration of monastic land granted immunity, and suggested that this was a deliberate policy on the part of the king to set up royal enclaves immune from outside interference: 'Quelques remarques sur l'organisation ecclésiastique de la Gaule du VIIIᵉ à la fin du IXᵉ siècle, principalement au nord de la Loire', *Settimane* 13 (1965), 451–86.
48. I have learnt much concerning Charles the Bald's ecclesiastical policy from Giles Brown's B. A. dissertation, 'Property, patronage, piety and politics: Charles the Bald and the church 840–877', Cambridge, 1980, and am grateful to him for allowing me to read it.
49. See J. Devisse, *Hincmar, archévêque de Reims* (Geneva 3 vols, 1976), and his exhaustive bibliography.
50. J. M. Wallace-Hadrill, 'History in the mind of Archbishop Hincmar', *The Writing of History in the Middle Ages, essays presented to R. W. Southern*, R. H. C. Davis and J. M. Wallace-Hadrill (eds) (Oxford 1981), 43–70.
51. McKeon, *Hincmar of Laon*, 132–155.
52. *Annales Bertiniani, s.a.*, 866, and see P. Grierson, 'The *Gratia dei rex* coinage of Charles the Bald', *Charles the Bald: Court and Kingdom*, 39–51, and E. Joranson, *The Danegeld in France* (Rock Island, Ill. 1923).
53. Grierson, 'The *Gratia dei rex* coinage'.
54. D. M. Metcalf, 'A sketch of the currency in the time of Charles the Bald', *Charles the Bald: Court and Kingdom*, 53–84.
55. J. Lafaurie, 'Deux trésors monétaires carolingiens: Saumeray (Eure-et-Loir) Rennes (Ille-et-Vilaine)', *Revue Numismatique* 7 (1965), 262–305 at 265–266.
56. *MGH Cap.* II, 310–28, esp. 314–18.
57. G. Tessier, *Recueil des actes de Charles II le Chauve* (Paris 3 vols, 1943–55), III, Introduction, and idem, *La diplomatie royale française* (Paris 1962).
58. A point made by Giles Brown, cited above, n. 48.
59. C. Brühl, *Fodrum, gistum et servitium regis* (Cologne and Graz 2 vols, 1968), 39–48 (with maps), and see summary by R. McKitterick, 'The palace school of Charles the Bald', *Charles the Bald: Court and Kingdom*, especially 387–8.
60. Examples of royal ostentation are to be found in *Annales Bertiniani, s.a.*, 864, 875, 876.
61. C. A. Bouman, *Sacring and Crowning* (Djakarta and Groningen 1957).
62. J. L. Nelson summarizes the argument in 'Inauguration rituals', *Early Medieval Kingship*, I. N. Wood and P. Sawyer (eds) (Leeds 1977), 50–71.
63. Compare the oaths made to Louis the Stammerer in 877 (*MGH Cap.* II, 365) and Charles the Bald's statement in 858 (*MGH Cap.* II, 296) discussed, with translation of the oaths, by L. Halphen, *Charlemagne et l'Empire Carolingien* (Paris 1968) 415 and 417; Eng. trs. (1977), 339–44.
64. *Annales Bertiniani, s.a.*, 856. Compare Asser's *Life of Alfred* W. H. Stevenson (ed.) (Oxford repr. 1959), c. 13 and c. 14, 11–13. See also P. Stafford, 'Charles the Bald, Judith and England', and J. Hyam, 'Ermentrude and Richildis', *Charles the Bald: Court and Kingdom*, 137–51 and 153–68 respectively.
65. But see M. J. Enright, 'Charles the Bald and Aethelwulf of Wessex. The alliance of 856 and strategies of royal succession', *Journal of Medieval History* 4 (1978), 291–303.

66. E. Kantorowicz, 'The Carolingian king in the Bible of San Paolo fuori le Mura', *Late Classical and Medieval Studies in Honor of A. M. Friend, Jnr* (Princeton 1955), 287–300.
67. J. Hyam, cited above n. 64.
68. R. McKitterick, 'Charles the Bald and his library' and see Chapter 8.
69. M. Viellard-Troïekouroff, 'La chapelle du palais de Charles le Chauve', *Cahiers Archéologiques* 21 (1971), 89–109.
70. E. Kantorowicz, *Laudes Regiae* (Berkeley and Los Angeles 1958), 65–111.
71. H. Kessler, *The Illustrated Bibles from Tours* (Princeton 1977), 125–38, and D. Bullough, '"Imagines regum" and their significance in the early medieval west', *Studies in Memory of D. Talbot Rice* (Edinburgh 1975), 223–76.
72. R. Deshman, 'The exalted servant: the ruler theology of the Prayer book of Charles the Bald', *Viator* 11 (1980), 385–417.

CHAPTER EIGHT

Scholarship, Book Production and Libraries: The Flowering of the Carolingian Renaissance

The main ateliers for intellectual and artistic activity in the second half of the ninth century were the principal monasteries and episcopal cities, many of which had first emerged as centres of learning and culture under the aegis of a former member or protégé of the court of Charlemagne. Alcuin for example had been appointed abbot of St Martin's at Tours and had established a school there; Theodulf was bishop of Orleans and abbot of Fleury; Leidrad became archbishop of Lyons and made every effort to establish schools and educate the clergy in his diocese, and Adalhard, Charlemagne's cousin, was abbot of Corbie, which by the beginning of the ninth century had built up an important library and developed one of the most productive scriptoria in the kingdom.

The evidence for these centres dictates the way one may discuss them, for it is in the form of extant manuscripts produced or possessed by a monastery or cathedral, catalogues of books in their libraries in the ninth century, or the work of particular scholars associated with them. The cathedral centres include Auxerre, Augsburg, Eichstätt, Freising, Cologne, Constance, Liège, Lyons, Mainz, Metz, Rheims, Salzburg, Strasbourg, Trier, Verona and Würzburg. The main monastic centres were: in the Bodensee and upper Rhine, St Gall, Reichenau, Murbach, Weissenburg and Lorsch; in the Rhineland and Hesse, Echternach, Cornelimünster, Prüm, Hersfeld and Fulda; in Saxony, Corvey and Werden; in Bavaria, Niederaltaich, Benediktbeuren, Wessobrun, Tegernsee, Mondsee and Kremsmünster (the two last now in Austria); in west Francia, Ferrières, Tours, Corbie, St Riquier, St Vaast, St Bertin, St Amand, St Wandrille, St Denis and St Germain-des-Prés; in Italy, Bobbio and Novalese. All these centres have been identified by books associated with them in some way. Although we know the existence of all these centres our information about some of them is extremely meagre. For only three of the cathedrals (Freising, Cologne, Würzburg) and seven of the Frankish monasteries (St Gall, Reichenau, Murbach, Lorsch, Fulda, St Riquier and St Wandrille) are there Carolingian lists of books possessed by them extant, though we can add to these the catalogues of Charlemagne and Wulfad, bishop of Bourges, and the lists in the wills of Eberhard of Friuli and Eccard of Mâcon. A number of manuscripts may also be associated with scholars such as Lupus of Ferrières and Florus the Deacon of Lyons, because of their handwriting or distinctive annotations. For a number of other centres there is a wealth of information to be gained from the surviving manuscripts. There is still a great deal of work to be done on these manuscripts before a full assessment of the intellectual and cultural achievement of the Carolingians in the middle decades of the ninth century will be possible, but some indication of the nature of the intellectual and artistic activity of these centres as well as of the court of Charles the Bald can be given here.

I

The *Gesta abbatum Fontanellensium*, a history of the abbots of St Wandrille composed in the middle of the ninth century, records gifts of books made to the abbey by abbots Wando (747–54), Gervold (787–807) and Ansegisus (823–33). The gifts included works by Augustine, Jerome, Gregory the Great, Isidore and Bede. Gervold also started a school at St Wandrille which was placed under the direction of Harduin. Harduin taught arithmetic in the school and established a scriptorium. Under his auspices more books were acquired for the library, some possibly acquired in St Wandrille's scriptorium. The gradual accumulation of books over a number of decades by gift and possibly by copying texts is fairly typical of the means by which Carolingian cathedral and monastic libraries were formed. Unfortunately nothing more is known of the books and in 859 the monks fled before the Vikings and did not return for a century. The only scholars associated with St Wandrille are the abbots Einhard (*c.* 816–?823) and Ansegisus whose main work was probably not done at the abbey.

Like St Wandrille, our information about St Riquier is incorporated in a history of the abbey, the eleventh-century chronicle by Hariulf. It preserves the inventory made in 831 of all the possessions of the abbey – vestments, church plate, estates, tenants, rents received and 256 books. Books of the Bible and commentaries upon them by Jerome, Augustine, Gregory, Origen, Fulgentius and late Christian writers as well as some contemporary theology form the bulk of the collection, but there were also some school and liturgical texts. Very few books from St Riquier survive, so this inventory and the existence of schools associated with St Riquier are all that is known about the intellectual life of the abbey; they indicate that the standard education was available at St Riquier but no notable scholar seems to have been educated there.

At Fulda on the other hand the high reputation of its school attracted students from many other monasteries. Walafrid Strabo from Reichenau and Lupus from Ferrières were among many Carolingian scholars who had been taught by Hraban Maur, abbot of Fulda and archbishop of Mainz, himself a former pupil of Alcuin. Hraban has left a vast corpus of exegetical and didactic writing, including the *De institutione clericorum*, the *Excerptio de arte grammatica Prisciani* and the encyclopaedia *De rerum naturis*.[1] His method of composition was to

201

provide a complete dossier of learned opinions on a given subject. His *De Institutione Clericorum* of 819, for example, outlines principles for the priesthood and clerical life as well as providing an account of the liberal arts, and is heavily dependent on the *De doctrina christiana* of Augustine. Ganz has suggested that it should be regarded as a first reader in the works of the great church fathers, designed for 'rapidly growing libraries'.[2] Hraban was not a mere compiler; he made slight but instructive alterations to the texts he used and added his own comments. He believed wholeheartedly in the necessity of studying whatever pertains to words and proper speech so that fullest understanding of the written word of Scripture would be attained. Like other Carolingian scholars Hraban bent over backwards in the effort not to be original. One should be learned and acquire knowledge, but originality was not something the Carolingian scholar would have appreciated; those like Gottschalk and John Scottus Eriugena who departed from orthodoxy and attempted to produce original thought were regarded with deep suspicion and incomprehension by their contemporaries.

Hraban's own stress in his studies and writing, that the object of study was the greater understanding of the Scriptures and the word of God, is the fullest affirmation of the principles for the revival of learning established under Charlemagne and expressed in the *De litteris colendis*, a copy of which was addressed to Baugulf, abbot of Fulda. In the late eighth century a list of twenty volumes belonging to Fulda was entered on f. 7ᵛ of Basle K. III. 159, a copy of Isidore of Seville's *De natura rerum*, and a further catalogue dated to the first half of the ninth century formed part of a Lorsch manuscript, Vat. pal. lat. 1877 (ff. 34–44). These lists indicate that by the mid-ninth century Fulda had a respectable collection of theological works, a large number of monastic rules and the works of Alcuin and Hraban Maur. By identifying Hraban's sources in his writings some notion of the books he used can be formed, though we cannot assume that these books, mostly commentaries by Augustine, Bede and Jerome, were at Fulda. It is possible that Hraban sometimes worked with borrowed books, sources for which may have been the libraries of Mainz and Lorsch.

Only a few eighth- and ninth-century volumes from Mainz itself survive. Those now in the Vatican are mostly collections of canon law, though one of them, Vat. pal. lat. 1447, contains the Old Saxon poem *Heliand*. Mainz's Anglo-Saxon connections are evident in the script of its manuscripts – at first insular minuscule predominated in the books produced in the Mainz scriptorium, but gradually a distinctive large and bold Caroline minuscule was introduced.[3] The greater part of the library at Lorsch on the other hand survives, and the connection between Fulda and Lorsch was particularly strong during the abbacy of Samuel (837–56) who had been a fellow student of Hraban Maur and remained a close friend.

Lorsch was a family monastery founded by Count Chancor in the seventh century. It became a royal monastery in 772 and built up its immense wealth thereafter. It moved quickly into the forefront of Carolingian ecclesiastical and secular politics and served as the necropolis for many later Carolingian kings. In time it became an important monastery for the Ottonians.[4] Quite apart from the surviving manuscripts, Lorsch is especially well documented, for no less than three ninth-century catalogues exist, numbering some 450 books. These catalogues, seen in conjunction with the extant manuscripts from the Lorsch scriptorium, reflect clearly the interdependence of scriptorium and library in a monastery.[5] It was, moreover, of crucial importance that the abbot or the master of the school should be devoted to learning and promote the activity of the scriptorium as well as donating books to the library. Lorsch was fortunate in this respect. Abbot Ricbod (784–804) had been a student of Alcuin and had some connection with Charlemagne's court. It is possible that the school at Lorsch was established by Ricbod as well as the scriptorium. Adalung, abbot of Lorsch (804–37) and of St Vaast from 808, was also connected with the court and in 823 went to Rome as an envoy for Louis the Pious. The abbey developed still further under Abbot Samuel and the librarian Gerward, who had been *bibliothecarius* to Louis the Pious and who gave his own collection of twenty-seven volumes to Lorsch. Lorsch's third library catalogue witnesses to their work. It was compiled under Abbot Eigilbert and it is on this that the fame of the Lorsch library is based. The library was rich in its patristic theology and biblical exegesis as well as school-books, but also possessed a remarkable collection of classical authors, including a sixth-century copy of Virgil and the works of Cicero, Seneca, Persius, Juvenal, Pliny, Sallust and Aristotle. It is not known whether many Lorsch monks went to Fulda to be educated in the school under Hraban and Rudolf as the Reichenau and Weissenburg novices did, but Theotrich, abbot from 864–76, seems to have done so. From the last few years of the reign of Louis the German onwards there is no material relating to intellectual life at Lorsch at all.

St Gall, founded on the site of the hermitage of the Irish monk Gall by Othmar in 720, developed very slowly. Unlike Lorsch it had no rich or aristocratic family at its back, nor did it become a royal monastery until 818. On the other hand, judging from the numerous small donations of land and property made to it, St Gall held an important place in the affections and interests of the Alemannian population.[6] In the course of the ninth century, however, after it had become a royal monastery, St Gall's intellectual life developed rapidly, and like Lorsch, this was due to a series of zealous abbots and masters of the school. There too the relationship between scriptorium and library may be seen very clearly in the catalogues produced in the second half of the ninth century. The oldest book list is dated between 850 and 860, with additions dating from about 880 which note the loss of a book, a book the library needs, or a book lent to another centre for copying or use in the school. The notes sometimes refer to the quality of the book and whether it is written in a beautiful hand, or make fierce remarks on the lies and falsehoods a work contains, its unreadableness or its uselessness for study. Jerome on the Hebrew names, Isidore of Seville's *Liber Differentiarum* and the *Synonyma* are censured in this way; the annotator had a particular aversion to collections of excerpts from earlier authors' writings and described them as *mendacissima et inutilia*. A further feature of the St Gall catalogues is that a separate list is made of the books written in 'Irish script'.

There are extra lists recording gifts made to the abbey by Grimald, abbot from 841–72. He gave a large number of liturgical books to the library as well as Vegetius' *De Re Militari*, Boethius' *De Consolatione Philosophiae*, pseudo-Cyprian's *De duodecim abusivis saeculi*, a Life of Charlemagne and the poetry of Virgil. Under Hartmuot, abbot from 872–83, many books were written in the abbey's scriptorium and added to the library, and Hartmuot also bequeathed his personal collection of books to the library. St Gall in the ninth and tenth centuries had a particularly fine collection of classical authors – Terence, Lucretius, Sallust, Cicero, Caesar, Virgil, Horace, Ovid, Vitruvius, Persius, Lucan, Quintilian, Statius, Juvenal. The St Gall manuscripts also provide evidence for the revision of the Bible and liturgy (the oldest exemplar of Alcuin's Bible is at St Gall), as well as for the monastic life (the oldest copy of the pure text of St Benedict's Rule is also in the St Gall library). Many Old High German texts are also to be found in the St Gall collection, but these will be discussed more fully in Chapter Eleven. Most Carolingian libraries have been dispersed but the manuscripts of St Gall can still be seen *in situ*, as can those of Würzburg and Lyons.

The earliest list of books in the library at Würzburg was entered in an Anglo-Saxon hand in about 800 on f. 236[r] of Oxford Bodleian Laud misc. 126.[7] The thirty-five books listed include the Acts of the Apostles, the Dialogues, Moralia in Job, Pastoral Care and Homilies of Gregory the Great, Bede's Ecclesiastical History, letters and theological treatises by Jerome and Ambrose, works on the spiritual life and the grammars of Augustine and Boniface. A later, German, hand noted that a commentary had been lent to Holzkirchen and that four books, *speculum, omelia sancti gregorii maiora pars, liber proverbium, beatitudines*, had been lent to Fulda. Laud misc. 126 itself was borrowed by another monastery.

The large number of Würzburg manuscripts surviving from the eighth and ninth century show every sign of having been used, especially for teaching. The bishops of Würzburg, moreover, like the abbots of Lorsch, Reichenau, St Gall and Fulda, promoted both the scriptorium and the library. Under Burchard, the first bishop of Würzburg (742–53), there was a scriptorium to supply the necessary books and it is probable that Burchard saw that Taubersbischofsheim, Ochsenfurt and Kitzingen were supplied with books as well. Three extant manuscripts can be dated to the period of office of the next incumbent, Megingoz, a time when Würzburg was part of the Bonifacian circle of monasteries, but under Berowulf (768/9–800) Chrodegang's Rule for canons was introduced and a closer connection with the Carolingians was formed. Charlemagne is supposed to have sent people to be taught in the cathedral school which blossomed under Berowulf; the first bishops of Paderborn, Hathumar and Badurad, were taught there, and it should be remembered that the only surviving copy of the letter addressed to Baugulf abbot of Fulda, *De litteris colendis*, is in a Würzburg manuscript. The catalogue cited above was probably made during Berowulf's incumbency. About his successors Liuttrit (800–3) and Egilwart (803–10) nothing is known, but under Wolfgar (810–32), who was favoured by Louis the Pious, Würzburg's possessions increased. Over twenty extant manuscripts were produced during his reign and one can recognize in them, according to Bischoff and Hofmann, a transition period, both palaeographically and in the history of the library.[8] As well as insular script we have the first certain examples of Würzburg Caroline minuscule. Pastoral and liturgical works predominate as well as many books of the Old Testament, and some canon law for the first time.

Humbert, bishop from 833–42, was in Würzburg by 815 and seems to have been a suffragan bishop of Mainz before being elevated to the Würzburg see. Humbert was a friend and correspondent of Hraban Maur as well as a great admirer of his biblical commentaries. He systematically built up the library's holdings of books of the Bible and commentaries upon them, favouring the works of Bede and Hraban. Humbert commissioned, for example, copies of the Hraban commentaries from Fulda, and sent a large supply of parchment for the work.[9] Humbert's successor Gozbald (842–55) was also zealous in building the library and promoting the activity of the school. Thirty-five books were produced or acquired during his reign. The collection of Old Testament books and commentaries upon them was completed and some New Testament books and commentaries were added, as well as some patristic theology and a few school-books, including Cicero's *De Inventione* and *Rhetorica ad Herennium*, Isidore's *Etymologiae* and Cassiodorus' *Institutiones*. In 855 the cathedral was burnt and this seems to have marked the end of the rapid growth of Würzburg's library.

Lyons re-emerged as a centre of learning under Leidrad. A letter to Charlemagne reports that he has attended to the rebuilding of churches, and their farm buildings and to the teaching and education of his clergy, to the liturgy and to the library.[10] Leidrad and his successors Agobard, Amolo and Remigius all gave books to the library. Under Agobard, Lyons became a centre for theological studies.[11] This had a lot to do with Florus the Deacon, who was associated with the church of Lyons from about 825; he served Agobard, Amolo and Remigius faithfully and is notorious for his vituperative attack on Amalarius, an intruder installed briefly in the see of Lyons, who attempted to foist his liturgical forms on the cathedral clergy. Many manuscripts from Lyons contain the distinctive annotations of Florus, particularly texts of Augustine.[12] Many of these signs are indicating passages to be excerpted for other clerics to copy. Florus' own works indicate the wide range of his reading which would only have been possible with a large library at his disposal. As well as the Carolingian manuscripts produced and acquired by Lyons in the ninth century, a number of earlier uncial and half-uncial manuscripts, many of them containing annotations dating from the sixth to the ninth centuries, were at Lyons in Florus' day. None of these can be definitely ascribed to a Lyons scriptorium, but they are thought to be of Burgundian origin at least. They may well reflect the zeal with which the Lyons bishops and scholars like Florus gathered books together from the surrounding region in order to use them for excerpting and expounding. There is little doubt that Florus was helped with the identification and selection and compilation of texts by his students and other clerics of the cathedral church. Hildig, for example, helped with the composition of a work sent to Bishop Bartholomew of Narbonne, and Manno, the prior of St Oyen, wrote some of Florus' compilation on the letters of Paul.

In other words, the Lyons evidence suggests that a number of people could contribute to the compilation of a work, and this is something that Ganz has noted from Corbie manuscripts as well.[13] Ganz has shown how a group of manuscripts at Corbie was used in the preparation of a patristic dossier on the Pauline epistles and how some of the manuscripts used for these projects were exchanged between centres. BN lat. 1748 for example was given to St Denis, and BN n.a. lat. 1448 has links with Tours. Although the works annotated by the monks of Corbie were predominantly theological, Corbie's library was remarkable for its wealth of classical texts. Something of this is evident from Hadoard of Corbie's florilegium or *Collectaneum*. This work contains excerpts from the 'Leiden Corpus' of Cicero's works as well as Cicero's Tusculan Disputations, *De Officiis, De Amicitia, De Oratore* and *De Senectute*.[14] Other authors excerpted for this collection were Sallust, Macrobius, Servius, Hortensius, Martianus Capella and Publilius Syrus. Hadoard, described in the preface to the *Collectanea* as the *custos librorum*, is thought to have stimulated the production of manuscripts in the Corbie scriptorium in the middle of the ninth century. Most of the classical texts produced by Corbie were written during the middle decades of the ninth century. These included Aristotle's Categories, Priscian, Livy, Cicero, Servius' Commentary on the Aeneid, Columella, Vegetius, Marius Victorinus, the Aratea, Terence, Statius' *Thebaid*, Martial, Ovid (*Amores, Heroides*), Martianus Capella, Boethius' *De Musica, De Geometrica* and *De Arithmetica*, Caesar, Pliny, Sallust, Seneca and many others. They also acquired classical texts from elsewhere. After 850, Tours, Ferrières, Fleury, Auxerre and Lorsch possessed comparable treasures.

Without a catalogue to help, as is the case for most of the monastic and episcopal centres of the west Frankish kingdom, it is more difficult to determine which of the books written in a centre's scriptorium were intended for the library and arising from this, which books were acquired from other centres. The earliest surviving catalogue of the library of Laon, for example, is that made by Montfaucon and published in his *Bibliotheca Bibliothecarum Manuscriptorum Nova* in Paris in 1739. He lists 364 titles, of which possibly as many as 119 were from the tenth century or earlier. Contreni is satisfied that Montfaucon's catalogue, and the one made by Bugniâtre just before the French Revolution, represent the contents of the library in the ninth and tenth centuries, for the manuscripts of this date show 'unmistakable signs' that they were in use in Laon at this time.[15] The 'unmistakable signs' are annotations written by Laon scribes, or ex-libris or ex-dono entries of people associated with Laon. Laon's ninth-century library was put together by two generations of masters and bishops. Twenty books are known to have been given to Laon by Dido, bishop from 882–93, Rodulf of Laon gave four books and Bernard and Adalelm of Laon gave twenty-two. Martin Scottus, a master at Laon and an Irishman, also gave books to the library; no ex-dono or ex-libris notes are written into his books, but his handwriting can be identified in Laon 38, a collection of the minor prophetical books of the Bible, Laon 273, a copy of Wicbod's

Quaestiones in Octateuchum, Laon 444, the famous Greek and Latin glossary, and Laon 468, a handbook for the study of Virgil, as well as at least twenty others in Laon's library which were not his personal possessions. Hincmar, bishop of Laon and recalcitrant nephew of Hincmar of Rheims, also procured books for the cathedral library. The scriptorium of Laon, although evidently a very modest affair, furnished texts for use in the school, and was probably active from the late eighth to the early tenth centuries. But it did not provide for all Laon's needs; many of Laon's manuscripts can be attributed to other scriptoria, such as those of St Amand, Rheims and Corbie.

While Laon's library seems to have been formed largely from imports and gifts, and there is only slight evidence for a scriptorium there, centres such as Tours, Cologne, Rheims, Lyons, Orleans, Corbie and St Amand produced a large number of books for use in their churches, cloisters and schools, as well as for the libraries and churches of other centres. Studies of all these centres, with the exception of St Amand have been published. By looking at the development of St Amand's library, scriptorium and school in some detail, we can gain some idea of the stages by which a monastery became an intellectual centre of importance. [16]

St Amand enjoyed some eminence in the eighth and ninth centuries. Amand, a missionary from Aquitaine, founded the monastery later called St Amand in 634 on a tract of land at the confluence of the Elno and Scarpe rivers apparently given to the saint for this purpose by the Merovingian ruler, Dagobert. Some evidence survives to suggest that later Merovingian and the first Carolingian kings retained an interest in the abbey. It was a royal abbey; it was part of the king's domain, the abbacy lay within his gift and he could dispose of some of its lands. St Amand's abbots for the most part were prominent men of the kingdom, and from the beginning of the ninth century, closely connected with the crown. Rotfrid, abbot until 847, had been one of Charlemagne's ministers; Adalhard, abbot until 864, was related by marriage to Charles the Bald; Carloman, abbot until 870 was Charles the Bald's son and Gauzlin (d. 885) was archchaplain at the palace of Charles the Bald. The next abbot, brother of Count Odo of Paris, ruled for the last year of his life as king of the Franks. Both the lands St Amand possessed and the manuscripts it produced attest to the abbey's great wealth. The manuscripts in particular reflect the rich intellectual and artistic tradition at St Amand from the late eighth to the early tenth centuries; the abbey participated fully in the Carolingian Renaissance.

The codices written at St Amand and now in centres other than Paris or Valenciennes are distributed in ones and twos and represent two different categories of book produced in the scriptorium for export. Beautifully written and decorated Gospel books and sacramentaries and one glorious Bible were commissioned from St Amand or presented to another centre or individuals by the abbey. Possibly as many as eight Gospel books, the Bible and eight sacramentaries from St Amand in this category are extant. The texts of these books were often adapted according to the needs of the church or abbey for which the books were intended. Leningrad Q.v.I.41, for example, is a sacramentary produced at St Amand for the diocese of Tournai; BN lat. 2291 was first used at St

Amand then adapted for use at St Denis, and Vienna 958, a prettily decorated fragment of eight folios, was copied for the diocese of Liège. The Ghent Livinus Gospels seem to have been presented by St Amand to St Bavo's in Ghent, and BN lat. 2, the Second Bible of Charles the Bald, was given to the king soon after 870. Most of these sumptuous volumes were written in the second half of the ninth century, a period when the abbey enjoyed its greatest prestige and wealth under the patronage of Charles the Bald.

The St Amand codices in Paris and Valenciennes represent the books once possessed by the abbey, in many cases since the ninth century. Not all these manuscripts were written at St Amand, and only a small proportion of them belong to the Carolingian period. From among the volumes at St Amand in 1700 and 1790, it has to be determined which were there in the ninth and tenth centuries. Fortunately there are two, possibly three, medieval catalogues of the library of St Amand, the earliest of which can be dated to the turn of the tenth century. The most comprehensive catalogue however is the *index maior*, compiled between 1150 and 1160.[17] Of the 278 books of the pre-1150 period it lists eighty-seven that have been identified among extant manuscripts. How then may one identify manuscripts written at St Amand and what was in its library during the Carolingian period?

There are a number of different features of a manuscript which may be considered: the make-up of each book and its collation, how the leaves are prepared for writing, the ink used, the script, scribal habits and techniques such as the use of abbreviations and display scripts, the lay-out, the decoration, and the text itself. For some manuscripts the binding is often important as well, especially as a clue to provenance. Six of the St Amand manuscripts have ninth-century leather bindings; two of these are on books written elsewhere. Not enough is known yet about ninth-century tooling and binding techniques to establish that these bindings were made at St Amand itself, but Vezin has argued on the basis of a number of bindings in the Bibliothèque Nationale in Paris that Corbie at least produced its own bindings for its manuscripts.[18] Of the remaining St Amand bindings, none is earlier than the twelfth century. St Amand developed a distinctive Caroline minuscule, and this is the surest way of identifying books written in the abbey's scriptorium. The best St Amand books observe a strict hierarchy of scripts; uncials, rustic capitals or square capitals are used for headings and title pages, minuscule for the text. A further feature of St Amand books is the distinctive decoration, often described as Franco-Saxon or Franco-insular; this mostly consists of animal and vegetable ornament and interlace patterns in the insular manner. Human figures are rarely part of the illustrations.

The chronological development of the script, the number of scribes at work and the particular scribal habits of the scriptorium of St Amand cannot be described in detail here. Nor can the organization and text of the contents of each codex, especially in relation to any other copy of a particular text. The impression gained so far from the manuscripts extant is that the activity of the scriptorium was fairly constant from the end of the eighth century until the middle decades of the tenth century. The first products in the last years of the eighth century and early years of the ninth were a number of patristic works on theology, including Cyprian, Origen and Lactantius and school-books such as Alcuin's abridgement of Priscian's grammar. Already with the Gospel book given to St Bavo's of Ghent in about 800 the practice had begun of producing fine liturgical books for other centres, a practice which dominated the book production of St Amand in the second half of the ninth century, when most of its Gospel books and sacramentaries were produced. Production of school-books, works on grammar and rhetoric and others among the liberal arts continued throughout the century, perhaps concentrated more from the mid-ninth century onwards, which accords well with what is known about the teaching activities of Milo and Hucbald, masters of the school of St Amand at the time. There was also a constant stream of patristic and contemporary biblical exegesis and theology.

Eighty-one of the extant manuscripts associated with St Amand in the eighth, ninth and tenth centuries were probably in the abbey library during this period. Eight more books which are known to have been given by Hucbald of St Amand to the library are now lost. About half the books in St Amand's library were written in the abbey's scriptorium. The relatively high proportion of books in the library which were written somewhere else could be due to the zealous acquisition of books after the Viking raids of 882. Some of the books, those that the monks had not been able to carry away with them when they fled for refuge to St Germain-des-Prés in Paris, may have been destroyed at this time, but this remains sheer speculation. [19] That the splendid late seventh- or early eighth-century uncial copy of the Chronicle of Eusebius, written at Luxeuil, Jerome's Commentary on Jeremiah (Valenciennes 59), a volume of 182 folios which took its scribe Agambert 30 days to write, and Lactantius' treatise *De falso religione* (Valenciennes 147) both written at Fleury at the beginning of the ninth century, or the *Martinellus* written at Tours in the first half of the ninth century, were in St Amand's library in the ninth century remains to be established. At least the books Hucbald of St Amand gave to the library were there by 930, the year of his death.

Although St Amand's scriptorium produced many sacramentaries and Gospel books for other centres, the only biblical books extant from its library, both produced at the beginning of the ninth century, were written elsewhere, the Gospels in north-east France (Valenciennes 69) and the Book of Revelation or Apocalypse, illustrated with delightful drawings, in the middle Rhine region by an *indignus presbyter* called Otoltus. The library possessed volumes of patristic exegesis by Augustine, Ambrose, Jerome and Gregory and by the medieval authors, Bede, Heiric of Auxerre and Claudius of Turin, as well as a large collection of patristic theology, especially works of Augustine. There were also volumes of the writings of Lactantius, Gregory Nazianzenus and Cyprian, and of the late Roman authors Cassiodorus and Isidore. The codex containing the writings of Gregory Nazianzenus is more famous now for the insertions made soon after 881 on leaves at the back – not in St Amand script but possibly by a visitor to the abbey – of the *Ludwigslied* and the Eulalia sequence, the former in Old High German and the latter the first extended piece of writing extant in Old French. Contemporary theology, canon law and hagiography were all represented; there was the Penitential of Halitgar of Cambrai, Alcuin's theological and didactic works, the *De institutione laicali* of Jonas of Orleans, and the theology of Lupus of Ferrières and Smaragdus of St Mihiel. The largest section of all is that of the grammatical and didactic treatises, poetry and classical literature used in the school. Not only were there the histories of Jordanes, Orosius and Eusebius, but also no less than eight collections of grammatical treatises and commentaries, some of them quite rare in the Carolingian period, works of the classical authors such as Virgil, Horace, Cicero, Terence, Pliny, Apuleius, Plato, Porphyrius and Pythagoras, but also a number of late antique and Carolingian treatises on metrics, music, rhetoric and dialectic by Boethius, Bede, Isidore of Seville and Alcuin. Among the Christian poets read at St Amand were Prudentius, Sedulius and Milo. Many of these manuscripts moreover have been glossed, an indication of their being used for teaching and study.

The library at St Amand thus served three important functions. It provided the monks and the scholars among them, with their reference and reading matter; the school was furnished with the texts it needed; exemplars of certain authors could be lent to other centres for copying. It was dependent on the abbey scriptorium for the greater proportion of its stock, but was in close contact with other scriptoria which could provide the books it needed.

II

The communication between the monastic and episcopal centres of the Frankish kingdoms is one of the most important aspects of intellectual life in the Carolingian period, and has still not been investigated in any detail. One important means of communication and the creation of a sense of spiritual brotherhood was the confraternity book. This was a list of the monks and clerics from different centres who formed a bond or brotherhood of prayer; that is, each centre would possess such a list and all the monks in each monastery would pray for everyone listed in the book. It used to be thought that confraternity books were of Anglo-Saxon origin, but these brotherhoods were first formed on the Continent in the seventh century. Schmid thinks it more likely that their use became more widespread under Anglo-Saxon influence, simply because of the bonds of prayer between Anglo-Saxon monasteries in England and Germany. There were also books for the dead.[20] At Attigny in 762 the confederations of prayer were organized on a synodal basis, and many of the connections between different monasteries date from the connection established at Attigny. The most famous confraternity book is that of Reichenau. It survives in the original manuscript, compiled by the Reichenau monks in 826, and contains 40 000 names from more than 100 abbeys, canonries and nunneries in east and west Francia and Italy, including St Gall, Kempten, Wessobrun, Augsburg, Ottobeuren, Freising, Niederaltaich, Chiemsee, Weissenburg, Münster-im-Gregoriental, Prüm, Lorsch, Cologne, Constance,

Corvey, Werden, Bremen, Luxeuil, St Germain-des-Prés, St Denis, Meaux, Rouen, Jumièges, St Bertin, Flavigny, Lyons, Vienne, Novalese, Nonantula, Brescia and Benevento. The Anglo-Saxon foundations and Echternach were not included, but many bishops and laymen, including twenty-five members of the Carolingian family, were. These lists were kept up to date; the Reichenau list, for example, was continued throughout the ninth century and the names of the monks of Remiremont were added under Abbot Alawich (934–58).[21]

As one might have expected, Reichenau's earliest connections, apart from twelve or so going back to the prayer companies formed at Attigny, were with other monasteries founded by Pirmin – Murbach, Pfäfers, Hornbach, Maursmünster, Schwarzach, Neuweiler and Gengenbach. Similarly, the foundations of Boniface and his disciples were closely connected, as were the establishments in northern France associated with Amand and his disciples. These connections are also evident in the intellectual sphere, for it is clear that these centres circulated their library catalogues between one another. A copy of the Reichenau catalogue, now Geneva Bibliothèque Publique et Universitaire MS 21, was sent to Murbach, and another Reichenau list (Donaueschingen Fürstliche Bibliothek MS 191) appears to have been made for Constance. The collection of Lorsch catalogues in Vat. lat. 1877 included a mid-ninth-century Fulda catalogue. Lupus of Ferrières asked Usuard, a monk of St Germain-des-Prés, to send him a description of the resources of his monastery and referred in another letter to a catalogue of Einhard's books of which he had a copy, asking to borrow some of the books listed so that he might transcribe them.[22] The famous list of books belonging to Wulfad of Bourges may well have been intended for circulation among his friends.[23]

Lupus of Ferrières (805–c. 862) is in fact the most striking illustration of the gregariousness of Carolingian scholarship and the importance of the connections formed between different centres. His letters contain many references to the lending of books as well as discussions of various intellectual matters with his friends in different religious communities. He is an example of the best that the educational tradition established earlier in the century could produce. Lupus was trained by Aldric at the monastery of Ferrières, who taught him grammar and rhetoric, and then became the pupil of Hraban Maur at Fulda, where he studied theology. While at Fulda he received his commission to compile a corpus of germanic laws for Eberhard of Friuli and wrote the Life of Wigbert. He and the monk Gerolf also corrected Hraban's exposition on the Book of Numbers.

It was probably at Fulda that Lupus became acquainted with Einhard. His first letter to Einhard introduces himself and is the letter of a young man writing to express his admiration for the work of an older scholar.[24] Lupus was of the opinion that the style of Einhard's Life of Charlemagne compared favourably with that of the classical authors whom he had already learnt to love. He also asked to borrow some of Einhard's books, particularly the De Rhetorica of Cicero, for he wished to compare it with his own copy and the Fulda copy.[25] Lupus evidently visited Einhard a number of times and a close friendship grew up between them, so that it was Lupus who attempted to console Einhard on the death of the latter's wife Emma. We learn from another letter that Lupus could not yet return Einhard's copy of the Attic Nights of Aulus Gellius because Hraban Maur was hanging on to it and refusing to let go until a copy was made for him.[26] (A Fulda copy was made and is still extant).

Other friendships formed by Lupus were with Probus of Mainz, Gottschalk of Orbais and the monks Marcward, Eigil and Ansbold of Prüm. In his letters to all his friends he revealed his interest in books, philology and textual matters and in many he asked for copies of particular texts to be made for him as well as discussing pronunciation and points of grammar and metre. Immo, for example, wrote to ask Lupus what books he had written or read while he was in Germany,[27] Altuin near Mainz was asked for a book others were keen to see as well,[28] Reginbert was sent a book, Adalgaud was asked about a copy of Cicero's Tusculan Disputations that he was having copied for Lupus,[29] and Marcward of Prüm was requested to send a monk to Fulda to ask Hatto the abbot to lend him Suetonius' Lives of the Caesars so that it could be copied at Prüm for Lupus.[30]

One of Lupus' most interesting requests, indicating as in many other letters that he had actually seen, or seen a note about, a particular book, was to Orsmar, archbishop of Tours (837–46), urging Orsmar to obtain for him the commentaries of Boethius on the *Topica* of Cicero. This book, says Lupus, is in the library of St Martin's and is a papyrus manuscript. He promises to take very good care of it if he is allowed to borrow it.[31] Another 'manuscript of venerable antiquity', containing Jerome's commentary on Jeremiah was requested from Pope Benedict III (855–8), as well as Cicero's *De Oratore* and Quintilian's *Institutiones Oratoriae* 'which are contained in one rather small volume'.[32] Lupus even sent to England for books. He asked Altsig, abbot of York, to send him the *Quaestiones* on the Old and New Testament by Jerome, referred to by Cassiodorus, Jerome on Jeremiah and Quintilian. Lupus told Altsig that these texts would be copied by Lantramn at St Josse and returned to York as soon as possible.[33] Lupus also copied manuscripts for himself, and is perhaps best known for his work as scribe and text critic. From the extant manuscripts which he copied and annotated we are able to see how he read a book and how he copied and collated his texts. He worked over Cicero's *De Oratore* (BL Harley 2736) as well as the *De Inventione*, Books IV and V of Livy, the letters of Symmachus, the Attic Nights of Aulus Gellius and Donatus' commentary on Terence. Many scriptoria were responsible for the production of the twenty odd manuscripts in which corrections attributed to Lupus have been found. Fleury, Auxerre, Tours, and Ferrières have been suggested as the likely origin for most of these, a suggestion which serves to stress the importance of contact between one centre and another.[34]

Apart from the references in the letters of Carolingian scholars of books passing between them, different monastic centres exchanged books. The Würzburg catalogue, for example, notes that a commentary has been lent to Holzkirchen and that four books have been borrowed by Fulda. Some ninth-century books also show signs that they were lent or given to other centres. A portion of Berne Burgerbibliothek MS 212 for example, containing the poetry of Porphyrius and Carolingian *carmina figurata* by Alcuin, Joseph and Theodulf of Orleans, was written at St Amand and the rest was written at Mainz. Further evidence for a connection between Mainz and St Amand is the collection of treatises by Lactantius produced at St Amand at the turn of the eighth century (Vat. pal. lat. 161). A manuscript of Quintus Curtius (BN lat. 5716) was given by 'Haimus monachus' to Count Conrad in return for borrowing the text of Hraban's exposition of Ecclesiastes in order to copy it. Four of Laon's library books were products of the St Amand scriptorium, a *Liber Pontificalis* copied at St Amand (Leiden Voss lat. Q. 60) was at Rheims by the second half of the ninth century and St Amand copies of Origen (Copenhagen Gl. Kgl. S. 1338) and Jerome on St Matthew (Vat. pal. lat. 176) were in the library of Lorsch by about 850. Monasteries dependent on St Gall borrowed books from St Gall's library, and St Gall itself borrowed books from Reichenau (for example Karlsruhe Landesbibliothek Aug. XIX, XXVI, XXIX). A copy of Jerome's commentary on Ezekiel (Bamberg A. II. 53) from Reichenau appears to have been borrowed by St Denis.

The examples given could be multiplied but they serve to show how great the co-operative effort in the production, preservation and exchange of books and precious texts was in the Carolingian period. There was also collaboration in producing new texts. A group of scholars in one or more centres, such as the monks of Fulda, and of Corbie, have left indications in a number of manuscripts that they used them to prepare a collection of excerpts from patristic authors on particular subjects. Ganz has noted from his close examination of the annotations in the Corbie manuscripts of the ninth century that there is what he thinks clear evidence for a comprehensive project of biblical commentary carried out on a co-operative basis in different monasteries.[35] As he says, this, if so, argues for a far greater co-ordination and contact between monasteries than has hitherto been assumed, as does the other evidence from library catalogues and manuscripts cited above. The controversy over Gottschalk's theory of double predestination, moreover, provides an example of the way in which scholars from various centres contributed opinions on a particular topic. Gottschalk of Orbais had proposed a theory of double predestination, according to which a few 'elect' were predestined to eternal blessedness and the rest to eternal damnation, though not necessarily to sin. He thus restricted both the saving will of God and the universal nature of the Redemption. Gottschalk's views were opposed by a number of the leading scholars of the kingdom, not just because his views were heretical but also because they detracted from the church's position as intermediary and that of the clergy as dispensers of God's grace. Charles the Bald himself asked Lupus to explain the issue, in response to which Lupus wrote a short exposition for Charles and later a longer tract on free will, predestination and the Redemption. Hincmar of Rheims consulted Lupus and Prudentius of Troyes and addressed a treatise to the king on the subject. Ratramnus of Corbie and John Scottus Eriugena also made their contributions.[36]

Charles the Bald's interest in the controversy over Gottschalk's theories raises the question of the part the court played in Carolingian culture in the second half of the ninth century. Again it is from books associated with Charles the Bald, that is, either dedicated to him or possessed by him, that the most can be learnt about the court. It is clear that he possessed a library of his own and he may well have inherited some at least of the books in the libraries of his father and grandfather.[37] Charles the Bald's books reveal that he patronized the centres of learning and book production. From Tours for example he received the beautiful *De Arithmetica* of Boethius and the Vivian Bible (now Bamberg Staatliche Bibliothek Class. 5 and BN lat. 1 respectively); from St Amand another Bible decorated in the Franco-Saxon style (BN lat. 2) and from the atelier which produced the *Hofschule* manuscripts, discussed in more detail below, he received or commissioned a Gospel book, Prayer book, sacramentary, Psalter and antiphonary. Individuals dedicated their works to him: Freculph of Lisieux wrote the second book of his world history specifically for Charles in 829 and revised Vegetius' *Epitoma rei militari* for the king; Nithard was commissioned to write his history of the quarrels between the sons of Louis the Pious in order that there might be a 'true and official' record; Ratramnus and Paschasius Radbert of Corbie presented their tracts on the Eucharist to the king and, as we have seen, a number of treatises on predestination were addressed to him by Lupus of Ferrières, John Scottus, Ratramnus and Hincmar of Rheims. Hincmar also dedicated three short works – *De cavendis vitiis et virtutibus exercendis*, *De regis persona et regio ministerio* and *De coercendo et exstirpando raptu viduarum* to Charles.

Charles the Bald was keenly interested in theology, the history of his own house and hagiography. He commissioned a martyrology from Usuard of St Germain-des-Prés in about 865 and was presented with Milo's Life of St Amand (and his poem *De Sobrietate*), the Life of Mary of Egypt and the tale of Theophilus in Latin translation, and Heiric of Auxerre's Life of St Germanus. On the question of image worship Jonas of Orleans contributed his *De cultu imaginum*. He seems also to have possessed Einhard's Life of Charlemagne, and two poems on the history of the Franks. Charles the Bald's patronage and appreciation of learning was probably due to his having been taught for nine years in his youth by no less a scholar than Walafrid Strabo of Reichenau.[38]

Yet although Charles' interest in intellectual matters is not in question, there is very little evidence that he had about him at court a group of scholars as Charlemagne had done. Of the scholars who dedicated their works to him, only Lupus of Ferrières, John Scottus and Hincmar of Rheims seem to have spent any time at court. In particular the evidence for the existence of a palace school in the sense of a place where younger scholars might further their education is meagre and ambiguous. I have argued elsewhere that the evidence for the palace school of some kind, headed by a certain Manno, dates from the mid-860s and the 870s, and that the most likely place for this school to have been was Compiègne, Charles the Bald's favourite palace (so far as we can determine from his itinerary).[39] I have also suggested that the atelier which produced the *Hofschule* manuscripts may also be located at Compiègne. Charles the Bald's court certainly was prominent in the promotion of Carolingian culture, but the web of his patronage also extended far and wide in his kingdom. In the third quarter of the ninth century royal patronage was of as fundamental importance for intellectual and artistic activity as the zeal of individual bishops and abbots in their sees and monasteries. Not all the Frankish abbeys and bishoprics were centres of fine book painting, ivory carving or metalwork, but those that were and the significance of the work they produced deserve to be considered in some detail.

III

Absent from most assessments of Carolingian art is an attempt to place it in the context of the long development of Gallo-Roman and Merovingian art. It is usually stated that Carolingian art marked a completely new phase – a revival of classical or late antique forms and techniques but a break with the Merovingian traditions. We need to determine the extent to which this is true.

A fundamental principle of book painting and decoration of any sort at all is the relationship between the text or content of the book and the decoration. Decoration in books could take two forms. First, the use of ornamented patterns, decorated initials, arrangement of the text on the page and the use of different letter forms. Second, the use of pictures to illustrate or to comment on the text. Originally, book illumination was probably intended as a form of punctuation. It made the text clearer, emphasized certain passages, and provided a visual aid with which the reader could be helped to remember details, or in the case of narrative and exegetical pictures, whole events or situations. Early decoration in the fourth and fifth centuries, therefore, tended to mark out the text to give it extra form and structure, such as the large initial beginning each page of the fourth-century Virgilius Augusteus (Vat. lat. 3256). The elaboration of the decorative initial, however, seems to have developed in scriptoria north of the Alps, in the Frankish kingdoms.[40] It is certainly a western phenomenon; in no manuscript before the end of the seventh century from the eastern Mediterranean are ornamental initials to be seen.

Decorative principles at first were simple, lines and circles, zigzag lines and filling in the letter space with colour and so on. The letters a, d, c, e, m and q in particular lent themselves most readily to decoration. In Merovingian Gaul letters were at first either ornamented (graphic half-initial) or filled with decoration (full initial), simply coloured, drawn with the pen and embellished with abstract designs. Gradually a further type developed, that of the substitute ornament, in which there was a play between the natural form of the letter and that of the decorative motif. Zoomorphic and vegetable ornament appeared in Merovingian manuscripts by the mid-seventh century; the curves of letters assumed the curved bodies of birds or fish, and the charm of these birds and fish is such that they often take over completely a page of the text. It is important to remember, however, that the decorated initial by itself did not constitute the only decoration of the book page, but that ornamented initials are to be seen in harmony with the script on the page as a whole; script and decoration were designed to balance and complement one another, and different letter forms – display capitals, capitals, uncials and minuscules – contributed to the design.

Book decoration in the Merovingian period was one in which animal, vegetable and abstract ornament was predominant. A new decorative feature appeared in the middle of the eighth century. The Gundohinus Gospels (Bibliothèque Municipale Autun MS 3) were completed in 754, the third year of the reign of Pippin III. The Gospels were commissioned by a woman called Fausta and a monk Fuculphus. The drawings in this manuscript are rather crude, linear and flat, done in ink with a pen, with the colour filled in with a light wash. What was significant about the drawings in these Gospels was the depiction of the human figure – the four Evangelists and Christ. In other manuscripts of the second half of the eighth century historiated initials begin to appear, that is, initials with figures in them which relate to the text.

The appearance of the human figure in manuscript decoration in the mid-eighth century has been described as the 'beginning of Carolingian art' and it has to be accounted for.[41] Is the representational art of the early Carolingian period a result of a Carolingian revival of Mediterranean forms, or was there an earlier development of representational art in the Merovingian kingdom from which Carolingian art, even if only in part, could have evolved? As might be expected, both Mediterranean and Merovingian art forms were influential. Representational art does not appear in Merovingian books, but in sculpture, on sarcophagi, jewellery, stone crosses and grave slabs, and quite possibly in mosaics and wall paintings as well, there is ample evidence for the human figure. There are the *orantes* figures on Agilbert's tomb at Jouarre, the two thieves on either side of the truncated cross base in the Hypogeum of Merobaudes near Poitiers, Daniel in the lion's den on the seventh-century sarcophagus from the abbey of Charenton-sur-Cher and on the grave slab at Baume, the sacrifice of Isaac on another Baume grave slab and the hunting scene on the seventh-century sarcophagus from Toulouse to mention only a few.

The Christian faith was quite clearly the main inspiration for these figures, with the exception perhaps of the hunting scene, but the stone sculpture also reveals that the Merovingians inherited a whole tradition of decorative and ornamental art from Germanic and from Gallo-Roman culture, of which the habits of figural composition, based in part on late antique techniques, formed an element. A certain similarity between Gallic and Oriental sculptural styles, in the use of low relief and a growing emphasis on non-figural and asymbolic ornament has also been observed. Although the origin of the latter trends in art styles is almost certainly the eastern Mediterranean, the beginnings of these trends had been a very long time before the Merovingian period. There is no need to assume a direct stylistic influence from the eastern Mediterranean in the Merovingian period. Still less is there a need to assume that the Merovingian artists were incapable of creating anything skilled or beautiful out of their own heads and with their own hands. It is quite possible that one artist may have seen an Eastern work of art or piece of craftsmanship and copied it within his own idiom, but this does not seem to me to constitute a valid reason to talk in terms of Mediterranean influence on Merovingian art. Certain trends in sculpture, painting and ornament, as Edward James has stressed, are associated with the use of a whole new aesthetic of art, which spread throughout the Mediterranean in part due to the spread of the Christian faith.[42] It would be more constructive and more accurate to think in terms of parallel developments rather than direct influence.

Both Merovingian book decoration and Merovingian figural and ornamental carving and sculpture influenced the earliest Carolingian art, but the precedents for figural representation in Carolingian book painting were the late antique and early Christian book illuminations. In the earliest illustrations in papyrus rolls, before the codex became the more usual form of book, drawings and diagrams to supplement, illustrate and emphasize the text were closely related to the column of writing. As well as literary texts, scientific treatises obviously required illustration and there are a number of early medical, herbal, mathematical and astronomical treatises adorned with diagrams and line drawings. The illustration could either be on the left-hand side of the writing column, on the right-hand side, or interrupt the text as it does in the Heracles Papyrus (London Egypt Exploration Society collection, Pap. 2331), dated to the third century AD, with a concise drawing without a frame. The method was adopted in codices as well, and there are examples in Carolingian copies of earlier manuscripts such as the Berne Physiologus (Berne Burgerbibliothek 318) and the Paris Terence (BN lat. 7899).[43] The increasing use of the codex in preference to the roll opened up far greater possibilities for the illustrator. Later, more elaborate systems of illustration tended to connect picture and text in a less intimate way, and the addition of frames increased this tendency; the earliest extant miniatures in a painted frame date from the fourth century. Illustrations could depict one scene from a text or present a composite narrative sequence of pictures within a single frame as in the Ashburnham Pentateuch, a wonderful seventh-century copy of the first five books of the Bible (now BN n. a. lat. 2334). From the sixth century, book production passed more and more into the hands of the church. Early Continental Gospel books had little in the way of decoration (in contrast to insular books) other than the decorated initials and canon tables, but texts of the Old Testament lent themselves to more copious decoration. Thus the appearance of the human figure in Carolingian book art of the mid-eighth century had clear antecedents in both Merovingian figural sculpture and late antique and early Christian book art.

In their techniques and types of images, that is, in their iconography, the mid-eighth-century Carolingian books mark the beginnings of a new phase in the development of manuscript illumination. An important inspiration for Carolingian art was the Christian faith; not only were the stories from the Old and New Testaments illustrated, but there is the veneration and devotion which inspired scribes and artists to make the books works of art and holy objects in themselves. Whereas in the Merovingian kingdom the range of books produced and of those that were decorated was mostly confined to theological and liturgical texts, in the Carolingian period a great many different kinds of book were produced. These were Christian texts for the most part but non-Christian and

217

secular texts were copied as well. The Christian books included copies of the Gospels, Epistles of St Paul, Revelation or the Apocalypse, complete Bibles (called pandects), the liturgical books used for the celebration of the Mass and offices of the church, the works of the Christian fathers and later Anglo-Saxon and Carolingian authors. There were also the works of the early Christian poets, the most popular of which was the *Psychomachia* of Prudentius. Among the secular and non-Christian texts decorated were copies of the laws, royal, customary and ecclesiastical, grammars and treatises on time, metrics, geography, medicine and astronomy. The Carolingian illustrations for all these books formed the beginnings of a definite iconography for books of this kind which was to be copied and developed throughout the Middle Ages.

The iconography of Carolingian Gospel books and sacramentaries or Mass books was particularly influential. Gospel books, that is, the books containing the Gospels of Matthew, Mark, Luke and John, all in the Vulgate text of Jerome, and Gospel lectionaries, which contained the sections from the Gospels read in church throughout the liturgical year, were the most important to the Christian church. They were offered a special and different kind of reverence than that offered Bibles or copies of the New Testament. Gospel books possessed a liturgical function. They were altar books, kept on the altar in the church and used during the celebration of the liturgy. Most Carolingian Gospel books are of great magnificence and beauty, with richly decorated pages and sometimes bound in wonderful jewelled or ivory covers, depicting scenes described in the Gospel story. The decoration of Gospel books is completely dependent upon their content. Jerome's preface and his dedicatory letter to Pope Damasus and the canon tables (a numerical analysis of the correspondence between the four different accounts of events in the life of Christ) precede the Gospel texts themselves; and all, particularly the canon tables, were decorated in a distinctive way. The canon tables were usually arranged in columns under a series of decorated arches, which varied considerably in intricacy and style; Nordenfalk has interpreted the ornamental canon tables in Gospel books as a 'monumental decor symbolic of the unity of Christian doctrine'. In the most elaborate Gospel books there is further prefatory material before each Gospel, including the list of chapters and the prologue or *argumentum* to each Gospel, usually ascribed to Priscillian. In some Gospel books, such as those of the Ada school, interpretations and events recorded in these prologues provide the subject-matter for the illustrations rather than the Gospel narrative. As well as this arrangement of texts there were sometimes additional ornamental pages, which would include the *incipit* or beginning of the Gospel itself, an evangelist portrait and often a purely ornamental page or pages as a frontispiece to the book.

The custom of depicting the evangelist author at the beginning of his Gospel seems to have developed from the classical and late Roman representations of the author, the 'author portrait'. Portraits, or imaginary likenesses, of Virgil, Cicero, Livy, Terence and so on, depicted holding or writing their books, were placed at the beginning of a copy of their works before the text began. The evangelists in Carolingian and insular Gospel books were also depicted writing

218

or carrying their books and are either accompanied or replaced by their symbols. These symbols are a portrayal in art of the scene from Revelation 4 : 2: 'And immediately I was in the spirit and behold a throne was set in heaven and one sat on the throne . . . and round about the throne were four beasts full of eyes before and behind. And the first beast was like a lion, the second beast like a calf, the third beast had a face as a man, and the fourth beast was like a flying eagle.' The beasts were associated by the third- and fourth-century exegetes, Jerome and Augustine among them, with the four evangelist authors of the Gospels. The beast with the face of a man was Matthew, the lion was Mark, the calf, Luke and the eagle, John. The earliest appearance of these symbols as frontispieces to the Gospels seems to be in insular manuscripts, such as the Book of Durrow and the Lindisfarne Gospels. By the ninth century, the Continental tradition of representing the evangelist with his symbol was predominant. They were usually enclosed in arches similar to those in the frontispieces of Merovingian decorated manuscripts.

The other decorated pages in Carolingian Gospel books need to be considered in the context of those produced by the artists associated with the court of Charlemagne. Their work is usually divided into two groups: the 'Ada Gospels' group and the 'Coronation Gospels' or 'palace school' group, and can be dated between 780 and about 820. The iconography of the evangelist portraits in the Ada school manuscripts has engendered a massive literature, because of the supposed 'models' for the way in which the evangelists are depicted. Rosenbaum's is typical of the sort of argument produced:

'Most of the evangelist pictures of the Ada school depend on the cycles of Evangelist pictures in three Mediterranean manuscripts – a sixth century manuscript probably from Ravenna, now lost, a second, iconographically related to the first but probably made in Rome in the first half of the eighth century [hypothetical] and a seventh century manuscript in the Greek style and perhaps made in Rome [also hypothetical]. The Godescalc, Abbeville and Trier manuscripts represent more or less the original series in their entirety.'[44]

This sort of argument, in which one is asked to believe that something one can see is derived from so much that is merely supposed to have existed, is unsatisfactory. Certainly early medieval artists liked copying and adapting, but defining their adaptations in terms of hypothetical 'lost models' will not do. The 'model' problem is a recurrent one in Carolingian art history. Unfortunately not one single page from a book which could have served as a model has been preserved. One should perhaps steer a more cautious course and talk not in terms of direct models, but of conventions in Gospel book decoration and the representation of the evangelists. Most art historians are happy to accept the development of techniques and conventions in Byzantine art and I cannot see why the same should not apply to western painting. In other words, Carolingian artists were painting within a tradition, not copying direct from models. In a sense, Carolingian art is like Carolingian literary composition; it draws on a host of older forms and creates a new form.

As far as technique is concerned we cannot be certain how much the Carolingians inherited from their Merovingian predecessors, but they obviously learnt a lot from them. Certainly in the Ada Gospels St Luke or the Soissons Gospels St Mark there is a wonderfully delicate use of colour and moulding of the drapery, but there is still a lack of a true sense of perspective. The faces are flat and linear. The architectural framework in the Soissons Gospels echoes decorative forms of the classical period in that it has classical marbled columns supporting late Roman capitals. Generally the evangelists of the Ada school codices are statuesque and solid, with draperies falling in heavy folds due to their own weight. They are richly decorated manuscripts, most of them written in gold letters on purple dyed parchment.

The Carolingians also added to the corpus of Gospel book decorations. In the Soissons Gospels is a representation of Heavenly Jerusalem, forming the frontispiece to the whole book.[45] In the bottom portion of the picture is a representation of the city, behind a structure of classical columns; above there are the four evangelist symbols representing the harmony of the Gospels, and above them, in the smallest section of the painting there are the saints who look upwards to the top of the painting where the Lamb, symbol of Christ, stands. The artist has set the most important part of the picture, and the central figure of the Christian faith, high up in a tiny roundel, yet it dominates the composition. In the same manuscript is the Fountain of Life, which first appeared in the Godescalc Lectionary commissioned by Charlemagne and Hildegard in 781. This manuscript celebrated the fourteenth year of Charlemagne's reign and the baptism of his son Pippin by Pope Hadrian. The picture is a representation of the Baptistery in the Lateran in Rome where Pippin was baptized; it allegorizes the Christian symbolism of baptism, the death, burial and rebirth as a Christian and makes of it the fountain of life which is referred to in connection with baptism by a number of patristic commentators as well as by Carolingian exegetes. Some of the elements such as harts drinking illustrate Psalm 42, associated with baptism in the liturgy.[46] Thus the Carolingian artist was drawing on his knowledge of Christian interpretation of Scripture and theology for his image.

In the sacramentary iconography this knowledge is also apparent. The central prayer of the Mass, the canon, begins with the words *Te Igitur*. In the Sacramentary of Gellone, the artist made the T into a crude but impressive picture of the crucifixion. The motif recurs in later Carolingian sacramentaries. A more exegetical approach was that of the artist of the Drogo Sacramentary (BN lat. 9428). The ends of the T strokes were filled in with various scenes of Old Testament sacrifices and sacrificial animals – Abraham and Isaac, Melchisedech and Joshua – as a reminder of the continuity between the Old Testament and the supreme significance of the sacrifice of the Mass itself.

In a completely different vein are the illustrations of the so-called palace school manuscript of which the 'Coronation Gospels' in Vienna are the best-known example. They are of unequivocally Byzantine inspiration, with an ease of form and movement lacking in the Ada school manuscripts. The author portraits of the evangelists are the only illustrations. The style of painting has been described as illusionistic; there is a classical use of highlights and the pictures are set in a landscape rather than in an architectural setting. The paintings seem to have been done by a Greek called *Demetrius presbyter* (the Vienna Gospels are inscribed with his name) fully within the Hellenistic tradition. In the Vienna Gospels, moreover, the evangelist symbols are absent. The artist used a painterly technique, modelling the face and features and indicating highlights and reliefs with washes of colour. The use of highlights in the classical manner is in fact one of the most important techniques adopted by the Carolingians and later medieval painters from classical painting. These Byzantine-inspired portraits were later to be imitated at Rheims in the second and third decades of the ninth century.[47]

Generally, the Gospel books and sacramentaries of the early Carolingian period illustrate a development from the flat linear art of the Merovingians to the use of the illusion of three-dimensional painting, with depth, realistic human figures and an ability to place a figure within a structure or in space. Decorative motifs were those employed in both insular and Merovingian manuscripts, and new ones were evolved. The court school codices are notable for their lavish and innovatory use of colour, with purple dyed vellum, gold and silver paint for the script, and many bright, and expensive, pigments. The growing elaboration of the frame is also a Carolingian contribution.

Psalter illustrations of the Carolingian period emphasize further the relationship between text and illustration. Decorations of Psalters were very rarely actual illustrations of the text, but were usually in the form of Old and New Testament pictures placed at the beginning of the volume, or a series of illustrations either incorporated into the body of the text or placed before each of the first Psalms said at Matins throughout the week or the first Psalm for Sunday evening. A further variant was marginal illustration, but this was more usually found in Greek manuscripts. Carolingian Psalter illustrations may be roughly divided into four types: the simply decorative, such as we find in the Corbie Psalter (Amiens Bibliothèque Municipale 3); the exegetical, which portrays commentaries of the Fathers who have ascribed some meaning to a particular word or phrase from a Psalm rather than the Psalm phrase itself, as in the Stuttgart Psalter and some of the Utrecht Psalter illustrations; the prophetic, which illustrate those verses in the Psalms which were interpreted by the Fathers as foretelling the coming of Christ or events in his life, death and Passion, such as Psalm 116, vv. 4–6; and the literal illustration in which words in the text were simply translated into images.

The Utrecht Psalter contains many examples of this literal type of illustration. The manuscript, in England from the tenth to the eighteenth centuries and now in the University library at Utrecht, was produced at the Rheims monastery of Hautvillers between 816 and 835. It contains 166 drawings executed in bistre outline and in a very striking style, known as *frissonant*, animated with little figures living, as Wormald put it, in a 'world of ecstasy, tearing wind and unceasing violence'.[48] The excitement and animation of the figures is quite remarkable, the scenes are hectic and set in a landscape of rocky hills and delicately drawn trees. Some have argued that the Utrecht Psalter, like a number of the other manuscripts produced in the Rheims scriptorium, is a copy of a late antique codex. Certainly the script (rustic capitals) and the drawings are full of late antique features; there is a habit of personification, for example, with river gods, the sun and the moon in human form, and scenes of rustic occupations, but the manuscript is now recognized as a Carolingian masterpiece. In Wormald's words: 'It is clear that the Utrecht Psalter does not represent the style of any particular archetype but is characteristic of the Carolingian Renaissance, at once eclectic and antiquarian, but nevertheless and paradoxically, new.' Psalters such as the Utrecht and Stuttgart Psalters illustrate more clearly than any other book paintings of the Carolingian period that two of the principal sources for Carolingian book art were the actual text of the Bible and the commentaries upon it.

The early schools of book painting, the Ada school and the palace school, were associated with the court of the Frankish king, but in the course of the ninth century a number of ateliers emerged, based on some of the great monasteries and diocesan centres. The Hautvillers–Rheims school of book painting, for example, is being studied by Florentine Mütherich. Among the manuscripts, apart from the Utrecht Psalter, that have been attributed to it so far are the Ebbo Gospels (Epernay BM MS 1), Hincmar Gospels (Rheims BM MS 7), the Berne Physiologus and the Paris Terence. Studies of the two latter manuscripts have argued that the fourth-century style of book painting provides the closest relative to them, and that there were a number of late antique manuscripts at Rheims which the artists had seen. It is also possible that the artist or artists responsible for the Coronation Gospel group of manuscripts had some influence on the artists of the Rheims school. Hautvillers itself seems to have been patronized by Archbishop Ebbo and possibly Archbishop Hincmar as well; another archbishop, Drogo of Metz, patronized artists at Metz. Their finest work is the Drogo Sacramentary, mentioned earlier; an astronomical manual and a number of beautiful ivory carvings are also thought to be from the Metz workshop.

During the abbacies of Fridugisus, Adalhard and Vivian (804–51), Tours developed a well-deserved reputation for the production of fine books. Tours was sacked by the Vikings in 903, so that a great deal of our knowledge about Tours manuscripts is based upon what they exported to other centres. Two hundred manuscripts of the Tours scriptorium survive, of which sixty are illuminated. The best known are the Moutier Grandval Bible (BL Add. 10546), the Stuttgart Gospels, the Bamberg Bible, the Vivian Bible (BN lat. 1) the St Gauzelin Gospels in the cathedral library of Nancy, the Lothar Gospels (BN lat. 266) and Boethius' *De Arithmetica* (Bamberg misc. class. 5). All Tours painting reveals a particular care with colour – using it to indicate shadows, to model folds in clothes and facial features – and the prominence given to the human figure in decoration. Some 'influence' from Rheims has been detected in the Tours style. Tours produced three of the four extant Carolingian illustrated Bibles. They were illustrated with narrative picture cycles showing several separate episodes in the same picture, so that in the illustration to Genesis for example, the serpent tempting Eve, Eve offering the apple to Adam, and Adam and Eve discovering their nakedness form one composition. Tours was generally bold in its book decoration, with a lavish use of gold and silver and many bright and subtle colours. Tours, moreover, was a centre which benefited from royal patronage. The Lothar Gospels were commissioned by the Emperor Lothar, with the approval of his brother Charles the Bald, to mark their reconciliation at Péronne in 849, while the glorious Vivian Bible, like the Bamberg Boethius, was presented by Tours to Charles the Bald. Another gift to the king was the Bible of San Paolo fuori le Mura, written in 869 or 870 by the scribe Ingobert, possibly at Rheims. The decoration is magnificent, and combines reminiscences of the work of most of the leading Frankish ateliers of the second half of the ninth century – Tours, Rheims, the Franco-Saxon school and the so-called palace school of Charles the Bald.

The Franco-Saxon manuscripts were decorated in a style that is reminiscent of insular decoration, with interlace and animal ornament. The main centre of the Franco-Saxon school was the monastery of St Amand in Flanders, whose importance as an intellectual centre has already been discussed. The Bible St Amand presented to Charles the Bald in about 870 (now BN. lat. 2) is the most beautiful example of the atelier's work. It was austere in its decoration; it contains no human figures, no royal portrait, but instead exhibits the taste for the strictly decorative which is characteristic of the Franco-Saxon school. The seventy-four decorated initials are intricately patterned with interlace design, often with zoomorphic finials. The colour is rich and bold and the contours of the letters are sometimes outlined in the red dots usually associated with insular decoration. Unlike Tours, Rheims and Metz, as far as we know, the Franco-Saxon style was not confined to St Amand; we can speak in terms of a regional style and tradition of decoration variously interpreted by artists of different ateliers. St Omer and St Vaast, for example, also produced books decorated in the Franco-Saxon manner, and manuscripts such as Oxford Add. c. 153 and Laud lat. 27 indicate that in the tenth century the style was being copied elsewhere in Flanders and in lower Saxony. St Amand itself remained the principal centre for the Franco-Saxon style until well into the twelfth century.

The atelier which produced decorated books almost exclusively for Charles the Bald himself was the so-called *Hofschule* or palace school. No less than twelve richly decorated and distinctive manuscripts dated between 860 and 877 were ascribed to the *Hofschule Karls des Kahlen* by Wilhelm Koehler, and seven of them may be associated directly with the king. They include the Psalter of Charles the Bald (BN lat. 1152), his Prayer book in the Schatzkammer der Residenz in Munich, an antiphonary (BN lat. 17436), a Psalter written entirely in gold and silver tironian notes, the notarial shorthand (Wolfenbüttel 3025), a sacramentary fragment (BN lat. 1141) and the *Codex Aureus* (Munich Clm 14000). The Paris Psalter, the Prayer book and the *Codex Aureus* contain portraits of Charles enthroned. There is no agreement about the identity of the king portrayed in the sacramentary fragment. The most characteristic decorative motif in this group of manuscripts is the acanthus leaf; lines of folds and of leaf shapes and patterns are picked out in white and gold, and there is a lavish use of gold leaf. All the manuscripts have a ruddy appearance, with brown, red and green predominating. The artist Liuthard was responsible for the painting in Charles the Bald's Psalter, and his work is to be seen in two other manuscripts of the *Hofschule*, Darmstadt Landesbibliothek 746 and the Munich *Codex Aureus*. The Munich *Codex Aureus* represents a culmination of the *Hofschule* style. Every square millimetre on the decorated page is filled with rich colour and ornamental detail. The portrait of the king, enthroned and flanked by faithful retainers and angels, glitters with gold leaf. The decorated borders throughout the book vary considerably in intricacy, with sequences of patterns being employed and gold used to pick out every detail.

As I have stressed elsewhere, the distinguishing feature of the *Hofschule* group is its eclecticism:[49] the painting and decoration reflect stylistic influences from various centres, including Rheims, Tours and Metz. This eclecticism is what one might expect from a group of artists from different centres gathered together by a patron in order to produce books for his personal use. A similar eclecticism has been observed in a group of ivory carvings with strong affinities with the *Hofschule* manuscripts, and it is possible that both ivory carvings and books were produced in the same centre, Compiègne.

After the reign of Charles the Bald, the production of richly decorated books seems to have decreased and no further schools of book painting, apart from the Franco-Saxon style and that of St Gall, have been identified until the Ottonian schools of the late tenth century.

The rapid development of a distinctively Carolingian art in the course of the ninth century, which I have outlined, may be linked with the revival of education and learning, but it is going too far to say, as Gaehde does, that 'the aim of the artistic revival proclaimed at court was the renewal of classical art'.[50] No such aim in general terms was declared, or at least, there is no evidence for it, nor was an artistic 'revival' 'proclaimed at court'. There are undoubtedly many classical elements in Carolingian art, such as the tradition of narrative picture cycles, the verisimilitude in anatomy, the illusion of the third dimension, the personification of the elements or mythological characters, the technique of highlighting and the employment of classical decorative motifs such as the acanthus leaf and late Roman capitals, putti and vine leaves. There is, however, insufficient evidence to posit a wholesale revival of classical art; classical art forms were used to form part of a new unity created by the Carolingian artists.

The main ateliers of Carolingian book painting in the second half of the ninth century benefited much from royal, noble, episcopal and abbatial patronage. Wealth was needed to produce books like this, just as the books themselves were symbols of wealth and favour. Centres such as Tours, Rheims and St Amand became so renowned for their book illustrations that manuscripts were commissioned from their workshops from all over the kingdom. Yet we should beware of talking too glibly about Tours, Rheims, Franco-Saxon or palace school styles of painting and the influence they had on one another. In the first place this is an extraordinarily disembodied view of art. These styles did not just exert 'influence' passively but were the work of men and women who saw images and interpreted them imaginatively and thoughtfully, who were almost certainly literate and versed in at least the Scriptures, if not all the exegesis on

Scripture, as well. In the second place Carolingian art is the painting, metal-work and sculpture of groups of individuals who learnt much from one another, all of whom were working within a distinct tradition which owed as much for sources and inspiration to the Carolingian heritage of classical, Merovingian, early Christian and late antique forms and conventions as it did to the Carolingian artists' interpretation of the texts they had to illustrate and their own creative imagination and considerable artistic skill. If 'Renaissance' be interpreted as a period in which a quantity of work of very high quality was produced and which, although based on the preceding centuries of development nevertheless produced new ideas and forms, then Carolingian art during the period 750–900 can certainly be considered as one manifestation of the Carolingian Renaissance.

NOTES

1. *PL* 111, cols 9–614. See E. Heyse, *Hrabanus Maurus Enzyklopädie De rerum naturis* (Munich 1969), M. Rissel, *Rezeption antiker und patristischer Wissenschaft bei Hrabanus Maurus* (Berne 1975), and P. Lehmann, 'Illustrierte Hrabanus Codices', 'Fuldaer Studien' cited above, chapter 6, n. 10 (Munich 1927), 13–47.
2. D. Ganz, review of Rissel, *Beiträge zur Geschichte der deutschen Sprache und Literatur* 101 (1979), 432–5.
3. W. M. Lindsay and P. Lehmann, 'The early Mainz scriptorium', *Palaeographia Latina* 4 (1925), 15–39.
4. H. Büttner and J. Duft, *Lorsch und St Gallen in der Frühzeit* (Stuttgart and Constance 1965).
5. B. Bischoff, *Lorsch im Spiegel seiner Handschriften* (Munich 1974).
6. A. Bruckner and R. Marichal, *Chartae Latinae Antiquiores* I and II (Olten and Lausanne 1954 and 1956), Büttner and Duft, *Lorsch and St Gallen*, J. M. Clark, *The Abbey of St Gall* (Cambridge 1926), and P. Lehmann, *Mittelalterliche Bibliothekskataloge Deutschlands und der Schweiz* I (Munich 1918).
7. E. A. Lowe, 'An eighth century list of books in a Bodleian manuscript from Würzburg and its probable relationship to the Laudian *Acts*', *Speculum* 3 (1928), 3–15.
8. B. Bischoff and J. Hofmann, *Libri sancti Kiliani* (Würzburg 1952).
9. *MGH Epp.* V, Ep. 26, 440, lines 15–20; Hraban's answer, ibid., Ep. 27, 441–2.
10. *MGH Epp.* IV, 542–4.
11. E. Boshof, *Erzbischof Agobard von Lyons* (Cologne 1969).
12. C. Charlier, 'Les manuscrits personnels de Florus de Lyon et son activité littéraire', *Mélanges E. Podechard* (Lyons 1945), 71–84.
13. D. Ganz, 'The literary interests of the abbey of Corbie in the first half of the ninth century', Oxford D. Phil. thesis, 1980.
14. C. Beeson, 'The Collectaneum of Hadoard', *Classical Philology* 40 (1945), 201–22 and B. Bischoff, 'Hadoardus and the classical manuscripts from Corbie', *Studies in honor of Anselm A. Albareda* (New York 1961), 41–57.
15. J. J. Contreni, 'The formation of Laon's cathedral library in the ninth century', *Studi Medievali* 13 (1972), 919–39, and *The Cathedral School of Laon: its Manuscripts and Masters* (Munich 1978).

16. I am preparing a full-length study of the scriptorium and library of St Amand from the eighth to the tenth centuries; what follow therefore are preliminary observations rather than final conclusions.
17. L. Delisle, *Le Cabinet des Manuscrits de la Bibliothèque Impériale* (Paris 4 vols, 1868–81), I, 448–58.
18. J. Vezin, 'Les reliures carolingiennes de cuir à décor estampé de la Bibliothèque Nationale de Paris', *BEC* 128 (1970), 81–113, and see K. Christ, 'Karolingische Bibliothekseinbände', *Festschrift Georg Leyh* (Leipzig 1937), 82–104 and G. D. Hobson, 'Some early bindings and binders' tools', *The Library*, 4th series, 19 (1938–39), 202–49.
19. A. Boutemy, 'Le scriptorium et la bibliothèque de Saint Amand d'après les manuscrits et les anciens catalogues', *Scriptorium* 1 (1946), 6–16.
20. K. Schmid and O. G. Oexle, 'Voraussetzungen und Wirkung des Gebetsbundes von Attigny', *Francia* 2 (1974), 71–122.
21. K. Beyerle, 'Das Reichenau Verbrüderungsbuch als Quelle der Klostergeschichte', *Die Kultur der Abtei Reichenau* K. Beyerle (ed) (Munich 2 vols, 1925), II, 1107–217; O. G. Oexle, *Monastischen und geistlichen Gemeinschaften im westfränkischen Bereich* (Munich 1978), and J. Autenrieth, D. Geuenich and K. Schmid, *Das Verbrüderungsbuch der Abtei Reichenau: Einleitung, Register, Faksimile. MGH Libri Memoriales et Necrologia* N. S. I (Hannover 1979).
22. Lupus, Epp. 40 and 1.
23. M. Cappuyns, 'Les *Bibli Wulfadi* et Jean Scot Erigène', *Recherches de Théologie Ancienne et Mediévale* 33 (1966), 137–9.
24. Lupus, E. 1.
25. Lupus, Epp. 4 and 5.
26. Lupus, Epp. 1 and 5.
27. Lupus, Ep. 7.
28. Lupus, Ep. 8.
29. Lupus, Ep. 21.
30. Lupus, Ep. 35.
31. Lupus, Ep. 53.
32. Lupus, Ep. 100.
33. Lupus, Ep. 87 and compare Epp. 65, 69, 77, 87, 88, 95, 100, 101, 104, 106, 108, 110, 113, 122, 133.
34. E. Pellégrin, 'Les manuscrits de Loup de Ferrières', *BEC* 115 (1957), 5–31.
35. D. Ganz, 'The literary interests of the abbey of Corbie'.
36. J. Bouhot, *Ratramme de Corbie* (Paris 1976). See also J. Jolivet, 'L' Enjeu de la Grammaire pour Godescalc', *Jean Scot Erigène et l'Histoire de la Philosophie* (Paris 1977 – Colloques Internationaux du Centre National de la Recherche Scientifique No. 561), 79–87, and D. Ganz, 'The debate on predestination', *Charles the Bald: Court and Kingdom*, M. T. Gibson and J. L. Nelson (eds) (Oxford 1981), 353–73.
37. See R. McKitterick, 'Charles the Bald (823–877) and his library: the patronage of learning', *EHR* 95 (1980), 28–47.
38. See B. Bischoff, 'Eine Sammelhandschrift Walahfrid Strabos (Cod. Sangall. 878)', *Aus der Welt des Buches. Festgabe Georg Leyh* (Leipzig 1950), 30–48.
39. R. McKitterick, 'The palace school of Charles the Bald', *Charles the Bald: Court and Kingdom*, 385–400.
40. C. Nordenfalk, *Die Spätantike Zierbuchstaben* (Stockholm 1970).
41. For example, J. Hubert, *Carolingian Art* (London 1970), 71–4.
42. E. James, *The Merovingian Archaeology of Southwest Gaul* (Oxford 2 vols, 1977).

43. K. Weitzmann, *Illustration in Roll and Codex: A Study of the Origin and Method of Text Illustration* (Princeton 1947), and *Ancient Book Illumination* (Cambridge, Mass. 1959).
44. E. Rosenbaum, 'The evangelist portraits of the Ada school and their models', *Art Bulletin* **38** (1956), 81–90 (my parentheses).
45. Compare *Revelation*, 21: 2.
46. Compare *Revelation*, 21: 7.
47. J. Beckwith, 'Byzantine influence on art at the court of Charlemagne', *KdG* III (1965), 288–301.
48. F. Wormald, *The Utrecht Psalter* (Utrecht 1953), 8.
49. R. McKitterick, 'Charles the Bald (823–877) and his library: the patronage of learning', *EHR* **95** (1980), 28–47.
50. J. Gaehde and F. Mütherich, *Carolingian Painting* (London 1977), 9.

CHAPTER NINE

Normandy, Brittany and Flanders

Normandy, Brittany and Flanders emerged in the ninth and tenth centuries as regions with strong Carolingian connections, but possessing a large measure of autonomy. That their populations, at least in the cases of Normandy and Brittany, were predominantly non-Frankish, makes their development rather different from that of the principalities to be considered in the following chapter.

I

Land ceded to the Vikings by the Frankish King Charles the Simple between 911 and 918 formed the nucleus of the ducal state of Normandy, and was the culmination of sixty years of Viking raiding in the Frankish kingdoms. Although there were probably Norwegians and Swedes among the bands of warriors who attacked Francia, Aquitaine and England, the majority are thought to have been Danes. All the raids were for plunder in the form of loot, ransoms, bribes, tributes (sometimes called 'Danegeld' by modern historians) and captives. There is also evidence that the Vikings were playing a vital part in the slave trade in Western Europe at this time, keeping the market well supplied. Many of these raids were undoubtedly carried out arbitrarily by opportunist pirates. Others, particularly the 'great invasion' of 856–62 and the siege of Paris in 885–6, were clearly the outcome of careful planning, based on sound information about the lie of the land, centres of wealth and settlement, and the congregations of people on religious festivals.[1]

The first recorded attack by the Danes on the Frankish kingdom, led by Chocolaicus (Hugleikr or Hygelac) against King Theudebert was noted by Gregory of Tours, and Venantius Fortunatus reported the defeat in Frisia in 574 of a party of Danes, Saxons and Jutes by the Franks.[2] Thereafter the Northmen (*Nordmanni*) disappear from Frankish sources until the eighth century. It is possible that Charles Martel's onslaught on the strong kingdom of Frisia and its annexation by the Carolingians exposed the Danes to the Franks (or the

Franks to the Danes) and Charlemagne's extension of his conquests north into Nordalbingia and Saxony may have precipitated defensive aggression on the Danes' part, though there is nothing to indicate that Charlemagne wished actually to conquer them. Whatever the cause, the first recorded Viking raid on Carolingian Gaul was off the coast of Aquitaine, and in 800 Charlemagne asked his son Louis to organize the coastal defences in that region.[3] This may have been a band of pirates unconnected with the Danish king, but in 804 the Danes, led by King Godofrid, embarked on hostilities against the Franks in Schleswig, sometimes referred to in the Royal Frankish Annals as the Danish march. The Obodrites were particularly vulnerable and in 808 they were attacked by the Danes and their commercial centre Reric was destroyed. Both Charlemagne and Godofrid constructed defences; Charlemagne had a fleet of ships built and made some moves to set up defences on the Elbe, and Godofrid may have built a portion at least of the massive rampart known as the *Danevirk* across the base of the Jutland peninsula.[4] Two years later the Danes ravaged Frisia (it was in the path of their sea route south) and imposed a tribute on the natives. In the same year Godofrid was murdered and was succeeded by his son Hemming.

The chief written sources for the history of Denmark in this period are Frankish, and it is difficult to determine the extent of the authority wielded by the Danish kings and whether the ones we hear about were petty kings among many or rulers of stature. There appear to have been at least two rival families claiming to rule Denmark. Succession to the kingship appears to have been a combination of election, assertion and hereditary right; it may be significant that it is usually the monarch's brother's son or sons who claim to be the heir or heirs, though the claim had to be made good. The kingship appears to have been remarkably unstable, and it is not until the tenth century that any kind of royal base (Jelling) or dynasty (house of Gorm), emerges. In the early ninth century furthermore, the policy chosen towards the Franks was crucial for the king's position. Hemming made an elaborate peace with Charlemagne – confirmed by an exchange of oaths between twelve Danish and twelve Frankish magnates – but died soon afterwards. The succession was disputed between Sigifrid, nephew of Godofrid, and Anulo, nephew of Hemming. Both were killed, but Anulo's supporters made Anulo's brothers Harald and Reginfred, kings. These two in their turn sued for peace with Charlemagne, and possibly in consequence were driven from Denmark by the four or five sons of Godofrid who returned from their exile in Sweden and made themselves kings. Reginfred was killed in the first attempt to regain the throne, but Harald appealed to Louis the Pious for assistance. With the help of the Obodrites, Louis restored Harald to his former position in Denmark in 819, which he was required to share with two of Godofrid's sons. The arrangement was an uneasy one and lasted only until 827, when the sons of Godofrid drove Harald out, and the eldest, Hohrich (Rorik) emerged as ruler of Denmark.

In 826, Harald himself with his wife, son and followers had been baptized in the church of St Alban's at Mainz and given the territory of Rüstringen on the mouth of the Weser in upper Frisia. This was the first portion of Frankish land to be ceded to a Dane; Louis may have intended Harald in Rüstringen to defend the coast of Frisia from attacks from the north. The area stayed in Harald's hands, and then those of his son Godofrid, until 856. The first phase of the conflict between the Danes and the Franks therefore was in the political context of the threat Charlemagne presented to the Danes and Louis the Pious' attempt to intervene directly in Danish affairs by supporting a claimant to the throne. Through Ebbo, archbishop of Rheims, and the Corbie monk Anskar, Louis had also tried to interfere in the religious sphere, by promoting the Christian mission to Denmark. He may have hoped thereby to turn pagan enemies into Christian allies.

For the rest of his reign, Louis had to put up with some impertinences from the Danish raiders, though their king Hohrich was at pains to disclaim responsibility for their activities, particularly the attack on the commercial centres of Walcheren and Dorestad between 835 and 837. There is reason to suppose that Louis' authority and his defences were sufficiently respected to keep the Danes at bay for the time being. Louis dismissed Hohrich's request in 838 to be ceded Frisia and the land of the Obodrites as ludicrous, and peace was concluded between them in 839. After Louis' death, however, the Vikings took advantage of the quarrels between his sons, as did many of the Frankish magnates, and increased their activities.

The attacks on Frisia come into a different category from those on the rest of the Frankish kingdom, for here there was conflict between rival groups of Danes. There is also a hint in the sources that the Frisians themselves were not exactly energetic in their efforts to resist Danish attempts at conquest. Frisians participated in Viking raids and some Frisian counts served the Danish kings. Frisia extended down the coast from the Weser to the Zwin and had been conquered by Charles Martel and Pippin. When Harald was installed in Rüstringen in 826 he may well have had some sort of responsibility to defend Dorestad; if he had, he did little to fulfil it. Between 835 and 837 Hemming son of Halfdan sacked Walcheren and Dorestad and received tribute from the Frisians, and towards the end of the reign of Louis the Pious two nephews of Harald and Hemming – Harald and Rorik – received Dorestad *iure beneficii* from the Emperor Lothar and became allies to Lothar in his conflict with his brothers.[5] In 841 Lothar gave Walcheren and other territories (probably Zeeland) to Harald, and Rorik held Dorestad, possibly in return for undertaking to defend the towns from Viking attack. In other words, from 841 the Carolingians no longer directly controlled these two trading centres. In Frisia, moreover, two different Danish leaders and their followers maintained semi-independent positions with regard to the Carolingian rulers as well as to those of Denmark. Both Harald and Rorik went so far as to assert claims to rule Denmark, and Rorik extended his territory in Frisia until he dominated much of the lower coast. Indeed some of the Viking raids recorded in the Annals of St Bertin may in fact be those of Rorik in his efforts to increase his territory. Later ravages of Frisia by the Vikings recorded in the annals, such as the Seine Vikings' sack of Dorestad in 863 are thus primarily attacks on rival groups of Danes, even though the Emperor Lothar was under some sort of obligation to defend the area as well.[6] Expeditions officially backed by the king of the Danes on the other hand tended to concentrate on Germany. In 845 for example, Hohrich sent '600 ships' up the Elbe and Hamburg was sacked before the Danes were driven off by Louis the German and his Saxons.[7]

The Viking raids on Francia started in grim earnest in 841 and from then until 892 hardly a year passed without an annalist recording a Viking attack. It is clear that the raids caused much misery, terror and destruction, even if only on a local level. The modern tendency is to play down the ravages of the Vikings in Frankish territory and convey the impression that they were merely, in Wallace-Hadrill's memorable caricature of the modern view, 'long-haired tourists who occasionally roughed up the natives'.[8] Emotional reports such as that of the much-quoted Ermentarius, monk of Noirmoutier, may well have been exaggerated by terrified chroniclers who had had to flee before the pirates and who had witnessed the carnage, the looting and burning of everything they held dear, and the capture of their friends and relatives. But murdered bishops – Frobald of Chartres, Baltfrid of Bayeux, Ermenfrid of Beauvais, Lista of Coutances, Madalbertus of Bourges and the bishop of Nantes and all his clergy – Franks taken into slavery (including Adalelm, bishop of Sées) and monks fleeing to safety with their relics and treasure,[9] are eloquent witness to the havoc wreaked by the pagans. Sawyer has contended that the numbers of the raiders and their ships have been exaggerated as well, but his argument is curiously lopsided; he accepts as trustworthy all the small figures provided in the annals, but rejects the large ones simply because they are large.[10] It is possible that we have overestimated the size of the average Viking ship and the number of men any one could carry after the booty, captives, food, drink, weapons and horses had been loaded. That is, that the large numbers of ships described by the annalists may be manned by far fewer men than is usually supposed. On the other hand large, round figures sound as if they are invented to impress. Whether the raiding parties were composed of thousands or of hundreds of men, the point is, surely, that they were relatively large forces as far as the Franks were concerned, attacking small groups of people. The Vikings were masters at attacking the defenceless – monks, people going to market, and merchants. Once they started wintering on Frankish soil, moreover, the Vikings could conduct raids throughout the winter. This was not playing the game, for the Frankish host was only summoned in the spring and did not usually operate during the winter months.

From our vantage point we can distinguish three main groups of Vikings under various leaders, operating on the Loire, Seine and Somme rivers respectively. For the Franks, however, there can have been little to distinguish the bands. Nor did each group of Vikings necessarily confine themselves to one region; the Seine Vikings in 853 sacked Nantes. Most of the raids were launched against the kingdom of Charles the Bald and were directed at towns and the principal monasteries – Rouen in 841, Quentovic in 842, Nantes in 843, Saintes, Beauvais, Angers, Tours in 852–4, Bayeux, Evreux, Noyon, Amiens, Thérouanne in 858–64, Angoulême and Poitiers in 863. The annals suggest that not all Franks were surprised by these raids. At Quentovic in 842 for example, the Vikings burned everything except 'those buildings which they had been bribed to spare', and in 847 Prudentius of Troyes accuses some of the citizens of Bordeaux of betraying the town to the Danes. In 853, because the raid on St Martin's had been known about beforehand, the body of St Martin and the treasure had been conveyed to safety, and in 863 the Northmen burned the church of St Hilary at Poitiers though they had been bribed to spare the city.

In some cases Franks actually joined forces with or used the Vikings to gain their own ends. We have already seen that Lothar hoped to use Harald and Rorik as allies and it is suggested that the Westfolding Vikings who sailed up the Loire in 842 and sacked Nantes on St John's Day, killing the bishop and his clergy and taking many of the city's population captive, were invited by Count Lambert, ambitious to secure Nantes for himself, and that Lambert provided Frankish pilots to guide the Viking ships upstream. In 862, Saloman, the ruler of the Bretons, hired twelve Danish ships (probably 'Loire Vikings') to assist him against Count Robert the Strong on the Loire. Robert in his turn made an alliance with the 'Seine Vikings' against Saloman. Pippin II of Aquitaine may have gone to the lengths of turning pagan as well as joining the Loire Vikings in 857, and Charles the Bald himself in 860 paid Weland, leader of the Somme Vikings, to conduct his pirates against the Seine Vikings ensconced on the island of Oscellus in the river Seine. The money for Weland took so long to collect that Weland raised his price by 2000 to 5000 pounds of silver and demanded wine and food too. Despite this, Charles the Bald himself managed to make a profit from this particular piece of fund raising; it by no means drained the treasury. Some Vikings furthermore joined Charles the Bald's army; Berno, chief of one group of pirates on the Seine swore fealty to Charles the Bald in 858. The evidence suggests in fact that the Vikings were far from being an unknown horde of occasional marauders. From the middle of the ninth century, their fortunes were bound up in Francia and they were a part of its political life.

For the first twenty years of the raids, the Franks seem to have been extraordinarily passive and offered very little resistance. The usual response to a raid was to run away. One important instance indicates that the king and counts were failing in their duty to defend their domains. In 859 some of the common people living between the Seine and Loire rivers formed an association among themselves and fought valiantly against the Seine Vikings, until they were killed by 'our' more powerful people (that is, by Frankish magnates!).[11] Ermentarius also lamented that no one in authority was prepared to make a stand. The men of Poitiers succeeded in killing some Vikings when they were attacked, and the booty they captured was donated to the church of Poitiers. Occasionally the Vikings demanded tribute from the local people – gold, silver, wine, corn and livestock – as the price of peace. It was often the citizens of a town who took the initiative in negotiating with the raider in a desperate attempt to salvage their property. In 888 for example, the citizens of Meaux decided to deal with the Vikings 'who were known to them' themselves, came to an agreement with them, and opened the town gates. But it availed them little; after a few days the citizens were rounded up and sold into slavery.[12] The Vikings themselves were employed as mediators; Sigifrid, grandson of Rorik and a Christian, for example. mediated between Carloman and the Vikings in 884.[13]

The only defensive strategy was the resort to paying tribute, that is, paying the Vikings vast sums of gold and silver to go away, thus buying time and preventing the possibility of a slaughter on the battlefield such as the Franks could ill afford. The respite thus gained was unfortunately short, for the Danes naturally enough came back for more. Tribute was paid in 845, 853, 860/1, 862, 866, 877, 884, 889, 897, 923/4 and 926.[14] The sums of the 7 payments of which we have details amounted to almost 40,000 pounds of silver, let alone the food and drink that often went with it. The burden of paying tribute probably fell most heavily on the vassals of the king.

After 862 however, there was some attempt to build defences against the Vikings in the form of fortified bridges on the principal rivers, especially the Seine, and at the assembly of Pîtres in 864 Charles the Bald requested that fortresses be built. He also ordered the demolition of any fortification that had been constructed without royal authorization, ostensibly to prevent their being used for the oppression of the people but perhaps fearing that they would be used against him as well as against the Vikings. In 869 Charles ordered the inhabitants of Le Mans and Tours to fortify their towns for the benefit of the population in the surrounding countryside. Earlier in the ninth century the towns had not built defences and had even dismantled the town walls. Ebbo, archbishop of Rheims, for example, had received permission from Louis the Pious to destroy the walls and gate of Rheims in order to reconstruct the cathedral. At Melun in 859, Wenilo, archbishop of Sens, was authorized to use stones from the town walls for the church. Justification for destroying the walls was always in terms of the need for building materials; it was Flodoard who first suggested that the destruction of town walls was a symbol of the Franks' sense of security. This explanation, however, does not accord with archaeological reality. Walls were still being dismantled after the Viking raids had started. Février furthermore makes the point that the walls may well have been of limited military value anyway, while the cathedrals would have constituted strong refuges.[15] The development of suburban areas of the town was altering the town structure, and the holiness of a city, together with its patron saint, was regarded as a defence against attack. The relics of saints Germanus, Geneviève, Cloud and Marcel guarded the town of Paris in 886, and it is significant that lives of the patron saints such as Hincmar's Life of St Remigius were being written and rewritten at precisely this time in order to reinforce the sensibility of the saint's protection. Another instance of the importance of a saint and his relics is the priority the latter were given when church treasures were removed to safety.

In the 870s and 880s more strongholds were built, not always authorized by the king. In 883 Fulk, archbishop of Rheims, rebuilt the walls Ebbo had destroyed, using material from the ruined church of St Denis (destroyed by the Northmen) for the purpose. At Metz, Bishop Robert restored the walls in 883,

In 885 Bishop Geilo of Langres did the same for his city. In 898 Charles the Simple gave the bishop of Noyon permission to raise the old ramparts of Tournai and restore those of Noyon. Most of the walls that were rebuilt followed the old foundations, though sometimes their embrace was enlarged to include suburban monasteries. Bishops and abbots, taking advantage in many cases of their immunity, were active at this stage in the defence and fortification of their towns. Ralph, abbot of St Vaast for example, fortified his abbey and the town of Arras. Counts also contributed to the defences as the king's ability to prevent them doing so lessened. No records of requests for permission to build fortifications are known after the death of Charles the Simple.

The extent to which the Vikings were involved, whether wittingly or unwittingly, in Frankish politics, the rivalries between the sons of Louis the Pious and the most powerful of the Frankish magnates, and the particular difficulties of Charles the Bald are most clearly illustrated by the 'great invasion' of 856–62. The circumstances of these years have been reconstructed from the ambiguities of the annal entries by Lot and Levillain, so need only be summarized here.[16] In July 856, Sidroc appeared at the mouth of the Seine and sailed with his followers up the river as far as Pîtres, where they were reinforced by Berno and his men. The Vikings wintered on the island of Oscellus (Oscelle) in the Seine opposite Jeufosse, and in December burnt Paris and all the churches except those of saints Stephen, Vincent, Denis and St Germain-des-Prés, for which the Vikings had been paid 'much silver' to spare.[17] Again there is this curious incidence of negotiations with the inhabitants of a town before an attack. The Vikings had chosen their moment well. Charles the Bald, as we have seen, was fighting hard to salvage his position at this stage, and contending not only with the dissident, mostly Neustrian, counts who had made approaches to Louis the German, and with Aquitainians, but also with the Viking attackers on the Loire who had been joined in 857 by Pippin II of Aquitaine. Indeed, so insecure was Charles the Bald's position that he was at first unable to muster an army, and it was not until October that he managed to summon a host, helped by supporters, Adalhard, son of Unruoch, Rudolf, Charles the Bald's Welf uncle, and counts Ricoin, Augier and Berengar. This army achieved little and the Vikings retreated to their island, from which they launched attacks on the surrounding countryside.

During 857 the Vikings left the Seine basin but by early 858 they had returned. In January St Wandrille was burnt and the monks fled. In April Louis, archchancellor and abbot of St Denis, with his brother Gauzlin was captured. His ranson was enormous. King, bishops, abbots, counts and other 'powerful' people were obliged to contribute 688 pounds of gold and 3250 pounds of silver.[18] At Verberie in May Berno the Viking leader swore an oath of fidelity to Charles though we do not know whether he then joined the Frankish army. In the same month Charles negotiated with his nephew Lothar II for assistance against the Vikings. On 1 July Charles arrived with his army before Oscellus where he was joined the following month by Lothar. Lot sees the seige of Oscellus as of the utmost importance for the defence of the kingdom against the Vikings. Had Charles the Bald been successful it would have delivered a crushing blow to the Danes as well as strengthened his authority. As it was, Charles was obliged to raise the siege on 23 September in order to go and meet his brother Louis the German who had entered the kingdom on the invitation of the dissident Neustrian counts.

The Vikings in the meantime continued to enjoy themselves in the Seine basin and exterminated the defensive league formed against the pagans by the local inhabitants of Neustria. Beauvais and Noyon were attacked early in 859. At this stage the Somme Vikings enter the picture. The area between the Somme and Scheldt rivers had been left relatively unscathed so far but in the autumn of 859 Weland's army disembarked at the mouth of the Somme and wintered in Francia. In order to prevent the Somme and Seine Vikings joining forces Charles the Bald offered 3000 pounds of silver to Weland to drive the Seine Vikings from the kingdom. While the money was being raised Weland went and amused himself in England. At the end of spring 861, his army returned to Francia, blockaded the Seine Vikings on Oscellus and eventually succeeded in making them leave. The following year another group was forced by Charles the Bald to withdraw to the open sea. In February 862 Weland made his submission to Charles the Bald and he and his wife and son received baptism; he was killed in a duel a year later by a pagan Viking.

Although Charles the Bald had not won any striking military victories over the Vikings, he had succeeded in ridding the kingdom of the worst of the raiders. Yet the lack of military resources or skill was a dangerous weakness. It is clear from the records of the subsequent half-century that the man who could organize effective resistance against the invaders could command and extend a strong political position within the kingdom. Hugh the Abbot, and Robert the Strong, count of Angers, for example, achieved notable successes against the Vikings and were, in Robert's case at least, the founders of their families' success. Robert himself was killed in a skirmish at Le Mans in 866 but his descendants became kings of France. Arnulf of Carinthia achieved notable successes against the Vikings which helped him secure his position in the eastern kingdom. The Carolingian Louis III of the west Frankish kingdom also showed himself to be a warrior of great promise, winning the battle of Saucourt against the Vikings in 881. The Old High German poem *Ludwigslied*, written to commemorate this victory, is a vigorous expression of Louis' valour as the Christian warrior against evil, and the Annals of St Vaast record that as a result of Saucourt the Vikings 'began to fear Louis'. It was a great misfortune for the Carolingian house that Louis was killed in a fall from his horse when pursuing a girl with amorous intent. Soon afterwards, Odo, while still count of Paris, was one of the leaders of the defence of the city of Paris, besieged by Sigifrid's great army in 885–6. The heart-rending miseries suffered by the inhabitants and the valour of Odo are vividly described in *Bella Parisiacae Urbis* by Abbo, a monk of St Germain-des-Prés. Odo, hard pressed, besought Charles the Fat for assistance. The Emperor opened negotiations with the Danes, granted them the Seine passage which the Parisians had fought so bravely to defend, gave them leave to winter in Burgundy and promised them 700 pounds of silver which Odo was obliged to collect and hand over the following year. Odo's reputation was untarnished by this humiliation. On the contrary; it and his prowess in subsequent years were material in elevating him to the kingship in 888.

For the years between the siege of Paris and the establishment of Normandy, our principal source is the Annals of St Vaast, but these run to 900 only. What appears to be a concentration of Viking activity in the Aisne and Scheldt areas may simply be due to the preoccupation of these annals. From their accounts of the raids it appears that the Vikings never actually left the kingdom at all after at least 880 or so, and their winter quarters were established further and further south at Ghent, Courtrai, Condé sur l'Escaut, Argova, Amiens and Paris. The Vikings whose 'departure' Odo bought in 897 simply went down to the Loire for the winter and returned the following spring. After 899 we know nothing concerning the Seine and Somme Vikings until 911 when a battle near Chartres is recorded between Charles the Simple and the Vikings led by Rollo. English sources are no help here. What may have happened is that on their return from Aquitaine in 898, or even as early as the 880s, the Seine Vikings had begun to congregate in the lower Seine area, so that by 911 Charles the Simple ceded territory that had already been appropriated and set-tled by the Vikings. The Loire Vikings on the other hand remained a separate entity; it was they who sacked Tours in 903. In 921 the Loire Vikings were ceded Nantes by Robert of Neustria, and again by Ralph in 927, and held it until 937.

The part of Neustria which became Normandy (see Map 12) may never have been very densely settled by the Franks and remained somewhat removed from the centre of the Carolingian world.[19] It is significant, for example, that no new monasteries were founded in the region between 715 and the tenth century and that only occasionally were the abbeys and monasteries of the ecclesiastical province of Rouen granted to members of the royal household. Einhard, for example was abbot of St Wandrille from 816 to 823. Rouen and its bishops were the only ones to retain some importance in the Carolingian world. This impression may be, however, due to the paucity of our sources from the Nor-mandy area. After the monks of St Wandrille had fled from their monastery our source of information dries up, and for the next century we are dependent upon a few references in later narrative sources and charters. The Annals of Flodoard, compiled sometime before 957, contain the earliest account of the foundation of Normandy. The panegyric by Dudo of St Quentin on the dukes of Nor-mandy, written between 1015 and 1026, which purports to tell the story of the origins of Normandy, has been completely discredited as far as his infor-mation about the early rulers of Normandy in concerned,[20] as has William of Jumièges, writing c. 1130, who abridged Dudo's account in his De ducum Normannorum Gestis. The earliest Norman charter to survive dates from Richard I's reign (942–96).

Until the second half of the tenth century therefore, there are almost no literary sources concerning Normandy or the rule of the Viking principes there. The archaeological evidence is also virtually non-existent. Place name evidence, however, has yielded some clues concerning the process of settlement by the Vikings in the Normandy area. It establishes that the Scandinavian settlements were both heterogeneous and sporadic. The river valleys of the Orne, Dives, Risle and so on were settled by different groups of Scandinavians rather than a single settlement at Rouen expanding outwards. Moreover, settlement continued for some decades, with Northmen coming from Scandinavia and the British Isles to live in Normandy. Linguistic evidence also suggests that the Northmen came as lords over a Frankish population in the first instance. Only about 300 Scandinavian loan words were incorporated into the French language and a third of these concern seafaring. Women seem to have been the main agents of linguistic change. Only three of the eighty-two Scandinavian personal names known in Normandy were female, and these three women were members of the ruling family. The evidence suggests a rapid acquisition by the Vikings of the Frankish language and Frankish customs and culture, an assimilation undoubtedly accelerated by their conversion to Christianity and by intermarriage.[21]

It is not known when Rollo arrived in the Viking kingdom. Dudo says that he took Rouen in 877, but most historians are agreed that Rollo probably did not appear in Francia until the early tenth century. The possibility exists however, that Dudo is preserving a belief that Vikings had been established in the Rouen area from about this time. Rollo is thought to have been Norwegian rather than Danish, and later Icelandic sources identify him with Hrolfr the Ganger (walker), son of Ragnvald earl of Moer, who had a career as a Viking before settling in Francia.[22] He married a Christian woman and his son William, according to the Lament of William Longsword, was born overseas.

Nothing more is known about the 'Treaty of St Clair-sur-Epte' concluded in a personal interview between Charles the Simple and Rollo than Dudo tells us, and he has been accused of inventing the meeting. That a cession of territory in the lower Seine, extending as far west as the mouth of the Seine on the coast and near the source of the Eure inland is affirmed by a charter of Charles the Simple dated 14 March 918. The charter assigns land to St Germain-des-Prés from the *pagus* of Mersean, except that territory within the *pagus* already ceded to 'the Northmen of the Seine, namely to Rollo and his followers, for the defence of the kingdom' (*praeter partem ipsius abbatiae quam annuimus Nottmannis Sequanensibus videlicet Rolloni suisque comitibus pro tutela regni*).[23] Flodoard adds the information that Rollo received baptism and the Frankish name Robert with the cession of this territory.

Rollo seems to have been made a count in 911, with the traditional duties assigned to a Carolingian count, namely, protection and the administration of justice. He was certainly subordinate to the Frankish king. With the proliferation of titles accorded the leader of the Normandy Vikings in later sources, some historians have suggested that Rollo was made a duke, but Werner has argued that there was no Norman *marchio* before 960–6, and no duke before 987–1006, that is, after Hugh Capet had gained the throne of France.[24]

The latest reference to Carolingian administration in Normandy is in 905, when a Count Odilard was still functioning in the region of Rouen and may have been the count of Rouen himself. Evidently Rollo took his place. In 867, the Cotentin and Avranchin had been ceded to Salomon of Brittany with all the fiscs, *villae* and abbeys but not the bishopric, in exchange for which Salomon had promised fidelity, peace and assistance against his enemies to Charles the Bald. Rollo appears to have received his territory on similar terms as the Bretons had received the Cotentin, except that the bishoprics were also ceded. (The grants of land to Vikings in Rüstringen and Frisia may also have been on these terms.) In exchange, Rollo was to defend the Seine from other Vikings, accept baptism and become the *fidelis* of the Frankish king. That there were other groups of Vikings in the region, particularly in the western part of Normandy, is clear. The west stayed pagan longer; it was a century before a bishop was appointed to the Cotentin. In the region of the Bassin and Bayeux the Scandinavian language lasted longer than anywhere else and Richard I was able to call on the leaders of the west Normandy Vikings for assistance in his efforts to establish his position free of the Carolingian Louis IV (see Ch. 12).

The arrangement made in 911 proved successful, though the Normans under Rollo conducted some raids in the Seine river valley in 923. In 924 they were ceded Le Mans, Bayeux, L'Huernin and the Bassin by King Ralph, and in 933 the Cotentin and Avranchin, hitherto part of Breton territory, were ceded to William Longsword, Rollo's son, who commended himself to Ralph. The area of Normandy by 933 corresponded to the area of the archdiocese of Rouen, with the seven *civitates* of Rouen, Bayeux, Avranches, Evreux, Sees, Lisieux and Coutances. The fortunes of the bishops of Rouen and of the *principes* of Normandy were in fact closely associated from the very beginning.

William Longsword, Rollo's son and successor, was the principal architect of Normandy's development. He married the daughter of Herbert of Vermandois but his children were born of a Breton concubine. William had supported Louis IV and attempted to establish his protection over Brittany, gaining at least the Cotentin and Avranchin in 933. There remains some doubt about William's claim to the whole Breton peninsula. When in 942 William was murdered at the instigation of Count Arnulf of Flanders, his son Richard, still a minor, succeeded him. Louis IV and Hugh the Great each tried to sieze Normandy, and Louis took charge of Richard. He then ensconced himself at Rouen and Hugh took Bayeux, which still had a Scandinavian leader called Sictric. Richard escaped from his custody at Laon, retook Rouen, and called on another Viking leader, Harald of the Bassin, for help. The Normans under Richard were able to re-establish their autonomy and from 947 Richard governed in relative peace. In 965 he swore allegiance to the Carolingian king Lothar at Gisors. Richard's official marriage was to Emma, daughter of Hugh the Great; they had no children, but by his common-law wife Gunnor, a Dane, he had many. Richard II, son of Gunnor and Richard I, succeeded his father in 996, another son Robert was archbishop of Rouen from 989 to 1037 and Emma their daughter became queen of England on her marriage to Aethelred, a position she maintained after his death in 1016 by marrying Cnut. Gunnor's nephews and other relatives furthermore formed the core of the new aristocracy which developed in the course of the eleventh century.[25] Unfortunately we know little about the internal organization and history of Normandy until the reign of Richard II, and this falls outside our period.

The church in Normandy had suffered badly as a result of Viking depredations from the middle of the ninth century. Its parlous condition in the tenth century is suggested by Orderic Vitalis and there is no reason to doubt what he says.[26] There are, for example, gaps in the episcopal lists. There was no bishop at Lisieux from 862 to 990, Avranches was vacant from 862 to 990 and Sées from 910 to 993. Bayeux and Evreux were also without a bishop for most of the second half of the ninth century and the tenth century. Ecclesiastical organization, especially in the western part of Normandy, seems to have broken down long before the end of the ninth century; only Coutances and Rouen had an almost unbroken succession of bishops, but five successive incumbents of Coutances resided at Rouen. It was almost a century after the foundation of Normandy, between 988 and 990, before the bishoprics were restored. In other words the Christianization of the Scandinavians in Normandy was a very gradual process. When the church was restored, it was under the protection of the Norman rulers, and they exploited it much as their Carolingian predecessors had done. The monasteries' fate was similar. The monks of Jumièges and St Wandrille had fled in the middle of the ninth century and not one monastery seems to have remained in Rollo's time. Intellectual and cultural life ceased to exist and was not revived until the late tenth century. Rollo is supposed to have made gifts to various churches after his baptism, but these gifts cannot be documented. Ancient rights to property on the other hand seem to have been respected. The domain of Bonneval belonging to St Denis, for example, was restored to that abbey by Richard I. William Longsword made some grants to the church and is associated with the restoration of Jumièges. In 966 Lothar confirmed by charter the restoration of the monastery of Mont-St-Michel by Richard I, who also made gifts to St Taurin of Evreux, St Omer and Jumièges and rebuilt the church of Fécamp. The reforms of Gerard of Brogne were brought from Ghent to St Wandrille and Mont-St-Michel by Mainard, but it was not until Richard II's reign that Cluny's influence began to be felt through William of Volpiano, and monastic life in Normandy began to flourish once more only in the course of the eleventh century.

Almost nothing is known of the early institutions of Normandy. Yver has outlined the possibilities and suggested that to a considerable extent Norman institutions were based on Carolingian institutions.[27] He argues for continuity between the former Frankish administrative structure in the Normandy region, but other scholars have suggested that the Normans revived Carolingian institutions which they observed in the Carolingian Francia of their own day. In the Edict of Pîtres of 864 the area of Normandy was still divided into *pagi* or counties, administered by counts. Even in Charles the Simple's reign, if no later, the existence of a count or counts indicated in the charter of 905, cited above, suggests a certain measure of survival of Carolingian administration to that date. Yver concludes that after Charles the Simple the local administration ceased to be answerable to the central authority but did not necessarily cease to exist. The few sources we have concerning Normandy give the impression of a land ravaged and depopulated, particularly among the 'upper' classes. According to Flodoard Normandy was still divided into *pagi* in the tenth century, though he could simply have been using terms to which he was accustomed rather than describing the existing divisions. In 968, however, the *pagi* referred to are exactly the same as the Carolingian *pagi*, apart from the Cotentin where the Scandinavian settlement appears to have been densest. Even the frontiers of Normandy followed the boundaries of the *pagi* for much of its length, though Holt points out that the Epte river was a military and strategic boundary rather than an administrative one.[28] Similarly, the church restored the old Carolingian diocesan boundaries. Yver has presumed, probably rightly, that the local administration of the *pagi* owed obedience to the *comes Normannorum* at Rouen. The title of count was only accorded the count of Rouen or his closest relatives; the local administrators of the *pagi* were no longer called counts but viscounts. In other words the basic administrative structure of Normandy was essentially Carolingian in its origins but was modified by the Normans. Yver also argues that the judicial, financial and regalian rights were derived from a Carolingian source, but this remains uncertain.

Although ecclesiastical and administrative divisions seem to have survived, and it is clear that the Norman rulers later emulated their Frankish superiors in the organization of their administration, writing office, taxes and so on, there is no evidence that a lay Frankish family preserved its property and position throughout the settlement period. It is here that the most complete break with the Carolingian past was made. Dudo tells us that Rollo made laws; if he promulgated any, none has survived. Scandinavian influence on the laws that have survived remains rather indeterminate. The laws of outlawry and wreck, the marriage *more Danico*, the notion of the peace of the house and some of the units of measurement seem to have been Scandinavian in origin. The fidelity sworn to the Norman counts by their subjects certainly involved military service, but no tenure associated with this service and called a fief exists before the mid-eleventh century.

Two things are clear. Normandy rapidly became wealthy from Richard I's time onwards. Rouen developed as a commercial entrepôt and markets and fairs are often referred to in the sources. Rouen had been included in the list of mints made at Pîtres in 864 and from William Longsword's reign, money of the Carolingian type was being minted there. Under Richard I the money minted in the count's name acquired the character of currency – specimens have been found as far afield as Scotland, Denmark, Pomerania, Poland and Russia, indicating the possibility at least that some trading contacts were being established and maintained. Secondly, Normandy's principal political connections developed west and north with England and Denmark and even further afield, rather than with the kingdom of France in the eleventh century. Nevertheless the relationship with the Carolingian and Capetian kings remained of abiding importance to the rulers of Normandy.

II

Brittany or Armorica had been part of Roman Gaul (see Map 13). The Armorican peninsula was also theoretically part of the ecclesiastical province of Tours, though this was only effective, if at all, for the regions of Rennes, Nantes and Vannes. When Clovis established himself in Gaul he and his successors are supposed to have made themselves overlords of Brittany, and by this time, as far as we can tell, Britons or Bretons, probably from Cornwall and Wales, had already settled in the western part of Armorica. None of the various explanations provided for the settlement of Armorica from Britain is satisfactory; nor can the date at which the Britons arrived be determined. In default of archaeological evidence, the arguments for the settlement of Armorica are almost wholly linguistic. On the basis of the little information we have, the settlement is usually thought to have taken place between about 300 and 600 AD and was probably a gradual process, but the first unequivocal references to Britons settled in Armorica date from the sixth century, in, for example, the records of the Council of Tours for 567 and in the *Historia Francorum* of Gregory of Tours.[29]

In the Merovingian period western Armorica, that is, the part of the peninsula most densely settled by Bretons, seems to have been divided into three regions – Dumnonia (Dumnonée) in the north, Cornubia (Cornouaille) in the south-west and Bro Weroch (Bro Erech) in the south-east. Sixth-century sources make a distinction between Romania, that is, Nantes, Rennes and part of Vannes in eastern Brittany, and Britannia, the region further west, but there is little information about relations between them. From the sixth until the mid-ninth century indeed, the eastern region appears to have been under Frankish control. Although there are few clues as to how effective this was, some Frankish institutions – commendation, *fideles*, *vassi*, the *mallus* and *scabini* are known to have existed there in the ninth century and coins were minted at Rennes in the time of Charlemagne (before *c.* 790), Louis the Pious (when there was also a mint at Nantes) and probably Charles the Bald and Charles the Simple as well.[30] It is also significant that the medieval linguistic boundary excluded Rennes and Nantes and the area east of these two centres from the Breton region.

Very little is known about Brittany in the pre-Carolingian period apart from the information supplied by Gregory of Tours. The only source for Breton social organization at this time is the *Excerpta de libris romanorum et francorum*, usually known by their old title, the *Canones Wallici*.[31] From this text the main classes of society can be identified as the freemen and slaves. The principal social group was the kin (*parentes*), the elected head of which was the *major*. The kin was responsible for law and order and land was owned by the family jointly. The older men of the kin acted as judges and the practice of compurgation was common in trials. The settlers also brought with them their own language and their own Christian organization. Although we know so little about early Brittany, enough evidence of Celtic institutions such as the *enepuuerti* (morning gift), *loth* and *cofrit* (charges on land) and *machtiern* (local ruler), as well as the differences in liturgical observance and monastic custom, survives to suggest that the non-Frankish element was strong. This has considerable implications for the nature of Brittany's relations with Francia and for Brittany's subsequent political development.

During the reign of Pippin III the Breton march, comprising the counties of Vannes, Rennes and Nantes, was established, backed up by the county of Le Mans. The counts put in charge of the marcher territory – Roland, killed at Roncesvalles, Guy (Wido) and Lambert – were Frankish nobles and members of the same family. Both Pippin and Charlemagne mounted campaigns against the Bretons; the Annals of Metz report that Pippin 'subjugated' the Bretons (but see Ch. 3), and it was to enforce the payment of a tribute supposedly demanded by Pippin that Charlemagne sent an army into Brittany in 786. The seneschal Audulf led the army; he conquered many Bretons in their refuges in strongholds, swampland and forest and brought the Breton leaders before Charlemagne at Worms the same year. In 790 the march of Brittany was included in the territory Charlemagne assigned to his son Charles. Breton incursions into Frankish territory continued, and in 799 another campaign was mounted, led by Count Guy of the Breton march. The Royal Frankish Annals triumphantly announce the conquest of Brittany, a little prematurely, for another Frankish contingent was sent to Brittany in 811 to deal with the 'treacherous Bretons'. Whatever Brittany's actual state of dependence or independence from the Carolingians, the Frankish sources describe the Bretons as a treacherous tribe, always breaking their promises to the Franks.

It was left to Louis the Pious effectively to establish some form of Frankish control in Brittany. Four campaigns were mounted, in 818, 822, 824 and 825. Louis took part in the one from Vannes in 818 and another from Rennes six years later (the counts of both these areas were subordinate to the count of the march). The resistance to Louis' armies seems to have been led by a certain Morvan who had asserted his sole authority 'against the usual custom of the Bretons' and his successor Wihomar.[32] Hitherto Brittany had been politically fragmented, with a number of rulers and no clear notion, so far as we can tell, of any one of these being superior to the rest. It may be that Carolingian aggression precipitated the emergence of one ruler, but Louis the Pious, with his appointment of the Breton Nominoë in *c.* 831 as sole ruler in Louis' name as Louis' *missus imperatoris in Brittania* certainly assisted the development of Brittany into a single political entity, and the uniting of the 'Celtic west' with the Gallo-Frankish east. It was a move, moreover, directed by Louis' circumstances in 830. This year witnessed the first major rebellion against Louis' authority, one of the principal ringleaders of which was Lambert, count of the Breton march. By appointing Nominoë, possibly in the first instance as a replacement for the count of the march, Louis was not only extending Carolingian influence into Brittany in the same way that he had tried to direct the affairs of the Obodrites and Danes; he was also providing himself with an ally.

Nominoë was a member of the local aristocracy about whom almost nothing is known before he was singled out by Louis. He seems originally to have been count of Vannes, where he possessed lands. When Louis the Pious died in 840,

Nominoë remained faithful to Lothar and interfered in the disputes between Lothar and Charles the Bald. The rivalries between the brothers enabled Nominoë to extend his position in the Breton march. When his son Erispoë killed Count Reynald of Nantes, Charles the Bald in retaliation attacked Nominoë. The Franks were routed in a battle near Redon on 22 November 845. The following year Charles the Bald made peace with Nominoë, oaths were exchanged and the Bretons achieved a considerable measure of autonomy. Nominoë occupied Rennes and Nantes and made incursions into Anjou, the Vendômois and even as far as the Bassin. He also tried, possibly in imitation of the Carolingians, to use the church to bolster his authority. The monastery of Redon, for example, was founded in 832 and Nominoë encouraged Louis the Pious to take an interest in it. Redon remained an important foundation for the Breton rulers; it was under their protection and received many grants and gifts from them.[33] Although Julia Smith has made a convincing case for the attempt to establish Dol as the metropolitan of a Breton province, and thus make the Breton church independent from the Frankish province of Tours, being made by Salomon (857–74) rather than Nominoë himself,[34] it seems clear from the evidence that under Nominoë, from about 848, co-operation between the Breton and Frankish clergy ceased, Nominoë interfered in episcopal appointments within Brittany[35] and the Breton church became increasingly isolated. It is difficult to estimate the extent to which Charlemagne may have interfered in the ecclesiastical affairs of Brittany, but Louis certainly promoted the monastic reforms of Benedict of Aniane there. Redon observed the Benedictine Rule (it was introduced by a monk from Glanfeuil), and in a charter of 818 to Landévennec, Louis enjoined the monks to adopt the Roman tonsure and observe the Rule of St Benedict.[36]

Nominoë was succeeded by his son Erispoë in 851. Although he seems to have sworn fidelity to Charles the Bald and was confirmed in the possession of the lands occupied by his father, he adopted the same aggressive policy towards Charles as Nominoë had done. He defeated the army of the Frankish king at Jengland on the east bank of the river Vilaine and obtained the cession of Rennes, Nantes and the *pays de Retz*.[37] Erispoë's own position was threatened by the leader of a rival branch of the family, Salomon, who was egged on by Charles the Bald. Nevertheless a *rapprochement* was obtained between the Breton and the Frankish ruler and a marriage alliance contemplated between Erispoë's daughter and Louis the Stammerer. It may be that the threat of Viking attacks promoted these more cordial relations, but they came to an abrupt end with Salomon's assassination of Erispoë in a church in 857.

Salomon remained the ruler of Brittany for the next seventeen years, allying himself to anybody who was opposed to Charles the Bald, and not scrupling to turn against his allies should their position become too strong and therefore a threat to his supremacy in eastern Brittany, as he did in the cases of Louis the Stammerer and Robert the Strong of Neustria, when they were appointed to the lower Loire region by Charles the Bald. In 863 Salomon swore fidelity to Charles and promised to pay the old tribute; in return Charles made him lay abbot of St Aubin of Angers and granted him the land between the Mayenne and Sarthe rivers. In 866 however, Salomon revolted and inflicted such a telling defeat on Charles the Bald at the battle of Brissarthe, with the help of his Viking allies, that he seems to have been able to dictate terms. As well as being confirmed in the possessions of the territory ceded in 863, Salomon was ceded the county of Coutances (Cotentin and Avranchin) with all the fisc lands, royal manors and abbeys, though not the bishopric.[38] Salomon in his turn promised to be a loyal ally thereafter and help Charles against his enemies; he kept his promise. It has been suggested that Salomon's revolt in 866 was an attempt to force Charles the Bald to acknowledge him as a ruler of some standing rather than a mere royal official or *missus* like Nominoë, and that it is connected with Salomon's request to Pope Nicholas I that the archiepiscopal pallium be sent to Festinian, bishop of Dol.[39] Salomon is certainly the first of the Breton rulers to style himself king. The title *rex* appears in both his own and in private charters and increasingly after 858 transactions are dated to the year of Salomon's rule rather than to that of the Frankish king. In one charter indeed he is referred to as the king of the whole of Brittany and the greater part of Frankish Gaul.[40]

Whether the authority of Nominoë, Erispoë and Salomon actually extended over the whole of the Breton peninsula is not absolutely certain, mainly because the evidence for the western region is so sparse. All the available evidence suggests, however, that these men did exercise authority over the whole of Brittany, negotiated with the Frankish kings on behalf of the region and were responsible for co-ordinating its defence. Nominoë's letter from the Frankish bishops acknowledging him as a *rector* of the Bretons established by God[41] and the fact that Erispoë is sometimes referred to as king indicate, Wendy Davies has suggested, that there was a gradual development towards, rather than a sudden development of, kingship.[42] La Borderie and many older historians have regarded the ninth century as a period in which a Breton monarchy emerged, though modern historians are inclined to place this in Salomon's reign rather than Nominoë's. Some administrative structure existed. That tribute could be collected under Nominoë and Salomon implies that there was some administrative machinery, and counties, including Vannes, Bro Weroch, Cornouaille, Poher, Léon, Goello, Rennes and Nantes, were used as administrative units, while Rennes and Nantes acted as the bases for the principal ruler. Counts were appointed at the head of the counties and met at assemblies on the Carolingian pattern. Both Nominoë and Salomon moreover used *missi* or deputies to make grants or preside in court. At a local level there was the system of *machtierns*, for which there is a wealth of evidence in the Cartulary of Redon.[43] The *machtiern* was a very small scale hereditary ruler, who possessed civil functions rather than military ones and who was usually associated with the primary unit of social organization, the *plebs* or *plou*. Davies suggests that the capacity of the principal ruler of Brittany to govern was limited by his ability to establish individual relationships with the *machtierns*.[44] This local network of government seems to have died out during the Viking occupation, or at least the distinctive terminology of it ceases to be used, for virtually no *machtierns* are recorded after the late 930s.

Until 907, the Vikings do not seem to have presented so great a threat to the Bretons that they could not be dealt with. Both Erispoë and Salomon allied themselves at times with the Loire Vikings, as well as defeating them in a battle in 853 and assisting Charles the Bald against them in 874. In 875, Pascwethen, Salomon's son-in-law and successor, called in the Vikings to help him against his co-ruler, Gurwant, Erispoë's son-in-law. They were replaced by another pair of rulers, Alan, count of Vannes, Pascwethen's brother, and Judicaël, Gurwant's son. It is not clear what this joint rule actually entailed, or whether it was understood in territorial terms. One ruler may have had the eastern region and the other the western, but this is mere conjecture. Judicaël was killed fighting the Vikings and Alan the Great became sole ruler from 888 to 907. Alan, with the assistance of Count Berengar of Rennes, inflicted several defeats upon the Vikings, notably at the Battle of St Lô; this success was even recorded in the Anglo-Saxon Chronicle. Under Wrmaelon (907 – c.914), however, the Northmen escalated their attacks on Brittany. In 913 the monastery of Landévennec was utterly destroyed, and other major raids are recorded for 912, 914 and 919. It is likely that the Northmen responsible for the ravaging of Brittany were those established in the lower Loire valley and ceded Nantes by Duke Robert in 921. Certainly between 919 and 937, the period during which the Loire Vikings are known to have been based on Nantes, there were no native rulers of Brittany. Some Bretons resisted, many fled into Francia, Burgundy and Aquitaine. The monks of Landévennec, for example, took the relics of Winwaloe (Guenolé) to Montreuil-sur-Mer and were joined by the monks of Quimper, and Mabbo, bishop of Léon, confided the relics of St Paul to Fleury. Many members of the leading families such as Mathedoi, count of Poher, took refuge at Edward the Elder's court in England.

As with the rest of the material relating to the Northmen, that concerning their activities in Brittany is fragmentary, inconsistent and ambiguous. We have little information about the years of 'Viking rule' in Brittany; no Viking personnel, for example, seem to have been installed there. It has been conjectured, moreover, that the Seine Vikings in Normandy were ceded Brittany along with Normandy in 911. William Longsword certainly claims overlordship of Brittany but this is after he has been ceded the Cotentin and Avranchin by King Ralph. It is possible that because they know Viking territory was extended to include the Cotentin and Avranchin in 933, territory formerly ceded to the Breton ruler Salomon in 867, modern historians have misunderstood the relations between the Seine Northmen or Normans and the Bretons. It is more likely that the Bretons simply lost control over this region in the early years of the tenth century, and the Cotentin Vikings moved in. It is significant that the restoration of Breton rule in Brittany in 937–9 coincides with the demise of the Loire Northmen's 'principality' based on Nantes. There may well have been raids on Brittany conducted by the Cotentin Northmen, but this was before their land was incorporated into the territory of the Norman ruler based at Rouen. The Loire Northmen's attacks on Brittany, led by Ragnold, are to be seen in the context of the attempt by these Vikings to carve out territory for themselves on the lines of Normandy.

Between 936 the Breton exiles in England, backed by King Athelstan (who provided a fleet of ships) and probably led by Alan II (called *Barbetorte* or Twistedbeard), son of Count Mathedoi, made a successful bid to recover Brittany. By 939 Brittany was restored to Breton rule, but it was the rule of a duke based at Nantes rather than of a king, and this duke may not have been the sole ruler of Brittany. The Chronicle of Nantes paints a vivid picture of Alan's return to Nantes after he had driven the Northmen from the city. He had to hack his way through thickets of thorns and brambles to get to the church and found it standing half-ruined and roofless. Alan set to work to rebuild the church and ordered a rampart of earth to be raised around it. The Chronicle adds that the counts, viscounts and *machtierns* who had fled into the Frankish lands began to return to Brittany.[45]

The position of the Breton ruler in relation to the Frankish king at this time is not clear, though the title of duke implies that he was subordinate to the Frankish king. It is possible that Louis IV approved and encouraged the efforts of Alan II to regain Brittany. On the other hand, the sources are silent about relations between the Franks and Bretons. From 898 to 1108, for example, no surviving royal charter refers to a Breton locality.[46] It seems that Brittany's external concerns were confined to relations with its immediate neighbours.

With the restoration of a Breton ruler at Nantes, Breton politics were open to Frankish influence. One way in which this was exerted was through the connections built up between the ducal and comital families of Brittany and the Loire region, particularly the counts of Blois–Chartres and of Anjou. Alan II himself was far from dominant in Brittany, for the counts of Rennes at least refused to acknowledge either Alan or his successors as overlord. In the tenth century the counts of Rennes and the dukes of Brittany were engaged in a constant struggle for supremacy which bore little relation to events in the rest of Alan's territory (this probably included the counties of Vannes, Poher and perhaps the rest of south-west Brittany). The counts of Rennes may have had direct control or else some sort of suzereainty over the rest of Brittany, but little is known about north Brittany in the tenth century.

Alan II died in 952 and was succeeded by his legitimate son Drogo, a minor, born of the union with the sister of the count of Blois and Chartres, Theobald the Cheat or Trickster. Alan's widow quickly married her brother's rival, Fulk the Good of Anjou. The rivalries of the counts of Blois–Chartres and Anjou spilled over into Brittany, in that the count of Rennes was backed by the count of Blois–Chartres and Alan's successors at Nantes by the count of Anjou. Conan I, count of Rennes, triumphed and assumed the ducal title, forcing Judicaël of Nantes to pay homage to him. However, the influence of the counts of Blois became so oppressive that the Breton ruler tried to ally himself to the ruler of Normandy to counterbalance it. By 1030, Alan III had to pay homage to Duke Robert of Normandy, and in 1066 Bretons were among the warriors in William the Conqueror's army. Thereafter an important connection developed between the dukes of Brittany and northern England.

The origin of the Breton connection with England is very obscure and impossible to trace before the reign of King Alfred. Asser twice refers to the

246

Bretons; the different nationalities hired by Alfred to protect his kingdom included the Bretons, and among the list of areas to whose monasteries Alfred sent gifts was Armorica.[47] The Anglo-Saxon Chronicle, particularly from 892 onwards, is almost exclusively concerned with the activities of the Viking army. The curious thing about the notices at this point is the bias, for the only defeat of the Vikings recorded is that inflicted at the Battle of St Lô. The Chronicle entries for 885 and 887 also note various changes of rule in the Frankish kingdoms. In 885 for example, Charles the Fat came to the throne and 'held all the kingdom except for Brittany as Charlemagne had done'. It is possible that, if the Anglo-Saxon chronicler was writing after the Battle of St Lô, then the source he was using may have been not only Continental, but Breton.[48]

Breton exiles fled to England, and particularly after 913, many Breton ecclesiastics arrived there. It may well be that England was regarded as the natural refuge for Bretons, though they also took refuge in Francia as far east as Paris. The cult of many Breton saints, such as Samson, Gildas, Winnoc and Malo was followed in England from the beginning of the tenth century,[49] some new monasteries were founded and dedicated to Breton saints, and many major English ecclesiastical centres, including Newminster abbey at Winchester, Wilton abbey, Milton Abbas and Padstow, acquired their relics.[50] England may also have been an object of the Breton book export trade in the late ninth and the tenth centuries, for some Gospel books, Psalters and grammars produced in Brittany in the second half of the ninth century are in England by the tenth. With the restoration of a Breton ruler in Brittany however, contact with England diminishes.

Monasticism of the Celtic type had been introduced by the Breton settlers, though it is not known when the great monasteries of Brittany – Dol, Tréguier, St Pol-de-Léon, St Malo, St Brieuc or Landévennec were established. Redon, the main monastic centre of the south-east, was founded in 832. The principal sources for ecclesiastical life in Brittany are the saints' Lives compiled in the ninth century, and their main value is the light they shed on conditions in the ninth century rather than the earlier period.[51] The Lives of Conwoion, founder of Redon, Samson, Turiau, Malo, Paul Aurelian, Winwaloe (Guenolé) all seem to be part of the same burst of intellectual activity in the ninth century. Riché has identified a particular interest in using rare words from glossaries and late Latin texts and a delight in building up words from Greek roots, as well as a common body of material which the authors of these Lives had read, such as Virgil's *Aeneid*, the *Collations* of John Cassian and the works of Augustine, Cassiodorus, Isidore of Seville and Gregory the Great. In other words, the saints' Lives establish that the authors had a common educational background and had been educated in the same way that scholars in the rest of the Frankish kingdoms had been educated. A notable feature of the Lives moreover is the stress given to the education of the saint. He is described as going to school with an important master. Riché argues that this has nothing to do with the sixth or seventh centuries, when most of these saints are supposed to have lived, but reflects conditions taken for granted in the ninth-century authors' own time.

Manuscript evidence can be added to that provided by the saints' Lives for the literary culture of Brittany in the ninth century. Enough manuscripts have survived to indicate that Brittany, and especially the monastery of Landévennec, was an important centre for book production. All kinds of books, from basic texts to works of advanced learning such as Munich Clm 18961, a miscellany of philosophical texts,[52] were produced, and many seem to have been exported to other centres. The script and decoration of some of these Breton manuscripts reveals their different sources of inspiration. The eleven surviving Breton Gospel books, for example, may be divided into two categories: those in which there are human evangelist portraits in the Carolingian manner, and those in which the evangelists are transformed into bizarre hybrids and given the heads of their symbols.[53] In one representative of the latter group, Oxford Auct. D. 2.16, both types of evangelist portrait are portrayed; there are two St Marks and two St Johns. Although some insular influence is evident in the decoration of the manuscripts, the script in which they are written is Caroline minuscule. Both saints' Lives and manuscripts indicate therefore, that Brittany participated in the Carolingian Renaissance.

When Brittany was restored to Breton rule in 937–9, Breton cultural life had also to be re-established, but it never seems to have reached quite the same level. The Breton ecclesiastical centres had exported clergy, relics and books out of Brittany and very few returned. Breton annotations in surviving Carolingian manuscripts give us some idea of the geographical extent of this exodus,[54] and books written in Landévennec and other major Breton centres are still extant in a number of French départementale libraries, such as Angers, Boulogne and Orleans (the last of these due to Fleury's connection with Brittany). Certainly as far as the church and ecclesiastical life are concerned, Brittany attached itself more and more to the Frankish and Latin tradition of the Continent. New contacts were built up by the Breton church, and Frankish clergy came from the Loire valley, especially from the monastery of Fleury, to help in the reconstruction of ecclesiastical life. Brittany remained however, outside Cluny's sphere of influence.

The Viking occupation of east Brittany seems to have marked a transition period in Brittany's development. Although some of these can be demonstrated in the political, ecclesiastical and cultural spheres, there are only conjectures, as distinct from evidence, concerning social changes. After the Viking period, nearly all our sources relate to eastern Brittany and the counties of Rennes and Nantes. If the history of Cornouaille and Léon were better known, then the general impression of Breton history in the tenth century, with its scarcity of Celtic survivals, might be modified.

III

Flanders has been described as the first real territorial principality to emerge in the Frankish kingdoms, though there is some dispute about its origins (see

Map 14).[55] Whether or not Charles the Bald should be credited with its creation, it is clear that the Viking invasions in the years following 879 gave Baldwin II the opportunity to assert himself in the region, and it is Baldwin II who is generally accepted as the first count of Flanders. Flanders itself is distinguished from the rest of Francia in that the original Frankish settlement had been more durable and the region remained more Germanic than south of the Canche, which was more heavily Romanized. This difference manifested itself in the linguistic boundary between Germanic and Romance speech which developed in the course of the early Middle Ages.[56] Even in Charles the Bald's time the language spoken in the Canche region was still Germanic, and this meant that the area between the Scheldt and Canche possessed a certain unity.

In 843, Flanders became part of Charles the Bald's west Frankish kingdom. Like the Normandy area, Flanders had been divided by the Carolingians into a number of *pagi* or *comitati*, including Waas, Flanders (*pagus Flandrensis* – very different in territorial extent from the county of Flanders which emerged in the second half of the ninth century), Thérouanne, Boulogne, Ghent, Courtrai, Mempisc, Artois, Melantois, Pévèle and Ostrevant, but from the time of Louis the Pious it was more normal for a number of these *pagi* to be entrusted to one count. Baldwin I, possibly of Lotharingian origin and of the same family as the counts of Laon, was originally count of Ghent and Waas, and Ingelram supervised the counties of Ostrevant, Pévèle, Melantois, Caubont and Tournai in 853. The accumulation of a number of counties in the hands of one count was a feature of Charles the Bald's reign, as we have seen, and in the case of Baldwin I, as in the cases of Robert the Strong, Eccard, Bernard of Gothia, Bernard Hairyfeet, Vulgrin and Hugh the abbot, Charles the Bald's concessions provided the basis for the growth of the territorial principality under his successors. In 864, thanks to the intervention of Pope Nicholas I, who persuaded Charles the Bald to acknowledge Baldwin's marriage to his daughter Judith (the couple had eloped in 860, aided and abetted by Judith's brother Louis), Ternois and Flanders were added to the counties Baldwin already held, as well as the lay abbacy of St Peter's Ghent. Dhondt has argued that the strengthening of Baldwin's position by Charles the Bald was part of an attempt to defend the kingdom against the Vikings.[57] The low indented coast, navigable rivers and safe harbours made Flanders particularly vulnerable to Viking attack, though there is some ambiguity about the nature of Baldwin I's relations with the Northmen; Hincmar of Rheims' letter to the Viking leader Rorik, asking him not to intervene in Flemish affairs, suggests that not all Baldwin's relations with the Vikings were those of enmity.[58] His son Baldwin II (879–918), moreover, seems to have offered very little resistance to the 'Great Army' of Vikings, when, fleeing from the danger presented by King Alfred, they occupied the Ysar–Scheldt region. Baldwin II is thought to have sat it out in the sand dunes on the coast near Bruges until the Vikings departed. He then took advantage of the Frankish king's inability to re-establish royal authority in the area to extend his own power. How much he had inherited of his father's responsibilities is uncertain. His subsequent activities suggest he had to assert a claim to every part of the territory once controlled by Baldwin I, rather than simply inheriting and building upon it. In other words, hereditary right was established only gradually. Baldwin II seized control of Flanders, Mempisc, Rodebourg, Ghent, Waas and Courtrai, the core of late medieval Flanders, but was limited in his expansion south by the marcher region created by Carloman in 883. Carloman had conferred on Ralph, related to Baldwin by marriage (Ralph's father Eberhard of Friuli had married Charles the Bald's sister Gisela), the responsibility for the defence of this region with authority over the counties of Artois and Ternois and the lay abbacies of St Bertin and St Vaast; Ralph fortified the abbey of St Vaast and organized the defence of Arras.[59]

On Ralph's death in 892, Baldwin II started to make himself master of his territories and ecclesiastical establishments as well as of the other possessions of Eberhard of Friuli's children in Mempisc and Ostrevant. The count's acquisition of these rich lands, and the wealthy abbeys of St Vaast, St Bertin and St Amand, was an important addition to his power. Thereafter Baldwin II extended his territory south to the Boulonnais, Artois, Ternois and Tournai, though he was obliged to renounce Artois in 899. The rapidity with which Baldwin II claimed the area administered by his father as his by right and made it secure for his heir is a measure of the inability of the Frankish kings to prevent him from doing so. The Annals of St Vaast suggest that both Odo and Charles the Simple recognized Baldwin's territorial power. Yet he did encounter some resistance, particularly in his bid to be made the lay abbot of St Bertin and St Vaast.

Indeed, the struggle over St Bertin and St Vaast is an indication of how essential control of the great monasteries was to a ruler's position. Odo tried to make his position more secure by increasing the monastic possessions of his house, and his brother Robert, count of Paris, was abbot of St Martin at Tours, Marmoutier, St Aignan in Orleans, St Germain-des-Prés, St Amand and St Denis. Archbishop Fulk of Rheims was a bitter opponent of Odo's possession of the crown and sought to get Arnulf of east Francia to replace him. Baldwin II and Ralph, abbot of St Vaast and St Bertin, were allies of Fulk in this but it came to nothing. Folcuin of St Bertin tells us in his *Gesta abbatum Sithiensium* that when Ralph died Baldwin sent to Odo to ask him to grant him the abbacy of St Bertin. The monks of St Bertin also sent messengers to the king to prevent this from happening. Their messengers met those of Fulk of Rheims on the same errand, and they agreed to try and get Fulk made the abbot. They succeeded, for the arrangement had the added advantage, as far as Odo was concerned, of being a means of winning over Fulk to his side. Battle was actually joined over St Vaast. The Annals of St Vaast report that the castellan of St Vaast had notified Odo of Ralph's death and asked for Baldwin to be made the abbot, against the wishes of the monks. Baldwin occupied St Vaast and held it when Odo besieged it. Baldwin then came to an agreement with Odo's brother Robert, and got the abbacy as the price of peace between him and Odo.

In the cases of both St Bertin and St Vaast therefore, the abbacy was a means for Odo to buy, as he thought, powerful support. Charles the Simple, however, renewed the dispute. He besieged St Vaast, demanded the monastery back and gave it to Fulk who promptly handed it over to Count Altmar. Baldwin then went after St Bertin. He had Fulk murdered, as well as Count Herbert of Vermandois, and in 900 St Bertin was granted to Baldwin II by Charles the Simple. Although Baldwin was unable to retain his hold on all his conquests, the county of Flanders at his death in 918 extended from the Scheldt to the sea and to the Canche and included the Boulonnais, Ternois and Tournaisis. Baldwin was the master of this region; royal authority there was reduced to nothing.

Baldwin II married Aelfthryth, daughter of King Alfred of England, and had two sons by her, Arnulf and Adalulf. When Baldwin II died in 918 his sons divided his territory between them; Adalulf got the abbacy of St Bertin, Ternois and the Boulonnais, and Arnulf took all the other counties. Both brothers remained in touch with their cousin Athelstan, and in between 925 and 933 the embassy from Hugh the Great to ask for Athelstan's sister Eadhild in marriage was led by Adalulf. When Adalulf died in 933 Arnulf appropriated his brother's portion of the county regardless of the claims of his nephews. Count Arnulf extended Flemish domination still further, profiting from the difficulties of the Carolingian ruler, but he also supported and paid homage to Louis IV. Arnulf's greatest rival was William Longsword of Normandy with whom he disputed control of Ponthieu between the Canche and Somme, and Montreuil-sur-Mer at the mouth of the Canche. Arnulf resorted to his father's methods to rid himself of his opponent, and in 942 he had William assassinated. Soon afterwards Arnulf added Montreuil and part of Ponthieu to the county of Flanders. An attempt to seize Amiens however, was successfully fended off by Hugh the Great. Some of the territories acquired by Baldwin and Arnulf included possessions in Mempisc and Ostrevant formerly owned by Eberhard of Friuli and his children. The rich abbey of St Amand also came under the control of the counts of Flanders.

Most of Arnulf's political and military strength was concentrated in the richer and more cultivated south of his domain. He completed the series of *castra* begun by his father and grandfather and it is assumed that defenders of these strongholds were appointed, perhaps with the duty of administering justice as well. There was probably an element of calculation in his marriage to Adela, daughter of Herbert II of Vermandois, though Herbert may himself have thought of the marriage as opening up possibilities for his own family. Yet the marriage is also significant in that it confirms the alienation of Flanders from its English connections. In 939, an English fleet sent to help Louis IV against his rebel magnates had ravaged the Flemish coast, with the result that Count Arnulf joined the rebels and for the rest of his reign there is no more evidence of friendly relations between the English and Flemish courts. Flanders became a haven for Englishmen out of favour at home, such as Dunstan.[60] Adela and Arnulf produced a son, Baldwin III, but he died before his father, leaving an infant heir, Arnulf II. In order to secure the succession to his territories by his grandson, Arnulf appealed to King Lothar, offering Artois, Ostrevant, Ponthieu and Amiens in exchange for his support. Despite the king's support, the position of the count of Flanders deteriorated rapidly after Arnulf I's death in 965. When Arnulf II became count in 976 and paid homage to the king, he was unable to exert any authority in the Boulonnais and Ternois. Courtrai,

Ghent and Waas also broke away. The counts or viscounts of these *pagi* may well have been vassals of Arnulf II in theory, but were certainly not in practice. On Arnulf II's death in 988, Hugh Capet married his son Robert to Arnulf's widow Susanna, and Flanders came temporarily under Capetian control. Throughout the second half of the tenth century only the counts of Flanders among those north of the Seine had refused to acknowledge the supremacy of the Robertians, but the precarious position of Arnulf II deprived the counts of the ability to resist any longer.

Unlike Brittany and Normandy, Flanders seems always to have been governed in the Carolingian manner. Dhondt has argued that the region was a march, and that the true function of the count of Flanders was in fact that of a marquis.[61] There are no surviving charters from Baldwin II's reign so we do not know what title he assumed. Regino of Prüm describes his power as that of the leader of a *ducatus*, an expression he employs in relation to other marcher counts.[62] Folcuin on the other hand, writing at the end of Arnulf II's reign, describes the Flemish principality as a *marca* and gives both Baldwin II and Arnulf I the title *marchisus*, a title also used of them in royal *acta*.

Perhaps the most striking imitation by the counts of Flanders of Carolingian policies was their attempt to control the church in their region. Most of Flanders was converted to Christianity in the course of the seventh century by natives of the region, as well as by missionaries from Aquitaine such as Amand, and the monasteries founded by him and his disciples and colleagues – St Bertin, St Amand (Elnone), Marchiennes, St Vaast at Arras, St Bavo's and St Peter's at Ghent became important religious and intellectual centres. The principal bishoprics were Cambrai, Thérouanne and Tournai. During the ninth century these ecclesiastical centres suffered from lay appropriation as well as the depredations of the Vikings, and in some of them religious standards fell rather low. Among eight abbots appointed to St Bertin between 820 and 883 for example, only one was a monk and one canon actually bought the abbacy from Charles the Bald for 30 pounds of gold. Thérouanne, Cambrai and Tournai were sacked by the Vikings, Arras cathedral was burnt in 883 and both St Amand and St Bertin were pillaged. Folcuin of St Bertin was particularly bitter about Baldwin II's activities as count-abbot of St Bertin. He informs us that Baldwin built fortifications round the monastery and that he took more from the church than he gave. 'May he be damned', adds Folcuin, 'by all present and future monks.'

Arnulf I however, for all his greed and ruthlessness, restored, with the aid of the monastic reformer Gerard of Brogne, the discipline of the monasteries in his lands. The reforms entailed the re-establishment of monastic life and reintroduction of monks to houses that had become occupied by canons or clerics. It aimed to instil a new vigour into religious life and make it conform more closely to the Rule of St Benedict. Gerard of Brogne was made abbot of St Peter's Ghent in 941 and St Bertin in 945. St Amand was reformed in 952, St Bavo's Ghent in 953 and St Vaast at about the same time. The progress of reform depended greatly on the count's patronage; Arnulf indeed seems to have retained the title of count-abbot over St Bertin from 944 and to have seen to its protection. Transmar, bishop of Tournai, had written in 941 begging him to restore the purity of the religious life at St Bavo's, and in 937 the relics of the saint, carried away for safety to St Omer in 846 and then to Laon in 853, were restored to St Bavo's. In a diploma of 8 July 941, Arnulf I declared himself moved by the example of Judas Maccabeus, the restorer of the temple of Jerusalem, and by the exhortations of pious people, to restore to St Peter's Ghent, with the authorization of the king of Francia and of the diocesan bishop Transmar, a small amount of land that he thought would be sufficient for their needs for the moment. Later Arnulf gave more land to the monastery and added to its collection of relics. He expressed the desire that the monks should serve God, follow the Rule of St Benedict and elect their abbots freely, and in the following year, Bishop Transmar at the request of the count and the abbot of St Peter's, restored all the monastery's ancient liberties.

In 952 Count Arnulf convoked an assembly of prelates, including Bishop Fulbert of Cambrai, Bishop Ralph of Noyon – Tournai, Gerard, abbot of Brogne and Hildebrand, abbot of St Amand, with the intention of reforming the abbey of St Amand.[63] The prior Leudric was made abbot and the temporal was restored by Arnulf from the benefices he and his predecessors had usurped. The position of St Amand is of some interest and fairly typical of the fate of the wealthiest abbeys under the counts. St Amand as we saw in Chapter Eight made a substantial contribution to the intellectual and artistic achievements of the Carolingian Renaissance as well as being an important centre for book production. Before Arnulf I extended his territories to include Ostrevant, the north of this *pagus* had been an hereditary benefice of Count Eberhard of Friuli's children. Adalhard, Eberhard's brother, was abbot of St Amand from 861 to 864 and the abbey had been a royal abbey, reformed by Louis the Pious in 821 and patronized by Charles the Bald. In south Ostrevant a rival family was in control. Arnulf succeeded in exploiting this rivalry and extending his own authority over the whole of Ostrevant and the abbey of St Amand and replaced the Carolingian kings as its patron. From 965 until 994 the abbey passed again into royal hands. Thereafter it came under the control once more of the counts of Flanders and the lands restored by Arnulf I were seized by Baldwin IV.[64]

Although there were still monks at St Bertin in the middle of the tenth century, religious discipline there was lax, and Count Arnulf appealed to Gerard of Brogne for assistance. He sent reforming monks to the abbey in about 944. Some of the St Bertin monks were so enraged at this intrusion that they fled to King Edmund in England, who settled them at St Peter's Bath. Gerard made one of his nephews, Hildebrand, abbot of St Bertin, and the monastery became a model for the neighbouring houses to copy. Arnulf also returned some land and retained a proprietary interest in the community. He seems to have retained the title of count-abbot over St Bertin from 944 and to have seen to its protection, as well as enjoying some of the comforts the monastery could offer. Folcuin tells the story of how Oduldus, a monk of St Bertin and charged with the supervision of the vintage in the abbey's properties on the Rhine, returned with eight barrels of new wine. Arnulf with his wife and son arrived to stay at the monastery soon afterwards, and Arnulf promptly ordered that the entire vintage should be reserved for his exclusive use. In order not to be accused of greed or theft he gave the monastery the church of Pétresse. The monastic reforms promoted by Gerard of Brogne and Count Arnulf were introduced into England through Dunstan, who had been exiled to Flanders in 956 and who spent his time there at the monastery of Ghent. Monks of Ghent moreover were called upon to assist in drawing up the *Regularis Concordia*. Dunstan was also friendly with Abbot Fulrad of St Vaast and the ecclesiastical contact thus established between England and Flanders was maintained.[65]

IV

The attempt to model themselves on the Carolingians in their control over the secular and monastic church is a common element in the policies adopted by the rulers of Normandy, Brittany and Flanders, as is the basic structure of the administration in Normandy and Flanders at least. The relations of all three with England at an important stage of their histories, however, is an indication of the peculiar, and peripheral, position these three territorial principalities enjoyed in relation to the rest of the Frankish lands throughout the Carolingian period. Only occasionally did events within these territories impinge on the affairs of the Carolingian house. The development of several powerful territorial principalities within the west Frankish kingdom, on the other hand, concerned the Carolingian rulers more nearly. It was eventually, as we shall see in the next chapters, to effect a radical transformation of the political structure of the country.

NOTES

1. I owe the latter point to Alfred Smyth.
2. Gregory of Tours, *Historia Francorum*, III.3 and Venantius Fortunatus, *Carmina* VII and IX. 1, *MGH AA* IV, 160 and 203.
3. *Annales regni Francorum, s.a.*, 800.
4. On the most recent theories concerning the *Danevirk*, see J. Graham Campbell, *The Viking Age* (London 1981), 208–10.
5. *Annales Fuldenses, s.a.* 837 and compare W. C. Braat, 'Les Vikings au pays de Frise', *Annales de Normandie* 4 (1954), 219–27.
6. *Annales Xantenses, s.a.*, 846.
7. *Annales Fuldenses, s.a.*, 845.
8. J. M. Wallace-Hadrill, *The Vikings in Francia* (Reading 1975), 5.
9. See P. Gasnault, 'Le tombeau de saint Martin et les invasions normandes dans l'histoire et dans la légende', *Revue d'Histoire de l'Eglise de France* 47 (1961), 51–66, and G. de Poerck, 'Les reliques de Saint Maixent et Léger aux IXe et Xe siècles et les origines de l'abbaye d'Ebreuil en Bourbonnais', *Revue bénédictine* 72 (1962), 61–95. See also P. Riché, 'Conséquences des invasions normandes sur la culture monastique dans l'occident franc', *Settimane* 16 (1969), 705–21, A. d'Haenens,

'Les invasions normandes dans l'empire franc au IXe siècle', ibid., 233–98, idem, *Les invasions normandes en Belgique au IXe siecle* (Louvain 1967), and *Les invasions normandes. Une catastrophe?* (Paris 1970).

10. P. Sawyer, *The Age of the Vikings* (London 1971), 123–6.

11. *Annales Bertiniani, s.a.*, 859.

12. *Annales Vedastini, s.a.*, 888.

13. Ibid., *s.a.*,884.

14. See the discussion by E. Joranson, *The Danegeld in France* (Rock Island, Illinois 1923), but compare S. Keynes, *The Diplomas of King Aethelred 'the Unready'* 978–1016 (Cambridge 1980), 202–3 and N. Brooks, 'England in the ninth century: the crucible of defeat', *TRHS* 29 (1979), 1–20.

15. P. A. Février, *Histoire de la France Urbaine* I *La Ville Antique*, G. Duby (ed.) (Paris 1980), 516–21 and F. Vercauteren, 'Comment s'est-on défendu au IXe siècle, dans l'empire franc, contre les invasions normandes?', *Annales du XXXe congrès de la Fédération Archéologique de Belgique* (Brussels 1936), 117–32.

16. F. Lot, 'La grande invasion normande 856–862', *BEC* 69 (1908), 1–62.

17. *Annales Bertiniani, s.a.*, 855–6.

18. Ibid., *s.a.*, 858.

19. L. Musset, *Les invasions: Le second assaut contre l'Europe chrétienne (VIIe – XIe Siècles)* (Paris 1965), and 'Naissance de la Normandie', *Histoire de la Normandie* M. de Bouard (ed.) (Toulouse 1970), 75–130.

20. H. Prentout, *Essai sur les origines et la fondation du duché de Normandie* (Caen 1911), and *Etude critique sur Dudo de St Quentin* (Paris 1916).

21. On these points see J. C. Holt in his forthcoming book on the Normans. I am grateful to him for allowing me to read the relevant portions. See F. Stenton, 'The Scandinavian colonies in England and Normandy', *TRHS* 4th series 27 (1945), 1–12 and D. C. Douglas, 'The rise of Normandy', *Proceedings of the British Academy* 33 (1947), 101–31.

22. See D. C. Douglas, 'Rollo of Normandy', *EHR* 57(1942), 417–36.

23. Charles the Simple, *Recueil*, No. 92.

24. K. F. Werner, 'Quelques observations au sujet des débuts du 'duché' de Normandie', *Droit privé et institutions régionales. Etudes historiques offertes à Jean Yver* (Paris 1976), 691–709.

25. D. C. Douglas, 'Les évêques de Normandie', *Annales de Normandie* 9 (1958), 87–102.

26. Ordericus Vitalis, *Historia ecclesiastica* III M. Chibnall (ed.) (Oxford 8 vols, 1969–81) II, 9.

27. J. Yver, 'Les premiers institutions du duché de Normandie', *Settimane* 16 (1969), 299–366 and M. Fauroux (ed.) *Recueil des Actes des ducs de Normandie 911–1066* (Caen 1961).

28. A point made by J. C. Holt in his forthcoming book.

29. C. De Clercq (ed.) *Concilia Galliae* (Turnhout 1963), 179; Gregory, *Historia Francorum*, IV, 20; V, 16; V, 21; IX, 18; X, 9. Compare Sidonius Apollinaris, I.7.5 letter of 469, III.9.2 letter of 470 and Jordanes, *De origine et actibusque Getarum*, *MGH AA* V, 118.

30. J. Lafaurie, 'Deux trésors monétaires carolingiens: Saumeray (Eure et Loire) Rennes (Ille et Vilaine)', *Revue Numismatique* 7 (1965), 262–305.

31. L. Bieler (ed.) *The Irish Penitentials* (Dublin 1963), 136–59 and see L. Fleuriot, 'Un fragment en Latin de très anciennes lois bretonnes armoricaines du VIe siècle', *Annales de Bretagne* 78 (1981), 610–60.

32. Ermold the Black, *In honorem Hludowici*, lines 99–103 and see *Annales regni Francorum, s.a.* 818 and 824.

33. Cartulary of Redon, 189–192 (Salomon's charter of 17 April 869); Fr. trs. J. Delumeau (ed.), *Documents de l'Histoire de la Bretagne* (Toulouse 1971), 84–5.

34. J. M. H. Smith, 'The 'archbishopric' of Dol and the ecclesiastical politics of ninth century Brittany', *Studies in Church History* 18 (1982).

35. See F. Lot, 'Le schisme breton du IXe siècle', *Mélanges d'Histoire Bretonne* (Paris 1907), 58–96.

36. Cartulary of Landévennec I, 75–6.

37. *Annales Bertiniani, s.a.*, 851, 856 and 857.

38. Ibid., *s.a.*, 867.

39. Smith, 'The 'archbishopric' of Dol', and her references. Compare *MGH Epp* VI, 639–40, 646–7, 648–9 and 619–22.

40. Cartulary of Redon, No. 241.

41. Lupus, Ep. 81.

42. W. Davies, 'On the distribution of political power in Brittany in the mid-ninth century', *Charles the Bald: Court and Kingdom*, M. T. Gibson and J. L. Nelson (eds) (Oxford 1981), 87–105, esp. 91.

43. See the evidence cited by Davies, ibid., 93–105.

44. Ibid., 99.

45. Chronicle of Nantes, XXVII–XXXI; Fr. trs. Delumeau (ed., *Documents de l'Histoire de la Bretagne*, 87–90.

46. J. F. Lemarignier, *Le gouvernement royale aux premiers temps capétiens 987–1108* (Paris 1965), 49.

47. Asser, *Vita Alfredi*, c. 102.

48. I owe this point to David Dumville.

49. See F. Wormald, *English Kalendars before* A.D. 1100 (London, Henry Bradshaw Society vol. 72, 1934).

50. L. Gougaud, 'Les mentions anglaises de saints bretons et de leurs reliques', *Annales de Bretagne* 34 (1919–21), 272–7, and see too D. Rollason, 'Lists of saints' resting places in Anglo-Saxon England', *Anglo-Saxon England* 7(1978), 61–93, and F. Lot, 'Date de l'exode des saints hors de la Bretagne', *Annales de Bretagne* 15 (1899), 60–76. The chronology of much of the 'exodus' is confused.

51. P. Riché, 'Les hagiographes bretons et la renaissance carolingienne', *Bulletin philologique et historique* (1966), 651–9, in J. Delumeau (ed.), *Histoire de la Bretagne* (Toulouse 1971), 133–50, and 'Translations de reliques à l'époque carolingienne: histoire des reliques de Saint Malo', *MA* 4th series 31 (1976), 201–18.

52. C. Ineichen-Eder, 'Theologisches und philosophisches Lehrmaterial aus dem Alkuin-Kreise', *DA* 34 (1978), 192–201.

53. C. R. Morey, E. K. Rand and C. H. Kraeling, 'The Gospel Book of Landévennec in the New York Public Library', *Art Studies* 8 (1931), 225–86, and J. Alexander and F. Wormald, *An Early Breton Gospel Book* (Cambridge, The Roxburghe Club 1977). See also W. M. Lindsay, 'Breton scriptoria. Their Latin abbreviation symbols', *Zentralblatt für Bibliothekswesen* 29 (1912), 264–72.

54. L. Fleuriot, *Dictionnaire des gloses en vieux breton* (Paris 1964).

55. J. Dhondt, *Etudes sur la naissance des principautés territoriales* (Bruges 1948), 50; H. Sproemberg, *Die Entstehung der Grafschaft Flandern* (Berlin 1935), and 'Judith, Königin von England, Gräfin von Flandern', *Revue Belge de Philologie et d'Histoire* 15 (1936), 397–428. But compare F. L. Ganshof, *La Flandre sous les premiers comtes* (Brussels 1949) and *La Belgique Carolingienne* (Brussels 1958), and L. Vanderkin-

dere, *La formation territoriale des principautés belges au Moyen Age* (Brussels 2 vols, 1902).

56. A. Joris, 'On the edge of two worlds in the heart of the new Empire: the romance regions of northern Gaul during the Merovingian period', *Studies in Medieval and Renaissance History* **3** (1966), 1–52, and J. Dhondt, 'Essai sur l'origine de la frontière linguistique', *Antiquité Classique* 16 (1947), 261–86. See also R. Fossier, *La terre et les hommes en Picardie jusqu'à la fin du XIIIᵉ siècle* (Paris and Louvain 1968).

57. Dhondt, *Naissance des principautés territoriales*, 277–84.

58. Flodoard, *Historia*, III, 23.

59. On Ralph see P. Grierson, 'La maison d'Evrard de Frioul et les origines du comté de Flandre', *Revue du Nord* 24 (1938), 241–66.

60. P. Grierson, 'Relations between England and Flanders before the Norman Conquest', *TRHS* 4th series 23 (1941), 71–112.

61. Dhondt, *Naissance des principautés territoriales*, 280. See also E. Klebel, 'Herzogtümer und Marken bis 900', *DA* 2 (1938), 1–53.

62. Regino, Chronicle, *s.a.* 818.

63. *Annales Elnonenses, s.a.*, 952.

64. H. Platelle, *Le temporel de l'abbaye de Saint Amand, des origines à 1340* (Paris 1962), 110–19.

65. T. Symons, '*Regularis Concordia:* History and Derivation', *Tenth Century Studies*. D. Parsons (ed.) (London and Chichester 1975), 37–59 especially 45–46. See also E. de Moreau, *Les Abbayes de Belgique* (Brussels 1952).

CHAPTER TEN

Odo and the Emergence of the Robertians

I

As soon as he heard of his father's death, Louis the Stammerer, Charles the Bald's eldest son, granted out abbacies, countships and estates 'according to what each man demanded' in a desperate but successful attempt to win support.[1] Thus his position was conserved only at the price of new concessions of *honores* and benefices to the nobility. A number of nobles, including his father's archchancellor Gauzlin (Fr. Josselin), counts Conrad of Paris, Bernard Hairyfeet of the Auvergne, Boso, Bernard of Gothia and the Welf Hugh the Abbot resisted Louis' claims but were bought off; Gauzlin, for instance, was given the abbacy of St Denis. Some of these nobles, once bought, were required to deal with others still hostile and were able to strengthen their own positions by so doing. In this way Bernard Hairyfeet, Count Theudebert and others among Louis the Stammerer's adherents acquired most of Bernard of Gothia's territory after the latter had been condemned and excommunicated for his revolt against the king and spoliation of church property in August 878. Bernard Hairyfeet's power indeed was further enhanced after Louis the Stammerer's death as a result of the campaign against Boso of Provence, for he established himself on some of the territories taken from Boso.

Louis the Stammerer was crowned by Hincmar, archbishop of Rheims, at Compiègne on 8 October 877, but within sixteen months he was dead. The succession was disputed. Louis had left three sons: Louis III and Carloman by an early marriage with Ansgard, sister to Count Odo son of Harduin, and Charles (later nicknamed the Simple) born posthumously of a union with Adalheid, daughter of Count Adalhard. The legality of both marriages and the legitimate claims of all three boys were not in question, but what was a matter of concern to a large group of nobles in Neustria and Francia was the power and influence of the Welf Hugh the Abbot, made great by his nephew Charles the Bald. As we saw earlier, aristocratic factions dominated Frankish politics in the second half of the ninth century, and it was the efforts of one faction, led by Gauzlin, a Rorgonid, and Count Theudebert of Vermandois, to force Hugh the Abbot to share his 'regency' of the kingdom with them which settled the succession question. Gauzlin had entered Charles the Bald's chancery in 860. He acted as *missus* in 865 and in 867 assumed the headship of the chancery in succession to his half-brother Louis, abbot of St Denis. He had in the meantime been granted the abbacies of Jumièges, Glanfeuil, St Amand and St Germain-des-Prés and in 884 he was elevated to the see of Paris.

Hugh the Abbot wished only one of Louis the Stammerer's sons, Louis III, to be king, for it was in his interests to prevent partition of the kingdom. It was probably Hugh who had prompted Louis the Stammerer to revoke his earlier wish to be succeeded by Louis III and Carloman and to designate Louis III only as his heir. It seems that many other nobles, including Gauzlin, felt they would have a better chance to wield political influence if there were two kings.[2] Consequently they decided to call in Louis the Younger of the east Frankish kingdom (who was known personally to Gauzlin) with the idea that a 'foreign' Carolingian king would either offset Welf influence or force Hugh the Abbot to recognize the claim of Carloman. Louis the Younger's first advance towards the west had the desired effect. In September 879 Hugh had both Louis III and Carloman crowned and anointed at Ferrières by Archbishop Ansegis of Sens, and early in 880, at Amiens, the nobles divided the kingdom between the two Carolingians: Louis III's portion comprised Francia and Neustria, and Carloman ruled Burgundy, Aquitaine and Gothia (see Map 15). Hugh the Abbot, while continuing to be pre-eminent in the southern kingdom and exerting considerable influence over both kingdoms, had to share his power in the north with a number of other nobles, including Gauzlin who, according to a new interpretation of the charter evidence, was sufficiently high in standing, despite his ambivalent position earlier in relation to Louis, to become Louis III's archchancellor.[3] The invitation to Louis the Younger however, had unfortunate consequences; it was only by obtaining the cession of the Lotharingian territories acquired by Charles the Bald at Meersen in 870 that Louis renounced his claim to the succession to the west Frankish kingdom at Remiremont in 880.

II

During the period of indecision following Louis the Stammerer's death, a third claimant to the throne of the west Frankish kingdom, Boso, had appeared, backed by most of the nobles and bishops of Burgundy and Provence. When Charles the Bald married Richild in 869, her brother Boso immediately received a number of favours, including both countships and abbacies. In 871 he had been made count of Vienne, and count of Bourges a year later. After arranging an exchange with Count Theudebert of Vermandois, Boso also acquired the countship of Autun, so that the territory he eventually governed comprised most of Burgundy and Provence, including the regions of Viennois and Lyonnais. When Charles the Bald was crowned Emperor in 875, he made Boso his *dux et missus Italiae sacrique palatii archiminister*. In other words, Boso ruled Italy for Charles and once there took the opportunity of marrying Ermengard, the daughter of Emperor Louis II. Boso by 877 was one of the most prominent men in the west Frankish kingdom. It was Boso who escorted Pope John VIII to Troyes when the latter visited the Frankish kingdom and he was also one of those appointed to safeguard the interests of Louis III, Louis the Stammerer's eldest son.

Boso, possibly egged on by his wife, clearly had great ambition as well as ability. He had suggested to John VIII that he might be a suitable candidate for the imperial title (John had apparently thought so as well) and began to assert himself soon after Louis the Stammerer's death. In July, Boso and his wife made a donation to the abbey of Montierender in which Boso described himself as *Ego Boso dei gratia id quod sum* and *proles imperialis* and which was recognized by a chancellor just as if it were a royal diploma.[4] On 15 October at Mantaille near Vienne, Boso was raised to the kingship. In the *acta* of the assembly at Mantaille, no mention was made of any territorial limitation to Boso's kingdom.[5] It was not a breakaway kingdom; Boso did not create himself king of Provence but king in opposition to the two teenage Carolingians. Boso's brother Richard, Bernard of Mâcon and Count Theudebald were among his lay supporters, and about two-thirds of all the Provençal and Burgundian bishops (of Aix, Arles, Gap, Riez, Avignon, Marseilles, Orange, Toulon, Vaison, Vienne, Lyons, Tarentaise, Die, Grenoble, Maurienne, Valence and Viviers, Autun, Chalon, Mâcon, Besançon, Lausanne, Uzès, Agde) and the abbot of St Claude were all at Mantaille when he was made king.

That Boso's support was largely from the Provençal region has led some later historians to include Boso among those who set up independent principalities in revolt against the Carolingians. This, as Bautier has argued, is mistaken.[6] Boso's bid for power is indicative of the support a strong man with pretensions to rule the whole Frankish kingdom could command from the noble and ecclesiastical magnates as well as, possibly, a group unwilling to submit to the machinations of either Hugh the Abbot or Gauzlin and his party. Provence and Burgundy furthermore, happened to be the areas in which Boso had accumulated lands and offices. Bautier points out that eastern Provence seems to have remained aloof and that it is possible that the lay and ecclesiastical magnates in this region recognized the sovereignty of Charles the Fat. This, if so, would certainly explain why Charles the Fat was hostile to Boso's claims.

As soon as he was crowned, Boso set out to consolidate his position. He appointed the powerful bishop of Autun, Adalgar, as his archchancellor, and made Geilo, abbot of Tournus, the bishop of Langres (and thus won over that diocese). The archbishop of Vienne imprisoned the hostile bishop of Geneva (who had not taken part in Boso's election) and someone else more sympathetic was consecrated in his place. There was also some collusion between Boso and his Lotharingian countrymen who had rallied round Hugh, Lothar II's bastard, in his attempt to claim the right to rule Lotharingia.

Boso's elevation and Hugh of Lotharingia's pretensions had the effect of uniting all the Carolingian cousins – Louis the Younger, Charles the Fat, Louis III and Carloman – and their supporters against them. Hugh was soon dealt with but Boso presented a more serious obstacle to Charles the Fat, as well as to Carloman and Hugh the Abbot. Charles seized the Italian lands of Boso's mother-in-law Engelberga, kidnapped Engelberga herself, appropriated the temporal of the archbishopric of Besançon and occupied Lausanne. By 881, Boso had lost the Jura and transjurane region to Charles the Fat. From the west Frankish side, Boso was deprived of many of his *honores* and benefices: the abbey of Montieramey was given a regular abbot and received a royal donation. Others among Boso's supporters were enticed away from his side; the county of Autun, for instance, was conferred on Richard, Boso's brother, who supported Carloman from then onwards (see Map 16). In 882 Vienne was attacked by a west Frankish army led by Richard who captured Boso's wife and daughter. Abandoned by the Pope, his brother and his chancellor who had decided to back Charles the Fat and Carloman respectively, and forsaken by his bishops and counts (who had probably recognized that further resistance was hopeless), Boso disappears from the sources. He died in obscurity on 11 January 887.

III

Although still in their teens, the west Frankish kings Louis III and Carloman showed some hopeful signs of developing into good soldiers and efficient rulers. Yet for the years of their short reigns they were too much under the thumbs of their noble 'advisers' to assert themselves with any force. Behind Hincmar of Rheims' quarrel with Louis III over the episcopal elections to Noyon and Beauvais indeed can be seen the opposition of Hincmar's aristocratic opponents, especially Gauzlin. On the death of Raginelm, bishop of Noyon in 880, the clergy and people elected Hedilo, Hincmar's candidate, to succeed him. Louis III wanted to put one of his palace clerics in Raginelm's place, but Hincmar insisted that the king had no right to interfere in church matters and especially in the episcopal elections. Hincmar's candidate was duly ordained but as luck would have it his subsequent behaviour cast doubt on Hincmar's choice. Undeterred, Hincmar supported the candidacy of Ralph for the see of Beauvais after the death of Bishop Odo (the king had proposed another palace clerk called Audacher or Odoacer), and again it was Hincmar's protégé who was consecrated.

Louis III won a decisive victory against the Vikings at Saucourt in 882 but was killed soon afterwards, as has been related earlier (p. 235), in a fall from his horse while chasing a pretty girl. His brother Carloman then ruled the west Frankish kingdom alone until he was killed in a hunting accident in December 884. During his reign as sole ruler his chief adviser was Archbishop Hincmar of Rheims; it was for Carloman that Hincmar composed the *De ordine palatii* shortly before his own death in 882.

Carloman's young brother Charles the Simple was still only five years old on his brother's death and clearly unfit to assume the leadership of a kingdom beset by Viking raiders. The west Frankish nobility and clergy turned to

Charles the Fat, Emperor since 881 and now the sole ruler of the east Frankish kingdom.

Charles the Fat, Louis the German's youngest son, had become Emperor more or less by default and proved an ineffectual defender of both Rome and Italy. After the death of John VIII the Papacy itself was beset and disgraced by bitter faction fighting; in the sixteen years between 882 and 904, for example, there were no less than twelve popes, none of them of good calibre. The reunification of the Frankish kingdoms under Charles the Fat in 884–5 has sometimes been celebrated, with no justification at all, as the last glorious moment of the Carolingian Empire. Notker Balbulus' *Gesta Karoli Magni*, presented to Charles the Fat after 883, provides some insight into the political atmosphere of the east Frankish kingdom at least at the end of the ninth century, as well as some indication of the extent to which the position of Emperor and the achievement of Charlemagne had become idealized,[7] yet it tells us little of the specific issues of west Frankish politics. The reconstitution of the Empire was far from being a real unification; it was more a temporary cobbling together of three separate kingdoms under the nominal headship of one man, though an ill-defined notion of the general 'moral' superiority of the Emperor may thereby have been preserved. Charles the Fat's elevation was far from being the ideal solution for the west Frankish kingdom and simply precipitated some years of confusion.

When Charles the Fat abdicated under pressure in 887 (he died soon afterwards) he left no real heir, for his attempt to have his illegitimate son Bernard recognized as such had failed. This was not necessarily because he was illegitimate but more likely to have been a reflection on his ability. At an assembly at Tribur, presided over by the chancellor Liutward, Arnulf, Carloman of Bavaria's illegitimate son, was elected king. In the west Frankish kingdom, however, there was no obvious successor. Charles the Simple was still only nine years old and the reason for which he had been passed over in 884 was still valid. Richer said of the situation that the Franks deliberated about the choice of the next king not in the spirit of rebellion but pressed by a common desire to fight against the enemy menacing them.[8] For the first time since the Carolingian rise to power a non-Carolingian, the Robertian Odo, count of Paris, was raised to the kingship. How this came about needs to be considered in the context of the development of the territorial principalities and the rise to power of particular noble families within the west Frankish kingdom.

IV

Both the Annals of Fulda and Regino of Prüm describe and comment upon the fragmentation of 'Europe, that is, Charlemagne's Empire' in 888. The Annals of Fulda say many petty kings (*multi reguli*) – Berengar in Italy, Rudolf, son of Conrad the Welf in upper Burgundy, Guy (Wido) and Louis in Gaul and Provence, Odo, son of Robert the Strong in Neustria and Ramnulf in Aquitaine, were acting as if they were kings. Regino observed how each region had made a king for itself 'out of its own guts' after the death of Charles the Fat and comments that there was really nothing to choose between the west Frankish nobles as far as power, family or offices held were concerned, and that no one was sufficiently distinguished among his peers for the rest to wish to submit to his authority.[9] What actually happened in the different regions of the west Frankish kingdom after 888 and who were the *reguli* referred to by Regino and the Fulda annalist?

Berengar of Friuli was, through his mother Gisela, a grandson of Louis the Pious and had ruled Friuli since 875. On Charles the Fat's death, Berengar had had himself crowned king of Italy at Pavia. Despite recognition from the east Frankish ruler Arnulf, Berengar found if difficult to maintain his position in Italy and encountered particularly forceful opposition from the ruler of Spoleto. Berengar retreated to north-east Italy and based himself at Verona while Guy of Spoleto, who had made an unsuccessful bid for the throne of the west Frankish kingdom (below p. 268), now had himself proclaimed king of Italy at Pavia and on 21 February 891 was crowned Emperor by Pope Stephen V. Guy had his young son Lambert made king three months later (and in 892 co-Emperor) in order to secure his family's position. But the Widonid (Guideschi) triumph was short-lived. Guy himself died suddenly in 894 and it was the east Frankish king Arnulf who was crowned Emperor in his place in February 896. Arnulf was unable to maintain his position in Italy; Berengar remained master of north-east Italy and Lambert, Guy's young son, reasserted himself and ruled the rest of Italy south of the Po. On Lambert's death in 898, Berengar was recognized once more as king of Italy, though Spoleto, Tuscany and Rome were more or less independent of his authority.

In 915 Berengar himself was crowned Emperor. By this time the grandiose title can have meant little more than an indication that the holder of it was under some sort of obligation to protect the Pope. Berengar throughout his reign was beset by rival dukes in Italy, quite apart from spasmodic attacks by Magyars. After 920 he was opposed by Count Adalbert of Ivrea and Odalrich, his count of the palace. No sooner had he dealt with these two than his position in Italy was challenged by Rudolf, the Welf ruler of upper Burgundy. Berengar was subsequently obliged to cede Rudolf part of his kingdom, though the rulers of Tuscany would recognize the authority of neither. Berengar himself was murdered in 924 and Rudolf forced to give up all pretensions to Italy soon afterwards. Thereafter Italy was riven by factional rivalries, dominated by pro-Franco-Burgundian and pro-east Frankish parties. The Frankish count of Arles, Hugh, retained at least the title of king in Italy between 926 and 948 but the interest of the east Frankish ruler Otto I in Italian affairs became increasingly apparent. By 951 Otto had established his rule in Italy. Otto's authority was successfully resisted for some time by Berengar II and Adalbert, grandson and great-grandson of Berengar I, but with Otto I's coronation as Emperor in Rome on 2 February 962, their power was broken. Italy lay no longer within the Carolingian, or even the west Frankish, sphere of influence.[10]

Rudolf, one of the *reguli* mentioned by the Fulda annalist and Regino in their comments on the events of 888, was the son of the Welf Conrad (brother of the Empress Judith) and had succeeded his father as count in the transjurane region of Burgundy (that is, between the Saône and the Alps) centred on Geneva. On 6 January 888 he had himself proclaimed king and anointed in the church of St Maurice d'Agaune and seems to have thought in terms of reconstituting the kingdom of Lothar II rather than claiming the whole of the west Frankish kingdom.[11] To this end he had himself anointed by Archbishop Arnulf of Toul. The parallels with Charles the Bald's attempt to seize Lotharingia in 869 are obvious, even to the swift retreat Rudolf had to beat in the face of east Frankish opposition to his pretensions. Thereafter, Rudolf's territory was limited to his patrimony in upper Burgundy. Arnulf's hostility to Rudolf remained unabated. Not only did Arnulf patronize the creation of the kingdom of lower Burgundy and Provence in 890; he also set up his illegitimate son Zwentibold as king in Lotharingia in 895. Rudolf I's son Rudolf II (912–937) attempted to expand the territory he had inherited but, like his father, he was halted in the east by Burchard I of Swabia. Rudolf made the best of the situation and married Burchard's daughter Bertha. In the south he enjoyed a temporary success in Italy. During the winter of 921–2 he installed himself at Pavia and, after Berengar of Friuli's death in 924, he proclaimed himself king of Italy. The death of his father-in-law Burchard in 926, however, deprived Rudolf of the military support he needed to maintain his position. He was obliged to relinquish the crown of Italy to Hugh of Arles and return to Burgundy. An opportunist, Rudolf turned to Germany and in 926 he appeared at the Liudolfing Henry I's court at Worms and formed some kind of connection (possibly vassalage) with that ruler.

On Boso of Provence's death in 887, his wife had fled with their son Louis to the court of her uncle Charles the Fat. In June 887 Charles adopted Louis. This was in recognition that he was the grandson of the Emperor Louis II rather than because he was the son of the black sheep Boso. Three years later, at the Council of Valence, Louis was elected by the lay and ecclesiastical magnates of Provence as their king, with the acquiescence of Arnulf, king of the east Franks. Bautier has argued that Arnulf's agreement to the creation of a kingdom for Charles was an acknowledgement that Louis, as Louis II's grandson, had a right to a legitimate territory.[12] It would be unusual for a Carolingian to be quite so philanthropic; Arnulf approved the new kingdom because it suited him. He probably intended it to include the 'illegal' kingdom created by Rudolf I in upper transjurane Burgundy (which it never did) or at least to act as a counter to Rudolf.

Louis of Provence also directed his attention towards Italy, to his cost. He may well have dreamt of regaining his grandfather's dominion in Italy. Although Louis succeeded in having himself crowned Emperor in 901, his authority actually extended no further than Provence. In Italy itself, moreover, he ran foul of Berengar of Friuli. In 902 Louis was only able to buy his safe retreat across the Alps with a promise never to return to Italy. When in 905 he broke this promise and advanced to Verona, Louis was overcome by Berengar who had the Provençal ruler's eyes put out. Louis, thereafter known as Louis the Blind, retreated to Provence and lived for another twenty years after this savagery had been inflicted upon him.

During that time the effective ruler of Provence was Louis' cousin Hugh, count of Arles and grandson through his mother Bertha of Lothar II of Lotharingia. Louis of Provence ceded Hugh the title of *dux* of Provence and *marchio* of the Viennois. Hugh attempted, with rather more success than either Louis or Rudolf of Burgundy, to dominate Italian politics and on 9 July 926 he was crowned king of Italy. This did not prevent him from retaining his influence in Provence. When, on Louis the Blind's death, Provence was claimed by both the west Frankish king Ralph and Rudolf of Burgundy, Hugh ceded the lands he had administered as count under Louis of Provence to Rudolf in 933 in return for Rudolf's undertaking to keep out of Italy.[13] Louis the Blind's son Charles Constantine seems to have been content to hold only the county of Vienne, which, with Lyons, came under the authority of the west Frankish king Ralph. On Rudolf II's death in 937 Hugh tried to regain what he had ceded to him four years earlier. He seized Rudolf's widow Bertha, married her, and betrothed her seven-year-old daughter Adelaide to his son Lothar, seemingly determined to confine Rudolf's son Conrad, who had been formally elected and crowned king of upper Burgundy at Lausanne, to the Welf patrimony in transjurane Burgundy. For a short time the 'kingdom of Arles' extended, in theory at least, from Basle to Marseilles. At this point Otto I, to whose father Rudolf II had commended himself, intervened, with the result that Conrad 'the Pacific' had his suzerainty over Louis of Provence's kingdom approved and recognized, and the orientation of at least transjurane Burgundy towards Germany was settled. The king of the west Franks had also been persuaded to renounce all claims to Provence by the cession of the dioceses of Uzès and Viviers, and on Hugh of Arles' death in 948 the southern portion of the kingdom of Provence also recognized Conrad as king.

Conrad (937–93) remains a relatively colourless character. He controlled the see of Lyons and, after the death of Charles Constantine, the county of Vienne. The relationship with Otto was cemented by marriage; Otto wed Conrad's sister Adelaide and Otto's niece Matilda (the daughter of Louis IV of the west Frankish kingdom) became Conrad's wife in 966 (but see below, p. 322). By the mid-tenth century, the kingdom of Burgundy–Provence extended from Basle to the Mediterranean and embraced the Rhône valley. The region, although within the German sphere of influence, remained autonomous for a century. On Rudolf III's death in 1032 it became part of the Empire. Provence itself on the other hand rapidly became more or less impervious to royal intervention. After the death of Hugh of Arles, Conrad had nominated a number of counts as his agents in Arles, Avignon and Apt and appointed viscounts in Cavaillon and Marseilles. These counts were not natives of the regions they were to administer but inevitably quickly identified their interests with their regions and their offices soon became hereditary. The Provençal portion of the kingdom of Burgundy was dominated by the descendants of the brothers Counts Boso and William of Arles and Avignon respectively. They enjoyed regalian rights; that is, they disposed of the royal fisc, protected the church, mustered military forces and administered justice. A further group of officials were the *castellani* in charge of the fortified places. The local aristocracy regained control of the principal bishoprics and monasteries; at Marseilles for example, three members of the same comital family held the bishopric between 948 and 1078. The dioceses of Senez, Antibes, Avignon and Cavaillon were also controlled by the local ruling family. Thus the real rulers of the region in the tenth century were the local nobles.

V

Another of the Fulda annalist's petty kings had set himself up in Neustria, the region between the Seine and the Loire. With the Breton march, this area was of great importance both tactically and politically to the Carolingians.[14] Charlemagne had made his eldest son Charles the ruler of the *ducatus Cenomannicus* centred on the episcopal city of Le Mans, and this position was subsequently held by other members of the Carolingian family. The Breton march in the early decades of the ninth century was administered by the leaders of the Widonid family. Guy (Wido), son of Lambert I, was count of the Breton march in 799 and is described as a *missus* in 802. His sons Guy and Lambert II were appointed count of Vannes (813–32) and count of the Breton march (818–34) respectively. Lambert II was a partisan of Lothar in 833 and consequently lost his office in 834. Lambert asserted his independence against Charles the Bald in 843, established himself in the lower Loire (based on Nantes) and distributed the *honores* of the Breton march among his supporters. Some agreement seems to have been reached, for Lambert was charged by Charles the Bald with the defence of the region he had commandeered. After 846, however, the main focus of the family's activities appears to have shifted to Italy. It is as the Guideschi rulers of Spoleto that the Widonids, as we have seen, played a prominent part in Italian politics for the next century. Count Vivian, the lay abbot of Tours, was in the meantime appointed to administer the lower Loire west of Tours in place of the Widonids.

Another family, the Rorgonids (see above p. 184) dominated the county of Maine, and administered the region as the king's officials when Charles the Bald decided against entrusting the *ducatus Cenomannicus* to his unsatisfactory son Louis the Stammerer. When in 862 the Rorgonids instigated the revolt of Louis the Stammerer against his father, the direction of the *ducatus Cenomannicus* and the Breton march was conferred on Robert the Strong, count of Angers Thus the whole region of Neustria was under one man.[15] In 865, Charles the Bald decided to place Louis the Stammerer in charge of Neustria and gave him the title of king, the county of Angers and the abbacy of Marmoutier. The last two named were almost certainly taken from Robert the Strong who was compensated with the counties of Autun and Nevers. Within a year Charles the Bald had regretted the appointment of his son; the Neustrian command and the defence of the region against the Northmen were re-entrusted to Robert the Strong. In addition, Robert was made the lay abbot of St Martin of Tours and the *honores* of the region were distributed among his followers.

It is Robert the Strong who gave his name to the Robertian family which was to play such a prominent part in Frankish politics from the end of the ninth century, and which, as the Capetians, ruled France from 987 to 1789. Robert the Strong was one of Charles the Bald's 'new men' and little is known of his family before Robert first appears in the sources.[16] There seems to have been some connection with the Mainz region and also consanguinity with the family of Count Odo of Tours. Tours was in fact for a long time the heart of Robertian territory. Robert the Strong had two sons, Odo and Robert. When Robert was killed at Brissarthe in 866 while fighting the Vikings, the two boys were still children. Although they were given some of their father's possessions, namely the counties of Blois and Nantes, the bulk of the Robertian land and all his offices were handed over to the Welf Hugh the Abbot, together with the responsibility to conduct the defence against Viking attack.

It was not until the death of Hugh the Abbot in 886 that Odo, eldest son of Robert the Strong, was able to regain his father's offices and lands (namely, the Loire counties of Angers, Tours, Blois and Orleans and many rich abbacies, including that of St Martin of Tours). These were restored to him by the Emperor Charles the Fat after Odo, as count of Paris (since 882), had distinguished himself in the defence of his city when it was besieged by the Vikings during the winter of 885–6. Odo, with his adherents, was among those who had backed Charles the Fat's rule in the west Frankish kingdom. Charles, according to Regino of Prüm, placed Odo in charge of the *ducatus regni*, hitherto administered by Hugh the Abbot. It is important to note that Odo was not made *dux* as such (the title *dux* was only used from the tenth century). That such an appointment was possible was due indirectly to Hugh the Abbot, who had greatly extended the position he had acquired in 866. He became virtually the official defender of the kingdom, fighting Vikings in both the Loire and Scheldt regions, and accustomed the Franks to the existence of a magnate based in Neustria of great military ability, landed wealth and power. A few charters witness to Odo's patronage of the monastery of Tours.[17] Odo was by this time abbot of Tours, and his patronage of the monastery could be interpreted as an attempt to put some of his own possessions out of the reach of his enemies or rivals. Quite apart from the counties acquired in 886, Odo had managed to build up a large concentration of power in the north of the kingdom, as the number of his vassals indicates.[18]

When Charles the Fat was deposed in 887 therefore, Odo in many ways, despite his not being a Carolingian, was, as the most powerful noble of proven martial ability who had been trusted by the Emperor, the most obvious candidate for the throne. Certainly part of the nobility in Neustria, including many of Odo's own vassals, and in Francia (the area between the Meuse and the Seine) thought so (they were led by Count Theuderic of Vermandois), but they encountered forceful opposition from Fulk, archbishop of Rheims, and his supporters. Our sole information about Fulk's origins and early career is derived from Flodoard, who tells us that Fulk was of noble birth and related to the

Widonids.[19] Fulk was one of the party who accompanied Charles the Bald to Rome in 877 and was probably therefore a member of the palace chapel. In 877 Fulk was made abbot of St Bertin and did his utmost to construct fortifications for his abbey. Soon after the death of Hincmar in December 882, Fulk, backed in all probability by Hugh the Abbot, was consecrated archbishop of Rheims and received the pallium from Pope Marinus.[20] It is clear that Fulk had every intention of continuing Hincmar's policies with regard both to Rheims and the king, and that his political machinations were not entirely motivated by his loyal attachment to the Carolingian family.

Fulk's candidate for the throne indeed was his own relative Guy of Spoleto,[21] though it is not clear how warm Fulk's support was; it certainly cooled rapidly. It is also uncertain how much Wido's attempt to gain the throne was on his own initiative rather than being prompted by Fulk. Guy had gathered to himself some adherents from among the Franco-Burgundian nobility and was crowned king at Langres in early March 888 by Bishop Geilo. In the meantime Odo forestalled Fulk and his cronies, Baldwin II, count of Flanders, and Ralph, abbot of St Bertin, by personally seeking Arnulf's recognition at Worms in gundy.[22] Guy retired back to Italy, accompanied by some of his Burgundian supporters, in order to contest Berengar of Friuli's authority there. Fulk had sought to win over the east Frankish ruler Arnulf to Guy's cause and once Guy had retreated asked Arnulf himself to rule the western kingdom. (It is possible that Fulk's attempts to conciliate Arnulf, both in 888 and in 892, had something to do with Fulk's wish to re-establish Rheims' control over the diocese of Cambrai and lands belonging to Rheims which had been since 843, apart from a brief period between 870 and 880, part of the kingdom of Lotharingia.) Odo forestalled Fulk and his cronies, Baldwin II, count of Flanders, and Ralph, abbot of St Bertin, by personally seeking Arnulf's recognition at Worms in August 888. The Annals of Fulda state that Odo wanted Arnulf's recognition and commended himself to him because he knew he could hardly expect a peaceful reign without it. If the annalist was right, then this is the first indication we have of the close interest on the part of the east Frankish ruler in west Frankish affairs. The relationship established between Arnulf and Odo at Worms in 888 does not seem to have been anything more than a formal recognition on Odo's part of Arnulf's superiority; Odo did not undertake any of the usual obligations of a vassal and the political autonomy of the west Frankish kingdom remained undisturbed.[23]

By his acknowledgement of Odo Arnulf was, however, guaranteed the right to exert an influence in the west Frankish kingdom, and the idea that all the Frankish kingdoms were part of a loose unity, upheld on Charles the Fat's selection as king, was preserved. Peace betweeen the two kingdoms, moreover, was assured. At the end of 888, Odo met legates from Arnulf who, according to the Annals of St Vaast, presented him with a crown. At Rheims on 13 November Odo was crowned again, possibly with this crown, by Archbishop Fulk. Odo's recoronation may have had little to do with Arnulf's recognition but more with Fulk's decision to accept Odo and stake Rheims' claim to constitute kings, thereby implying that the archbishop of Sens' coronation was insufficient. Rheims had no clear right yet to consecrate kings, though Hincmar had tried to assert it; of the twelve Frankish kings anointed between 840 and 987, only five (Louis the Stammerer, Charles the Simple, Louis IV, Lothar and Louis V) were anointed by the archbishops of Rheims. Fulk's move is a further instance of the rivalry between the sees of Sens and Rheims which was to become so marked in the second half of the tenth century.

One of the difficulties in tracing the developments of Odo's reign with any precision is the meagreness of the sources. An essential source for the history of Odo's reign is the pro-Robertian Annals of St Vaast which cover the period 874–900. It has the disadvantage, however, that it is concerned almost exclusively with events in the north of the kingdom. Richer, writing in about 998, is on the other hand, despite his muddled chronology, of importance for the small amount he tells us about Odo's activities in Aquitaine. Regino's Chronicle and the Annals of Fulda refer to Odo occasionally in relation to Arnulf; and Flodoard, writing his history of the church of Rheims in about 948, throws interesting light on the political relations between Fulk and the Robertian king. Abbo's poem on the siege of Paris, written in 888 or 889, gives a glowing picture of Odo's valour and the high hopes for the new king at the beginning of his reign rather than useful information. Only the fifty-four (fifteen more are known to have existed) charters issued during Odo's reign are of real value in estimating the effectiveness of Odo's kingship as well as for mapping his movements.[24]

For much of the first few years of his reign, Odo vindicated his election as king by conducting the defence of his kingdom against the Vikings. He won a notable victory against the pirates in June 888, but further raids are recorded, later that year on Meaux as well as in 889, 890 and 891. In 889, Odo was obliged to pay tribute to the Vikings (for what tactical reasons is not known, but he may have wished to deploy his army elsewhere) and in 892 the Vikings left Francia.[25]

Odo also attempted to consolidate his position in the west Frankish kingdom and turned his attention to Aquitaine, Septimania and the Spanish march, the only regions to have failed so far to acknowledge Odo's suzerainty. Since 877, royal authority in Aquitaine had weakened and a number of powerful noble families had emerged who had little inclination to be subservient to the Carolingian kings. When Odo came to the throne the count of Gothia and of the Auvergne was William the Pious (886–918), who had inherited these counties after the death of his father Bernard Hairyfeet in 886. Wifrid the Hairy was count of Barcelona and of the Spanish march, and most of the rest of Aquitaine was ruled by Ramnulf II, count of Poitiers, the last mentioned in the Fulda annalist's catalogue of petty kings. Ramnulf, grandson of Louis the Pious through his mother Hildegard, had acquired considerable power in Aquitaine. It is possible that he had entertained hopes of gaining the throne of the west Frankish kingdom for himself.[26] As Charles the Simple had been resident at his court since 888,[27] Ramnulf may also have nurtured an ambition to press Charles the Simple's claim: Ramnulf's partisanship therefore was vital to Odo.

Early in 889, Odo set out for Aquitaine and in June called an assembly at

Orleans. A number of charters – the largest series his chancery produced – were solicited by the participants, and these certainly give the impression that a number of the lay and ecclesiastical magnates of Aquitaine and Septimania rallied to Odo, if only to acknowledge him as a remote patron and source of protection and favour.[28] It was during this visit that Odo appears to have gained the acknowledgement of his kingship from Ramnulf II and William of the Auvergne. By the end of 889, Odo had been recognized in the dioceses of Langres, Chalon-sur-Saône, Mâcon and most of the former kingdom of Carloman. During a later visit to Aquitaine in 892–3, moreover, his charters witness to the fact that Odo intervened effectively in Berry, Le Puy, Brioude, Auvergne, Limoges, Angoulême and Périgueux. Richer comments that the king concerned himself with matters of 'public interest' as well as with the affairs of the nobility. Odo's efforts to extend Frankish royal authority in Aquitaine were the last to be made by any west Frankish ruler during the Carolingian period which met with much success. It was to be three centuries before Aquitaine was once more close to the French crown.[29]

Odo made no alteration to the nature and function of Carolingian kingship. He did not attempt to continue his administration of the regions over which he had been count before his elevation to the throne. These, together with the abbacy of St Martin, he relinquished to his brother Robert, who, because Odo's only son had died in infancy, became in effect Odo's heir.[30] The first time Robert is called *marchio* (marquis) in the sources is in 893, and by this time the title no longer meant count of the march but the king's official over all the counts in the part of the kingdom assigned to him (in this case, Neustria).[31] Odo continued to shower offices and honours on Robert and has been accused, both by contemporaries and modern scholars, of using his royal power to enhance the position of his own family, as if this were a new practice. But the Carolingians had also done so. Nevertheless, the nature of Odo's activities as king generally suggest that his entrusting of so much to Robert, his most loyal follower, was not just promoting family interests but was Odo's best way of making his position secure. When Ramnulf II, count of Poitou died, for example, Odo attempted to give the office to his brother. But this provoked the revolt in Aquitaine not only of the Robertian cousin Ademar, but also of the uncles of Ramnulf's young son Ebalus (Fr. Ebles) Gauzbert and Ebalus, lay abbot of St Denis and St Germain-des-Prés, Odo's chancellor.

There had already been other indications that Odo was not going to be allowed to rule unopposed and here Regino's comment about the equality of power among the Frankish nobles is pertinent.[32] In 890, Louis of Provence, with Arnulf's approval, had been elected king in Provence and a group of Frankish nobles had again invited Guy of Spoleto to take over the west Frankish kingdom. Fulk did not support his relative this time and nothing came of the scheme. In 892, Baldwin II had declared himself against Odo and with the connivance of Count Waltger of Laon had entrenched himself in that city. The immediate cause of this revolt seems to have been Baldwin's disappointment over not being given the abbacy of St Vaast on the death of the former abbot Ralph. The consequences of this dispute have already been related (above

p. 250), but the incident is of further interest. Fulk, with remarkable two-facedness, threatened Baldwin with excommunication and reproached him for betraying his oath of fidelity to the king.[33] After Odo recaptured Laon he had Waltger, his unfaithful count, beheaded. According to a haughty letter from Archbishop Fulk to Bishop Dido of Laon, Waltger had also been refused the last rites by his bishop. Fulk protested at the fate of Waltger's soul (there is little pity for his body) and upbraided Dido for withholding his blessing.[34] It is clear that Fulk blamed Odo for forcing Dido to act contrary to his vows and nursed a grievance against Odo for his coercion of one of his suffragans.

Friction between Odo and Fulk was enhanced further by Fulk's contest with Odo over the episcopal election to the see of Langres in which Fulk succeeded in gaining the see for Teutbald, a member of the Carolingian family, and overrode the claims of Argrim, an adherent of Odo.[35] It was Fulk who led the third and most serious revolt against Odo in January 893. He was joined by Askeric, bishop of Paris (who had been appointed chancellor in Ebalus' place on 30 September 892), Herbert (a grandson in the male line of Bernard, king of Italy, who had been blinded on Louis the Pious' orders in 817), some minor northern counts and probably some members of the family of Adelheid, Charles the Simple's mother. On 28 January, 893, Fulk crowned Charles the Simple, now thirteen years old, at Rheims. Fulk and Herbert probably calculated on governing the kingdom themselves while Askeric maintained the chancery. In response to an eloquent letter from Fulk promising him superiority over the kingdom of Charles the Simple, his cousin, Arnulf was induced to recognize Charles,[36] and from Flodoard we learn that Fulk also succeeded in gaining the approval of Pope Formosus, though Fulk himself had not hitherto enjoyed very cordial relations with Rome. Formosus nevertheless seized the opportunity to deliver sententious, and gratuitous, advice on how best to rule the kingdom.[37] There seems to be no clear evidence that Odo was formally deposed; even Fulk did not say Odo had usurped the throne but simply that he had abused royal power.[38] Fulk may have been referring to Odo's advancement of his family interests, but it is more likely that he had in mind Odo's attempts to interfere in ecclesiastical affairs.

Suprisingly placid at the news of this coup, Odo remained in Aquitaine for another nine months. One can only conclude that Odo was fairly confident that support for Charles the Simple and Fulk was confined to the far north of the kingdom, in Flanders, Vermandois and the cities close to Rheims, and that the settlement of Aquitainian affairs had a higher priority. Neustria in the meantime remained loyal to Odo, as did a number of the bishops in Francia, such as Dido of Laon and Honoratus of Beauvais, some counts and possibly the monastery of St Medard of Soissons. In the south-east Franco, bishop of Nevers and Adalgar, bishop of Autun (who replaced Askeric as chancellor) were among Odo's staunch supporters. Odo also gained the acknowledgement at least of Richard the Justiciar who had at first joined Fulk's party.

Richard, count of Autun and brother of Boso of Provence, exploited the situation created by Fulk's coup and formed an alliance with his nephew and most powerful vassal Manasses in order to oust Robertian influence from the area of Burgundy he administered. (This comprised the counties of Avallon, Auxerre, Langres, Mâcon, Chalon-sur-Saône, Autun, Auxois, Lassois, Barrois, Tonnerrois, the country between the Saône, Vingeane and Tille rivers, and after 895, Sens and Troyes.) Under Richard the area became an autonomous and hereditary 'duchy'. His reputation for political acumen and ruthlessness was enhanced by successes against the Vikings and the internal organization he imposed within his territory. It was for the latter he later earned the epithet 'the Justiciar'. Richard, confident in his strength and position by 895, was prepared to recognize Odo as king. After Odo's death Richard gained supremacy over the counts of Burgundy and the title and functions of *marchio*. He dominated the bishoprics and counties of Burgundy and his residence acquired the character of a court. In the last year of his life (921) his charters give him the title *dux et princeps*. The emergence of the *marchio* and *dux* in Burgundy was one of the most important long-term consequences of the struggle between Odo and Charles the Simple.

Once assured of the fidelity of Ademar, the new count of Poitou, and the neutrality of William of the Auvergne, Odo returned to Francia and besieged Rheims. Charles the Simple fled, though he continued to contest Odo's right to the throne for the next two years. He was backed briefly by Zwentibold of Lotharingia in 895, but the ranks of his supporters dwindled away steadily. In his desperation, Charles even contemplated an alliance with the Vikings, but was dissuaded from taking such a drastic step by Fulk on the grounds that it would alienate what Frankish support Charles had left.[39] Odo swiftly gained the upper hand and in 895 succeeded in regaining Arnulf's recognition. Here the Annals of Fulda and Regino report that Odo went to Arnulf bearing gifts. The gift of Charles the Bald's magnificent *Codex Aureus* (Clm 14000) and the bejewelled gold ciborium (now in the Schatzkammer der Residenz in Munich) is probably to be associated with this visit rather than with that of 888 as it usually is.[40] That the annals specifically refer to gifts being made in 895 and do not do so in 888 is of course not necessarily conclusive, but Odo's position was far less secure in 895 and his need of Arnulf's support the greater.

By the end of 895 Charles the Simple had lost all his adherents. Even Archbishop Fulk, Herbert (made count of Vermandois by Odo in 896) and Baldwin of Flanders had been won over. Peace was concluded between Odo and Charles the Simple in 896-7. Charles recognized Odo's right to rule and was allotted the city of Laon and its environs as a refuge. The Annals of St Vaast's version of the agreement of 897 is usually interpreted as an undertaking on Odo's part to propose Charles the Simple as his successor; it is notable that Robert, Odo's brother, was subsequently loyal in his support of Charles. On his death-bed, Odo begged all the magnates to stay loyal to Charles.[41] He died on 1 January 898 and was buried at St Denis.[42]

VI

In the earlier part of his reign Odo had continued to employ the traditional

Carolingian forms of administration. He called a succession of assemblies and synods – at Orleans in June 889, Meung-sur-Loire in July 891 and at Verberie in the summer of 892 – and maintained the system of counts as royal agents revocable, movable and non-hereditary. There are instances of his successful exercise of royal rights in relation to the counties, such as his execution of Count Waltger and the appointment of Ademar to the county of Poitou, but like Charles the Bald, Odo relied heavily on a number of powerful men, the *marchiones*, with authority over a large area comprising a number of counties, such as his brother Robert in Neustria. The itinerary indicated by his charters reveals that Odo more often than not resided in walled towns or abbeys close to towns rather than in the rural palaces as his predecessors had done.

Odo also took over the Carolingian royal chancery. Ebalus, abbot of St Denis, Askeric, bishop of Paris, Adalgar, bishop of Autun and a former notary in the chancery of Charles the Bald, and Walter, archbishop of Sens, acted as his chancellors in turn while the chancery was run in the early years by Throannus, later bishop of Orleans. On Odo's succession, some mistakes in charter protocol and format suggest that notarial training and chancery practice had grown rather lax since Charles the Bald's death. Throannus appears to have succeeded in imposing new discipline in the chancery, for later charters are much improved, and better than they were to be ever again under the last Carolingians. Tironian notes appear for the last time in a charter dated 13 June 889, which suggests that this branch of notarial knowledge died out after that. Even in Odo's time Heriveus and Arnulf, the notaries who succeeded Throannus, were less rigorous in their standards than their predecessor.

The greater proportion of Odo's charters are those making gifts to episcopal churches, monasteries and *fideles*, though he also restored rights to property, confirmed the possession of property given by an earlier ruler and confirmed royal protection and immunity. In most cases where Odo confirmed the latter two privileges to monasteries he also conceded the right to elect the abbot freely, but he did not do so in the cases of Vézelay, St Germain of Auxerre, St Vaast and St Martin of Tours. These were abbacies usually granted to a layman. Most of Odo's charters were drawn up in response to requests, but one, for his *fidelis* Ricbod, was a spontaneous gift on Odo's part. The document, which survives in the original (London BL Add. Charters 8516) is remarkable in that it bears a splendid wax seal in perfect condition containing a profile portrait of a king.[43] This is the sole surviving seal from Odo's reign. With four possible exceptions, the surviving charters of Odo's reign appear to have been drawn up in the royal chancery rather than in the abbey concerned.[44] Of further interest is the extension of immunity to the *castellae* constructed by such abbeys as St Vaast, Vézelay and St Philibert of Tournus.[45] Land and houses were acquired as refuges furthermore by suburban monasteries inside the town walls of Tours, Auxerre and Sens by the monasteries of St Martin, St Germain and St Columba respectively.[46] Both Langres and St Philibert were granted the right to mint coins,[47] but generally Odo did not concede regalian rights.

The number of charters issued from Odo's chancery decreased considerably in the second part of his reign, but so it does for the later part of the reigns of every other Carolingian king, simply because it was at the beginning of a new reign that the ecclesiastical magnates sought the renewal of their privileges and grants. Nevertheless the drop is dramatic; twenty-five charters were produced between June 889 and June 890 and only eight charters were produced after 893. Altogether the charters issued by Odo suggest that the king was still in a position to be generous even if he was careful in the exercise of his munificence. The geographical distribution of the charters – Neustria (14), Spanish march and Septimania (13), Burgundy (11) and the ecclesiastical province of Rheims (9) – witness to the soliciting of royal favour in all parts of the west Frankish kingdom and to a continuing respect for royal authority. The charters also reveal something of Odo's policy towards the church.

Odo had promised at his coronation in 888 to preserve the privileges of the church, to maintain law and justice, to protect the church against predators and oppressors and defend ecclesiastical property with the strength given him by God.[48] The bishops in their turn promised aid and counsel. Both parties kept their promises to some extent. Odo's administration was run by bishops and clerics and their support was crucial for the maintenance of his authority. The church was the chief beneficiary of the grants of land and privileges made by Odo during his reign. Odo also used the church as all the Frankish rulers had used it: lay abbacies of important and wealthy monasteries were granted to the leading magnates among his followers, just as Odo himself had acquired the abbacies of St Martin of Tours and Marmoutier from Charles the Fat while still count of Paris. That charters of St Julian of Brioude, under the lay abbacy of William of the Auvergne, are dated according to Odo's regnal years, has been interpreted as indicating that St Julian too was loyal to Odo. The Robertians seem in fact to have consolidated their power with the acquisition of lay abbacies, though the evidence for this is equivocal. After Odo's elevation to the throne, Odo gave his countships and his abbacies to his brother Robert; Robert thus became abbot of St Martin and of Marmoutier at Tours[49] and St Aignan at Orleans. When Ebalus, abbot of St Denis and St Germain-des-Prés, was killed in 892, Odo himself seems to have become abbot of St Denis, as Charles the Bald had done before him, while St Germain-des-Prés was granted to Hucbold. St Hilary of Poitiers was granted to Bishop Ecfrid of Poitiers in 892. Between 903 and 918 at least, Robert is named as abbot of St Germain, after 903 he is also abbot of St Denis and at about the same time he is mentioned as abbot of St Amand and of Morienval. What is not clear is whether it was Odo who gave Robert these abbacies between 888 and 898 or Charles the Simple after 898.

The Annals of St Vaast imply that there was a close relationship between Odo and St Vaast in the earlier part of his reign. Odo's chief opponents also controlled powerful abbacies, such as those of St Bertin, St Germain of Auxerre, St Crépin at Soissons and St Columba of Sens. After Fulk's coup, Charles the Simple endeavoured to reduce the number of monasteries controlled by the Robertians; he tried for example, but without success, to appoint Fulk to the abbacy of St Martin which was held by Robert. Odo also attempted to put his own candidates in particular sees, such as Langres and Chalon-sur-Saône, though here he was outwitted by Fulk. Other bishops, such as Dido of Laon and Honoratus of Beauvais, remained Odo's staunch supporters throughout his reign.

The merits of Odo's reign should not be exaggerated, though it was far from being a failure. He left the west Frankish monarchy in a stronger position than it had been on his accession, as well as suggesting a pattern for its survival. Odo maintained much of the structure of the Carolingian administration, achieved a number of notable successes against the Vikings which halted their advance southwards, and secured, at the price of recognizing Arnulf as a superior, west Frankish independence of the east Frankish kingdom. Yet Odo's election by the nobles in 888 and the subsequent necessity for the support of the lay and ecclesiastical magnates for the maintenance of his position developed still further the relationship between king and nobility which we saw in its rudimentary stages under Charles the Bald. It was still not clearly defined. The structure of the kingdom itself was altering; the west Frankish kingdom was becoming a collection of territorial principalities, ruled by *marchiones* who in their turn had authority over the counts in their respective regions. The *marchiones* acted as intermediaries; the king's rule in the territorial principalities – Brittany, Flanders, Aquitaine, Burgundy, Provence and Neustria – was no longer direct. Yet the monarchy was retained, and apart from a short period between 923 and 936, it was the Carolingians who sat on the throne for the next century, even though a precedent had been set for non-Carolingian rule. Moreover, while Odo's reign had meant the establishment of Robertian power and influence and the acquisition by them of royal fiscal lands alienated by Odo to Robert, the Robertian family was not always in the ascendant thereafter. As we shall see in the last chapter of this book, the Robertians were simply among a large group of principals in the political developments of the west Frankish kingdom in the tenth century.

NOTES

1. *Annales Bertiniani, s.a.*, 877.
2. K. F. Werner, 'Gauzlin von Saint-Denis und die westfränkische Reichsteilung von Amiens (März 880). Ein Beitrag zur Vorgeschichte von Odos Königtum', *DA* 35 (1979), 395–462.
3. Ibid.
4. R. Poupardin (ed.), *Recueil des Actes des rois de Provence* (Paris 1920), No. 16, 31–33.
5. *MGH Cap.* II, 365–7. Compare the hostile account in *Annales Bertiniani, s.a.*, 879.
6. R. H. Bautier, 'Aux origines du royaume de Provence. De la sédition avortée de Boson à la royauté légitime de Louis', *Provence Historique* 23 (1973) 41–68.
7. H. Lowe, 'Geschichtsschreibung der ausgehenden Karolingerzeit', *DA* 23(1967), 1–30, and 'Das Karlsbuch Notkers von St Gallen und sein zeitgeschichtlichen Hintergrund', *Schweizerische Zeitschrift für Geschichte* 20(1970), 269–302.
8. Richer, I, 4.

9. On Regino see the comments by D. Bullough, 'The continental background to reform', *Tenth Century Studies*, D. Parsons (ed.) (Winchester 1975), 20–36, and the studies by H. Lowe, 'Regino von Prüm und das historische Weltbild der Karolingerzeit', *RhV* 17 (1952), 151–79 and K. F. Werner, 'Zur Arbeitskreise Reginos von Prüm', *Welt als Geschichte* 19 (1959), 96–116.

10. For a succinct summary of Italian politics in the tenth century, see C. Wickham, *Early Medieval Italy 400–1000* (London 1981), 168–81. See too E. Hlawitschka, *Franken, Alemannen, Bayern und Burgunder in Oberitalien (774–962)* (Freiburg 1960).

11. See the exchange between Hlawitschka and Schlesinger in *HZ* 208 (1969), 775–85 and L. Boehm, 'Rechtsformen und Rechtstitel der Burgundischen Königserhebungen im 9.Jht. Zur Krise der Karolingische Dynastie', *HJ* 80 (1961), 1–59, esp. 9–10.

12. Bautier, 'Aux origines du royaume de Provence'.

13. Liutprand, *Antapodosis*, III, 48. See also R. Poupardin, *Le royaume de Provence sous les Carolingiens 855–933* (Paris 1901), 59 and J.-P. Poly, *La Provence et la société féodale 879–1116* (Paris 1976), 30–8.

14. J. Boussard, 'Les destinées de la Neustrie du IX⁰ au XI⁰ siècles', *Cahiers de civilisation médiévale* 11 (1968), 15–28.

15. F. Lot, 'Le Loire, l'Aquitaine et la Seine 862–866: Robert le Fort', *BEC* 76 (1915), 473–510.

16. See K. F. Werner, 'Untersuchungen zur Frühzeit des französischen Fürstentums (9–10 Jht.)', *Welt als Geschichte* 19 (1959), 146–93.

17. Ibid.; his patronage continued after he became king. See Odo, *Recueil*, Nos. 9, 19, 41, 55 and 56.

18. See Werner, 'Untersuchung', 169–81.

19. Flodoard, *Historia*, IV, 1.

20. See the discussion by G. Schneider, *Fulk, Erzbischof von Reims 882–900* (Munich, 1973), 22–49.

21. *Annales Vedastini*, *s.a.*, 888.

22. Ibid., and see Abbo, *Bella Parisiacae urbis*, II, lines 442–51.

23. Flodoard, *Historia*, IV, 5 records that Fulk called Odo 'Arnulf's man'.

24. See the excellent edition by R. H. Bautier of Odo's charters.

25. See the entries in the *Annales Vedastini* for these years.

26. *Annales Fuldenses*, *s.a.*, 888, and E. Favre, *Eudes comte de Paris et roi de France* (Paris 1893), 122, n. 1 and compare 152.

27. *Annales Vedastini*, *s.a.*, 889.

28. Compare R. H. Bautier, 'Le règne d'Eudes (888–898) à la lumière des diplômes expédiés par sa chancellerie', *Académie des Inscriptions et Belles Lettres. Comptes rendus de séance de l'année* 1961, 141–57.

29. L. Auzias, *L'Aquitaine Carolingienne 778–987* (Toulouse–Paris 1937), and W. Kienast, 'Die Wirkungsbereich des französischen Königtums von Odo bis Ludwig VI (888–1137) in Südfrankreich', *HZ* 209 (1969), 529–65.

30. On Odo's son see K. F. Werner, *Handbuch der europäische Geschichte* I, T. Schieder (ed.), (Stuttgart 1976), 744, n. 4.

31. The famous charter in which Robert is described as *dux francorum* (Odo, *Recueil*, No. 53) is apparently a forgery; thus there are no grounds for supposing that this title was granted to Robert.

32. Regino, *Chronicon*, *s.a.*, 888.

33. Flodoard, *Historia*, IV, 7 and compare Favre, *Eudes*, 141–3.

34. Flodoard, *Historia*, IV, 6.
35. Ibid., IV, 1 and see Schneider, *Fulk von Reims*, 82–9, 94–5. Fulk also had his own nominee Mancio, of evil repute, appointed to the see of Châlons-sur-Marne in 893. Even the Pope thought this was going too far; see Flodoard, *Historia*, IV, 6.
36. Ibid., IV, 3 and Favre, *Eudes*, 163.
37. Flodoard, *Historia*, IV, 3.
38. Ibid., IV, 3.
39. Ibid., IV, 5.
40. See P. E. Schramm and F. Mütherich, *Denkmale der Deutschen Könige und Kaiser* (Munich 1962), Nos. 52, 60 and 61; O. Werckmeister, *Der Deckel des Codex Aureus von St Emmeram. Ein Goldschmiedewerk des 9. Jahrhunderts* (Baden-Baden and Strasbourg 1963) and R. Otto, 'Zur stilgeschichtliche Stellung des Arnulfs-Ciborium und des Codex Aureus aus St Emmeram in Regensburg', *Zeitschrift für Kunstgeschichte* 50 (1952), 1–16.
41. *Annales Vedastini. s.a.*, 897.
42. The 2nd and 3rd of January have also been proposed as possible dates by R. H. Bautier, *Recueil des Actes d'Eudes* (Paris 1967), clvii, n. 1.
43. Odo, *Recueil*, No. 3, 12–15 and illustrated Plate I.
44. The exceptions are Odo, *Recueil*, Nos. 36, 41, 35 and 16. See Bautier's Introduction, lxvi–lxvii.
45. Odo, *Recueil*, Nos, 20, 10 and 13.
46. Ibid., Nos. 41, 11 and 25.
47. Ibid., Nos. 15 and 13.
48. Bouquet, *Recueil*, IX, 314.
49. See K. Voigt, *Karolingische Klosterpolitik* (Stuttgart 1917), 109, n. 1.

CHAPTER ELEVEN

Learning and Monasticism in the Tenth Century

A thorough reappraisal of the period *c.* 880 to *c.* 1050, usually regarded as the darkest and most unproductive of times, is not possible at present, owing to the amount of work that still needs to be done or assessed on such general issues as monasticism and monastic renewal, book production, the extent of lay patronage and new intellectual developments in the spheres of philosophy and logic, mathematics and music. Far from being sterile, this was a vital period of transition; many of its achievements and institutions had their roots in the earlier Carolingian period and bore fruit in the eleventh and twelfth centuries.

I

Between the death of Charles the Bald and the consolidation of authority by the Saxon kings in east Francia and Germany towards the end of the tenth century, the political situation was such that kings at least were rarely in as strong a position as their forebears had been to act as patrons. The last pieces of literature actually associated with the Carolingian court appeared in the reigns of Louis the Stammerer and Carloman and these are of a purely practical nature, such as the *De ordine palatii* of Hincmar of Rheims. We know nothing of the education of Louis III and Carloman, and although according to Richer Charles the Simple had been instructed in the liberal arts, possibly at Rheims, we know of no works dedicated to him, nor do we have any indication of a literary culture associated with his court. Charles' son Louis IV was brought up in England, but his literary education was neglected. Although Louis may not have been completely illiterate, he knew no Latin. His wife Gerberga on the other hand, sister to Otto I, was both intelligent and educated. She commissioned from Adso of Moutier-en-Der, for example, a work entitled *De ortu et tempore antichristi*, and it was no doubt due to his mother's influence that her son Lothar undertook some studies under the supervision of his maternal uncle,

Bruno, archbishop of Cologne. No intellectual activity, however, can be traced to the courts of Lothar, Louis V or indeed Charles of Lorraine. As for the Capetians, although Hugh the Great and Hugh Capet were pious and favourable towards monasticism, the Capetian court appears not to have promoted letters to any degree until the reign of Robert the Pious (d. 1031). The fate of the royal library of the Carolingians which, according to Charles the Bald's Capitulary of Quierzy in 877, was divided into three between Louis the Stammerer, St Mary's monastery at Compiègne and St Denis, is unknown, though gifts from it appear to have been made by Odo to Arnulf at least. If kings no longer interested themselves in culture, the monasteries and cathedral chapters which had emerged in the course of the ninth century as centres of both cultural and political influence still maintained learning and scholarship. In the territorial principalities there was noble and episcopal patronage as well, which was particularly evident in the promotion of monasticism.

II

The reforms of Benedict of Aniane and Louis the Pious are often assumed to have died with them; but, as we saw in Chapter Five, there is evidence that particular houses adopted either the canons' ordinances or those for monks published in 816 and 817 and that the Rule of St Benedict became established as the most important guide for the monastic life, even though a diversity of monastic custom undoubtedly continued. The nature of our sources makes it difficult to chart the observance of any particular monastery throughout the ninth century, and this sort of study has in fact rarely been undertaken, so that it is not possible to determine with any exactitude the extent to which monasticism as a whole was in need of reform by the tenth century. In particular cases, such as St Bertin, there is evidence that discipline had grown lax and there was also probably some feeling that canons occupied too many of the main monasteries – they were installed at St Denis and Tours among others – and that a pure monastic observance ought to be reintroduced.

In the second half of the ninth century we hear little about religious leaders who could inspire their brethren with a pure monastic ideal. Nevertheless, the texts of the founding charters of some houses established at this time, such as Charles the Bald's charter for Compiègne, or Gerald's foundation at Aurillac, or of charters making grants to particular houses, suggest that there was still as much fervour for the monastic life and the opportunity to save one's soul as there had been in the first half of the ninth century. Indeed, the monastic renewal in tenth-century Burgundy and Lotharingia itself, generally interpreted as proof of the decline in religious life, could be regarded as testimony to considerable vigour. Yet the policies of the Carolingian rulers, particularly Charles the Bald and his successors, meant that too many monasteries had had vital revenues and lands appropriated, and too many had come into the power of laymen. A lay abbot, as Felten has stressed, was not necessarily an evil for the monastery concerned, but the religious life and discipline of a community could be adversely affected by too great an involvement in secular affairs.[1]

The Viking attacks had undoubtedly disrupted the religious life of many centres in that the monks fled to safer retreats and in some cases, such as St Wandrille or Jumièges, abandoned their original home for many decades. Other monasteries, however, sustained and recovered from seemingly disastrous blows.[2] St Amand, for example, was sacked in the great raids of 882 and the monks took refuge at St Germain-des-Prés in Paris. When they returned to their monastery the monks of St Amand resumed life once more; the library seems to have been preserved largely intact, and the school flourished. Prüm was sacked and burnt in 882, and was given the royal domain of Neckrau by Charles the Fat in compensation for its losses. In 892 Prüm was attacked again, the abbot and monks fled and those left behind were massacred or taken captive. Yet the abbey continued to exist.

Reform in this context often meant no more than a man devoted to the monastic ideal founding a new house or by his piety and fervour inspiring with new zeal the brethren in the community of which he was already a member. In other words, reform in the early tenth century meant that monastic life was given a new sense of purpose and direction by energetic young religious; monasteries aligned themselves into new groups and found new patrons. In none of the accounts of the tenth-century saints who spread their conception of the religious life in their native regions – Gerard of Brogne, John of Gorze or Odo of Cluny – is there any hint that they had to combat great vice, worldliness or ignorance. We hear rather of their dissatisfaction and of how, for example, Odo and his friend Adhegrin found that none of the religious communities they visited quite lived up to their expectations of, and hopes for, the monastic life. It is important to remember moreover that the reinvigoration of monastic life in Burgundy and Lotharingia came from within, and that its agents built on existing religious practice. At Baume under Abbot Berno for instance, a monastery restored by Berno after its devastation by Vikings, Odo and Adhegrin found contentment.

According to John of Salerno, Baume observed the 'customs of Benedict of Aniane'.[3] This statement is of the greatest significance, for there is no reason to suppose that Baume and Berno's other foundation, Gigny, were the only monasteries in which Benedict's customs, that is the ordinances of 816/17, had been preserved; it was also the customs of Baume that were transferred to Cluny. That Cluny's tenth-century customs were based upon those of Benedict of Aniane has recently been challenged and the differences between Cluny's observance and that proposed in the 816/17 decrees stressed.[4] We are somewhat hampered in assessing Cluny's customs in its early years by the fact that the earliest extant customary dates from the early eleventh century, but from what we can gather of the liturgical observance at Cluny the balance between work, prayer, food, sleep and reading maintained in the 816/17 decrees was lost; and manual labour was redefined to embrace prayer and praise, the heavy work was done by lay brethren, serfs and servants, and the monks spent far more time in the church.[5] John of Salerno records the regular and extended observance of silence at Cluny as well as the practice of singing 138 psalms through each day rather than each week. It is unlikely that the Baume customs transmitted to Cluny would have been free of modifications in the liturgy, daily routine and diet, but in its emphasis on the Rule of St Benedict as the basis of its organization, the insistence on uniformity and the position of the abbot and the prior, and within the context of the varied response to the 816/17 decrees which had allowed a number of older Frankish customs to persist, Cluny was the true heir to the reforms of Louis the Pious and Benedict of Aniane. In this respect it was vital for the continued strength of the Carolingian monastic ideal.

Abbot Berno had achieved fame for his piety and efficient administration at Baume, and his advice was sought by Duke William of Aquitaine when the latter wished to found a monastery. The site chosen by Berno was the favourite hunting-lodge of the duke, situated in the diocese of Mâcon on lands which had belonged to William's sister Ava. William of Aquitaine had no thought of monastic reform when he founded Cluny. His donation charter, usually dated 11 September 910, states clearly that the foundation was to ensure his salvation and prayers for his soul and for the souls of the members of his family. The land was given on condition that a regular monastery be established in honour of the apostles Peter and Paul, and that the monks there, under the authority of Abbot Berno, should live according to the Rule of St Benedict.[6] William also granted the monks the freedom to elect Berno's successor from among their number and the monastery was commended to the protection, not of any lay ruler or member of William's family, or to any bishop, but to the apostles Peter and Paul and their representative the Pope. Cluny in fact was to enjoy full immunity in the technical sense, though the actual word was not used in the charter. No secular prince, count, bishop or pope was to enter the possessions of Cluny, or to sell, diminish, exchange or in any other way take anything from the monastery's property.

Much has been made of the clause making Cluny answerable to the Pope alone and free from all secular interference. The precise legal position as a result of this provision, however, is not at all clear. In practice the links established between the new monastery and Rome seem to have been very limited, and it was the elimination of future family or outside lay interference, seen against the background of the royal and noble encroachments on and interference in the affairs of the monasteries during the past century, which can be counted as the most important feature of the foundation charter.[7] As Cowdrey has pointed out, the Cluny foundation charter contained almost nothing for which there was not already a precedent.[8] The three main provisions concerning proprietorship, protection and immunity, had, as we have seen, developed gradually in the course of the ninth century. They had originally been directed towards bolstering royal authority, but as the king's power of enforcement decreased, alternative protectors were found. Members of the nobility became proprietors with greater frequency, though royal protection remained much sought after, until, in the time of Pope Nicholas I (858–67) and John VIII (872–82), the Pope's protection began to be solicited more often. In 863, for example, Gerard of Roussillon founded Vézelay, entrusted the new monastery to saints Peter and Paul, made the Pope its protector and in effect granted it immunity. Nicholas I recognized these provisions and John VIII issued privileges of a similar type for the monasteries of St Gilles de Rhône and Charroux. From the foundation of Vézelay onwards, many monasteries in Francia, Burgundy, Germany and the Spanish march, including Cluny, became the 'property' of St Peter. That Cluny ultimately became famous for its relationship with the Holy See was due not so much to the clause in its foundation charter as to what Cowdrey describes as the 'cultivation of its liberty' by the Popes and the succession of long-lived saintly abbots who ruled the abbey in the first two centuries of its history. A clearer definition of the terms of Cluny's foundation charter emerged in due course, for its rights were confirmed no less than six times in the first fifty years of its existence. Not until the eleventh century, however, was Cluny freed from the spiritual jurisdiction of the bishop.

In its early years, Cluny was a small, poorly endowed and insignificant community. When Berno died in 926 he disposed of the direction of the abbacies in his charge as if they had been his property; Wido or Guy was designated abbot of Gigny, Mouthier-en-Brisse and St Lanthier, and Odo became abbot of Cluny, Nasay and Deols. Odo had studied under Remigius of Auxerre, and learnt dialectic, logic and the liberal arts in Paris before going to Tours and finally to Baume, where he became the master of the monastery's school. Odo's writings, particularly the *Occupatio* and the *Collationes*, reveal that his monastic ideal was dominated by an almost mystical sense of intimacy with Christ, king and shepherd, and by the conviction that every aspect of the monk's daily life – the liturgy and praise, the observance of silence, celibacy, withdrawal from the world, cultivation of the state of innocence and the community of brethren blessed by the Holy Spirit – was in some sense an anticipation of the world to come and a foretaste of eternity.[9] St Martin the holy warrior was central to Odo's conception of sainthood; he wrote a number of works about St Martin, including a sermon for the saint's feast day and a hymn in his honour, and he was asked by Abbot Baldwin of St Paul's in Rome to gloss the Dialogues of Sulpicius.[10] In his life of Gerald of Aurillac, Odo depicted the Christian saint who was virtuous as a warrior for Christ rather than virtuous in spite of being a soldier. Erdmann indeed regarded Odo's attitude and his portrayal of Gerald as crucial in the sacralization of warfare and the warrior which culminated in the crusading ideal.[11]

Under Odo, Cluny began to emerge as a centre of monastic zeal and to inspire other houses with the example of its observance and religious fervour. Odo himself was called upon to direct the reinvigoration of monasteries in Burgundy and elsewhere, work which enhanced Cluny's influence rather than increasing its wealth or temporal power. Elisardius, for example, summoned Odo to Fleury, where discipline had grown lax. There Odo began to persuade the monks to give up eating meat, to eat sparingly and to possess nothing of their own. Odo also renewed the monastic discipline of the monasteries of St Gerald of Aurillac, St Pons of Thonières, St Austremoine (Clermont), St Peter le Vif at Sens, St Martin at Tulle, St Peter of Lezat, St Saviour at Sarlat, St

Martial of Limoges, St Sore de Gervouillac and St Julian at Tours. Cluniac influence was also extended to the eastern Pyrenees and into Italy. Odo was asked to take Lezat (founded 940) near Toulouse under his jurisdiction, and after his death his disciple Adasius was left in charge. In 965 Count Sunifred of Cerdanya requested Gari the abbot of Lezat to take the monastery of Cuixá (since 950 under the jurisdiction of the Holy See) into his care, and the abbot made Cuixá the centre of a new monastic congregation. A reforming abbot was also established by Gari at the monastery of St Hilary in Carcassonne. Pope John XV confirmed in 993 the position of the congregation of the monasteries of Lezat, Mas-Garnier, St Hilary, Alet and Cuixá under the jurisdiction of Gari as abbot general. Although this congregation was not dependent on Cluny, it had been inspired by Cluny and was Cluniac in spirit and methods. Members of the Cuixá congregation founded other monasteries in northern Italy. After Gari's death in 998, however, the congregation fell apart and the five main abbeys regained their independence, though Cuixá itself retained a few daughter houses.[12]

Alberic, count of Rome, invited Odo of Cluny to revive the religious life of his city in 936.[13] Forty-seven religious communities had been recorded in the city in 806, but between 844 and 915 the Popes had been obliged to entrust to secular clergy that which had hitherto been the province of monks. The three main basilicas of Rome – St Peter's, Santa Maria Maggiore and St John Lateran – were each served by three or four monasteries, but since sometime before Odo's arrival they had been staffed by canons rather than monks. No attempt was made by Odo to change the organization of these or of the five Greek monasteries remaining in Rome at this time: his activities were confined to the Latin monasteries and direct intervention is only recorded at the churches without the walls of St Paul, St Laurence and St Agnes. Baldwin was appointed abbot of St Paul's by Odo, and John, later abbot of Salerno and Odo's biographer, was made prior. The Cluniac reform in Rome seems to have made little impact apart from on those houses ruled by Baldwin and John (Monte Cassino and Salerno), and between 946 and 955 Pope Agapetus II appealed to Einold, abbot of Gorze in Lotharingia, for assistants to continue the work begun by the Cluny monks. Promotion of the reform was taken up by Count Alberic and his relatives with the co-operation of the papacy, and the rest of the Roman nobility soon followed their example. Monasteries became increasingly better endowed, the calibre of the postulants improved as the monastic life came to be held in better repute, and the Lateran administration was gradually able to free itself from lay control. Elsewhere in Italy Odo's successors at Cluny maintained a foothold. Maiol for example, with the collaboration of Queen Adelaide, wife of Otto I, founded the monastery of San Salvatore in Pavia in 971 and reformed San Pietro Ciel d'Oro in the same city in 983. Pavia continued to be a centre of Cluniac life throughout the eleventh century.

In 927, King Ralph confirmed Cluny's autonomy and granted the monastery the right to mint coins. Louis IV in 939 confirmed these privileges, adding freedom from market tithes, immunity and the right to devote the tithes to the maintenance of the hostel for pilgrims and travellers. The material prosperity of Cluny was increased under Abbot Aymard (944–65), both by exploiting existing properties better and by acquiring new ones. The fame of Cluny was now such that it attracted gifts from pious gentry, and Aymard and his successor Maiol (965–94) continued to consolidate Cluny's estates and promote the religious life of the monasteries in Gaul and Italy, including Lérins, Marmoutier, St Germain d'Auxerre, St Maur des Fosses, St Peter le Vif at Sens and St Bénigne of Dijon. In 966 Otto I and Queen Adelaide entrusted Sant' Apollinare in Classe to Maiol, and in 994 he was asked by Hugh Capet to restore monastic discipline to St Denis, but he died during the journey thither. Maiol's successor Odilo (994–1049) led Cluny to fame and power. Not until the eleventh century, however, did Cluny begin to exert the enormous influence and acquire the particular characteristics of organization, with its vast network of dependent daughter houses, which have made it famous. Until then, Cluniac houses were united only loosely and erratically in association with Cluny: some houses adopted Cluniac customs, others were directly under the jurisdiction of Cluny's abbot, others were controlled by Cluny in so far as their abbots were generally elected with the authorization of the abbot of Cluny.

The monastic revival in lower and upper Lotharingia, in contrast to Cluny, was closely associated with secular affairs; the relationship with the diocesan bishop was very important, for the principal patrons of the revival were the leading members of the aristocracy and the bishops of the province of Trier. Whereas Cluny had been a new enterprise, most of the Lotharingian developments constituted an attempt to improve an existing situation. Of significance too is the role played by the cathedral chapters; without their support and their personnel, the monastic revival would probably not have been possible. Many of the monasteries involved, particularly those of Flanders, were essential to the strengthening of the patron's political position. The principles of the initiators of the monastic revival in Lotharingia differed little from those of the leaders of Cluny (though it was not until the eleventh century that Cluniac influence reached Lotharingia through the work of William of Dijon), and were close in spirit to the reforms of Louis the Pious and Benedict of Aniane.

A number of different groups of monasteries instituted a reform in the discipline and organization of their communities in an effort to restore the Benedictine monastic rule, free communities from the evils of lay control and instil the brethren with a new religious fervour. Most of Gerard of Brogne's activity, for example, was concentrated in Flanders where his patron was Count Arnulf I. Gerard (d. 958) founded a small monastic community on his own property near Namur in 913 or 914, and obtained for his house the relics of Eugenius of Toledo. Very little is known of the early years of Gerard's foundation, apart from the fact that he built a church, but he seems to have had a close connection with St Denis, and it was in Paris that he was ordained deacon in 922 and priest five years later. Wollasch has suggested that St Denis interested itself in Gerard's foundation from the start and that it would provide an opportunity for St Denis to exert its political and religious influence in the Brogne region.[14] Gerard may well have imported some St Denis monks into Brogne. The vicissitudes of Lotharingia's political position had repercussions for Gerard's foundation and eventually loosened the connection with St Denis. Brogne was then commended to the protection of the bishop of Liège, a bishopric that was later to become part of the Ottonian kingdom, so that Brogne's affiliations thereafter tended to be towards east rather than west Francia. It is clear that Gerard had no reforming intentions in his original foundation, but his way of life and his own personal piety must have been such as to attract attention and admiration.

In 931 or 932 Gerard was summoned to restore monastic life to the canons living in the former Benedictine monastery of St Ghislain by Gilbert (Gislebert) of Hainault, at that time a supporter of Henry the Fowler. On Gilbert's death in 939 Gerard moved to Ghent at the request of Count Arnulf of Flanders, who entrusted him with the reform of St Bavo's and St Peter's in Ghent, St Bertin and St Amand. Gerard in effect became 'abbot of Flanders'. The monks of Brogne itself played very little part in Gerard's work of restoration; his chief helpers were Womar, abbot of St Peter's Ghent, Womar's successor Adalwin, and Agilo of Tours. If the direct influence of Gerard can be discerned in only a few monasteries, his indirect influence is certainly evident in Normandy, and through Dunstan, in England. Monks from both Fleury (reformed by Cluny) and Ghent (reformed by Gerard), both of which claimed inspiration from Benedict of Aniane, were at the Council of Winchester in 970 or 973, and their customs were incorporated into the *Regularis Concordia* drawn up at that meeting.[15]

To restore Benedictine observance was the aim also of the monasteries of the dioceses of Trier, Metz, Toul and Verdun in the ecclesiastical province of Trier.[16] The decay of monastic life due to secularization and the weakness of the central power is rather better attested in upper Lotharingia than elsewhere. Lothar I had been obliged to cede a number of abbeys to his followers: Adalhard, for example, was abbot of Echternach and St Maximin between 849 and 855, canons were introduced into both houses and Echternach remained in lay hands. In 856 and 863 and again from 922 to 933 Gorze had been subjected to a lay abbot. St Maximin of Trier was usurped by laymen until 933 or 934, after which it was restored by Abbot Ogo. St Martin's of Trier, St Arnulf's of Metz, Moyenmoutier and other monasteries had similar histories. Even noblewomen possessed monasteries; Theutberga, wife of Lothar II, owned the convent of St Glossinde in Metz and Richardis received the monastery of Etival from Charles the Fat. Many Lotharingian houses were occupied by canons; Echternach and St Arnulf's had been so since the middle of the ninth century, St Vanne of Verdun since 870, Moyenmoutier from 896 and Salone, Bonmoutier and Étival from about the same time. Nevertheless the picture was not entirely black; there were undoubtedly some centres in which religious life in all its dignity and regularity was preserved, for otherwise a concerted renewal could not have been effected.

Clerics from the cathedral chapters of Metz and Toul, discontented with the situation in the church in upper Lotharingia, came together in 933 at Gorze, the monastery founded by Chrodegang, to establish a communal life. Monastic life was restored by the newly appointed regular abbot Einold, formerly a member of the cathedral chapter of Toul, who, with his eight companions, determined to establish a house of austerity and strict observance of the Rule of St Benedict. The move was encouraged by Bishop Adalbero I of Metz who confirmed the aims of the community in his charter of 933, but the permanent loss of the lands once attached to Gorze had to be accepted. The community was distinguished by its great religious fervour, especially under abbots Einold and John. In 934 Gauzlin, bishop of Toul, founded a reform monastery at St Evre in Toul and monks from both Gorze and Toul were dispatched to other houses. Bishop Richer of Liège (920–45) and Ragnar II of Hainault, for example, promoted the revival of monasticism at St Hubert, Stavelot–Malmédy and Lobbes helped by Gorze monks. Gorze influence also extended to Waulsort, an Irish foundation; its first abbot Maccalan had been, for a short time at least, a monk at Gorze. Not only was the religious life revived in decayed foundations; new abbeys were founded, including Hastière, Gembloux (946), Muno (945), Waulsort (c. 946), St Laurence of Liège (before 972) and Ronquière (after 977). The Lotharingian revival soon spread its influence eastwards into Germany; Prüm and Reichenau were reformed by Abbot Immo of Gorze and Lorsch, Fulda and Corvey by Poppo of Stavelot in the eleventh century, while in Lotharingia itself the movement was given further impetus by Richard of St Vannes (1005–46).[17]

Both in their religious life and in the training grounds they offered for servants of the new kings of Germany, the monasteries and sees of Lotharingia were crucial for the preservation of the Carolingian achievement and its transmission to new heirs.[18] No less so were the monasteries and cathedral chapters of western Francia, Burgundy and Aquitaine, where monasticism and a rich spiritual life remained based upon the sound literary and religious culture cultivated in the schools. For example, Cluny's first four abbots had all been trained in the great schools of Francia. In these schools the most important of the subjects studied were philosophy and logic, music and mathematics.

III

The development of philosophy and the introduction of logic into theological discussion in the Frankish kingdoms was a gradual but continuous one from the late eighth to the tenth centuries, and was based on the study of a few texts: the writings of Boethius and Augustine and a few antique books on logic, of which the most widely used was the Categories of Aristotle. Three Latin versions of the Categories were available in the early Middle Ages: a close translation of it made by Boethius, a composite translation comprising the *lemmata* of Boethius' Commentary on the Categories with missing passages supplied by an anonymous translator, and a paraphrase known as *the Categoriae Decem* attributed erroneously to Augustine. It was from this last version that Carolingian scholars, including Ratramnus of Corbie, John Scottus Eriugena, Heiric of Auxerre and Remigius of Auxerre, knew the teaching of Aristotle. Other important texts were the *Isagoge* or Introduction to Aristotle's Categories by Porphyry, translated into Latin by Marius Victorinus and by Boethius, Boethius' own two commentaries on the *Isagoge* and the Categories, Augustine's *De Trinitate*, Book IV of Martianus Capella's *De Nuptiis*, Cassiodorus' *Institutiones* and three of Boethius' five *Opuscula Sacra*. Boethius' treatises adopted a logical approach to doctrinal controversy and were particularly influential for their explanation of how the concepts embodied in the *Categoriae Decem* were to be understood.

Aristotle's Categories and the various commentaries on and translations of it were quite simply a discussion of how all things which exist may be classified. He devised ten categories or classes into which everything could be divided: 'Of things said without any combination, each signifies either substance or quantity or qualification or a relative or where or when or being-in-a-position or having or doing or being-affected.'[19] It was a way of discussing being which gave prominence to the relationship between things, other things and their properties, and in which the function of particular words within a sentence assumed great importance. As far as the early medieval thinkers were concerned, the Categories were particularly relevant in discussions about God and his nature. Could the Categories be used to describe Him? Were there such things as Universals, that is, what was the relation of genera and species to individuals? How was essence to be discussed and what was the soul's relationship with God? The introduction of the method of thinking embodied in the Categories, and transmitted in the Carolingian period through the *Categoriae Decem*, was vital for the organization of thought in the later Carolingian period. The manuscript tradition alone attests to its wide dissemination in the ninth and tenth centuries, and that the text was closely read is indicated by the extensive glosses many of these manuscripts contain.

It seems to have been Alcuin who introduced both Boethius' discussions of logic and the *Categoriae Decem* into general circulation in the Frankish kingdom, or at least, it is in his writings that the earliest extant evidence of these works being read is to be seen.[20] Whether Alcuin did this at the court of Charlemagne, as Marenbon asserts, or at his school at Tours, as seems more likely, is not certain.[21] But Alcuin's teaching seems to have constituted the first attempt in the Carolingian period not only to understand logic and its techniques but also to apply them to the study and elucidation of theology. His own *De Dialectica* is a succinct, if derivative, manual on logic, and the early ninth-century manuscript Clm 6407, containing fifteen passages concerning the Trinity, the existence of God, the Categories and exercises in syllogistic method, as Marenbon has demonstrated, is evidence that the level of sophistication was greater than is generally allowed. Alcuin's pupils Fridugis, Candidus, Ricbod, Amalar of Trier and Hraban Maur undoubtedly passed on what elements of his teaching they could, but the continuity between Alcuin and John Scottus Eriugena and the school of Auxerre, where philosophy and logic began to come into their own, is assumed as yet rather than proven. The transmission of the Munich passages, however, is one indication of how a particular method of thinking and the texts concerned were handed down, as are the glosses on the different manuscripts of *Categoriae Decem*. Indeed the glosses continue to be added until the twelfth century. Much also was passed on through the work of John Scottus Eriugena and his followers.

Eriugena is thought to have been born in Ireland in about 810, but we know nothing of his life before he is first mentioned as being at the court of Charles the Bald in 843.[22] Prudentius, bishop of Troyes, described him as a holy man who came from Ireland and who had received no ecclesiastical orders. Probably before he arrived in the Frankish kingdom, Eriugena had acquired a knowledge of Greek. Whether he had done so in Ireland or elsewhere is not known, but it is most likely that he learnt it from the Greek monks at one of the many Greek monasteries in Rome. Eriugena's translations of a number of Greek Christian Neoplatonic writings, including those of Maximus the Confessor, pseudo-Dionysius the Areopagite and Gregory of Nyssa, would be sufficient to distinguish him from his contemporaries, had he not also left a remarkable corpus of philosophical writings.

The first public expression of Eriugena's views as a theologian and philosopher came at the request of Archbishop Hincmar of Rheims, who wanted him to refute the views of Gottschalk. Eriugena's response was the *De divina praedestinatione*, which refuted Gottschalk's views primarily on philosophical grounds. Eriugena had faith in man's power and responsibility for determining the course of his action by free will. To John, God in his oneness of essence and will was the Good. Nothing not good, that is, sin and evil, could come from God, for this would be a contradiction of his nature. Neither sin nor Hell therefore were real, as they could not come from God. Sin was the perverse action of the human will; its punishment was the soul's consciousness of lacking good.

These views and the metaphysical system they implied were a little beyond Eriugena's contemporaries; it was a way of thinking in which most of them were not interested. His Frankish colleagues, among them Prudentius of Troyes, Florus of Lyons and Hincmar of Rheims, thought indeed that his tract smelt of heresy and the work was condemned at the councils of Valence and Langres in 856. Despite this controversy Eriugena's reputation as a scholar seems to have been little impaired. He was commissioned by Charles the Bald to translate the writings of pseudo-Dionysius the Areopagite from the Greek text sent to Louis the Pious by the Emperor of Byzantium in 827.

In his *Periphyseon* or *De Divisione naturae*, written *c.* 860–2, Eriugena attempted to place Christianity on a Christian Neoplatonic foundation, and his thought in this respect, particularly his idea of procession from God and return to him, owed a great deal to the work of the Christian Neoplatonists he had translated. Despite the originality of his writing and the perplexing inconsistencies in his thought, Eriugena was far from being an isolated figure, for as Marenbon has stressed, Eriugena's methods and ideas were read, copied, developed and distorted by a sizeable band of followers.[23] Eriugena himself, with all his confusions and contradictions, was fully within a developed tradition of philosophy. He shared the interest of his contemporaries in the problems of essence, the Categories and the Universals, and examined these problems in terms of the philosophical tradition he had inherited. Reason was set to grapple with abstract problems.

Evidence for Eriugena's influence survives in the form of notes and glosses in a number of manuscripts and the diffusion of copies of the *Periphyseon*; from this evidence a number of Eriugena's followers may be identified. Two individuals, known rather ignominiously as i^1 and i^2, made notes in a total of thirteen manuscripts which reveal a close knowledge of, and sympathy with, Eriugena's thinking.[24] Other members of Eriugena's circle were Sedulius Scottus, Martin of Laon, Wulfad bishop of Bourges and Heiric of Auxerre. In the cases of the last two named, Eriugena's influence was considerable. Eriugena dedicated his *Periphyseon* to Wulfad and addressed him as his 'collaborator in philosophical disputes'. In the list of books owned by Wulfad were a number of Eriugena's works – his translations of the works of pseudo-Dionysius, the *Ad Thalassium* of Maximus the Confessor, and the list itself was written on the last page of Eriugena's translation of the *Ambigua*.[25] Heiric of Auxerre probably became acquainted with Eriugena and his work at Soissons between 863 and 865. His sermon on the prologue to the Gospel of St John is heavily reminiscent of Eriugena's own homily on the same subject. Heiric discussed why St John described Christ's coming as the Word, and his interpretation is for the most part an exercise in linguistic and philosophical analysis.[26] Heiric's Life of St Germanus of Auxerre also shows Heiric's fascination with Eriugena's ideas, but he best reveals himself as a follower of Eriugena and interpreter of his thought to subsequent generations of scholars in his glosses on school texts. Those in BN lat. 12949, a copy of the *Categoriae Decem*, for example, are usually attributed to him.[27] This glossing of texts became the normal method of philosophical discussion in the circle of Eriugena and at Auxerre, whereas in Alcuin's time the method used had been excerption and compilation, with the selection of particular texts and the changes made to certain passages indicating the thought of the compiler. The new glossing method introduced in the second half of the ninth century retained its importance until the middle of the twelfth century, thanks to the school of Auxerre and its pupils.

The monastery of St Germain of Auxerre rather than the cathedral church of St Stephen was the main centre of learning in that see, though there was a close association between the two institutions. The monastery, for example, supplied the see with a number of its bishops, Heribald (d. 857), Wala (d. 879) and Wibald (d. 887). A history of the see of Auxerre was written by two monks of St Germain, and the bishops in their turn were generous in their patronage of the monastery. Auxerre's interests in classical literature and grammar, biblical exegesis and philosophy combined to make Auxerre one of the most important and influential of the Carolingian centres of learning in the late ninth and the tenth centuries.[28]

The three chief luminaries of the monastery were Haimo (d. 866), Heiric (d. 877–83) and Remigius (d. 908). Haimo's reputation was based upon his skill as an exegete and preacher and he also seems to have been a teacher of genius. Heiric, brought up from infancy at Auxerre and taught also by Lupus of Ferrières,[29] succeeded Haimo as master of the monastery's school in 865 or

866. His main works were the long poem about St Germanus: the *Collectaneum*, a *florilegium* composed largely of extracts from classical authors, particularly Valerius Maximus; a homiliary distinctive for the originality of its interpretations of scripture; and the glosses (mostly inspired by Eriugena) on the *Categoriae Decem* referred to above. Remigius of Auxerre, the last great scholar of that monastery, was Heiric's pupil and himself taught at Rheims during the archbishopric of Fulk (882–900). He wrote a variety of commentaries on school texts such as the *De consolatione Philosophiae* of Boethius, the grammars of Donatus and Priscian, and the *De Nuptiis* of Martianus Capella, as well as exegetical works on the Bible. One great service Remigius rendered was to discuss and quote extensively from the work of Haimo, Heiric and John Scottus Eriugena, and thus preserve for us information that would otherwise have been lost. In his commentary on Boethius, Remigius anticipates the problem of the collision between Christian doctrine and ancient theories of the origins of the Universe, yet still at this stage the potential conflict between secular learning and Christianity was circumvented. Logic, syntactical argument and pure reason were not to be fully applied to Christian doctrine until the eleventh century, but Auxerre nevertheless made a vital contribution to the development of Western thought by its promotion of these intellectual tools; at Auxerre are to be detected the rudimentary beginnings of the scholastic method of argument.[30]

Auxerre, like other Frankish monasteries and cathedral schools, spread its influence through its teaching and through contacts with other centres. A colleague of Remigius' at Rheims who was also possibly taught by Heiric was Hucbald of St Amand (c. 840–930). Hucbald had been taught by his uncle Milo of St Amand and succeeded his uncle as master of the school at St Amand in 872. At the request of the abbot of St Bertin, Hucbald became head of the school there, and Fulk of Rheims subsequently engaged him, with Remigius of Auxerre, to revive the school at Rheims. After Fulk's assassination in 900, Hucbald returned to St Amand where he taught until his death at the unusually ripe old age of ninety. Evidence of Hucbald's learning and activity as a scholar survives in the form of the books he owned and in works attributed to him. According to the twelfth-century catalogue of the library of St Amand, Hucbald gave no less than eighteen of his books to St Amand, some of which are still extant. A few, such as the grammar of Marius Victorinus or Plato's *Timaeus* in the translation of Chalcidius, were probably written in the abbey scriptorium, while others, such as his copy of Alcuin's *De Fide* and Augustine's *De Trinitate* he presumably collected on his travels. One indeed he bought from a Viking pirate. Hucbald is one of the few Frankish individuals about whose library we have some information. His collection may be compared with those of Wulfad of Bourges, Hincmar of Rheims, Dido of Laon, Einhard, Eberhard of Friuli or Eccard of Mâcon. As well as the books already mentioned, Hucbald possessed Marius Plotius on metrics, Isidore of Seville and Alcuin on rhetoric, Augustine and Alcuin on the Trinity, Augustine's *De Anima*, the letters of Augustine and of Jerome and the Chronicle of Isidore of Seville. The books now lost included collections of exegesis by Gregory the Great and Hraban Maur, Martianus Capella's *De Nuptiis*, Priscian's grammar and a commentary on the Rule of St Benedict.[31] It is a diversified collection, reflecting both the pedagogic and personal interests of the owner, interests which included, as his own writings indicate, philosophy and music.

Valenciennes BM MS 167, a copy of the *Enchiridion* of St Augustine, contains two fragments of philosophical import which in fact comprise part of a *florilegium* of carefully chosen extracts from books I and II of the *Periphyseon* of John Scottus Eriugena. A preference is shown in the selection for texts which contain definitions or which take up a particular position on certain controversial points. The extracts are written in a hand dated to the turn of the ninth century and the compiler of this philosophical *florilegium* has been tentatively identified with Hucbald by Mathon, though Marenbon doubts this attribution.[32] The manuscript itself was not written at St Amand, and this would cast further doubts on Hucbald's authorship. Hucbald has also been credited with the glosses on the *Isagoge* of Porphyry in BN lat. 12949, a collection of logical texts quite extensively glossed. These glosses consist for the most part of Boethius' commentary on the *Isagoge* augmented with passages chosen from other philosophical works and commentaries. As well as some poems and saints' Lives and glosses on the *computus*, Hucbald wrote the treatise *De Harmonica Institutione* which discussed the tonal system underlying ecclesiastical plainchant and incorporated such tenth-century musicology as existed. Some scholars regard this treatise as a practical manual for teaching and learning music. Others stress that Hucbald's work was more for those interested in a way of discussing different aspects of the chant. It is for his treatises on music and his own compositions that Hucbald was particularly remembered in his own monastery, and has his own small but significant place in the history of music.[33]

IV

The Romans had adopted Greek theory and practice as far as both vocal and instrumental music were concerned and made few contributions of their own. Indeed, the later Roman writers on music, Martianus Capella, Boethius and Cassiodorus, drew on and preserved the Greek musical tradition. The barbarian kingdoms of the early Middle Ages inherited what the Romans had preserved, and thus the concept of the scale, a theory of acoustics and various principles of instrument construction were known. Music was taught in the early medieval schools as a theoretical discipline. It comprised harmonic theory, rhythm, metrics and some philosophical speculation, and was part of the *quadrivium*, with Boethius' *De Musica* as the main textbook, augmented by Augustine's *De Musica* and the relevant portions of Cassiodorus' *Institutiones* and Isidore of Seville's encyclopaedia. These remained the main material for the study of music until the early ninth century. As well as transmitting Greek theory,

Boethius' text preserved Greek musical notation; although he also used Roman letters to illustrate different acoustic points he did not propose a new notational system.

Of further importance for the development of western music, particularly from the fourth century onwards, was the cantillation of prayers, lessons and responses and the singing of psalms. This means the singing of phrases on a single note with the melodic formulae in which the last words of a phrase are sung acting as punctuation. The singing of psalms and responses in any Anglican choral evensong or Matins today gives some idea of what this would have sounded like. This liturgical singing in the churches was descended from the vocal music of the synagogue. There were also chants for the Mass and the Office, rather more melodic than the cantillated psalms and responses; the main chants were in existence by the sixth century. Thus by the ninth century in the Frankish kingdoms there were two sources of musical knowledge: music theory based on that of the Greeks, and the actual playing and singing of music, though it is largely from the ecclesiastical context, especially from the liturgy of the mass, that most of our evidence for musical practice comes. This evidence is in the form, on the one hand, of such musical treatises as survive, and on the other, of notated manuscripts. The main problem for working out what the music in the oldest of these manuscripts sounded like is the form of musical notation employed.

The earliest musical notation survives in manuscript fragments from the late eighth century and is found in greater frequency throughout the ninth and tenth centuries. It took the form of neumes, that is, signs representing a note or notes thought to derive from the acute and grave accents used to regulate the voice when speaking, which indicated the progression of the melody. They gave no idea at all however of intervals or pitch, nor was the duration of notes normally specified, though some St Gall manuscripts give letter abbreviations for words relating to the interpretation of rhythm from an early stage. Neumes therefore could only be used by those who knew the melody already, and served simply as reminders, showing clearly the number of notes to be sung, the manner of grouping them and melodic contour, but indicating only gradually in the course of the later ninth and the tenth centuries, as the neumes were heighted, the rise or fall of pitch. This means that the neumes were written either higher or lower according to their position in the scale of sounds. Hucbald of St Amand made a contribution to the development of notation in that he tried, with his layout of staff notation, a precursor of the daseian notation of later music treatises, to establish a system whereby the pupil would be able to see what the pitch was for each syllable to be sung, even if he had never seen nor heard the music before, and pointed out the inadequacies of merely directional neumes. Gradually, neumes were spaced according to the intervals and a diastematic notation evolved during the tenth century in which, instead of the rise or fall in pitch being expressed by the form of the sign and the direction in which it was traced, the musical value of a sign depended on its position in relation to a real or imaginary line. The first indication of this development was that notation began to be arranged around one line which seems to have varied according to the pitch of the notes rather than according to mode; a second line was added (the two were normally F and c′) and gradually the staff or stave of four lines was formed. The four-line stave system was perfected in the eleventh century by Guy of Arezzo, who fixed the clefs and the number of lines. In other words, throughout the tenth century there is a steady transition from neumes written without lines to diastematic neumes. Lines and staves changed the form of the neumes by requiring them to be written very exactly on the desired degree of the staff; a point was added to indicate the place and the point or note thus became the essential part of the sign, just as it is in modern musical notation. The form of the neumes and notes, moreover, varied from place to place, so that the origin of a particular piece of musical notation can often be determined. It is also important to stress that the speed of the development of notation described in general terms above also differed quite considerably in different parts of the Frankish kingdoms. At St Gall, for example, unheighted notation lasted until at least the eleventh century when St Martial of Limoges' notation was already heading towards the full stave.

Most of the ecclesiastical music for which we have notation from this early period was designed for the voice and was sung, and it is not known to what extent such instruments as the organ or the cithara (sometimes called a cittern – it was a wire-stringed instrument played with a plectrum) were used in church music, or indeed whether brass or wind instruments were played there as well as in non-ecclesiastical circles. In 757 Pippin III received an organ as a present from Constantine Copronymous, and a hydraulis or water organ was built for Louis the Pious in about 826. Organs were being constructed in Germany towards the end of the ninth century, for a treatise survives dating from that time which discusses the measurements of organ pipes.[34] Dunstan is supposed to have promoted the installation of the organ in England, and in about 950 a wonderful organ with 26 bellows and 400 pipes was constructed at Winchester. Dunstan himself could play the organ, psaltery, harp and chime bells.

The ecclesiastical chant, based on Ambrose's four modes, had developed rapidly after the fourth century, and in the time of Gregory the Great four more modes were added; plainchant or plainsong has become so much associated with Pope Gregory I that it is often referred to as Gregorian chant. Roman chant was promoted by Pippin III and Chrodegang of Metz and soon became the norm in all the churches of the Frankish kingdom. The Carolingians made their own important contribution to the development of the chant with the composition of tropes. Tropes were regular additions in the form of melodies or of both melodies and texts made to parts of the liturgy. A special form of trope was the sequence, a long melody added to the *jubilus* or Alleluia, itself originally an addition to the responds. The melody was broken up into strophes to enable the singer to breathe; when singing it was natural for these strophes to be repeated and eventually for words to be added. Our earliest known sequences were written by Notker Balbulus of St Gall, who apparently copied the idea from a visiting monk from Jumièges who took refuge at St Gall from the Vikings.[35] Notker relates how he found sequences in the antiphonary the

Jumièges monk had brought with him and in his turn supplied suitable texts for the melismas then in use at St Gall. He is no longer thought to have invented the sequence. The sequence became an enormously popular musical form all over western Europe, with the two main schools of musical composition centred on St Gall in the east and St Martial of Limoges in the west. Liturgical drama in the early Middle Ages appears to have been a direct development from the tropes added to the Introits for Christmas and Easter such as *Hodie cantandus*, a trope composed c. 900 which prefaces the Introit of the Mass for Christmas and is arranged in dialogue form, and the *Quem quaeritis*, a trope prefixed to the Mass for Easter based on the story of the two Marys coming to the tomb on Easter morning and finding it empty. The performance of this short tableau with words and music is described at length in the *Regularis Concordia* of 970 or 973, after it had been performed in Winchester cathedral.[36] During the tenth and eleventh centuries liturgical drama developed rapidly.

About secular music we are less well informed, for the music of Latin secular songs from this early period survives mostly in unheighted neumes, though some of it was later rewritten with staff notation. Of vernacular songs we have evidence only from the end of the eleventh century onwards. A genre of literature which was certainly set to music in a great many cases was the *planctus* or lament. [37] Laments survive, for example, on the deaths of Charlemagne and of Hugh, abbot of St Quentin and on the Battle of Fontenoy of 842. There are also various settings of classical and late antique texts, such as odes of Horace, poems by Boethius, passages (particularly of direct speech) from Statius' *Thebaid*, and lines from the *Aeneid*. The distinction between secular and ecclesiastical music (not all the latter was liturgical chant) was hazy or non-existent at first, but in the course of the tenth and eleventh centuries a body of secular song was built up, the most important representatives of which are the songs of the Goliard poets.

Monophonic music as represented by plainsong, and polyphony, that is, part music in which the parts move independently but in harmony with the other parts, probably developed side by side throughout the Middle Ages, though in the ninth and tenth centuries polyphony was still in its primitive form, known as *organum*. This was the parallel movement of the melody in fourths, fifths and octaves, which had probably originally been a vocal convenience in that people sang at a pitch which suited the compass of their voices. The first discussions of *organum* are in musical treatises dating from the late ninth and early tenth centuries, though it is usually assumed that the practice itself can be dated earlier. Gradually the parallel movement was modified, some free *organum* with contrary motion and some 'imperfect' intervals such as thirds or sixths introduced and movement in cadences tried; polyphony thereafter developed rapidly. The earliest source of polyphony as practised is the eleventh-century Winchester Troper in Corpus Christi College Cambridge MS 473.

The later Carolingian period also witnessed the first stage in the reconciliation of the Greek musical theory as it was taught in the schools and music as it was practised in the churches. The existing tradition of writing about music combined with the primitive state of musical notation meant that the methodical exposition of ecclessiastical chant was difficult for those who attempted it. Gradually only those elements of the classical musical tradition found to be relevant to existing musical practice were retained, and music treatises became increasingly practical in their application. Some attempts to write musical treatises for their students were made by Hraban Maur, who produced a compilation based on Cassiodorus and Isidore, and Aurelian of Réomé who gave details about the structure of melodic formulae having modal significance.

But the most important contributions to musical theory and practice were made at the beginning of the tenth century by Remigius of Auxerre, in his commentary on the musical portion of Martianus Capella's *De Nuptiis*, Hucbald of St Amand, Regino of Prüm and Otger, the author of the *Musica Enchiriadis*.[38] Hucbald himself was once credited with the authorship of the *Musica Enchiriadis*, but it is now agreed that he is only responsible for the *De harmonica institutione*. In his work Hucbald used many examples from the most common of the chant melodies sung in his own day to illustrate his points about intervals, the formation of the scale and the rudiments of melody, as well as endeavouring to improve the precision of musical notation. He also showed himself aware of the difference between *organum* and monody with which latter subject his own work was concerned. His book may have been intended for beginners, though some scholars have disputed this and suggested that it was intended for those already familiar with the chant. Hucbald certainly seems to have been the first to discuss Greek musical theory and methods, as transmitted by Boethius, in relation to contemporary musical problems. A few of his musical compositions – Offices for the feasts of saints Andrew, Peter, Theodoric and Cilinia, a trope for the Gloria beginning *Quem vere pia laus*, and possibly two other offices – have survived.

Regino of Prüm also drew upon both theory and practice; in his treatise he borrowed from Cicero, Boethius, Cassiodorus, Isidore of Seville and Aurelian of Réomé and he made a tonary, that is, a systematic arrangement of antiphons and responses according to the mode in which they were to be sung. The *Musica Enchiriadis* ascribed to Otger (no more is known of him than his name) was the first treatise on music to discuss polyphony, while the *Dialogus*, once ascribed to Odo of Cluny but now attributed to an Italian monk living *c* 1000, was the first comprehensive attempt to use letters to indicate pitch in the way that became standard for the rest of the Middle Ages.[39]

By the second half of the tenth century, music, with all its new emphasis on the relation between music theory and practice, was taught at a number of schools as part of the curriculum. At Rheims, for example, in the time of Gerbert (972–80) the teaching of music, with astronomy and mathematics, made the school famous, and students came from all over Western Europe to study there. Gerbert apparently directed the school of chanters at Rheims, and among his students a number were composers of sequences, including Robert the Pious, king of France from 996 to 1031. New finger techniques for playing the organ were suggested and Gerbert insisted that practice on actual instruments was essential for the study of music, something that would probably not have been advocated a century earlier.

V

Little is known about the school of Rheims before Hucbald and Remigius taught there in the 880s, though the activity of the city's scriptoria and the existence of a cathedral library during the ninth century are rather better attested, particularly during the archbishoprics of Ebbo and Hincmar. The school of Rheims in Gerbert's time, however, is described by Richer in his account of the career of Gerbert, later Pope Sylvester II.[40] Gerbert (c. 940–1004) spent the first part of his life at the monastery of St Gerald of Aurillac where he was grounded in grammar; in 967 he left to pursue his studies in Spain, possibly at the monastery of St Maria de Ripoll. It was there that he acquired his interest and proficiency in mathematics and astronomy. (The conquest of Spain by the Arabs in 711 had meant that advanced Arabic science and Arabic translations of Greek works were introduced.) In 972 Gerbert became secretary to Archbishop Adalbero of Rheims and taught the arts of the *quadrivium* in the cathedral school while continuing his studies in rhetoric and dialectic. According to Richer, Gerbert made a number of innovations at Rheims; he introduced the use of the abacus for mathematical calculations and popularized the use of the arabic numerals one to nine (the zero was introduced later). There is in fact some evidence that the abacus was already in use in the Rhineland before Gerbert's time, and from the little we know about intellectual contacts between the Lotharingian monasteries and the Arabic science of Spain, it is certainly possible that Gerbert was not the first to communicate the fruits of Arabic learning.

As we noted in Chapter Six, arithmetic or *computus* was studied only at an elementary level in the ninth century, but by the tenth century it is clear that mathematics was being taught at a rather more sophisticated level; towards the middle of the century practical reckoning seems to have been taught to school children in Germany and England. At Rheims, the interest in mathematics was keen, though those who practised it found it very difficult. Gerbert corresponded with a number of friends on mathematical subjects; he expounded in a letter to Constantine of Fleury, for example, rules for using the abacus, and in other letters he discussed various passages on numbers in the *De Musica* of Boethius.[41] A number of treatises besides Gerbert's *Regulae Abaci* were written on numbers and the use of the abacus, and although these tend to be dismissed as jejune, they do constitute evidence that a fresh approach was being made to elementary mathematics, that theoretical and practical knowledge were compared and that the problems of practical calculation, addition, subtraction, multiplication, division and fractions, began to be related to mathematical theory, just as the theoretical and practical knowledge of music had begun to be related.

For the study of astronomy, again according to Richer, Gerbert introduced the astrolabe and the planetarium, and in a letter to Constantine of Fleury, Gerbert explained the construction of a hemisphere and how it could be used for making astronomical observations.[42] Rheims was clearly an important centre for the study of astronomy as well as music and mathematics. Aimon of Fleury's Life of Abbo abbot of Fleury (987–1004) tells how Abbo was educated at Fleury in grammar, arithmetic and dialectic and sought knowledge of the other arts at Paris and Rheims. Only at Rheims was he able to find instruction in astronomy; he learnt music at Orleans and taught himself geometry and rhetoric from manuscripts he found at Paris and Fleury. Subsequently under Abbo the school and library of Fleury in its turn attracted many students and Abbo became famous for his teaching of arithmetic, astronomy and dialectic. A number of his teaching manuals on these subjects, such as his *Liber de Computo*, the *Quaestiones grammaticales* and works on dialectic, mathematics, astronomy and canon law, survive. Through Fleury's close relationship with Ramsey abbey in England (Abbo himself had spent two years teaching there and at other ecclesiastical centres in the country) some of the Continental developments, in learning as well as in monasticism, reached England.

Another school famous for its music and the teaching of the liberal arts was St Gall. Like Reichenau and Trier, St Gall was crucial not only in preserving the achievements of the ninth century into the tenth and eleventh centuries, but also in transmitting them to the newly emerging centres of Ottonian Germany. St Gall first emerged as a centre of learning under Abbot Gozbert (816–37). Under Grimald, abbot from 841–872, who had been court chaplain and chancellor to Louis the German, and Hartmuot (872–83), St Gall retained its reputation and enjoyed a productive period of scholarship.[43] It was during Hartmuot's abbacy that St Gall's connections with other great abbeys and sees, particularly Fulda, Reichenau and Mainz, were forged. Grimald was a friend of Hraban Maur, Otfrid of Weissenburg and Walafrid Strabo. Among the masters of St Gall were Iso, Hartmuot, Werimbert, Engilbert and the Irishmen Moengal and Marcellus, some of whom had been trained elsewhere but had returned to St Gall to teach. The most celebrated scholars produced by St Gall in its first period of greatness were Notker I Balbulus and Salomo II, bishop of Constance. Notker Balbulus is best remembered as the author of the *Gesta Karoli Magni*, written for Charles the Fat, which contained a collection of lively anecdotes about Charles the Fat's predecessors, especially Charlemagne. Notker also wrote a treatise on rhetoric, and, as we have seen, introduced the sequence to St Gall. The St Gall library catalogue of 850–60 with additions made in about 880 is a rich source of information concerning the range of interests at St Gall and the subjects taught in its school[44] (see above, pp. 203–4).

St Gall had another productive period in the tenth century under Salomo III, bishop of Constance and abbot of St Gall from 890 to 920; it was particularly important then for its teaching of the *trivium* – grammar, rhetoric and dialectic. The *Glossarium Salomonis*, an encyclopaedia of contemporary scientific knowledge, dates from this time. Salomon was a powerful ally of Louis the Child (900–11) and of Conrad. After the Saxon line gained the East Frankish throne in 919, St Gall declined in importance, but from 978 to 1022, under abbots Immo and Burckhardt, it revived again. The intellectual leaders of St Gall then were Notker II the Physician and Notker III Labeo; their work shows that the St Gall school tradition and its musical interests had survived its political and economic vicissitudes unimpaired.

Notker Labeo was a polymath like Gerbert of Rheims, versed in all the arts and disciplines – theology, grammar, dialectic, rhetoric, mathematics, astronomy, music and poetry. It is his translations and adaptations of Latin school texts for which he is best remembered, though his work is now more treasured by philologists than anyone else. Old High German texts in the ninth century had been largely religious in nature, translations of prayers, the Gospels, the Rule of St Benedict and so on, [45] but Notker put his native language to new service; he translated and adapted into Old High German the first two books of Martianus Capella's *De Nuptiis*, Boethius' Latin translation of the Categories and *De Interpretatione* of Aristotle and his commentaries upon them and Boethius' *De consolatione Philosophiae*. These have survived, but translations Notker made of the *Disticha Catonis*, Virgil's Bucolics and the *Andria* of Terence are no longer extant. Notker also composed a number of school-books, some in Latin – *De Arte Rhetorica, De Partibus Logicae, De Disputatione* and a *Computus* – for which he provided a German translation or German notes, and one in German from the start, the *De Musica*, and translated a number of religious texts, including the Psalms and Canticles, the Lord's Prayer, the Apostles' creed and the *Quicunque vult*. A translation he made of the Book of Job has not survived. It is clear from the modifications Notker made to his texts as he translated them, such as reordering the words so that they might be the more easily construed, and adding synonyms, glosses and notes, that his revised German versions were intended as aids to understanding. All his translations of school texts for example were accompanied by exegetical commentaries in German, based on, or even translations of, the commentaries on these same books made by Remigius of Auxerre.[46] All his comments and observations provide a clear record of his teaching. Notker's abbot, Burkhard II (1001–22) was the last great abbot-patron of the learning of his monastery; after his death intellectual life at St Gall seems to have declined.

Throughout its history, St Gall numbered Irishmen among its brethren, and was in fact one of the main havens for the Irish who came to the Continent from the eighth to the twelfth centuries, though the impact of the Irish 'colony' at St Gall upon the community or the intellectual life of the surrounding region, like the Irish contribution to European culture from the ninth to the twelfth centuries, has not yet been adequately assessed. The most important sources of information concerning the presence and activity of Irish scholars in the Frankish kingdom are the extant manuscripts written on the Continent in insular script of the Irish type, or in Irish glosses inserted into Continental manuscripts.[47] Occasionally there are references to the Irish in narrative sources and a few of their works survive.[48] From this evidence it appears that Irish monks were known in Gaul from the late sixth century onwards, and by the eighth century they had established a number of centres such as Péronne (*Perrona Scottorum*) in Picardy founded by Fursey, Fosses, Mazerolles and Honau, while a few individuals are associated with particular sees such as Würzburg (Kilian, Colman and Totman) and Salzburg (Virgil).

The presence of Irishmen in large numbers is implied by such documents as the charter issued by Charlemagne to Honau which states that the Frankish king has granted freedom to all Irish pilgrims and forbids anyone to carry off their property or to occupy their churches,[49] or the clause of the acts of the Reform Council of Chalon in 813 which legislates specifically against wandering Irish bishops.[50] A number of Irish scholars were associated with the court of Charlemagne. Alcuin refers to an Irish poet called Joseph in one of his letters[51] and some of Joseph's poems survive in Berne Burgerbibliothek MS 212. Dicuil was at Charlemagne's court by 814 and still at the court of his son in 825. He dedicated a treatise ón astronomy to Louis the Pious, wrote on grammar and is best remembered for his geographical treatise *Liber de mensura orbis terrae*, based almost entirely on classical treatises on the subject, particularly Pliny. Clemens and Cadac are referred to in relation to the court;[52] Clemens was described as a master at the court of Louis the Pious and wrote a treatise on grammar. Dungal, a learned Irishman, was placed in charge of Lothar's reorganization of education in Italy in 825 and taught at Pavia.

It was probably as a result of the Viking raids on Ireland that Irish pilgrims and scholars began to arrive in the Frankish kingdom in greater numbers towards the middle of the ninth century. At the Council of Meaux in 845 and again in 858, the Frankish bishops asked Charles the Bald to help restore the hospices for Irish pilgrims.[53] Berne Burgerbibliothek MS 368 contains marginalia which refer frequently to many of these refugees and pilgrims, including Sedulius Scottus, John Scottus Eriugena, Fergus, Dubtach, Suadhar, Mac Ciallain, Taircheltach, Robartaich and Cathasach. Heiric of Auxerre in the preface to his *Vita Sancti Germani* referred to the great multitude of Irishmen who had come to the kingdom of Charles the Bald.[54] Particular sees and monasteries – Cambrai, Laon, Liège and St Gall – seem to have provided refuges.

Sedulius Scottus, for example, arrived at Liège in about 848 and was given a warm reception by Bishop Hartgar (840–54) who became his patron, as did Hartgar's successor Bishop Franco (854–901). Sedulius solicited other clerical, noble and royal patrons with verses and treatises, among whom were Gunther, archbishop of Cologne, Adventius, archbishop of Metz, the Emperor Lothar and Count Eberhard of Friuli. Sedulius was primarily a grammarian and an exegete, but he has left, besides his poems, the *Liber de rectoribus christianis*, an interesting treatise on kingship, possibly written for Louis II or Lothar II, which envisages a close relationship between the ruler and his bishops, some exegesis and a *Collectaneum* or commonplace book of excerpts from classical authors which provides valuable evidence of his reading and the books available to him.[55] A number of other Irish scholars seem to have joined Sedulius for a time in Liége and a number of manuscripts are associated with the Liége 'colony', but of Sedulius himself we hear no more after 874. Intellectual life at Liège on the other hand went from strength to strength in the tenth century, and was particularly noted for its cultivation and teaching of the arts of the *quadrivium* in the time of Notker (*c.* 930–1008). Liège and its cathedral school is counted among the most important of the intellectual centres which preceded the development of the universities.[56] At Soissons there is evidence of Irish visitors and another 'colony' of *Scotti* was at Laon. As Contreni has stressed, the description of an Irish 'colony' at Laon should be understood to mean that the careers of a number of Irish scholars, including Probus of Mainz, Adalelm, Cathasach, Fergus, Eriugena and Martin, touched Laon at one time or another.[57]

All of them, with the sole exception of Martin of Laon, are known to have taught and studied elsewhere in the Frankish kingdom as well, and to have had connections with such centres as Péronne, St Amand, Reichenau, Auxerre, Rheims, St Gall, Schüttern and the court of Charles the Bald. Martin of Laon (819–75) presided over the cathedral school of Laon until his death. From twenty-one manuscripts containing his handwriting, a Continental script with some insular symptoms, Contreni has been able to delineate the intellectual profile of one of the most interesting scholars of the second half of the ninth century, whose methods were retained at Laon until well into the tenth.[58] Martin was a collector, annotator and copyist of books and ultimately a benefactor of the cathedral library at Laon. He was a teacher rather than an original thinker, who supervised the scriptorium, taught grammar, and was learned also in law, medicine, computation and history. He possessed some proficiency in Greek and compiled a Greek–Latin glossary and a Latin grammar (extant in Laon Bibliothèque Municipale MS 444). He was consulted on Greek matters by other Frankish scholars, including, possibly, Lupus of Ferrières. Other manuscripts Martin compiled or copied are teaching manuals. Among Martin's students were Manno, later a master of the 'palace school' of Charles the Bald, and Bernard of Laon. Martin was undoubtedly acquainted with the most famous and brilliant of the Irishmen in ninth-century Europe, John Scottus Eriugena, whose works and influence were discussed in detail above. Laon remained an important school until at least the death of Adalelm in 930.[59] Of the Irishmen who arrived on the Continent in the tenth century, some came to Lotharingia to found or to join religious houses. Waulsort, for example, was founded and endowed in 946 by Eilbert and his wife Heresuind for the benefit of 'certain servants of God coming from Ireland and wishing to live under the Rule of St Benedict'.[60] It was stipulated that the abbot of Waulsort was always to be an Irishman so long as he could be elected from the brethren of the community. Cadroe, its first abbot (d. 978) played a not inconsiderable part in the monastic movement in Metz; he was summoned by Bishop Adalbero and reformed the monasteries of St Clement and St Felix. Cadroe was succeeded by Forannan, another Irishman. Others among his compatriots are associated with the development of learning in Lotharingia and Germany: the Life of Bruno archbishop of Cologne by Ruotger, for example, records that Bruno was taught by a learned Irish bishop called Israel, and Gerard, bishop of Toul, was said to be amiably disposed towards both Greek and Irish clerics. Nor did Irish immigration cease, for the eleventh and twelfth centuries saw the foundation of a number of *Schottenklöster* in Germany, the most famous of which were the monasteries of St Peter and St James, Regensburg and St James, Würzburg.

VI

In the two and a half centuries during which the Frankish kingdoms were ruled by the Carolingians a school curriculum was formed and a Christian educational tradition with clearly defined aims established. Knowledge was avidly sought, books copied and libraries formed. On the foundations laid down in the eighth and early ninth century, later generations of scholars in many different parts of the Frankish kingdom promoted, with the support of royal, noble and ecclesiastical patronage, increased critical and creative artistic and intellectual activity. Just as Caroline minuscule took shape in the course of the eighth century, came to full maturity in the ninth and evolved gradually into a new script (the Gothic) in the course of the tenth and eleventh centuries, so, as knowledge was transmitted from master to pupil and exchanged between centres, Carolingian learning was augmented and built upon, emphases altered, new works were assimilated and new techniques and modes of thought were applied to familiar fields of study. Arithmetic, astronomy, music, geometry and philosophy were tackled with new zest and interest, conquered, and became in their turn part of the school curriculum and the basis for future development. Although it is true to say that Ottonian Germany was the cultural heir of the Carolingians, so was Capetian France with its great schools of Rheims, Fleury, St Amand, Auxerre, Laon, Paris and Chartres, all of which had first emerged in the ninth and tenth centuries.

In the three chapters devoted to the intellectual and cultural development of the eighth, ninth and tenth centuries it has only been possible to sketch in the barest outline of the rich achievement of these centuries and merely to suggest how solid a foundation the Carolingians had prepared for European scholarship in every field. Their work may seem less glamorous and exciting to those accustomed to the sophistication of the twelfth- and fifteenth-century Renaissances, but within its own context, Carolingian culture was vital, pioneering and creative.

NOTES

1. Felten, cited above, chapter 5, n.25.
2. A. d'Haenens, 'Les invasions normandes dans l'empire franc au IXe siècle', *Settimane* 16 (1969), 233–98.
3. *Vita Odoni*, I, 23.
4. B. Rosenwein, 'Rules and the Rule at tenth century Cluny', *Studia Monastica* 19 (1977), 307–20.
5. See the full discussion by J. Evans, *Monastic Life at Cluny 910–1157* (Oxford 1931), 78–97.
6. J. H. Pignot (ed.), *Histoire de l'Ordre de Cluny depuis la fondation jusqu'à la mort de Pierre le Vénérable* (Autun and Paris 3 vols, 1868), I, 34; Eng. trs. in Evans, *Monastic Life at Cluny*, 4–6. On Cluny see E. Sackur, *Die Cluniazenser in ihrer kirchlichen allgemeingeschichtlichen Wirksamkeit bis zur Mitte des elften Jahrhunderts* (Halle 2 vols, 1892–94), J. Wollasch, H. E. Mager and H. Diener, *Neue Forschungen über Cluny*

und die Cluniazenser, G. Tellenbach (ed.), (Frieburg 1959), and K. Hallinger (ed.), *Gorze-Kluny* (Rome 1950).

7. On Cluny's legal position see G. Letonnelier, *L'Abbaye exempte de Cluny et le Saint-Siège*, Archives de la France monastique 22 (Paris and Ligugé 1923).

8. H. J. E. Cowdrey, *The Cluniacs and the Gregorian Reform* (Oxford 1970), 4–8.

9. K. Hallinger, 'Zur geistigen Welt der Anfänge Klunys', *DA* 10 (1954), 417–45; Eng. trs. in N. Hunt (ed.) *Cluniac Monasticism and the Central Middle Ages* (London 1971), 29–55.

10. B. Rosenwein, 'St Odo's St Martin: the uses of a model', *Journal of Medieval History* 4 (1978), 317–32.

11. K. Erdmann, *Die Entstehung des Kreuzzugsgedanken* (Stuttgart 1965); Eng. trs. M. W. Baldwin and W. Goffart (Princeton 1977).

12. A. M. Mundó, 'Moissac, Cluny et les mouvements monastiques de l'Est des Pyrénées du Xᵉau XIIᵉ siècles', *Annales du Midi* 75 (1963), 551–70; Eng. trs. Hunt (ed.) *Cluniac Monasticism*, 98–122.

13. B. Hamilton, 'The monastic revival in tenth century Rome', *Studia monastica* 4 (1962), 35–68. See also J. Leclercq, 'Nouveaux aspects de la vie clunisienne à propose des monastères de Lombardie', *Studia Monastica* 22 (1980), 29–42.

14. J. Wollasch, 'Gerard von Brogne und seine Klostergründung', *Revue Bénédictine* 70 (1960), 62–82.

15. T. Symons, '*Regularis concordia*: History and Derivation', *Tenth Century Studies*, D. Parsons (ed.) (London and Chichester, 1975), 37–59.

16. K. Hallinger, *Gorze-Kluny*.

17. See E. de Moreau, *Les Abbayes de Belgique* (Brussels 1952), and J. Leclercq, 'Jean de Gorze et la vie religieuse au Xᵉ siècle', *Saint Chrodegang* (Metz 1967), 133–52.

18. J. Fleckenstein, 'Königshof und Bischofschule unter Otto der Grosse', *Archiv für Kulturgeschichte* 38 (1956), 38–62. See also J. W. Thompson, 'The introduction of Arabic science into Lorraine in the tenth century', *Isis* 12 (1929), 184–93.

19. J. Ackrill, *Aristotle's Categories and De Interpretatione* (Oxford 1974 reprint of 1963 edn), 4.

20. M. T. Gibson (ed.), *Boethius, His Life, Thought and Influence* (Oxford 1981), especially the essays by Barnes, Lewry and Gibson; H. Chadwick, *Boethius* (Oxford 1981)

21. J. Marenbon, *From the Circle of Alcuin to the School of Auxerre. Logic, Theology and Philosophy in the early Middle Ages* (Cambridge 1981).

22. M. Cappuyns, *Jean Scot Erigène, sa vie, son oeuvre, sa pensée* (Louvain 1933), 66, and compare J. J. Contreni, *The Cathedral School of Laon from 850–930. Its manuscripts and masters* (Munich 1978), 83–5.

23. Marenbon, *From the Circle of Alcuin*, esp. 88–115.

24. On their identity, see L. Traube, 'Paläographische Forschungen: Autographa des Johannes Scottus', *Abhandlungen der königlichen Bayerischen Akademie der Wissenschaften*, philol.-philos.-hist. Klasse 26.1 (1912); E. K. Rand, 'The supposed autographa of John the Scot', *University of California Publications in Classical Philology* 5 (1920), 135–41, and T. A. M. Bishop, 'Autographa of John the Scot', *John Scot Erigène et l'Histoire de la Philosophie* (Paris 1977 – Colloques Internationaux du Centre Nationale de la Recherche Scientifique No. 561), 89–94.

25. M. Cappuyns, 'Les *Bibli Wulfadi*', cited above Chapter 8, n. 23.

26. E. Jeauneau, 'Dans le sillage de Jean Scot Erigène', *Studi Medievali* 3rd series 11 (1970), 937–55.

27. E. Jeauneau, 'Les écoles de Laon et d'Auxerre au IXᵉ siècle', *Settimane* 19 (1972),

495–522 especially 513, notes 63 and 64; compare Marenbon, *From the Circle of Alcuin*, 121–3.

28. Jeauneau, 'Les écoles de Laon et d'Auxerre'.
29. *MGH Poet.* III, 427. Compare R. Quadri, *I Collectanea di Eirico di Auxerre* (Freiburg 1966).
30. M. T. Gibson, 'The continuity of learning *circa* 850–*circa* 1050', *Viator* 6 (1975), 1–13.
31. L. Delisle, *Le Cabinet des Manuscrits de la Bibliothèque Impériale* (Paris 4 vols, 1868–81), I, 448–58.
32. G. Mathon, 'Un florilège érigènien à l'abbaye de Saint Amand au temps d'Hucbald', *Recherches de Théologie Ancienne et Médiévale* 20 (1953), 302–11 and Marenbon, *From the Circle of Alcuin*, 103. See also A. van de Vyver, 'Hucbald de Saint Amand, écolâtre, et l'invention du nombre d'or', *Mélanges Auguste Pelzer* (Louvain 1947), 61–79.
33. C. V. Palisca (ed.), *Hucbald, Guido and John on Music. Three Medieval Treatises*, trs. W. Babb (New Haven and London 1978); R. Weakland, 'Hucbald as musician and theorist', *Musical Quarterly* 42 (1956), 66–84 and 'The compositions of Hucbald', *Etudes Grégoriennes* 3 (1959), 155–62; J. Smits van Waesberghe, 'Neue Komposition des Johannes von Metz (um 975) Hucbald von St Amand und Sigeberts von Gembloux', *Speculum Musicae Artis. Festgabe für Heinrich Husmann* (Munich 1970), 285–303.
34. P. Piper (ed.), *Die Schriften Notkers und seiner Schule* I (Freiburg and Tübingen 1882), 857; and see G. Reese, *Music in the Middle Ages* (London 1941), 123. See also J. Smits van Waesberghe, 'La place exceptionelle de l'ars musica dans le développements des sciences dans le siècle carolingien', *Revue Gregorienne* 31 (1952), 81–104.
35. J. Duft, 'Le "presbiter de Gimedia" apporte son Antiphonaire à St Gall', *Jumièges. Congrés scientifique du XIIIᵉ centénaire* (Rouen 2 vols, 1955), II, 925–35 (and see the articles in the same volume by Orbin, Chailley and Hesbert). C. Hohler, however, has suggested that it may be wrong to translate *Gimedia* as Jumièges, and believes that sequence composition began in Italy and that Notker got an antiphonary from a monk in an Italian monastery rather than from one at Jumièges, *Journal of the Plainsong and Medieval Music Society* 2 (1976), 66.
36. E. K. Chambers (ed.), *The Medieval Stage* (Oxford 2 vols, 1902), II, 14–15; Eng. trs. Reese, *Music in the Middle Ages*, 194–5.
37. Studied by J. Yearley, 'The mediaeval Latin *planctus* as a genre', D.Phil. dissertation, University of York, 1982. I am grateful to her for allowing me to see her dissertation before completion.
38. These treatises are listed and discussed in Reese, *Music in the Middle Ages*, 125–7.
39. M. Huglo, 'L'auteur du "Dialogue sur la Musique" attribué à Odon', *Revue de Musicologie* 55 (1969), 119–71.
40. Richer, III, 43–66.
41. Text of letters on the abacus included in N. Bubnov, *Gerberti Opera Mathematica* (Berlin 1899) 25–8, 32–5, 29–30, 30–1, 23–4, 6–8 (Eng. trs. Lattin, Nos. 2, 3, 4, 5, 6, 7). On the abacus, see also G. R. Evans, '*Difficillima et ardua*: theory and practise in treatises on the abacus 950–1150', *Journal of Medieval History* 3 (1977), 21–38 and A. Murray, *Reason and Society in the Middle Ages* (Oxford 1978), 162–7.
42. Eng. trs. Lattin, No. 2, based on Bubnov, *Gerberti opera mathematica*, 25–8.
43. J. Clark, *The Abbey of St Gall* (Cambridge 1926), and H. Büttner and J. Duft, *Lorsch und St Gallen in der Frühzeit* (Stuttgart 1965).

44. P. Lehmann, *Mittelalterliche Bibliothekskataloge Deutschlands und der Schweiz* I (Munich 1918), 66–88.
45. See McKitterick, *Frankish Church*, 184–205.
46. J. Knight Bostock, *A Handbook on Old German Literature*, 2nd edn. (Oxford 1976), 281–98.
47. Clark, *Abbey of St Gall*, 18–54, and B. Bischoff, 'Irischen Schreiber im Karolingerreich', *Jean Scot Erigène* (above, n. 24), 47–58. H. Löwe (ed.), *Die Iren und Europa im früheren Mittelalter* (Stuttgart 2 vols, 1932); the proceedings of a conference held in Tübingen in 1979, however, constitute a significant contribution to our knowledge of Irish activity on the Continent.
48. Material relating to the Irish on the Continent is listed by J. F. Kenney, *The Sources for the early History of Ireland* (Shannon 1968 reprint with updated notes). This provides the foundation for a much needed reassessment of Irish activity and influence on the Continent in the early Middle Ages.
49. *MGH Dip. Kar.* I, No. 77, 110–11.
50 *MGH Conc.* II, i, 282.
51. Alcuin, Ep. 8, 7 and 77 resp.; Eng. trs. Allott, Nos. 9, 31 and 158.
52. B. Bischoff, 'Theodulf und der Ire Cadac Andreas', *HJ* 74 (1955), 92–8.
53. *MGH Cap.* II, No. 293, c. 40, 408, and ibid., No. 257, 260–3. Compare *PL* 126, cols 9–25.
54. *MGH Poet.* III, 429 lines 24–6.
55. S. Hellmann, *Sedulius Scottus* (Munich 1906).
56. G. Kurth, *Notger de Liège et la civilisation au Xe siècle* (Paris 1905).
57. J. J. Contreni, 'The Irish "Colony" at Laon during the time of John Scottus', *Jean Scot Erigène*, 59–67.
58. J. J. Contreni, *The Cathedral School of Laon* (above, n. 22).
59. See *MGH SS* XIV, 505–41 and *MGH Diplomatum regum et imperatorum Germaniae* I (Hannover 1884), 160–1; A. Gwynn, 'Irish monks and the Cluniac reform' *Studies* 29 (1940), 409–29.
60. *Vita Brunoni*, c. 7., *MGH SS* IV, 254–275.

CHAPTER TWELVE

The Last Carolingians

The Carolingians fought hard for their kingship in the tenth century. Not one of them was an effete or useless ruler, and there is no justification for the parallel that has sometimes been drawn between them and the Merovingian *rois fainéants* (do-nothing kings). Too much weight furthermore has been accorded by historians to Gerbert's statement in a letter, dated 980, that the real ruler of the west Frankish kingdom was not Lothar the king but Hugh Capet the Robertian leader. Gerbert, for all his learning and his later papal dignity as Pope Sylvester II, was a wily and ambitious politician with his stakes in the east Frankish kingdom. It is unlikely that his statement was an accurate one as far as Lothar's position was concerned, but even if it were, it is hardly a reliable description of the Carolingian position in relation to the Robertians throughout the tenth century. The last Carolingians should not be reduced to the status of a brief preface to the history of the Capetian monarchy. Under the last Carolingians, who reigned for almost a century after Odo's death (apart from a brief period under the 'stop-gap kings' Robert and Ralph from 922 to 936), the political structure of the west Frankish kingdom changed; the territorial principalities were consolidated and the nobility at all levels secured a greater degree of independence within their own localities at the expense of royal authority. Yet this should not be exaggerated as a 'decline' or as a failure on the part of the Carolingians. Their policies and efforts to maintain their position did much to secure the future of the monarchy.[1]

The narrative sources for the tenth century have contributed greatly to the negative picture of the last Carolingians simply because none are directly associated with the Carolingian family; all are written from parochial or at best regional points of view. There are thus major areas where we are either ignorant of the details or even existence of Carolingian activity, or else we are informed by hostile, or at best neutral, commentators. There is moreover a marked decrease during the tenth century in the number of narrative sources of major interest or importance. The St Vaast Annals end in 900; Regino of Prüm's Chronicle, already noted for the value of its political commentary, ends in 906; Flodoard's Annals cover the period 919–66, and in them he incorporates a wide variety of material, whereas his history of Rheims, based primarily on the documents in the Rheims archive, provides an invaluable source of information only about the archbishops of Rheims in the later ninth and the tenth centuries. Flodoard's first loyalty, however, was to Rheims; he was no more pro-Carolingian than he was a partisan of the house of Vermandois.[2] For the second half of the tenth century, the main narrative source is Richer's history, written in 995 or 996 (the autograph manuscript, BN lat. 5354, is still extant). Richer, a disciple of Gerbert and Archbishop Adalbero and writing some time after the ascent of the Robertians to the throne, was unlikely to be notably favourable to the Carolingians. His history, moreover, is of little independent value for the years before 970.[3] Gerbert's letters contain much information about the later years of Lothar's reign and the brief reign of Louis V, but Gerbert was a hostile witness. Other information is patchy, diffuse and often ambiguous, though a great deal of useful information, particularly with regard to the nature, extent and exercise of royal authority within the west Frankish kingdom, can be derived from the royal charters. Modern treatment of the last Carolingian kings has followed the main primary sources closely in detail, areas of ignorance and prejudice. It is high time that the full range of regional sources and the regional studies and syntheses by such scholars as Werner, Lemarignier and Duby were fully exploited,[4] and the developments of the tenth century, especially in the political and ecclesiastical spheres, properly appreciated.

Despite the need for a thorough reappraisal of the tenth-century Frankish kings, only an outline of their careers can be attempted here. The relations between the kings and the great nobles under Charles the Simple, Robert, Ralph, Louis IV and Lothar, the importance of the see of Rheims, the question of Lotharingia and the role of the east Frankish kings in west Frankish affairs (especially after 956) are the principal themes in the political vicissitudes of the west Frankish kingdom in the tenth century which determined the fate of the Carolingian kings. In some respects the east Frankish kings and the see of Rheims became of primary importance only in the second half of the tenth century, but both, with the questions of Lotharingia and the west Frankish nobility, were interrelated themes at recurrent intervals throughout the tenth century. For the sake of clarity and convenience therefore, I consider these themes in the context of each king's reign.

I

Charles the Simple, then aged nineteen, succeeded Odo in 898 with the full support of Odo's brother Robert, who later in the spring swore to Charles an oath of fidelity, as did Richard of Burgundy, William of the Auvergne and Herbert of Vermandois. Baldwin of Flanders made his submission later. There is no indication in the meagre shreds of information we have for the years between 900 and 919 that Charles' position was troubled by any major internal opposition to his authority. These years are marked rather by two events of great significance: the establishment of Rollo and the Seine Vikings in the lower Seine basin and the acquisition of Lotharingia.

Viking raids had increased after Odo's death. We can only assume that the Franks resisted these raids effectively, for we are ignorant of the background to Charles' treaty with the Viking leader Rollo in 911 (discussed above, pp. 237–8). That the Seine Vikings had been occupying the lower Seine region round Rouen for some years and that Charles the Simple's treaty represents a realistic recognition of this is implicit in the evidence we have. Yet it is remarkable that relatively little – a countship, a small extent of territory and an obligation to protect the Franks from further Viking attack – was conceded, especially when one considers how often the Vikings had held the kingdom to ransom in the past (see Map 17). Charles the Simple apparently had the upper hand; he must have gained it during the years 903 to 911 when the sources are silent about the Vikings, and he may well deserve the credit for reducing the Vikings to a position of relative meekness, willing to negotiate a treaty on Charles' terms, and to accept the overlordship, even if only nominal, of the Frankish king. Dudo's heart-rending description of the battle-weary Vikings before the agreement was reached with Charles makes much better sense if we view Charles in this more positive light.[5]

In the same year as the agreement with Rollo, Charles became the king of Lotharingia.[6] Under Arnulf, Lotharingia had enjoyed a considerable measure of independence. After he had made his bastard Zwentibold the subking in Lotharingia, for example, Arnulf himself issued no more charters for the region. This special position continued under Louis the Child, who succeeded his father Arnulf in 899, for the Lotharingian chancery under Radbod, archbishop of Trier, remained separate from the east German chancery which was under the direction of the archbishop of Salzburg.[7] The Lotharingian nobles moreover do not seem to have been fully integrated into the east Frankish kingdom; they did not participate in east Frankish assemblies, their religious interests were centred on the abbeys and bishoprics of Lotharingia (reform was promoted on a local basis) and many of them had both land and kindred in the west Frankish kingdom. They were, moreover, anxious to preserve some measure of independence; Louis the Child's appointment of the Franconian Gebhard (d. 910) as *dux* in Lotharingia had alienated the support of a number of Lotharingian nobles such as Gerard and Matfred (both of whom had been banished by Louis) and Ragnar Longneck, count of Hainault who had been, since 898, a *fidelis* of Charles the Simple. Ragnar in particular had been obliged to play second fiddle to Gebhard, though after the latter's death he was the leading magnate and called himself *comes et missus dominicus*.

When after Louis the Child's death in 911 Gebhard's son Conrad was elected king of the east Frankish kingdom by the magnates of Saxony, Thuringia, Bavaria and Alemannia, the Lotharingians decided to turn to Charles the Simple instead. The Lotharingian nobles were both resentful and suspicious of the Franconian Conrad and it is possible, as Eckel suggested, that they thought their interests would be better served if they were ruled by a weak king.[8] It is by no means certain, however, that Charles the Simple's reputation was poor at this stage or that he was regarded as an ineffectual ruler. In fact, because of the way he had dealt with the Vikings, it was probably good. It is conceivable that Charles may have represented to them the hope of protection against Franconian aggrandizement and that some lingering sense of identity with the west Frankish kingdom as well as loyalty to the Carolingian house contributed to the nobles' decision. Charles himself, moreover, had nurtured his connection with Lotharingia for some years, since 898 in fact; his first wife Frederuna, whom he married in 907 and who bore him six daughters, was a Lotharingian. We should not underestimate the uncertainty with which the election of Conrad, the first non-Carolingian king of the east Franks, and the new political situation this created, must have been viewed.

For Charles, the acquisition of Lotharingia meant a crucial extension of the royal domain and of the area in which royal authority could be exercised directly (see Map 18); it was the restoration of the old Frankish heartland to the Carolingians, and Charles' revival of the title *rex francorum* (it had fallen out of use) celebrated this. It is clear from Charles' charters moreover that he devoted much energy and interest to Lotharingian affairs after 911.[9] A third of the extant charters issued by Charles after 911 relate to Lotharingia. They record concessions to churches, monasteries and individuals as well as assemblies of magnates. The assembly held at Herstal in 916, for example, was attended almost exclusively by Lotharingians.[10] The Lotharingian royal palaces of Thionville, Gondreville, Herstal, Aachen and Metz feature prominently on the royal itinerary after 911.

Because of the dearth of sources it is difficult to know what the west Frankish nobles felt about the acquisition of Lotharingia, how they reacted to the king's prolonged absences in Lotharingia or what precisely the king's relations with his nobles were at this time. It is likely, however, that Robert of Neustria's position at least was enhanced, in that he acted as a sort of second-in-command to the king. Certainly the royal diplomas witness to the cordiality of the relations sustained between the king and Robert until 920, for without exception they employ phrases expressing the king's trust in and reliance on the chief among his *fideles*.[11] Lotharingian lands and offices granted to Lotharingians should not have caused west Frankish resentment. What does seem to have roused the west Frankish nobles to protest was, on the one hand, the growing influence over the king of the Lotharingian Hagano (described in a charter of 921 as a cousin of the king through the latter's mother) and, on the other hand, the king's granting of west Frankish favours to the Lotharingian nobles. This was not accompanied by the conferring on the west Franks of any favours from Lotharingian resources. That the acquisition of Lotharingia made Charles potentially too strong for the west Frankish nobles' comfort can probably be discounted, for there is no evidence to suggest that Charles made any attempt to encroach on the positions or possessions of the counts and *marchiones*.

Whether the revolt of the nobles, led by Robert, against Charles in 920 was a specific protest against the favouritism shown to Hagano, or a general expression of dissatisfaction with Charles the Simple's preoccupation with Lotharingia is not to be ascertained from the laconic report in Flodoard's Annals, but the refusal of anyone but the archbishop of Rheims to send troops to assist Charles against the Magyars in 919 suggests that some nobles at least had adopted by then a policy of non-co-operation. Flodoard states that at Soissons in 920 all the Frankish counts deserted Charles because he would not renounce his favourite, the upstart Hagano.[12] Only Heriveus, the archbishop of Rheims, remained loyal and provided Charles with a refuge for seven months. After this Charles and his nobles were reconciled and Charles was restored to his kingdom. Some Lotharingian nobles, led by Gilbert (Gislebert) son of Ragnar Longneck, then declared their independence of Charles' authority. On Ragnar's death in 915 Charles had declined to make Gilbert a *marchio* as his father had been. The Lotharingian nobles clashed with Charles over the election to the bishopric of Liège. Charles wished to give the bishopric to Richer, abbot of Prüm, because the other candidate, Hilduin, had defected to Gilbert.[13] The people of Liège, however, elected Hilduin and he was consecrated by Archbishop Hermann of Cologne. Charles succeeded in regaining the submission of Gilbert and his followers, though Hilduin was left unmolested in his see. The most serious aspect of the revolt was that Gilbert had invoked the aid of the new ruler of the east Franks, the Saxon Henry I the Fowler. Charles, after quelling the resistance of the Lotharingian Count Ricoin, made a treaty with Henry at Bonn in 921. The two kings met on terms of equality, expressed clearly in the titles each accorded the other at their meeting: *rex francorum occidentalium* (Charles) and *rex francorum orientalium* (Henry).[14] Charles did not renounce Lotharingia.

In the meantime Charles had ignored his 'nobles' request to remove Hagano and the Lotharingian count remained in favour. Some charters of 920 and 921 were actually issued with Hagano acting as intermediary, and in one the monks who received the grant were required to offer up prayers in perpetuity, not only for members of the royal family, but for Hagano as well![15] The last straw for the west Frankish nobles was Charles' conferral on Hagano of the abbacy of Chelles (a royal nunnery) of which he arbitrarily deprived his aunt Rothild, the abbess, who also happened to be related to the Robertians.[16] How much hurt family pride was expressed in the nobles' reaction and how much Charles' perverse promotion of his favourite had provided the excuse for revolt cannot be gauged exactly, but it is certainly the case that all the relations of Rothild, led by Robert and his son Hugh (Rothild's son-in-law) now united in their opposition to Charles. Charles panicked and fled to Lotharingia, but returned with some soldiers to fight the warriors of Robert and Hugh. Flodoard's account reveals unequivocally that the west Franks' hostility was directed almost exclusively at Hagano, for it was his possessions which were attacked and pillaged. Charles and Hagano fled in secret to Lotharingia once more and in their absence, Robert was elected king and crowned at Rheims by Walter, archbishop of Sens, under the very nose of Archbishop Heriveus who lay on his death-bed (and died three days later). Charles naturally enough disputed Robert's title and met him in battle at Soissons on 15 June 923. Robert was killed but the forces led by his son Hugh and by Herbert of Vermandois defeated the king's army and Charles retreated. He attempted to form an alliance with the

Vikings on the Seine but was forestalled. On 13 July 923 a new king, Ralph, the eldest son of Richard 'the Justiciar' of Burgundy (d. 921), was elected king and anointed in the church of St Médard at Soissons by Walter, archbishop of Sens.

II

Ralph appears to have been a compromise candidate. Presumably neither Hugh nor Herbert would have countenanced the election of the other and to have elected Hugh would also have incurred the danger of establishing the Robertians as hereditary rulers. On election, Ralph, the first Frankish king whose family lands lay outside Francia, did not relinquish his position in Burgundy (as Odo had relinquished the countship of Paris to Robert). Instead he based his power there, especially in the counties of Autun, Avallon and Lassois. In his absences from Burgundy his wife Queen Emma administered the counties on his behalf.

The position of Ralph was precarious in 923; only the counts of Neustria and Francia (including Hugh's vassals the viscounts and counts of Tours, Chartres, Angers and Blois) acknowledged him. Normandy, Brittany, Aquitaine and Lotharingia remained aloof. Among those who had acknowledged Ralph, Herbert of Vermandois for one soon defied the king. After Ralph's coronation, Herbert beguiled Charles the Simple into meeting him at the Castellum Theuderici (Château Thierry) and promptly took him prisoner. Charles remained Herbert's captive and royal pawn until he died in 929. Contemporaries, according to Flodoard, were disgusted by the treacherous capture of Charles but made no move to rescue him. There is some indication indeed that some, including Ralph himself, were aware of Herbert's intentions beforehand.[17] Nevertheless, Herbert's action proved to be as much against King Ralph as against Charles; the house of Vermandois, indeed, represented the gravest threat both to the position of the monarch and to Robertian predominance among the nobles until 943.

Herbert I, count of Vermandois and lay abbot of St Quentin, was a direct descendant in the male line of Bernard of Italy, Charlemagne's grandson. Herbert's father Pippin seems to have had a county in the Paris region and in the muddled years between 840 and 843 served Lothar for a time before defecting back to Charles the Bald on the settlement in 843, no doubt because his own family lands were in the western kingdom. Two of Pippin's sons, Pippin and Herbert, also served Charles the Bald and all three sons held counties. Herbert, though a count by 889, cannot be associated with the county of Vermandois before 896. The Vermandois possessions moreover were somewhat dispersed in the region north of the Seine and centred on St Quentin. Other estates and offices were acquired gradually; the countship of Troyes, for example, was gained in 931. The bishopric of Soissons seems to have been controlled by the counts of Vermandois between 900 and 932, and they maintained their hold on the abbey of St Medard of Soissons until 1084; Herbert III was himself its lay abbot.[18] That Herbert was a Carolingian was of some importance for the side he chose to be on during Odo's reign, but his temperate support of Carolingian legitimacy and Charles the Simple between 888 and 898 was with more than half an eye on the opportunities for advancing his own position; blood kinship with the Carolingians was exploited when it suited him. Herbert I was assassinated in about 902 by a vassal of Baldwin II of Flanders, but he bequeathed both his ambition and his unscrupulousness to his son Herbert II (902–43). Richer described Herbert as a man in a position to do much harm and eager to do it.[19] Herbert II's chance to extend Vermandois dominance came with the downfall of Charles the Simple. With Charles secured, Herbert II turned his attention to the methodical expansion of his territory north of the Seine. He seized Péronne and then Rheims.

The archbishop of Rheims had played a central role in Frankish politics in the time of Hincmar; and Fulk, Hincmar's successor, had maintained, though not so successfully, Rheims' importance in relation to the king. Fulk's murder in 900 signalled the foundering for some decades of the archbishopric's influence and prestige. Heriveus, archbishop from 900 to 923, was a staunch supporter of Charles the Simple. He came to the king's aid with 1500 warriors in 919, and in 920 he provided the king with a refuge after the first revolt of the nobles. Heriveus was also, according to Flodoard, a pious, wise and effective archbishop. He succeeded in recovering lands granted out by his predecessor, as well as promoting the religious life of his diocese and province. He supported the attempt to convert the Vikings in Normandy to Christianity. After his death, the church of Rheims became one of the principal objects of the struggle between the king and the nobles. Heriveus' successor Seulf was King Robert's nominee. He spent much of his short incumbency (922–5) endeavouring to recover Rheims' land from the brothers and nephews of his predecessors, being aided and abetted in this by Herbert of Vermandois, who hoped thereby to gain control of the lands of Rheims. Seulf was rash and feeble enough to promise Herbert that his successor would not be elected without Herbert's sanction. He died rather too soon afterwards and Flodoard says that it was generally thought that he had been poisoned by Herbert's servants.[20]

For the next twenty years the count of Vermandois retained his grip on Rheims, a grip gained with shocking ease and countenanced by the Pope himself. After Seulf's decease, Herbert went to Rheims to organize the election of his successor, convoked an assembly attended by the bishops of Châlons and Soissons (the latter was under Herbert's thumb) and the people and clergy of Rheims, and persuaded them to elect his five-year-old son Hugh as the new archbishop of Rheims. It is remarkable that so uncanonical an election was countenanced at all, and is indicative of Herbert's strength north of the Seine. Because Herbert held Charles the Simple, King Ralph's acquiescence was received (Herbert later assisted Ralph against the Vikings) and Pope John X authorized the new appointment as well as endorsing Herbert's position as the lay administrator of the temporal of Rheims. Abbo, bishop of Soissons, was selected to conduct the services and regulate spiritual affairs as the baby archbishop's proxy. (Odalric, bishop of Aix-en-Provence, later took over the spiritual direction of Rheims after he had been driven from his own see by the Saracens.) The incident hardly adds to the Papacy's reputation at this period. Herbert quickly exploited his new position. Rheims' land was conferred on his supporters and the clergy were terrorized. Flodoard, the historian of Rheims, was one of those who suffered; because of his disapproval of the irregularity of Hugh's election, Flodoard was deprived of his benefices. By 931, Ralph decided the time had come to break Herbert's hold on Rheims. He besieged the city and forced a new archbishop, Artald, on the people. Artald was consecrated in the presence of eighteen bishops, and Hugh, still only eleven years old, was declared deposed. The Pope, John XI this time, was as co-operative as ever, and in 933 the pallium was sent to Artald, who remained undisturbed in the see until 940.

On the death of Count Roger of Laon in 926, Herbert endeavoured to add Laon to the Vermandois possessions and asked that his son Odo be made count of Laon. Ralph, however, was disinclined to be as co-operative over Laon as he had been when Herbert seized Rheims. Laon was vital strategically for the king's hold of the north. Quite apart from being a favoured royal residence it was a splendid stronghold, for it was on top of a large, steep-sided, flat-topped hill which rose abruptly out of the surrounding plain. (For the modern traveller approaching Laon, the city and its glorious cathedral are still an imposing spectacle.) Laon therefore was granted by Ralph to Roger's son (also called Roger). The count of Vermandois, reinforced by soldiers from Lotharingia and Saxony, thereupon launched an offensive against Laon and Ralph, and proclaimed the unfortunate Charles the Simple king at St Quentin in 927. Laon was stoutly defended by Queen Emma. Herbert was eventually obliged to capitulate, as he had failed to muster sufficient support for his cause, and Charles was returned to his prison. Flodoard tells us that Ralph visited Charles in prison, besought his forgiveness and gave him presents, including the royal palace of Attigny; Richer repeats this story but both may well have confused the earlier concessions Odo had made to Charles and ascribed them to Ralph as well.[21]

Ralph's ally against Herbert after 929 was the Robertian Hugh the Great, brother-in-law to Ralph and Herbert's nephew (Hugh's mother Beatrice was Herbert's sister). Hugh, under the pretext of aiding the king, systematically broke down the power of his greatest rival. He besieged Amiens and captured St Quentin, but failed to secure Péronne. Herbert acquired a powerful ally in Arnulf of Flanders and also tried to entice away those of Hugh's vassals who lived north of the Seine. With Hugh's help therefore, Ralph was able to subdue Vermandois and Herbert finally made his submission to the king and received back some of his domains (which had been occupied by Hugh). This setback to Hugh's achievements against Herbert undoubtedly rankled; much of his work had been negated by the king whose ostensible supporter he had been. A formal reconciliation was later effected between Hugh and Herbert, though the former refused to relinquish St Quentin and was only persuaded to do so by the Lotharingian and Saxon army.

As well as the defiance of Herbert II of Vermandois and the growing strength and ambivalent support of Hugh the Great, Ralph had to contend with raids into Francia by the Vikings (tribute was paid in 924) and into Champagne by the Magyars. The Bassin and Maine were ceded to the Seine Vikings in 924 and the Loire Vikings were granted leave to settle round Nantes in 924–7. In 928 William Longsword swore fidelity to Ralph and was ceded the Cotentin and Avranchin five years later. Loss of Frankish territory in the west was paralleled in the east, for in 925 Ralph lost Lotharingia to Henry I. Henry made Gilbert son of Ragnar *dux* in Lotharingia and gave him the hand of his daughter Gerberga in marriage. Lotharingia thereafter was in the east Frankish orbit, though the Carolingians, as we shall see, made several efforts to retrieve it. Yet Ralph's policies in the western and eastern reaches of his kingdom were not those of desperation or weakness but more the outcome of a realistic appraisal of the possibilities. Ralph was concerned above all to retain what he had rather than fight to maintain a hold on peripheral regions in which rival interests were already firmly entrenched. He was active in asserting royal authority within the Frankish kingdom apart from Lotharingia, and in demanding submission from the nobles.

In Aquitaine, for example, the nobles delayed their recognition of Ralph for some years. By the end of the ninth century, Aquitaine, that is, Poitou, Auvergne, Septimania, Gothia and Gascony, was dominated by Ramnulf II, count of Poitou (d. 890) and by William the Pious, count of Auvergne and Gothia (d. 918). Ramnulf was succeeded first by his bastard Ebalus and then by Ademar, who ruled as count from 893 to 935 and was succeeded by William 'Towhead'. William of the Auvergne was succeeded by his nephew William II (d. 927), while Raymond Pons of Toulouse became the count of Gothia. An Aquitainian revolt against Ralph petered out after the cession of Berry and William II's oath of fidelity in 924, but it was not until 932 that Raymond Pons of Toulouse acknowledged Ralph as king. Ralph was also temporarily suzerain of the Rhône valley and received the oath of fidelity from his cousin Charles Constantine, count of Vienne, in 933.

Despite his preoccupation with his Burgundian patrimony (particularly evident from his charters), the cessions of territory and privileges he was obliged to make to many of the nobles (Hugh the Great for example was ceded Maine) and the fact that the counts of Vermandois, Neustria, Aquitaine, Normandy and Burgundy were able to strengthen their positions at the expense of the monarchy during his reign, Ralph managed to gain the recognition of his suzerainty from the Scheldt to Navarre, though he never exercised his authority effectively south of the Loire. Yet the coherence of the west Frankish kingdom was now dependent to far greater an extent than ever before on the fidelity of the nobles and a satisfactory balance of power among those nobles. This was Ralph's legacy to Louis IV.

III

When Charles the Simple was deposed in 923, his wife Eadgifu fled with their son Louis to the court of her father Edward the Elder (d. 924) in England. Louis had made no move to advance his claim to the throne when his father died in 929. When Ralph died in January 936 he left no direct heir. His brother Hugh the Black succeeded him in Burgundy but did not make a bid for the crown. Other possible candidates among the nobility were Arnulf of Flanders, William Longsword of Normandy, Herbert, count of Vermandois and the Robertian Hugh the Great. It is from Ralph's death that Hugh the Great's rise to pre-eminence in the Frankish kingdom dates, and we need to see what resources he had at his disposal which made this possible.

By 923 when Hugh succeeded his father Robert, the Robertians commanded the region corresponding to ancient Neustria between the Loire and the Seine, except for the portions ceded to the Vikings between 911 and 933.[22] Hugh also possessed land in the Touraine, Orleanais, Berry, Autunois, Maine and north of the Seine as far as Meaux, and held the countships of Tours, Anjou and Paris. Many powerful viscounts and counts were his vassals and deputies such as Bernard, count of Senlis, Herluin, count of Montreuil, Hilduin of Montdidier, the counts of Tours, Blois and Angers and the viscounts of Paris, Chartres and Orleans. Some of these vassals themselves rose in time to great pre-eminence among the Frankish and French nobility. Besides the counties, a number of wealthy monasteries were also in Robertian hands. Hugh himself was lay abbot of St Martin of Tours, Marmoutier, St Germain of Auxerre (after 937), St Denis, Morienval, St Riquier, St Valéry and possibly St Aignan of Orleans, St Germain-des-Prés and St Maur des Fosses. He was certainly the richest, most powerful and independent of the territorial princes north of the Loire.

Some indication of the impression he could make on his contemporaries is given by the account of the gifts Hugh sent to King Athelstan on his betrothal to Athelstan's sister Eadhild in 926. As well as spices and perfumes never smelt in England before, precious jewels (including emeralds), a vase made of onyx, horses richly caparisoned and a gold crown encrusted with gems, Hugh presented Athelstan with no less than three priceless relics – the sword of Constantine in whose hilt one of the nails of the Passion was mounted, the Holy Lance 'which Charlemagne had won in the war against the Saracens' (which hitherto had been part of the treasure of the church of Sens) and the standard (*vexillum*) of St Maurice which Charlemagne had brought back from Spain.[23] These were fabulous gifts, the sort that a king would make. The marriage to Eadhild and the connection Hugh thereby formed with the English court should not be forgotten in any consideration of Hugh's activities with regard to the succession in his own country in 936. Hugh was after all negotiating with his sister- and brother-in-law for the return of his nephew by marriage to rule the west Frankish kingdom.

Hugh the Great seems to have made no move to claim the throne for himself, possibly because he estimated accurately the opposition he would encounter from the rest of the Frankish nobility. According to Flodoard, Hugh negotiated with Eadgifu, Charles the Simple's widow and her brother Athelstan, now king in England, and recalled Charles the Simple's fifteen-year-old son Louis (often called in later sources *transmarinus* or *ultramarinus*, Fr. *outremer*, because of his English blood and English exile). No doubt Hugh calculated that he would be able to exert effective power within the kingdom as the young monarch's uncle, chief adviser and supporter. Louis IV and the Frankish legates, with an escort provided by Louis' uncle King Athelstan, arrived at Boulogne where they were met by Hugh the Great and other west Frankish nobles. At Laon on 19 June 936, Louis was anointed king by Artald, archbishop of Rheims 'in the presence of twenty bishops and all the great men of the land'. Flodoard, whose description this is, was exaggerating the extent to which Louis' elevation was recognized, for it was some years before, and in a few cases not until after a bitter struggle that, he was acknowledged as king by the territorial princes outside Francia.

Hugh the Great's sanguine expectations were at first fully justified. Soon after Louis' coronation, Hugh and Louis marched on Burgundy in order to win recognition from Hugh the Black and the other Burgundian counts. This they did with the added bonus for Hugh the Great of the northern portion of Burgundy, including the archdiocese of Sens. In other words, Hugh had turned the establishment of the king's position to his own advantage. Two charters of Louis, moreover, dated 25 July 936 and 25 December 936, make clear the prize Hugh received for his kingmaking, for in them he is called *dux francorum* and second only to the king in the realm.[24]

The meaning of the title *dux francorum* as far as the authority it conferred is concerned is ambiguous. It was certainly a power recognized and conceded by the king, but there is some dispute as to whether this power was the superior authority Hugh exercised over Francia or whether it implied viceregal authority over the whole kingdom. Both these interpretations may be possible; Werner, for example, has suggested that the position of *dux francorum* could have been that of intermediary between the king and each of the *marchiones* as well as being that of the *marchio* of Francia. What is clear is that there was no ethnic element involved.[25]

Hugh's satisfaction with his exalted position in the kingdom and the exertion of his influence over Louis was short-lived, for in 937 Louis quit Hugh's residence in Paris, ensconced himself at Laon with his mother Eadgifu, appointed Artald, archbishop of Rheims, as his archchancellor and formed an alliance with Hugh the Black of Burgundy.

For the next few years, and indeed throughout his reign, Louis was preoccupied with disputes with his chief nobles, particularly Hugh the Great, Herbert of Vermandois, Arnulf of Flanders and William of Normandy. Vassals supposedly loyal to Louis broke their oaths and were promiscuous in their fidelity to the king's opponents. There were many shifting alliances between the nobles and the king; Hugh the Great, for example, joined forces with his former rival Herbert of Vermandois. Each side enjoyed some successes, though it is a comment on the respect Louis inspired that major enterprises in Francia were only embarked upon when he was safely out of the way in Burgundy or elsewhere. Louis showed that he was no man's puppet. As well as his efforts to establish his authority in Burgundy between 940 and 942, Louis endeavoured to capture some of the strongholds north of the Seine and to win over some of the lesser counts. A number of fortresses – Montigny, Touzy (with its neighbouring farms) Corbigny, Visar and Chausot – were taken. Louis succeeded in gaining the allegiance of Odo, one of the sons of Herbert of Vermandois, whom he had made count of Laon after he had driven out Herbert (he had seized Laon while Louis was in Burgundy). In 940 William Longsword swore an oath of fidelity to the king.

By 942, peace was restored between the king and all his nobles. The balance of power among the nobility, however, was altered radically with the murder of William Longsword in 942 by henchmen of Count Arnulf of Flanders, and the death of Herbert II of Vermandois the following year. Both left heirs in their minority. Louis quickly made peace with the four sons of Herbert and seized his opportunity to exert an influence in Normandy. In 944 he managed to get himself recognized by the Normandy Vikings as regent for William's son Richard I (942–96). For a time Louis' Viking allies proved invaluable in helping to pay back in kind some of the excesses of Hugh the Great's vassals. Hugh had continued to goad the king through counts Bernard of Senlis, Theobald of Blois and Herbert of Vexin, who had, for example, besieged Louis' castle of Montigny. Bernard had also kidnapped the horses and dogs on a royal hunt and pillaged the villages round Compiègne. But in 945 Louis was taken prisoner by his Viking allies and only rescued from them, in exchange for Louis IV's youngest son, by Hugh the Great. This was to exchange the frying pan for the fire, for Hugh, instead of releasing Louis, committed him to the custody of Theobald of Blois where he languished for a year. Attempts were made to rescue him by, among others, his uncle Edmund of England, and representations were made to Hugh to free the king. Hugh's response was to convoke an assembly to discuss the matter, and there he agreed to release the king.[26] His capitulation was no doubt hastened by the arrival in the kingdom of an east Frankish army under Conrad the Pacific, king of Burgundy. The army had been sent by Otto I in response to an appeal from his sister Gerberga, Louis's wife, in order to secure Louis' release. It subsequently assisted Louis to recover the archbishopric of Rheims from the Vermandois' possession.

In 940, Artald, archbishop of Rheims and chancellor of the kingdom, had been conceded the county of Rheims and the right to mint coins. Louis probably hoped thereby to exploit Rheims' resources as well as strengthening the archbishop's ability to resist the house of Vermandois. Thereafter, it is not always clear how the archbishop maintained secular authority over the city and its environs, nor whether there were any lay counts of Rheims. Despite Louis' precautions, Herbert of Vermandois and Hugh the Great attacked Rheims, drove out Archbishop Artald (who took refuge in the monastery of St Remigius) and convoked a synod of the bishops and clergy of the province of Rheims. This synod deposed Artald, and Herbert's son Hugh, now twenty and an ordained deacon, was reinstated as archbishop. Pope Stephen VIII, preserving the tradition of papal compliance, sent the pallium to Hugh in 942. Artald contemplated an appeal to Rome but settled instead for the two abbacies – of St Basle and Avenay – given him by Archbishop Hugh.

As an archbishop in his own right Hugh proved to be a capable ecclesiastic. Flodoard's praise of him is all the more remarkable in that Flodoard suffered with his fellow priests when Artald was removed. To avoid acknowledging Hugh, Flodoard had arranged to make a pilgrimage to the shrine of St Martin at Tours, but just as he was sneaking off he was caught, accused of plotting against Hugh the Great and Herbert of Vermandois, deprived of his estates and his parish of Cormicy, and held in semi-captivity among the canons of Rheims from October 940 to March 941. He was then, thanks to the inter-cession of Hugh the Great, restored to favour and his parish. This did not prevent Flodoard rejoining Artald's staff on the latter's restoration to his see in 946. The canonical legality of any of the changes in the incumbency of Rheims between 925 and 946 was very doubtful to all observers. At the Council of Ingelheim in 948, convoked after Artald's restoration by the combined forces of Otto I of the east Frankish kingdom and Louis IV, presided over by Otto, Louis and the papal legate Marinus, and attended almost exclusively by Lothar-ingian and east Frankish bishops (apart from the bishops of Rheims and Laon), Hugh was declared an usurper, deposed and excommunicated. It is of interest that the proceedings were translated from Latin into *teutisca lingua* (the German tongue) for both Otto's and Louis' benefit; neither understood Latin. Pope Agapetus II subsequently ratified the Ingelheim decision at a synod in Rome. Ex-archbishop Hugh had taken refuge at Mouzon but in September 948 a Lotharingian army attacked Mouzon and destroyed it. At a countil held at Trier soon afterwards, Archbishop Hugh's hangers-on and Hugh the Great were excommunicated.[27]

To account for the involvement of the east Frankish ruler and the magnates of Lotharingia in west Frankish affairs and the quarrel over Rheims, we need to retrace our steps to Louis' assertion of independence from Hugh the Great in 937.

In the east Frankish kingdom, Henry I had died in 936 and after a disputed succession between his two sons, Otto and Henry of Bavaria, Otto I had been crowned king. By marrying Otto's sister Hadwig in 938, Hugh the Great formed an exploitable relationship with the east Frankish ruler and thereby anticipated the subsequent east Frankish interference. This was provoked by Louis IV's interest in Lotharingia. Many Lotharingian nobles had remained sympathetic to the west Frankish kingdom after 925, despite their incorpo-ration into the east Frankish political structure. Of importance to both eastern and western kingdoms, moreover, was the contiguity of Lotharingia to the ecclesiastical province of Rheims. Cambrai, one of its bishoprics, was actually in Lotharingian territory, as were some of the estates of the churches and mon-asteries of Rheims. It is even possible that the east Frankish ruler had taken an interest in who occupied the see of Rheims as early as 931, for Herbert of Vermandois commended himself to Henry I as well as securing the support of Ralph and the Pope for his seizure of Rheims. After Otto's accession, Gilbert duke of Lotharingia and a Count Eberhard rebelled against Otto I's suzerainty and sought an alliance with Louis IV. At first, according to Flodoard, Louis was unwilling to offend Otto, but the temptation to recover Lotharingia and augment his strength was too great. In 939 he received the oaths of fidelity from Duke Gilbert (who had assisted Hugh the Great and Herbert of Vermandois against Louis only the year before), and the counts Theudebert of Holland, Otto of Verdun and Isaac of Cambrai, and between 938 and 940 he conducted raids into Lotharingia as far as the Rhine. His greatest success was the capture of Verdun after which the bishops of Verdun, Toul and Metz commended themselves to him. In retaliation, and possibly at the instigation of Hugh the Great and Herbert, Otto I (whose allies in the west Frankish kingdom were Herbert, Hugh, Arnulf of Flanders and William Longsword) entered Francia and encamped his army on the Seine. He received homage from Herbert and Hugh at Attigny and obliged Hugh the Black of Burgundy (still loyal to Louis) to submit to him. He then recrossed the Rhine. Resuming the offensive, Louis and Archbishop Artald re-entered Lotharingia, with the result that a truce was agreed between Otto and Louis.

By this time, Louis had complicated matters by becoming Otto's brother-in-law. After Gilbert of Lotharingia had been drowned in the Rhine in 939, Louis, without Otto's permission, had promptly married his widow (Otto's sister Gerberga, who was seven years older than Louis), and had her crowned as his queen. The marriage, coming so soon after that of Hugh the Great to Gerberga's sister Hadwig, can only have been a carefully calculated move on Louis' part, not only to neutralize the effects of Hugh's link with Otto but also to maintain a toehold in Lotharingia itself, through Gerberga's possessions in her former husband's territory. Gerberga proved a great support to Louis. She participated in public affairs both while her husband lived and during the minority of their son Lothar. She acted as intermediary in relaying requests for charters to Louis and two diplomas are recorded as having been drawn up in the queen's presence.[28] In 951 she received from her husband the domain of Anthony and the abbey of St Mary at Laon which the queen mother Eadgifu had held before her.[29] Gerberga was entrusted with the defence of Laon in 941 and of Rheims in 946, and she accompanied the king on his expeditions to Aquitaine in 944 and Burgundy in 949. Even more positive was her activity while Louis was being held prisoner by Hugh the Great's vassal Theobald in 945–6, for it was she who sought help from her brother Otto and from her husband's uncle.[30] Again in 949 Gerberga besought her brother's assistance, on her husband's request, when Hugh attacked their residence at Rheims. Thus Gerberga played an active diplomatic role just as Charlemagne's mother Bertrada and Empress Engelberga had done before her. Both Gerbert's letters and the Annals of Flodoard moreover, often show queens and noblewomen diplomatically, administratively and militarily active in the later tenth century. It should be stressed, however, that what evidence we have about earlier Frankish queens suggests that their tenth-century sisters were emulating their example rather than initiating a new role for queens. Although some of their activity was due to their responsibility for the royal purse of the palace, how prominent a political role she played also seems to have depended very much on the personality of the woman herself.[31]

Peace was concluded between Otto and Louis in 942, and friendly relations were maintained between them for the rest of Louis' reign. Louis made no further attempts to annexe Lotharingia. Henry of Bavaria, Otto's younger brother, received it to administer, though he was subsequently replaced by Count Otto of Verdun. Some have attempted to see in Otto's initial alliance with the Frankish nobility a wish to preserve the instability of the west Frankish kingdom and prevent its king from extending his power. There may be some truth in this (and see Bruno's policies, below p. 320), but a powerful and strong ally on the throne of the west Frankish kingdom would surely have been a more attractive alternative. The eastern and western kingdoms were not natural enemies but two parts of a whole. The old agreement with the east Frankish ruler Arnulf in 888 should not be forgotten, for there is much in the Ottonian attitude towards the west Frankish kingdom which is reminiscent of the relationship that had once existed between Arnulf, Odo and Charles the Simple. Lotharingia, however, was to remain a bone of contention between the two Frankish kingdoms.

For the remaining years of his life after the Lotharingian episode Louis struggled to maintain his authority within the Frankish kingdom, and against Hugh the Great. Peace was finally concluded between Louis and Hugh in 950, through the mediation of Conrad the Pacific (acting for Otto), Hugh the Black, Adalbero of Metz and Bishop Fulbert. This peace was precariously maintained, despite severe provocations from Hugh, such as the erection of forts in Francia from which his relatives and vassals could ravage the surrounding countryside. Louis built forts of his own at Montfelix and Vitry, and was obliged to call on Otto I to assist him to preserve the peace several times between 947 and 954. Were it not for his untimely death Louis IV might have achieved much. After a long struggle to maintain his position in the face of determined, self-seeking and truculent nobles, during which he had for a time had the upper hand, Louis had just reached the point at which he could have begun to consolidate his rule when he was mortally wounded in a fall from his horse and died at Rheims, aged thirty-three, on 10 October 954.

It is perhaps the most significant comment on the respect Louis had won for himself that his thirteen-year-old son Lothar was made king without opposition. Gerberga had the sense to appeal to Hugh the Great to ensure that Lothar was raised to the throne. With Hugh again assuming the role of protector, Lothar was elected king by an assembly of the lay and ecclesiastical magnates of Francia, Burgundy and Aquitaine on 12 November 954, and crowned and anointed by Archbishop Artald in the church of St Remigius at Rheims.[32]

IV

Lothar (954–86) was the ablest of the last Carolingian kings; he built on the work of his father and succeeded not only in raising the prestige of the Carolingian monarchy within and without the west Frankish kingdom but also in continuing the development of a new and positive form of kingship in relation to the nobility and the church. The sources for Lothar's reign, however, are decidedly meagre, and for the years between 958 and 966 virtually non-existent. For the years after 980 almost the only information available is that provided by Richer's history and Gerbert's letters, both hostile sources and deliberate distorters of Lothar's motives and activities. Nevertheless several important developments can be discerned.

At the beginning of his reign, Lothar was burdened with the protection of Hugh the Great. With Lothar's consent, and presumably as a reward for securing Lothar's accession, Hugh was made *dux* of Burgundy and Aquitaine in 954 (see Map 19). This meant that William Towhead, count of Poitou, and Gilbert, count of Chalon, the rulers of Aquitaine and Burgundy respectively, became effectively Hugh's vassals. Gilbert at least accepted this association and married his daughter to Hugh's son Odo. Hugh's dominance of Lothar, however, does not seem to have been as great as it had been of Louis IV, and in any case it did not last long, for in June 956 he died. He left three sons, Hugh Capet (the sobriquet was applied only from the twelfth century), Odo and Otto-Henry, of whom only Hugh had reached his majority. Thereafter Lothar ruled his kingdom himself, though Gerberga's brother Bruno, archbishop of Cologne, played a prominent role as protector of the king and arbitrator in west Frankish affairs for the next nine years. Twice, in 958 and 959, for example, Bruno intervened militarily to assist Lothar in Burgundy. The connection with Bruno, fostered by Gerberga, meant a further involvement of the east Franks in west Frankish affairs which was to influence Lothar's policies profoundly. Bruno, moreover, was not disinterested. He was not only the archbishop of an important east Frankish see, duke of Lotharingia and uncle of Lothar; he was also the uncle of Hugh the Great's three sons (they were the offspring of Hugh's second marriage to Hadwig, Bruno's other sister) and seems to have sought to strike an equitable balance between Robertian and Carolingian interests. He actually reinforced the Robertian position. On Bruno's prompting, for example, Hugh Capet and Odo, on commending themselves to Lothar in 960 and becoming his *fideles*, were made *dux francorum* and *dux burgundionum* respectively, and when Odo died in 965, the third brother, Otto-Henry, succeeded him in Burgundy.

Rather than the nobles joining forces against the king as they had done in the past, counts jockeyed for position in the kingdom north of the Loire and attempted to extend their positions; they looked to the king for support. In 960, Odo of Burgundy spent Easter with Lothar at Laon, along with other nobles of Francia and Burgundy. After Easter a royal assembly was held at Soissons, an indication both of the continuation of the traditional means of Carolingian government and of Lothar's wish to establish direct contact with his nobles.[33] Some members of the assembly then moved against Richard I of Normandy, whose soldiers had been raiding Neustria.

Staunch allies of Lothar, among many in Francia, were the sons of Herbert II of Vermandois and their brothers-in-law, the counts of Anjou and Blois. The sons of Herbert had initially given Lothar some trouble. In Burgundy in 959, for example, Count Robert seized the *castellum* of Dijon. He was driven out by a contingent of warriors sent by Bruno, retook it and was expelled once more by Lothar who established a garrison there. After the death of Artald, archbishop of Rheims, in 962, Herbert revived the question of the succession to the see, for he wanted his brother Hugh restored. On Lothar's orders a synod was summoned at Meaux which was attended by the bishops of the provinces of both Sens and Rheims. Bishops Rorico of Laon and Gibuin of Châlons were particularly opposed to the restoration of the deposed and excommunicated Hugh, but Bruno, until persuaded to change his mind by Gerberga, was amenable. The synod resolved to be bound by the Pope's decision. On appeal, Pope John XII rule that Hugh could not be reinstated as archbishop. Odalric, a canon of Metz and a Lotharingian, was elected instead. He proved to be a good ecclesiastical choice; he succeeded in persuading the house of Vermandois to restore to Rheims lands its members had purloined, such as Epernay.[34] Apart from these two incidents early in Lothar's reign, friendly relations between the Vermandois brothers and the king appear to have been maintained. In 957, Robert, count of Troyes, Meaux and Châlons and Albert, count of Vermandois, had commended themselves to the king. Herbert also became Lothar's ally and secured the counties of Troyes and Meaux after his brother Robert's death, while Lothar seems to have made him count of the palace. Marriage and ecclesiastical preferment strengthened the bond; Count Albert married Lothar's halfsister Gerberga, and in 979, Liudolf, Albert's son, was appointed bishop of Noyon. The Vermandois together dominated the *pagi* of Vermandois, Soissonais, Noyonais, Omois, Tardenois, Beauvaisis, part of Laonnais, Bourgogne, Meaux, Troyes and Tournaisis.

The Vermandois were connected by marriage to the counts of Blois and Anjou, but this did not prevent them from quarrelling. Theobald of Blois, for instance, ravaged the Soissonais and Laonnais and seized the *castellum* of La Fère. He was obliged by Rorico, bishop of Laon, to surrender it again. Herbert and Adalbert of Vermandois also clashed with Ragnold of Roucy (d. 967). The latter had taken Montfelix, a *castellum* of Herbert's. Ragnold is an interesting instance of the rapid rise of a warrior and his heirs to a position of prominence and trust, though Ragnold himself seems to have provoked a number of his contemporaries as well as the Vermandois brothers and Odalric, archbishop of Rheims, who excommunicated Ragnold for his depredations of Rheim's property. Ragnold, a Viking, may have been installed originally as the military chief in the county of Rheims on Artald's restoration in 946. Certainly between 947 and 953 Ragnold fought the archbishop's enemies and constructed a fort at Roucy on the strategically vital axis of the road between Rheims and Laon. But he may simply have been a powerful and protective vassal of the church of Rheims; there is no evidence to suggest that Ragnold was count of Rheims. Ragnold supported Lothar on his expedition to Aquitaine in 955 and besieged the monastery of St Radegund at Poitiers. Ragnold married Alberada, another of Lothar's half-sisters. Their son Gilbert was count of Roucy and possibly count of the palace. Gilbert's brother Bruno was made bishop of Langres by Lothar in 981 and his son Ebalus became archbishop of Rheims in 1021 in succession to his cousin Arnulf.[35]

The counts of Anjou and Blois, both vassals of Hugh the Great, also rose rapidly and expanded their control into Brittany, Normandy and the Rhemois. By the eleventh century the counts of Anjou controlled the Touraine, Vendôme and Saintonge. The earliest recorded member of the house, Fulk the Red, was originally from the Loire region and was mentioned in charters as a vassal first of Odo and then of Robert. He was viscount of Anjou after 898 and count by 941. He also held the county of Nantes after 914. Fulk the Red's younger son Fulk the Good was count from 942 to 960; his heir was Geoffrey Greymantle (960–87). Geoffrey, despite being a vassal of Hugh the Great and Hugh Capet was a loyal subject of King Lothar. His brother Guy was made bishop of Le Puy by Lothar in 975 and his sister Adelaide was married to the young King Louis V in 982. In 965, Geoffrey Greymantle and Baldwin of Flanders joined in complaining to Lothar about the incursions made into their territory by Richard I of Normandy and his Vikings. With Theobald of Blois' help, Lothar captured Evreux, but what kind of consequences this had is not known. Theobald later came to terms with Richard at an assembly at Jeufosse on 15 May 966.

Because he had fallen out with Hugh Capet, Theobald count of Blois, nicknamed the Trickster, became a vassal of King Lothar in 963. He gained control of the counties of Chartres and Châteaudun and in 964 was excommunicated by Archbishop Odalric of Rheims for taking Coucy and other Rheims' estates. Odalric succeeded in recovering Coucy from Theobald but granted it to Theobald's son Odo I, who made his submission to the archbishop. Theobald's loyalty to Lothar was somewhat ambivalent (he fully lived up to his nickname), but Odo I of Blois was a staunch supporter of the king and married Lothar's niece Bertha. The counts of Anjou and Blois had their own vassals, and they too attempted to improve their condition. Hadouin, a vassal of Theobald for example, entrenched himself in the Rheims fortress of Coucy and was only driven out by King Lothar himself, to whom Hadouin was obliged to submit.

As well as forging bonds of fidelity with a number of the nobles of Francia, Lothar made some attempt to establish his authority in the peripheral regions of the Frankish kingdom, though we have little idea how effective or enduring this proved. Lothar strengthened his position in the south-east in 964 by marrying his sister Matilda to Conrad the Pacific; Conrad remained one of Lothar's allies. As Matilda's dowry, Lothar ceded the counties of Lyons and Vienne. Lothar also tried to bring Flanders under his direct control. He was acknowledged as suzerain by Count Arnulf to whom Lothar gave the title *marchio*. Arnulf in his turn gave Lothar his Flemish territories in trust for his grandson, also called Arnulf. On the elder Arnulf's death in 965, Lothar entered Flanders and the Flemish nobles submitted to him. Lothar however, rather than ruling Flanders directly, chose to return Flanders (with the possible exception of Arras) to the administration of Baldwin who was acting as regent for the younger Arnulf, though he remained the suzerain. In Aquitaine Lothar was again obliged to compromise. In 955 he and Hugh the Great had successfully besieged Poitiers and Lothar had been persuaded to cede Aquitaine as well as Burgundy to Hugh, though the royal gift did not make Hugh's authority effective in either of these regions. William II, who succeeded in 963, maintained peaceful relations with both Hugh Capet and Lothar, and on the marriage of his sister Adelaide to William II in 970 Hugh Capet renounced all pretensions to Aquitaine. In 982, Lothar made a renewed effort to restore royal authority to Aquitaine by making it a subkingdom. He married his fourteen-year-old son Louis V to Adelaide, widow of Count Stephen of Gevaudun (and sister of the count of Anjou) who was about twice Louis' age and had them crowned king and queen of Aquitaine at Orleans. The plan failed as quickly as the marriage; after two dismal years of bickering Louis returned to his father's court. Cutting his losses, Lothar accorded William II the title of *dux aquitanorum* which presumably gave him a similar status to the *dux francorum* and *dux burgundionum*, but this time an ethnic element was involved. By 987 the Poitevin dynasty was securely installed in Aquitaine and preserved good relations with Hugh Capet after he became king.

Marriage alliances and ties of kinship seem to have been of importance in the policies of the king and the nobles described above, yet it is important to be wary of reading too much significance, or too modern a significance, into the shreds of evidence that we have. Our understanding of the relationships of the nobility and the nobles' consciousness of their membership of a family or kin group is largely determined by the nature of the evidence. The sources are particularly limited moreover in the information about the family origins of individuals, for it is usually only when a member of the family acquired office that he appears in the public records. It is not at all certain that family structures were as coherent and kinsmen as loyal to each other as is usually assumed, or whether single political reasons can be assigned to the noble and royal alliances of the tenth century.[36]

Certainly the wish to promote a political alliance or re-establish political control of some kind can be read into some of the marriages among the upper nobility or royal families in the ninth and tenth centuries, such as the marriage between Louis V and Adelaide, but the estates over which Adelaide had control must have increased her attractiveness to her would-be father-in-law, as did her kinship with Lothar's ally the count of Anjou. Primarily political motives were also behind Hugh Capet's promotion, after he became king, of the alliance between his young son Robert and another 'elderly' widow, Susanna of Flanders. Yet even in the cases of advantageous alliances with clear political implications, such as Louis IV's marriage to Gerberga, Lothar's to Emma, Hugh the Great's to Eadhild and then to Hadwig, or Charles the Bald's to Richild, it seems that these marriages created ties which could be exploited if and when it suited. They could also provide the excuse for quarrels or for the sequestration or acquisition of territory. There are too many cases of brother fighting or betraying brother or brother-in-law within the Robertian, Carolingian, Angevin and Vermandois families to make it possible to affirm the sanctity of kinship ties.

The most important consideration in marriage alliances was land. Theobald the Trickster probably acquired, on his marriage to Luitgard, daughter of Herbert II of Vermandois, the estates of Bray-sur-Seine, Melun and Chalautrela-Grande in the county of Troyes and possibly more lands in the Vexin. In about 960, Robert, count of Troyes, gained the use of the counties of Chalon sur-Saône and Beaume on his marriage to Adelaide, daughter of Gilbert of Dijon. Adelaide, however, kept possession of these counties; when she died she left them to her daughter Adelaide, who married Lambert, count of Autun. The elder Adelaide's sister married Odo, son of Hugh the Great and this assisted the Robertians to gain a foothold in Burgundy. Some women therefore were inheriting property and retaining possession of it even if their husbands administered or enjoyed the use of it during their lifetimes. How common this practice was, or whether it could only happen in the absence of male heirs, has not yet been established. Some evidence from Aquitaine is of interest though it cannot be regarded as typical, or even possible, within the kingdom as a whole; examples exist of women acting as guardians of property not only during the minority of their sons but also after they had reached their majority. Garsind, widow of Count Raymond Pons of Toulouse, directed the county in the name of her son William; Adelaide, widow of Matfrid, viscount of Narbonne, was required by her husband's will to administer the viscounty in the name of her son Raymond, provided she did not remarry. Her own will of 990 indicates that she continued to administer the viscounty until her death.[37] Marriage alliances could symbolize the end of enmity or seal a pact; they permitted the extension of the man's domain and could sometimes enable him to acquire the control of territory once administered by his wife's father or former husband; they could bring about warmer relations between neighbours or cause undying enmity. Some 'new men' moreover, such as Ragnold of Roucy, acquired added status and power by marrying the daughter of a well-established and wealthy family.

V

Lothar was first involved in Lotharingian affairs in 956 when Ragnar III, count of Hennegau and Brabant, seized the land Gerberga had received as dowry on her marriage to her first husband Gilbert of Lotharingia. In concert with Bruno, Lothar captured Ragnar's fort on the Chier and took his family prisoner. The latter was only restored to Ragnar, with his soldiers, on his handing back Gerberga's land. The following year Bruno exiled Ragnar to Bohemia. It may be that these lands of Gerberga's, nowhere specified (but they included Meersen), constituted the initial excuse for Lothar's subsequent claims in Lotharingia. Even after Gerberga's death and her bequest of these lands to the abbey of St Remigius of Rheims, they remained technically part of the west Frankish kingdom even though they were situated in Lotharingia. Flodoard moreover supplies the puzzling comment that when Lothar was in Cologne for Easter 959, 'he received assurances concerning the kingdom of Lotharingia'. Perhaps these 'assurances' related to Gerberga's lands or to other west Frankish estates in Lotharingia, apart from those of the church of Rheims, about which we are ignorant.

Under Bruno, east Frankish influence in Lotharingia increased steadily. Non-Lotharingians were elected to the bishopric of Trier and even to that of Cambrai, despite its being a suffragan see of Rheims. Two of its bishops, Berengar (956–60) and Tetdo (972–76), were Otto I's candidates and came from Saxony; neither could speak the local dialect. Cambrai eventually managed to free itself from too forceful a lay encroachment and developed into an episcopal principality.[38] The Lotharingian nobles also resented east Frankish dominance and in 959, some, led by Immo, revolted against Bruno. In consequence, Frederick of Bar, count of upper Lotharingia, was appointed governor of Lotharingia. With the death of Bruno (965) and that of Gerberga (969), west Frankish involvement in Lotharingian affairs became less close, though the link with the east Frankish kingdom was strengthened on Lothar's marriage, possibly arranged by Gerberga, to Emma, the daughter of Otto I's wife Adelaide by her first husband, Lothar of Italy.

After Otto I's death in 973, Lothar fell foul of Otto II over Lothar's claims to some at least of Lotharingia, or so a rather oblique passage in Richer's History suggests. Richer refers to the region of *Belgica* as the one in which Lothar was particularly interested, but this region clearly does not correspond to the region defined as *Belgica* by Richer at the beginning of his book.[39] That Lothar later concentrated on Verdun may be an indication of the area with which he was concerned. Lothar and his nobles may also have been irritated, as Richer suggests, by Otto's taking up residence at Aachen. Richer omits to mention, however, that Lothar's invasion of Lotharingia was provoked by Otto II. In 977 Otto reinstalled Ragnar III in the county of Hennegau and made Lothar's younger brother Charles, who had been exiled from the west Frankish kingdom for maliciously slandering Queen Emma (he claimed she had committed adultery with Bishop Adalbero of Laon), his vassal and duke of lower Lotharingia. Otto also acquired Hainault and Cambrai. When Lothar consulted his nobles at an assembly at Laon, the proposal to attack Lotharingia won enthusiastic support. In 978 he and his army invaded Lotharingia, captured Aachen and sacked the royal palace, though they failed to capture Otto II as they had hoped to do. Lothar's success seems to have taken him by almost as much surprise as it had the east Franks. Unfortunately he lacked the resources to follow up his conquest and after remaining three days in Aachen he retreated. Richer records the story that before he left, Lothar, in a rather futile gesture of defiance, turned the bronze eagle Charlemagne had put on the roof of the palace to face east once more.

In direct retaliation, Otto invaded Lothar's kingdom, burnt the royal palaces of Compiègne and Attigny, ravaged the Laonnais, Soissonais and Rhemois, took Laon, and had Charles of Lotharingia, Lothar's brother, proclaimed king by Bishop Theudebert of Metz. Otto then moved to attack Paris but was driven off by the west Frankish army, and his vanguard was almost totally wiped out on the banks of the Aisne. However unreliable Richer may be, he cannot obscure the massive support for Lothar in his own kingdom, but he adds the information that Archbishop Adalbero of Rheims was sympathetic towards Otto and provided him with guides to conduct him safely from the kingdom.[40]

Lothar's reaction to the proclamation of his brother as king was to have his own son Louis crowned co-ruler by Adalbero on 8 June 979, a move favoured by Hugh Capet.[41] Thus the succession was assured. In June 980 peace was concluded between Otto II and Lothar at Margut and Lothar renounced his pretensions to Lotharingia. According to Richer this peace settlement enraged and alienated Hugh Capet and some of those who had hitherto supported Lothar, for they felt it was a negation of all their efforts.[42] Whether this was his reason or not, it is certainly from 980 that Hugh appears as Lothar's opponent, though he did not remain so. Hitherto relations between Robertian and Carolingian had been good,[43] though Hugh Capet had steadily built up Robertian strength. He had continued his policy of establishing connections by marriage with other leading members of the Frankish nobility. His sister Emma, for example, married Richard I of Normandy, though she died childless in 968, and Hugh himself married Adelaide, daughter of William Towhead of Poitou. But at Easter in 982 Hugh Capet went to Rome and there made a successful bid to win Otto II's friendship. Because Hugh knew no Latin, proceedings had to be conducted through an interpreter.[44] Hugh and Lothar were later reconciled.

On 7 December 983 Otto II died, leaving a three-year-old son, Otto III. Lothar's hopes of annexing Lotharingia (or a part thereof) were nourished once more, for, in the disputed succession in the east Frankish kingdom between Henry of Bavaria and Otto III and his supporters, both sides courted Lothar's favour.[45] Lotharingia appears to have been the prize offered by Henry while Lothar, supported by Adalbero, archbishop of Rheims, and Gerbert, the master of the Rheims school, offered himself as *tutor* and guardian of Otto III (he was as closely related to the infant as Henry of Bavaria) with the clear intention of acquiring the government of Lotharingia as well. Some Lotharingian nobles swore fidelity to Lothar. In May 984, the Empress Theophanu assumed the guardianship of her son Otto III herself.

Archbishop Adalbero played a prominent part in the subsequent events. Like Odalric, his predecessor, Adalbero had been a canon of Metz. He was the brother of Godfrey, count of Verdun, and had been educated at Gorze. In the first few years of his incumbency he was an exemplary archbishop; he restored canons and a canons' rule to the cathedral and regular monks to the monastery of St Theuderic, as well as installing Gerbert as a master in the cathedral school at Rheims. Like all Rheims' archbishops, he endeavoured to safeguard the temporal of the see, yet he spared the funds to embellish the cathedral church and build a new church dedicated to St Denis. After 969 Adalbero was archchancellor to King Lothar. Where Adalbero differed at first from his predecessors in the see was in his seeming reluctance to embroil himself in politics, even when Lothar invaded Lotharingia in 978. The change in his conduct after 984 is usually attributed to the influence of Gerbert who had arrived back in Rheims in 984, fully committed to serving the Empress Theophanu and her son Otto III. Gerbert's letters are full of his intrigues and investigations on their behalf.[46]

Lothar invaded Lotharingia again in 985, captured Verdun, an important trading centre, and took a number of prisoners, among whom were Godfrey, count of Verdun, and his son Frederick (Adalbero of Rheims' brother and nephew). Verdun remained in Carolingian hands for two years, though most other Lotharingian nobles remained loyal to Otto III. In response, and no doubt in his perplexity, Adalbero adopted a policy of non-co-operation with Lothar; he openly defied the king in allowing another nephew, also called Adalbero and formerly a cleric of Rheims, to be made bishop of Verdun and refused to demolish the walls round the monastery of St Paul. Adalbero was summoned to an assembly to be held at Compiègne on 11 May 985 in order to answer charges of treason, on the grounds that he had permitted his nephew to leave Rheims and assisted in making him bishop without Lothar's permission. Although the Compiègne assembly never actually met, Adalbero's aggrieved defence survives, evidently composed for him by Gerbert.[47] In it, Adalbero insists that he had simply ordained his nephew priest 'lest our church be censured for raising a subdeacon to episcopal rank' and that he had remained faithful to Lothar. Something more than a dispute between king and bishop over prerogative was involved. Gerbert's letters make abundantly clear how involved Adalbero was in intrigue against Lothar, and Lothar, as Adalbero himself feared, had probably got wind of this.[48] Any further actions on Lothar's part were cut short by his sudden death on 2 March 986, at the age of forty-four. Richer thought it worth noting that Lothar was given a magnificent funeral.

The succession of Louis V was not disputed. Unfortunately Louis appears to have been of a petulant and self-willed disposition and his short reign was almost entirely occupied with his quarrel with Archbishop Adalbero of Rheims. Queen Emma, Louis' mother, had received the oaths of fidelity from the west Frankish nobles and seemed ready to play a similar role in relation to her son as Gerberga had enacted with Lothar. She was in favour of peace with the east Franks over Lotharingia and to this end appealed to her mother Queen Adelaide. It is arguable that had Louis V been less anxious to assert his independence of his mother's guidance he would have retained the support of the archbishop of Rheims. But Louis quarrelled with his mother, banished Bishop Adalbero of Laon (implying that he believed the old scandal of illicit relations between the bishop and his mother) and, with the support of Hugh Capet, besieged Rheims. Adalbero of Rheims agreed to answer formal charges of treason at a council to be convened at Compiègne in March 987, but it was postponed to May, and on his way there, Louis V was killed in an accident. Hugh Capet assumed the presidency of the assembly at Compiègne which had been summoned to deal with Adalbero, and the archbishop was unanimously acquitted. Adalbero then made a stirring speech about the problem of the succession, proposing that the nobles should elect one from their number to be king and that they should reassemble later when they had had a chance to consider their choice. Accordingly, the assembly was reconvened at Senlis at the end of May. The grand justification for the election of Hugh Capet which Richer puts in the mouth of Adalbero cannot be accepted as the words of the archbishop, but Richer probably records correctly the important role the archbishop played in securing Hugh's selection in preference to Lothar's brother, Charles of Lotharingia.[49] Hugh was elected king with the support of his brother Otto-Henry of Burgundy, Richard of Normandy and William of Aquitaine. At Noyon he was proclaimed king and on 3 July 987, he was crowned and anointed by Archbishop Adalbero. Charles of Lotharingia made a claim to the throne in 988 and based himself at Laon, gathering together considerable support. But in 989 he surrendered and died in captivity, probably in 991.[50]

VI

What did Hugh Capet have to gain by becoming king? How much authority and wealth was left to the monarchy by 987? To answer these questions, it is necessary to survey the exercise of authority by the Carolingian kings throughout the tenth century.

Some indication of the remaining strength of royal authority may be gained by an examination of the extent to which the kings reserved the power of royal intervention in episcopal and abbatial elections, maintained the system of *missi dominici* and issued legislation. After 898 there is certainly much less evidence of successful royal intervention in ecclesiastical elections. As late as 918, however, Charles the Simple granted freedom of election to the monks of St Maximin of Trier;[51] Louis IV did the same for the monks of Cuixá in 937 and Lothar followed suit for the monks of St Bavo, Ghent in 956.[52] Charles the Simple also appointed lay abbots to Chelles (but compare above, p. 309), St Martin and St Vaast, though neither Louis IV nor Lothar have left charters indicating that they did so. The sees of Laon and Rheims as well as those of Lotharingia appear to have been subject to the king's influence, especially once the hold of the house of Vermandois on Rheims had been loosened. Hugh Capet moreover maintained the royal relationship with Rheims established by the Carolingians.

The main obstacle to the kings' direct intervention in episcopal and abbatial elections was the intermediary power of the local counts, *marchiones* and dukes. It was they who now intervened in church affairs, though some still sought the king's confirmation of their actions. More usually, however, the royal confirmation was sought in cases of grants of land and privileges such as immunity to churches and monasteries, reform of monasteries and grants to individual *fideles*. Local rulers also solicited charters from the king. The royal charters indeed reveal that even this seeking of confirmation by intermediaries was decreasing rapidly. The greater proportion of the confirmations made by Charles the Simple, for example, were no longer confirmations of the grants of his predecessors but confirmations of grants made by his counts and viscounts (as well as, in a few cases, by the queen).[53] To these the king simply added the final seal of approval, though sometimes conditions were attached, such as the obligation for the beneficiaries regularly to offer up prayers for the king. There are still a number of confirmations of this nature among the extant charters of Louis IV,[54] but the number seems to have decreased by the time of Lothar and Louis V. This suggests that the counts and viscounts were no longer bothering to seek royal confirmation for their grants and thus that royal influence in this sphere had weakened. From the time of Louis IV, personal requests for grants from the king also became much less frequent and charters were solicited to a much greater extent by intermediaries. It is notable that these intermediaries were lay or ecclesiastical magnates either with some interest in the region concerned (such as Hugh the Great, Bernard, count of Beauvais, Arnulf of Flanders, Raymond of Toulouse, Wifrid of Barcelona, William Towhead of the Auvergne, Hugh the Black of Burgundy and the bishops of Tours, Mâcon, Noyon, Chalon and Metz) or else were close to the king, such as the queen herself.[55]

Louis III and Carloman were the last Carolingian kings to make any pretence of maintaining a centralized administration. The *missi dominici* had formed an essential feature of such a system. As Charles the Bald and subsequent rulers delegated power, land and responsibility to the counts, so the office of *missus dominicus* ceased to be distinguishable from that of the count set over a number of counties. It should also be remembered that the *missatica* boundaries had more or less coincided with ecclesiastical divisions, so that it is likely that certain archbishops now continued to exercise the old functions of the *missus dominicus* as part of their archiepiscopal responsibilities.

Although it is very likely that the regional administration of the west Frankish kingdom remained essentially the same as it had been under the first four Carolingian kings (see below p. 332), its direction and supervision altered. It was no longer supervised directly by the king or agents appointed by him but by an hereditary lay nobility and by the ecclesiastical magnates who were bound to the king by ties of fidelity – feudal ties – of varying degrees of closeness, and observed with varying degrees of constancy and scrupulousness.

The distribution of the royal *fideles* themselves reflects the alteration in the orientation of the administrative structure. The general oath of fidelity Charlemagne had imposed on all his subjects (discussed above pp. 88–9) had ceased to be sworn by the tenth century. Instead there was an oath sworn by some of the counts, bishops, abbots and royal vassals; other subjects swore fidelity to the counts rather than directly to the king, and were thus the king's vassals only through an intermediary.

Narrative and documentary sources reveal moreover that by no means all the lay and ecclesiastical magnates were the *fideles* of the kings in the tenth century; nor did those who became *fideles* of the king necessarily do so at the beginning of his reign.[56] From Folcuin we learn, for example, that on his restoration to the kingdom, Louis IV had received an oath of fidelity from Hugh the Great, Herbert II of Vermandois and probably Arnulf of Flanders when he landed at Boulogne in 936.[57] The other territorial princes – Hugh the Black of Burgundy, William Towhead of Poitou, Raymond Pons of Gothia and William

Longsword of Normandy – are not mentioned and we know from other sources that they swore homage to Louis some years later. Hugh the Black did so in 938 after Louis had broken with Hugh the Great; William of Normandy followed suit in 940, William Towhead and Alan of Brittany swore homage in 942 and Raymond Pons in 944 (though he had acknowledged Louis as king since 937). Not only was homage tardy; fidelity was intermittent and political loyalty fragile. Nobles rebelled and simply renewed their oaths on reconciliation. Hugh the Great for example, who had sworn fidelity in 936, was obliged to make peace with the king and renew his oath in 946, and again in 950.

The royal charters amplify and confirm the information about *fideles* of the king supplied by the chroniclers. In the 111 charters produced by the last 3 Carolingian kings between 936 and 987, the king not only accords particular titles to his magnates such as *dux, comes* or *marchio*, he also adds where appropriate the appellation 'our *fidelis*'. Charles the Simple described 47 different men, including 6 of the territorial princes and many counts as his *fideles*, whereas 90 other magnates are not qualified as such. Louis IV described 13 different men as his *fideles*, while 55 other magnates mentioned in his charters are not so described. Lothar refers to 14 different individuals (including Hugh Capet and his own wife Queen Emma) as his *fideles*, while 40 men are without this appellation. There are no references to *fideles regis* in the two extant charters of Louis V.

A necessary qualification to these observations is that while we can recognize as a *fidelis* someone described in a charter as *fidelis noster*, it is not necessarily the case that someone not so described is not a *fidelis*. Under Charles the Simple for example, Robert of Neustria is sometimes called a *fidelis* and sometimes not. This kind of evidence therefore, has to be interpreted very carefully, however much confidence we may have in the redactors of the charters; cases where the discrimination is precise and can be checked against the narrative sources are the only ones in which we can be at all confident. Nevertheless, it is clear that there was a continuing decline throughout the tenth century in the number of lay or ecclesiastical magnates as well as those of lower social standing taking an oath of fidelity to the king and becoming his *fideles*. About a half of the magnates mentioned in Charles the Simple's charters are described as *fideles*, whereas for Louis IV the proportion is a third and has sunk to a quarter under Lothar. Under the last three Carolingians there were areas where there were no *fideles* at all, such as Gothia and the Spanish march, though these areas do not seem to have lost their sense of being part of the *regnum francorum*. Royal *fideles* could be recruited also from outside the borders of the Frankish kingdom; Lothar for example had *fideles* in Lotharingia and Vienne. Yet the greater proportion of the kings' *fideles* were in Francia, that is, the area under the direct authority of the king.

The circle of royal *fideles* was thus very small by 987, but the feudal bond and mutual obligation between man and lord were becoming more widespread and more common. The great magnates and the counts in fact were becoming intermediaries in the receipt of the oath of fidelity just as they were becoming the intermediaries and the regional governors in the administrative sphere (see

Map 20). Hugh the Great, for example, had succeeded in separating from royal
fidelity most of the counts within his own territory. In Burgundy, the king's
contact with the population was through the duke. A charter of Louis IV concerning the introduction of Cluniac reforms into the monastery of St Martin,
Autun and requested by Hugh the Black and the leading nobles of Burgundy
was approved by Louis IV and the west Frankish nobles. The text is precise
about who among the nobles was a *fidelis* of the king. All the nobles of the
west Frankish kingdom are so described, but on the Burgundian side only
Hugh the Black is called a *fidelis*.[58]

VII

Dhondt maintained that after 888 the Carolingian kings issued no more capitularies. Although this is true (or at least, none have survived), it is important
to remember that it is precisely from the late ninth and the tenth centuries
that a large proportion of the fullest collections of capitularies dates. BN
lat. 10758, pp. 137–340, for example, was compiled during the episcopate
of Fulk in the diocese of Rheims and forms with the preceding 136 pages
(compiled under Archbishop Hincmar) a comprehensive collection of legal and
historical material, including Einhard's Life of Charlemagne, the *Lex Salica*,
and the capitulary collection of Ansegisus. Other large late ninth- and tenth-century collections, such as Vat. pal. lat. 582, Clm 19416, Clm 3853, Berlin
Phillipps 10190, Wolfenbüttel Blankenberg 130.52, BN lat. 4995 and BN
lat. 3878, to mention only a few, have not yet been studied in detail. Of the
284 manuscripts listed by Werminghoff as containing Carolingian capitularies,
no less than 120 are dated by him to the turn of the ninth, the tenth or the
turn of the tenth centuries, or contain both ninth- and tenth-century sections.
Some of the ninth-century manuscripts among the remaining 164 codices may
well have been compiled after 877, but detailed work on the manuscript tradition and palaeography of the capitulary collections generally is needed before
this can be ascertained.

We must infer from the extant manuscripts that some of the older capitularies continued to be referred and resorted to, and acted upon, after new capitularies ceased to be issued, and that new compilations of older capitulary
material were made with that very purpose in mind. Archbishop Hincmar certainly presented Louis the Stammerer with a long series of articles taken from
earlier capitularies in 881,[59] and later kings may well have had similar collections compiled which may be among the extant manuscripts. Of the 65 known
(59 extant) manuscripts containing the capitulary collection of Ansegisus, 7 are
dated to the ninth century (including one, Yale 413, dated to the end of Charles
the Bald's reign and probably made for the king), 11 are dated to the late ninth
or early tenth century, 19 to the tenth century and 5 to the late tenth or early
eleventh centuries. The remaining 22 date from the eleventh century or later.
It should also be noted that some of these codices such as Berlin lat. qu. 931

come from the east Frankish kingdom and some, such as BN lat. 4628A and BN lat. 4634 (from St Denis, and St Mary and St Stephen at Sens respectively), can be associated with particular monasteries within the territorial principalities.

This distribution of an official collection acknowledged by both Louis the Pious and Charles the Bald, added to that of the extant manuscripts which include capitulary material, is significant. It suggests at the very least a continuing interest in the contents of the capitularies and the possibility that in the tenth century they were still regarded as relevant and applicable. In other words, the Frankish kings after 877 and throughout the tenth century did not issue capitularies of their own simply because those already issued had acquired the status of a law code and were still being used. No doubt some of the post-tenth-century manuscripts can be attributed to a more academic interest in their contents, though this cannot be readily assumed. Work is needed, however, to establish the origin and correct date for all the manuscripts containing capitularies, including those of the Ansegisus collection, and to determine their regional distribution. It may then be possible properly to assess the relationship between the continued copying of older capitulary legislation and Carolingian administration in the tenth century, as well as ascertaining the extent to which regional administration continued on much the same lines in the tenth century as it had in the ninth. From the few regions studied so far, such as Poitou or the Mâcon, it is clear that the regional structure of Carolingian administration was preserved, but a more comprehensive knowledge should be possible. Hitherto, the effectiveness or survival of administration in the Frankish kingdoms has been dismissed on the basis of the lack of evidence,[60] but such an argument from silence is unsatisfactory and has failed to take into account the evidence that does exist.

From the chronicles and chancery documents of the Frankish kings, as well as from surviving manuscripts, the maintenance of the traditional forms of Carolingian government is evident. *Placita* or general and regional assemblies, the most important means of maintaining contact between counts and the king, were still being held and the royal court still functioned and issued judgements.[61] The significance of Lothar's assemblies, for example, was noted above. One important development was that the territorial princes also held assemblies in their own regions.[62] For the personal physical presence of the sovereign in the territorial principalities however, that of the count or duke was substituted. Regional rulers often made their petition through intermediaries, as did the counts of Barcelona and Roussillon, rather than coming to the king in person. When the regional nobles ceased to come to court to do homage to the king then an essential element in the Carolingian system was lost.

The itineraries of the tenth-century kings, mapped by the date clauses in their charters, indicate that the kings' movements were no longer so wide-ranging as they had been hitherto. Apart from occasional sorties into Lotharingia, Aquitaine and Burgundy, the kings remained much more in Francia, and tended to favour one or two residences much more than any other, to which only single visits were paid. Compiègne, Attigny, Laon and Tours-sur-Marne were, apart from his Lotharingian palaces, the residences most frequented by Charles the Simple. Laon and Rheims and Laon and Compiègne respectively were the palaces most favoured by Louis IV and Lothar.

The distribution of beneficiaries corresponds roughly to the progress of the royal itinerary; individuals and establishments in Francia (and Lotharingia under Charles the Simple) received many more grants than those in Neustria and Burgundy. This distribution became more marked with each successive king, though a common feature, as Kienast pointed out, is the relatively large number of diplomas destined for Aquitaine and Catalonia. Most of these were solicited by intermediaries rather than by the bishops and counts of these regions in person. It implies at least a continuing appreciation of the benefits of royal patronage and protection, if not an acknowledgement of royal author- ity. The grants Charles the Simple and his successors made in Neustria and Burgundy probably represent attempts to exert royal influence and conciliate potential followers as well as rewards given to existing ones. This is apparent from Charles the Simple's grant of the abbacies of St Martin at Tours (despite Robertian possession of it) and St Vaast to Fulk and the famous grant of Chelles to his favourite Hagano.[63] Louis and Lothar also confirmed a number of charters from Flanders, including those concerning the reforms introduced by Gerard of Brogne. They also authorized the reforms at St Martin, Autun and at Mont- St-Michel.[64] Louis IV patronized Cluny and her daughter houses and made the community a number of grants of land.[65]

From the grants of land, revenue and privileges made to monasteries, churches and individuals in Charles the Simple's reign, it seems that the king could still afford to be generous. Charles made 36 grants to bishoprics and monasteries and 12 to individuals out of a total of 123 extant charters, though some of these were simply confirmations of grants made by his predecessors. Charles actually founded a new monastery at Corbeny on 22 February 906[66] and was able to provide his wife Frederuna with a handsome dowry on his marriage to her in 907, by granting her the new monastery as well as the cell of St Peter in the *comitatus* of Laon and the church at Craonne.[67] In 915 Charles gave land at Compiègne for the construction of a church in honour of St Clem- ent and conceded land on the Oise and in the Beauvaisis as well as serfs at Compiègne.[68] Charles granted out land in Francia and Neustria and occasion- ally from domains elsewhere. Even under Louis IV and Lothar, new grants continued to be made, though on a greatly reduced scale. Louis IV, for exam- ple, made 15 grants to churches and monasteries (notably to Cluny) and 2 to individuals, and Lothar made 5 grants to monasteries and one grant to an individual. Under Lothar an unusually large number of monasteries had land restored to them that had been despoiled or granted elsewhere, and immunity was granted to eight.[69] Charles ceded to Cambrai the right to mint coins. Louis granted the *comitatus* of Rheims and the right to mint coins to the archbishop and Lothar conceded similar privileges to the bishop of Langres. The monas- teries of Paris, Soissons and Compiègne were more favoured than the others.

The extant diplomas of Charles the Simple (124 issued in a 26-year reign), Ralph (27 in 13 years), Louis IV (54 in 18 years) Lothar and Louis V (58 in 33 years) indicate that charter production diminished steadily and the chancery itself was gradually reduced in size. Archchancellors headed the chancery between 898 and 987, but they ceased to supervise the redaction of diplomas and became honorary officials who advised the king and who often held the title of archchaplain as well. The chief notary, often now referred to as chancellor, was in charge of the chancery, but he does not seem to have written the documents himself; this was done by a number of anonymous scribes. The royal writing office was undoubtedly itinerant with the king and these circumstances may have affected the redaction. Some at least of the surviving charters were actually drawn up outside the royal chancery by the beneficiaries;[70] this practice may well have increased and could account for the lower number of diplomas issued from the royal chancery. A separate chancery was maintained in Lotharingia from 911 to 920.

Under Louis IV the royal chancery was less closely supervised and started to relax the rigidity of the Carolingian formularies and the details of the expedition of charters; the diplomas are full of errors and omissions. Great diversity among the formulae used in the charters of Lothar and Louis V suggests that this laxness increased. For a time under the notary Gezo there was a tightening up of discipline but it relaxed again under Adalbero (later bishop of Laon); the spelling of the royal name became particularly indecisive, though the formulae remained constant.[71] Under Arnulf, disorder increased rapidly; even the date clause was sometimes omitted entirely. It is interesting that Charles the Simple's charters reverted in their formulae to the charters of Pippin III, Carloman and the early years of Charlemagne's reign. From Charles the Simple's time the invocation formula: *In nomine sanctae et individuae trinitatis* is almost constant. The methods of redaction, preparation of the parchment, arrangement of the text, layout and type of script remained the same in the tenth-century charters as they had been throughout the ninth century.

VIII

The diminuation of the area over which the king exercised direct authority is also evident in the coinage.[72] In many respects, the tenth-century coinage of the west Frankish kingdom was a continuation of that of the ninth, though royal control of the coinage was rapidly being lost. The mints of the territorial princes, however, conformed to the general system and in some cases used the royal name and monogram on their coins. The most characteristic feature of the tenth-century coinage is the poverty of the types and their poor execution; legends are often off the flan and the designs are clumsily traced. Odo had maintained Carolingian coinage but royal control of the coinage weakened after the deposition of Charles the Simple in 922. Coins were struck in the name of Charles and of Ralph in twenty centres, mostly in Francia and Burgundy, but only eleven centres can be identified under Louis IV and Lothar, while only coins struck at Rheims are known for Louis V. Even here, the coin evidence can be deceptive. The presence of the king's name on a coin does not necessarily mean that the revenue from seigneurage went to the king, or that the mints were still within royal control. It is possible that the maintenance of the royal name on coins struck by the nobles or bishops constituted a symbolic acknowledgement of royal power, but use of a Carolingian king's name on coins from, for instance, Poitou as late as the twelfth century (in the name of Charles the Bald!) make one wary of leaping too readily to this conclusion. Originally a count had not had the right to mint coins by virtue of his office, but Carolingian legislation had placed the control of mints under the counts and as they acquired independence the profits of the mint and the control of its production came to be considered part of the comital office. There is no evidence that the king ever ceded monetary rights to the counts. The counts usurped them. Grierson has offered the suggestion that it was a 'certain sense of propriety' that prompted these counts to continue striking the coin in the king's name because it ensured general acceptance or at least ensured a uniformity of type.

Surviving tenth-century coinage appears to have been predominantly secular, though all our written evidence records concessions of the right to mint coins to bishops, such as Louis IV to Rheims and Lothar to Langres. Among the issues of coinage which it is possible to distinguish from royal issues, a few have the names of territorial princes. William II of the Auvergne (918–26) was apparently the first such to put his name on coins. Other pieces are extant from the mid-tenth century bearing the name of Hugh the Great and also of Theobald of Chartres. When Hugh the Great obtained his ducal title from Louis IV in 943, he, and after him Hugh Capet, struck coins at Paris, St Denis and Senlis. The Normans do not seem to have started to strike coins until late in the countship of William Longsword (927–42), but the striking of coins rapidly gathered momentum under Richard I (942–96). The counts of Auxerre produced their own coinage in about 920. Clerics usually put the king's name on their coinage, but the bishops of Le Puy at the end of the century and the abbot of St Martin at Tours struck coins with distinctive designs. Charles the Simple also issued coins in Lotharingia after 911. Lafaurie has argued that the maintenance of a particular king's name on the coinage of bishops or abbots simply records the name of the king who granted the right to mint coins to that bishop or of the king who renewed the right.[73]

As far as the landed wealth of the last Carolingians is concerned, there is much uncertainty, but the royal domain was probably more substantial than is usually assumed.[74] They were by no means reduced to penury and there is no trace in the pro-Capetian sources of the ridicule Carolingian sources heaped on the Merovingians. Indeed, Hugh Capet's official view was that he was not an enemy of the Carolingians but continued their rule in the absence of a direct heir. Charles the Simple's wealth must still have been considerable, though royal land had almost certainly passed from Odo to Robert and thence to Hugh the Great. The Robertians retained their hold on St Denis for example, and a list survives of the treasures Odo removed from St Denis. These presumably remained in the Robertian family.[75] The palaces mentioned in Charles the Simple's charters cannot be assumed to be the only palaces remaining to him, but hitherto, estimates of the extent of the royal domain have been based entirely upon the extant charters. While these sometimes provide information about estates and more particularly the residences – Compiègne, Laon, Attigny and Rheims – favoured by the kings, they cannot be interpreted as a complete inventory of royal possessions. The royal domain of Hugh Capet might give some indication of the later Carolingian royal domain, but here one would have to be quite clear how much of this was originally Robertian family land. Lot enumerates the bishoprics and abbacies for which Hugh Capet and his son Robert had the right to nominate candidates. Of the bishoprics, only Langres, Le Puy, Bourges and Le Mans outside the ecclesiastical provinces of Sens and Rheims were royal, while most of the sees of Sens and Rheims were in royal control. The distribution of royal abbeys is similar. In Francia the king retained control of many (and here those that had long been in Robertian hands can be identified), but with a few exceptions he could not exert an influence over any of the abbeys either in the territorial principalities or in a number of counties. From Lot's description of Hugh Capet's royal domain, the Carolingians probably possessed extensive property in Francia as well as in some parts of Burgundy and possibly Lotharingia, while they were also the direct suzerains of a ring of counties on the rim of Francia.

If one compares the known lands and abbacies of the Carolingians to those of the Robertians in the second half of the tenth century the impression is that the latter's wealth was far greater than that of the Carolingians. Lot, however, stated that Robertian land on Hugh Capet's accession was less than that possessed by King Ralph in 923. Presumably the acquisition of the Carolingian royal domain increased Robertian wealth appreciably, and it is important to remember also that Hugh Capet's purposeful courting of church support, culminating in his securing that of the archbishop of Rheims, meant that he had a sizeable army of warriors at his disposal. Yet the strength of the Robertians was not so much due to their possessions as to their suzerainty over a number of powerful vassals, including the counts of Anjou and Maine. The last Carolingians, especially Lothar, also had many allies among the nobility and clergy. Even to compare the king's power and wealth with those of one of his nobles, however, is a comment on the relative weakness of the monarchy, or it would be if there was enough evidence to make a comparison feasible.

It may seem that the record of the policies of the last Carolingians and their efforts both within the kingdom and in the peripheral regions to extend their position is at odds with the shrinking of the area over which their authority and administration were directly effective. This is an illusion; although bold, Lothar's policies apart from Lotharingia were confined on the one hand to establishing direct relations with the nobles of Francia, and on the other to forging links based on commendation and fidelity, feudal links, with the territorial princes, and a special place for the king within the kingdom of the Franks. This was his legacy to Hugh Capet. In every way, Hugh Capet represented a continuation of the Carolingian kingship that had developed in the course of the tenth century.

NOTES

1. Each of the last Carolingian kings is the subject of a monograph: A. Eckel, *Charles le Simple* (Paris 1899), P. Lauer, *Robert I et Raoul de Bourgogne, rois de France 923–936* (Paris 1910) and *Le règne de Louis IV d'Outremer* (Paris 1900), F. Lot, *Les derniers Carolingiens. Lothaire, Louis V et Charles de Lorraine 954–991* (Paris 1891). All these, however, discuss the events in each king's reign on a year to year basis and can be confusing.

2. See G. A. Bezzola, *Das Ottonische Kaisertums in der französischen Geschichtschreibung des 10. und beginnenden 11. Jahrhunderts* (Graz and Cologne 1956), 20–54.

3. R. Latouche, 'Un imitateur de Sallust au Xe siècle, l'historien Richer', *Annales de l'Université de Grenoble* 6 (1929), 289–305.

4. For example, G. Duby, *La société aux XIe et XIIe siècles dans la region mâconnaise* (Paris 1971) and E. Magnou-Nortier, *La société et l'église dans la province écclésiastique de Narbonne de la fin du VIIIe à la fin du XIe siècle* (Toulouse 1974).

5. I am grateful to Eleanor Searle for her illuminating comments on Dudo.

6. For Charles the Simple's earlier involvement in Lotharingia, see Eckel, *Charles le Simple*, 90–7; W. Kienast, *Deutschland und Frankreich in der Kaiserzeit 900–1270* (Stuttgart 3 vols. 1974–75), I, 50–2.

7. T. Schieffer, *Die Lothringische Kanzlei um 900* (Cologne and Graz 1958) and E. Hlawitschka, *Lothringien und das Reich an der Schwelle der deutschen Geschichte* (Stuttgart 1968).

8. But see Eckel, *Charles le Simple*, 74–5 and 91–7.

9. See for example, Charles the Simple, *Recueil*, Nos. 5, 67–72, 74, 76, 81, 84, 100, 103, 106 and 114. See No. 95 for the use of *rex francorum*.

10. For example, ibid, No. 84.

11. For example, ibid., Nos. 81, 92 and 105; see also Nos. 13, 45–50, 54, 57, 63, 65, 77, 82, 89, 94, 98.

12. Flodoard, *Annales, s.a.*, 922.

13. R. Parisot, *Le royaume de Lorraine sous les Carolingiens 843–923* (Paris 1899), 633–40.

14. Bouquet, *Recueil, IX, 323* and see H. Büttner, *Heinrichs I Südwest- und Westpolitik* (Stuttgart 1968).

15. Charles the Simple, *Recueil* Nos. 106, 112 and especially 108; see also Flodoard, *Annales, s.a.*, 912.

16. Flodoard, *Annales, s.a.*, 922.

17. K. F. Werner, *Handbuch der Europäischen Geschichte* I, T. Schieder (ed.) (Stuttgart 1976), 742, and Kienast, *Deutschland und Frankreich*, 74–5.

18. K. F. Werner, 'Untersuchung zur Frühzeit des französichen Fürstentums (9–10 Jht)', *Welt als Geschichte* 20 (1960), 87–119.

19. Richer, *Historia*, I, 47.

20. Flodoard, *Historia*, IV, 19.

21. Richer, *Historia*, I, 55 and Flodoard, *Annales, s.a.*, 928.

22. Lauer, *Louis IV*, 2–8.

23. *MGH SS* X, 460 or W. Stubbs (ed.), *Rerum Brittanicarum Scriptores* 90, 150, reprinted in P. E. Schramm and F. Mütherich, *Denkmale der deutschen Könige und Kaiser* (Munich 1962),95–6. See L. Hubbard Loomis, 'The holy relics of Charlemagne and King Athelstan: the lances of Longinus and St Mauricius', *Speculum* 25 (1950), 437–56 and 'The Athelstan gift story; its influence on English chronicles

and Carolingian romances', *Publications of the Modern Languages Association* **68** (1952), 521–37.

24. Louis IV, *Recueil*, Nos. 1 and 4.
25. F. L. Ganshof, 'A propos de ducs et de duchés au haut moyen âge', *Journal des Savants* (1972–73), 13–24 (a review of W. Kienast, *Der Herzogstitel in Frankreich und Deutschland (9–12 Jht)* (Munich 1968).)
26. Flodoard, *Annales, s.a.*, 946.
27. Flodoard, *Historia*, IV, 35.
28. Louis IV, *Recueil*, Nos. 32, 33, 38, 47 and 53.
29. Flodoard, *Historia*, IV, 35. Louis seems to have done this out of pique on his mother Eadgifu's marriage to Herbert, after 967 count of Meaux and Troyes, a son of Herbert II of Vermandois.
30. Flodoard, *Historia*, IV, 35 and *Annales, s.a.*, 945.
31. See J. Verdon, 'Les femmes et la politique en France au Xe siècle', *Economies et sociétés au moyen âge. Mélanges offerts à Edouard Perroy* (Paris 1973), 108–19 and M. L. Portmann, *Die Darstellung der Frau in der Geschichtsschreibung des früheren Mittelalters* (Basle and Stuttgart 1958).
32. Flodoard, *Annales, s.a.*, 956.
33. Ibid., *s.a.*, 961.
34. Ibid., *s.a.*, 962.
35. P. Desportes, 'Les archévêques de Reims et les droits comtaux aux Xe et XIe siècles', *Economies et sociétés au moyen âge*, 79–89. On Rheims generally see A. Dumas, 'L'église de Reims au temps des luttes entre Carolingiens et Robertiens 880–1027', *Revue d'Histoire de l'Eglise de France* **30** (1944), 5–38.
36. See the literature cited by C. Bouchard, 'The origins of the French nobility: a reassessment', *American Historical Review* **86** (1981), 501–32 and M. Heinzelmann, 'La noblesse du haut moyen âge (VIII–XI). Quelques problèmes à propos d'ouvrages récents', *MA* 4th series **31** (1976), 131–44. See also G. Duby (ed.), *Famille et parenté dans l'occident mediéval. Colloques de l'Ecole Francais de Rome* **30** (Rome 1977).
37. P. de Vic, *Histoire générale de Languedoc* (Toulouse 5 vols, 1730–45), V, Nos. CI and CIII.
38. L. Trenard (ed.), *Histoire des Pays-Bas francais* (Toulouse 1972), 83–4.
39. Richer, *Historia*, III, 81; compare I, 9 and III, 102.
40. Ibid., IV, 33 and compare III, 78.
41. See Lot, *Les derniers Carolingiens*, 108–9.
42. Richer, *Historia*, III, 81.
43. As is indicated, for example, in the charter: Lothar and Louis V, *Recueil*, No. 36.
44. Richer, *Historia*, III, 85.
45. Gerbert, Ep. 39; Eng. trs. Lattin No. 24.
46. See in particular Gerbert Epp. 37–39, 42, 45, 47, 48–52, etc.; Eng. trs. Lattin, Nos. 45–49, 51, 53–60, etc. See H. Zimmermann, 'Frankreich und Reims in der Politik der Ottonenzeit', *MIÖG Ergänzungsband* **20** (1962), 122–46.
47. Gerbert, Epp. 53 and 57; Eng. trs. Lattin, Nos. 63 and 64.
48. Ibid., Ep. 52; Eng. trs. Lattin, No. 59.
49. Richer, *Historia*, IV, 11 and 12.
50. See K. F. Werner, 'Die Legitimität der Kapetinger und die Entstehung des *Reditus regni Francorum ad stirpem Karoli*', *Welt als Geschichte* **12** (1952), 203–25 and J. Ehlers, 'Die *Historia francorum Senonensis* und der Aufstieg des Hauses Capet', *Journal of Medieval History* **4** (1978), 1–26.

51. Charles the Simple, *Recueil*, No. 74.
52. Louis IV, *Recueil*, No. 41; Lothar, *Recueil*, No. 1 and see also for Compiègne in 974 (No. 34) and confirmed in 984 (No. 51).
53. Charles the Simple, *Recueil*, Nos. 28, 30, 35, 38, 54, 78, 87 and 91.
54. Louis IV, *Recueil*, Nos. 5, 36, 40, 42.
55. See the list for example in Louis IV, *Recueil*, Introduction, XXIV–XXVIII.
56. See J. Lemarignier, 'Les fidèles du roi de France 936–987', *Recueil de travaux offert à M. Clovis Brunel* (Paris 2 vols, 1955), II, 138–62. I follow Lemarignier in my discussion of *fideles*.
57. *Gesta abbatum Sithiensium, MGH SS* XIII, 626.
58. Louis IV, *Recueil*, No. 23.
59. *PL* 125, col. 1084–5.
60. Werner, cited above, Chapter 4, n. 21 and J. Campbell, 'The significance of the Anglo-Norman state in the administrative history of western Europe', *Beihefte der Francia* 9 (Munich 1980) 117–34.
61. For example, Flodoard, *Annales, s.a.*, 944, 961, etc.
62. For example, Hugh the Great, Flodoard, *Annales, s.a.*, 945.
63. Charles the Simple, *Recueil*, Nos 1 and 17 and Flodoard, *Annales, s.a.*, 922.
64. Louis IV, *Recueil*, Nos. 33 and 36 and Lothar and Louis V, *Recueil*, No. 24.
65. Louis IV, *Recueil*, Nos. 10, 27, 28, 29, 37 and compare 33.
66. Charles the Simple, *Recueil*, No. 53.
67. Ibid., Nos. 56 and 80.
68. Ibid., No. 95.
69. Lothar and Louis V, *Recueil*, for example Nos. 5 or 8.
70. Charles the Simple, *Recueil*, Nos. 2, 34, 40, 60, 64, 65, 67, 75, 94, 97, 105, 106 and 116; Louis IV, *Recueil*, Nos. 3, 7, 9, 27, 44 and see Introduction, XXI–XXIII; Lothar and Louis V, *Recueil*, Nos. 1, 29, 56.
71. R. T.Coolidge, 'Adalbero of Laon', *Studies in Medieval and Renaissance History* 2 (1965), 1–114 especially 11–16. See also the introductions to the charters of all the last Carolingian kings.
72. Here I rely on P. Grierson, *Monnaies du Moyen Age* (Fribourg, 1976).
73. J. Lafaurie, 'Numismatique: Des Carolingiens aux Capetiens', *Cahiers de civilisation mediévale* 13 (1970), 117–37. The abbey of St Martin of Tours, for example, was granted the right to mint coins in 919.
74. See the discussion in F. Lot. *Études sur le règne de Hugues Capet et la fin du Xe siècle* (Paris 1903), 187–239.
75. Schramm and Mütherich, *Denkmale der deutschen Könige und Kaiser*, 95.

Bibliography of Principal Sources

ABBO, *Bella Parisiacae Urbis*, H. Wacquet (ed.), *Le siège de Paris par les Normands* (Paris 1964).

Actus pontificum Cenomannis in urbe degentium, G. Busson and A. Ledru (eds), Archives historiques du Maine (Le Mans 1901).

ADAM of Bremen, *Gesta Hammaburgensis ecclesiae pontificum*, B. Schmiedler (ed.),*MGH SS rerum germanicarum* (Hannover and Leipzig 1917) and reprinted in R. Buchner (ed.), *Quellen des 9. und 11. Jhts zur Geschichte der Hamburgischen Kirche und des Reiches* (Darmstadt 1978); Eng. trs. F. J. Tschan (New York 1959).

ADEMAR of Chabannes, *Chronicon*, J. Chavanon (ed.), *Ademar de Chabannes, Chronique* (Paris 1897); *Commemoratio abbatum Lemovicensium*, H. Duples Agier (ed.), *Chroniques de St Martial de Limoges* (Paris 1974).

ADREVALD et al., *Miracula sancti Benedicti*, E. de Certain (ed.) (Paris 1858).

AGOBARD of Lyons, *Opera Omnia, PL* 104; *Carmina, MGH Poet.* II.

AIMOIN of Fleury, *Historia Francorum*, Bouquet (ed.), *Recueil*, III and XI; *Miracula sancti Benedicti*, see under Adrevald; *Vita Abboni, PL* 139.

ALCUIN, *Opera Omnia, PL* 100 and 101; also *Epistolae, MGH Epp.* IV (Eng. trs. S. Allott, *Alcuin of York*, York 1974); *De Rhetorica* (Eng. trs. W. S. Howell, *The Rhetoric of Alcuin and Charlemagne*, Princeton 1941); *De Orthographia*, H. Keil (ed.), *Grammatici Latini* VII (Leipzig 1865–88); Poems, including *De sanctis eboracensis ecclesiae, MGH Poet.* I (Eng. trs. of the York poem in Allott, *Alcuin of York*); On music, see under Gerbert, M; see also C. Chase, *Two Alcuin Letter books from the British Museum MS Cotton Vespasian A.XIV* (Toronto 1975).

ANGILBERT, *Carmina, MGH Poet.* I; *Opera omnia, PL* 99; *De ecclesia centulensi, MGH SS* XV.

Annales Alamannici, MGH SS I, 22–60.

Annales Bertiniani, F. Grat, J. Vielliard and S. Clemencet (eds), *Annales de Saint Bertin* (Paris 1964) (Germ. trs. and Latin *MGH* text in Rau, *Quellen*, II).

Annales Elnonenses, P. Grierson (ed.), *Les Annales de Saint-Pierre de Gand et de Saint-Amand* (Brussels 1937).

Annales Fuldenses, F. Kurze (ed.), *MGH SS rerum germanicarum* (Hannover 1891) and in Rau, *Quellen*, III.

Annales Guelferbytani, *MGH SS* I, 23–46.

Annales Laureshamenses, *MGH SS* I, 22–40.

Annales Laurissenses Minores, *MGH SS* I, 112–23 and 630.

Annales Mettenses Priores, B. von Simson (ed.) (Hannover and Leipzig 1905).

Annales regni Francorum, F. Kurze (ed.),*MGH SS rerum germanicarum* (Hannover 1895 and 1950); Eng. trs. B. W. Scholz, *Carolingian Chronicles* (Ann Arbor 1970); Germ. trs. Rau, *Quellen*, I.

Annales Vedastini B. von Simson (ed.), *MGH SS rerum germanicarum* (Leipzig and Hannover 1909); Germ. trs. Rau, *Quellen*, II.

Annales Xantenses, B. von Simson (ed.), *MGH SS rerum germanicarum* (Leipzig and Hannover 1909); Germ. trs. Rau, *Quellen*, II.

ARATOR, *De actibus apostolorum*, A. P. McKinlay (ed.) (Vienna 1951).

ARNULF, Charters, P. Kehr (ed.), *MGH Dip. Regum germaniae ex stirpe Karolinorum* III. *Arnulfi Diplomata* (Berlin 1956).

ASSER, *Vita Alfredi*, W. Stevenson (ed.) (Oxford 1904 and revised edn 1959); Eng. trs. A. S. Cook (Boston 1906) and S. D. Keynes and M. Lapidge, *Alfred the Great. Asser's 'Life of King Alfred' and other contemporary sources* (Harmondsworth Books 1983).

ASTRONOMER, *Vita Hludowici*, *MGH SS* II, 607–48 and Rau, *Quellen*, I; Eng. trs. A. Cabaniss, *Son of Charlemagne* (Syracuse 1965).

AUGUSTINE, *De civitate Dei* (many trans. and edns); *De doctrina christiana* (Vienna 1863); Eng. trs. D. W. Robertson (Indianapolis 1958).

AURELIAN of Réomé, see under Gerbert, M.

AVITUS, K. R. S. Peiper (ed.), *MGH AA* VI, 2 (Berlin 1883).

Becker, G., *Catalogi bibliothecarum antiqui* (Bonn 1885).

BENEDICT, *Rule*, with Eng. trs. J. McCann (ed.) (London 1952).

BOETHIUS, *De Musica*, G. Friedlein (ed.), *Boetii de institutione arithmetica libri duo, de institutione musica libri quinque* (Leipzig 1867).

BONIFACE of Mainz, *Epistolae*, M. Tangl (ed.), *MGH Epp. Selecti I Bonifacii et Lulli Epistolae*, 2nd edn. (Berlin 1955); Eng. trs. E. Emerson, *The Letters of St Boniface* (New York 1940) and C. H. Talbot (selections) *The Anglo-Saxon Missionaries in Germany* (London 1954 and 1981).

Capitularia regum francorum, A. Boretius and V. Krause (eds), *MGH Cap.* I and *Cap.* II (Hannover 1883–97).

CARLOMAN II, see under LOUIS II the Stammerer.

Cartulary of Landévennec, A. de la Borderie (ed.), *Cartulaire de l'abbaye de Landévennec* (Rennes 1888).

Cartulary of Nîmes, E. Germer Durand (ed.), *Cartulaire du chapître de l'église cathédrale Notre Dame de Nîmes 876–1156* (Nîmes 1872).

Cartulary of Redon, A. de Courson (ed.), *Cartulaire de l'abbaye de Redon en Bretagne* (Paris 1963).

Cartulary of Toulouse, C. Douais (ed.), *Cartulaire de l'abbaye de Saint-Sernin de Toulouse 844–1200* (Paris 1887).

CATO, Dionysius, *Disticha Catonis*, M. Boas (ed.) (Amsterdam 1952).

CHARLEMAGNE, charters, *MGH Dip. Kar.* I.

CHARLES the Bald, G. Tessier (ed.), *Recueil des actes de Charles II le Chauve roi de France* (Paris 3 vols, 1943–55).

CHARLES the Simple, P. Lauer (ed.), *Recueil des actes de Charles III le Simple, roi de France 893–923* (Paris 1940–49).

CHRODEGANG of Metz, *Regula canonicorum*, W. Schmitz (ed.) (Hannover 1889).

Chronicon Moissiacense, MGH SS I, 280–313.

Chronicon Namnetense, R. Merlet (ed.),*Chronique de Nantes* (Paris 1896).

Chronicon de Normannorum gestis in Francia 820–911, MGH SS I, 532–6.

CLAUDIUS of Turin, *Libri tres de cultu imaginum* and other works, *PL* 104.

Codex Carolinus, W. Gundlach (ed.), *MGH Epp.* I, 469–657.

Cologne episcopal register, F. W. Oediger (ed.), *Die Regesten der Erzbischöfe von Köln im Mittelalter* I 313–1099 (Bonn 1954–61).

COLUMBANUS, *Opera*, G. Walker (ed.), *Sancti Columbani Opera* (Dublin 1970).

Conciliar decrees of the Frankish church, A. Werminghoff (ed.), *MGH Conc.* II, ii (Hannover 1880).

CONRAD, T.Sickel (ed.), *Diplomatum regum et imperatorum Germaniae I Conradi I, Heinrici I et Ottonis I. Diplomata* (Hannover 1879–84).

Corpus consuetudinum monasticarum I, K. Hallinger (ed.) (Siegburg 1963).

DHUODA, *Liber Manualis. Dhuodane quem ad filium suum transmisit Wilhelmum*, P. Richè (ed.), *Dhuoda. Manuel pour mon fils* (with Fr. trs.) (Paris 1975).

Diplomata Karolinorum, facsimile edition of the surviving original charters, P. Lauer and F. Lot (eds) (Toulouse 10 parts, 1936–49).

DUDO of St Quentin, *De moribus et actis primorum Normanniae ducum*, J. Lair (ed.) (Caen 1865); extracts in *MGH SS* IV.

DUNGAL, *Opera omnia, PL* 105.

EDDIUS STEPHANUS, *Vita Wilfridi*, B. Colgrave (ed.) (with Eng. trs.) *The Life of Bishop Wilfrid* (Cambridge 1927).

EINHARD, *Vita Karoli*, O.Holder Egger (ed.), *MGH SS rerum germanicarum* (Hannover 1911 and 1947), and Rau, *Quellen*, I; Eng. trs. L. Thorpe, *Einhard and Notker the Stammerer, Two Lives of Charlemagne* (Harmondsworth 1969).

Epitaphium Arsenii, see under PASCHASIUS RADBERT.

ERCONRAD, *Translatio sancti Liborii episcopi*, with Fr. trs. A. Cohausz, V. Mellinghoff-Bourgerie and R. Latouche (eds), *La translation de saint Liboire de diacre Erconrad* (Le Mans 1967).

ERMOLD the Black, *In honorem Hludowici*, E. Faral (ed.) (with Fr. trs.), *Poème sur Louis le Pieux et épitres au roi Pepin* (Paris 1964).

FLODOARD, *Annales*, P. Lauer (ed.), *Les Annales de Flodoard* (Paris 1905) (Fr. trs. M. Guizot, *Collection des mémoires relatifs à l'histoire de France* 6 (Paris 1924); *Historia Remensis ecclesiae, MGH SS* XIII (Fr. trs. M. Guizot, *Collection* 5 (Paris 1824).

FOLCUIN, *Gesta abbatum sancti Bertini Sithiensium, MGH SS* XIII (narrative sections only) and B. Guérard, *Cartulaire de Saint Bertin* (Paris 1840).

FREDEGAR, *Chronicon*, J. M. Wallace-Hadrill (ed.), *The Fourth Book of the Chronicle of Fredegar with its continuations* (with Eng. trs.) (London 1960).

GERBERT of Rheims (later Pope Sylvester II), *Epistolae*, J. Havet (ed.), *Lettres de Gerbert, 983–997* (Paris 1889), and F. Weigle, *Die Briefsammlung Gerberts von Reims, MGH Der Briefe der deustchen Kaiserzeit* II (Berlin, Zurich and Dublin 1966); Eng. trs. H. Lattin (New York 1961).

Gerbert, M., *Scriptores ecclesiastici de musica* (Typ. S. Blasianis, 1784).

Gesta abbatum Fontanellensium, F. Lohier and J. Laporte (eds) (Paris and Rouen 1936).

Gesta domni Aldrici Cenomannicae urbis episcopi a discipulis suis, R. Charles and L. Froger (eds) (Mamers 1889).

Gesta episcoporum Autissiodorensium, MGH SS XIII.

Gesta episcoporum Cameracensium, L. C. Bethmann (ed.),*MGH SS* VII.

Gesta episcoporum Mettensium, see under PAUL the Deacon.

GREGORY of Tours, *Historiae francorum*, H. Omont and G. Collon (eds) (Paris 1886–93 and 1913), and W. Arndt, *MGH SS rer. merov.* I; Eng. trs. L. Thorpe (Harmondsworth 1974) or O. Dalton (Oxford 2 vols, 1927).

GUY of Arezzo, on music, see under Gerbert, M.

HARIULF, *Chronicon Centulense*, F. Lot (ed.), *Chronique de l'abbaye de Saint-Riquier* (Paris 1894).

HENRY I, see under CONRAD.

HILDEMAR, Exposition on the Rule of Benedict, R. Mittermüller (ed.), *Vita et regula SS. P. Benedicti, una cum expositione regulae a Hildemaro tradita* (Regensburg, New York and Cincinnati 1880).

HINCMAR of Rheims, *De ordine palatii*, T. Gross and R. Schieffer (eds), *MGH Fontes Iuris Germanici antiqui in usum scholarum separatim editi* (Hannover 1980) (with Germ. trs.); Eng. trs. D. Herlihy, *The History of Feudalism* (London 1970), 208–228; *Epistolae, MGH Epp.* VIII and *PL* 125.

Historia francorum senonensis, MGH SS IX.

HRABAN MAUR, *Carmina MGH Poet.* II; *De institutione clericorum, PL* 107, cols 293–419; *De laudibus sanctae crucis*, facs. ed. K. Holter (Graz, 1973); *De Universo, PL* 111, cols 9–614; *De Musica, PL* 110, cols 495–500.

HUCBALD, On Music. For Latin text, see under Gerbert, M., Eng. trs. W. Babb, *Hucbald, Guido and John on Music* (New Haven and London 1978); *Opera omnia, PL* 132.

ISIDORE of Seville, *Etymologiae*, W. M. Lindsay (ed.) (Oxford 2 vols, 1910); *Liber de natura rerum*, J. Fontaine (ed.) (Bordeaux 1960).

JOHN of Gorze, *Vita Chrodegangi, MGH SS* X.

JOHN of St Arnulf, *Vita Johannis abbatis Gorziensis, MGH SS* IV.

JOHN of Salerno, *Vita Odonis*, J. Mabillon (ed.), *Annales ord. S. Benedicti* V (Paris 1685); Eng. trs. G. Sitwell (with the Life of Gerald of Aurillac) (London 1958).

JOHN SCOTTUS ERIUGENA, *Commentarius in evangelium Johannis*, with Fr. trs. E. Jeauneau (ed.) (Paris 1972); *Annotationes in Marcianum*, C. E. Lutz (ed.) (Cambridge, Mass 1939); *Carmina, MGH Poet.* III; *Expositiones in ierarchiam coelestem*, J. Barbet (ed.) (Turnholt 1975); *Periphyseon* (or *De divisione naturae*) with Eng. trs. I. P. Sheldon-Williams (ed.) (Dublin 1968–72, 2 vols so far of 4 projected).

JONAS of Orleans, *De institutione regia* J. Reviron (ed.), *Jonas d'Orléans et son De Institutione Regia. Etude et texte critique* (Paris 1930); *De institutione laicali*, PL 106, cols 117–280.

JUVENCUS, *Evangeliorum libri quattuor*, C. Marold (ed.) (Leipzig 1886), and I. Huemer (Vienna 1891).

Lehmann, Paul, *Mittelalterliche Bibliothekskataloge Deutschlands und der Schweiz* I (Munich 1918).

Lex Salica, K. A. Eckhardt (ed.), *Lex Salica, 100 Titel Text. MGH Leges nationum germanicarum*, 4, ii (Hannover 1969) and *Pactus Legis Salicae, MGH Leges nationum germanicarum*, 4, i. (Hannover 1962).

Liber Historiae Francorum, B. Krusch (ed.), *MGH SS rer. merov.* II; Eng. trs. B. Bachrach (Laurence, Kansas 1973).

Liber Pontificalis, L. Duchesne (ed.) (Paris 1886).

Library catalogues, see under Becker and Lehmann.

LIUDGER, *Vita Gregoriii abbatis Traiectensis, MGH SS* XV, 63–79; Germ. trs. W. Wattenbach, G. Grandaur and M. Laurent (Leipzig 1888).

LIUTPRAND, *Antapodosis*, J. Becker (ed.), *Die Werke Liudprands von Cremona, MGH SS rerum germanicarum* (Hannover–Leipzig 1915); Eng. trs. F. A. Wright, *The Works of Liutprand of Cremona* (London 1930).

LOTHAR and LOUIS V, L. Halphen and F. Lot (eds), *Recueil des actes de Lothaire et de Louis V, rois de France 954–987* (Paris 1908).

LOUIS the Child, T. Schieffer (ed.), *MGH Dip. regum germaniae ex stirpe Karolinorum* IV. *Zwentiboldi et Ludowici infantis Diplomata* (Berlin 1960).

LOUIS I the Pious, Bouquet (ed.), *Recueil*, VI. (charters).

LOUIS II the Stammerer and LOUIS III, *Recueil*, F. Grat, J. de Font Reaulx, G. Tessier and R. H. Bautier (eds), *Recueil des actes de Louis II le Bègue, Louis III et Carloman II rois de France, 877–884* (Paris 1978).

LOUIS IV, P. Lauer (ed.), *Recueil des actes de Louis IV, roi de France 936–954* (Paris 1914).

LOUIS V, see under LOTHAR.

LUPUS of Ferrières, *Epistolae*, L. Levillain (ed.), *Loup de Ferrières. Correspondence* (Paris 1964), with Fr. trs.; Eng. trs. G. W. Regenos (The Hague 1966).

MARTIANUS CAPELLA, *De nuptiis philologiae et Mercurii*, A. Dick (ed.) (Leipzig 1925); Eng. trs. W. H. Stahl, R. Johnson and E. L. Binge (New York 2 vols, 1971 and 1977).

Merovingian royal charters, facs., P. Lauer and C. Samaran (eds), *Les diplômes originaux des mérovingiennes* (Paris 1908).

Musica enchiriadis, see under Gerbert, M.

NITHARD, *De dissensionibus filiorum Ludowici Pii*, with Fr. trs., P. Lauer (ed.) (Paris 1926); Eng. trs. B. W. Scholz, *Carolingian Chronicles* (Ann Arbor 1970).

Norman dukes' charters, M. Fauroux (ed.), *Recueil des actes des ducs de Normandie de 911 à 1066* (Caen 1961).

Notitiae, C. Manaresi (ed.), *I Placiti del 'Regnum Italiae'*, (Rome 1955).

NOTKER BABULUS, *Gesta Karoli*, H. F. Haefele (ed.), *MGH SS rerum germanica-rum*, Nova series XIII (Berlin 1959) and Rau, *Quellen*, III with Germ. trs.; Eng. trs. L. Thorpe, *Einhard and Notker the Stammerer. Two lives of Charle-magne* (Harmondsworth 1969).

NOTKER LABEO, on music, see under Gerbert, M.

ODILO of Cluny, *Epitaphium domine Adalheide auguste*, H. Paulhart (ed.), 'Die lebensbeschreibung der Kaiserin Adelheid von Abt Odilo von Cluny', *MIÖG, Ergänzungsband* 20 (1962).

ODO, R. H. Bautier (ed.), *Recueil des actes d'Eudes, roi de France 888–898* (Paris 1967).

ODO of Cluny, supposed author of *Dialogus de Musica*, see under Gerbert, M.

OTTO I, see under CONRAD.

OTTO II, *MGH Dip. regum et imperatorum Germaniae*. II. i. *Ottonis II Diplomata* (Hannover 1888).

PASCHASIUS RADBERT, *De corpore et sanguine domini*, B. Paul (ed.) (Turnholt 1969); *Epitaphium Arsenii* or *Vita Walae* and *Vita Adalhardi*, PL 120; Eng. trs. A. Cabaniss, *Charlemagne's Cousins: Contemporary Lives of Adalhard and Wala* (New York 1967).

PAUL the Deacon, Poems, K. Neff (ed.), *Die Gedichte des Paulus Diaconus* (Mun-ich 1908); *Gesta episcoporum Mettensium*, G. H. Pertz (ed.), *MGH SS* II; *His-toria langobardorum*, G. Waitz (ed.), *MGH SS rerum langobardorum*; Eng. trs. W. D. Foulke (Philadelphia 1907).

PIPPIN I and PIPPIN II of Aquitaine, M. Prou and L. Levillain eds, *Recueil des actes de Pépin I et de Pépin II rois d'Aquitaine 814–848* (Paris 1926).

POETA SAXO, P. Winterfield (ed.), *MGH Poet. IV.*

PRISCIAN, *Institutionum grammaticarum libri XVIII*, H. Keil (ed.), *Grammatici Latini*, II and III (Leipzig 1855).

PRUDENTIUS, *Psychomachia*, M. Lavareune (ed.), *Psychomachie, texte, traduction, commentaire avec une introduction historique* (Paris 1933); Eng. trs. H. Isbell, *The Last Poets of Imperial Rome* (Harmondsworth 1977), 127–52.

RALPH, see under ROBERT I.

RALPH GLABER, *Historiarum sui temporis Libri V*, M. Prou (ed.) (Paris 1886); Fr. trs. M. Guizot, *Collection des mémoires relatif à l'histoire de France* 6 (Paris 1824).

RATRAMNUS of Corbie, *De Corpore et sanguine domini*, J. N. Bakhuizen van den Brink (ed.) (Amsterdam 1974).

REGINO of Prüm, *Chronicon*, F. Kurze (ed.), *Reginonis abbatis Prumiensis Chronicon cum Continuatione Treverensi, MGH SS rerum germanicarum*, and Rau, *Quellen*, III; on music, see under Gerbert, M.

REIMBERT, *Vita Anscharii, MGH SS rerum germanicarum*; Eng. trs. C. H. Robin-son, *Anskar the Apostle of the North* (London 1921).

REMIGIUS of Auxerre, *Commentum in Martianum Capellam*, C. E. Lutz (ed.), (Lei-den 2 vols, 1962–65); on music, see under Gerbert, M.

RICHER, *Historia Francorum*, with Fr. trs. R. Latouche (ed.), *Richer, Histoire de France 888–995* (Paris 1967).

ROBERT, *Recueil*, J. Dufour (ed.), *Recueil des actes de Robert I et de Raoul rois de France 922–936* (Paris 1978).

RUOTGER, *Vita Brunonis archiepiscopi Coloniensis*, I. Ott (ed.), *MGH SS rerum germanicarum*, N. S. X. (Weimar 1951); also in R. Buchner (gen. ed.), *Ausgewählte Quellen zur deutschen Geschichte des Mittelalters* 22 (Darmstadt 1973), with Germ. trs.

SEDULIUS SCOTTUS, *Liber de rectoribus christianis* and *Collectaneum*, S. Hellmann (ed.) (Munich 1906).

SIDONIUS APOLLINARIS, *Epistolae et Carmina*, with Eng. trs. W. B. Anderson (ed.) (London and Cambridge, Mass. 1936 and 1963).

SNORRI STURLUSON, *Heimskringla*, F. Jonssón (ed.) (Copenhagen 1911 and reprinted Oslo 1966).

Supplex Libellus, J. Semmler (ed.), in K. Hallinger (ed.), *Corpus consuetudinum monasticarum* I (Siegburg 1963), 319–27.

THEGAN, *Vita Hludowici, MGH SS* II, 590–604 and Rau, *Quellen*, I (with Germ. trs.).

THEODULF, *Carmina, MGH Poet.* I; *Libri Carolini sive Caroli Magni de Imaginibus, MGH Conc.* II, *Supplementum* H. Bastgen (ed.) (A new edition with Eng. trs. is being prepared by Ann Freeman). *Capitulare ad presbyteros parochiae suae, PL* 105, cols 223–40 and Second statute, C. de Clercq (ed.), *La législation religieuse franque* (Paris and Louvain 1935), 321–51; and H. Sauer, *Theodulfi capitula in England: die altenglischen Übersetzungen zusammen mit dem lateinischen Text* (Munich 1978).

Vita Abboni, see under AIMOIN.

Vita Adalhardi, see under PASCHASIUS RADBERT.

Vita Alfredi, see under ASSER.

Vita Anscharii, see under REIMBERT.

Vita Brunonis, see under RUOTGER.

Vita Chrodegangi, see under JOHN of Gorze.

Vita Gregorii, see under LIUDGER.

Vita Hludowici, see under ASTRONOMER and THEGAN.

Vita Karoli, see under EINHARD.

Vita Odonis, see under JOHN of Salerno.

Vita Walae, see under PASCHASIUS RADBERT.

Vita Wilfridi, see under EDDIUS STEPHANUS.

WALAHFRID STRABO, *Carmina, MGH Poet.* II; *Carmen de visionibus Wettini*, text and Eng. trs. D. A. Traill (Berne 1974); *Hortulus*, facs. edn, transcription and Eng. trs. R. Payne and W. Blunt (Haarlem 1966).

WIDUKIND, *Res gestae Saxonicae*, H. E. Lothmann and P. Hirsch (eds), *MGH SS serum germanicarum i.u.s* (Hannover 1935); also in A. Bauer and R. Rau, *Quellen zur Geschichte der sächsischen Kaiserzeit* (Darmstadt 1977) with Germ. trs.; selection with Fr. trs. in R. Folz, *La naissance du Saint Empire* (Paris 1967).

WILLIAM of Jumièges, *Gesta Normannorum ducum* J. Maix (ed.) (Rouen and Paris 1914); Fr. trs. M. Guizot, *Collection des mémoires relatifs à l'histoire de France*, 29 (Paris 1886).

ZWENTIBOLD, see under LOUIS the Child.

A Note on Further Reading

The Carolingians were far from forgotten throughout the Middle Ages; they, and Charlemagne in particular, were the subject of many epic poems, such as the *Song of Roland*, trs. D. Sayers (Penguin Classics 1957). But it was not until the sixteenth century that scholarly and antiquarian interest in the Franks grew, and the study of the Franks became closely connected with the general development of the study of medieval history in Europe. I have discussed this in some detail in 'The study of Frankish history in France and Germany in the sixteenth and seventeenth centuries', *Francia* 8 (1980), 556–72, while the historical scholarship of the Bollandists and Maurists in the seventeenth century and the founding of the *Monumenta Germaniae Historica* in the early nineteenth century have been described by D. Knowles, *Great Historical Enterprises* (London 1962). On further developments in the study of Frankish history, J. W. Thompson, *A History of Historical Writing* (New York 1942), B. Lyon, *Henri Pirenne* (Ghent 1974) and D. Bullough, *'Europae pater*: Charlemagne and his achievement in the light of recent scholarship', *EHR* 85 (1970), 59–105, are useful.

English language publications concerning the Carolingians concentrate for the most part on the reign of Charlemagne. Standard works, full of invaluable references, are D. Bullough, *The Age of Charlemagne*, 2nd edn. (London 1973), H. Fichtenau, *The Carolingian Empire* (Oxford 1968), L. Halphen, *Charlemagne and the Carolingian Empire* (Amsterdam, New York and Oxford 1977) translated from the 1968 French edition, though the actual text remained that of the 1947 edition), F. L. Ganshof, *The Carolingians and the Frankish Monarchy* (London 1971), *Frankish Institutions under Charlemagne* (New York 1968) and *Feudalism* (London 1964). Always of value for their insight on the ideological aspects of the Carolingian period are K. F. Morrison, *The Two Kingdoms: Ecclesiology in Carolingian Political Thought* (Princeton 1964) and W. Ullmann, *The Carolingian Renaissance and the Idea of Kingship* (London 1969). Written from a rather different point of view but no less valuable is J. M. Wallace-Hadrill, *Early Germanic Kingship in England and on the Continent* (Oxford 1971). P. Llewellyn, *Rome in the Dark Ages* (London 1971) provides a background for the Carolingians' relations with the Papacy. Later Carolingian history is not as well served in English as the earlier period, but J. L. Nelson and M. T. Gibson (eds), *Charles the Bald: Court and Kingdom* (Oxford 1981) breaks new ground. An important contribution to our knowledge of the aristocracy is the collection of essays edited and translated by T. Reuter, *The Medieval Nobility* (Amsterdam, New York and Oxford 1978). K. Leyser, *Rule and Conflict in an Early Medieval Society. Ottonian Saxony* (London 1979) is essential reading on the tenth century, and has an excellent bibliography. On medieval religious sensibility, J. Sumption, *Pilgrimage* (London 1975) and P. J. Geary, *Furta Sacra* (Princeton 1978) are both helpful and interesting.

Those students who wish to pursue further matters discussed in this book should follow up the references provided in the notes. For information about work in progress or published since this book was completed they should consult the review and received book sections of the leading journals of medieval studies such as *Speculum*, published by the Medieval Academy of America, and *Deutsches Archiv für die Erforschung des Mittelalters* published by the *Monumenta Germaniae Historica*. Other Continental journals, especially *Le Moyen Age*, *Frühmittelalterliche Studien*, *Francia* and *Bibliothèque de l'École des Chartes* regularly publish articles on the Carolingian period. The *Revue d'Histoire Ecclésiastique* publishes a comprehensive bibliography each year, which despite the journal's title, does not confine itself to ecclesiastical history. Many monographs and surveys of the Carolingian period, moreover, include good bibliographies. For the Germanic background to the period, for example, L. Musset, *The Germanic Invasions* (London 1975) provides an excellent guide, as does P. Riché to the intellectual and cultural developments preceding the Carolingian Renaissance in *Education and Culture in the Barbarian West* (Columbia, South Carolina 1976). On general aspects of culture and on art and architecture in particular, J. Hubert, J. Porcher and W. Volbach, *Carolingian Art* (London 1970) and W. Horn and E. Born, *The Plan of St Gall* (Berkeley 1979) provide comprehensive bibliographies as well as a wealth of illustrations. For the entire Carolingian period the most useful bibliography is that provided by E. James, *Gaul 400–1000* (London 1982). Of immense value to the student, and packed with descriptions of manuscripts and artefacts from the Carolingian period as well as many descriptive essays, is the 1965 Council of Europe exhibition catalogue, *Charlemagne, Oeuvre, Rayonnement et Survivances* (Aachen 1965). The annual Spoleto conference proceedings, *Settimane di Studio dell Centro Italiano di Studi sull' alto Medioevo* (Spoleto 1954–   ), especially 1, 2, 4, 16, 17, 19, 20 and 27, are essential.

Genealogical Tables

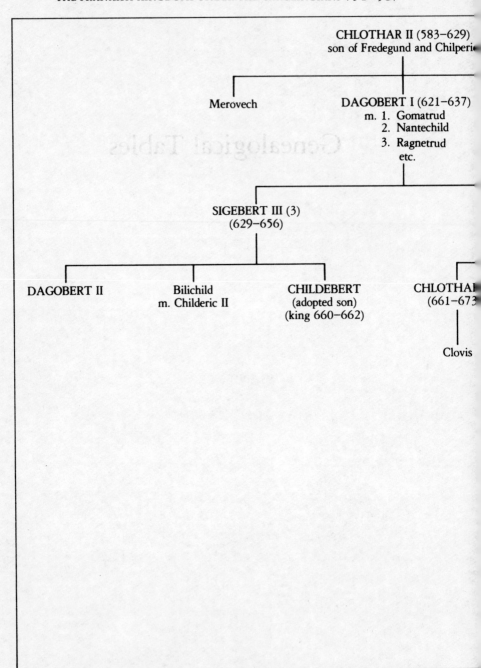

Table 1. The later Merovingians

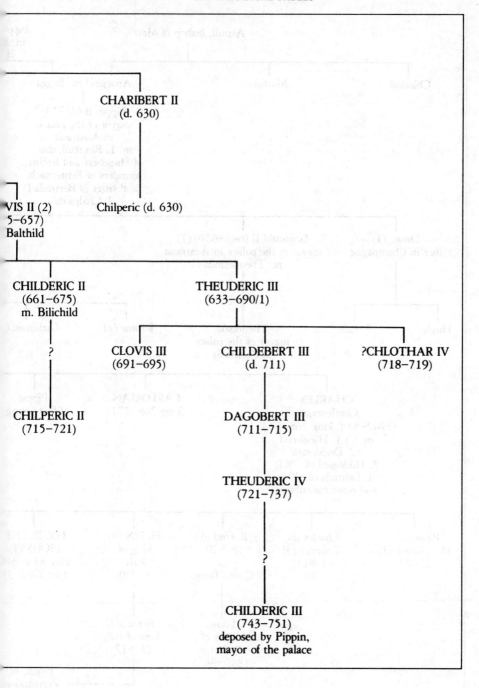

CHARIBERT II
(d. 630)

VIS II (2)
5–657)
Balthild

Chilperic (d. 630)

CHILDERIC II
(661–675)
m. Bilichild

THEUDERIC III
(633–690/1)

?

CLOVIS III
(691–695)

CHILDEBERT III
(d. 711)

?CHLOTHAR IV
(718–719)

CHILPERIC II
(715–721)

DAGOBERT III
(711–715)

THEUDERIC IV
(721–737)

?

CHILDERIC III
(743–751)
deposed by Pippin,
mayor of the palace

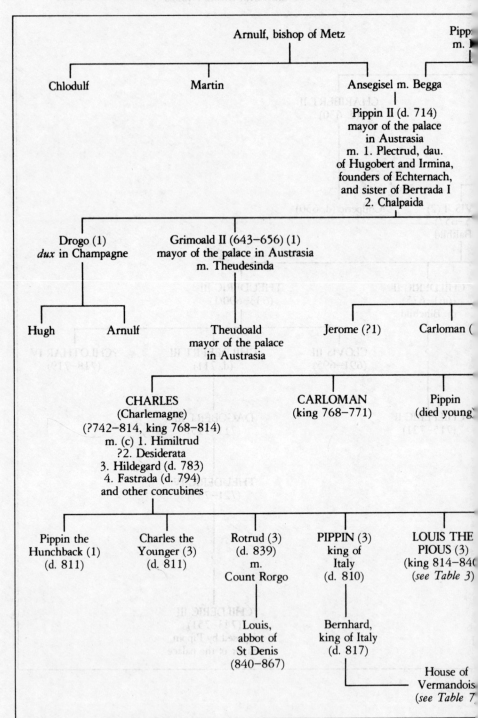

Table 2. The early Carolingians

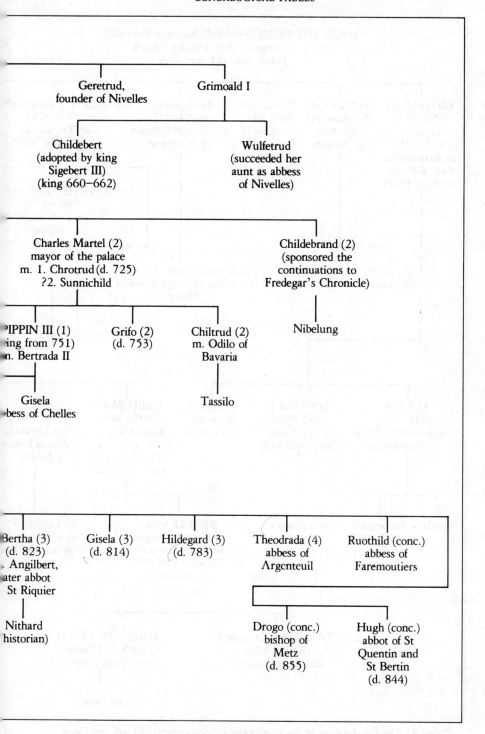

Geretrud,
founder of Nivelles

Grimoald I

Childebert
(adopted by king
Sigebert III)
(king 660–662)

Wulfetrud
(succeeded her
aunt as abbess
of Nivelles)

Charles Martel (2)
mayor of the palace
m. 1. Chrotrud (d. 725)
?2. Sunnichild

Childebrand (2)
(sponsored the
continuations to
Fredegar's Chronicle)

PIPPIN III (1)
king from 751)
m. Bertrada II

Grifo (2)
(d. 753)

Chiltrud (2)
m. Odilo of
Bavaria

Nibelung

Gisela
abbess of Chelles

Tassilo

Bertha (3)
(d. 823)
, Angilbert,
ater abbot
St Riquier

Gisela (3)
(d. 814)

Hildegard (3)
(d. 783)

Theodrada (4)
abbess of
Argenteuil

Ruothild (conc.)
abbess of
Faremoutiers

Nithard
historian)

Drogo (conc.)
bishop of
Metz
(d. 855)

Hugh (conc.)
abbot of St
Quentin and
St Bertin
(d. 844)

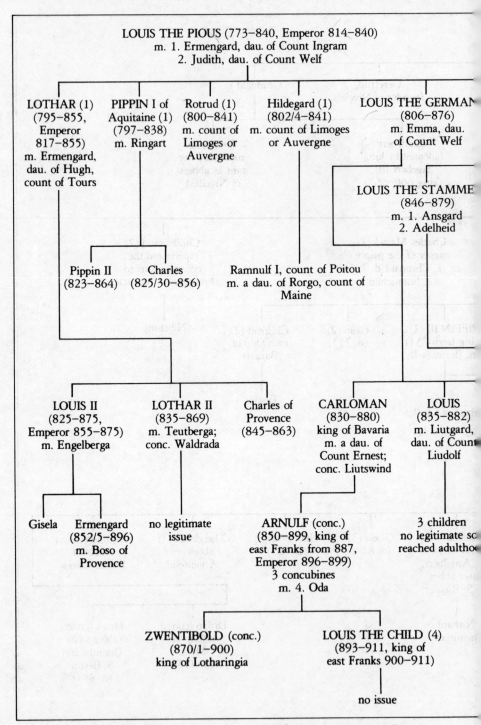

Table 3. The Carolingians in the ninth century: descendants of Louis the Pious

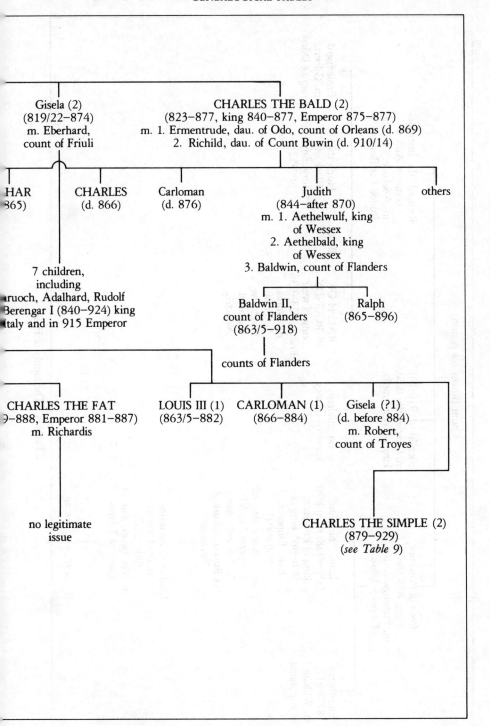

Gisela (2)
(819/22–874)
m. Eberhard,
count of Friuli

CHARLES THE BALD (2)
(823–877, king 840–877, Emperor 875–877)
m. 1. Ermentrude, dau. of Odo, count of Orleans (d. 869)
2. Richild, dau. of Count Buwin (d. 910/14)

HAR
365)

CHARLES
(d. 866)

Carloman
(d. 876)

Judith
(844–after 870)
m. 1. Aethelwulf, king
of Wessex
2. Aethelbald, king
of Wessex
3. Baldwin, count of Flanders

others

7 children,
including
aruoch, Adalhard, Rudolf
Berengar I (840–924) king
Italy and in 915 Emperor

Baldwin II,
count of Flanders
(863/5–918)

Ralph
(865–896)

counts of Flanders

CHARLES THE FAT
9–888, Emperor 881–887)
m. Richardis

LOUIS III (1)
(863/5–882)

CARLOMAN (1)
(866–884)

Gisela (?1)
(d. before 884)
m. Robert,
count of Troyes

no legitimate
issue

CHARLES THE SIMPLE (2)
(879–929)
(*see Table 9*)

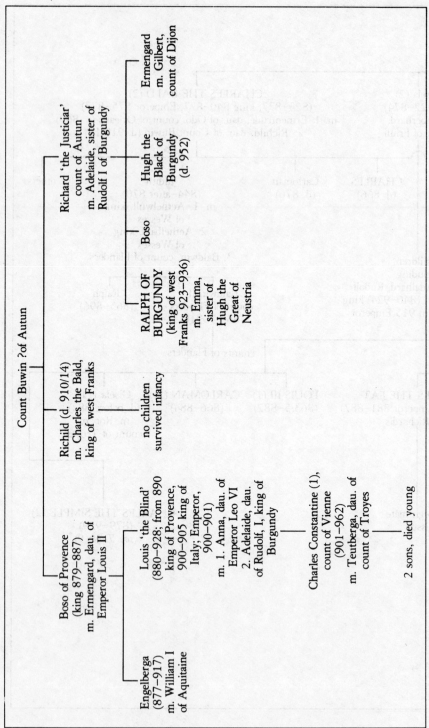

Table 4. The family of Boso

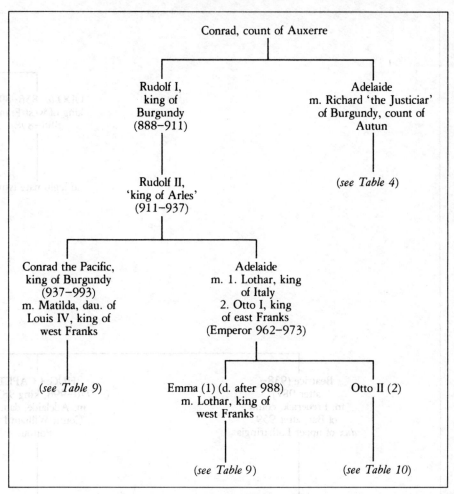

Table 5. House of Rudolf I, king of Burgundy

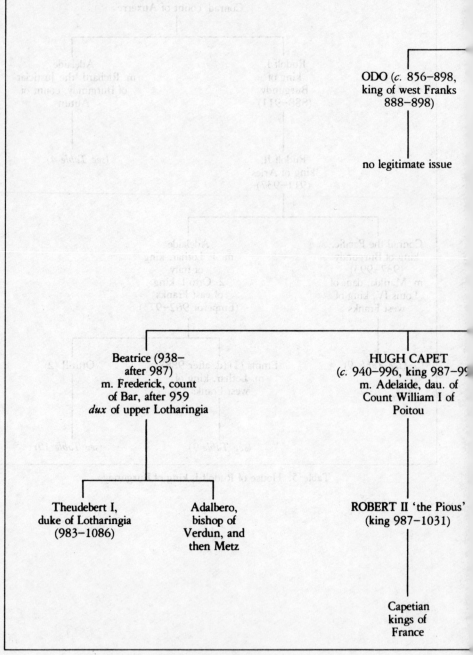

ODO (*c.* 856–898,
king of west Franks
888–898)

no legitimate issue

Beatrice (938–
after 987)
m. Frederick, count
of Bar, after 959
dux of upper Lotharingia

HUGH CAPET
(*c.* 940–996, king 987–99
m. Adelaide, dau. of
Count William I of
Poitou

Theudebert I,
duke of Lotharingia
(983–1086)

Adalbero,
bishop of
Verdun, and
then Metz

ROBERT II 'the Pious'
(king 987–1031)

Capetian
kings of
France

Table 6. The Robertians

358

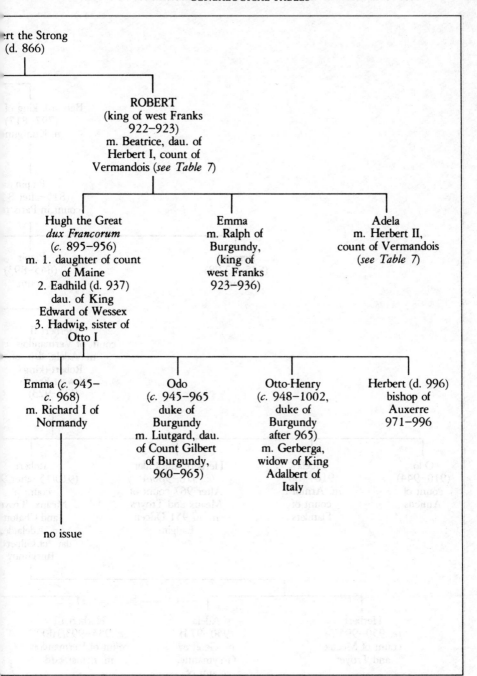

rt the Strong
(d. 866)

ROBERT
(king of west Franks
922–923)
m. Beatrice, dau. of
Herbert I, count of
Vermandois (*see Table 7*)

Hugh the Great
dux Francorum
(*c.* 895–956)
m. 1. daughter of count
of Maine
2. Eadhild (d. 937)
dau. of King
Edward of Wessex
3. Hadwig, sister of
Otto I

Emma
m. Ralph of
Burgundy,
(king of
west Franks
923–936)

Adela
m. Herbert II,
count of Vermandois
(*see Table 7*)

Emma (*c.* 945–
c. 968)
m. Richard I of
Normandy

Odo
(*c.* 945–965
duke of
Burgundy
m. Liutgard, dau.
of Count Gilbert
of Burgundy,
960–965)

Otto-Henry
(*c.* 948–1002,
duke of
Burgundy
after 965)
m. Gerberga,
widow of King
Adalbert of
Italy

Herbert (d. 996)
bishop of
Auxerre
971–996

no issue

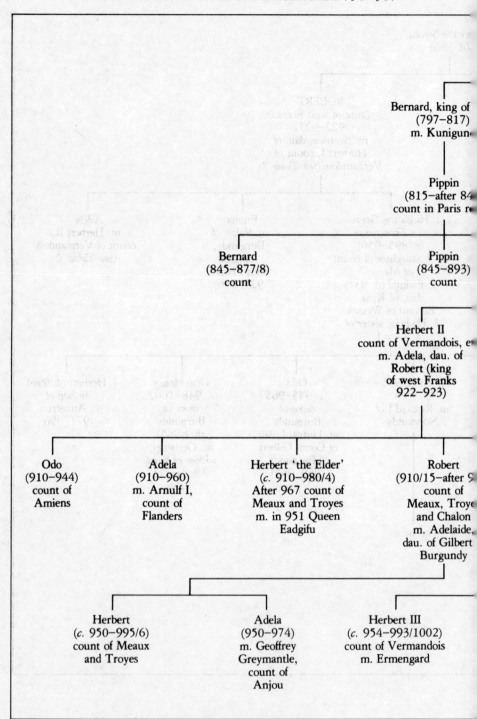

Table 7. The house of Vermandois

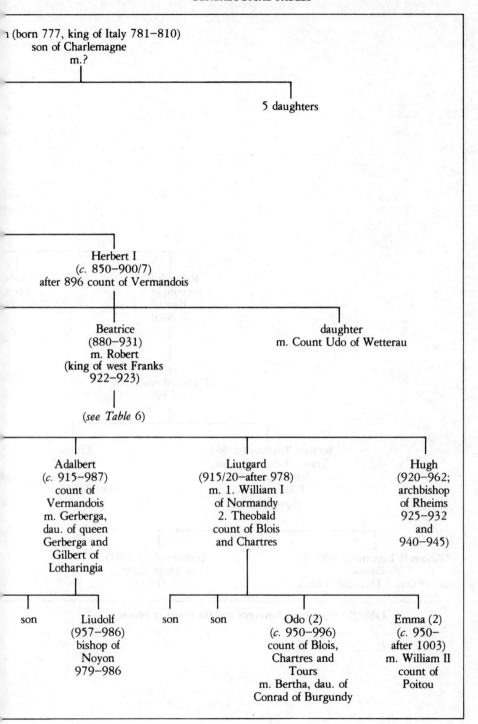

ı (born 777, king of Italy 781–810)
son of Charlemagne
m.?

5 daughters

Herbert I
(c. 850–900/7)
after 896 count of Vermandois

Beatrice
(880–931)
m. Robert
(king of west Franks
922–923)

daughter
m. Count Udo of Wetterau

(see Table 6)

Adalbert
(c. 915–987)
count of
Vermandois
m. Gerberga,
dau. of queen
Gerberga and
Gilbert of
Lotharingia

Liutgard
(915/20–after 978)
m. 1. William I
of Normandy
2. Theobald
count of Blois
and Chartres

Hugh
(920–962;
archbishop
of Rheims
925–932
and
940–945)

son

Liudolf
(957–986)
bishop of
Noyon
979–986

son

son

Odo (2)
(c. 950–996)
count of Blois,
Chartres and
Tours
m. Bertha, dau. of
Conrad of Burgundy

Emma (2)
(c. 950–
after 1003)
m. William II
count of
Poitou

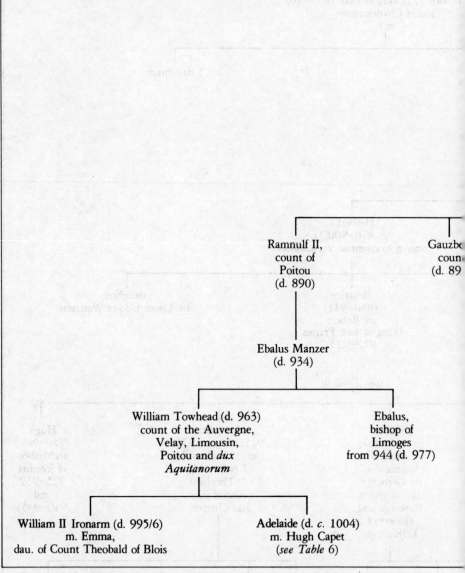

Table 8. Aquitaine, Auvergne and the house of Poitou

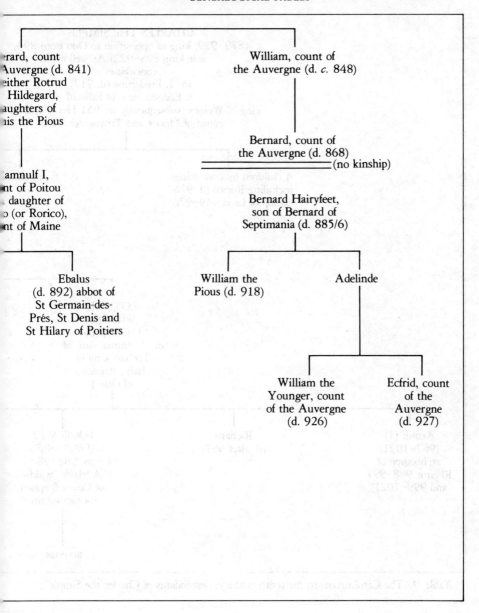

erard, count
Auvergne (d. 841)
either Rotrud
Hildegard,
aughters of
is the Pious

William, count of
the Auvergne (d. c. 848)

Bernard, count of
the Auvergne (d. 868)
━━━━━━━━━━━━(no kinship)

amnulf I,
nt of Poitou
daughter of
o (or Rorico),
nt of Maine

Bernard Hairyfeet,
son of Bernard of
Septimania (d. 885/6)

Ebalus
(d. 892) abbot of
St Germain-des-
Prés, St Denis and
St Hilary of Poitiers

William the
Pious (d. 918)

Adelinde

William the
Younger, count
of the Auvergne
(d. 926)

Ecfrid, count
of the
Auvergne
(d. 927)

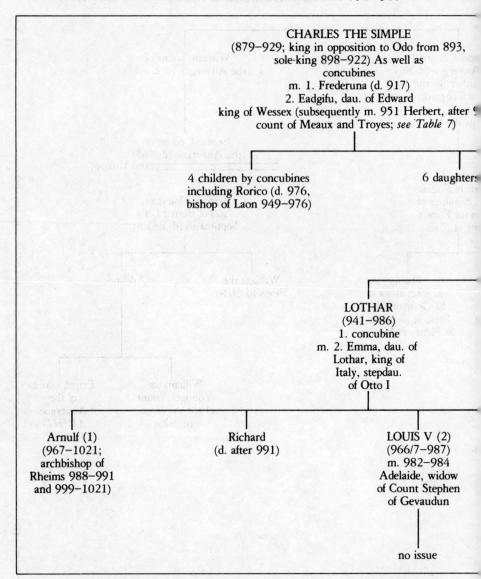

CHARLES THE SIMPLE
(879–929; king in opposition to Odo from 893,
sole-king 898–922) As well as
concubines
m. 1. Frederuna (d. 917)
2. Eadgifu, dau. of Edward
king of Wessex (subsequently m. 951 Herbert, after ?
count of Meaux and Troyes; *see Table 7*)

4 children by concubines
including Rorico (d. 976,
bishop of Laon 949–976)

6 daughters

LOTHAR
(941–986)
1. concubine
m. 2. Emma, dau. of
Lothar, king of
Italy, stepdau.
of Otto I

Arnulf (1)
(967–1021;
archbishop of
Rheims 988–991
and 999–1021)

Richard
(d. after 991)

LOUIS V (2)
(966/7–987)
m. 982–984
Adelaide, widow
of Count Stephen
of Gevaudun

no issue

Table 9. The Carolingians in the tenth century: descendants of Charles the Simple

364

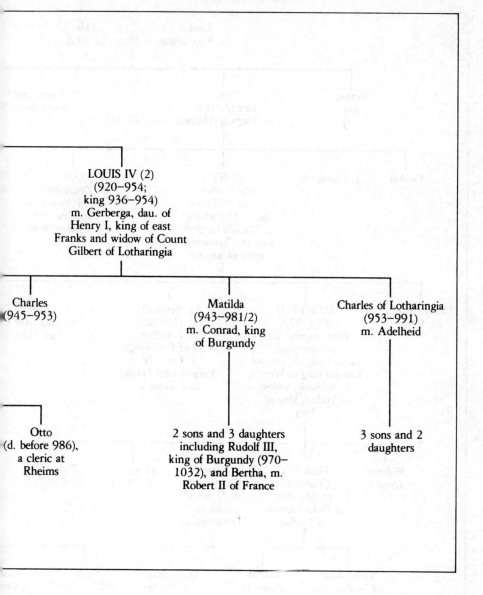

LOUIS IV (2)
(920–954;
king 936–954)
m. Gerberga, dau. of
Henry I, king of east
Franks and widow of Count
Gilbert of Lotharingia

Charles
(945–953)

Matilda
(943–981/2)
m. Conrad, king
of Burgundy

Charles of Lotharingia
(953–991)
m. Adelheid

Otto
(d. before 986),
a cleric at
Rheims

2 sons and 3 daughters
including Rudolf III,
king of Burgundy (970–
1032), and Bertha, m.
Robert II of France

3 sons and 2
daughters

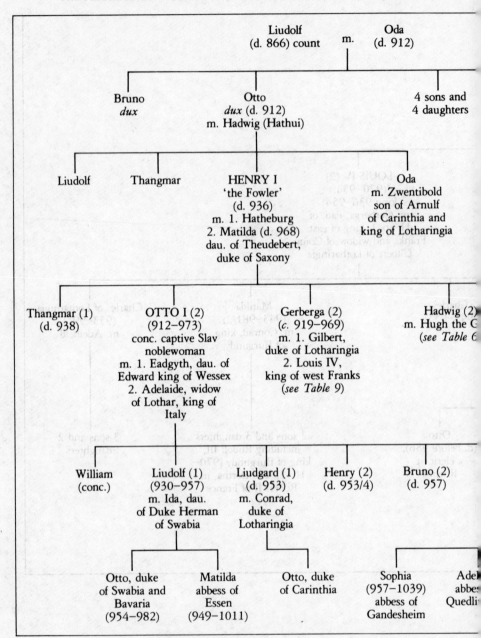

Table 10. The Ottonians

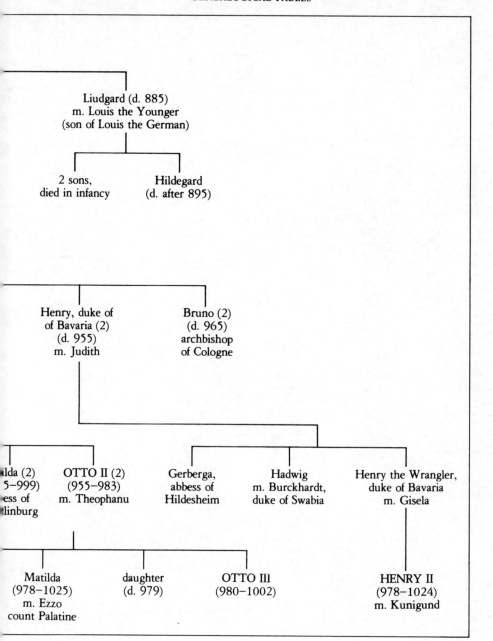

Liudgard (d. 885)
m. Louis the Younger
(son of Louis the German)

2 sons,
died in infancy

Hildegard
(d. after 895)

Henry, duke of
of Bavaria (2)
(d. 955)
m. Judith

Bruno (2)
(d. 965)
archbishop
of Cologne

ilda (2)
5–999)
ess of
linburg

OTTO II (2)
(955–983)
m. Theophanu

Gerberga,
abbess of
Hildesheim

Hadwig
m. Burckhardt,
duke of Swabia

Henry the Wrangler,
duke of Bavaria
m. Gisela

Matilda
(978–1025)
m. Ezzo
count Palatine

daughter
(d. 979)

OTTO III
(980–1002)

HENRY II
(978–1024)
m. Kunigund

Maps

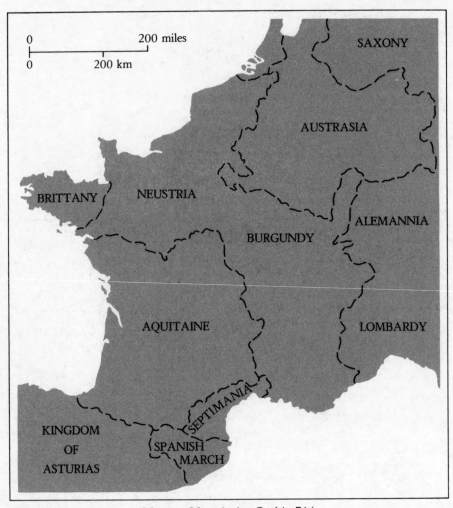

Map 1. Merovingian Gaul in 714

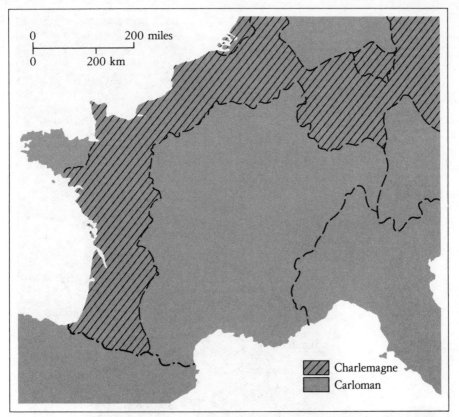

0	200 miles
0	200 km

Charlemagne

Carloman

Map 2.   Frankish Gaul 768–771

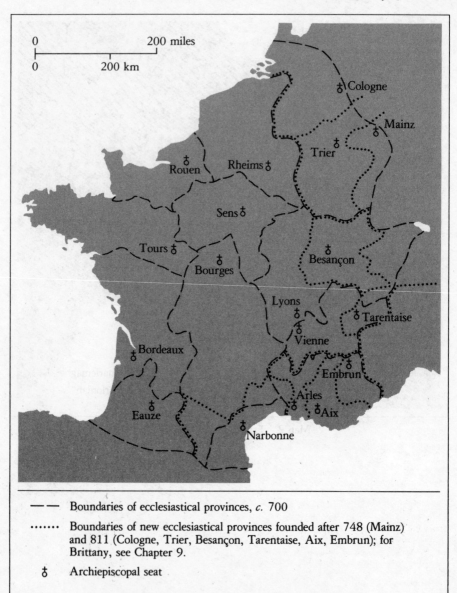

Map 3.   The ecclesiastical provinces of Frankish Gaul

RHEIMS
Thérouanne
Cambrai
Amiens
Noyon
Laon
Soissons
Beauvais
Senlis
Châlons

ROUEN
Bayeux
Évreux
Lisieux
Sées
Avranches
Coutances

TOURS
Alet
Rennes
Le Mans
Léon
Quimper
Vannes
Nantes
Angers

TRIER
Maastricht
Cologne
Metz
Verdun
Toul
Strasbourg
Speyer
Worms
Mainz

In 748 the
metropolitanate was
restored to Mainz and
in 811 it was restored
to Cologne, so that
the ecclesiastical
provinces, with the
new bishoprics
established in
Germany, thereafter
consisted of

TRIER
Metz
Toul
Verdun

MAINZ
Worms
Speyer

Strasbourg
Constance
Chur
Paderborn
Augsburg
Eichstätt
Halberstadt
Hildesheim
Würzburg

COLOGNE
Liège
Utrecht
Tongres-Maastricht
Münster
Bremen
Minden
Osnabrück

SENS
Paris
Meaux
Troyes
Auxerre
Nevers
Orleans
Chartres

BORDEAUX
Saintes
Angoulême
Périgueux
Agen
Poitiers

EAUZE
Dax
Labourd
Auch
Béarn
Comminges
Oloron
Aire
Bigorre
Conserçens
Lectoure
Baxas
(information from
this province is very
sparse during the
Carolingian period)

NARBONNE
Carcassonne
Elne
Agde
Béziers
Maguelonne
Nîmes

ARLES
Uzès
Gap
Vaison
Orange
Trois Châteaux
Digne
Nice
Sisteron
Antibes
Fréjus
Riez
Toulon
Aix
Marseilles
Apt
Glandève
Carpentras
Vence
Alais
Vivier (later in
province of Vienne)
Die (later in
province of Vienne)
Embrun

Not all these
bishoprics had
incumbents
throughout the
Carolingian period. In
811 Embrun became
a metropolitanate
and consisted of

EMBRUN
Digne
Vence
Nice
Orange
Cavaillon
Trois Châteaux

Aix was a
metropolitanate by
the end of the
eighth century
and consisted of

AIX
Apt
Riez
Fréjus
Gap
Sisteron
Antibes

LYONS
Mâcon
Autun

Chalon
Langres
Besançon
Basle
Lausanne
Sion (later in province
of Tarentaise)

In 811 Besançon
was made a
metropolitanate and
consisted of

BESANCON
Bellay
Constance (later in
province of Mainz)
Civitas Helvetiorum
(Windisch, Avenches,
Lausanne)

VIENNE
Geneva
Tarentaise
Grenoble
Maurienne
Valence
Die
Viviers

Tarentaise was made
a metropolitanate in
811 and consisted of

TARENTAISE
Aoste
Sion

BOURGES
Limoges
Clermont
Javols
Velay
Cahors
Rodez
Albi
Toulouse

SALZBURG
(not shown)
Passau
Freising
Regensburg

**HAMBURG-
BREMEN**
(not shown)

became an
archdiocese
after 831

0   200 miles

0   200 km

York

ENGLAND

London

Winchester   Canterbury

Exeter

Utre
Duurstede

Ghent

Boulogne   Courtrai
     R. Scheldt
Thérouanne   Tournai
Arras   Cambrai
Amiens   St Quentin
Compiègne   Laon   Soissons
Rouen   Beauvais   Rhe
R. Seine   Senlis   Verberie   Verc
Tréguier   Coutances   Lisieux   Ver
Bayeux   Pontoise
Léon   Avranches   Évreux   Paris   Meaux
Alet   Sées   Châlons   Ponthion
BRITTANY   Rennes   Chartres   Melun   Tro
Quimper   **NEUSTRIA**   Étampes   Sens   I
Le Mans   Orleans   **BURGUN**
Vannes   Vendôme   Auxerre
Angers   Tours   Blois   Fontenay   I
Nantes   Bourges   R. Loire   Nevers   Aut
Poitiers

Mâcon

Saintes   Clermont   Lyons
Angoulême   Vienne
Périgueux   Brioude   **PROVENCE**
Bordeaux   Le Puy   Gre
     GASCONY   Cahors   Rodez   Viviers
     Orange
   Uzès   A
Béarn   Toulouse   Nîmes   A
   Maguelonne   R. Rhône
Pamplona   Bigorre   Carcassonne   Béziers
Comminges   **SEPTIMANIA**   Narbonne
Burgos   **NAVARRE**   Elne   Ma
   Urgel   Ampurias
  R. Ebro   Huesca   **SPANISH**
Saragossa   **MARCH**   Gerona
Lerida
Barcelona
S P A I N   Tarragona
Tortosa

AQUITAINE

Map 4.   The 'Carolingian Empire' in the period of its greatest expansion, 814–840

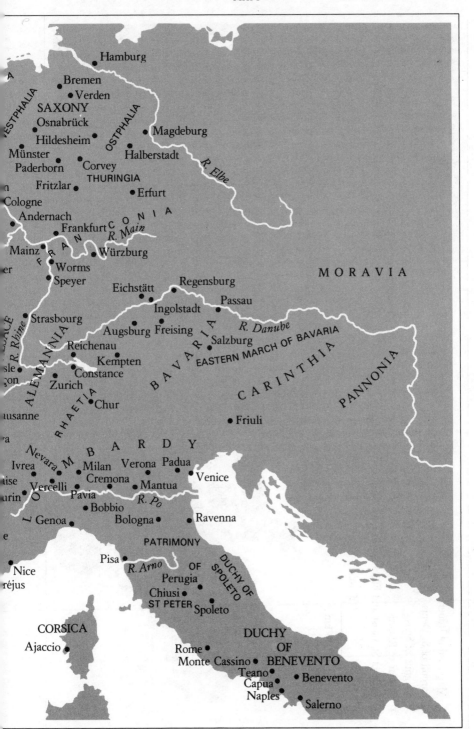

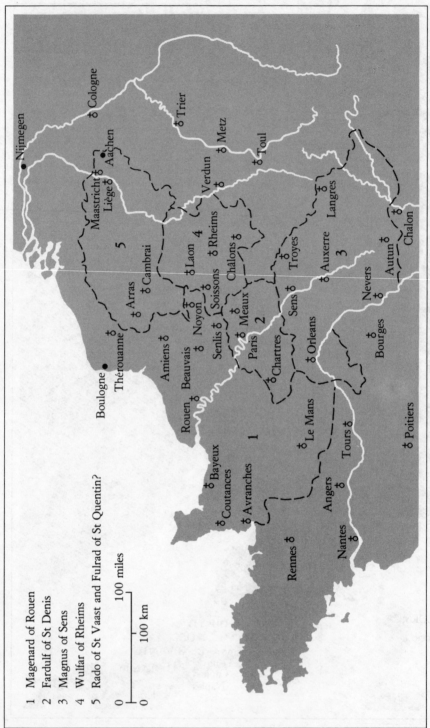

1 Magenard of Rouen
2 Fardulf of St Denis
3 Magnus of Sens
4 Wulfar of Rheims
5 Rado of St Vaast and Fulrad of St Quentin?

Map 5. The *missatica* of the Frankish kingdoms in 802

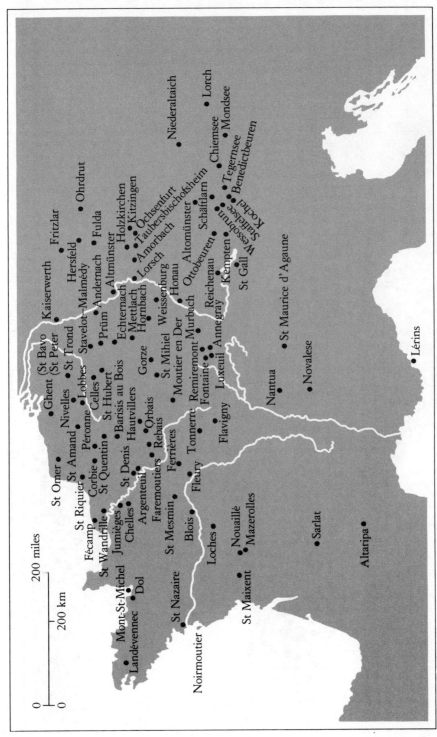

Map 6. Principal monasteries of the Frankish kingdom, c. 817 (except those attached to episcopal sees, shown on Map 7)

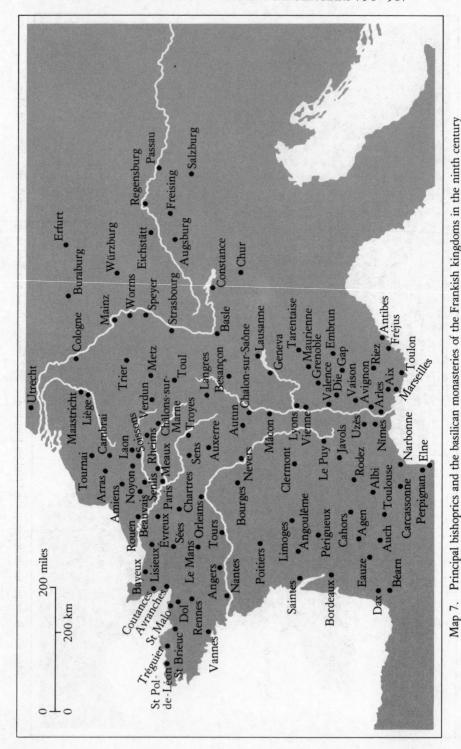

Map 7. Principal bishoprics and the basilican monasteries of the Frankish kingdoms in the ninth century

Amiens
St Martin

Angers
St Sergius

Arles
Hilarianum
St Aurelian
St John
St Peter

Arras
St Vedast

Augsburg
St Afra

Autun
St Symphorian

Auxerre
Sts Cosmo and Damian
St Germain
St Martin
BVM
St Eusebius
St Julian

Besançon
St Columba
St Paul
Jussianum

Bourges
St Martin
St Symphorian
BVM
St Sulpicius

Cahors
St Amand
St Stephen

Cambrai
St Medard

Chalon-sur-Sâone
St Marcel

Eichstätt
St Salvator

Cologne
St Severin
St Cunibert
BVM

Langres
St Geosmes

Laon
St Vincent
St Salaberga
BVM

Le Mans
BVM
St Vincent
St Audoen
St Germain
St Peter de la Conture
Les Andelys

Limoges
St Martial
St Yrieix
St Martin
Solignac

Lyons
Ainay
Insula Barbara (Ile Barbe)
St George
St Michael
St Peter

Maastricht
St Servatius

Mainz
St Alban
Altmünster
St Nicomède

Marseilles
St Victor
St Cassian

Meaux
St Favo

Metz
St Stephen
St Arnulf
St Glossinde
St Felix
St Martin
St Symphorian

Noyon
St Eligius
St Godebertha

Orleans
St Anianus
St Aignan

Paris
St Denis
St Germain-des-Prés
St Laurent
St Eligius
St Maur des Fossés

Poitiers
BVM
St Hilary
Holy Cross (Sainte Croix)
Ligugé

Regensburg
St Emmeram

Rheims
St Remigius
St Peter les Dames
St Peter in the city
St Theuderic (Thierry)

Rouen
St Peter

Salzburg
BVM
St Peter

Sens
St Peter le Vif
St Columba
St Remigius

Soissons
BVM
St Medard

Speyer
St Germain

Tours
Marmoutier
St Martin
St Peter
BVM
St Julian
St Monegund
St Venantius

Trier
St Maximin
St Echarius
St Symphorian
BVM

Utrecht
St Salvator

Vienne
St Peter
St Andrew the Great
St Andrew the Less
St Marcel

Würzburg
BVM
St Andrew
St Kilian

Note: BVM = Monasteries
dedicated to the
Virgin Mary

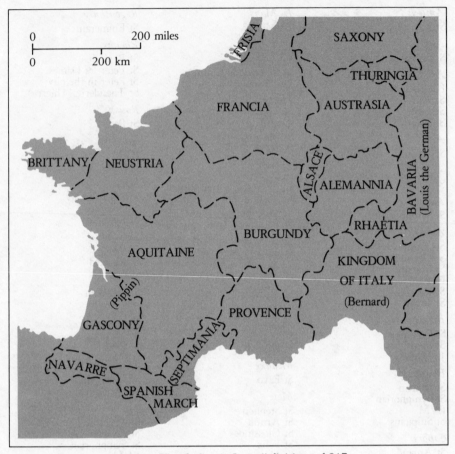

Map 8.   The *Ordinatio Imperii* divisions of 817

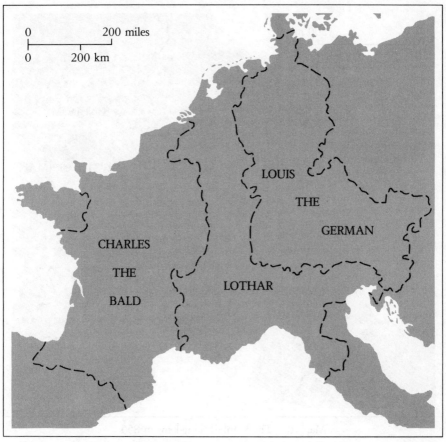

Map 9. The partition of Verdun, 843

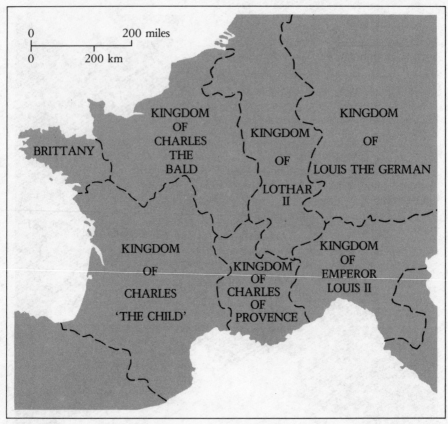

Map 10. The Frankish kingdoms in 855

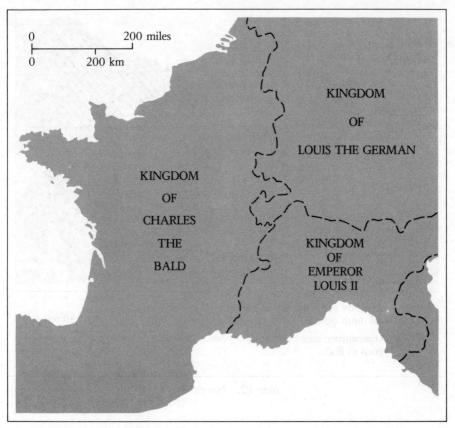

Map 11. The partition of Meersen, 870

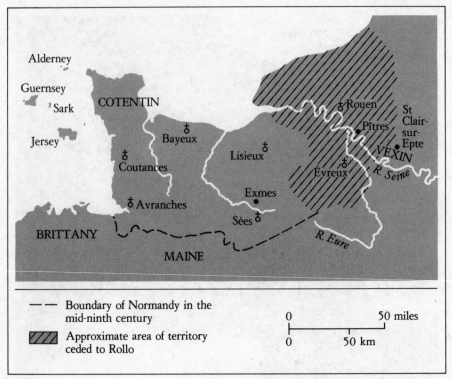

Map 12. Normandy

—— Boundary of Normandy in the
mid-ninth century

Approximate area of territory
ceded to Rollo

0   50 miles

0   50 km

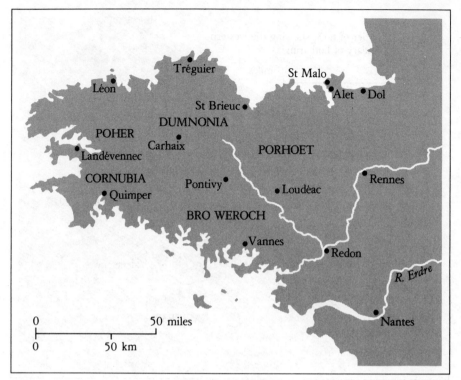

Map 13. Brittany

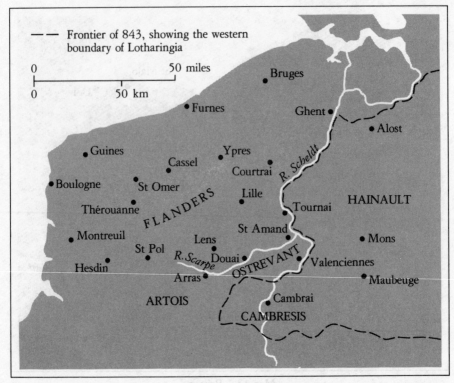

Map 14. Flanders

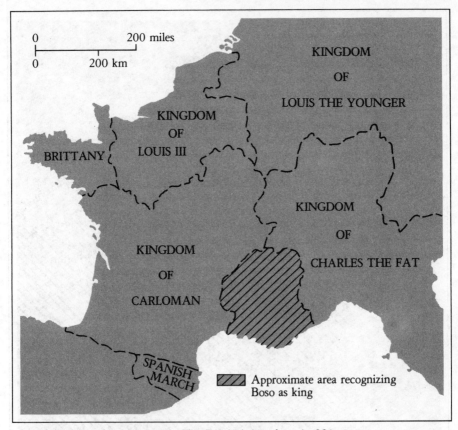

Map 15. The Frankish kingdoms in 880

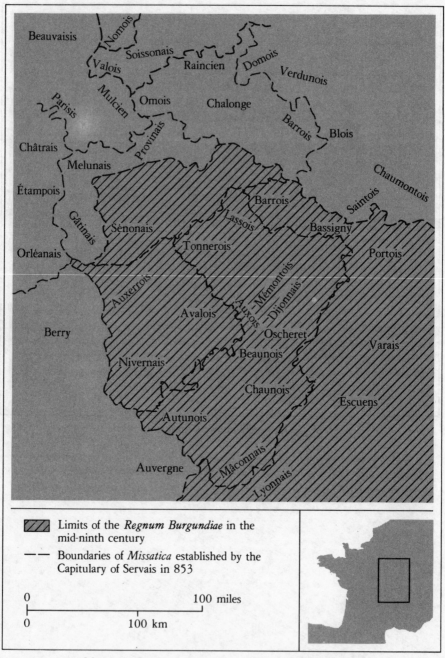

Map 16. Burgundy: principal *pagi* in the ninth century

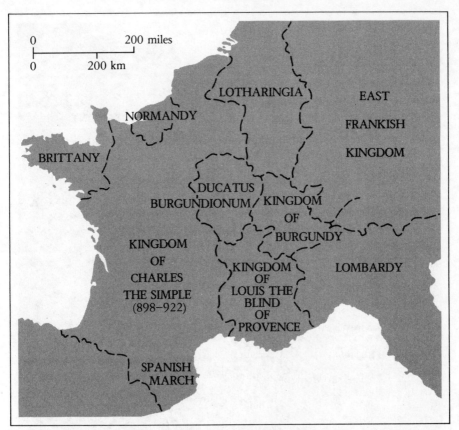

Map 17. The Frankish kingdoms *c.* 912

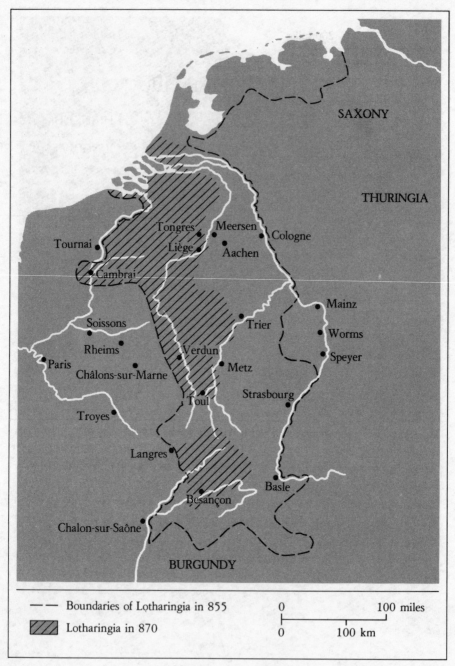

Map 18. Lotharingia

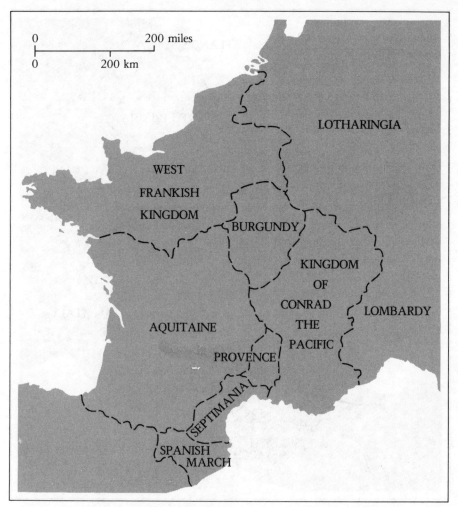

Map 19. The Frankish kingdoms in 950

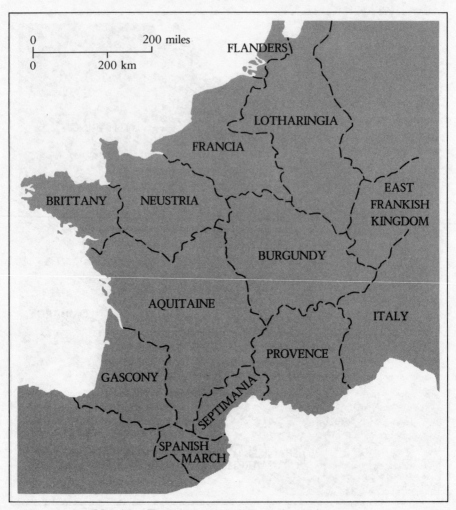

Map 20. Territorial principalities in the tenth century

Index of manuscripts

General index